Special Edition

USING
COREL
WORDPERFECT
SUITE 7

Special Edition

Using
Corel
WordPerfect
Suite 7

Written by Bill Bruck with

Brian Underdahl

Special Edition Using Corel WordPerfect Suite 7

Library of Congress Catalog No.: 96-71441

ISBN: 0-7897-0999-6

98 97   6 5 4 3

Interpretation of the printing code: the rightmost double-digit number is the year of the book's printing; the rightmost single-digit number, the number of the book's printing. For example, a printing code of 96-1 shows that the first printing of the book occurred in 1996.

Screen reproductions in this book were created using Collage Plus from Inner Media, Inc., Hollis, NH.

Credits

PRESIDENT
Roland Elgey

PUBLISHING DIRECTOR
David Solomon

EDITORIAL SERVICES DIRECTOR
Elizabeth Keaffaber

MANAGING EDITOR
Michael Cunningham

DIRECTOR OF MARKETING
Lynn E. Zingraf

ACQUISITIONS MANAGER
Elizabeth South

PRODUCT DEVELOPMENT MANAGER
Lisa Wagner

PRODUCT DIRECTOR
Carolyn Kiefer

PRODUCT DEVELOPMENT SPECIALISTS
Kevin Kloss
Joyce Nielsen
Janice A. Snyder

MEDIA DEVELOPMENT SPECIALIST
David Garratt

PRODUCTION EDITOR
Sarah Rudy

EDITORS
Margo Catts
Kate Givens
Brian Sweany
Nick Zafran

ASSISTANT PRODUCT MARKETING MANAGER
Christy M. Miller

TECHNICAL EDITORS
Robert Hartley
Lorrie Maughan
Christine Peterson

TECHNICAL SUPPORT SPECIALIST
Nadeem Muhammed

ACQUISITIONS COORDINATOR
Tracy Williams

OPERATIONS COORDINATOR
Patty Brooks

FORMATTING COORDINATOR
Michelle Newcomb

BOOK DESIGNER
Ruth Harvey

COVER DESIGNER
Dan Armstrong

PRODUCTION TEAM
Stephen Adams
Marcia Brizendine
Kevin Cliburn
Melissa Coffey
Erin Danielson
Bryan Flores
Jessica Ford
Trey Frank
Jason Hand
Daniel Harris
Clint Lahnen
Steph Mineart
Casey Price
Erich Richter
Laura Robbins
Sossity Smith

INDEXERS
Cheryl Dietsch
Debra Myers
Tim Taylor

Composed in *Century Old Style* and *Franklin Gothic* by Que Corporation.

About the Authors

Bill Bruck, Ph.D. is a WordPerfect Certified Instructor and owner of Bill & Associates, a computer training and performance consulting firm in Falls Church, Virginia. BB&A delivers customized training services in major applications suites and other applications to clients nationwide. Bill's consulting work focuses on helping businesses get the most from their microcomputers through work flow re-engineering, office automation, and ensuring staff can use software tools by creating learning labs, implementing assessment tools, and conducting instructor-led training.

A counseling psychologist by training, Bill comes from academia, having taught at the University of Florida, Seattle University, and West Georgia College. He is currently professor of psychology at Marymount University in Arlington, Virginia. Bill is also an author of several other Macmillan books on WordPerfect, GroupWise, and PerfectOffice.

Brian Underdahl is an author, independent consultant, and custom application developer based in Reno, Nevada. He's the author or co-author of over 25 computer books, as well as numerous magazine articles. He has also acted as a product developer and as a technical editor on many other Que books. His e-mail address is 71505,1114 on CompuServe.

Acknowledgments

I would like to extend my thanks and acknowledgment to my co-authors for the first edition of this book, Judy Felfe, Steve Mann, Sue Plumley, Patrice-Anne Rutledge, and the co-author for this edition, Brian Underdahl. Their hard work has formed the basis for this new edition.

User Programs personnel at Corel, Michael Bellefeuille and Michelle Murphy were very helpful; various anonymous Corel technical support staff have been uniformly courteous, knowledgeable, and helpful with a variety of questions and concerns.

Thanks to technical editors Robert Hartley, Lorrie Maughan, and Christine Peterson, and to Que staff, including David W. Solomon, Elizabeth South, Carolyn Kiefer, Joyce Nielsen, Janice A. Snyder, Sarah Rudy, Patty Brooks, Lisa Wagner, Tracy Williams, David Garratt, Michelle Newcomb, and Kevin Kloss for their support and the work they have put in to get this book to press.

Finally, my deepest appreciation to my wife, Anita Bruck, for putting up with my continued absences while writing this book, and for her support and encouragement throughout this project.

We'd Like to Hear from You!

As part of our continuing effort to produce books of the highest possible quality, Que would like to hear your comments. To stay competitive, we *really* want you, as a computer book reader and user, to let us know what you like or dislike most about this book or other Que products.

You can mail comments, ideas, or suggestions for improving future editions to the address below, or send us a fax at (317) 581-4663. For the online inclined, Macmillan Computer Publishing has a forum on CompuServe (type **GO QUEBOOKS** at any prompt) through which our staff and authors are available for questions and comments. The address of our Internet site is **http://www.mcp.com** (World Wide Web).

In addition to exploring our forum, please feel free to contact me personally to discuss your opinions of this book: I'm **104521,2411** on CompuServe, and I'm **ckiefer@que.mcp.com** on the Internet.

Thanks in advance—your comments will help us to continue publishing the best books available on computer topics in today's market.

Carolyn Kiefer
Product Director
Que Corporation
201 W. 103rd Street
Indianapolis, Indiana 46290
USA

Contents at a Glance

Table of Contents

II | Using Corel WordPerfect

VI | Using Other Suite Applications

Introduction

Corel WordPerfect Suite 7 is the most popular retail software suite of desktop applications you can buy. Its powerful, integrated software set includes many best-of-class applications, including the latest versions of WordPerfect for word processing, Corel Quattro Pro for spreadsheet analysis, and Presentations for drawing and presenting graphics. In addition, you receive tools such as QuickConnect, QuickFinder, and Envoy to help integrate and publish your work.

With the power of Corel WordPerfect Suite comes both ease of use and sophisticated features. Individuals can load it on their stand-alone machines at home, and let QuickTasks and the PerfectExpert guide them through sending correspondence, making family budgets, and maintaining a Christmas list. Multinational corporations can load the Corel WordPerfect Suite on LANs, and conduct enterprise computing via the Internet and corporate intranets using the Suite's built-in Internet features. Businesses can also maintain corporate documents electronically through Envoy, keep corporate financial spreadsheets in Corel Quattro Pro, and create custom interfaces and automated tasks.

Who Should Use this Book?

Corel has created an easy-to-use and easy-to-learn product in the WordPerfect Suite. However, the sheer number of included applications, richness of features, variety of shortcuts, and power of its automation functions imply that both the new and experienced user will not be able to take full advantage of the WordPerfect Suite by mere experimentation. This book can increase understanding and decrease learning time for everyone using the Corel WordPerfect Suite 7.

For newcomers, this book offers a conceptual overview of the Suite, step-by-step instructions for common functionality, and a thorough introduction to each of the included applications.

More experienced users will appreciate coverage of the new features offered by Suite 7, along with the sections on Suite customization and integration. Discussion of creating and moving files from and onto the Internet will also be of great value.

Many readers will find that they use one application extensively, and the others occasionally. For these users, this book will be their only point of reference for those applications used occasionally. It will also serve as a first point of reference for their major application. Other users will also want to buy a Que book devoted exclusively to that major application, such as *Special Edition Using Corel WordPerfect 7*, or *SE Using Corel Quattro Pro 7*.

How this Book Is Organized

This book is organized into seven major parts that take you from the basic design of WordPerfect Suite 7, through using each application, and into advanced integration and customization of the suite:

Part I: Working with Corel WordPerfect Suite 7

Part II: Using Corel WordPerfect

Part III: Using Corel Quattro Pro

Part IV: Using Corel Presentations

Part V: Using Internet Applications

Part VI: Using Other Suite Applications

Part VII: Integrating and Customizing Corel WordPerfect Suite 7

Part I, "Working with Corel WordPerfect Suite 7," provides a conceptual overview of the Suite. It shows you how to perform simple functions, explains how common tools such as the spelling checker and Grammatik work, and discusses common file management issues.

Parts II through VI are devoted to the specific applications that make up Corel WordPerfect Suite 7, including the bonus applications. You can turn directly to these sections if you have specific questions to answer or tasks to accomplish.

Part VII, "Integrating and Customizing Corel WordPerfect Suite 7," discusses ways in which individual applications work together. You find out how to use QuickTasks to perform common functions, how to transfer data between applications, and how to create and edit toolbars and custom menus.

Conventions Used in this Book

The conventions used in this book have been developed to help you learn to use Corel WordPerfect Suite 7 quickly and easily. Most commands can be entered with a mouse, the keyboard, or buttons on the toolbar and Power Bar—for example, choosing menu options or dialog box commands. Instructions are written in a way that enables you to choose the method you prefer. For example, if the instruction says "Choose File, Open," you can click the File menu, then click the Open option. Alternatively, you can press Alt+F to access the File menu, then press O; or use the arrow keys to highlight Open, then press Enter. Finally, you can use the mouse to click the Open file button on the toolbar.

When you need to hold down the first key while you press a second key, a plus sign (+) is used for the combination:

    Alt+F or Ctrl+M

The Shift, Ctrl, and Alt keys must all be used in this way.

When two keys are pressed in sequence, they are separated with a comma. For instance, the Home key is never held down while pressing another key, but it is often pressed before pressing another key. "Press Home, up arrow" means to press and then release the Home key, then press and release the up-arrow key.

When a letter in a menu or dialog box is underlined, it indicates that you can press the Alt key plus that letter (or that letter alone in submenus and dialog boxes) to choose that command. In "Choose File, Open" you can access the menu by pressing Alt+F; then with the File menu selected, you can choose Open by pressing the letter O. Often, the underlined letter is the first letter in the word; at other times it is not. For instance, to choose Edit, Preferences, you would press the Alt key and hold it down while you press the E key.

If there are two common ways to invoke a command, they are separated with a semicolon (;). For instance, you can access the Print dialog box in two ways, as indicated by these instructions: "Choose File, Print; or press Ctrl+P."

Many times, the quickest way to access a feature is with a button on the toolbar. In this case, the appropriate toolbar button is shown in the margin next to the instructions.

Bold text is used to indicate text you are asked to type. *Italic* text is used for new terms. UPPERCASE letters are used to distinguish file names. On-screen messages appear in monospace type.

N O T E Notes provide additional information that might help you avoid problems, or offer advice or general information related to the current topic. ▪

 Tips provide extra information that supplements the current topic. Often, tips offer shortcuts or alternative methods for accomplishing a task.

CAUTION
Cautions warn you if a procedure or description in the topic could lead to unexpected results, or even data loss or damage to your system. If you see a caution, proceed carefully.

TROUBLESHOOTING

I'm having a specific problem with a WordPerfect feature. Look for troubleshooting elements to help you identify and resolve specific problems you might be having with WordPerfect, your system, or network.

What About Sidebars?
Sidebars are sprinkled throughout the book to give you the author's insight into a particular topic. The information in a sidebar supplements the material in the chapter.

Margin cross-references like the one here direct you to related information in other parts of the book.

▶ **See** "Building a Spreadsheet," **p. xx**

Internet references such as the following point you to sites on the Internet where you can find additional information about a topic being discussed:

ON THE WEB

http://www.corel.com   Corel's Internet Web Site.

We, the authors, hope you enjoy using *Special Edition Corel WordPerfect Suite 7*, and that you find this book to be a valuable tool as well as an ongoing reference to assist you in the learning process.

Working with Corel WordPerfect Suite 7

CHAPTER 1

Introducing Corel WordPerfect Suite 7

With Corel WordPerfect Suite 7, you have purchased the latest version of the world's best retail-selling word processor, Corel WordPerfect, and a collection of other best-of-class applications including Corel Quattro Pro and Corel Presentations. But Corel WordPerfect Suite 7 is much more than a collection of applications. It is a true integrated suite of products aimed at making tasks you do at the office or at home easier. ■

Suite applications

Find out what applications are contained within the Suite.

Desktop Application Director

Learn to use the Desktop Application Director (DAD) to easily start Corel WordPerfect Suite 7 programs from the Windows 95 taskbar.

Choose your application

See which application is best for your particular task.

Extend your desktop

Find out how Corel WordPerfect Suite 7 integrates with your network, corporate intranet, or the Internet.

What Is Corel WordPerfect Suite 7?

Corel WordPerfect Suite 7 is a collection of applications for common home and office tasks, integrated with the Desktop Application Director, that includes a scripting language for cross-program applications.

What's Included in the Suite?

The Corel WordPerfect Suite 7 is designed for the Windows 95 operating environment and it ships with the following applications:

- Corel WordPerfect 7
- Corel Quattro Pro 7
- Corel Presentations 7
- Corel Desktop Application Director 7
- CorelFLOW 3
- Corel Barista
- AT&T's WorldNet℠ Service Software including Netscape Navigator Internet Browser
- Starfish's Sidekick 95
- Starfish's Dashboard 95
- Envoy 7
- IBM's VoiceType Control
- INSO's Quick View Plus
- Corel Screen Saver
- 150 Typographical Fonts
- 10,000 Clip Art Images

Corel also publishes Corel WordPerfect Suite 7 Professional, which is targeted to a more specialized audience. The Professional Suite includes the same applications in the standard version of Corel WordPerfect Suite 7. You can use *Special Edition Using Corel WordPerfect Suite 7* to learn these core applications in the Professional version. In addition, the Professional Suite adds the following software: Corel Time Line, CorelDRAW! 6 (illustration module only), Corel A to Z, Borland's Paradox 7.0, Groupwise 4.1 e-mail client license, Corel InfoCentral 7, and VisualDTD. These additional products are beyond the scope of this book.

What Are the Operating Requirements?

To use Corel WordPerfect Suite 7, Corel recommends the following minimum system configuration:

- Operating System: Windows 95
- CPU Type: PC 486/25 processor; 486/66 recommended
- Memory: 8 M RAM; 16 M recommended
- Graphics: VGA monitor
- CD-ROM Drive Speed: Double-speed CD-ROM drive recommended to access all applications, fonts, and clip art
- Audio: 8-bit Sound Blaster or 100% compatible sound card
- Hard Drive: 30 M; 220 M hard disk space required depending on configuration
- Mouse or Tablet
- Corel WordPerfect Suite 7 for Windows 95 works with virtually any network, including Novell NetWare, Windows for Workgroups, Banyan Vines, and LAN Server.

TROUBLESHOOTING

My screen and menus are a little different than some of the figures and instruction sets in the book. This book was written against Version 7.0.1.0 of the product dated 6/28/96.

Understanding the Design Goals

The Suite isn't just a bunch of stand-alone applications bundled and marketed together. It is a true *suite* of products that are integrated together, and aimed at home and business functionality.

Thus, understanding Corel WordPerfect Suite 7 isn't merely a matter of learning the features of individual applications. In fact, before you learn about the functions of all the applications, it's important to understand the basic design goals of Corel WordPerfect Suite 7. These may be divided into the following areas:

- Ease of learning and use
- Integrated working environment
- Extension of your desktop

Understanding Ease of Use Features

The Corel WordPerfect Suite 7 has been developed with extensive input from Corel WordPerfect's usability testing procedures. Two features that have been incorporated into the Suite as a result of this research are a consistent user interface, and the extensive availability of help in a variety of formats.

Consistent Interface   A consistent interface means that the way you work in one application should parallel how you work in another. In Corel WordPerfect Suite 7, this can be seen in several areas:

- *Menu similarity.* As you can see in Figure 1.1, menus are similar in Corel WordPerfect Suite 7 applications. Not only are the names on the menu bar similar, the selections within each menu item parallel each other as much as possible, taking into consideration the differences in each application's features.

FIG. 1.1
Menus are similar in Corel WordPerfect Suite 7 applications.

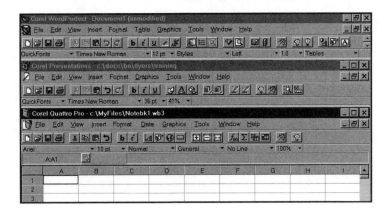

- *Toolbar similarity.* In menus that are parallel within each application, the same buttons are used for basic tools across applications. These include:

Table 1.1   Common Corel WordPerfect Suite 7 Buttons

Icon	Function
	New Blank Document. Create a blank document in a new window.
	Open. Open an existing document into a new window.
	Save. Save the current document.
	Print. Print the current document.
	Cut. Move the selection to the Clipboard.
	Copy. Copy the selection to the Clipboard.
	Paste. Insert the Clipboard contents at the insertion point.
	Undo. Reverse the last change.
	Bold. Turn on/off Bold.
	Italic. Turn on/off Italic.
	Browse the Web. Launches your Web browser.
	Ask the PerfectExpert. Launches help system and allows you to ask questions.

■ *Dialog box similarity*. In addition, similar dialog boxes are used wherever possible throughout Corel WordPerfect Suite 7. For instance, the same Open dialog box is used in Corel WordPerfect, Corel Quattro Pro, and Corel Presentations.

PerfectExpert and Guide Me Through It   Corel WordPerfect Suite 7 provides extensive and easy-to-follow help with two powerful features: PerfectExpert and Guide Me Through It.

With PerfectExpert, you can ask questions in plain English, and Corel WordPerfect will find the help topics most closely related to your request. In addition, you can play video clips showing you commonly used features, or access QuickTasks (discussed later).

Guide Me Through It helps you accomplish a task by taking you through a series of choices. For instance, the Create Table dialog box found within the Corel WordPerfect PerfectExpert help system (see Figure 1.2) asks you a series of questions related to creating your table, then creates the table with you.

FIG. 1.2
The Create Table dialog box of the Table guide helps you create tables in Corel WordPerfect.

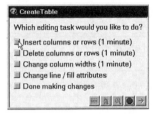

Similarly, as you progress through the PerfectExpert in Corel Presentations, you are guided through the steps needed to create an effective presentation. After you select the template that provides the "look" for your presentation, the PerfectExpert asks what type of presentation you are going to make (see Figure 1.3).

FIG. 1.3
The Slide Show PerfectExpert gives you advice on constructing Presentation shows for different purposes.

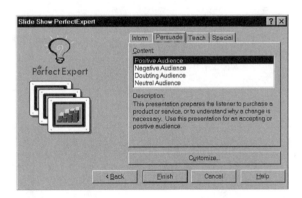

Depending on your choices, the Slide Show PerfectExpert shows you what types of information should be included in the presentation. This is accomplished through the presentation of an outline that you can complete with your own presentation's data (see Figure 1.4).

▶ **See** "Learning About QuickTasks," **p. 706**

Understanding the Integrated Working Environment

Perhaps Corel WordPerfect Suite 7's most powerful feature is the integrated working environment it provides. With Corel WordPerfect Suite 7, you can concentrate more on the tasks you need to do, and less on the application(s) in which you need to do them.

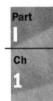

FIG. 1.4
The Slide Show PerfectExpert even suggests an outline of what information to include in your presentation.

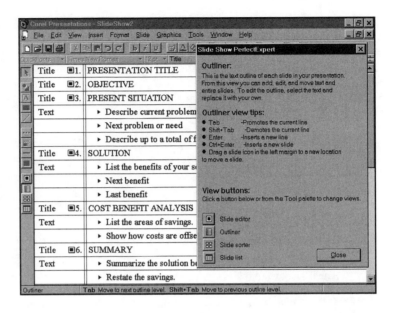

Of course, part of an integrated working environment is the common look and feel of applications. However, with Corel WordPerfect Suite 7, this is only the beginning. Corel WordPerfect Suite 7 offers features that include:

- QuickTasks
- Common tools for file management and writing
- The Desktop Application Director (DAD)

QuickTasks You can think of a QuickTask as a Guide that operates across applications. QuickTasks provide guided, step-by-step instructions for common tasks such as:

- Creating a letter, memo, or fax
- Creating an agenda, calendar, or newsletter
- Sending a file via e-mail or faxing the current document
- Creating a Web page
- Creating a grading sheet
- Creating a budget or loan amortization

Even apparently simple QuickTasks can involve several applications. For example, the Create Letter QuickTask uses Corel WordPerfect to write the letter, Address Book 7 to obtain the recipient's address, your e-mail package to mail it (if available), or Envoy to publish it if desired (see Figure 1.5).

▶ **See** "Learning About QuickTasks," **p. 706**

FIG. 1.5

QuickTasks help you work easily and quickly with multiple applications to complete common tasks like creating and distributing a letter.

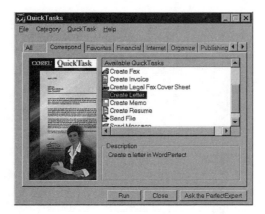

Common File Management Tools   File management is the art of creating an electronic filing system that enables you to store files securely and find files quickly. Corel WordPerfect Suite 7 offers you tools to assist you in your electronic filing tasks.

 ■ *Common file management dialog boxes.* Corel WordPerfect Suite 7 applications have common file management dialog boxes (see Figure 1.6). These dialog boxes all have file management capabilities built in. From these dialog boxes you can copy, move, rename, print, and change file attributes, plus create, remove, and rename folders. In fact, there is a file management dialog box—QuickFinder—that is available to you from any application by clicking its button on the Windows taskbar.

FIG. 1.6

Corel WordPerfect Suite 7 applications use common file management dialog boxes, such as the one pictured, for file management.

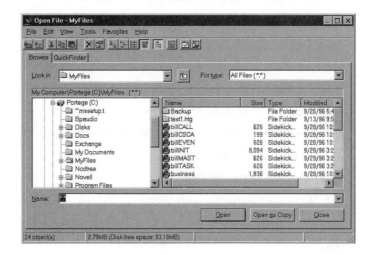

- *QuickFinder*. Corel WordPerfect Suite 7 also includes the powerful QuickFinder indexing program. It enables you to build indexes of your data files. Using these indexes, you can search for files with specific words in them (for example, Wilson Accounting Group). Almost immediately, all files with these words are listed. You can even search for files containing synonyms of target words (accounting, budgeting), word forms (account, accounted, accounting), and common misspellings (acount).

Common Writing Tools   The Corel WordPerfect Suite 7 also provides you with writing tools that make the art of writing easier, and your document more professional-looking. These tools are not only available in Corel WordPerfect, but in Corel Presentations. They include:

- *Speller*. The speller will correct common spelling errors, and catch irregular capitalization, words containing numbers, and repeated words. In Corel WordPerfect, the speller will also remember words you have told it to ignore in a document, so that future spelling checks of that document will continue to ignore the words. (Spelling tools are also available in Corel Quattro Pro.)
- *Thesaurus*. The thesaurus provides you with synonyms and antonyms of selected words. It groups synonyms according to the word's meaning and part of speech (noun, adjective, verb).
- *Grammatik*. Grammatik is Corel WordPerfect Suite 7's grammar checker. Not only does it flag more than a dozen types of errors, it will actually rewrite sentences for you! You can select from among 10 predefined checking styles, depending on the style of writing you use, or create your own.
  ▶ **See** "Using the Writing Tools," **p. 45**
- *QuickCorrect*. Would you like for Corel WordPerfect Suite 7 to correct your spelling as you type? Would you like common abbreviations like LKSB to automatically expand as you type to your firm's name of Luskin, Brankowitsch, Serrandello and Buskin? QuickCorrect is for you! Not only can QuickCorrect correct spelling and abbreviations, it can also automatically capitalize the first word of sentences, correct irregular capitalization, and place the correct number of spaces between sentences.

These writing tools are discussed further in Chapter 3, "Using Common Corel WordPerfect Suite 7 Tools."

DAD   DAD, the Desktop Application Director, provides convenient access to the Corel WordPerfect Suite 7 applications. DAD installs application icons right on the Windows 95 taskbar, as shown in Figure 1.7.

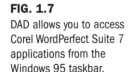

FIG. 1.7
DAD allows you to access
Corel WordPerfect Suite 7
applications from the
Windows 95 taskbar.

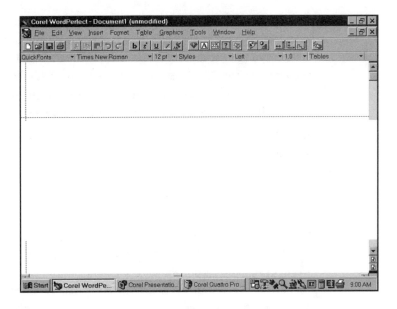

You can read more about DAD Bars in Chapter 2, "Getting Started with Corel WordPerfect Suite 7."

Extending Your Desktop

While Corel WordPerfect Suite 7 is a powerful desktop tool, its power is increased when you *extend your desktop* to your network, corporate intranet, or the Internet. The Suite's ability to extend your desktop can be seen in many areas, including:

■ Performing common network tasks within applications

■ Publishing documents with Envoy

■ Internet integration

■ Data sharing

■ Integrated code

Perform Common Network Tasks Whether you are running Novell, Banyan, Windows 95, Windows NT, or another common network operating system, Corel WordPerfect Suite 7 enables you to perform common network tasks, such as attaching to file servers, from any file management dialog box.

Document Publishing As time goes on, companies are publishing more and more documents electronically. For instance, master copies of personnel manuals or technical manuals can be maintained electronically on a corporate intranet. They can then be updated as needed by responsible parties, and the updated information is available instantly to all users.

Corel WordPerfect Suite 7 includes Envoy—a powerful document-publishing application that allows you to distribute documents across LANs, intranets, the Internet, or on disk. Files can contain bookmarks and hypertext links to assist users in jumping to areas of interest. Documents are "bonded" so that users cannot change them, but can highlight or add notes to areas of interest.

Envoy even includes a runtime viewer, so that documents can be read and annotated by others who do not have Envoy on their computer.

Internet Integration   Corel WordPerfect, Corel Quattro Pro, and Corel Presentations are all able to convert files to the HTML format for publishing on the World Wide Web. You can add links to Internet files in your documents, so that a reader can click them and go immediately to a related file on the Internet. The Suite even extends the Help system to access help files that are maintained by Corel on the Internet.

In addition, the Suite comes with Netscape Navigator for browsing the Web, sending and receiving Internet e-mail, and a newsreader for participating in group discussions on the Internet. Also included is a sign-up process with AT&T WorldNet Services to provide you with an Internet account.

Data Sharing   You can also extend your desktop by sharing data between applications with three Corel WordPerfect Suite 7 applications. Data sharing features include:

- *Shared file formats.* Whether you need to bring a Corel WordPerfect outline into a Corel Presentations slide, or clip a memo graphic from Corel Presentations and insert it into a Corel Quattro Pro notebook, you will find it easy to do.

- *OLE 2.0.* The latest version of Microsoft's Object Linking and Embedding (OLE) is available in three Corel WordPerfect Suite 7 applications: Corel WordPerfect, Corel Quattro Pro, and Corel Presentations. OLE 2.0 enables you to drag and drop objects such as drawings or charts from one application window to another. It also enables you to edit objects like Corel Presentations drawings from within Corel WordPerfect by merely double-clicking the object.

    ▶ **See** "Learning Techniques for Linking and Embedding," **p. 726**

Code Integration   The Corel WordPerfect Suite 7 uses the concept of shared code to maximize performance and minimize use of system resources. Common tools such as the Speller, Thesaurus, Grammatik, QuickCorrect, and QuickFinder are shared between applications, thus saving disk space. Moreover, no matter which application calls them, they are only loaded once, saving system resources.

Determining Which Application to Use

Most people have a "home base" program where they generally start out, and do most of their work during the day. For most, this is Corel WordPerfect, though many people spend most of their time in Corel Quattro Pro. In the past, people would often try to use their "home base" program well past the limits of its innate capabilities—for example, writing memos in their spreadsheets.

To some extent, software manufacturers have encouraged this trend. However, today when working in an integrated suite environment, you will find yourself more often using multiple applications to produce common documents. For instance, a newsletter may be created in Corel WordPerfect with Corel Quattro Pro spreadsheets or charts and Corel Presentations graphics. It may be published electronically with Envoy on your LAN and converted to HTML to be published again on the Internet.

Corel WordPerfect Suite 7 sometimes seems to offer an abundance of riches. There are often so many ways to do things that you may get confused! For instance:

- You can maintain a personal calendar or to-do list in Sidekick or use a QuickTask to create a calendar in Corel WordPerfect.
- You can maintain contact information with the Suite's Address Book or Sidekick, create an address list within Corel WordPerfect to use in conjunction with templates, or keep addresses in Corel Quattro Pro.
- You can create charts and graphs in Corel Presentations, Corel Quattro Pro, and CorelFLOW.

While these multiple ways of doing things may seem confusing at first, there are some simple criteria you can use to determine which way to go:

- *Use the right amount of horsepower.* The Address Book is not very feature-rich, and can contain only about 1,000 records before slowing down. Sidekick and Corel Quattro Pro can maintain more addresses comfortably, but they don't integrate with Corel WordPerfect as well as Address Book does. On the other hand, contacts maintained in Sidekick can be easily linked to Sidekick appointments and tasks.

  In general, match the power of the feature to your needs.
- *Minimize the number of applications you use.* If almost all your work in done in Corel WordPerfect, then perhaps the Address Book that links to it will suffice. Similarly, if you work in Corel Quattro Pro a lot, and have no other reason to use Corel Presentations, you may wish to do your charting in the spreadsheet, rather than moving to a second application.

In general, use the KISS principle—Keep It Simple, Stupid! Minimizing the number of applications you use keeps it simple.

■ *If you work alone, use what's familiar.* Even if there is more power in a Sidekick contact list than in one maintained in Address Book 7, or a Corel Presentations chart has more features than a Corel Quattro Pro one, you may be wise to stick with the applications you know and love, rather than try to do things a new way—if you work alone.

■ *If you don't work alone, ignore the last rule.* When I go into organizations as a consultant, I often find people using an application to do something it wasn't designed for. For instance, I often find people keeping time and billing information in Corel WordPerfect, rather than in a spreadsheet. Why? Because that's what they know, and so as more people started using the system, that's what they had to use as well.

If there will be a number of people involved in a business process, make sure that you pick the application best suited to the task, rather than using the one that the original person was most familiar with.

For example, if you have a need to send document drafts to several people for annotation, don't just assume that it should be done in Corel WordPerfect, because "everybody knows it." (Many probably don't know how to use the comment feature effectively, anyway!) Consider the advantages and disadvantages of publishing the document in Envoy versus distributing it in Corel WordPerfect before making a final decision.

Getting Started with Corel WordPerfect Suite 7

Using the Desktop Application Director (DAD)

Learn to use the Desktop Application Director to quickly launch Corel WordPerfect Suite programs from the Windows 95 taskbar.

Understanding common window elements

See how all the Corel WordPerfect Suite applications have common menus, toolbars, Power Bars, and QuickMenus to make using several applications easier.

Using help systems

Learn about the tremendous variety of help systems Corel WordPerfect offers, from traditional Windows help, through animated demos, automated Guides, and connections to online help through the Internet.

Well, here you are. You've got Corel WordPerfect Suite 7 loaded and you're ready to get started. Let's do it! In this chapter, you learn about those elements of Corel WordPerfect Suite 7 that are similar throughout the Suite and make the Suite easy to learn and use. ■

Introducing DAD

DAD is the Desktop Application Director that enables you to launch Corel WordPerfect Suite 7 programs easily from the taskbar. Though we're not privy to the inner workings of Corel, it is safe to assume that DAD is no relative of Microsoft's MOM, and that the similarity of acronyms is purely coincidental.

In learning to use the Corel WordPerfect Suite 7, it is thus appropriate that you start by learning how to use DAD to launch the Suite applications. Using DAD involves three aspects:

- Ensuring that DAD appears on your taskbar
- Launching applications with DAD
- Adding or removing applications from DAD

Displaying DAD

When DAD is installed, you see icons for various Corel WordPerfect Suite tools in the notification area of your taskbar, along with whatever icons, windows, and other applications put in your taskbar, as shown in Figure 2.1. Table 2.1 shows the DAD icons and their names.

FIG. 2.1
The installation of Corel WordPerfect Suite 7 puts DAD icons in the notification area of your Windows 95 taskbar.

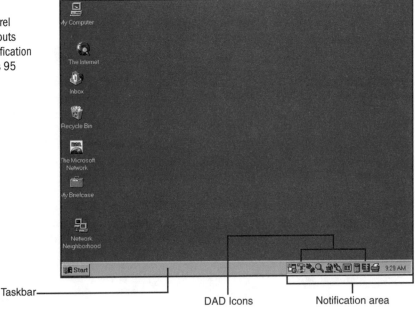

Taskbar

DAD Icons

Notification area

If you do not see any of these icons, DAD is probably not installed, or not in the startup folder.

 T I P If you have installed the Suite, but not started Windows 95 again, you will not see the DAD icons. If you've just installed the Suite, restart Windows to see the DAD icons.

Table 2.1   DAD Buttons

Icon	Name
	QuickTasks
	Corel QuickConnect
	QuickFinder
	Corel Address Book 7
	Corel WordPerfect 7
	Corel Presentations 7
	Corel Quattro Pro 7
	Envoy 7

TROUBLESHOOTING

I know that the Suite is on my machine, but the DAD icons do not appear on the Windows 95 taskbar. Someone has removed the necessary files from the Startup folder in the Windows directory. You can start the Suite by clicking the Start button in Windows 95. The Suite will appear as a menu item at the top of the Start menu, or inside the Programs menu list. When you select the Corel WordPerfect Suite 7 menu item, another list appears of the applications that you may use. You can start any of the programs from this point. (If you wish to see how to add the DAD icons back into the Windows 95 taskbar, see the section "Adding DAD to the Windows 95 Taskbar," as follows.)

Starting DAD   If the DAD icons don't appear on the taskbar, and you want to start DAD, click the Start button on the taskbar, then click Corel WordPerfect Suite 7, Accessories, Corel Desktop Application Director. The Corel WordPerfect Suite icons appear on the taskbar.

Starting DAD Automatically   When you installed Corel WordPerfect Suite 7, the setup program put the Desktop Application Director in the Startup folder, so that DAD loads automatically when you start Windows 95.

This is by far the best and quickest way to use the Corel WordPerfect Suite 7, especially because DAD does not use many Windows resources and it doesn't obscure any other application windows.

Adding DAD to the Windows 95 Taskbar   If the Suite icons don't appear automatically on your taskbar when you start Windows 95 and you would like them to, you can put DAD in the Startup folder as follows:

1. Click the Start button on the taskbar, then choose Settings, Taskbar. Click the Start Menu Programs tab. You see the Taskbar Properties dialog box shown in Figure 2.2.

FIG. 2.2
Change items in your Startup folder using the Taskbar Properties dialog box.

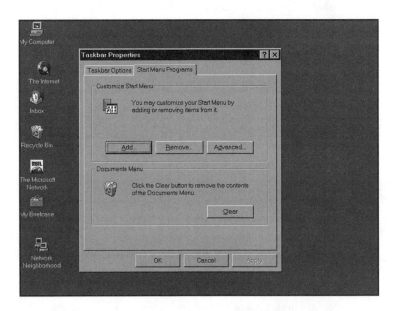

2. Click the Add button. You see the Create Shortcut dialog box shown in Figure 2.3.

FIG. 2.3

In the Create Shortcut dialog box, you can type the name of the program you want to add to your Startup folder, or click the Browse button to locate it.

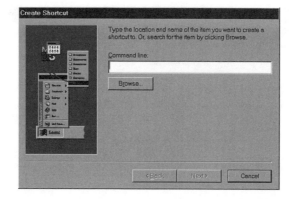

3. Click the Browse button. You see the Browse dialog box shown in Figure 2.4.

4. Navigate to the folder containing the application named Quick.

FIG. 2.4

You can Install DAD to the Startup folder by adding the application named Quick that is found in the Browse dialog box.

NOTE By default, the folder containing the application named Quick is the C:\COREL\OFFICE7\DAD7 folder for a stand-alone installation. If you are on a network, ask your network administrator for the location of this file. ■

5. Double-click the Quick application. You return to the Create Shortcut dialog box (refer to Figure 2.3) and see the Quick application in the Command Line box.

6. Choose Next. You see the Select Program Folder dialog box shown in Figure 2.5.

   ▶ **See** "Navigating the Filing System," **p. 68**

7. Scroll down until you see the Startup folder. Select it and click Next.

8. You see the Select a Title for the Program dialog box as in Figure 2.6. Accept the default name Quick, or choose a more descriptive name like DAD.

9. Choose Finish. You return to the Taskbar Properties dialog box shown in Figure 2.2.

FIG. 2.5
Select the StartUp folder from the Select Program Folder dialog box.

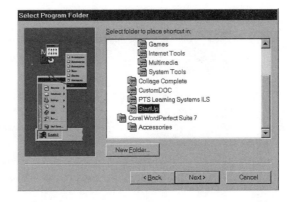

FIG. 2.6
In the Select a Title for the Program dialog box, you give a name to the shortcut you are adding to the Startup folder.

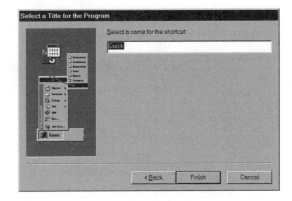

10. Choose OK to return to the Windows desktop.

11. You will need to restart your machine for the DAD icon to load and be visible in the Windows 95 taskbar.

The next time you start Windows 95, DAD will be loaded automatically.

Exiting DAD   Under normal circumstances, you should never need to close DAD. You will need to close DAD, however, if you want to add or remove Corel WordPerfect Suite 7 components using the Suite's Setup program.

To close DAD:

1. Right-click one of the Corel WordPerfect Suite 7 icons on the Windows 95 taskbar, such as the Corel WordPerfect, Corel Quattro Pro, or Corel Presentations icon.

2. Choose Exit DAD from the pop-up menu shown in Figure 2.7. The Suite icons disappear from the taskbar, and you have exited DAD.

FIG. 2.7
Exit DAD by right-clicking a
Corel WordPerfect Suite 7
application on the Windows
95 taskbar.

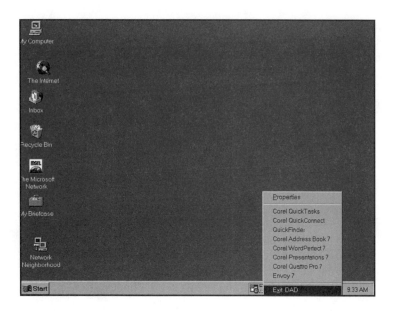

Launching Applications with DAD

To launch a Corel WordPerfect Suite application from DAD, click the appropriate icon for the desired application on the Windows 95 taskbar.

> **TIP** Occasionally, you may not know what application a button will launch. If you rest your mouse pointer on an icon for more than a second or so, you will see a pop-up QuickTip that tells you the name of the application.

You can also use DAD to switch between Suite applications that are already open. For instance, if you click the Corel WordPerfect icon on the DAD Bar, then click the Corel Presentations icon, both Corel WordPerfect and Corel Presentations will be open. If you click the Corel WordPerfect icon again, you will switch back to Corel WordPerfect.

Adding and Removing Applications from DAD

You can easily add or remove Corel WordPerfect Suite 7 applications from DAD, and thus, add or remove their icons from the taskbar.

To do so:

1. Right-click any Corel WordPerfect Suite 7 icon you see on the taskbar, then choose Properties. You see the DAD Properties dialog box shown in Figure 2.8.

2. Check or uncheck the applications to be added or removed from the taskbar.

FIG. 2.8
Add or remove Corel
WordPerfect Suite 7
applications from the taskbar
with the DAD Properties
dialog box.

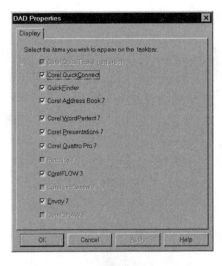

3. Click OK and you return to the Windows desktop and see the changed set of icons on the taskbar.

TIP If an application is not installed, it will be grayed out in this dialog box. The dialog box also lists programs in the Corel Office Suite 7, such as Paradox 7, Corel InfoCentral 7, and CorelDRAW 6.

NOTE The previous version of the Suite (PerfectOffice 3.0), permitted you to have multiple DAD bars, move their placement on the screen, and add non-Corel WordPerfect programs to them. Usability testing revealed that users preferred the simple icons on the taskbar that you find with the present version of DAD. ■

Understanding Common Window Elements

Throughout the Corel WordPerfect Suite 7 applications, you will see similar screen elements, such as the menu bar, the toolbar, and the Power Bar shown in Figure 2.9.

- *Menu bar.* Menu bars are similar throughout all Corel WordPerfect Suite 7 applications and have, to the extent possible, the same menu items.

- *Toolbar.* Toolbars appear in all Corel WordPerfect Suite 7 applications. In some, like Corel WordPerfect, Corel Presentations, and Corel Quattro Pro, more than one toolbar may appear on the screen at once.

Menu bar   **Toolbar**

FIG. 2.9

Each of the Corel
WordPerfect Suite 7
applications has similar
toolbars, and menu bars,
some of which are shown in
the Corel WordPerfect 7
screen.

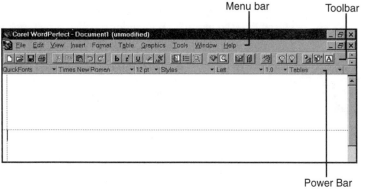

Power Bar

In all applications, you can rest the mouse pointer on the toolbar to see a QuickTip telling you what the tool is used for.

You can always invoke the toolbar feature by clicking the appropriate button. Buttons that are grayed out are for features that are not currently available. For instance, if you have nothing in the Clipboard, the paste icon will be grayed out because there is nothing to paste.

 T I P   In Corel WordPerfect, Corel Presentations, and Corel Quattro Pro, you can create and edit your own toolbars.

- *Power Bars.* Power Bars appear under the toolbar in Corel WordPerfect Suite 7 applications.

  By default, Power Bars show text, while toolbars display icons. You can change the display of the Power Bar from text to icons, if you like.

  Power Bars give you access to commonly used features, and depending on what function you are doing, items on the Power Bar may change. As with toolbars, Power Bar items that cannot be used at a given point in time will be grayed out.

Other screen elements that are shared across applications include:

- *Menus.* All the Corel WordPerfect Suite 7 applications have standard Windows 95 menus. In fact, as was discussed in Chapter 1, many of the menu items are identical from application to application.

  You can choose a menu item by clicking it with the mouse, or by using the shortcut key—holding down the Alt, Ctrl, or Shift key and pressing the underlined letter of the menu.

  Pull-down menus are used to organize the first level of commands. If a command offers a second level of command choices, a triangle appears beside the menu item, and a cascade menu appears at the side of the pull-down menu when the item is selected. If the menu item includes an ellipsis (...), the application needs more information to complete the command and displays a dialog box when the item is selected.

 T I P   In Corel WordPerfect and Corel Presentations, you can create and edit your own menus.

▶ **See** "Customizing Toolbars and Menus," **p. 733**

■ *QuickMenus.* You can right-click different parts of Corel WordPerfect Suite 7 application windows to see pop-up QuickMenus. QuickMenus offer context-appropriate options to help you do your work more quickly.

For instance, Figure 2.10 shows the QuickMenu that appears when you click in the text area of a Corel WordPerfect window.

FIG. 2.10
The QuickMenu, which displays when the text area of a Corel WordPerfect window is right-clicked, provides you with text-formatting options.

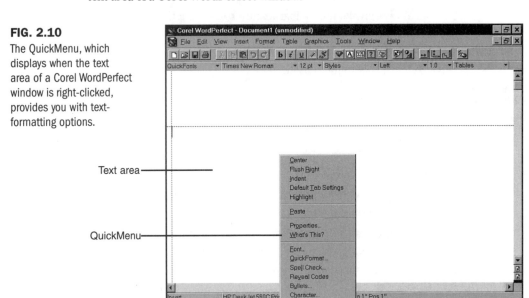

Text area

QuickMenu

Figure 2.11 shows the QuickMenu that appears when you click in the top margin.

N O T E   Technically, you click the *secondary mouse button* to access a QuickMenu. More than 98 percent of Windows users retain the default setting, or set their primary mouse button to be the left button, and the secondary mouse button to be the right mouse button. Therefore, in this book we refer to clicking the secondary mouse button as "right-clicking." If you have reversed the primary and secondary buttons for your mouse, make the appropriate adjustments throughout the book. ■

FIG. 2.11

The QuickMenu that appears when you click in the top margin provides options for adding headers and watermarks.

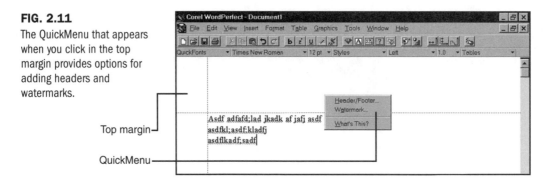

Top margin

QuickMenu

Using Help

The Corel WordPerfect Suite 7 offers many different ways to provide help to you. These include:

- Help Topics
- The PerfectExpert system
- Upgrade help
- Help online
- Context-sensitive help
- Reference manuals

Using Help Topics

Corel WordPerfect Suite 7 uses a standard Windows 95 help system; in other words, the Corel WordPerfect Suite 7 Help works the same way as it does in any other Windows 95 application.

To access the Help system, choose Help from the menu; or press F1. What you see differs somewhat depending on the application you are in, but is similar to the Corel WordPerfect Help dialog box shown in Figure 2.12. Five different types of help are offered: Contents, Index, Find, Show Me, and Ask the PerfectExpert.

> **N O T E** Some of the supplementary applications, such as Envoy, Dashboard, and Sidekick, do not implement all help features discussed in this section; in addition, Corel Quattro Pro's Help feature differs in some slight respects from those of Corel WordPerfect and Corel Presentations. If you understand the Help options in this section, however, you will easily be able to obtain help in the other applications. ■

FIG. 2.12

The Help Topics: WordPerfect Help dialog box provides tabs offering five different types of help.

Contents The Contents tab of the Help dialog box acts like a table of contents for your help system, displaying major categories of help topics. For instance, as shown in Figure 2.13, the How Do I section shows a list of common tasks for Corel Presentations. About the Features provides an alphabetical feature list, while What's New or Changed (not shown) and Troubleshooting (not shown) provide help on special topics. You also see help for Macros which provides specialized help with recording macros or programming them using PerfectScript.

FIG. 2.13

How Do I, which is available in the Help Topics: Corel Presentations Help dialog box, lists common tasks you perform in the application.

To use the Contents:

1. Choose Help, Help Topics, and ensure that you are in the Contents tab.

2. Double-click the major topic (like How Do I), then double-click the desired subtopic (like Basics).

3. You may see further subtopics (denoted by a book icon), or help documents (pieces of paper with a question mark on them). Double-click the subtopic or document you want to see.

Index If the Contents tab is like a table of contents for your help system that lists major topics, the Index tab works like the index you might find in the back of a book. It lists key words that you find throughout the help system, and enables you to quickly go to the help you need, even if it isn't a major help topic. The Index for Corel Quattro Pro is shown in Figure 2.14.

FIG. 2.14

The Help Index alphabetically lists all the keywords in the help system of each application, like the one shown here for Corel Quattro Pro.

To use the index feature, choose Help, Help Topics, and ensure that you are in the Index tab. Type the word you're looking for in the Type The First Few Letters Of The Word You're Looking For box. You see topics related to the desired term in the Index Entry box. Select the appropriate term, then click Display.

 The index feature is particularly helpful when the topic you want is not listed in the Contents.

Find The Find tab uses another Windows 95 help feature—an indexed list of every word in the help system. The first time you use the Find feature, a wizard asks you a few

Part
I
Ch
2

questions, then all the words in the help file are indexed. After this is done, a word list is created, and you can search for any word in the help file—not just the ones the help file authors included in the index. The Corel WordPerfect Help Find tab is shown in Figure 2.15.

FIG. 2.15
Use the Find tab in your application's Help Topics dialog box when the topic you want is not in the Contents or Index.

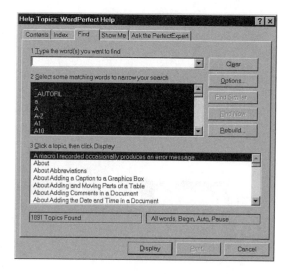

To use Find, choose Help, Help Topics, and ensure that you are in the Find tab. Type the word you want to find, then in the Select Matching Words box, select the term that best fits what you're looking for. You see a list of related topics in the Topic box. Select the most appropriate topic, then click Display.

 TIP While you are reading a Help screen, you can click an icon to see a definition of that icon. Underlined words are hypertext linked to other topics. If a word is hypertext linked, it means you can click that underlined word to jump to help on that topic.

 TIP In Help, a term with a dotted underline is a glossary term. You can click it to see its definition.

Using the PerfectExpert System

The PerfectExpert system is a new Help feature in Corel WordPerfect Suite 7. It allows you to ask questions in plain English and offers three ways to get information. You can see an animated demonstration, have a Guide assist you through the menu items, or use the Do It For Me feature to select a QuickTask to automatically perform a variety of tasks.

Ask the PerfectExpert   The Ask the PerfectExpert feature allows you to formulate queries in plain English. The PerfectExpert will interpret your question and display a number of help topics that may assist you.

To use the PerfectExpert, choose Help, Help Topics, then select the Ask the PerfectExpert tab. You see the Ask the PerfectExpert dialog box shown in Figure 2.16.

FIG. 2.16

PerfectExpert allows you to frame queries in plain English in the Ask the PerfectExpert dialog box.

Ask your question just as you would ask a help desk person, for example, type **How do I start page numbering with a new page?** When you click the Search button, you will see a number of topics that may assist you displayed at the bottom of the dialog box in Figure 2.16. Select the one that addresses your question most directly, then choose Display.

Play a Demo   If you have the CD version of Corel WordPerfect Suite 7, you can play a video demonstration of several Corel WordPerfect functions. To do so, ensure that your Corel WordPerfect Suite CD is inserted in your CD player, then choose Help, Help Topics. Click the Show Me tab, and select the Play a Demo option button. You see a list of available demonstrations in the list box, or if the CD is not loaded, you are prompted to load it, as shown in Figure 2.17. Select the demonstration you want to see, then click the Display button.

Guide Me Through It   You may prefer to obtain assistance in performing a new function in a real document that you are working on. If so, Guide Me Through It is for you. This feature shows dialog boxes that take you through the process step-by-step, and even show you where you will find the next step on each menu or dialog box.

FIG. 2.17

You can access demonstrations of Corel WordPerfect functions from the Show Me tab of the Help Topics dialog box if you have the CD version of Corel WordPerfect Suite 7.

To use Guide Me Through It, choose Help, Help Topics. Click the Show Me tab, and select the Guide Me Through It option button. You see a list of 25 topics from which you can choose, as shown in Figure 2.18. Select the desired topic, then click the Display button.

FIG. 2.18

The Show Me tab is where the Guide Me Through It feature is found. This feature helps you learn new features in real documents, showing you dialog boxes and prompts at each step.

In the first step of the Guide, you will be asked whether you want to be guided through each step of the task, or have the Guide do the steps for you. If you choose the first option, you will be told which menu item or dialog box option to pick, but you will need to actually perform the step, as shown in Figure 2.19.

FIG. 2.19
Guide Me Through It is
available for a number of
common tasks.

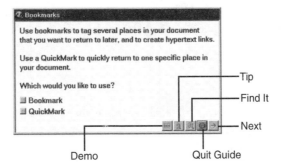

Tip

Find It

Next

Demo

Quit Guide

At different points in the process, buttons at the bottom of the Guide dialog box will be active, as shown in Table 2.2.

Table 2.2   Guide Me Through It Buttons

Button	Function
	Demo. Shows a CD-based demonstration of the function.
	Find It. Automates the selection of the next command.
	Tip. Provides a tip on choices you might want to make.
	Quit Guide. Stop the guide and return to your document.
	Next. Go to the next step.

If you choose Find It, the Guide will point to the necessary item and prompt you to click the mouse. For example, in the Bookmark guide, at the first point Find It is active, it will move the mouse pointer to the Insert Menu, open the menu, then move the mouse pointer to Bookmark and prompt you to click the bookmark entry.

Do It For Me   The Do It For Me button can be found on the Show Me tab of the Help Topics dialog box. This feature lists the QuickTasks, and allows you to start them. QuickTasks are discussed in detail in Chapter 33, "Integrating Your Work with QuickTasks."

Upgrade Help   If you are upgrading from a previous version of Corel WordPerfect, Quattro Pro, or Presentations, or from a competitive product, you may find the Upgrade Help very useful. Access Upgrade Help by choosing Help, Upgrade Help. You see the Upgrade Help dialog box.

Part
I

Ch
2

Choose the product from which you are upgrading. You see a list of features. Click the feature you want to find help on, and you see help in the text box on the right of the dialog box.

Using Help Online

With Help Online, you can immediately access the Corel documentation site on the Internet, or the Corel WordPerfect forum on Compuserve Information Services, if you have the proper configuration.

ON THE WEB

http://www.wordperfect.com/products/frame_wp7.htm   WordPerfect help can be found at this address.

The Corel Internet site contains links to the Reference Center, from which you can download manuals and system administration information. You can also follow links to Corel Technical Information Documents, as well as tips and tricks for using the Corel WordPerfect Suite effectively. To link to the Corel Internet site, you must have an Internet connection via your network or a dial-up connection, and a Web browser such as Microsoft Explorer or Netscape Navigator.

The Compuserve connection takes you to the users' forums that discuss the use of Corel WordPerfect Suite 7. To link to Compuserve, you must have a Compuserve account and the WinCIM software that connects you to Compuserve.

ON THE WEB

www.CorelNET.com   If you are linked to the Internet, you may want to investigate this address, which hosts a number of moderated discussion groups.

If you are attached to a network that has a high-speed connection to the Internet, you will find Help Online especially valuable, as you can access it almost as quickly and easily as the Help files that are on your local hard disk or network.

To access Help Online:

1. Choose Help, Help Online. You see the Help Online dialog box shown in Figure 2.20.

2. Choose Internet or Compuserve in the Select A Service box.

3. Choose Connect. Your Web Browser or Compuserve software starts, and you are connected to the appropriate online service, such as the Netscape connection to Corel's Web site.

FIG. 2.20
You can choose to connect to the Internet or Compuserve for Help Online in the Help Online dialog box.

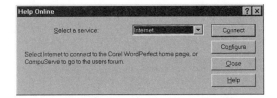

Using Context-Sensitive Help

Context-sensitive help is available throughout the Corel WordPerfect Suite 7 applications. In many dialog boxes, you will see a Help button like the one shown in the Corel WordPerfect Style List dialog box shown in Figure 2.21.

FIG. 2.21
Help buttons appear in many dialog boxes.

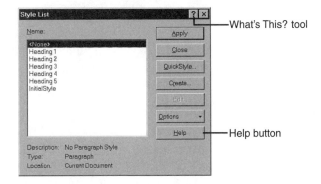

Choosing Help displays assistance for the function you are working on. In addition, even when there is no Help button, you can often receive context-sensitive help by pressing the Help key (F1).

Many dialog boxes also have a What's This? tool. If you click this tool, your mouse pointer changes to a pointer with a question mark. You can point at different objects in the active window or dialog box and click them to receive help on that specific object.

N O T E One other way that you can get context-sensitive help when you are not in a dialog box is to right-click an area of the active window to bring up the QuickMenu. The QuickMenu often has a What's This? choice. ▪

Reference Manuals

If you loaded Corel WordPerfect Suite 7 from CD, you have reference manuals online, in the *Reference Center*. You may have even installed them to your local hard drive or network workspace.

To access the Reference Center, choose Start, Corel WordPerfect Suite 7, Accessories, Reference Center. You see the Reference Center dialog box shown in Figure 2.22.

FIG. 2.22
The Reference Center provides reference materials for Suite applications.

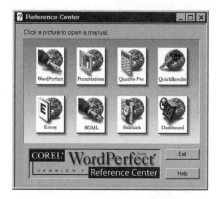

Double-click any icon. The reference book is brought up in the Envoy viewer. You can click items in the table of contents to go to the area of interest, read the book cover to cover, or even search for specific keywords throughout the electronic manual.

▶ **See** "Viewing and Annotating Envoy Files," **p. 587**

If you purchased the product individually (as opposed to being in an organization that has a site license), you also have paper manuals. These include the Corel WordPerfect Suite 7 Quick Results booklet (a task-oriented introduction to the Suite), a clip art book that provides thumbnail pictures of all the clip art included with the Suite, and a fonts pamphlet that shows you what the included fonts look like. ●

CHAPTER 3

Using Common Corel WordPerfect Suite 7 Tools

Even if you will be using only one or two Corel WordPerfect Suite 7 applications, you will want to skim through this chapter. Writing tools appear throughout Corel WordPerfect Suite 7. This chapter and Chapter 4, "Managing Files," detail the commonalities you will find. ∎

Using a QuickTask

Learn how to use QuickTasks, Visual Basic applications that integrate Corel WordPerfect Suite 7 applications to perform common tasks.

Using QuickCorrect

Find out how you can correct your spelling as you go.

Using Spell Checker, Thesaurus, and Grammatik

Learn how to use powerful tools to improve your writing including a spelling checker, a thesaurus that doubles as a dictionary, and an electronic editor that helps make your writing more concise and persuasive.

Using QuickMenus

Find out how to access common functions quickly with QuickMenus.

Using QuickTasks

As you learned in Chapter 1, QuickTasks are Visual Basic applications that integrate Corel WordPerfect Suite 7 applications to assist you in performing common office tasks.

To use a QuickTask, follow these steps:

1. Click the QuickTasks button on the Desktop Application Director (DAD) bar. Alternatively, if you are not using the DAD bar, choose Start, Corel WordPerfect Suite 7, Accessories, Corel QuickTasks. You see the QuickTasks dialog box shown in Figure 3.1.

   ▶ **See** "Displaying DAD," **p. 24**

FIG. 3.1

QuickTasks walk you through common office functions with the click of a mouse.

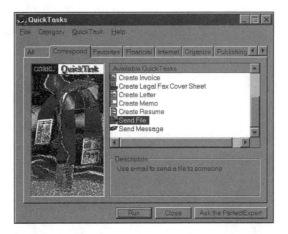

2. Choose the tab for the category of QuickTask that you want to use.
3. Select the QuickTask in the Available QuickTasks list box. A description of the QuickTask appears in the Description area.
4. Choose Run. Any appropriate application(s) will be loaded, and you can follow the prompts to accomplish the task.

N O T E Some QuickTasks assume that you do, in fact, have other elements of the system installed on your system. For example, the Send File QuickTask assumes that an e-mail system has been installed and the Create Time Line QuickTask uses CorelFLOW. If you have done a custom install and not included all of the features of Corel WordPerfect Suite 7, or have not installed all of the Bonus Applications on the CD, then some QuickTasks will give you an error. You will need to install those missing applications to accomplish such tasks through QuickTasks. ■

Refer to Chapter 33, "Integrating Your Work with QuickTasks" for a more detailed description and examples of QuickTasks.

▶ **See** "Taking a Guided Tour of Some QuickTasks," **p. 711**

Using the Writing Tools

Corel WordPerfect Suite 7 offers you powerful tools to assist you in producing a document that looks like it was crafted by a professional. These tools include QuickCorrect, Spell Checker, Thesaurus, and Grammatik.

Using QuickCorrect

Part

I

Ch

3

QuickCorrect is an intelligent writing tool that helps you avoid common spelling and grammar errors as you type. It maintains a list of commonly misspelled words, and automatically corrects them as you type.

You can also use QuickCorrect to automatically expand abbreviations, if you add the abbreviation to your list of common misspellings.

QuickCorrect is presently found in Corel WordPerfect, Corel Presentations, and Corel Quattro Pro.

 T I P The same QuickCorrect dictionary is used in all applications. Thus, once you define an automatic correction, it will be made in all applications using QuickCorrect.

QuickCorrect enables you to maintain a list of abbreviations and commonly misspelled words, then automatically replaces these with the correct term or word as you type.

N O T E QuickCorrect uses your personal word list to store misspelled words and abbreviations. So, if you're on a network, the additions you make to QuickCorrect will not affect how other people's QuickCorrect works. ■

To use QuickCorrect, you need to know how to turn on QuickCorrect, maintain a list of misspelled words, and set options.

Turning on QuickCorrect   To turn on QuickCorrect:

1. Choose Tools, QuickCorrect. You see the QuickCorrect dialog box (see Figure 3.2).
2. Check the Replace Words As You Type check box, if it is not already checked. Now, any commonly misspelled words you have identified will automatically be replaced as you type.

FIG. 3.2

QuickCorrect will correct common spelling errors, found in the list in the QuickCorrect dialog box, on-the-fly, as you type.

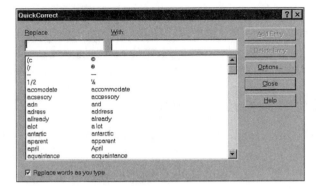

Maintaining the List of Commonly Misspelled Words   To add words to the commonly misspelled word list:

1. Access the QuickCorrect dialog box (seen in Figure 3.2).

2. Type a word you often misspell, or an abbreviation you want to have automatically expanded, in the Replace text box.

> **CAUTION**
>
> Be careful when you add abbreviations to this list. The abbreviation will *always* be replaced by its expanded term; thus, you will not be able to use the abbreviation in this or any other document.

3. Type the correct spelling, or the expanded term, in the With text box.

4. Click Add Entry. You see the term in the alphabetical list of commonly misspelled words.

▶ **See** "Using QuickCorrect," **p. 149**

Setting QuickCorrect Options   If you choose Options from the QuickCorrect dialog box, you see the QuickCorrect Options dialog box (see Figure 3.3). You can choose from among the following capitalization and punctuation options:

■ *Sentence Corrections.* You can automatically capitalize the first letter of each sentence, prevent the first two letters of a word from being capitalized, or change any double space within a sentence to a single space.

■ *End of Sentence Corrections.* You can change a sentence that ends with a single space to a double space, or change a double space to a single space.

 Though most people do not know it, current American typographical convention calls for a single space between sentences when using proportional fonts.

FIG. 3.3
QuickCorrect options found in the QuickCorrect Options dialog box even include capitalizing the first letter of sentences, and adjusting the number of spaces after a period.

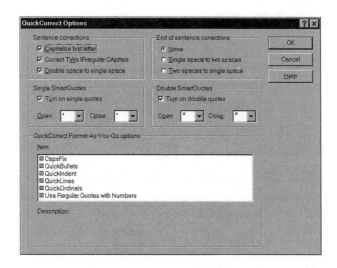

■ *Single SmartQuotes.* This option automatically changes apostrophes to single open and single closed quotes. (The first apostrophe is changed to a single open quote, the next to a single closed quote.)

 TIP Turning on Single SmartQuotes will not cause apostrophes used in possessive words (for example, Sam's) to be turned into SmartQuote symbols.

■ *Double SmartQuotes.* This option automatically changes the first " to a double open quote ("), and the next one to a double closed quote (").

N O T E With both the Single and Double SmartQuotes options, you can turn the option on by selecting the appropriate check box. You can also specify the character to be used for the SmartQuote symbols. ■

You may also make a selection from a list of other formatting options by clicking the box next to your choice to select it:

■ *CapsFix.* This option turns off your caps lock and corrects the capitalization if you accidentally have it turned on. (tHIS becomes This.)

■ *QuickBullets.* Changes lines beginning with numbers (1, I, a., and so on) to numbered lists, and lines beginning with characters such as * or o to bulleted lists.

■ *QuickIndent.* If you have a paragraph that begins with a tab, and at the beginning of the second or subsequent lines you press Tab, the entire paragraph will be indented. If you have a paragraph that is not tabbed on the first line, pressing Tab on the second or subsequent lines results in a hanging indent for the paragraph.

- *QuickLines.* Creates a horizontal line from margin to margin if you begin a line with — or ===.

- *QuickOrdinals.* Changes 1st into 1ˢᵗ.

- *Use Regular Quotes with Numbers.* This option enables you to use a straight single or double quote following a number.

TROUBLESHOOTING

How can I stop QuickCorrect from un-capitalizing PCs? It changes them to Pcs. You can do this in three ways: First, you can disable irregular case-checking by choosing Tools, QuickCorrect, Options, Correct TWo Irregular Capitals. However, you may want the feature on for other potential errors.

Second, you can position the insertion point back on the c of Pcs and change it to a C. QuickCorrect will not override this edit.

Third, you can add the term "Pcs" to the QuickCorrect dictionary, and replace it with "PCs."

Checking Your Spelling

You can access the spelling checker from Corel WordPerfect Suite 7 applications including Corel WordPerfect, Corel Quattro Pro, and Corel Presentations. The spelling checker is a common one, which means that all applications check from the same word lists.

N O T E Sidekick uses a different spelling checker than other Corel WordPerfect Suite 7 components. Envoy and Dashboard have no spelling checker. ■

The Spelling Checker checks words in your application against lists of words called *word lists.* There are three different types of word lists that the Spell Checker uses:

- *Main word list.* This is the word list that ships with the Corel WordPerfect Suite 7. If you purchase additional language modules, you will have additional main word lists for the other languages. You can also purchase additional word lists that have been created for specialty terms, like those in the legal field.

- *User word list.* When you add a word, it is added to a user-created list of words called the user word list. You may specify the file that these additional words are added to; thus, you can create any number of user word lists for different users or for different aspects of your job. The user word list is also the list that is used for the QuickCorrect feature.

- *Document word list* (in Corel WordPerfect only). When you use the Skip Always option in the Spell Checker, the word is added to a list of words that is stored with the document itself. Thus, when you check the spelling of the document again, these words are skipped.

Using the Spell Checker involves two skills:

- Setting the spelling check options
- Conducting a spelling check

 Setting Spell Checker Options   Before you start checking spelling, you can establish a few rules to govern how Spell Checker operates on the text. To set Spell Checker options, choose Tools, Spell Check or click the Spell Check button on the toolbar. You see the Writing Tools dialog box in Corel Presentations (see Figure 3.4) and Corel Quattro Pro, or the docked Spell Checker at the bottom of the screen in Corel WordPerfect.

Part

I

Ch

3

FIG. 3.4
The Writing Tools dialog box in Corel Presentations allows you to access the Spell Checker, Grammatik, and the Thesaurus.

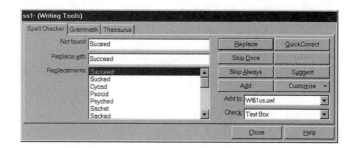

From the Spell Checker dialog box, if you choose Customize, you choose from several ways to customize the way the spelling checker works:

- *User Word Lists*. Allows you to add additional User Word Lists that should be used in spell checking your document.

- *Main Word Lists*. Allows you to add additional Main Word Lists to be used in spell checking your document.

- *Language*. Allows you to specify the language preference that should be used in spell checking your document.

- *Auto Start*. Starts spell checking when the Spell Checker dialog box is opened from within an application.

- *Beep on Misspelled*. Beeps when a misspelled word is found.

- *Recheck all Text*. Checks all text, not just text that has not yet been checked.

- *Check Words with Numbers*. When selected, Spell Checker stops at words containing numbers. (This was needed more often when people confused 1s and ls. In some types of modern writing—such as computer manuals—many terms do contain numbers, so you may want to disable this feature.)

- *Check Duplicate Words.* When selected, Spell Checker stops when the same word is repeated twice.

- *Check Irregular Capitalization.* When selected, Spell Checker stops at words with odd capitalization, such as ANd or tHe. (Again, computer writers writing Corel WordPerfect books probably wouldn't like this option!)

- *Prompt Before Auto Replacement.* If unchecked, automatically replaces words that are in a supplementary dictionary and have a replacement term.

Conducting a Spell Check   To conduct a spell check, follow these steps:

1. In Corel WordPerfect, Corel Presentations, or Corel Quattro Pro, make sure the text you want to check is on-screen.

2. Choose Tools, Spell Check or click the Spell Check button on the toolbar. You see the Spell Checker dialog box or Spell Checker at the bottom of the screen in Corel WordPerfect (see Figure 3.5).

FIG. 3.5

The Spell Checker is available in Corel WordPerfect, Corel Presentations, and Corel Quattro Pro.

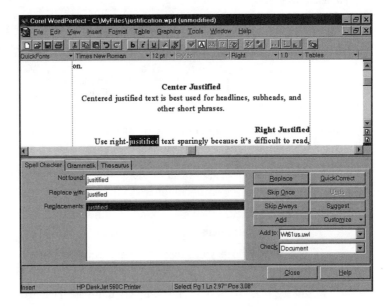

3. The spell checking procedure may start automatically, depending on how options have been set. If it does not, choose Start.

4. As the spelling check begins, you have the following options when the Spell Checker pauses at each misspelled word:

> *Replace.* Select a word in the Replacements list. It appears in the Replace With box. Alternatively, enter a word in the Replace With box. Click Replace. The misspelled word in the document is replaced with the specified word.

Skip Once. Skip the word this time, but stop if it appears again in the text being checked.

Skip Always. Skip the word wherever it appears in the text. (In Corel WordPerfect, this will also add the word to the document dictionary.)

QuickCorrect. If you select a word in the Replacements list, then choose QuickCorrect; the misspelled word and corrected word are added to the QuickCorrect list. (See the previous section "Using QuickCorrect" for details.)

Suggest. This displays any additional possible corrected words in the Suggest list box.

Add. This option adds the word to the selected user word list. The word is then always skipped when you spell check any other document.

Add To: Enables you to change the supplementary dictionary file that words are added to.

Check: Offers you the choice of checking the entire file or a portion of it.

▶ **See** "Using the Spelling Checker," **p. 148**

5. When the spelling check is completed, click Close to close the Spell Checker and return to your application.

Using the Thesaurus

You can use Corel WordPerfect Suite 7's Thesaurus to find synonyms and antonyms of selected words in Corel WordPerfect and Corel Presentations.

▶ **See** "Using the Thesaurus," **p. 151**

To use the Thesaurus, follow these steps:

1. Place your insertion point in the word for which you want to find a synonym or antonym. If you are in Corel Presentations, you should be in the Outline view or in the Slide view with a text box selected.

2. Choose Tools, Thesaurus. You see the Thesaurus in a docked dialog Writing Tools box in the lower half of the editing window (Corel WordPerfect) or in the Writing Tools dialog box (Corel Presentations), like the one in Figure 3.6.

TIP To undock the dialog box in WordPerfect, position your mouse pointer at the top of the dialog box until the pointer becomes a hand, then drag the dialog box to the middle of the screen.

3. Highlight the word you want to use as the replacement, and choose Replace. You return to your application, and the selected word is replaced with the one chosen from the Thesaurus.

Part
I

Ch
3

FIG. 3.6
Choose synonyms or
antonyms with the
Thesaurus.

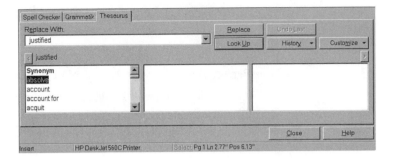

While you are in the Thesaurus, you can also double-click any suggested synonym. If it is
in the Thesaurus, you will see synonyms for *this* word in the next column. You then can
pick a replacement word and choose Replace.

If you repeat this process several times, you will need more than the three columns provided in the Thesaurus. You can then use the left and right buttons to move from column
to column, as shown in Figure 3.7.

FIG. 3.7
Find synonyms for related
words by double-clicking
them.

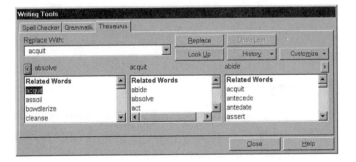

 If you have another language module, you may have alternate Thesaurus dictionary choices.

 TROUBLESHOOTING

**Why isn't the Thesaurus on the Corel WordPerfect toolbar like the Spell Checker and
Grammar Checker?** I don't know. However, if you use the Thesaurus a lot, you can easily put it on
the toolbar in Corel WordPerfect or Corel Presentations. To do so, right-click the toolbar, then
choose Edit. With the Edit Toolbar dialog box on the screen, choose the Tools feature category,
then choose Thesaurus, and click Add Button. The new button appears on your toolbar. Click OK
to return to the application.

Checking Grammar

Grammatik, Corel WordPerfect Suite 7's grammar checker, can prove to be an invaluable tool to help you refine your writing style. It can be accessed within Corel WordPerfect and Corel Presentations by choosing Tools, Grammatik.

To use Grammatik in a Corel WordPerfect Suite 7 application, follow these steps:

1. Open the file you want to check.

2. Choose Tools, Grammatik. You see Grammatik in the lower half of the window in Corel WordPerfect, as shown in Figure 3.8, or in a dialog box in Corel Presentations.

FIG. 3.8
Grammatik will not only flag potential errors, it will suggest corrections for you.

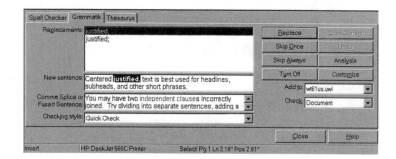

Part

I

Ch

3

3. Grammatik automatically starts checking your document for grammar and spelling errors. When an error is found, Grammatik will make a change (if possible). You may then choose:

   - *Replace* to accept the change to your document.
   - *Skip Once* or *Skip Always* to ignore the error one time or throughout the document.
   - *Add* to add the misspelled word to Grammatik's dictionary.
   - *Undo* to undo your last change.

4. When you are finished, click Close.

▶ **See** "Checking Grammar," **p. 152**

While you are in Grammatik, you may choose from the following options to customize the way the grammar checker works:

■ Choose Customize, Checking Style to select from among the 10 predefined styles.

 TIP

To see the specifications for each predefined checking style, select a checking style and choose Edit from the Checking Styles dialog box.

■ Choose T̲urn Off to turn off a particular grammatical rule, turn it back on, or save the set of rules as a new checking style.

You can see some very interesting statistics on your document by choosing Analy̲sis from the Grammatik window. You see a pop-up menu offering several choices, the most useful of which is B̲asic Counts. This feature tells you how many words, sentences, paragraphs, syllables per word, words per sentences, and so on, are in your document. F̲lagged indicates how many times each rule class was violated in your document. R̲eadability compares your document to a Hemingway short story, an IRS form, the Gettysburg Address, or any other document you specify in terms of reading level and complexity. Refer to the Corel online help for in-depth coverage of these features.

▶ **See** "Checking Grammar," **p. 152**

Using QuickMenus

QuickMenus are pop-up menus that appear when you click the right mouse button in selected areas within Corel WordPerfect Suite 7 applications. QuickMenus display context-sensitive options. For instance, the QuickMenu displayed when right-clicking a Corel Quattro Pro cell is shown in Figure 3.9. It offers the options most used while entering and formatting data in a spreadsheet.

FIG. 3.9
QuickMenus are accessed by clicking the right mouse button, and offer context-sensitive options.

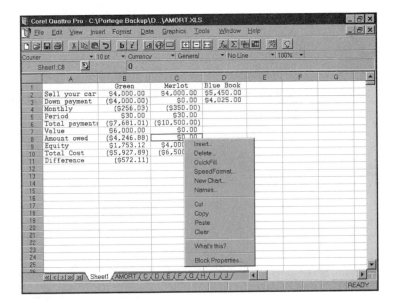

Alternatively, the QuickMenu accessible from the main Corel WordPerfect document window is shown in Figure 3.10. It provides options used in creating, editing, and formatting text.

FIG. 3.10

These options are available from the QuickMenu at the main editing window of Corel WordPerfect.

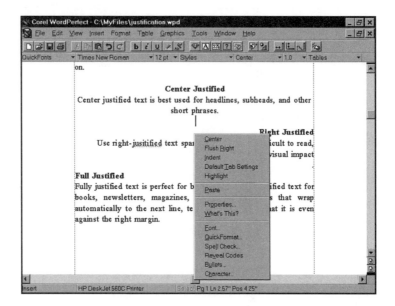

Using QuickMenus is often more efficient than selecting the same options from a menu or toolbar, because you do not need to move the mouse as much. Though it doesn't seem like much, you will quickly find that when you get used to QuickMenus, they can improve your efficiency significantly. ●

CHAPTER 4

Managing Files

Can you imagine an administrative assistant who stacks
all correspondence, outgoing letters, internal memos,
and other paperwork in one large drawer? What would
happen if everyone in a department did this, using a
large, common box? We can predict that this organization would not be able to function effectively!

Yet, many of us maintain our electronic files in an
equivalent shambles. In this chapter, you learn how to
use tools that enable you to create an effective electronic filing system. ■

Basic file management

Find out how to do basic file management operations such as saving,
opening, and closing files.

**Manage your electronic filing
system**

Create, rename, and remove folders;
also copy, move, rename, delete,
print, and assign attributes to files.

Find files

Find files quickly using Favorites
and QuickFinder.

Saving, Opening, and Closing Files

When you create a Corel WordPerfect document, Corel Quattro Pro spreadsheet, or Corel Presentations slideshow, you are working with a *file*. Files can exist in your computer's memory and on disks. You can think of these electronic files like their paper counterparts.

Your computer's memory is like the surface of a desk that for security reasons is cleared off at the end of the day, and everything on it put into the shredder. You can work on files while they are on your desktop. You can create files, add information to them, or send them to other people. But at the end of the day, unless you put them away, they will be destroyed. In many companies, paper files can't stay on the desktop after hours. Similarly, electronic files are destroyed when you turn off your computer, or exit the program that creates them.

N O T E   For those of you who aren't computer "techies," *memory* is the working area of your computer. When you are using programs, they are loaded into memory. When you open a file, it is loaded into memory. The programs and data that are in memory are lost when you turn off your computer.

Disks, whether they are floppy disks, local (in your own computer) hard disks, or network drives, are storage areas. You do not "run" programs from the disk. You load a program from the disk into memory when you open it. Then, when it is in memory, you can use it. Similarly, you load data from your disk into memory to access it. Data on disks is maintained even when you turn off your computer. ■

 T I P   Memory is the generic term for Random Access Memory, or RAM.

Your disk is like your file cabinet. You can keep files in it indefinitely—until it gets full. Then, you can add another file cabinet, until your office gets full of cabinets! The better idea is to purge files in your file cabinet periodically, so that you only keep the ones you need. Until you take a file from the file drawer and put it on your desk, however, you can't work on it. Similarly, electronic files can stay on a disk indefinitely, but until you load them into memory, you can't work on them.

In fact, the analogy can be carried further; you can think of each disk drive as a file cabinet. Each disk can contain folders—like file cabinets contain file drawers. Each drawer can contain hanging folders and/or loose sheets of paper, while electronic folders can contain subfolders and/or files. Each hanging folder can contain manila folders and/or sheets of paper, while electronic subfolders can contain other subfolders and/or files.

N O T E In Windows 95, the term "directories" that was used in previous versions of Windows and DOS has been changed to "folders." Users of previous versions can think of folders just as they used to think about directories. ▪

Thus, whether you are working in Corel WordPerfect, Corel Quattro Pro, Corel Presentations, or other Corel WordPerfect Suite 7 applications, you need to save your work if you want to be able to access it after you turn off your computer. You also need to be able to retrieve it from the disk into memory when you want to edit it again.

N O T E In most applications, files exist only in memory until they are saved. If you work on a spreadsheet and add 100 rows of information without saving your work, then the power goes off, you will lose that work. This is true in WordPerfect, Presentations, Quattro Pro, and CorelFLOW. Databases work somewhat differently. Once the database is created, each record is saved on the disk as it is created or edited. Thus, the most information you would lose in a power failure would be changes to the current record. ▪

Saving Files

Saving a file is like taking a copy of it from your desktop and putting it into a file drawer. To save a file means storing it on a disk—either a floppy disk, your local hard drive, or a network drive. After you save a file, it exists in two places—in memory and on the disk, until the program you used to create it is exited and/or the machine is turned off. Then you only have the file that you have saved.

 In all Corel WordPerfect Suite 7 applications, you can save the file you are working on by choosing File, Save. If the toolbar is displayed, you can also click the Save button.

N O T E A path plus a file name (the drive, folder, and file name) can be up to 255 characters long and can have an optional extension of up to three characters. The name can contain any combination of letters and numbers, except the following:

" / \ : * ? " < > | "

Don't use any other special characters, such as commas or backslashes. Also, don't use any of the following names, which are reserved by DOS for its own use: CLOCK$, COM1, COM2, COM3, COM4, CON, AUX, LPT1, LPT2, LPT3, LPT4, NUL, or PRN. ▪

CAUTION
Be careful in using long file names. Many network operating systems do not support file names longer than eight characters. Consider using no more than eight characters in your file names and no spaces, if you are using such a network.

The first time you save a file, you see a Save File dialog box (see Figure 4.1). Type the name of the file in the Name box and click Save to save your work.

FIG. 4.1

The first time you save a file, you see the Save File dialog box, enabling you to give the file a name.

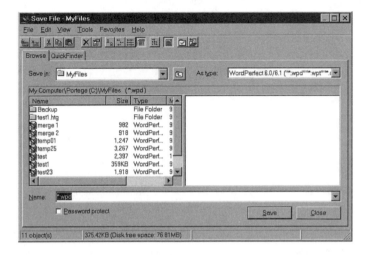

 T I P   As you start saving more and more files, you will want to create electronic folders to organize your files. If you don't choose a folder, your files are saved in the default folder at first. If you change the folder you are saving your files in, additional files will continue to be saved to that new folder until you exit the application. Then, the next time you open the application, files will be saved in the default folder again.

You can also save the file on a different drive and/or in a different folder as explained in the section, "Using File Management Dialog Boxes," later in this chapter.

When you continue working in the same document and want to save your work again, choose File, Save, or click the Save button on the toolbar again. You do not see a dialog box. The operation happens immediately. When you resave your work in this way, the first version is replaced on the disk by the second; thus, the earlier file is lost.

 T I P   Be sure that you don't mind losing your earlier version before pressing the Save button on the toolbar. Your new version will replace the old on the disk without prompting you to ensure you aren't making a mistake. If you want to save both versions, you must use Save As (see next paragraph).

To save both versions, you need to either save the second one with a different name, or in a different folder. You cannot have two files with the same name in the same folder. Choose File, Save As to rename the latter version. You will see the Save As dialog box, and you can rename the document or specify a different folder prior to saving it.

Opening Files

Opening a file is like taking a copy of it from your file drawer and putting it on your desk. It then exists in two places—in the file drawer and on your desk. When you make changes to it, the original is still safely in the file drawer. The original copy in the file drawer is only changed when you save the edited version again.

 Thus, when you open a file, you are retrieving a copy of the file from the disk to your computer's memory. In all Corel WordPerfect Suite 7 applications, you can open a file by choosing File, Open. If the toolbar is displayed, you may also click the Open button. In either case, you see an Open File dialog box similar to the one shown in Figure 4.2. Instructions for choosing files from this dialog box are found in the section "Using File Management Dialog Boxes" later in this chapter.

FIG. 4.2

Choose files to open from the Open File dialog box, which also provides many file management capabilities.

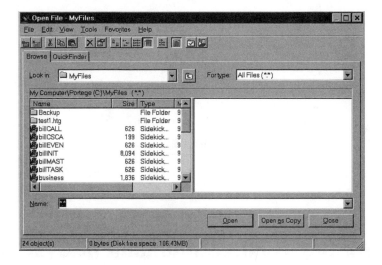

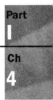

Part

I

Ch

4

N O T E The title bar of file management dialog boxes includes the current folder name, "Open File - MyFiles" or "Save File - Backup." What you see on the title bar will depend on what your default folder is. To prevent confusion, this book will refer to file management dialog boxes only by their function, for example, "Open File" or "Save File." ■

Closing Files

Closing a file is like taking it off of your desktop and shredding it. If you have saved it prior to closing it, it is in your file cabinet (or electronically, on your disk). Otherwise, it is gone for good.

Thus, when you close a file, you are erasing it from your computer's memory. In Corel WordPerfect Suite 7 applications, you close a file by choosing File, Close. If the file has been edited since it was last saved, you will be prompted to save it prior to closing it. Unless you want to lose your work, it's a good idea to do so!

N O T E When you close an application, you will also close any open files in that application. Thus, when you close an application that has modified, open files, you will be prompted to save them before the application closes. ▨

TROUBLESHOOTING

Why isn't there a button to close a file like there is to save or open a file? There is—but it's not on the toolbar.

- You can double-click the control menu button that is on the left side of the menu bar to close the active document.

  There are actually two control menu buttons. The one on the left of the title bar is the application control menu button. Double-clicking it closes the application. The lower one on the menu bar is the control menu button that controls the document.

- You can single-click the Close button (the button with the X on it) on the right side of the menu bar.

You can also put a button on your toolbar to close a document in most Corel WordPerfect Suite 7 applications.

▶ **See** "Creating and Editing Toolbars and Menu Bars" **p. 740**

Creating a File Management System

File management dialog boxes allow you to manipulate files and folders with ease. Before learning *how* to do this, however, it's a good idea to start by understanding *what* you might want to do.

In creating an electronic filing system, it's important to think through several issues:

- Which drive you should save your files on
- What folders you should have
- How you should name your files

Choosing a Drive

You will generally have up to four choices for types of disk drives to save your files on: floppy disks, local hard drive (the hard drive in your computer), network drives (if you're on a network), and the Internet or a corporate intranet (if you are so connected).

Floppy Drives   In the past, most people saved their work on floppy disks, and are used to doing this. It seems reasonable; you use a different floppy disk for each subject, and it's easy to stay organized. If someone else needs the file, you hand them the disk. This process keeps the hard disk from filling up.

A short piece of advice: *Stop thinking this way.*

If you exchange files often, you should be working on a network. Hard disks hold 10 to 20 times more than they used to; if your hard disk keeps filling up, you should either have a high-capacity hard disk, or better yet, archive and purge your files periodically like you do with your paper filing system. If you want to stay organized, use folders rather than individual floppies.

There are several reasons to use hard drives rather than floppy drives, which are explained in the following sections. Floppy drives are good in three circumstances:

- Taking files off-site to work on them.
- Archiving old files when you don't have access to a tape backup or other mass storage devices for archiving purposes.
- Creating backup copies of critical data that can be stored elsewhere and retrieved if necessary in a disaster recovery situation.

Part
I

Ch
4

Local Hard Drives   A local hard drive operates 10 to 20 times faster than a floppy, and has the advantage that all your files are available whenever you want them. As you start to become more familiar with working electronically, this latter advantage becomes more important. You will find yourself bringing up old files often, and cutting pieces out of them for your new work. Or, you may use them as the basis for template and style creation. You can also use your old files as a knowledge base, accessing work done by yourself or others in your work group to learn from what you've done before, or to track the history of a project.

The other reason you will want to save your work on a hard drive is that the QuickFinder indexing system discussed later will then index all of your files, so that you can immediately find all documents by specifying any text that is in them—no matter what folder you have put them in on your hard drive.

Local hard drives are an excellent place to store documents when:

■ You are working on a stand-alone computer

■ Your network administrator limits the amount of storage you have for documents

■ The files are ones that only you will use, and you regularly back up your hard drive

Network Drives   Saving files on network drives has all the advantages of saving them on local hard drives. There are a couple other considerations, however, that must be taken into account.

First, the network almost invariably is backed up regularly; often daily. (Ask your system administrator for details.) Because most people don't back up their local drive regularly, this may be reason enough to save files on the network.

Second, if you work in a work group, saving files on a network is the best way to start creating a "learning organization," a team of people who can build on each others' work.

There are three disadvantages to saving files on the network. First, if the network goes down, you will not have access to your files. Second, if you don't archive and purge your files regularly, the network drive will fill up rapidly. Third, some companies' network drive purge policies are time-based, meaning that if a certain file has not been actively used for a certain time period, that file is archived. If it is archived, it may still be accessible by request, but may require time or paper work for you to have the network administrator retrieve it; you will not have direct access to it.

T I P   Saving files to a shared workspace on a network is one of the best ways of getting workgroups to start sharing files electronically.

Internet Servers   You can also save files on an Internet server, if you have a Web site and sufficient permissions. This gives people throughout the world access to the files.

The Corel WordPerfect Suite 7 can assist you in *creating* Web pages (files that can be viewed with Web browsers such as Netscape Navigator); however, the Suite does not have programs designed for uploading such files to the Internet.

▶ **See** "Uploading Your Presentation," **p. 518**

Ask your Internet Service Provider or Network Administrator for procedures to be used in uploading your files to the Internet. Be aware, however, that when you upload files to an Internet Service Provider there may be fees attached for storage of those files.

Understanding Electronic Filing Systems

Once you have decided which drive(s) to save your files on, you will want to create a filing system—a set of folders and subfolders—in which to save your files.

If you are saving files on a network drive, you will have a workspace that contains only your data files. If you are working on a stand-alone computer, consider creating a main folder for all your data files. When you install the Corel WordPerfect Suite, the folder MyFiles is created. This can serve admirably as a main folder. If all your other folders are created as subfolders of MyFiles, you can easily back up your data files because they are all in one place. You can also keep all your data files separate from program folders, so that you can more easily search them.

N O T E Your electronic filing system should mimic your paper filing system. Thus, if you have different filing cabinets or file drawers that are organized by type of business, client, or employee, your main subfolders should be organized the same way. ■

Create subfolders under the main subfolders that mimic your hanging files, and if needed, create an additional layer of subfolders that mimics your manila files. You probably don't want to have more than four or five layers of folders, because navigating through them becomes time-consuming. Coordinate your folders with your file-naming conventions, as described in the next section.

Setting File-Naming Conventions

Just as you wouldn't want your office manager or employees to randomly put stickers on manila folders, you will also want to systematically think about how to name your files. Keep in mind that you can now make use of long file names with spaces in them, which are permitted by Windows 95.

Consider the following when creating file-naming conventions:

■ *Agree on file-naming conventions within the office.* Assign one person to be responsible for periodically checking file names in public workspaces, renaming files as needed, and notifying the owner of the file that the name has been changed. Create a job aid that outlines the file-naming conventions and distribute it to present and new employees.

■ *Coordinate file names with folders.* If you have a folder for each client, with subfolders for letters, briefs, and legal memos, you do not need to have the word "letter" or the client name in the file name, because a letter will be saved in the appropriate client folder and letters subfolder.

■ *Remember alphabetization.* Have the first word(s) of the file name be key words that you will want to alphabetize your files by. This may be type of file (letter), client name (Smith, John), or subject.

A typical file management dialog box is shown in Figure 4.3. In this case, the filing system is set up in such a way that all letters (to anyone) are in a Letters folder. Thus, the file-naming convention calls for the client's last name, followed by the number of the letter, followed by a few words describing the subject of the letter.

FIG. 4.3
A good file-naming system allows anyone in your office to quickly find a file you have saved.

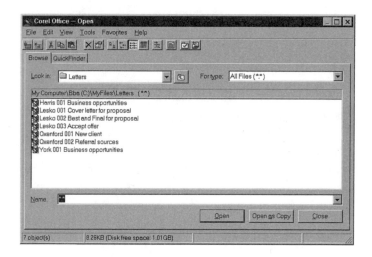

Using File Management Dialog Boxes

The Corel WordPerfect Suite 7 offers extremely powerful file management features through *file management dialog boxes.* You see a file management dialog box whenever you use any feature that offers you options while saving or retrieving files (for example, File Open, File Save As, Insert File, Insert Object, and so on). In fact, any time you can select a file using a Browse button, you will be taken to a file management dialog box, like the Save File dialog box shown in Figure 4.4.

N O T E Your dialog box may not resemble the one shown, because the way files may be displayed is determined by options you can set, as explained later. ■

File management dialog boxes allow you to quickly navigate throughout your filing system. More importantly, however, they allow you to manage your drives, folders, and files.

FIG. 4.4
All file management dialog boxes have options similar to the file management options shown in this Save File dialog box.

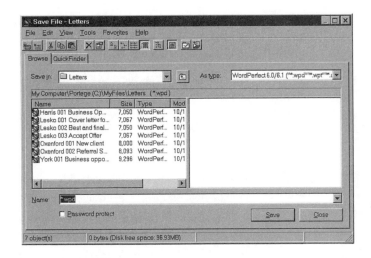

Setting File Management Dialog Box Options

Depending on their function, file management dialog boxes have slightly different options. However, you will see common options in all file management dialog boxes.

The toolbar is an excellent way to set dialog box display options. If the toolbar is not displayed, choose View, Toolbar. A check mark appears by the Toolbar entry (see Figure 4.5).

FIG. 4.5
File management dialog boxes have their own toolbars that you can display or hide.

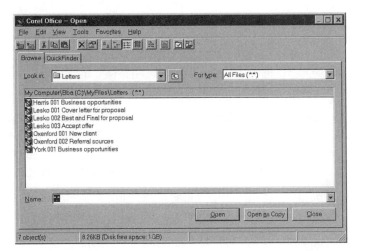

You can split the main window that shows your folders and files into two or three separate windows:

Part

I

Ch

4

- If you click the Tree View icon, you see your folders in the left window, and the subfolders and files contained in the selected folder in the window to its right. Using the Tree View is the easiest way to navigate through your filing system.

- If you click the Preview icon, you see a window on the right that shows you the contents of the selected file.

TIP Using Preview will slow down navigating through the system, so you should turn Preview on only when needed.

- You can also display the files in the selected folder in four ways: as large icons, small icons, a list of file names, or a single list of file names with details.

Large and small icons show you what type of file each file is (Corel Quattro Pro, Corel WordPerfect, and so on). They are not terribly useful if you only store files of one type in a folder. Moreover, they don't permit as much of the file name to show.

The file name list can be a very useful view because you see several columns of files in one screen, and can often locate your file much more quickly. The details view shows only one column of file names, but it does display the file size and date it was last saved, which some users prefer to see.

TIP Click a column such as file name or modified to put the files in alphabetical order based on that column. Click again for descending alphabetical order.

Navigating the Filing System

After you've used the Suite for a while, you will want to put your files in different folders to organize them. You can switch between drives and folders, and select one or more files with File Management dialog boxes.

Switching Between Drives and Folders   You will navigate through your filing system in two directions: up and down. Navigating down is easy; the subfolders of the currently selected folder will display in the window. For example, if the MyFiles folder has a subfolder called Letters, the Letters subfolder will display if the MyFiles folder is selected.

To navigate down to a subfolder, click it. For example, to navigate from the MyFiles folder shown in Figure 4.6 to the Letters subfolder, you would double-click it.

If you wish to go to a folder that is not a subfolder of the currently selected folder, you'll need to navigate up, then (possibly) down again, by navigating up to a common point.

For instance, say the MyFiles folder has several subfolders, including Letters and Memos. You are in the Letters subfolder and want to go to the Memos subfolder. You must first navigate up to the common folder, MyFiles, and then back down to the Memos subfolder. It may sound complicated, but it's actually quite easy once you've done it a few times.

FIG. 4.6
Navigate down to a subfolder like Letters in the example shown by double-clicking it.

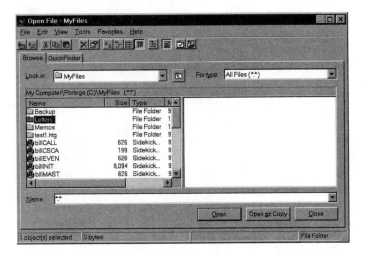

If you continue to navigate up, you will reach the drive itself. One level up from the drive is My Computer. From My Computer you can see all the drives on the computer, as well as folders for the Control Panel and Printers.

One level up from My Computer is the Desktop, from which you can see your computer, the Network Neighborhood, Recycle Bin, and your Briefcase (if it is installed).

 To see the folder, drive, or computer above the selected object, click the Up One Level button. For example, to navigate from a local hard drive to a network drive, you will continue to click the Up One Level icon until you reach the Desktop, then double-click Network Neighborhood, then double-click the appropriate workgroup and the network computer you are navigating to.

Selecting Files   Once you have navigated to the appropriate folder, you can type in the name of the file to be saved, or double-click the file to be opened.

On occasion, however, you will want to select more than one file —either to open multiple files or to perform file management tasks.

To select multiple adjacent files, click the first file to be selected, then hold down the Shift key and click the last file. To select non-adjacent files, click the first file to be selected, then hold down the Ctrl key while you click any additional files. The selected files are highlighted, as shown in Figure 4.7.

Part

I

Ch

4

FIG. 4.7
You can select multiple files, whether they are adjacent to each other or not, as shown in this example.

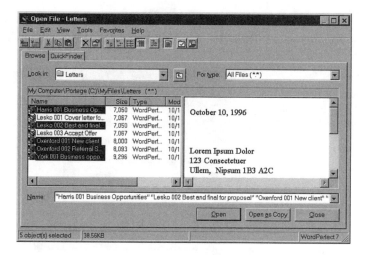

Managing Drives

You can map and disconnect network drives from Corel WordPerfect Suite 7 file management dialog boxes. This can be very useful if you work on a large network, and are not normally connected to all the available servers. When you need to open a file on a server you are not connected to, you can map to that server, then disconnect from it when you are done.

 TIP Mapping to a network drive assigns a letter to the drive. This makes the drive accessible to opening and saving files, and makes it possible to log on to the drive.

 To map to a network drive, access any file management dialog box. Click the Map Network Drive button. You see the Map Network Drive dialog box shown in Figure 4.8. Select the letter for the Drive you want to map to, then type the Path to the drive, and click OK.

 When you are finished, you can disconnect from the drive using the Disconnect Net Drive button.

 TIP The Reconnect at Logon option causes Windows to automatically remap the specified drive when you log into the system the next time.

Managing Folders

If you remember our original analogy, folders and subfolders are like the drawers, hanging folders, and manila folders in a file cabinet (disk drive). They are used to organize your work, and enable you to create a system for maintaining your files.

FIG. 4.8

You can map to network drives from the Map Network Drive dialog box, which can be accessed through any file management dialog box.

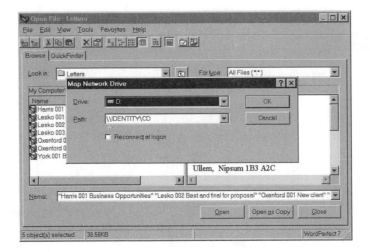

In order to manage the directories that make up your electronic filing system, you need to be able to create, remove (delete), and rename directories (folders). To create a new folder, do the following:

1. Access a file management dialog box.

2. Navigate to the folder that will be the parent of the new folder.

3. Choose File New, Folder. You see the new folder named New Folder under the original folder, with its name highlighted, as shown in Figure 4.9.

4. Type the name for the new folder and press Enter.

FIG. 4.9

You can create new folders in any file management dialog box.

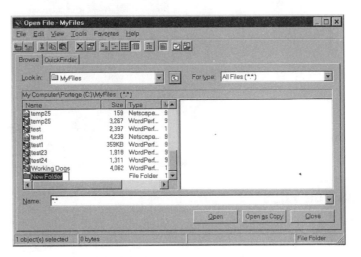

Part

I

Ch

4

TIP You can access these options to manage folders via a QuickMenu by right-clicking the directory list.

To rename a folder, select it, then choose File, Rename. The folder name is highlighted; type the new name and press Enter.

To remove a folder, select it, then choose File, Delete. The folder and its contents are deleted, and its contents are moved to the Recycle Bin.

CAUTION

Removing a directory with files in it deletes the files from the disk and puts them in the Recycle Bin. While they can be recovered, they will not automatically be put back into the right folder, even if you re-create it. Use this command with care.

You can also view and set the properties for a folder, including whether it is hidden, read-only, or shared (on a Microsoft network). To do so, select the folder, then choose File, Properties. You see the Properties dialog box for the Letter folder shown in Figure 4.10.

FIG. 4.10
You can view or set properties and file sharing options of a file from file management dialog boxes.

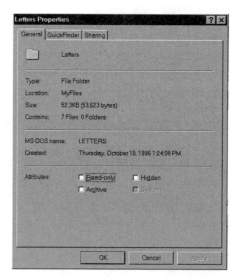

Managing Files

Once you have the backbone of your filing system—the folders—created, you will want to finish creating your filing system by renaming and moving files into your new filing system. Periodically, you will also want to archive and purge your filing system by moving files out of the folders and onto floppy disks or a tape backup unit.

With Corel WordPerfect Suite 7 dialog boxes, you can do these tasks and more. You can copy, move, rename, and delete files, and you can set their properties.

 T I P If you hold down the Shift key while you delete a file, it will not go into the Recycle Bin. However, once such a file is deleted, it is *gone* and the safety provided by the Recycle Bin is not there.

Copying and Moving Files The easiest way to copy and move files is by using the Tree View. In this view, you can copy and move files just as you would using Windows 95 Explorer.

 From any file management dialog box, click the Tree View button. Navigate through the folders in the left window until you see the folder containing the file(s) you want. Double-click this folder, if necessary, so that you see the desired file(s) in the right window.

In the left window, navigate to the destination folder using the scroll bars. If you need to open folders to see subfolders, click the plus sign to the left of the folder icon, rather than double-clicking the folder itself. This will ensure that the contents of the right window do not change.

When you can see the destination folder in the left window, select the file(s) you want to move or copy in the right window. Drag them from the right window to the icon for the destination folder in the left window.

If they are on the same drive, the files will be moved. To copy them instead, hold down the Ctrl key while you drag them. You see a plus sign on the icon as they are moved, as shown in Figure 4.11, indicating that the files are being copied.

Part

I

Ch

4

FIG. 4.11

Holding down the Ctrl key while dragging files is indicated by a plus sign in a box next to the cursor, and forces the files to be copied rather than moved.

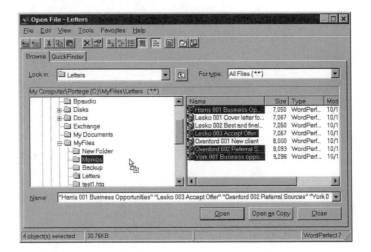

T I P To move files from one drive to another, drag them using the right mouse button rather than the left. When you have dragged the file to the new drive, you will see a pop-up menu, and can choose whether to move or copy the file.

N O T E You can also move or copy files by selecting them, then choosing Edit, Cut or Edit, Copy. Navigate to the destination folder and choose Edit, Paste. If you copy a file to the same directory, its name will have "Copy of" appended to the front of it. ▪

Setting File Attributes You can make a file hidden, read-only, or see when it was created, last modified, and last accessed. To do so, select the file, then choose File, Properties; alternatively, right-click the file and choose Properties. You see the Properties dialog box shown in Figure 4.12. Set the properties as desired, then click OK.

FIG. 4.12
You can set file properties or see when a file was created, modified, and/or last accessed in the file's Properties dialog box.

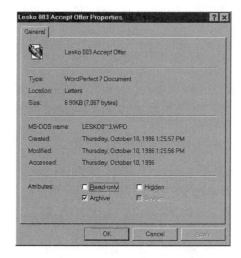

Renaming Files To rename a file, select it in a file management dialog box, then choose File, Rename; alternatively, you can right-click the file, then choose Rename. The file name is highlighted with a box around it. Type the new name and press Enter.

Deleting Files To delete one or more files, select them in a file management dialog box, as described previously. Press the Delete key. You see the Confirm File Delete dialog box shown in Figure 4.13. Confirm that you want to delete the files, and they are moved to the Recycle Bin.

FIG. 4.13
When you delete files, they
go to the Recycle Bin, where
you can undelete them if you
need to.

Finding Files

Sometimes, even with the powerful file management tools at your disposal, you forget
where you have filed an important document. Or someone else in your office comes to
you and says, "Can you get that memo that I did sometime last month? It was about Providence National Bank." In the past, this could have been a full day job, but not any more!

Corel provides you two powerful tools to make finding files a snap: Favorites and
QuickFinder.

CAUTION
Your files might not go to the Recycle Bin if the Recycle Bin properties have been modified. To check
your Recycle Bin settings, right-click the Recycle Bin icon on the desktop, then choose Properties.

Using Favorites

The Corel WordPerfect Suite 7 integrates tightly with the Favorites folder contained in
Windows 95.

The Favorites folder contains shortcuts to your most used folders and files. The Favorites
folder is common to all Windows 95 applications, so if you add a file to your Favorites
folder while you are in a non-Corel application like Microsoft Word, you will see it when
you access Favorites in Corel WordPerfect as well.

NOTE A shortcut is a small file that, as the name implies, is a shortcut to another folder or
file. It merely tells Windows 95 where the actual folder or file is located. When you
double-click a shortcut, it has the same effect as double-clicking the actual folder or file. ■

 To access your Favorites folder, you can be in any file management dialog box. Click the
Go To/From Favorites button. You see the contents of the Favorites folder. If you click the
button again, you return to the folder you were previously in.

 To add an item to the Favorites folder, select it, then click the Add to Favorites button. You
will be given the choice of adding the selected item, or the folder in which it resides.

To delete an item from the Favorites folder, go to the Favorites folder, select the item, press the Delete key, and confirm the deletion.

N O T E   Deleting an item from the Favorites folder merely deletes the shortcut to the item that resides in the Favorites folder, and leaves the item itself untouched. ■

Using QuickFinder

QuickFinder is unsurpassed at helping you find the files you need. QuickFinder searches through all the files on your hard disks (and network drives, if you so specify). It can even *index* your files by examining them during off hours, and making a list (*index*) of words that your files contain. That way, when you look for files containing "providence," you find them almost instantly!

 You can access the QuickFinder in two ways. From any file management dialog box, click the QuickFinder tab. If it is more convenient, you can also select the QuickFinder button from the task bar, where the Desktop Application Director puts it by default. In either case, you see the QuickFinder tab in the dialog box, shown in Figure 4.14.

FIG. 4.14
The QuickFinder tab is used to index your files, allowing you to search for files by the text they contain, and finding resulting files almost instantly.

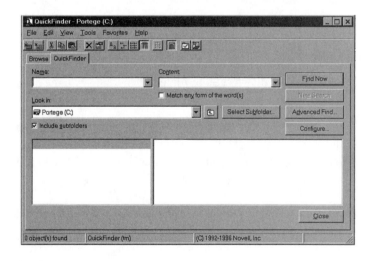

Finding Files   To search for a file with a specified word or phrase in it, follow these steps:

1. Access the QuickFinder dialog box. If you haven't indexed any files, you will see the QuickFinder Fast Search Setup Expert dialog box.

2. If you know the name of the file for which you are searching, enter it in the Name box.

You can put an asterisk before and/or after a word in the file name to search for a part of a file name, if you don't know the exact file name.

3. If you know a word or phrase that is in the document, enter it in the Co<u>n</u>tent box. If desired, check Match An<u>y</u> Forms of the Word(s) to have QuickFinder look for other verb forms of the word.

 4. Specify the drive and/or folder to look at. Click the Up One Level button to move up a level, or select the Su<u>b</u>folder button to move down one. Check Include <u>S</u>ubfolders to include subfolders in the search.

5. Choose F<u>i</u>nd Now to conduct the search. The files meeting your search criteria will be listed at the bottom of the QuickFinder dialog box. Double-click the desired file to open it.

You can also set advanced options by clicking the A<u>d</u>vanced Find button in the QuickFinder dialog box. You see the Advanced Find dialog box shown in Figure 4.15.

FIG. 4.15
The Advanced Find dialog box allows you to search for a document by looking for words specific to that document.

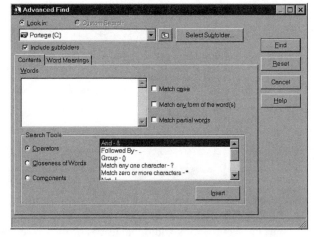

Construct searches using advanced logic by typing a word or phrase, then selecting an <u>O</u>perator such as And or Followed By, then typing another word or phrase. Alternatively, you can type a word or phrase, and choose <u>C</u>loseness of Words to specify how close the first word or phrase needs to be to the next. You can also choose Components to specify that the word or phrase must be on the first page of the document.

You can also search for synonyms of the specified word by clicking the Synonyms tab. As you type a word and choose Look Up, the synonyms appear in the Concept Net area, and you can create searches that simulate the "fuzzy logic" found in dedicated search engines.

N O T E There are several commercial software utilities that do nothing but index documents on your disk, and allow you to find them using a variety of criteria. The process of using advanced mathematical algorithms to find the most relevant documents is called "fuzzy logic." ▪

Configuring QuickFinder QuickFinder can search for files in two ways. If you configure QuickFinder to index your disk (or specific folders in it), an index file is created containing an alphabetical list of words, and the files they are in. Then, when you search for text, QuickFinder searches this index, and finds appropriate files very rapidly. This is called a Fast Search. If an index is not created, QuickFinder searches through files one by one, which is a very slow process.

To configure QuickFinder, click the Configure button in the QuickFinder window. You see the QuickFinder Manager dialog box shown in Figure 4.16.

FIG. 4.16
Configure QuickFinder in the QuickFinder Manager dialog box to do Fast Searches on your documents.

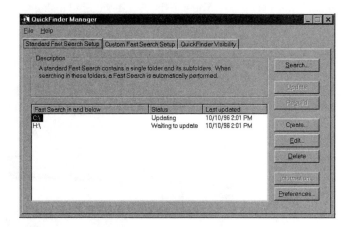

Any QuickFinder Fast Searches (indexes) are listed in the QuickFinder Manager dialog box. If you would like to index additional drives or folders, click the Create button. You see the QuickFinder Standard Fast Search dialog box shown in Figure 4.17.

FIG. 4.17
Configure QuickFinder to search through multiple drives or folders by creating new indexes in the QuickFinder Standard Fast Search dialog box.

Type in the drive and/or folder you want to search; or click the Browse button, and specify how often the index should be updated, or whether you will update it manually. Click the Options button to specify whether the search should include the full document or just the document summary.

 TIP Automatic updating is most convenient, but it may slow down your computer dramatically during the time it takes to update the index.

If you have set your options for manual update, you can update a Fast Search by accessing the QuickFinder dialog box, then choosing Configure to see the QuickFinder Manager dialog box. Select the Fast Search to be updated, then choose Update. Periodically, you will want to delete your index and reconstruct it completely. This makes sure that you don't get false "hits" from files that have been deleted. You can do this by selecting a Fast Search and clicking the Rebuild button instead of Update.

 TIP You can Edit a Fast Search to change the schedule by which it is updated, or Delete one entirely, if desired.

Part

I

Ch

4

Using Corel WordPerfect

CHAPTER 5

Getting Started with Corel WordPerfect

Of all the applications included with Corel WordPerfect Suite 7, Corel WordPerfect may be the one you use most. Besides producing letters and envelopes like an ordinary word processor, WordPerfect also creates memos, fax cover sheets, reports, newsletters, mailing labels, brochures, pages for the World Wide Web, and many other types of documents.

WordPerfect offers many features that help you complete your work quickly and easily. There are features that correct errors automatically, features that add visual interest to your documents, and features that help you organize and manage long documents. WordPerfect provides easy graphics handling, outlining, calculations of data in tables, the capability to create a mailing list, list sorting, and efficient file management. You can perform desktop publishing tasks such as formatting fonts, inserting drop caps, adding graphic borders, and adding shading. You can even prepare documents to be published on the Internet or a WordPerfect-based corporate intranet.

When you use WordPerfect, you're sharing a common look and feel with other applications in the

How to understand the WordPerfect screen

This chapter identifies items on the WordPerfect screen that provide you both document information and shortcuts for common tasks.

Entering text

Learn the differences between entering text with WordPerfect and with a typewriter.

Editing text

WordPerfect makes it simple to add new text, delete unwanted text, and move or copy text from one place to another.

How to save, close, and open documents

Learn to save your finished work on the disk and how to open stored files for further editing.

WordPerfect Suite 7. Switching to Corel Quattro Pro for spreadsheets is easily accomplished without drastically changing your work environment. You can even integrate and edit data from another application while remaining in WordPerfect.

For example, when you have embedded a Quattro Pro spreadsheet in a WordPerfect document, you can edit the spreadsheet after double-clicking the embedded object in your WordPerfect document. Then, when you finish editing the spreadsheet, you can return to the WordPerfect document by choosing File, Exit and Return.

This section of *Special Edition Using Corel WordPerfect Suite 7* presents you with an overview of the WordPerfect program. In this book, you learn how to utilize WordPerfect as a word processor for business tasks. For a more comprehensive examination of WordPerfect 7, refer to Que's *Special Edition Using Corel WordPerfect 7*. ■

Understanding the WordPerfect Screen

When starting WordPerfect, you see certain screen elements (as shown in Figure 5.1), including the title bar, menu bar, the WordPerfect 7 toolbar, the Power Bar, guidelines, the status bar, and the scroll bars.

FIG. 5.1
Using WordPerfect's screen elements can help you complete tasks quickly and efficiently.

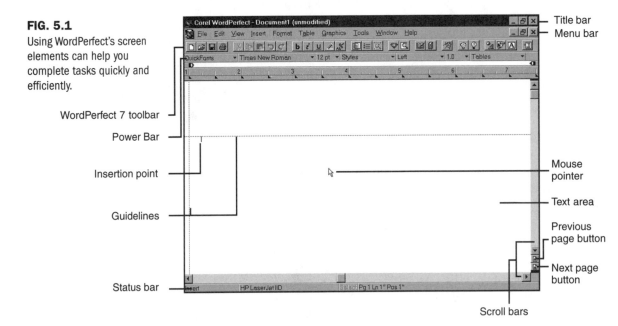

▶ **See** "Using Help," **p. 33**

Screen elements provide information on your document and allow you to quickly complete common tasks.

- *Title bar.* The title bar identifies the WordPerfect application window and the name of the document in the current document window.

- *Menu bar.* The menu bar gives you access to the most commonly used WordPerfect features. Each menu contains a specialized list of related commands. Choose commands from the Format menu, for example, to specify fonts, change margins, create a header or footer, and so on.

- *Toolbars.* By default, the WordPerfect 7 toolbar is displayed just beneath the menu bar. When you point to a button, its name is displayed beneath the pointer and its function is described in the pop-up Quick Tips window. Toolbars contain buttons you can use to perform common tasks, such as opening an existing document, saving a document, applying boldface, and spell checking. When scroll arrows are displayed at the right end of the toolbar, you can use them to see other buttons. When performing a specialized task, you can switch to a toolbar with buttons relative to that task (for example, when you're working with a table, you can display the Tables toolbar). You can switch between toolbars whenever you like, and even choose where they will appear on the screen.

- *Power Bar.* The Power Bar consists of a series of buttons that give you easy access to common text editing and text layout features. While there is only one Power Bar, you can still change its appearance and button configuration.

  ▶ **See** "Customizing Toolbars," **p. 734**

- *Margin Guidelines.* Guidelines are the blue lines that you see on the screen that indicate where your margins are. You will see other guidelines from time to time in addition to the blue guidelines you see when you first enter WordPerfect. You will see pink guidelines around headers and footers, black guidelines around cells in tables, and red guidelines around columns. Not only do these non-printing guidelines show you where various elements will appear, you can drag them to change the element's formatting. For instance, you can drag the blue guidelines to set margins in your document.

- *Text area.* The text area consists of a blank "page" in which you can enter text or place pictures, graphics, and so on. By default, the text area is displayed in Page mode—or, as it would appear on the printed page—including the margin space at the top of the page (depending on the zoom percentage, you may not see a full page of text at once). The insertion point is a blinking vertical line that indicates the position where text would be inserted if you were to type text.

Part

II

Ch

5

N O T E You can switch between ways of looking at your document, called views. The Page mode is most commonly used; it shows the page as it will print. The Draft mode hides headers, footers, and watermarks. Because it does not show a space between one page and the next, some people prefer to use this view when reading long text documents. The Two Page mode shows two complete pages, and is useful when examining your entire page layout. Switch between views by choosing View, then selecting Draft, Page, or Two Page. ▣

- *Status bar.* The status bar informs you of the status of many WordPerfect features. Use it to quickly identify whether you are in Insert or Typeover mode, to note the currently selected printer, and to locate the page, line, and position of your insertion point.
- *Scroll bars.* Use the scroll bars to move quickly to another area of the document. Previous Page and Next Page buttons appear at the bottom of the vertical scroll bar, and are used to move to the previous or next printed page of the document.

You can display or hide many of these elements to suit your working style. To display or hide the toolbar, Power Bar, status bar, and Ruler, do the following:

1. Choose View, Toolbars/Ruler. You see the Toolbars dialog box shown in Figure 5.2.

FIG. 5.2
You can easily display or hide screen elements to provide more assistance, or give you the "clean screen" look.

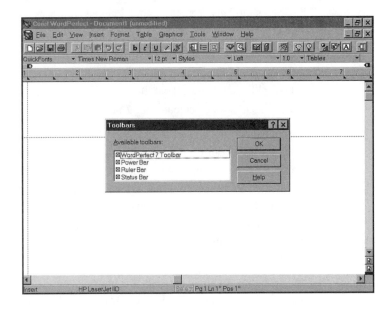

2. Check or uncheck the appropriate element to display or hide it.
3. Click OK.

N O T E You can specify how scroll bars are displayed by choosing Edit, Preferences, Display, and selecting the Document tab. ■

In addition, there are two other screen elements that you will see when you have typed text in your document: QuickSpots and the shadow cursor.

- ■ *QuickSpot.* As you move your mouse pointer over a paragraph, a table, or a graphic, a small gray square appears at the side of the element. Click the QuickSpot to see a menu of formatting choices appropriate to that document element.

  ▶ **See** "Formatting Text and Documents," **p. 103**

- ■ *Shadow Cursor.* As you move your mouse pointer over text, a gray bar appears in the text. This is called the shadow cursor, and it indicates where your insertion point will be if you click the mouse button.

Entering Text

When starting WordPerfect, you are supplied with a new, empty document window named Document1 in the title bar. You can begin to type at the blinking insertion point, initially positioned just below the top margin. As you type, text is entered at the insertion point.

This section describes the basic techniques of entering text, moving through a document, and selecting text for editing.

Typing Text

When typing text, type as you would in any word processor. WordPerfect automatically wraps the text at the end of a line, so you don't have to press Enter to begin a new line. It does so by inserting a *soft return* at the end of the line. A soft return is a line break that appears as needed.

Press Enter only to start a new paragraph or create a blank line. Pressing Enter inserts a *hard return* into your document. A hard return is a line break that stays where you put it, even if the line of text does not extend to the right margin. WordPerfect defines a paragraph as text that ends with a hard return, a hard page break, or a hard column break.

As you type, certain keys that you press—such as Enter, Tab, and Spacebar—create non-printing characters at the insertion point. You can view these non-printing characters by choosing View, Show +.

Figure 5.3 illustrates non-printing characters, with a document containing lines that wrap with hard returns and lines that wrap with automatic word wrap.

Part

II

Ch

5

FIG. 5.3
Paragraph marks and spaces are non-printing characters; they do not print, whether or not they are displayed.

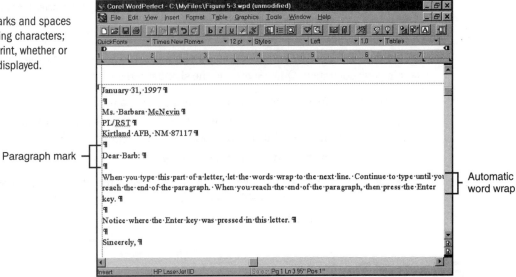

Paragraph mark →

Automatic word wrap

As you type, follow these guidelines:

- If you make a mistake, press the Backspace key to erase the character immediately preceding the insertion point.

- Alternatively, you may press the Delete key to remove the character immediately following the insertion point.

- When you're typing a sentence or phrase that extends past the end of the line, let the words wrap to the next line automatically (do not press Enter when you get to the end of the line, but rather only when you get to the end of the paragraph).

- Use the Tab key or the Indent feature (F7) to indent lines; don't use the spacebar.

- Press the Insert key to use Typeover mode, in which the text you type replaces existing text. Press Insert again to turn off Typeover mode. You can tell whether Typeover is active by looking at the status bar at the bottom of the screen.

Positioning the Insertion Point

To move the insertion point, move the mouse pointer to the new location, noting the position of the shadow cursor as you move the mouse. When the shadow pointer is where you want it, click the left mouse button. You can position the insertion point anywhere in the text area, but not past the end of the text.

To move the insertion point to a place that you don't see on-screen, use the scroll bar(s) to move to a new location. When the new location is visible on-screen, place the mouse pointer where you want to position the insertion point and click the left mouse button.

Another way to move the insertion point is by pressing keys on the keyboard. Sometimes, especially when you're already using the keyboard to type text, it's easier and faster to move the insertion point by pressing keys than by using the mouse. Table 5.1 lists common keys that you can use to move around in your document.

Table 5.1   Use Keyboard Shortcuts to Easily Move Around in Your Document

Key	Moves Insertion Point
→/←	Next or previous character
↑/↓	One line up or down
PgUp/PgDn	One screen up or down
Ctrl+→/←	One word to the right or left
Home/End	Beginning or end of line
Ctrl+Home/End	Beginning or end of document

Selecting Text

After you enter text, you may want to delete a word, sentence, paragraph, or other section of text, or you may want to boldface the text or change its font or size. Before you can perform some formatting or editing actions on existing text, you must first select the text. Selecting the text shows WordPerfect where to perform the action.

You can select text with the mouse, the keyboard, or a combination of both. Some of the most useful ways to select text include the following:

- To select a section of text of any length, position the shadow cursor at one end of the text and drag to the other end of the text with the mouse.
- To select a word, position the shadow cursor anywhere in the word and double-click.
- To select a sentence, position the shadow cursor anywhere in the sentence and triple-click.
- To select a paragraph, position the shadow cursor anywhere in the paragraph and quadruple-click.

Part
II

Ch
5

■ To select a sentence, position the mouse pointer in the left margin area. When you point the mouse in the left margin area, the pointer changes to a right-pointing hollow arrow, as shown in Figure 5.4. Click to select a single sentence; to select multiple sentences, keep holding down the left mouse button after you click and drag through the sentences or drag the mouse pointer in the left margin.

FIG. 5.4

To select text, position the mouse pointer in the left margin and click once.

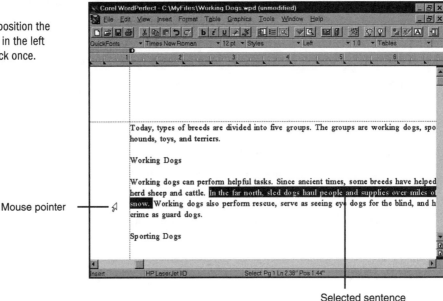

Mouse pointer

Selected sentence

■ To select a paragraph, position the arrow pointer next to the paragraph in the left margin area. The arrow pointer should be pointing to the right. If it is not, move it further into the left margin area until it points to the right. Double-click to select the paragraph. To select multiple paragraphs, keep holding down the left mouse button after you click and drag through the paragraphs.

■ For multiple selection options, position the right-pointing arrow pointer in the left margin area and right-click. Next, make a choice from the selection options on the QuickMenu.

■ To select a section of text of any length, position the insertion point at one end of the text. Next, position the shadow cursor at the other end of the text and hold down Shift while you left-click.

■ To select text with the keyboard, position the insertion point at the beginning of the text, then press and hold down the Shift key while you press the appropriate cursor movement keys. To select from the insertion point to the end of the line, for example, hold down Shift while you press End. To select the character immediately following the insertion point, hold down Shift while you press the Right Arrow ($\rightarrow$).

TROUBLESHOOTING

I began typing the text, but it didn't appear where I expected it to appear. Text that you type appears at the insertion point, not at the mouse pointer. Before you type text, position the insertion point by clicking where you want the text to appear.

I have trouble controlling the selection when I drag through text with the mouse. It takes practice to control the mouse when you select text by dragging through it. Consider using this method only when all the text you want to select is visible on the screen. When it is not, click at the start of the selection, then use the scroll bars to move to the end of the selection, then hold down the Shift key while you click at the end of the selection for maximum control.

I selected some text and made it bold, but when I started typing afterward the text disappeared. When text is selected, whatever you type replaces the selected text. It's a good idea to deselect text as soon as you finish performing any action(s) on the selection. To deselect text, click anywhere in the typing area. To recover your "lost" text, choose Edit, Undo.

N O T E   You can use the Shift key to extend (or shrink) a selection. Hold down Shift while you press an arrow key to extend (or shrink) the selection.

To deselect text, click the mouse anywhere in the text area, or press any of the arrow keys. ■

Part
II

Ch
5

Editing Text

You can easily make changes and corrections to your document. You can select any text and delete it, copy it, or move it. You can even undelete text you accidentally deleted, or undo other editing operations you do by accident. This section shows you how to make basic editing changes quickly and easily.

Deleting Text

To delete a small amount of text to the right of the insertion point, press the Delete key. Hold the Delete key to continue deleting text. Similarly, to delete a small amount of text to the left of the insertion point, press the Backspace key. Hold the Backspace key to continue deleting text.

To delete larger amounts of text, select it as described previously, then press the Delete key.

T I P If you erase text by mistake, you can recall it using the Undelete or Undo commands, as described later in the section "Undeleting Text."

Copying and Moving Text

One task you'll do a lot as you edit documents is copying and moving text. Copying text leaves the text in its original location, but makes a copy of it in another place. When you move text, it is deleted from the original location, and inserted at the new location.

If you're going to copy or move the text to another location, you can use one of two methods: the "cut-and-paste" method or the "drag-and-drop" method.

Using the Cut-and-Paste Method   To copy or move text from one area of the document to another area that is not visible on the screen, it is easiest to use the three-step cut-and-paste method.

In the first step, you select the text, then move or copy the text to the Windows Clipboard. Moving the text to the Windows Clipboard deletes it from its original location, and is thus called *cutting* the text. The text stays in the Windows Clipboard until you exit Windows or place something else in the Clipboard. (Thus, you can paste text from the Clipboard into your document any number of times, until you put something else in the Clipboard.)

To cut selected text, choose <u>E</u>dit, Cu<u>t</u>, or press Ctrl+X. Alternatively, click the Cut button. To copy selected text, choose <u>E</u>dit, <u>C</u>opy, or press Ctrl+C. Alternatively, click the Copy button. The text is placed in the Windows Clipboard.

T I P You can also right-click the selected text, then choose <u>C</u>ut or C<u>o</u>py from the shortcut menu.

Once you move text to the Clipboard, the second step is to show WordPerfect where you want to place the text. Do this by clicking where you want the text to appear in your document.

The third step is to paste the text from the Clipboard to the document. To do this, choose <u>E</u>dit, <u>P</u>aste, or press Ctrl+V. Alternatively, click the Paste button. The text is copied from the Windows Clipboard to your document. For more information about sharing data, see Chapter 34, "Transferring Data Between Applications."

N O T E   Copying text—or other elements in your documents, such as pictures and charts—is a way to share data between applications. The Windows Clipboard is common to all applications running under Windows. You can, for example, create text in Corel WordPerfect, copy it, and paste it in Corel Presentations. You can also copy a spreadsheet from Corel Quattro Pro and paste it into Corel WordPerfect. ▪

Drag-and-Drop Editing   Another technique for moving and copying text is called drag and drop. Drag and drop is especially handy for moving or copying selected text a short distance—a location, say, that is already visible on-screen. Drag and drop can also be used to move graphics.

To move or copy text using drag and drop, take the following steps:

1. Select the text you want to move.

2. Point to the selected text and hold down the left mouse button. The drag-and-drop pointer shown in Figure 5.5 appears if you are moving text.

 T I P   To copy the text instead of moving it, hold down the Ctrl key before you release the mouse button at the new location. When you hold down Ctrl, the drag-and-drop pointer includes a plus (+) sign.

FIG. 5.5

Use the drag-and-drop pointer to drag the selected text or graphic to a new location. When the insertion point is correctly placed, release the mouse button.

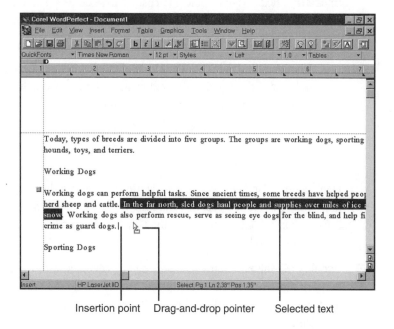

Insertion point   Drag-and-drop pointer   Selected text

3. Drag the pointer until the insertion point is at the new location, and then release the mouse button.

Converting Case

WordPerfect includes a useful command that you can use to change the case of selected text. Suppose you type a heading with initial caps at the beginning of each word and then decide that it would look better in all uppercase. You can use Convert Case to convert it to uppercase.

To change the case of existing text, take the following steps:

1. Select the text.

2. Choose Edit, Convert Case.

3. Choose Lowercase, Uppercase, or Initial Capitals.

Correcting Mistakes

Unless you're one of those people who fills out crossword puzzles with a pen, you'll find that the Undelete and Undo commands will become two of your best friends.

Undeleting Text   Use Undelete to restore deleted text. Undelete will restore any or all of your last three deletions. To use Undelete, take the following steps:

1. Position the insertion point where you want to restore the text.

2. Choose Edit, Undelete. The Undelete dialog box appears and the most recent deletion is displayed in the text window. If necessary, drag the dialog box out of the way so you can see the displayed deletion.

3. If the displayed deletion is what you want restored, choose Restore. Otherwise, choose Next or Previous to display the deletion that you want to restore, and then choose Restore.

Don't confuse Undelete with Undo; Undelete restores the last three deletions at the insertion point, but not necessarily where the text was deleted from. Undo can restore up to 300 of the last deletions to where the text was deleted from, but not where your insertion point happens to be.

Undoing Mistakes   Many mistakes can be reversed with the Undo command. Suppose that you move text to the wrong place. You can undo the move operation with Undo. Click the Undo button on the WordPerfect 7 toolbar to undo your most recent action, or choose Edit, Undo.

WordPerfect also provides a Redo command that you can use to reverse the last Undo. Click the Redo button on the WordPerfect 7 Toolbar to reverse your most recent undo action, or choose Edit, Redo.

The Undo and Redo commands work only on the last action you performed. However, WordPerfect provides a history of your edits and Undo actions. You can choose from among them, or even undo a series of actions by choosing Edit, Undo/Redo History.

Figure 5.6 shows the Undo/Redo History displaying the most recent actions. To undo the last four actions, click the fourth item from the top of the Undo list (this selects all of the first four items that are listed in the illustration), and then choose Undo.

TROUBLESHOOTING

I accidentally deleted text that I didn't mean to delete. Position the insertion point where you want to restore the text and choose Edit, Undelete. Display the correct deletion and then choose Restore.

I pasted text in the wrong place. Before you place anything else in the Clipboard, click the Undo button, and then position the insertion point in the correct location and press Ctrl+V, or choose Edit, Paste.

I accidentally get the drag-and-drop pointer when I don't want it. Press Esc before you release the mouse button. If it's too late, and the text has already been moved, use the Undo command to correct the mistake.

I tried to move selected text to another page with drag and drop, but it was very cumbersome to position the insertion point while dragging the selection. Try using cut and paste rather than drag and drop when moving or copying to a distant location.

FIG. 5.6
The Undo/Redo History lists a series of the most recent actions that you can undo (or redo).

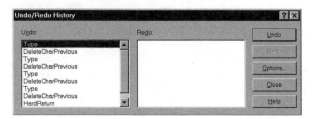

Saving, Closing, and Opening a Document

As you work on your document, you'll want to save it to the disk so that your work won't be lost if you turn off your computer or lose power. This section shows you how to save and close a document, open an existing document, and start a new one.

 See "Saving, Opening, and Closing Files," **p. 58**

Saving a Document

As in other WordPerfect Suite 7 programs, you save a WordPerfect document by assigning it a name and a location in your drive and folder list. After naming the file, you can save changes to the document without renaming it, or rename it to save both the original and new versions.

Naming a Document   You can save a file to a hard drive, floppy drive, or network drive, and give your file a name that has up to 255 characters and includes spaces. If you need to exchange files with someone using a different word processor, you can even save your file in another format (such as WordPerfect 5.1 or Microsoft Word).

> **CAUTION**
>
> Some programs and versions of network operating systems cannot use long file names. You need to think about where this file will be going in the future. If there is any chance that the document might be going through or to a system that doesn't handle long names, you might consider using the older "8.3" file-naming conventions: Keep your file name to eight characters or less, with an optional period and up to three more characters; and don't use spaces in the file name.

When you're ready to save your document for the first time, do the following:

1. Choose File, Save, or click the Save button on the WordPerfect 7 toolbar. WordPerfect displays the Save dialog box shown in Figure 5.7.

FIG. 5.7

The Save dialog box allows you to save your file to the disk.

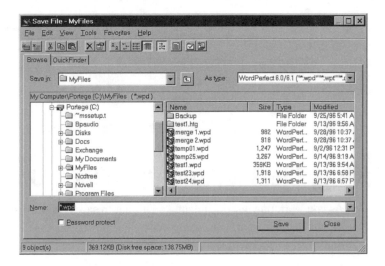

2. If you do not want to save your document in the default folder, navigate to the appropriate drive and folder by clicking the Save In box, then selecting the drive and folder you want.

3. If you want to save your file in another format, click the As Type box, and pick the desired format.

4. Type the name of the file in the Name box, then click the Save button. Your file is saved, and you return to the editing window. Notice that the title bar displays its location, name, and that it is unmodified.

   ▶ **See** "Using File Management Dialog Boxes," **p. 66**

When you save a document, the storage location defaults to the directory specified through Edit, Preferences, Files. In addition, the File Preferences dialog box specifies a default file name extension of .WPD.

▶ **See** "Customizing File Preferences," **p. 169**

Saving Changes to a Named Document   When you've saved your document by assigning it a name and a location on the disk, you can continue to work on it. The changes you make are not saved, however, unless you tell WordPerfect to save them.

 After modifying or editing an already-named document, choose File, Save, or click the Save button on the WordPerfect 7 toolbar. WordPerfect saves the changes and you are ready to proceed.

 Consider clicking the Save button whenever you are using your mouse to click a button on the toolbar. It's a very good idea to save your document before doing large-scale editing like a global search and replace.

Part
II

Ch
5

Renaming a Document   Occasionally, you will want to save your changes in a different file, so that you can keep track of the revisions you make to a document. You do this by renaming the document, so that both the original and the renamed version exist as separate files on the disk.

To rename your document, do the following:

1. With the document on the screen, choose File, Save As. You see the Save As dialog box shown in Figure 5.8.

2. If you do not want to save your document in the default folder, navigate to the appropriate drive and folder by clicking the Save In box, then selecting the drive and folder you want.

FIG. 5.8
You can rename your
document to save both the
old and new versions using
the Save As dialog box.

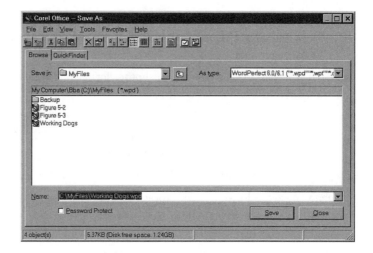

3. If you want to save your file in another format, click the As Type box, and pick the desired format.

4. If you want to change the name of your document, type the new name of the file in the Name box.

5. Click the Save button. Your file is saved, and you return to the editing window. Notice that the title bar displays the file's new name and that it is unmodified.

Closing a Document

When you finish working with a document, choose File, Close. The document is removed from the screen. If there are changes that haven't been saved, the system asks if you want to save them before closing the document.

If you intend to exit WordPerfect after working on the document, you do not need to close the document first. The document will be closed automatically when you exit WordPerfect, and you will be prompted to save the document if there are unsaved editing changes.

Opening a Document

When you open a document, a working copy of it is made from the disk onto the screen and your computer's memory. You can open up to nine documents at once, which can be very helpful when you need to bring information from several old documents into a new document.

If you prefer, you can open the document as a *copy*. If you do this, the document opens as a read-only file, and you will be unable to accidentally modify the original document. You will still be able to save the document, however, if you rename it.

To open a document, do the following:

1. Choose File, Open, or click the Open button on the WordPerfect 7 toolbar. WordPerfect displays the Open dialog box shown in Figure 5.9.

FIG. 5.9
The Open dialog box is where you select the file from the list of files, and then choose Open to open the document.

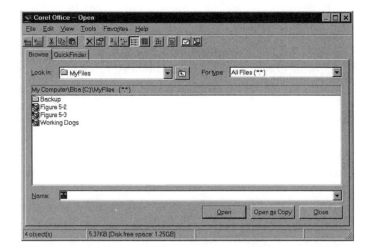

2. In the Open dialog box, select the file name from the list of files if you saved it in the default folder. Otherwise, you can change the drive and folder by clicking in the Look In box to navigate to the desired folder, then select the appropriate file name.

3. Click the Open button or the Open As Copy button, as desired. You see the document in the editing window, with its name on the title bar.

 TIP To open several files at once, hold the Ctrl key down while selecting each file you want to open.

 TIP If the file you want to open was recently edited, it will be listed at the bottom of the file menu when you choose File. You can select it from the File menu without accessing the Open dialog box.

Starting a New Document

All documents are based on *templates*. A template is a master document that contains formatting information, and can also contain text, macros, styles, and keyboard

Part
II

Ch
5

definitions. The *standard template* is where you save default formatting settings for future documents. The Standard template has the following characteristics:

- Uses an 8 1/2 by 11-inch portrait-oriented page
- Includes 1-inch top and bottom margins and 1-inch left and right margins
- Uses the initial printer font for the currently selected printer
- Uses left justification
- Supplies five heading styles that can be used to format different levels of headings in your document

 Starting a New, Blank Document   You can start a new document at any time. To start a new, blank document based on the standard template, click the New Blank Document button, or press Ctrl+N. You see a new, blank document in the editing window.

> **N O T E**   You do not need to close your old document before starting a new document, because WordPerfect can have up to nine documents open at once. If you cannot create a new document, check to see if the maximum number of documents is already open, or if your insertion point is currently in a substructure such as a header, footer, graphics box, and so on. ■

Starting a Document and Specifying a Template   A template is a basic document design that can include text as well as formatting. You can save time and work by using templates for your standardized documents, such as letters, memos, and fax forms. Many templates prompt you for information when you use them; this saves you the work of positioning the insertion point manually to fill in the information. Many templates for common office tasks ship with Corel WordPerfect.

▶ **See** "Using Templates," **p. 138**

TROUBLESHOOTING

I wanted to save a file with a new name, but when I clicked the Save button I didn't have a chance to change the name. To change the name, storage location, or file type of the document in the active document window, choose File, Save As. In the Save As dialog box, you can change any of these options.

I wanted to save a file in a different folder, but that folder isn't listed in the folder list. You may need to select a folder above the selected folder before you can see the desired folder name. For example, if C:\Myfiles\WPDOCS is the selected folder and you want to look at the files in C:\Myfiles\MEMOS, first you must select C:\Myfiles. Then, you can see (and select) the C:\Myfiles\MEMOS folder. Remember that you need to double-click a folder to select it.

I opened a document that was created in another file format, and now I want to save it.
Choose File, Save As. WordPerfect displays the Save As dialog box.

I can't open a file; in fact, New and Open are grayed out on the File menu. You already have
nine documents open, the maximum WordPerfect allows at once. Close an open document, then
try again. If this isn't the problem, your insertion point may currently be in a substructure such as
a header, footer, or graphics box. Click in the main body of the document, then try again.

Part
II

Ch
5

Formatting Text and Documents

Many of Corel WordPerfect Suite 7's features enable you to change the appearance of your documents, that is, to format your documents. You can boldface or italicize text, you can adjust the spacing between lines, or you can choose from many other formatting features to make your documents more readable and more attractive.

WordPerfect makes formatting quick and easy. You can use toolbar buttons and menu commands to make an ordinary business document eye-catching and readable. ■

Change the appearance of your screen

The WordPerfect screen can be customized in many ways. Learn about the three views of your document, how to zoom your screen, and how to display and hide screen features.

Working with the Reveal Codes screen

See how to use WordPerfect's famous Reveal Codes screen, to examine and modify the codes that make your document appear the way it does.

Format your text

See how you can easily specify fonts, size, appearance attributes, and the color of the text you print.

Format your paragraphs

Learn to specify line spacing, indents, margins, justification, and tab settings.

Format your page

Create headers and footers, print page numbers, choose paper size and orientation, and shrink your document to fit perfectly on one piece of paper.

N O T E When you format a document, WordPerfect records your commands in the form of embedded codes. You can avoid formatting problems if you remember to check the position of the insertion point before you make a formatting change. Unless you want to remove specific formatting manually (by removing the code that causes the formatting—discussed later in this chapter), you don't need to concern yourself with embedded codes. You can, however, see embedded codes whenever you want by choosing View, Reveal Codes.

In this chapter you learn to format text, lines, paragraphs, and pages using the easiest and fastest methods. ▓

Changing Screen Appearance

WordPerfect enables you to change your screen appearance in several ways to suit your working style. These include:

▓ Displaying or hiding screen elements

▓ Specifying viewing modes

▓ Setting the screen magnification

▓ Working with the Reveal Codes screen

The display or removal of screen elements, view modes, and magnification options are all set from the View menu. To select your view mode, choose View, then select Draft, Page, or Two Page. To work with the Reveal Codes screen on, you choose View, Reveal Codes.

Displaying Screen Elements

You can also remove or display various screen elements, such as the toolbar, Power Bar, Ruler Bar, status bar, and display of non-printing characters to customize the way your screen appears.

To remove or display the toolbar, Power Bar, Ruler Bar, or status bar, choose View, Toolbars/Ruler. You see the Toolbars dialog box shown in Figure 6.1. Click the elements you want to display, then choose OK.

FIG. 6.1

You can display or remove screen elements to customize the look of WordPerfect in the Toolbars dialog box.

To provide a totally "clean screen" look and remove all bars (including scroll bars and the title bar), choose View, Hide Bars. Your screen will look like the one in Figure 6.2. Press the Esc key to restore the original look of the screen.

FIG. 6.2

You can produce a completely clean screen look by choosing View, Hide Bars.

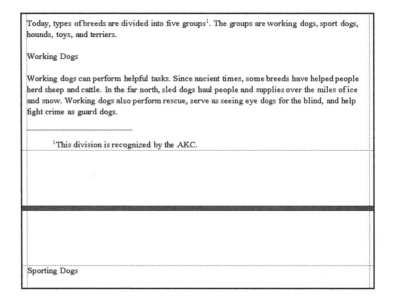

Today, types of breeds are divided into five groups[1]. The groups are working dogs, sport dogs, hounds, toys, and terriers.

Working Dogs

Working dogs can perform helpful tasks. Since ancient times, some breeds have helped people herd sheep and cattle. In the far north, sled dogs haul people and supplies over the miles of ice and snow. Working dogs also perform rescue, serve as seeing eye dogs for the blind, and help fight crime as guard dogs.

[1]This division is recognized by the AKC.

Sporting Dogs

You can also modify the viewing options to display non-printing characters such as spaces, hard returns, tabs, indents, and so on in the current and new document. Use the following steps:

1. Choose Edit, Preferences, Display.

2. Select the Symbols tab. You see the Display Preferences dialog box shown in Figure 6.3.

FIG. 6.3

You can specify which non-printing characters should display on your screen in the Display Preferences dialog box on the Symbols tab.

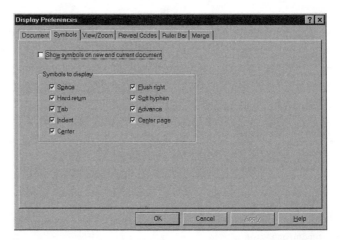

3. Check Sho_w_ symbols on new and current documents, then check the specific symbols you wish to display.

4. Click OK to exit the Display Preferences dialog box.

5. Click Close to exit the Preferences dialog box and return to your document.

Using View Modes

WordPerfect offers three different viewing modes that you can use while you are editing your document: Page view, Draft view, or Two Page view. Each view offers its own advantages for text editing and formatting. Changing the view affects the on-screen appearance of the document; it doesn't affect the actual formatting of the document or the way it will print out.

When you work in a document, you're working in Page view by default. You can use the View menu to switch to another view whenever it suits you.

 T I P   You can modify the viewing options to change the default view from Page view to Draft view by choosing Edit, Pr_e_ferences, _D_isplay, and selecting the View/Zoom tab.

Page View   In Page view, what you see on-screen is the page just as it will print, as shown in Figure 6.4. This is a true WYSIWYG (What You See Is What You Get) view of your document. Page view displays headers, footers, page borders, top and bottom margins, and footnotes. Page view is well suited for applying finishing touches to the text and page layout, although many people like to use this view for entering and editing text as well. Working in Page view is slightly slower than working in Draft view, however, on faster computers this difference may be imperceptible.

 Draft View   It's fastest and easiest to enter and edit text when you work in Draft view. In Draft view, you see text just as it will print, including variations in font face, font size, and graphics elements, as shown in Figure 6.5. You can scroll smoothly from the bottom of one page to the top of the next page without jumping past the gap between the bottom margin of one page and the top margin of the next page. Whenever you want to see everything on the page just as it will print, including margin space, headers, footers, page numbering, and page borders, you can switch from Draft view to Page view. You can do this easily by clicking the Page/Zoom Full button on the toolbar, then clicking it again to return to your current view mode.

FIG. 6.4
Page view shows you everything on the page just as it will print; this is a true WYSIWYG view.

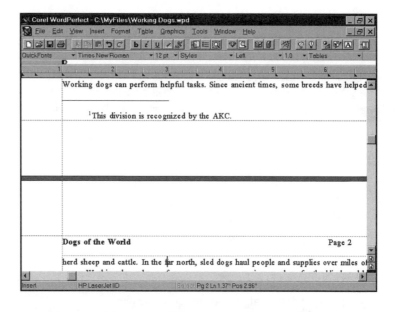

FIG. 6.5
Draft view enables you to enter and edit text smoothly and easily.

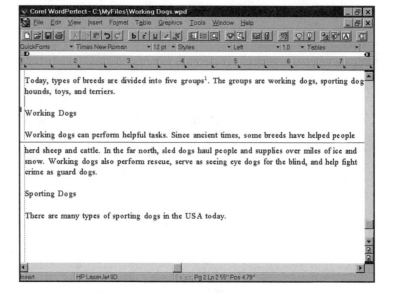

Two Page View   Use Two Page view when you want to see two pages on-screen at once. Two Page view is best suited for looking at facing pages (when you're printing on both sides of the paper) and for seeing more of the document layout than you can see in Page view. You can see where text will fit on a page best with the Two Page view, and ascertain how much white space exists on each page.

Part
II

Ch
6

You can edit your document in Two Page view just as you can edit it in Draft view or Page view, although the text is extremely small. Working in Two Page view is even slower than working in Page view.

 T I P You can modify the viewing options to change the default view mode from Page view to Draft view or even Two Page view by choosing Edit, Preferences, Display, then selecting the View/Zoom tab.

Magnifying the View

In addition to the choice of views, WordPerfect provides various magnification options for viewing a document. You can magnify the view from 25 to 400 percent when you are in the Draft or Page view. If you have a 15-inch or larger monitor, you may want to use a smaller magnification. The letters on the screen will still be readable, but you will be able to see more of the page.

Setting magnification does not affect the way the document is formatted or how it will print out; it only affects its on-screen display.

To change the magnification factor, click the Magnification button on the Power Bar. You see a drop-down menu like the one in Figure 6.6. Choose your magnification from the menu, or select Other to select a setting that does not appear.

FIG. 6.6
Using the Magnification button on the Power Bar, you can change the magnification factor of the screen without affecting the document format or the way it prints out.

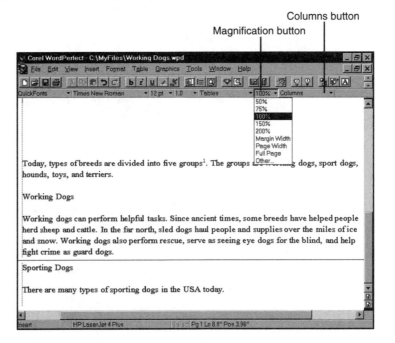

TIP If you cannot see the Magnify and Column buttons on the Power Bar, consider changing the font size of the Power Bar buttons. Right-click the Power Bar and choose Options. Pick a font like Arial that has smaller point sizes available if the default font does make smaller sizes available (refer to Figure 6.6).

When you select Other, the Zoom dialog box will appear, as in Figure 6.7. This same box appears when you choose View, Zoom from the menu bar. You can click one of the preset magnification levels in the box, or you can set your own level from 25 to 400 percent by clicking the up or down arrows in the spin box at the bottom of the Zoom dialog box.

FIG. 6.7
In the Zoom dialog box, you can change the magnification factor of the screen to preset levels or set your own level.

 TIP To quickly switch between full page and your default magnification, use the Page/Zoom Full button on the WordPerfect toolbar.

 TROUBLESHOOTING

I can't see all of the text on a line on-screen at once. Change the level of magnification with the Zoom button or after choosing View, Zoom. Experiment with 100 percent, Margin Width, and Page Width to see what best suits the situation.

It takes too long to scroll through a document. Maximize the speed at which you're working by using Draft view mode (open the View menu to change the view mode).

When I scroll from the bottom of one page to the top of the next page, the screen takes a big jump and it's difficult to get a continuous view of the text from one page to the next. Open the View menu to change from Page view to Draft view.

Part
II

Ch
6

Working with the Reveal Codes Screen

TheReveal Codes screen gives you a behind-the-scenes look at your document. Unless you have formatting problems, there is no need to look at the Reveal Codes screen.

Working with Reveal Codes on, however, is an excellent method of becoming familiar with codes and formatting. That way, when something does appear differently on the screen than you expected, you will be able to spot the problem code immediately. Remember that WordPerfect records your formatting commands in the form of embedded codes. The Reveal Codes screen shows you those embedded codes along with your text. Sometimes, the most efficient way to solve a formatting problem is by working in the Reveal Codes screen and by removing the code that causes a problem. This section shows you how to work in the Reveal Codes screen.

Accessing the Reveal Codes Screen   The position of the insertion point determines the placement of codes and where their formatting takes effect. When you select a subtitle and apply boldfacing, for example, boldface codes are embedded at either end of the subtitle. When you change tab settings, a tab set code is embedded at the beginning of the current paragraph.

When you display the Reveal Codes window—by choosing View, Reveal Codes, by pressing Alt+F3, or by dragging one of the Reveal Codes bars up or down—the screen is split into two windows, as shown in Figure 6.8.

FIG. 6.8
Formatting codes are visible in the Reveal Codes window at the bottom of the screen.

Insertion point in editing window

Insertion point in Reveal Codes window

InitialStyle code

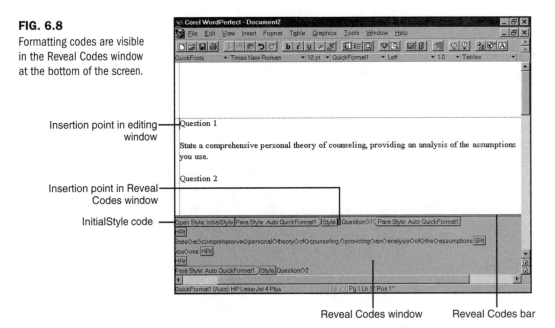

Reveal Codes window   Reveal Codes bar

N O T E   Every document contains an [Open Style:InitialStyle] code at its beginning. This code cannot be removed, but it can be edited. Formatting in the InitialStyle is a reflection of formatting in the InitialStyle for the current template. ▪

The following pointers will help you work in the Reveal Codes window:

- To remove a code, drag it out of the Reveal Codes window, or position the insertion point in front of the code and press Delete.

- There are two kinds of codes: open and paired. Open codes are contained in rectangular boxes. Paired codes are contained in boxes with points at the right (for a Start code) or left (for an End code). Open and paired codes are discussed more fully in the following section.

- To edit a code (so you can change the value it contains), double-click the code in the Reveal Codes window. To edit a margin code, for example, double-click the code. You are taken to the Margins dialog box, where you can specify a new value.

Open and Paired Codes   Most character formatting commands are inserted as paired codes—they always have a Start and an End code, for example, a Start Bold and End Bold code. When you select text and then apply the formatting, you are inserting a Start code at the beginning of the block, and an End code at the end of it. When you set your insertion point without selecting text, and then apply the formatting, you are inserting a Start code immediately followed by an End code, with your insertion point between them. The End code is pushed ahead as you type new text.

Some formatting codes, like type face and size, are *open* codes. If you set your insertion point and apply the formatting without selecting text, an Open code is placed in the document, and all text from then on takes that attribute. If you select text before inserting one of these open codes, WordPerfect puts the open type face or size code at the beginning of your blocked text, then automatically also puts an open code for the original type face or size at the end of it.

 Chapter 8, "Customizing Corel WordPerfect," shows you how to customize Corel WordPerfect to suit the way you work. You'll learn to customize display preferences, file preferences, environment preferences, toolbar and Power Bar preferences, Status Bar preferences, and summary preferences.

Part
II

Ch
6

Formatting Characters

With WordPerfect, you can format your text with a variety of font attributes such as font face, size, and appearance. The most frequently used features can be easily accessed via the WordPerfect toolbar and the Power Bar.

T I P Another way to format characters is with the WordPerfect Style feature, discussed in Chapter 9, "Organizing and Formatting Large Documents."

Font Attributes

Font attributes that you can specify include the following:

- *Font Face.* The font face is the typeface of text. Common faces are Times New Roman and Courier. Windows offers many TrueType font faces in addition to those that are built into your printer that will display on the screen just as they print out. Choose the font face that suits your work. For an informal flyer you could choose a light italic font, such as Brush. For a more formal effect, you could choose Shelley, or Caslon Openface.

- *Font Size.* Font size is measured in points. A smaller point size results in a smaller print; a larger point size results in a larger print. All text you enter in a new document that is based on the Standard template is in your printer's initial typeface and size. Most font faces are scaleable, meaning that you can change the font size.

N O T E Font size points and picas are typesetter's measurements used for measuring spacing, line thickness, and other font attributes. There are 12 points to a pica and 6 picas to an inch; therefore, there are 72 points to an inch. ■

- *Appearance.* WordPerfect allows you to specify common appearance attributes such as bold, italic, underlined, and double-underlined. You can also specify attributes including outline (letters appear with a clear fill), shadow, small caps, redline (for text that is new to this version), strikeout, and hidden (text that will not normally appear when the document is printed).

- *Position.* Text can be normal, superscripted (text set slightly above the line, r^2 for example), or subscripted (text set slightly below the line, as with H_2O).

- *Relative Size.* You can specify that text be normal, large, extra large, small, or fine. This will enlarge or reduce the text proportionate to the base font size you have selected.

- *Text Color.* You can choose the color of the text. It will display in color and, if you have a color printer, also print in color; although the display color and the printer color shade or tone may be somewhat different from each other.

- *Shading.* You can also specify the darkness of the color you have chosen. 100 percent black is black; 50 percent black is gray.

- *Underline Options.* You can specify whether the underline feature underlines spaces and/or tabs, or just the words.

You can apply formatting commands via the toolbar and Power Bar, or via the Font dialog box.

The easiest way to change the appearance of existing text is to select it, then click the Bold, Italic, or Underline buttons on the WordPerfect toolbar, or click the Change the Font or Change the Font Size buttons on the Power Bar (see Figure 6.9). Selecting a font face is shown in Figure 6.9. WordPerfect lists the four most recently used font faces at the top of the list so you can find them quickly.

FIG. 6.9
Selecting a font face may be done through the Font Face pull-down menu.

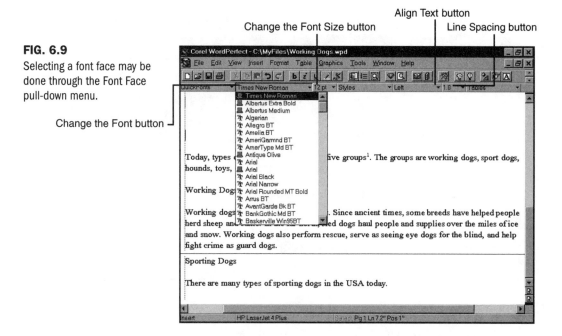

If you need more control over your text appearance, or to access features that are not on the toolbar and Power Bar, select the desired text, then access the Font dialog box by choosing Format, Font. You see the Font dialog box shown in Figure 6.10.

TIP You can also access the Font dialog box by double-clicking the Change the Font or Change the Font Size buttons (refer to Figure 6.9).

You format *new* text by positioning the insertion point, making the formatting changes with the toolbar or Font dialog box, and then typing the text. All text typed from that point on will be formatted according to your specifications until you change the formatting

Part
II

Ch
6

again. In addition, if you change the type face or size, the old text starting from the insertion point will take on the new attributes you specified.

When you format text, you put hidden control codes in your document. You can see these by selecting View, Reveal Codes.

FIG. 6.10
You can set a variety of text appearance attributes using the Font dialog box.

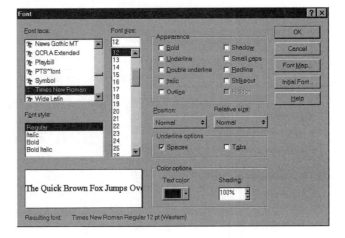

TROUBLESHOOTING

I just changed the font and font size of the text, and now I want to return it to its original format. Choose Edit, Undo/Redo History to undo the changes.

Choosing the Initial Document Font

To select the font that you want for all elements of a document, including headers, footers, footnotes, and graphic box captions:

- Choose Format, Font, then click the Initial Font button in the Font dialog box.

- Make your selections in the Document Initial Font dialog box (see Figure 6.11).

- Note that you can change the default initial font for the selected printer in this dialog box by selecting the desired font, then checking the Set As Printer Initial Font check box. When you change the default font for the selected printer, that font becomes the default font for the standard template.

 An easy way to reuse font attributes you have recently used is by selecting the text to be changed, then clicking the QuickFonts button. The last fonts you have used, along with their appearance attributes, are saved on the QuickFonts list, and you can pick the one you want to reuse.

FIG. 6.11

Set a variety of text appearance attributes using the Document Initial Font dialog box.

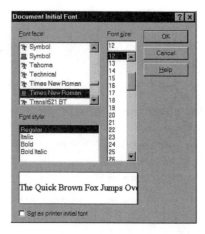

Formatting Lines and Paragraphs

Use Line and Paragraph formatting features for many of the appearance changes that you want to make in a document. For example, you can change line spacing, center text on a line, indent paragraphs, and change margins and justification.

Line and paragraph formatting features are available through the Format menu. Commonly used features are also available on the Power Bar and the toolbar.

TIP Use QuickFormat to quickly copy text formats, as discussed later in the section "Copying Formats."

Adjusting Spacing

You can adjust the spacing between lines of text within a paragraph when it suits your work, or you can adjust the spacing between paragraphs. Unless you change the defaults, or unless you're using some of the specialized templates, you're using single spacing between lines and between paragraphs.

Line Spacing Line spacing refers to the space between the baseline of one line of text and the baseline of an adjacent line of text, as shown in Figure 6.12. WordPerfect adjusts line spacing automatically to allow for the height of the largest font on a line (the line height). Enough extra white space is added to make the text readable.

WordPerfect's default line spacing is set to single spacing. When you specify a new number for the line spacing value, the current line height is multiplied by that number. If you choose a value of 1.5 for line spacing, for example, the height of a single-spaced line is multiplied by 1.5.

Part

II

Ch

6

FIG. 6.12

Line spacing affects
readability and page design.

Single line spacing

One-and-one-half line spacing

Double line spacing

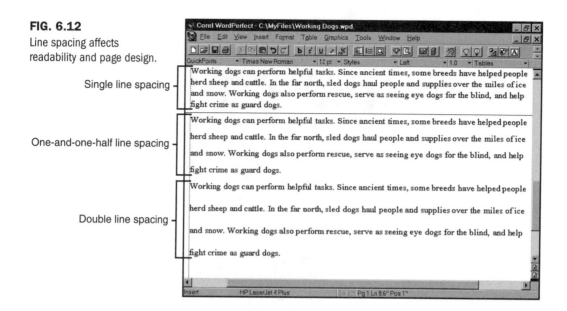

N O T E Line spacing refers to the spacing between lines that are separated by automatic word wrap. Paragraph spacing (discussed later) refers to lines that are separated by a hard return (an Enter keystroke).

To adjust line spacing, do the following:

1. Place your insertion point where the new line spacing should begin, or select the text to which it should apply.

2. Click the Line Spacing button on the Power Bar, and then choose a value from the line spacing list (refer to Figure 6.9). If you want a value that isn't on the list, choose Other. You see the Line Spacing dialog box shown in Figure 6.13, and can specify the line spacing—even to two decimals accuracy (for example, .98 or .35).

FIG. 6.13

Change the line spacing in
the Line Spacing dialog box.

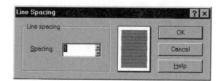

3. In the Line Spacing dialog box, enter a new value in the Spacing text box.

4. After entering the value you want for line spacing, choose OK.

TIP You can also access the Line Spacing dialog box by double-clicking the Line Spacing button, or by choosing Format, Line, Spacing.

NOTE Line spacing is inserted as a paired code if text is selected, and as an open code otherwise. ■

Paragraph Spacing   Adjust the spacing between paragraphs rather than lines when you want to adjust the white space between paragraphs (wherever there is an Enter keystroke). You commonly see paragraphs that are separated by a blank line. This appearance is the result of pressing Enter twice. You can add readability to your document with a different approach—by adjusting the spacing between paragraphs. When you set paragraph spacing to 2.0, for example, and you press Enter once at the end of a paragraph, the distance between the first paragraph and the second paragraph is 1.5 times the current line spacing value.

To adjust the spacing between paragraphs, choose Format, Paragraph, Format. The Paragraph Format dialog box is displayed, as shown in Figure 6.14. Enter a new value for Spacing Between Paragraphs and choose OK.

FIG. 6.14
In the Paragraph Format dialog box, add extra spacing between paragraphs for readability.

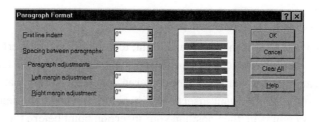

Text with paragraph spacing adjusted to 1.5 is shown in Figure 6.15.

Centering and Flush Right

You can position specific text on a single line with the Center or Flush Right command. Text that is centered is centered between the left and right margins. Title lines are commonly centered. Text that is flush right ends at the right margin; it extends "backward" to the left. Page headers and footers often have text that is flush right.

To apply Center or Flush Right:

1. Position the insertion point immediately before the text that is to be centered or flush right. (To center or flush right the entire line, position the insertion point at the beginning of the line.)

Part
II

Ch
6

2. Right-click with the mouse, then choose <u>C</u>enter or Flush <u>R</u>ight from the QuickMenu.

FIG. 6.15

With paragraph spacing set at 1.5 in the Paragraph Format dialog box, you just press Enter once between paragraphs to get a result that looks like this.

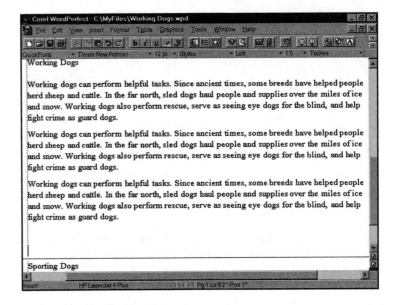

▶ **See** "Using QuickMenus," **p. 54**

When you apply Center or Flush Right, text following the insertion point is formatted with that feature. Thus, you can easily have some text on the same line that is at the left of the line, another few words that are centered, and some others that are flush right. To do so, you would position your insertion point before the text to be centered, then choose the <u>C</u>enter command, then position your insertion point before the text to be flush right, then choose the Flush <u>R</u>ight command.

 TIP To create text that is centered or flush right with a dot leader (a series of dots) before it, apply the Center or Flush Right command twice.

▶ **See** "Setting Justification," **p. 125**

The Center and Flush Right commands apply only to text on a single line. To make all text after the insertion point centered or flush right, use the Align Text button on the Power Bar (refer to Figure 6.9).

Indenting Text

You can indent one or more paragraphs to emphasize the text, format a long quotation, or create subordinate levels. There are four common types of indents that you can see in Figure 6.16.

FIG. 6.16

You can emphasize text with four types of indents.

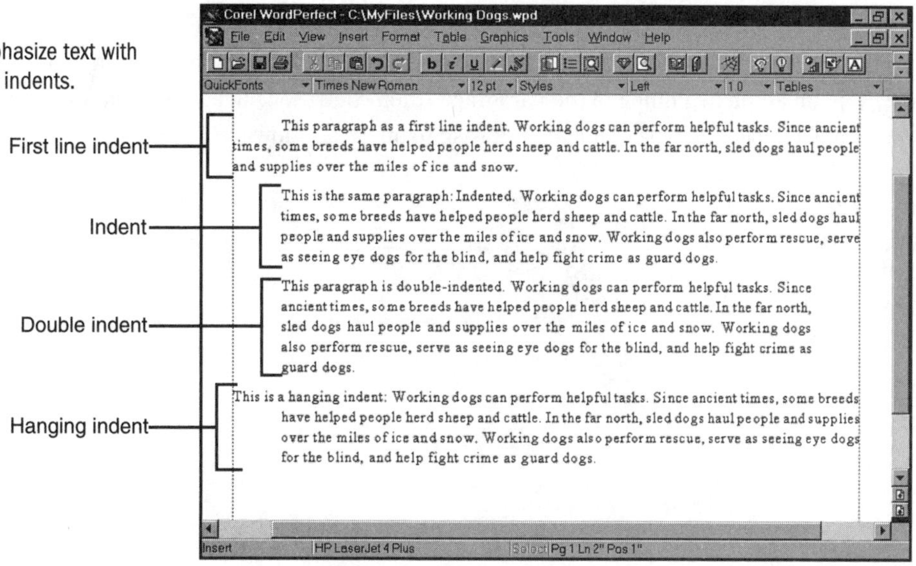

- *First line indent.* The first line of text is indented one tab stop from the left, as when you press the Tab key at the beginning of a paragraph. This is most often used for double-spaced text.

- *Indent.* This is WordPerfect's term for moving the entire paragraph one tab stop in from the left. This is often used to set off points you are making.

- *Double indent.* The entire paragraph is moved in both one tab stop from the left and from the right. This is often used for long quotations.

- *Hanging indent.* The first line extends to the left margin, but succeeding lines are indented in from the left by one tab stop. This is often used in bibliographies.

All of these indents affect the text from the insertion point, through the end of the paragraph.

To create a first line indent, you can press the Tab key at the beginning of each paragraph. You can automate this process by using the paragraph formatting feature; this is often done in conjunction with setting paragraph spacing. Do so by positioning your insertion

Part

II

Ch

6

point before the paragraphs to be indented, then choose Format, Paragraph, Format. The Paragraph Format dialog box is displayed (refer to Figure 6.14). Enter a new value for First Line Indent, such as .5, and choose OK.

N O T E Remember that a paragraph ends with a hard return (an Enter keystroke). ▉

To indent, double-indent, or hanging indent a single paragraph, position your insertion point at the beginning of the paragraph, then click the QuickSpot. Click the Indent button, and choose the type of indent you wish to apply, as shown in Figure 6.17.

FIG. 6.17
You can choose the type of indent you wish to apply from the QuickSpot menu.

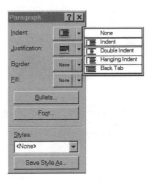

To indent several paragraphs at once, first select the paragraphs, and then follow the steps for indenting a single paragraph.

 Indenting is such a common task that you may wish to remember the hot key for it, F7.

CAUTION
Don't try to align paragraphs on-screen with the spacebar or Enter key. This probably won't look right and it causes editing problems.

Setting and Using Tabs

Unlike indents, which affect all text lines until the next hard return, tabs affect only the current line of text. Tabs are used primarily to indent the first line of a paragraph, to indent one-line paragraphs, and to line up columns of text or numbers.

By default, tabs are set at half-inch intervals across the page. When you use a feature that positions at the next tab stop (Tab, Indent, Hanging Indent, or Double Indent), the insertion point moves to the next tab stop on the right. You can customize tab stops to suit your work. For example, if you want less space between the bullets in a bulleted list and the text following the bullets, move the tab stop that aligns the text closer to the bullet. You can also set customized tabs to type in columns of text or numbers.

N O T E   By default, tabs are measured relative to the left margin, not from the left edge of the page. This means that when the left margin is changed, tab settings remain at the same distance from the margin. You can optionally set tabs in absolute measurements, from the left edge of the paper.

Another way to align columns of text or numbers is with a table. Tables make it easy to align text, and there are many formatting features that you can use to enhance the appearance of tables. ■

▶ **See** "Working with Tables," **p. 196**

Setting Tabs with the Ruler Bar   You can quickly set tabs using the Ruler Bar. New tab settings take effect at the beginning of the current paragraph. If you have selected text, the new tab settings apply only to the selection. If you have not, new tab settings apply to all text from the paragraph the insertion point is in until a different tab setting code is reached. Be sure to position the insertion point properly (or to select the text for which you want customized tab settings) before you adjust tab settings.

▶ **See** "Displaying Screen Elements," **p. 104**

Tab settings on the Ruler Bar are indicated by markers that hang down in the bottom area of the Ruler Bar. The shape of the marker indicates the type of alignment (left, center, right align, decimal align) and whether the tab stop has a dot leader. Figure 6.18 shows the Ruler Bar with customized tab settings for several types of alignment.

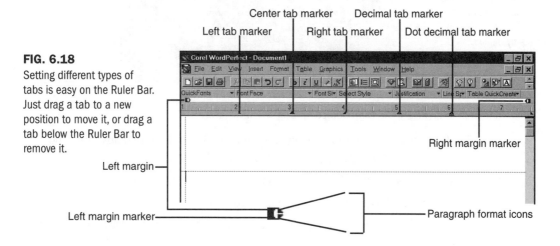

FIG. 6.18
Setting different types of tabs is easy on the Ruler Bar. Just drag a tab to a new position to move it, or drag a tab below the Ruler Bar to remove it.

Center tab marker   Decimal tab marker

Left tab marker   Right tab marker   Dot decimal tab marker

Right margin marker

Left margin

Left margin marker   Paragraph format icons

Part

II

Ch

6

Important items to remember about setting tabs include:

- Before you set new tabs, position the insertion point and clear all existing tab stops.

- To move a tab, drag it to a new position. As you drag, the position is indicated on the Status Bar.

- To insert a new tab (of the current type), click in the Tab area of the Ruler, beneath the numbered ruler scale where you want the marker to appear.

- To set a different type of tab, right-click in the Tab area and choose a type from the QuickMenu. For example, to set a tab that aligns a column of numbers, first right-click in the Tab area. Choose Decimal, and then left-click at the desired position on the ruler scale.

- To remove a tab, drag it below the ruler. To remove all tabs, right-click in the Tab area and choose Clear All Tabs from the QuickMenu.

Setting Tabs from the Tab Set Dialog Box   The Tab Set dialog box enables you to set tabs precisely, and to specify options that aren't available from the Ruler Bar. Before you adjust tabs, be sure to position the insertion point in the paragraph where you want the new tab stops to take effect, or select the text that you want formatted with new tab stops.

To display the Tab Set dialog box, choose Format, Line, Tab Set, or right-click in the Ruler Bar and choose Tab Set. WordPerfect displays the Tab Set dialog box shown in Figure 6.19.

FIG. 6.19
After positioning the insertion point, use the Tab Set dialog box to position tabs in precise positions. Positions in this box and on the Ruler Bar are set in inches by default.

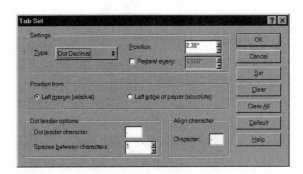

It is best to clear out old tabs before setting the new ones.

- To clear a single tab setting, specify the setting in the Position text box, then choose Clear or choose Clear All to clear all tabs.

- To set a tab using the Tab Set dialog box, take the following steps:

  1. Select a tab type from the Type drop-down list.

  2. Specify a position (in fractions of inches) that you want in the Position text box.

  3. Choose Set.

■ To clear existing tab stops and restore the default tabs, choose <u>D</u>efault.

■ Click OK when you finish working in the Tab Set dialog box.

 T I P Chapter 9, "Organizing and Formatting Large Documents," covers outlining and formatting with styles.

Setting Margins

You can change the margins at any point in a document. You may want to make the left and right margins smaller to add more room for text in columns, or you may want to set one-half inch top and bottom margins when you use page headers and footers. WordPerfect's Standard template uses 1-inch top and bottom margins and 1-inch left and right margins. Left and right margins can be set by dragging margin markers on the Ruler Bar; all four margins can be set from the Margins dialog box or with the guidelines. See the section "Using Headers and Footers" later in this chapter.

N O T E To make your margin change to all elements of the document, including text, page headers, and footers choose Fo<u>r</u>mat, <u>D</u>ocument, Initial Codes <u>S</u>tyle. Within the Styles Editor dialog box, choose Fo<u>r</u>mat, <u>M</u>argins, and set the Margins you want. Click OK. Click the <u>U</u>se as Default check box before you click OK to close the Styles Editor. ■

If no text is selected when you set left and right margins, changes take place from the beginning of the current paragraph. Similarly, when you set top and bottom margins, changes take place from the beginning of the current page. Margin changes apply to all following text until another margin code is reached. Alternatively, if text is selected when you change margins, margin changes apply only to selected text.

Setting Margins Using Guidelines   You can quickly adjust all four of the margins using the guidelines, as follows:

1. Select text or position your insertion point as needed.

2. To adjust the left or right margin, drag the appropriate guideline to the desired position. As you drag the guideline, you will see the margin setting in a tiny pop-up window, as shown in Figure 6.20.

Setting Margins with the Ruler Bar   If you prefer, you can also quickly adjust left and right margins using the Ruler Bar:

1. Select text or position your insertion point as needed.

2. If it is not already displayed, choose <u>V</u>iew, <u>T</u>oolbars/Ruler, and check Ruler Bar to display the Ruler Bar.

Part

II

Ch

6

3. To adjust the left or right margin, drag the appropriate margin marker to the desired position (symbols for the margin markers are identified in Figure 6.18). The left margin marker is the outside marker at the left end of the white space in the Ruler Bar; the right margin marker is the outside marker at the right end of the white space. As you drag a marker, its position is indicated on the Status Bar and a vertical dotted line marks its position.

FIG. 6.20

You can drag the guidelines to set margins. When you do, the margin setting appears in a small pop-up window.

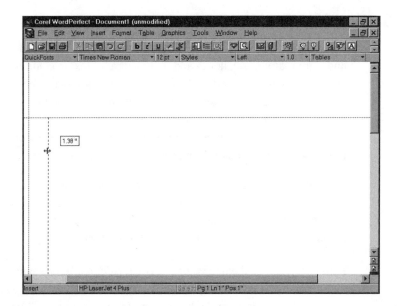

Setting Margins from the Margins Dialog Box   You can specify precise margins from the Margins dialog box using the following steps:

1. Select text or position your insertion point as needed.

2. To access the Margins dialog box, choose Format, Margins, or right-click in the left margin and choose Margins from the QuickMenu. The Margins dialog box is displayed as shown in Figure 6.21.

FIG. 6.21

Specify precise margins from the Margins dialog box.

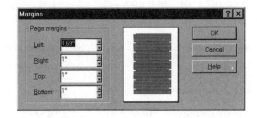

3. Enter the new margins settings in the appropriate text box areas.

4. When you finish adjusting margins, choose OK.

Setting Justification

Justification is the way that text is aligned relative to the left and right margins on the page. The way you justify text can make the text easy to read, decorative, eye-catching, formal and sophisticated, or casual and flexible. WordPerfect provides five main types of justification: Left (the default), Center, Right, Full, and All, as shown in Figure 6.22.

FIG. 6.22
WordPerfect offers five types of justification: Left, Center, Right, and Full are pictured here.

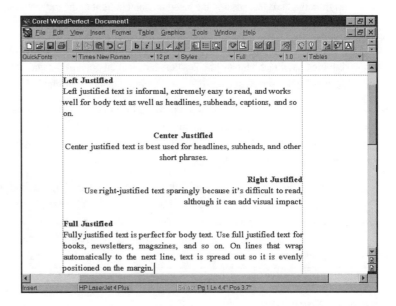

NOTE Full and All both produce text that is aligned with both the left and right margins. The difference is in how spaces are inserted. Full justification inserts spaces between words; All inserts spaces between words and between letters within words. All also aligns all lines of text including the last line, which ends with a hard return. ■

Part
II

Ch
6

If you have text selected when you set justification, the justification will apply only to the selected text. Otherwise, it will apply from the paragraph the insertion point is in until it reaches another justification command. To set justification:

1. Select text or position your insertion point as needed.

2. Click the Align Text button on the Power Bar (refer to Figure 6.9), and choose the justification style you desire.

N O T E If you want all your new documents to use a justification that is different from the default, change the default justification. Choose Format, Document, Initial Codes Style. Within the Styles Editor dialog box, choose Format, Justification, and select the justification that you want. Click the Use as Default check box before you click OK to close the Styles Editor. ▪

TROUBLESHOOTING

I used Double Indent to indent a quotation in my document but I want the text to go further in from the margins. Position the insertion point in front of the indented text and create another Double Indent. This indents the text by one more tab stop.

I set customized tab stops for columns of text and now, at the end of the document, my bulleted list doesn't look right. Position the insertion point at the end of the columns of text and restore the default tab settings (choose Format, Line, Tab Set, Default, OK).

I tried to adjust the customized tab settings that I created for columns of text but now the columns don't line up evenly. You can undo the damage with the Undo button, or with the Edit, Undo/Redo History. Before you adjust tab settings again, be sure to position the insertion point on the first line of the text that you want to adjust.

I used full justification in my document, and now there are big gaps between words. Try using All rather than Full justification, because All will put spaces between letters as well as between words. Another way to alleviate the problem is to turn on Hyphenation by choosing Format, Line, Hyphenation, Hyphenation On. For more information on using hyphenation, see Hyphenation in the WordPerfect online Help.

Copying Formats

QuickFormat makes it easy to copy formats from already formatted text without respecifying each format instruction. Suppose that you took pains to apply several font changes to a subtitle to make it look just right. Now you want to give the same look to other subtitles. Just show QuickFormat where to copy the formats, and it does all of the work for you. When you choose to format headings, WordPerfect automatically updates all related headings formatted with QuickFormat. If you change your mind about the font face in your heading, for example, you can change the font face in one of the headings, and your change is instantly reflected in the others.

N O T E You can apply more than one set of QuickFormat formats in the same document. ▪

To use QuickFormat, first select the text that contains the formats that you want to copy, or place the insertion point in the paragraph whose formats you want to copy. Next, click the QuickFormat button on the toolbar, or choose Format, QuickFormat. The QuickFormat dialog box is displayed, as shown in Figure 6.23.

FIG. 6.23
Choose Headings from the QuickFormat dialog box to copy paragraph formatting as well as fonts and attributes. Choose Characters to copy fonts and attributes only.

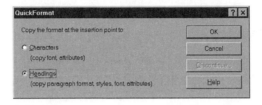

Select Headings to copy fonts and attributes as well as paragraph formatting. When you choose OK, the mouse pointer changes to a paint roller or a paint brush, depending on whether you chose to format characters (brush) or headings (roller). Figure 6.24 shows you the paint roller pointer while QuickFormat is active.

FIG. 6.24
Use QuickFormat to copy formats from one text area to other text areas.

Copy formatting from here...

to here, using QuickFormat

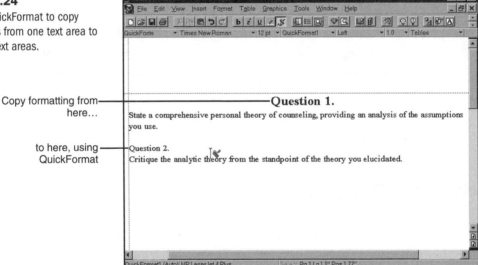

While QuickFormat is active, select any text to which you want to copy formats, or click in a paragraph to which you want to copy formats. Repeat this step as often as desired. When you finish copying formats, click the QuickFormat button to deactivate the feature. The new format is applied to all of the selected paragraphs and the pointer returns to its I-beam appearance.

Part
II

Ch
6

TROUBLESHOOTING

I indented a paragraph, but it doesn't look right. Remember that you should only use Indent once at the beginning of the paragraph to indent the entire paragraph. If you used Indent again anywhere else in the paragraph, this may be what caused your problem. Either delete the paragraph and retype it, or remove any extraneous [Hd Left Ind] codes (choose <u>V</u>iew, Reveal <u>C</u>odes to turn on Reveal Codes).

 I used QuickFormat to copy formats to text in several locations, but after I finished, I accidentally copied them to an extra place. When you choose Headings at the QuickFormat dialog box, it's easy to copy formats; simply click in the paragraph that you want to format. However, it's also easy to click inadvertently and to format text unintentionally before you remember to turn off QuickFormat. The damage is easily reversed by clicking the Undo button, even after you've turned QuickFormat off.

Formatting the Page

When you work with multiple-page documents, you may be concerned with the position of page breaks. You also probably want to use page headers and/or footers, and you might want to number pages. These topics can all be thought of as elements of page formatting. Page Size is also an element of page formatting, although this topic can just as easily apply to a single-page document as to a multiple-page document.

WordPerfect's page-formatting features are flexible and easy to use. You can change the appearance of the page to fit your text so that you present the most professional-looking document possible.

Working with Page Breaks

WordPerfect automatically divides your document into pages based on the formatting choices you make. These automatic page breaks are called soft page breaks. The position of a soft page break adjusts automatically as you edit a document and cannot be deleted.

Because it's often important to break a page at a specific location, WordPerfect offers ways to control where pages are divided. The simplest method for ensuring that a page break falls where you want it to fall, regardless of format changes, is to use the Page Break feature. A page break created with the Page Break feature is called a hard page break.

To create a hard page break, position the insertion point at the beginning of the first line that is to start on a new page, and press Ctrl+Enter, or choose Insert, Page Break. All text following a hard page break automatically repaginates.

In Draft view, a hard page break appears as a double line across the screen; a soft page break appears as a single line across the screen. In Page view, soft page breaks and hard page breaks look exactly alike; each of them appears as a heavy line across the page.

N O T E When you remove hard page breaks from a document, start at the beginning of the document and work your way toward the end of the document. When you remove a page break, all text from that position on repaginates automatically, and you can adjust subsequent page breaks accordingly.

> **CAUTION**
>
> When you use hard page breaks too often, your document cannot easily be edited, because the page breaks wind up in the wrong position. Use hard page breaks only when pages should always end at the hard page break—at the end of chapters, for example.

A hard page break can be removed. To remove a hard page break, position the insertion point just in front of the page break and press Delete, or position the insertion point just after the page break and press Backspace. The Make It Fit feature is a good way to avoid using hard page breaks.

Using Headers and Footers

A header or footer is information that appears at the top or bottom of every page (or just on odd or even pages). You can save yourself a lot of work by creating headers and footers in multiple-page documents.

WordPerfect's headers and footers are easy to use and very flexible. A header or footer can include one or more lines of text, automatic page numbers, the document path and file name, graphic lines, and other graphic elements, as well as formatting such as tables or columns.

The amount of white space at the top or bottom of the page changes only when you change the top or bottom margin, not when you use headers or footers. When you use headers and footers, there is less room on the page for body text. Soft page breaks adjust automatically to allow room for headers and footers.

Headers and footers are visible on-screen in Page view or Two Page view. Even though you can't see a header or footer on-screen in Draft view, it will print.

Part

II

Ch

6

WordPerfect provides two headers, Header A and Header B, and two footers, Footer A and Footer B, in case you want different headers or footers on odd and even pages. Unless you're printing on both sides of the paper, you only need one header or footer. The instructions that follow refer to Header A, but are the same as the instructions for Header B, Footer A, or Footer B. To create Header A, take the following steps:

1. Position the insertion point on the first page of body text, or on the page where you want the header to begin.

2. Right-click in the top margin, then choose Header/Footer; or Choose Format, Header/Footer. The Headers/Footers dialog box is displayed. Select Header A, if it's not already selected.

3. Choose Create. You are placed in a special editing screen for Header A (indicated in the title bar at the top of the screen). The Header/Footer feature bar is displayed just below the toolbar and the Power Bar. If you're working in Page view or Two Page view, you can see the body text on-screen while you're working with your header. The insertion point is placed at the beginning of the header area, as shown in Figure 6.25.

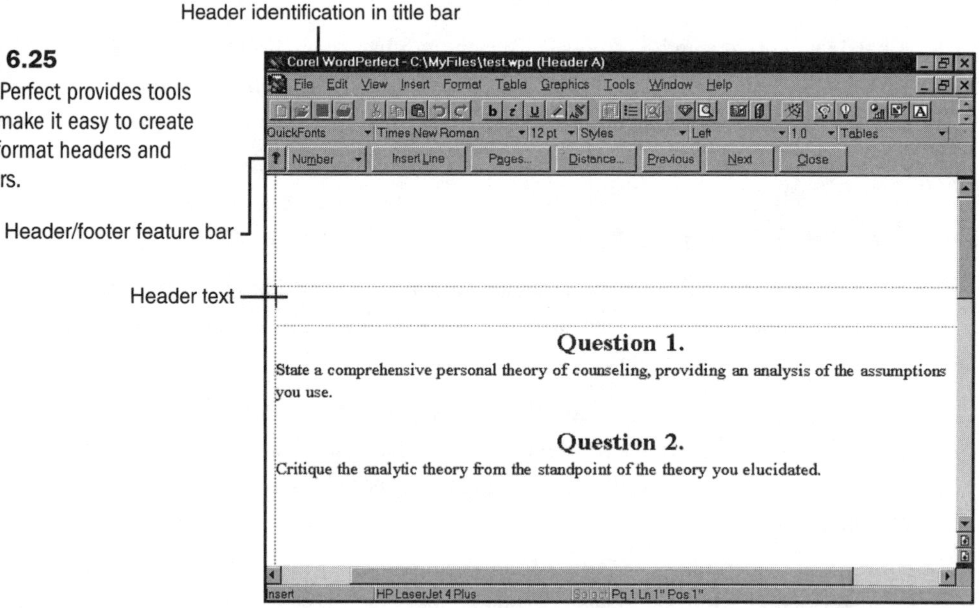

Header identification in title bar

FIG. 6.25
WordPerfect provides tools that make it easy to create and format headers and footers.

Header/footer feature bar

Header text

Corel WordPerfect - C:\MyFiles\test.wpd (Header A)

File Edit View Insert Format Table Graphics Tools Window Help

QuickFonts   Times New Roman   12 pt   Styles   Left   10   Tables

Number   Insert Line   Pages...   Distance...   Previous   Next   Close

Question 1.
State a comprehensive personal theory of counseling, providing an analysis of the assumptions you use.

Question 2.
Critique the analytic theory from the standpoint of the theory you elucidated.

Insert   HP LaserJet 4 Plus   Select   Pg 1 Ln 1" Pos 1"

- Choose Insert, Other, Path and Filename to insert the path and file name.

- Use the Center or Flush Right feature to place information appropriately within the header by clicking before the text, then choosing Format, Line Center or Flush Right.

- Choose Insert, Date, Date Text; or press Ctrl+D to insert the current date. Alternatively, choose Insert, Date, Date Code to insert a dynamic date.

4. Use the appropriate buttons on the feature bar (refer to Figure 6.25) to format and to add information to your header.

- Choose Number, Page Number to insert automatic page numbers at the insertion point.
- Choose Insert Line to insert a horizontal graphics line that extends from margin to margin at the baseline of text on the current line.
- Select Pages to specify whether the header or footer should be on odd pages, even pages, or all pages.
- Choose Distance to adjust the distance between text in the header and text on the page.
- Select Previous to edit the previous header or footer, if there is one.
- Choose Next to edit the next header or footer if there is one.

5. Use the WordPerfect menu bar, the toolbar, and the Power Bar as needed to format and edit your header.

6. When you finish working in the header editing screen, click the Close button on the feature bar.

Print a letter that makes your letterhead stationery more attractive and professional-looking by creating a header that prints on all pages after the first page. On the first line of the header is the name of the recipient, on the second line is the page number, and on the third line is the date. Figure 6.26 illustrates a header that follows this format. Although the header is being created on the first page of the letter, it will be suppressed on this page (see the section "Suppressing Headers, Footers, and Page Numbering," later in the chapter).

N O T E To edit a header or footer, switch to Page view by choosing View, Page. You will be able to see the header or footer at the top or bottom of the page. Click in the header or footer to edit it, or delete the text in it to delete it. ▪

Part

II

Ch

6

Numbering Pages

Although you can insert page numbers in headers or footers, you also have the capability to number pages with the Page Numbering feature. The page number prints in the top or bottom line of the text area. WordPerfect inserts a blank line to separate the number from other text on the page. In Page view, page numbering is visible on-screen. To suppress page numbering, see the later section "Suppressing Headers, Footers, and Page Numbering."

FIG. 6.26

With the Header/Footer feature bar, you can easily create professional-looking headers for page 2 (and the pages that follow) of a business letter.

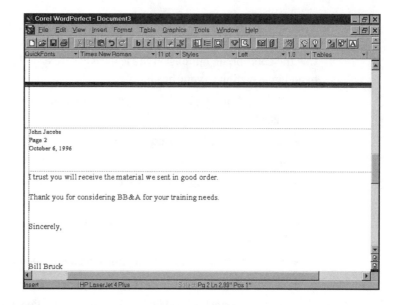

Choosing a Page Number Format   To use the Page Numbering feature, you must specify a format for the numbering. Choose Format, Page Numbering, Select. The Select Page Numbering Format dialog box is displayed. Figure 6.27 illustrates the Select Page Numbering Format dialog box with Bottom Center as the selected position. Dashes have been added on either side of the number by selecting the appropriate format in the Page Numbering Format box. Choose OK to close the dialog box.

FIG. 6.27

Add page numbers to your document with the Page Numbering Format feature.

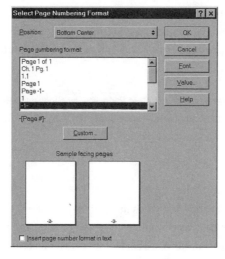

T I P "Select" is grayed out if the focus is currently in a header, footer, or graphic.

Changing the Page Number Value By default, WordPerfect uses the physical page number as the page number value. The page number value is the number that will print, whether you ask for page numbering in a header or footer or whether you ask for it with the Page Numbering feature. When you have a title page at the beginning of your document, you need to change the page number value on the first page of body text so WordPerfect thinks of that page as page 1.

To change the page number value, position the insertion point on the page to be renumbered, then choose Format, Page Numbering, Value/Adjust. You see the Value/Adjust Number dialog box shown in Figure 6.28. Set the page number, then click OK.

FIG. 6.28
You can change the initial page number to account for title pages and tables of contents in the Value/Adjust Number dialog box.

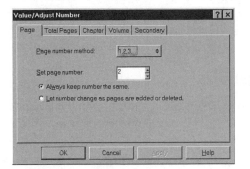

N O T E You can also set the number of your chapter, volume, or secondary pages using this dialog box. This can be useful when creating large manuscripts or books. You can insert your chapter, volume, or secondary page number in a header or footer by clicking the Number button on the Header/Footer Feature Bar. ▪

Suppressing Headers, Footers, and Page Numbering

To keep a header, footer, or page number from printing on a specific page, use WordPerfect's Suppress feature. Typically, a header or footer is created on the first page of body text, although it may be suppressed on that page. Headers and footers are usually suppressed on title pages at the beginning of new sections in a long document.

To suppress headers, footers, and page numbering, take the following steps:

1. Position the insertion point on the page where you want to suppress the header/footer/page numbering.

2. Choose Format, Page, Suppress. The Suppress dialog box shown in Figure 6.29 is displayed.

FIG. 6.29
Suppress headers, footers, or page numbering on the current page in the Suppress dialog box.

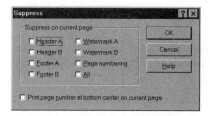

3. Click beside the features that you want to suppress on the current page.

4. Choose OK.

N O T E WordPerfect's Delay Codes feature provides you with a method for delaying the effects of headers and footers (and other types of formatting) for a specified number of pages. Use Delay Codes by choosing Format, Page, Delay Codes. Specify the number of pages to delay in the Delay Codes dialog box, then choose OK. Insert codes such as headers and footers, then click Close on the Delay Codes Feature Bar. ▓

Changing the Page Size

Whenever you start a new, empty document with the Standard template, you're using the Letter page size (8 1/2 × 11-inch paper in a portrait orientation). To use a different physical size or a different orientation, specify another page size with WordPerfect's Page Size feature. For example, if you need lots of page width for a table with many columns, you could choose Letter Landscape as your page size.

CAUTION
Your printer must be able to use the paper size you select and print that paper size in the orientation you select, or you may get unpredictable results.

To change the Page Size, take the following steps:

1. Position the insertion point on the first page where you want to specify a page size.

2. Choose Format, Page, Page Size. The Page Size dialog box appears (see Figure 6.30).

FIG. 6.30
Select your page definition in the Page Size dialog box.

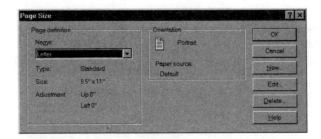

3. Select the paper size that you want from a list of predefined document types. Notice that the Page Definition area and the Orientation area give you information and a preview of the selected page size.

4. Choose OK. The selected page size takes effect on the current page.

TROUBLESHOOTING

I created a hard page break but now I have too many page breaks. Make sure you're working in Draft view so you can see which page breaks are hard page breaks (you can't remove a soft page break). Position the insertion point just in front of a hard page break and press Delete to remove it. Alternatively, turn on Reveal Codes so you can delete the code (see the previous section, "Working with the Reveal Codes Screen," in this chapter).

I asked for Page Numbering on the first page where I wanted it and the number that prints is not 1. Unless you change the page number value, the number that prints is the same as the physical page number. Position the insertion point on the page that you want numbered with a 1 and change the page number value to 1 (after choosing Format, Page Numbering, Value/Adjust).

Using Make It Fit

It's easy to make a document fit on the page when you use the Make It Fit feature. Instead of making endless trial-and-error adjustments to margins, font size, and line spacing, let Make It Fit do it all for you. You get a perfect fit every time. You tell WordPerfect what kind of adjustments to make; if you don't like the results, Undo them and try Make It Fit with another set of specifications.

To use Make It Fit, take the following steps:

1. In an open document, click the Make It Fit button. The Make It Fit dialog box is displayed (see Figure 6.31).

Part II
Ch 6

FIG. 6.31

The Make It Fit feature contracts or expands a document to a specified number of pages.

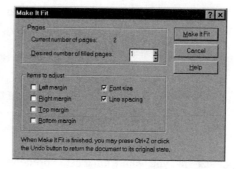

2. Specify the number of pages to fill in the Desired Number of Filled Pages box. For example, to make a document that is just barely too long for a single page fit on one page, specify 1 as the number of pages to fill.

3. Select the options that you want adjusted in the Items to Adjust area.

4. Choose Make It Fit.

5. Check the results to see if they're satisfactory. Remember that you can zoom back and forth from a Full Page view with the Page/Zoom Full button. If you don't like the results, click Undo and repeat these steps with different adjustments.

CHAPTER 7

Using Writing Tools and Printing

Corel WordPerfect supplies a variety of tools that make it easy to create professionally finished documents without errors. By simply selecting a template and filling in the blanks, you can quickly create fax forms, memos, daily planners, and many other standard documents. In addition to supplying you with preformatted documents, Corel WordPerfect provides a variety of powerful proofreading tools. You can check spelling and correct errors automatically. You can keep your text from being monotonous and repetitive by finding alternative words with the Thesaurus. You can use the grammar checker to suggest improvements to your writing style.

With all of these writing tools at your fingertips, you can create error-free, well-written documents that look as though they were created by a professional editor. Corel WordPerfect takes care of much of the tiresome detail work of formatting, manual proofreading, and evaluating your writing style.

Once you finish your document, you can print it. Corel WordPerfect provides features that make it easy to print envelopes and mailing labels as well as documents. ■

Use templates

Learn about templates that automate the preparation of many types of business documents.

Check your spelling

See how Corel WordPerfect offers sophisticated spell checking, including automatic correction of common errors, and an indicator that shows you misspellings as you type!

Use the Thesaurus

Corel WordPerfect's Thesaurus doesn't just provide synonyms. Use this complete dictionary to define common words.

Check your grammar

Learn to select the writing style you want, and let Corel WordPerfect tell you how you're doing.

Print your document, envelopes, and labels

Understand how to easily print part or all of your document to any available printer, as well as envelopes for your letters, and labels for common Avery styles.

Using Templates

Every new document that you create is based on a template. The standard template (the default template) is generic; you provide most of the formatting and all of the text. Other templates often provide text as well as formatting. Many templates are automated. Repetitive information is entered only once, and you can fill in the blanks with a minimum of effort. The template prompts you for necessary information (like the recipient's name), you answer the prompts, and the template places your input in the proper location.

 T I P Chapter 11, "Automating with Macros and Merge" shows you how to save time by automating repetitive processes that you do over and over.

Whenever you create a new document that should have a consistent, specialized appearance, it makes sense to use a template. It's well worth your while to explore Corel WordPerfect's templates, and to see which ones will save you time and work. In this section, you learn how to use templates and how to make minor modifications to a template so that it better suits your taste.

Understanding Templates

You already know that templates can contain text as well as formatting. Each template contains its own set of tools, including styles, abbreviations, macros, keyboards, toolbars, and menus. Templates can even have customized toolbars so that you have just the right tools close at hand when you create a document based on that template.

> **N O T E** Another way to customize your documents is by setting up Corel WordPerfect's defaults to resemble those of your most used document style. Chapter 8, "Customizing Corel WordPerfect," covers customizing Corel WordPerfect to suit the way you work. You will learn to change Display preferences, Environment preferences, File preferences, Summary preferences, and other preferences. In addition, you will learn to customize the default settings for new documents. ■

A typical memo template might contain the company letterhead and logo, and standard text in specific places on the page. A letter template, on the other hand, might consist of your company name and address, the date, a standard salutation, and a standard closure. An expense report template could include a table complete with formulas that automatically total each category of expense as well as the total expenses.

Although the template feature is complex, learning to make the feature work for you is easy. You can use Corel WordPerfect's predefined templates as is. You can easily make basic editing changes to existing templates, and you can easily create simple templates of your own.

 TIP You can also include tables and graphics in your templates to give your documents a professional appearance. Chapter 10, "Using Tables and Graphics," teaches you how to include tables, clip art, charts, and other graphic design elements in your Corel WordPerfect document.

Using Templates Supplied with Corel WordPerfect

There are a number of different templates supplied with Corel WordPerfect. In fact, there are templates supplied for business, education, legal documents, personal documents, publishing, and Web documents.

Some templates are further automated with dialog boxes that ask you a series of questions before constructing your document. That way, you can customize the document to your tastes and needs. These automated templates are called *experts*.

Using templates and experts can be an easy and even fun way to create great-looking documents, once you've started using them. To demonstrate how easy they are, the following steps show you how to use a common expert that most people need often, the Letter Expert.

1. Choose File, New. You see the Select New Document dialog box shown in Figure 7.1.

FIG. 7.1
Corel WordPerfect comes with templates to help you create many different types of documents.

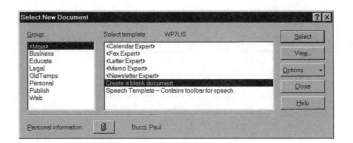

2. Ensure that the <Main> group is selected, then select <Letter Expert> in the Select Template box.

 TIP You can enter personal information that is used in all appropriate templates and experts by choosing Personal Information and entering or selecting information in the Address Book, which is discussed in Chapter 29, "Using Corel Address Book 7."

Part
II

Ch
7

3. Choose Select. After 10 seconds or so, the screen goes blank, then after a few more seconds you see the formatted letter in the background and the Letter Expert dialog box shown in Figure 7.2.

FIG. 7.2

The Letter Expert allows you to modify various elements of the letter you are creating.

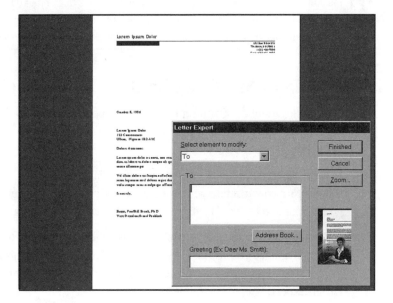

4. Fill in the recipient's name and address in the To box, and the greeting in the Greeting box.

T I P You can also use the Address Book for this information, as discussed in Chapter 29, "Using Corel Address Book 7."

5. In the Select Element to Modify drop-down list box, choose From. The Letter Expert dialog box resembles the one shown in Figure 7.3. Notice that you cannot change this element; it is brought in if you select Personal Information from the initial Select New Document dialog box. You can, however, modify your letter when it is completed, so for now accept whatever is in this window.

6. Choose Subject and Reference in the Select Element to Modify drop-down list box. You see the Letter Expert dialog box shown in Figure 7.4. If you want a Subject Line or Reference Line, mark the appropriate check box, then fill in the subject or reference of your letter.

7. Select Appearance in the Select Element to Modify drop-down list box. You see the Letter Expert dialog box shown in Figure 7.5. Choose from a variety of letterhead styles and text formats in the appropriate drop-down list boxes.

FIG. 7.3

Personal Information is brought into your letter if you used the Address Book to enter it in the Select New Document dialog box previously.

FIG. 7.4

The Letter Expert allows you to add a subject and/or reference line to your letter.

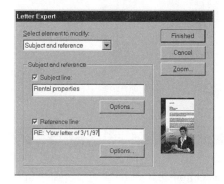

FIG. 7.5

You can choose from a variety of built-in letterhead styles and text formats for your letter.

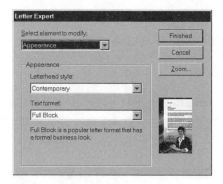

8. Similarly, select Closing in the Select Element to Modify drop-down list box to enter your closing (for example, Sincerely,), and whether to include writer's initials, typist's initials, and how many (if any) enclosures are with the letter.

9. Select Courtesy Copies to enter the names of people to whom the letter is cc:'d, or select Options to specify the date format, the punctuation after the greeting and closing, and whether the letter should be centered vertically on the page.

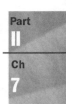

Part

II

Ch

7

10. When you have chosen all the options you need to, choose Finished. Wait a few seconds, then you see your letter as shown in Figure 7.6.

FIG. 7.6
Your finished letter appears on the screen.

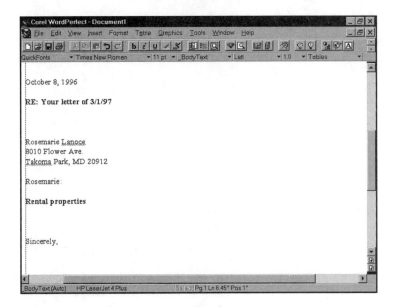

11. Replace any of the sample text with the appropriate information, and your letter is done.

Once you've used the Letter Expert, using other templates and experts is a snap. Merely choose File, New, pick the category of your template, then select the template or expert you want to use. You'll be prompted for certain information, then your document will be created. It's that simple.

For example, to create a meeting agenda, you may wish to use a template. To do so, choose File, New. Select the Business group, then choose the Meeting Agenda template. You see the Template Information dialog box shown in Figure 7.7.

FIG. 7.7
Many templates use a Template Information dialog box, which allows you to enter information that will be placed in the document you create.

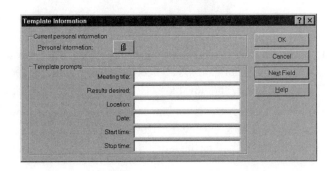

After you enter the information and choose OK, you see the meeting agenda, like the one shown in Figure 7.8.

FIG. 7.8
You can create a meeting agenda with a template.

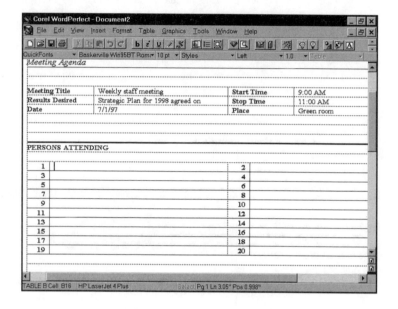

 TIP To find out more about an existing template, select it, then click the Vie_w_ button within the Select New Document dialog box. The Previewer window appears, showing you sample text and formatting.

Making Basic Editing Changes to a Template

When you customize the templates that ship with Corel WordPerfect for your use, you may find that you use nothing *but* templates for your business documents.

You can add text to a template that makes it specific to your organization, or change its formatting to give it a look and feel that you prefer. You can even add prompts that request information in a Template Information dialog box that pops up when the template is used.

N O T E Editing the template makes changes that are reflected in every new document that is created based on that template. This is different than editing the *document* that is created from the template. ■

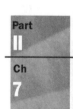

Part

II

Ch

7

CAUTION

Experts are templates that also include complex macros, which run when the template is used. These macros create the dialog boxes that you see. You can edit an Expert, but the macro may not run correctly if you accidentally delete an element from the template that the macro needs.

To make a simple change to the formatting of a template, you can use a procedure like the one below for editing the Meeting Agenda:

1. Choose File, New. Select the Business group, and select Meeting Agenda.

2. Choose Options, Edit Template. You see the template on the screen, like the one in Figure 7.9.

FIG. 7.9
You can edit a template to change all new documents based on that template. In this meeting agenda, a place for the organization's name has been added.

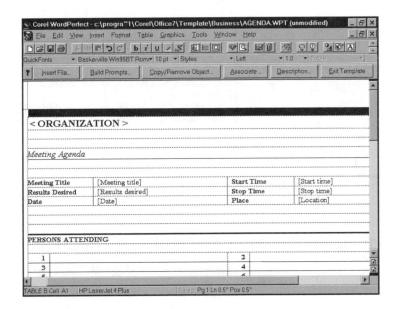

3. Make desired editing changes. For example:

- Replace Meeting Agenda with Case Conference Agenda.

- Choose Edit, Select, All, then choose Baskerville Win95BT from the Font button on the Power Bar.

4. When you are finished making changes, click the Exit Template button on the Feature Bar. You are prompted to save your changes, then the template closes. All future documents based on this template will incorporate these changes.

TIP Be careful when editing a template not to delete or modify any of the prompts without using the Build Prompts feature button. Any missing prompts or bookmarks will result in error messages the next time you use the template.

You can also add your own prompts to a template that the user will see in the Template Information dialog box when the template is first run.

For instance, you might want to add a prompt to the meeting agenda template to remind participants which papers they should bring with them. To do so:

1. Edit the template as described previously.

2. While you are editing the template, click the Build Prompts button on the Feature Bar. You see the Prompt Builder dialog box shown in Figure 7.10.

FIG. 7.10
Make templates more powerful by adding prompts to them in the Prompt Builder.

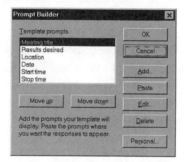

3. Choose Add. You see the Add Template Prompt dialog box shown in Figure 7.11.

FIG. 7.11
Specify the name of the prompt in the Add Template Prompt dialog box.

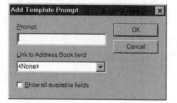

4. Fill in the name of the prompt and choose OK. The new prompt is added to the bottom of the list.

5. Select the Bring field. Place the insertion point in the template document where you want the "Bring" information to be inserted, then click the Paste button in the Prompt Builder dialog box. You see Bring in the template.

6. Choose OK. Wait while the template is prepared.

Part II
Ch 7

7. Exit the template and save changes as you normally would. When you next create a new document based on the template, you see the new prompt in the Template Information dialog box, as shown in Figure 7.12.

FIG. 7.12

New prompts appear in the Template Information dialog box.

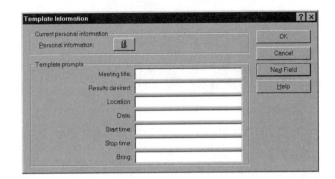

N O T E To create a new template, choose File, New. click the New Document button. At the Select New Document dialog box, choose Options, then New Template. If you have a previously saved document that you'd like to use for the template, use the Insert File button on the feature bar to insert the document into the template editing window. Create or modify text as desired, and set formatting features as needed. Give the document a new description and exit the template, making sure to choose Yes to the changes. ■

Checking Spelling

The Spelling Checker is the single most important proofreading tool you can use. No matter how long or short a document is, using the Spelling Checker is well worth the time it takes. How do you feel about the person who sends you a letter with a typo or a spelling error? Don't let this happen when someone else receives your letter.

The Spelling Checker looks for misspelled words, duplicate words, and irregular capitalization. When it finds a word with one of these problems, it stops and offers suggestions. You can choose to replace the problem word, skip to the next problem, or select one of several other options for each word where the Corel WordPerfect dictionary finds an inconsistency.

Corel WordPerfect includes two additional features that help you with your spelling. Spell-As-You-Go shows your spelling errors as you type; QuickCorrect corrects spelling mistakes as you make them.

Using Spell-As-You-Go

If Spell-As-You-Go is selected, spelling errors will be shown to you as you type. As soon as you press the spacebar after misspelling a word, the misspelled word will appear with a red underline.

To activate the Spell-As-You-Go feature, choose Tools, Spell-As-You-Go.

You can easily correct the word immediately by right-clicking it. You see a pop-up menu that provides alternate spelling choices, as shown in Figure 7.13.

FIG. 7.13
When you right-click a misspelled word, you see alternate spellings and other correction option choices.

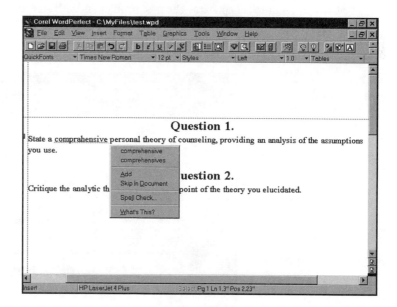

You can use the following options for the misspelled word:

- Click any alternate word choice to replace the misspelled word with a correctly spelled one.
- Choose Add to add the word to your spelling dictionary. It will never be marked as misspelled again.

CAUTION

Be careful in adding words to your dictionary. Don't add acronyms that would prevent the dictionary from finding a commonly misspelled word, and try not to add hundreds of words (such as names you'll only use infrequently) that can slow down your spell checking.

Part
II

Ch
7

- Choose Skip in Document to ignore future occurrences of the misspelled word in the current document.

- Choose Spell Check to start the Spelling Checker (see the "Using the Spelling Checker" section, next).

Using the Spelling Checker

 To start the Spelling Checker, click the Spell Check button, or choose Tools, Spell Check, and confirm that the Spell Checker tab is selected. The Spell Checker dialog box tab shown in Figure 7.14 appears. The first problem is both selected in the text and displayed in the dialog, with a list of suggestions for replacement. Table 7.1 describes the options available in the Spell Checker dialog box.

FIG. 7.14

Select a word in the Replacements list or enter the correct word in the Replace With text box to correct the mistake in the text.

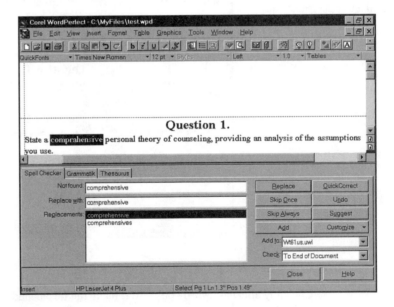

Table 7.1 Spell Checker Options

Option	Description
Not Found	Displays the word in question.
Replace With	Displays the suggested spelling. If this is incorrect, enter correct spelling in this text box.
Replacements	Selects a word in the Replacements list box to replace the misspelled word by clicking the word. It will then appear in the Replace With box.
Replace	Replaces the problem word with the text specified in the Replace With box.

Option	Description
Skip <u>O</u>nce	Skips this occurrence and moves to the next problem.
Skip <u>A</u>lways	Skips all occurrences of this word in this spelling check session.
QuickCorrect	Replaces the word with the word in the Replace <u>W</u>ith box, and adds the error and the replacement word to the QuickCorrect list. (See the following section, "Using QuickCorrect," for more information.)
U<u>n</u>do	Undoes the last correction.
S<u>u</u>ggest	Offers more suggestions for word replacement, if possible.
A<u>d</u>d	Adds the word to the supplemental dictionary named in the Add <u>T</u>o box. Use this option to add proper nouns (like your name or street address) so the Spelling Checker won't stop on them again.
Custo<u>m</u>ize	Customizes spell checking options.
Add <u>T</u>o	Specifies the dictionary to which words will be added (normally, your personal supplemental dictionary).
<u>C</u>lose	Closes the Spelling Checker.

If the problem word is a capitalization problem, Corel WordPerfect displays Capitalization instead of the Not Found box. Select the correct suggestion, or type it into the Replace With box, then choose <u>R</u>eplace.

If the problem word is a duplicate word, Corel WordPerfect displays Duplicate words instead of Not Found, and suggests that you replace the duplicate word with a single word. You can replace or skip to the next problem.

Choose Custo<u>m</u>ize from the Spell Checker dialog box to change the scope of the spell check or to customize the way the Spelling Checker works. Any settings that you change affect future Spell Check sessions.

 TIP If you select text before starting the Spelling Checker, only the selected text is spell checked.

Using QuickCorrect

QuickCorrect saves time and effort by correcting common spelling errors as you make them. QuickCorrect replaces the error with the correct spelling (or the correct capitalization) as soon as you move past the misspelled word. If, for example, you often type **teh** instead of **the**, QuickCorrect corrects the word as soon as you press the spacebar, or as soon as you press another punctuation key (such as a comma, period, or semicolon). In addition to correcting spelling errors, QuickCorrect can automatically correct other

Part
II

Ch
7

problems, like double spacing between words. You can also program QuickCorrect to replace open and close quotes with typesetter-style quotes called SmartQuotes.

QuickCorrect has a built-in list of common misspellings and their correct spellings. You can add your own common misspellings to the list. QuickCorrect is just one of Corel WordPerfect's many features that can be customized for the way you work.

To add items to the list of common misspellings and their corrections, or to change QuickCorrect options, choose Tools, QuickCorrect. The QuickCorrect dialog box is displayed as shown in Figure 7.15.

FIG. 7.15
The QuickCorrect dialog box is used to identify what common spelling errors should be automatically corrected and with what words they will be replaced.

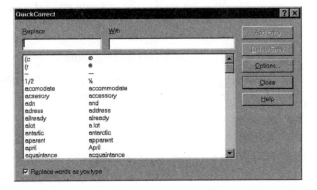

Add an entry by typing what you want to correct in the Replace box, typing what you want the correction to be in the With box, and then choosing Add Entry.

To change QuickCorrect options, click the Options button. The QuickCorrect Options dialog box appears, as shown in Figure 7.16.

FIG. 7.16
Use the QuickCorrect Options dialog box to tell QuickCorrect what kind of corrections you want made.

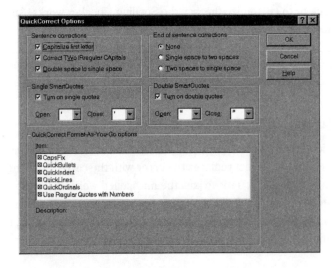

TROUBLESHOOTING

I have a lot of words that contain numbers, such as measurements, in my document. I want the Spelling Checker to skip these words. Choose Customize from the Spell Checker dialog box, then deselect Check Words with Numbers.

I want to remove a word that I inadvertently added to my dictionary. From the Spell Checker dialog box, choose Customize, User Word Lists. Highlight the appropriate word list, then highlight the appropriate entry in the Words/Phrase box, and choose Delete Entry.

Using the Thesaurus

Corel WordPerfect's Thesaurus can help you improve your composition skills. When you can't think of the word that means exactly what you want to say, or you think that you've used the same word too often, let the Thesaurus help you. The Thesaurus supplies a variety of alternatives (synonyms and antonyms) for the word you're looking up. You can choose the word you want from the list of alternatives and ask the Thesaurus to provide a replacement.

To find a synonym for the word *comprehensive*:

1. Place the insertion point in the word.

2. Choose Tools, Thesaurus, or press Alt+F1. The Thesaurus dialog box tab appears, as shown in Figure 7.17.

3. Alternatives for *comprehensive* appear in the first column along the bottom of the box. The alternatives are divided into categories, such as synonym, related words, and antonym. (Use the scroll bars along each side of the box to scroll down to see alternatives that are not visible.)

4. The right box contains definitions for various forms of the word (for example, verb, noun, adjective, and so on). Scroll through this box to view alternative definitions.

5. Figure 7.17 illustrates the Thesaurus after several lookups have been performed. If you perform more than three lookups, you can use the arrow buttons to scroll to columns that aren't visible. When you decide on the word that you want to use as a replacement, select it and choose Replace.

6. If you decide not to make a replacement, choose Close.

Part

II

Ch

7

FIG. 7.17
Find alternate words
or definitions with the
Thesaurus.

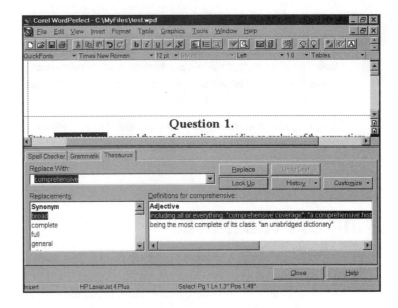

TROUBLESHOOTING

I looked up several meanings, and now I want to go back to the original word I looked up in the Thesaurus. Use the scroll bars to scroll back to the column of alternatives for the original word, or choose History on the Thesaurus menu bar and then choose the word that you want to go back to.

While I was using the Thesaurus, I thought of a different word that I wanted to look up. Can I do it without closing the Thesaurus and typing the word into the document? Type the word that you want to look up in the Replace With box, and then choose Look Up.

Checking Grammar

Grammatik is yet another proofreading feature that Corel WordPerfect provides for you. Even if you don't think you have problems with your writing style, Grammatik may help you. When Grammatik points out a potential problem and explains the logic behind the problem, you may realize that its suggestions offer real improvement. Grammatik is a built-in grammar checker that checks your document for correct grammar, style, punctuation, and word usage, and thus catches many errors that would be bypassed by the Spelling Checker. Grammatik checks both grammar and spelling; so you actually take care of grammar problems and spelling problems all at once.

When Grammatik reports a potential grammar problem, you can review the error and suggestion, then decide whether to change the text.

To proofread your document with Grammatik, choose Tools, Grammatik. Proofreading begins and the first item for review brings up the Grammatik dialog box tab, as shown in Figure 7.18.

FIG. 7.18
Grammatik checks your word usage, punctuation, and sentence structure as well as your spelling.

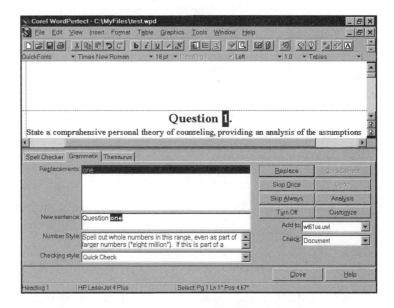

Correcting Errors

When Grammatik stops on a problem, you see information in the four boxes shown previously in Figure 7.18. The dialog box is dynamic, so the boxes and buttons will change slightly depending on the error that is found.

- The Replacements box shows choices for a new suggested word or phrase.
- The New Sentence box shows the new sentence as it will look.
- The Number Style box shows information on the grammatical rule that is being applied. This box will change depending on the error found.
- The Checking Style box shows you the type of grammar checking you have chosen to use.

When Grammatik finds an error, you can respond with the options described in Table 7.2.

Part
II

Ch

7

Table 7.2   Grammatik Options

Option	Description
Resume	This option appears after you pause Grammatik to edit the document. Click Resume to resume proofreading.
Replace	Replace the problem word or phrase with the suggested replacement that is listed in the New Sentence box.
Skip Once	Ignore the highlighted problem and move on to the next problem.
Skip Always	Ignore the highlighted problem for the rest of this proofreading session.
Turn Off	Turn off the current rule.
Add to	Add the word to the selected dictionary.
QuickCorrect	Add the misspelled word and its replacement to the QuickCorrect list.
Undo	Undo your last replacement.
Customize	Change Grammatik options, including the checking style.
Analysis	Perform an analysis as described below in the "Analyzing Your Writing" section.
Close	End the proofreading session.

In some cases the grammatical problem might require manual editing. When this occurs, click in the document window and, using the scroll bar if necessary, edit the problem in the document window. When you finish your manual editing, choose Resume on the Grammatik tab.

Changing the Checking Style

The Grammatik checking style determines what is identified as a potential problem. For example, in a formal checking style, a contraction (such as won't) is identified as a potential problem. You can change the checking style to one that's best for your work.

To change the checking style for this session and future sessions:

1. Choose Customize from the Grammatik dialog box.

2. Choose Checking Styles. You see the Checking Styles dialog box in Figure 7.19.

3. To examine the rules for any style, or to edit the style, select the checking style and choose Edit. You see the Edit Checking Styles dialog box shown in Figure 7.20.

FIG. 7.19
Choose the checking style most appropriate for your writing style and the style of the document being checked.

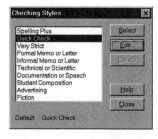

FIG. 7.20
Each editing style has different rules that are applied to the text being checked.

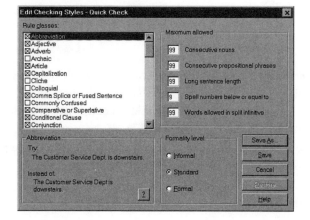

4. In the Edit Checking Styles dialog box, you can see which rule classes are selected for the style and other rules that apply to the style. To edit the style, change the rule classes by clicking the appropriate rules to add or delete the x in the box for that rule.

5. You may also select the numbers in any of the boxes in the Maximum Allowed section and type in new numbers.

6. Click the button of the Formality Level based on the type of document being checked and your writing style.

7. Save your changes with Save (to keep the same style name) or with Save As (to give the edited style a new name). You return to the Checking Styles dialog box.

8. Choose Close to return to the Grammatik tab.

Analyzing Your Writing

Grammatik can analyze your writing in a number of ways. If you choose Analysis from the Grammatik tab, you can choose to parse the selected sentence, show which part of speech each word in the selected sentence is, or show how many words, sentences, and so on are

Part
II

Ch
7

in your document. You can even compare the readability of your document to an IRS form, a Hemingway short story, or the Gettysburg Address.

TROUBLESHOOTING

Grammatik keeps stopping on contractions ("won't," "you're," and so on) and I want it to skip them. You can either change the checking style to a less formal style, or you can turn off the rule with the Turn Off button located on the Grammatik tab.

Printing

Whether you use Corel WordPerfect to create simple documents or desktop publishing masterpieces, printing is a task that you perform often. Because you are working in a WYSIWYG environment, what you print is not the mystery it was a few short years ago. If you're working in Draft view, you can see almost everything just as it will print. You can click the Page/Zoom Full button to get a quick look at a full page in Page view. Alternatively, you can use the View menu to switch to Page view.

Printing a Document

 To print the document in the active window, click the Print button, or choose File, Print. The Print dialog box is displayed, as shown in Figure 7.21.

FIG. 7.21
You can set all the print options in the Print dialog box.

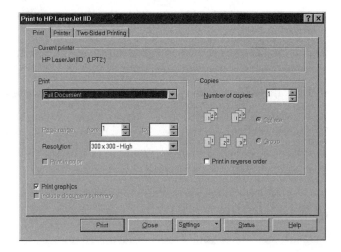

When you print a document, most often you will print using the default options in the Print dialog box, which print one copy of all the pages in the document. Switch between the Print, Printer, and Two-Sided Printer tabs of the dialog box to see all the print options. Table 7.3 describes options in the Print dialog box.

Table 7.3   Important Print Options in the Print Dialog Box

Option	Description
Print	Select which parts of the document to print (Full Document, Current Page, Multiple Pages).
Page Range	To print a part of a document, enter the beginning and ending pages to be printed from within the document.
Resolution	Choose from available resolutions for your printer.
Print in Color	Use the color printing capability of your printer (if available).
Print Graphics	Print graphs, table lines, clip art, and other graphic figures.
Include Document Summary	Print the document summary as well as the document.
Number of Copies	Specify the number of copies.
Collate/Group	Print all pages of one copy together (versus print all copies of each page together).
Print in Reverse Order	This option is useful for some printers that cannot collate copies.

 T I P   You can print files directly from the disk. Select all the files to be printed in the Open dialog box. Right-click them, then choose Print.

N O T E   If you have more than one printer on your system, you can choose which printer to use in the Printer tab of the Print dialog box.

The Two-Sided Printing tab allows you to set two-sided printing options. If your printer supports two-sided (duplex) printing, you can set options for this here. If it doesn't, you can still manually print two-sided documents by specifying that the printer print the odd, then the even pages. Also use this tab to set options for binding offsets (the white space on the inside margin of the document). ▧

Part

II

Ch

7

Printing an Envelope

Corel WordPerfect's Envelope feature automatically formats and addresses your envelope for you. If you have already typed the inside address into a letter, and you want an envelope for the letter, just choose Format, Envelope.

To address an envelope after typing a letter, follow these steps:

1. Choose Format, Envelope to open the Envelope dialog box shown in Figure 7.22.

FIG. 7.22
Corel WordPerfect's Envelope feature automatically formats and addresses your envelope.

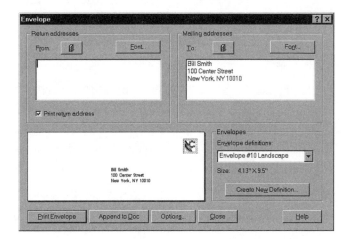

2. Check Print Return Address, then type your return address in the From box.

3. To change the font face or size used in the return address, choose the Font button in the return address section.

N O T E   The font on an envelope is automatically taken from the document initial font (Format, Document, Initial Font). To save yourself the work of changing fonts twice—once in the document text and once in the envelope window—make sure that the document initial font is what you want both for the letter and the envelope. ◼

4. To enter the mailing address (if the mailing address is not automatically selected), type the recipient's name in the To box.

5. As with the return address, you can change the font face or font size used in the mailing address.

6. Select the envelope size from the Envelope Definitions drop-down box.

7. If you want a USPS bar code printed on the envelope, or to change the vertical or horizontal position of the mailing address and/or return address, click the Options button, and make the appropriate selections.

8. To print the envelope immediately, choose Print Envelope; to add the envelope to the document, choose Append to Doc.

 TIP Choose Create New Definition to display the New Page Size dialog box. You can define a new envelope type, including its name, size, and orientation, in this dialog box. This is great for printing on odd-sized envelopes.

Printing Labels

Corel WordPerfect makes it easy to print labels by showing you each label on-screen exactly as it will appear on the printed sheet. All that you have to do is to find and select the brand name and item number on Corel WordPerfect's list of label types and then enter the names and addresses.

If you're printing three-across labels, you probably want to select a font that is smaller than the font you usually use for your documents.

Choosing a Label Definition   To choose a label definition, take the following steps:

1. Place the insertion point at the beginning of an empty document, or on a blank page.

2. Choose Format, Labels to open the Labels dialog box shown in Figure 7.23.

FIG. 7.23
Select the labels you want to print from Corel WordPerfect's list of label types.

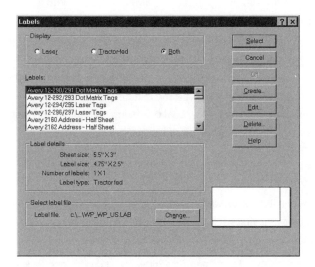

3. In the Labels list, choose the definition you want to use, then choose Select. An empty label is displayed on-screen.

Part
II

Ch

7

Centering Text on Labels   To center the name and address information vertically on each label, so that it doesn't start at the top edge of the label, use Corel WordPerfect's Center Page feature.

To center all names and addresses between the top and bottom of each label:

1. Position the insertion point at the beginning of an empty document, or on the first label.

2. Choose Format, Page, Center.

3. At the Center Page(s) dialog box, choose Current and Subsequent Pages.

4. Choose OK.

Entering Text on Labels   To understand how the Labels feature works, imagine that each separate label is a page, although there may be many labels on a single sheet of paper. Each label is treated as a logical page, although it may not be a physical page. This means that you can print page headers on each label, you can apply the Center Page(s) feature to all labels, and you can (and need to) create hard page breaks between labels. After choosing a label definition and determining if you want the labels centered:

1. Type the name and address as you want it to appear on the printed label.

2. At the end of each line press Enter to move to the next line, but only if there are more lines to be typed for this label. If the line you just typed is the last line for this label, press Ctrl+Enter to create a hard page break.

3. Continue typing names and addresses (or other label text) and inserting hard page breaks after each label, until you have typed all the labels that you want to print. As you add each label, it appears on-screen exactly as it will print. Be careful not to press Enter after you type the last line of each label; this adds an unnecessary blank line and distorts the vertical centering. After you add several names and addresses, your screen may look like Figure 7.24.

TROUBLESHOOTING

I have several lines of text that overflow to the second page of my document, and I'd like them to be on the first page. Choose Format, Make It Fit. At the Make It Fit dialog box, pick the options that you want adjusted and choose Make It Fit.

After I typed a letter, I told Corel WordPerfect to create an envelope, but the inside address didn't appear in the mailing address area. If your letter isn't in a standard business format, Corel WordPerfect may not be able to find the address inside of it and copy it to the mailing address. If this happens, close the Envelope dialog box, select the inside address, and access the

Envelope dialog box again. When you select a name and address before using the Envelope feature, the selected information appears automatically in the mailing address on the envelope.

Some of my labels aren't centered vertically, even though I used the Center on Page feature.
If you add extra Enters at the bottom of your labels, you may distort the vertical centering. Look in Reveal Codes for extra hard returns and eliminate them.

FIG. 7.24
See your labels on-screen just as they will print. Lines are ended by pressing the Enter key; labels are separated by hard page breaks.

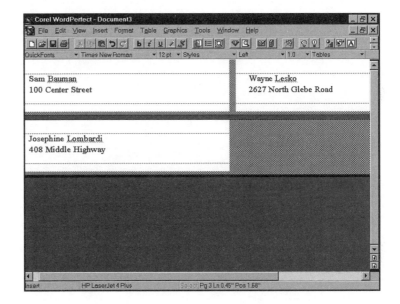

CHAPTER 8

Customizing Corel WordPerfect

Corel WordPerfect is flexible and can be customized in many ways to suit your working habits and preferences. Customizing the program involves changing any of its default settings, after which your new settings remain in effect until you change them again.

Many types of settings are customized through Preferences. To customize the screen display, for example, you first access Preferences. Other settings are customized through the features that are being customized. When you choose a default initial font for the selected printer, you choose it through the Document Initial Font feature. When you customize the writing style that Grammatik uses to evaluate your writing, you customize it through the Grammatik feature.

This chapter introduces you to some of the ways that you can customize Corel WordPerfect and tailor it to your own personal working habits.

▶ **See** "Formatting Characters," **p. 111**
▶ **See** Checking Grammar," **p. 152** ∎

Customize the screen display
Learn to choose which view and zoom percentage you want to see by default in new documents.

Customize the environment
Understand how to set user information about yourself, as well as options for setting QuickMarks that take you to where you were in the document when you last closed it.

Customize the location of files
Learn about specifying where files will be stored, as well as default file extensions.

Customize document summaries
See how to tell Corel WordPerfect to prompt you for document summary information when saving your file, as well as specify which fields the document summary should contain.

Using the Preferences Dialog Box

Because many of the features you will learn how to customize are accessed from one starting point—the Preferences dialog box—let's begin by looking at this dialog box. Choose Edit, Preferences. You see the Preferences dialog box shown in Figure 8.1

FIG. 8.1
Customize Corel WordPerfect to suit your taste by using the Preferences dialog box.

T I P Right-click the toolbar, Ruler Bar, status bar, or either scroll bar and choose Preferences from the QuickMenu—you'll go directly to the Preferences for that screen element.

Starting from the Preferences dialog box, you can customize Display preferences, Environment preferences, File preferences, and Summary preferences. These subjects are covered in detail in the following sections. Customizations of toolbars, the Power Bar, the status bar, the keyboard, the menu bar, and file conversions are summarized in the section "Customizing Other Preferences," later in this chapter.

Customizing Display Preferences

Use Display Preferences to customize the way various screen elements are displayed on-screen. Choose Display in the Preferences dialog box to open the Display Preferences dialog box. Figure 8.2 illustrates the Document tab of the Display Preferences dialog box. Deselect the Horizontal check box in the Scroll bars section of the Document tab if you don't want to display the horizontal scroll bar on-screen.

The selected tab (Document, Symbols, View/Zoom, and so on) determines the options that are available in the lower portion of the dialog box. When you select View/Zoom, for example, the available options involve the Default View mode and the Default Zoom percentage. Figure 8.3 illustrates the Display Preferences dialog box with the View/Zoom tab selected. Set the Default View to Draft view to hide the display of the top and bottom margins, along with any footers, headers, footnotes, and page borders.

▶ **See** "Using View Modes," **p. 106**

FIG. 8.2
Document options are
displayed in the Display
Preferences dialog box.

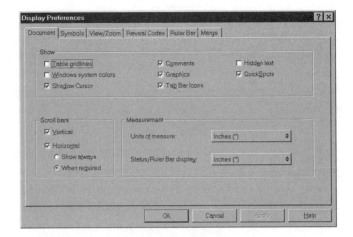

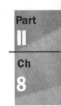

FIG. 8.3
View/Zoom options are
displayed in the Display
Preferences dialog box.

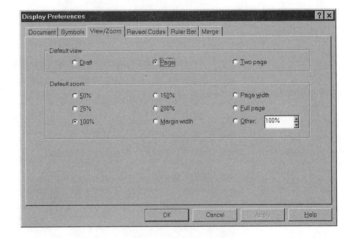

Some of the options that you can change through Display Preferences will speed up your work. As you increase the graphics display on-screen, you slow down the screen refresh rate; whatever you do to reduce graphical display will make your work go faster.

Display settings you can select to speed up your work include:

■ Choose Draft view rather than Page or Two Page view (View/Zoom Display Preferences).

■ Show Table Gridlines rather than table lines and table fill (Document Display Preferences).

■ Deselect Graphics to suppress the display of graphics in the editing window (Document Display Preferences); when Graphics is deselected, the position of graphics is still indicated in the document window.

All of the settings in this list can be temporarily changed from the View menu. If you've told Corel WordPerfect to work in Draft view by default, you can always use View, Page menu selection (or Alt+F5) to switch to Page view when you want to see headers, footers, and page borders. If you've told Corel WordPerfect to show table gridlines in your Display Preferences, you can use the View, Table Gridlines menu selection to see lines and fill styles in a table. And, when speed is not a priority, you can use the View, Graphics menu selection to display graphics.

View, Show ¶ options (Ctrl+Shift+F3) can help by showing you what keys you've pressed (you won't have to look in Reveal Codes). Although showing non-printing characters as symbols (spaces, hard returns, tabs, and so on) adds clutter to the screen, many of us can benefit from seeing these symbols. For example, if you can't tell by looking whether you pressed the spacebar once or twice, you'd know for sure by the number of dot symbols that represent spaces. Then, you can easily position the insertion point in the correct location and delete an unneeded symbol. See Figure 8.4 for an illustration of the Symbols tab options of the Display Preferences dialog box.

FIG. 8.4

You can tell Corel WordPerfect that you want to display non-printing characters and choose which characters you want to display as symbols from the Symbols tab of the Display Preferences dialog box.

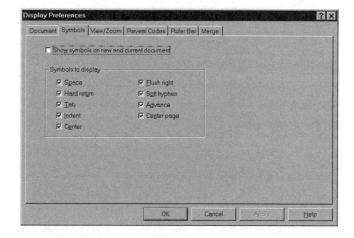

You can use the View menu to instruct Corel WordPerfect to hide or display non-printing characters temporarily. When you display non-printing characters, the characters that are displayed as symbols are the ones that are selected through the Display Preferences Symbols tab.

You can determine what suits you best only when you know what options are available. Once you know what your options are, you can think about how the various choices affect your work.

TROUBLESHOOTING

I changed my Preferences to display table gridlines and now when I format my table with table lines, they're not there. Your table lines are there; you'll see them when you choose View, Table Gridlines (to turn off the gridlines and display any defined table lines), or when you print the document.

I'd like to have my Ruler Bar on-screen all the time without having to ask for it. Under Display Preferences, choose Ruler Bar, then select Show Ruler Bar Guides.

Customizing Environment Preferences

The first time that you access Environment Preferences by choosing Edit, Preferences, Environment, you should see the name you entered during installation in the Name text box (see Figure 8.5). Enter your correct name, if it's not already entered correctly, your correct initials, and select a personal color. What you enter in the User Info for Comments and Summary area will be applied in document comments or summaries.

TIP All comments you make will display in your personal color. If several reviewers make comments on a document, it is helpful if they have different personal colors.

FIG. 8.5

Customize User Info, Language options, Beep On options, and other environment options through the Environment Preferences dialog box.

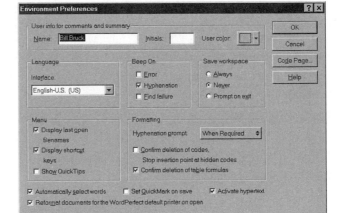

If you have purchased another language version of Corel WordPerfect and you want to use that language's formatting conventions, select the appropriate language from the drop-down list for the Interface option.

You can specify conditions under which Corel WordPerfect beeps at you with the Beep On options. For example, if you want to be beeped when a find operation is unsuccessful, select the Find failure option.

The Save Workspace options can be especially handy if you frequently want to work on the same document(s) that you were working on during your last work session in Corel WordPerfect. You can, for example, exit Corel WordPerfect while a particular document is still open, then start Corel WordPerfect and automatically open the same document all at once.

Menu options are all selected by default. If, for simplicity's sake, you'd rather not display any of the items listed in the Menu options area, then deselect the item(s) that you don't want to display.

▶ **See** "Formatting the Page," **p. 128**

In the Formatting area of the Environment Preferences dialog box, you can tell Corel WordPerfect how you want to be prompted for hyphenation. You can also specify whether you want to confirm the deletion of formatting codes and to note the position of these codes. Leave Confirm Deletion of Table Formulas selected to help you guard against the accidental deletion of table formulas.

When Automatically Select Words is selected, entire words are selected automatically as you drag through text with the mouse (you can still hold down the Shift key and press an arrow key to adjust the selection on a character-by-character basis).

If you work with long documents, by all means select the Set QuickMark on Save option (Environment Preferences). A QuickMark makes it easy to return instantly to the place where you were last working. When Set QuickMark on Save is selected, a QuickMark is created at the insertion point whenever a document is saved. The QuickMark is a temporary placeholder; there is only one QuickMark in a document. When you press Ctrl+Q, you jump to the QuickMark.

Hypertext links allow you to jump to another location in the same document or a different document, or to execute a macro. When the Activate Hypertext option is enabled, all hypertext links in your documents are automatically activated (although Hypertext can be activated on an as-needed basis).

 TIP

Hypertext links are often used in conjunction with publishing documents on the Web.

▶ **See** "Adding Hypertext Links," **p. 598**

An example of a personalized Environment Preferences dialog box is shown in Figure 8.5. A name has been added; Set QuickMark On Save has been deselected; and Activate Hypertext has been selected.

Customizing File Preferences

The Files Preferences dialog box, accessed by choosing Edit, Preferences, Files, includes options about where you save or access various types of files (see Figure 8.6). Figure 8.6 shows the Document tab of the File Preferences dialog box. The option Use Default Extension On Open And Save has been selected, and the default extension is specified as wpd. Files Preferences also includes choices on the default extension for new documents, and on automatic backup options.

FIG. 8.6

Tell Corel WordPerfect where you want to save and access files using the Files Preferences dialog box.

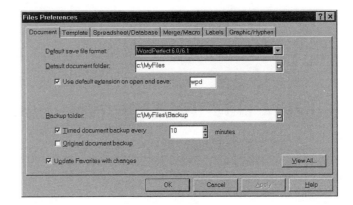

Corel WordPerfect expects to back up any open documents every 10 minutes; you can adjust the interval, but it's not a good idea to deselect the option for automatic timed backup. If your system freezes and you haven't saved changes, the timed backup can spare you a lot of grief.

When you install Corel WordPerfect on your computer, the location of files is defined for you by default (you can, however, specify your own locations during installation by using Custom Install rather than Traditional Install). Documents are stored in one location, templates in another location, and graphics in another location. Normally, this works exactly the way you want, so you probably wouldn't want to change these preferences, although you can change them if desired. When you're working with Files Preferences, you can see where a particular type of file is stored by selecting that file type (Document, Template, Spreadsheet/Database, and so on), or you can see all of the default storage locations at once by clicking the View All button. The Update Favorites With Changes option tells Corel WordPerfect whether or not to update the Favorites list of folder names in directory dialog boxes, such as the Open dialog box.

▶ **See** "Saving Files," **p. 59**

N O T E   Even though Corel WordPerfect backs up open documents for you, do not wait until you finish working on a document to save it. Save your work at regular intervals—every 10 minutes, for example. Automatic backup is a disaster recovery feature; it is not a substitute for regular file save operations. ■

Just as with Display Preferences and Environment Preferences, you can easily customize your Files Preferences to suit the way you work. Through Files Preferences, you can specify whether to use automatic file name extensions for documents (and for merge files); you can also change default storage locations and customize backup options.

   Chapter 11, "Automating with Macros and Merge," shows you how to set up and perform merge operations—both mail merge and keyboard merge.

Customizing Document Summaries

Would you like to include a general overview of a document with the document, or other reference information such as keywords that are used in the file? If the answer to either one of these questions is yes, then customize Corel WordPerfect's document summary preferences.

Including Summary Information with Individual Documents

Even if you don't customize summary preferences, you can include summary information with individual documents through the file menu. Choose File, Document, Properties to enter or change summary information for an individual document. The Properties dialog box appears, as seen in Figure 8.7. Any summary information that you enter is saved with the document when you save the document.

FIG. 8.7

Enter or change summary information for a document, or change the configuration for summaries in the Properties dialog box. Use the scroll bar to see other summary fields.

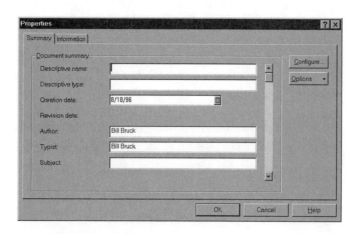

TIP Choose the Configure option in the Document Summary dialog box to specify which fields to use in summaries, and the order in which the fields appear.

To customize your Summary preferences for all documents, choose Edit, Preferences, Summary. The Document Summary Preferences dialog box appears (see Figure 8.8). By default, all three check box options are deselected; in this example, summary preferences have already been customized so that options are selected. You can use the Subject Search Text option to tell Corel WordPerfect how to identify a document subject. For example, when RE: is the specified subject search text, any text following RE: is automatically inserted in the Subject field in the document summary.

FIG. 8.8
Create summary information by default by customizing your document summary preferences.

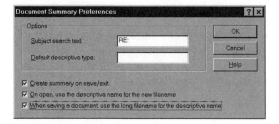

Creating Summaries on Save/Exit

When you specify that you want to Create Summary on Save/Exit, Corel WordPerfect automatically asks for summary information when you save a document for the first time. Although this might seem like a nuisance when you don't want to enter summary information, it only takes a single click (OK) or keystroke (Enter) to get past the request. This can be helpful when you are in a workgroup environment, and people use keywords when saving their documents.

TROUBLESHOOTING

I want to include a document number in my summaries, but there isn't a place to do it. In the Document Summary Properties dialog box on the Summary tab, you can customize document summary fields after choosing Configure. Document number is one predefined field that you can select. You can remove a field by dragging it off of the Selected Fields list, and you can drag a field to a new position in the list of selected fields.

I'd like to print the document summary for my document. Choose Include Document Summary in the Print dialog box (File, Print).

Customizing Other Preferences

You can customize Display preferences, Environment preferences, File preferences, and Summary preferences; you can also customize preferences for toolbars, the Power Bar, the status bar, the keyboard, the menu bar, writing tools, printing, and file conversions.

This section summarizes some of the changes you can make for each of these other types of preferences. See Chapter 35, "Customizing Toolbars and Menus" for more information.

 Double-click any of the status bar items to either toggle the action or open its related dialog box. Double-clicking the date or time item will add the date or time text to your document.

The following list summarizes some of the changes you can make for preferences that are not previously covered in this chapter. After selecting Edit, Preferences, the Preferences dialog box appears with the following options:

- *Toolbar.* Use Options to customize the appearance or location of toolbars; you can display text on toolbar buttons, a picture, or both. You can also specify the maximum number of rows to be used for displaying a toolbar (displaying two rows takes more screen space, but lets you display more buttons at once). You can also edit the toolbar to add, remove, or rearrange buttons.

- *Power Bar.* Adjust the appearance to display text only, a picture only, or both. You can add, remove, or rearrange buttons.

- *Status Bar.* Add items to the status bar, rearrange items, resize items.

- *Menu Bar.* Display, create, or manage another predefined menu bar, including any that you have created.

- *Keyboard.* Display, create, or manage another keyboard, including any customized keyboard that you have created for special-purpose work.

- *Convert.* Specify default delimiters, encapsulation characters, and characters to strip for ASCII text files (options that are most commonly used or referenced when merging with database data files). Specify Code Page options (options that are used when importing or exporting files from or to another language).

TROUBLESHOOTING

Help! I experimented with customizing the status bar and now I'd like to put it back the way it was. Choose Edit, Preferences to get to the Preferences dialog box. Then select Status Bar, and choose Default.

I frequently import database files in an ASCII-delimited format, and I'd like to have quotation marks stripped when the file is imported. Choose Edit, Preferences to get to the Convert Preferences dialog box. Specify quotation marks as characters to be stripped.

Customizing the Default Settings for New Documents

Whenever you open a new, empty document, you accept default settings that are associated with the standard template. Many other formatting defaults are included in these settings, including margin settings, the justification setting, and tab settings. If you prefer to work with settings that are not the same as these defaults, you can change the defaults for these other settings for new documents through the Document Initial Codes Style. This section shows you how to change the default settings for new documents that are based on the standard template.

▶ **See** "Using Styles," **p. 185**

To change the default settings for new documents that are based on the standard template, take the following steps:

1. Choose Format, Document, Initial Codes Style. The Styles Editor dialog box appears, with the Document Initial Style as the style to be edited (see Figure 8.9).

FIG. 8.9
Customize formatting for new documents in the Styles Editor dialog box.

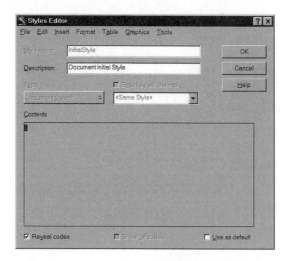

2. In the style Contents area, insert any format settings that you want as defaults for all new documents based on the Standard template. For example, if you prefer to work

with Full justification rather than Left justification, insert a formatting code for Full justification by selecting Format in the menu bar of the Styles Editor dialog box. Then select Justification, Full from the drop-down menu.

3. Select the Use As Default check box option.

4. Click OK.

After you customize the Initial Codes Style and specify that the formatting should be used as a default, all new documents based on the Standard template will use the customized settings. An illustration of the Initial Codes Style with customized settings is shown in Figure 8.10. The Use As Default check box option has been selected.

FIG. 8.10

When you customize formatting for new documents in the Styles Editor dialog box, make sure to select the Use As Default check box.

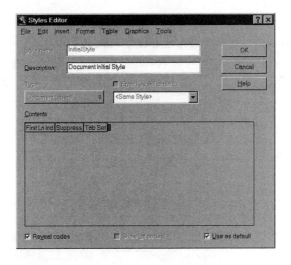

Organizing and Formatting Large Documents

When you produce a document with many pages—from 10 or 15 pages to hundreds of pages—you need special organizational and managerial techniques. Corel WordPerfect provides a number of features that help you manage long documents. You can use these features for short documents as well.

One organizational feature you can use in a large document is outlining. An outline gives you an overview of a document by organizing topics into a list that can have as many as eight different levels. The outline helps you determine what topics you want to cover and in what order the topics should be presented.

Corel WordPerfect's Styles feature helps you format long documents consistently and easily. With a single operation, you can apply a style that includes preformatted fonts, attributes, and even text. ■

Organize a simple list with bullets or numbers

One of the best ways to organize points you are making is with bulleted and numbered lists. Learn how to create these easily with Corel WordPerfect.

Use Corel WordPerfect's Outline feature

Understand how you can use WordPerfect as a thinking tool to organize your thoughts in an outline form, then open just the part(s) of the outline that you are working on.

Use Corel WordPerfect's built-in styles to format a document

Use Corel WordPerfect's built-in styles to easily format titles, headings, and body text, thus ensuring consistency of appearance and saving time and effort.

Create and edit your own styles

Once you start using Corel WordPerfect's styles, you'll want to start creating your own. This section shows you how to do so quickly and easily.

Using Bullets and Numbers

Corel WordPerfect's Bullets & Numbers feature gives you a quick and easy way to create an outline in a simplified format. Use the Bullets & Numbers feature to create lists like the ones shown in Figure 9.1. A bullet or number appears at the left margin, followed by an indent. Numbers increase automatically from paragraph to paragraph.

FIG. 9.1
Create bulleted and numbered lists easily with the Bullets & Numbers feature.

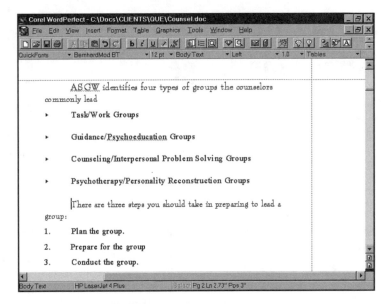

Take the following steps to create a simple list:

1. Position the insertion point at the left margin of the first line in the list.

2. Choose Insert, Bullets & Numbers. You see the Bullets & Numbers dialog box shown in Figure 9.2.

3. Select the style that you want for your list.

4. If you want another bullet or number to appear when you press Enter, make sure that the New Bullet or Number on Enter box is checked. If you want blank lines between items in the list, leave the check box empty.

5. Click OK. Corel WordPerfect inserts the first bullet (or number) followed by an indent into your document.

6. Type your text and press Enter.

7. If you told Corel WordPerfect to create a new bullet or number on Enter, you already have the next bullet or number. Continue typing text and pressing Enter

until you finish typing the list. Use the Backspace key to remove the extra bullet or number at the end of the list and to stop the sequence.

FIG. 9.2
One or two clicks at the Bullets & Numbers dialog box produces a number with an indent.

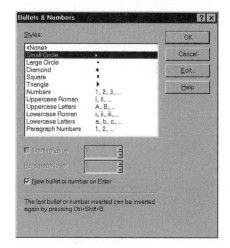

 8. If you left the New Bullet or Number on Enter check box empty, you can add a blank line if desired. When you're ready to create another bullet or number, click the Insert Bullet button.

TIP Use the Insert Bullet button to quickly create another bullet or number in the current style (you can change the current style at the Bullets & Numbers dialog box).

N O T E Corel WordPerfect gives you a choice of five types of bullet styles and six types of number styles with its Bullets & Numbers feature. You can customize any of the predefined styles. You can, for example, use a different Corel WordPerfect character as a bullet by editing one of the predefined styles and replacing the bullet character with the character of your choice. ▪

TROUBLESHOOTING

I created a numbered list and now I'd rather have a bulleted list. Select the entire list and choose a bullet style from the Insert Bullets & Numbers dialog box.

I created a numbered list and I want to add another item to the list. Insert the item, using the Bullet button to create a number at the beginning of the item. Numbers will resequence automatically.

continues

continued

I typed a list of items without bullets and now I'd like to add bullets at the beginning of each item. Select the entire list and choose a bullet style from the Bullets & Numbers dialog box.

Outlining a Document

An outline is more than Roman numerals that are typed in at the beginning of each new topic. Once you start an outline, the numerals, if there are any, are created and sequenced automatically. You have a choice of several outline styles, as you can see in Figure 9.3, or you can create your own style.

FIG. 9.3
Three different outline styles are applied to the same text.

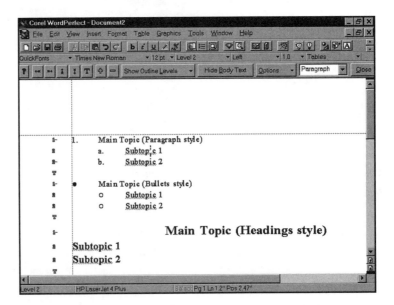

When you change your mind about the order of topics in your outline, you can easily rearrange topics. The rest of the topics resequence automatically when you rearrange topics—or when you add or delete topics. If you change your mind about the style of the outline, place the insertion point anywhere in the outline and choose a different style. To see only the most important topics in your outline, collapse the outline down to the first level.

Before you work with outlines, it helps to familiarize yourself with outline concepts and terminology, and with the Outline Feature Bar.

Understanding Outline Concepts and Terminology

The following concepts and terminology will help you work with outlines:

- An outline is a series of paragraphs, called outline items, in which each paragraph has an optional number or letter and a hierarchical level. The level number or letter type generally corresponds to the number of tabs or indents that separate the beginning of the topic from the left margin.

- An outline can include body text. Body text does not have a number and may not have the same level of indentation as the portions of the outline that surround it.

- An outline family is a group of related material consisting of all the numbered paragraphs and body text that are directly underneath the first item in the group.

- An outline style is a formatting style that uniquely defines the appearance of the number and text for each level of an outline.

Part
II

Ch
9

Understanding the Outline Feature Bar

The Outline Feature Bar shown in Figure 9.4 is your gateway to the commands that you use when you work with outlines. This section introduces you to the Outline Feature Bar. Table 9.1 describes individual buttons on the Outline Feature Bar.

FIG. 9.4
The Outline Feature Bar provides one-button access to Outline's capabilities.

Outline Feature Bar ——

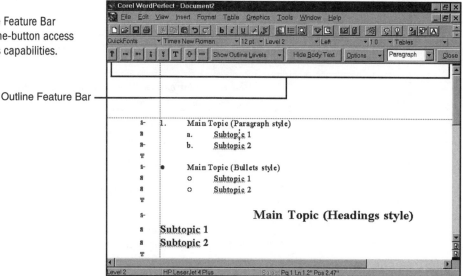

Table 9.1   Buttons on the Outline Feature Bar

Button	Function
?	*Feature bar help and options.* Provides menu access to Outline Feature Bar functionality, and provides outline help.
◄«	*Change the current outline item to the previous level.* Decreases an outline item's level number or letter by one (same as Shift+Tab).
»►	*Change the current outline level to the next level.* Increases an outline item's level number or letter by one (same as pressing Tab).
↨	*Move the current or selected family or item up; keep the same level.* Moves the outline item or selection text up one item without changing its level letter or number.
↨	*Move the current or selected family or item down; keep the same level.* Moves the outline item or selection text down one item without changing its level letter or number.
T	*Change the current or selected item to body text and back.* Toggles an outline item from body text to outline form or vice versa.
✚	*Show all levels of the outline family.* Shows/redisplays the collapsed family that is below the current outline item.
▬	*Hide all but the current level of the outline family.* Hides/collapses the family that is below the current outline item.
Show Outline Levels ▾	*Choose outline display level.* Hides all levels of the outline below the number selected.
Hide Body Text	*Turn the display of body text on and off.* Toggles the display of body text on or off (the button changes from Hide Body Text to Show Body Text).
Options ▾	*Choose outline options* (includes: Define outline, End outline, Change level, Set number, and Show level icons). Through various parameter selections permits you to determine the style of the outline, adjust the numbering, display/hide level icons in the left margin, and end the outline.

Button	Function
Bullets ▼	*Select an outline definition.* A drop-down list permits you to select an outline style (use this to change the current style).
Close	*Close the Outline Feature Bar.* Outlining in the text ends and the Outline Feature Bar disappears.

Part II
Ch 9

Creating an Outline

The general steps for creating an outline are as follows:

1. Position the insertion point at the left margin of the line that will be the first line in the outline.

2. If the Outline Feature Bar is not already visible, choose Tools, Outline. The Feature Bar appears, a Level 1 outline item is created in the document, and the insertion point is placed so you can enter your text.

> **N O T E** You will see letters and numbers in the left margin when you are in outline mode. The letter T indicates that the paragraph is text. A number (1, 2, 3, etc.) indicates that the paragraph is in outline level 1, 2, 3, etc. A "-" following the number indicates that the outline family is expanded; a "+" following the number indicates that the outline family is collapsed (there is text or sub-levels that are not shown). ■

3. If the style of the inserted outline item is not the one you want, use the Style Definition button to pull down a style list, then select another style.

4. Type the text, and then press Enter. The insertion point is automatically positioned at the same level to enter the text for the next item.

5. If you want to change the level of the next item before you enter text:
   - To increase the level, press Tab (increase level) or click the Increase Level button.
   - To decrease the level, use Shift+Tab (decrease level) or click the Decrease Level button.

6. To add body text to the outline, click the Body Text button. You can press Indent (F7) to align the text with the associated outline item.

7. After entering the last item's text, choose Options, End Outline, or click the Close button on the Outline Feature Bar.

> **N O T E** If you accidentally delete an outline number, either Undo the action, or Backspace to the end of the previous item and press Enter. ■

Collapsing and Expanding Portions of an Outline

Corel WordPerfect makes it easy to work with a portion of your outline by letting you display only the portion in which you're currently interested. Using the Outline Feature Bar, you have the following methods to control what portion of an outline is displayed:

- Hide/collapse individual families under their first outline item.
- Hide all outline items of a specified level and their families.
- Hide the entire outline excluding body text.
- Hide only body text.

When you're displaying just the portion that you want to work with, it's easy to edit (or reorganize) outline items. Because outline items are just normal text with an outline style applied to them, you edit text in outline items just as you do any other text.

Figure 9.5 is an example for the hiding and showing techniques that follow.

FIG. 9.5

This is a complete outline used in the hiding and showing examples. A minus sign by the level number icon indicates that the family can be collapsed (hidden).

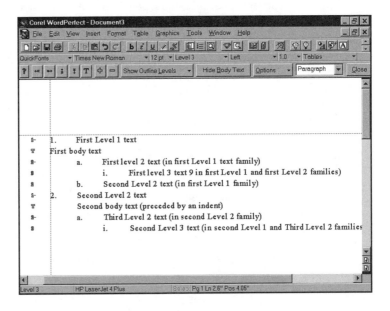

Hiding/Showing an Outline Family To hide an outline family—that is, to collapse the family so only its first-level item is visible—place the insertion point in the first level of the family and click the Hide Family button. Alternatively, place the mouse pointer to the left of the first level of the family, so that the pointer becomes a vertical, double-headed arrow; then, double-click.

Figure 9.6 shows the result of collapsing the first Level 1 family.

FIG. 9.6
A plus sign by the Level 1
number in the margin
indicates that this family
can be expanded.

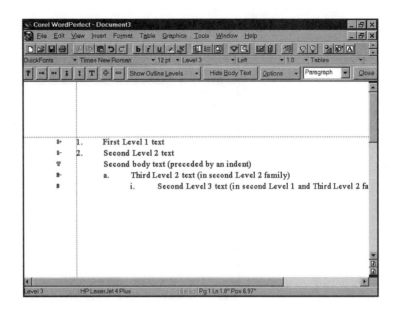

To show/redisplay a collapsed outline family, place the insertion point in the visible out-line item and click the Show Family button. Alternatively, place the mouse pointer to the left of the visible outline item so that the pointer becomes a vertical, double-headed arrow, and then double-click.

Hiding/Showing All Outline Families Under a Specified Level   To hide all the outline families under a specified level for the entire outline, place the insertion point in the outline. Then, choose the lowest number that you still want shown from the Show Outline Levels button's drop-down list.

Figure 9.7 shows the result of choosing 1 from the Show Outline Levels button's drop-down list (body text is also hidden).

To show/redisplay hidden levels, place the insertion point in the outline and choose the lowest level from the Show Outline Levels button's drop-down list.

Hiding Body Text, Displaying Hidden Body Text   To hide an outline's body text, place the insertion point in the outline and choose the Hide Body Text button. Body text is hidden and the button changes to a Show Body Text button.

To redisplay body text, place the insertion point in the outline and click the Show Body Text button. (The name on the button changes to Hide Body Text when the body text is visible.)

FIG. 9.7

An outline collapsed to Level 1 with body text hidden.

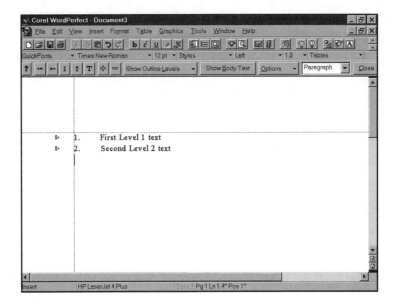

Modifying an Outline's Structure

You can modify an outline's structure by rearranging items and families, by inserting new families, or by deleting families. When the level icons are displayed (in the left margin), it's easy to select families for cutting, copying, and deleting. Another kind of change you can make is to switch an outline item to body text or vice versa. Corel WordPerfect automatically adjusts the numbering of the outline.

Adjusting Levels   To increase the level of an outline item, position the insertion point anywhere in the item and choose the Next Level button. Alternatively, position the insertion point at the beginning of the text in the item and press Tab.

To decrease the level of an outline item, position the insertion point anywhere in the item and click the Previous Level button. Alternatively, position the insertion point at the beginning of the text in the item and press Shift+Tab.

To increase or decrease several levels at once, position the insertion point anywhere in the outline item and choose Options, Change Level, and then specify a level number.

Changing to and from Body Text   To change an outline item to body text, position the insertion point in the item and click the Show Body Text button; or press Ctrl+H. The text is placed at the left margin. You may want to adjust its indentation with Tab or Indent (F7).

To change body text back to an outline item, place the insertion point anywhere in the body text and click the Show Body Text button again. The text becomes an outline item (you may want to adjust the level number and you may need to delete some extra tabs).

Changing an Outline's Style

To change an outline's style, take the following steps:

1. Position the insertion point anywhere in the outline.

2. If the Outline Feature Bar is not visible, choose Tools, Outline.

3. Pull down the outline styles list from the Outline Definition button and select the new style. The outline is formatted with the new style.

TROUBLESHOOTING

I want to print only the Level 1 items in my outline. Corel WordPerfect prints only what is displayed on-screen. Collapse the outline to Level 1 (and hide body text if you want), then print your document.

I performed several cut-and-paste operations and now my outline is a mess. I wish I could put it back the way it was. Choose Edit, Undo/Redo History. Select the last item that you want to undo (the lowest item that you want to undo in the Undo list). You can undo as many items as are on the list.

Using Styles

Use styles to format your documents and templates easily and quickly, and to give them a consistent and professional look. Styles are an extraordinarily powerful formatting tool. Instead of applying several separate formatting changes to a subtitle in a long document, you can apply them all at once with a style. You can apply the same style over and over again to every subtitle in the document. If you change your mind about any of the formatting, you have only one change to make—to the style itself. Styles are readily available for use in other documents; see the section "Sharing Styles Between Documents," later in this chapter for more information.

Because styles can incorporate nearly any Corel WordPerfect formatting feature—as well as text, graphics, and even other styles—their potential is nearly unlimited. You can save a great deal of time and work by learning to use styles, especially when you work with long documents.

TIP Chapter 10, "Using Tables and Graphics," also covers working with graphics lines, creating paragraph and page borders, creating drop caps, creating graphics boxes for figures and text, creating special text effects with text art, and creating watermarks.

This section introduces you to styles, shows you how to use Corel WordPerfect's built-in styles, and introduces you to creating and using your own styles.

Considering Types of Styles

One way to classify styles is by their location. Styles can be built into the current document, saved in a style file, or built into a template. Styles are also part of the Corel WordPerfect program and are called *system styles*. When you first access the styles list in a new document, immediately after installation of the program (see Figure 9.8), you see a list of the built-in system styles. When you or others using the system create a new style, it is added to the list. The styles that you create are called user styles.

A style is categorized as one of four types:

- *Character (paired)*. The formatting in a Character style takes effect at a specified position and it ends at a specified position. A Character style is suitable for formatting several words in sequence (a company name, for example).

- *Paragraph (paired)*. The formatting in a Paragraph style affects the current paragraph (or a series of selected paragraphs). A Paragraph style is ideal for formatting one-line titles and headings.

- *Paragraph (paired-auto)*. This type of style is like the Paragraph (paired) style, except that formatting in the style is automatically updated when you change any paragraph that is formatted with the style.

- *Document (open)*. When a Document style is applied, the formatting it contains stays in effect for the rest of the document (or, until there's another change for the same type of formatting).

Using Corel WordPerfect's Built-In Styles

You can easily format a document with built-in styles. You can even make a global adjustment to the effects of a style simply by changing the formatting of one paragraph where the style is applied when the style type is Paragraph (paired-auto). In this section, you will learn to format a document with built-in styles and to make an adjustment that affects all paragraphs that are formatted with a style.

To display the Style List dialog box in any document based on the Standard template (as shown in Figure 9.8), start a new document based on the Standard template. Then, choose Format, Styles, or double-click the Styles button (a single-click displays only a list of style names; a double-click displays the Style List dialog box).

FIG. 9.8

The Style List dialog box in a new empty document is based on the Standard template.

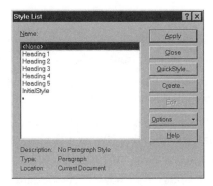

At the Style List dialog box, you can highlight each style name on the list and see the description and other information about that style below the list.

You can apply a style from the Style List dialog box; or, more easily, from the Styles button on the Power Bar.

The InitialStyle sets formatting defaults that affect the entire document. The Heading styles are designed to format the title and various levels of headings in a document; these styles contain font changes, centering, and Table of Contents markings. The number and bullet styles (if present) contain formatting for Bullets & Numbers styles.

Suppose that you have a document on-screen that is based on the Standard template. The document has a title and headings, as shown in Figure 9.9.

FIG. 9.9

A document before formatting with built-in styles.

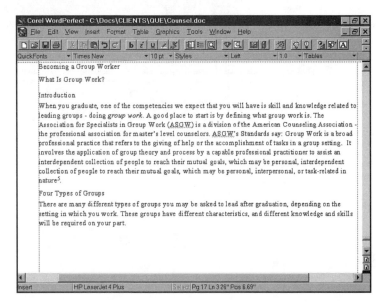

To apply and adjust built-in styles, take the following steps:

1. Format the title with the Heading 1 style. Position the insertion point anywhere in the title. Pull down the style list from the Styles button. Select the Heading 1 style.

   Formatting in the Heading 1 style is now applied to the entire paragraph (which is the entire title). The title is centered, bold, and very large.

2. Format the main heading with the Heading 2 style. Position the insertion point anywhere in the first main heading ("What is Group Work"). Pull down the style list from the Styles button and select the Heading 2 style.

   Formatting in the Heading 2 style now affects the entire paragraph. Repeat this step for every main heading in the document. When you finish, all main headings are formatted with a consistent appearance.

3. Format lower-level headings with the Heading 3 style. Position the insertion point anywhere in the first lower-level heading ("Introduction"). Pull down the style list from the Styles button and select the Heading 3 style.

   Repeat this step for every lower-level heading in the document. (In the sample document, the other Heading 3 is "Four Types of Groups.") All lower-level headings now have a uniform appearance. The example used above would now appear as shown in Figure 9.10.

FIG. 9.10
The document after formatting with built-in styles.

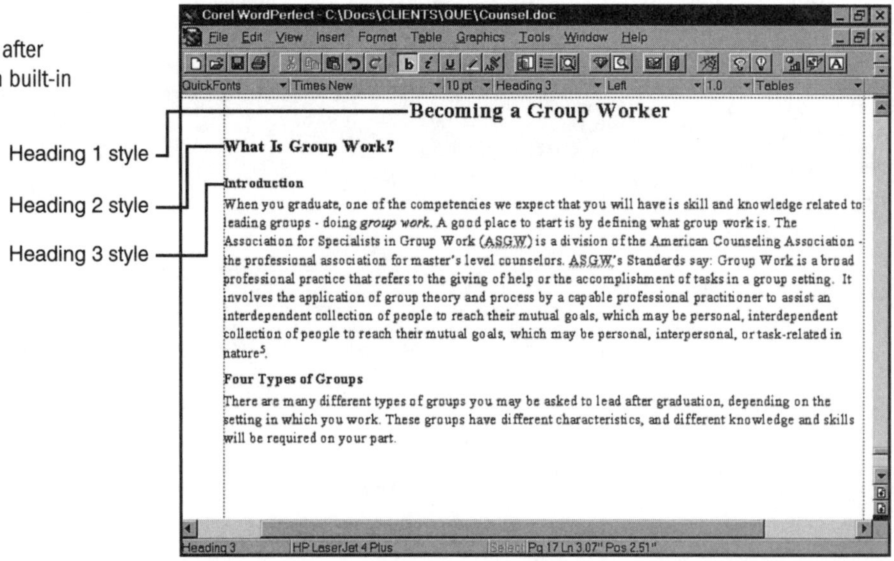

Heading 1 style
Heading 2 style
Heading 3 style

4. Make an adjustment that affects all paragraphs formatted with the Heading 3 style. Suppose you decide that your lower-level headings would look better in italic. Select any paragraph formatted with the Heading 3 style and click the Italic button.

Because Heading 3 is a Paragraph (paired-auto) type style, the change you made now affects all paragraphs formatted with the style (as in Figure 9.11).

FIG. 9.11
The same document after adjusting the formatting in one of the paragraphs formatted with the Heading 3 style.

New Heading 3 style

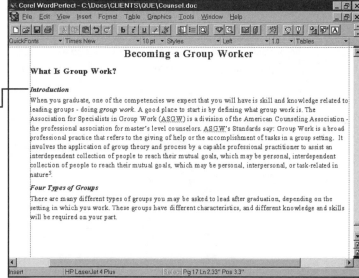

Creating and Using Your Own Styles

When you see and feel the power of styles, you'll be willing to put in some extra time and work learning how to create your own styles. Although the use of styles adds a level of complexity to your work, the results are well worth it. You'll save time formatting, your documents will have a professional, consistent appearance, and you'll be able to make global formatting adjustments quickly and easily.

In the next section, you'll learn to use QuickStyle to create a style from formatting, in effect, at the insertion point. Then, you'll learn to create a style from scratch in the Styles Editor window.

To learn more about styles, explore Corel WordPerfect's templates. Create a document based on a template as discussed in Chapter 7, "Using Writing Tools and Printing," then access the Style List dialog box, select a style, and choose Edit to see what codes it contains.

Creating a Style with QuickStyle   An easy way to create a style is to format some text as you want it to look, and then use the QuickStyle feature to copy the formatting into a style. With QuickStyle, you can create a Paragraph style that contains all of the formatting codes and font attributes in an existing paragraph; or, you can create a Character style that contains all the font attributes on an existing character.

To create a style with QuickStyle, take the following steps:

1. Format a section of text or a paragraph with the features that you want included in the style.

2. Position the insertion point anywhere in the formatted paragraph (to create a Paragraph style), or select the formatted text (to create a Character style).

3. Click the Styles button, and then choose QuickStyle; or, choose Format, Styles, QuickStyle. The QuickStyle dialog box is displayed, shown in Figure 9.12.

FIG. 9.12

Format text as you want it to look, then use the QuickStyle dialog box to copy the formatting into a style.

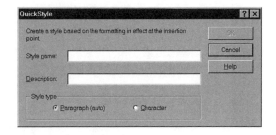

4. Enter a name for the style.

5. Enter a description for the style.

6. Select Paragraph as the style type if you want the style to affect an entire paragraph (a Paragraph style is ideal for formatting headings); select Character as the style type if you want the style to affect a passage of text of any length (a Character style is ideal for formatting a series of words—for example, a company name).

7. Click OK. The style is created and you are returned to the document window.

Creating a Style from Scratch   Maximize the power of styles by creating your own styles with exactly the formatting, text, graphics, and even other styles, that suit your work.

To create a style from scratch, you need to enter formatting codes (and any other contents for the style) in the Styles Editor window. Follow these steps to create a style from scratch:

1. Double-click the Styles button (on the Power Bar), or choose Format, Styles. The Style List dialog box shown in Figure 9.13 appears.

2. Choose Create. The Styles Editor window is displayed like the one shown in Figure 9.14.

FIG. 9.13
You can create a style from scratch using the Style List dialog box.

FIG. 9.14
A paragraph style named 1 Hdr, which will be used to format headings, is shown in the Styles Editor dialog box.

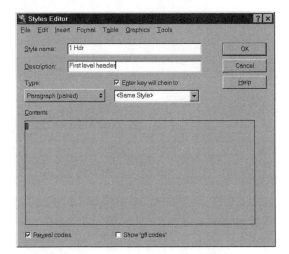

3. Enter a name for the style.

4. Enter a description for the style. It's helpful to describe the formatting used in the style or the purpose for which it will be used.

5. Change the type, if desired, by choosing a type from the Type drop-down list.

6. For a Paragraph or Character style, program the Enter key, if desired. This means that when you press the Enter key at the end of a paragraph in new text, the program will do what you have specified. The list of Enter Key Will Chain To options is a pull-down menu. When you apply the style to existing text, it doesn't matter how the Enter key is programmed. It does make a difference when you apply the style before typing text. The Enter Key Will Chain To options include:

- *None*. The Enter key simply turns off the style.
- *Same Style*. The Enter key turns off the style and then immediately turns it on again (useful for bulleted lists).
- *Style name*. The Enter key turns off the current style and turns on the Style name in this box (useful for linking Question & Answer styles).

7. Click in the Contents area and enter formatting codes (and any other contents) for the style.

8. If the style type is Paragraph or Character, you can specify formatting that takes effect after the text in the paragraph. For example, you might want to insert a graphics line after a heading that is formatted with the style.

 T I P Remember to use the menus in the Styles Editor dialog box, not the WordPerfect menus.

To specify formatting that takes effect after text in the paragraph, you must first select the Show '<u>O</u>ff Codes' check box option. A comment separates the ON and OFF areas in the style <u>C</u>ontents area. Put the codes you want to have after the paragraph after the comment code, like the paragraph border code in Figure 9.15.

FIG. 9.15
The Show '<u>O</u>ff Codes' item is selected in the Styles Editor dialog box and the <u>C</u>ontents area is divided into ON codes and OFF codes. You can include elements like graphic lines that should be inserted after the style is turned off.

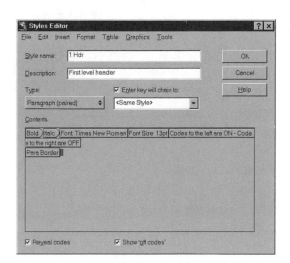

9. Click OK, and then click Close to return to the document window.

Applying a Style   You can apply a style either as you type or to existing text.

 TIP   If the style type is Paragraph (paired-auto) you don't have to edit a style with the Styles Editor. When you change any paragraph that is formatted with the style, the changes are automatically reflected in the style.

Part
II

Ch
9

To apply a style as you type, take the following steps:

1. Position the insertion point where you want the effects of the style to begin.
2. Click the Styles button on the Power Bar to display the style list.
3. Select the style that you want to apply.
4. If the style being applied is a Document type or a Paragraph type, you have finished applying the style.

   If the style being applied is a Character style, type the text that is to be affected by the style, then pull down the style list again and select "none" or another style from the list. This turns off the first style.

To apply a style to existing text, take the following steps:

1. If the style being applied is a Document style, position the insertion point where you want its effects to begin.

   If the style being applied is a Paragraph style, position the insertion point in the paragraph to be affected, or select the paragraphs to be affected.

   If the style being applied is a Character style, select the text to be affected.

2. Click the Styles button and select the style.

Editing a Style   Once you create and apply a style, you may change your mind about formatting in the style. Styles are very flexible; as soon as you change the style, the changes take effect wherever that style is applied.

To make any changes that should apply to the document as a whole (except for the Document Initial Font), edit the Initial Style. Every document contains the Initial Style code at the beginning of its text (you can't remove the code). When you edit the Initial Style, therefore, your formatting takes effect at the beginning of the document. Because the Initial Style is a Document (open) style, its formatting stays in effect for the rest of the document, or until it is overridden by other formatting of the same type. You might, for example, insert justification and margin codes in the Initial Style.

NOTE   Formatting codes that appear in the body of a document, or in other styles that are applied in the document, override similar formatting in the Document Initial Style. ■

To edit a style:

1. Double-click the Styles button to open the Style List dialog box.

2. Select the style you want to edit and choose <u>E</u>dit. The Styles Editor window appears.

3. Make any desired changes, then click OK and Close.

Sharing Styles Between Documents   Styles are automatically saved with the document containing them. You can save the styles in a document as a separate style file (so you don't have to keep the document that originally contained them) and then retrieve the style file into the style list of another document. If you want customized styles to be available in all new documents based on a particular template, copy the styles to the template, or create the styles while you edit the template.

- To save styles in the current document to a separate style file: access the Style List dialog box, choose <u>O</u>ptions, Save <u>A</u>s, and then type a name for the style file and click OK.

- To save a style in the current document to the current template: display the Style List dialog box, select the style name, choose <u>O</u>ptions, <u>C</u>opy, <u>T</u>emplate, and then click OK.

- To retrieve styles from a style file (or from another document): display the Style List dialog box, choose <u>O</u>ptions, R<u>e</u>trieve, and then enter a file name (and path) and choose OK. You will be asked whether you want to overwrite current styles (with incoming styles that have the same names). Answer <u>Y</u>es or <u>N</u>o to complete the retrieve operation.

TROUBLESHOOTING

I created a style to format the company name but when I apply it, it formats the entire paragraph. Change the style type from Paragraph to Character.

I want to use the styles I created in my Report file in a new document. With the new document on-screen, access the Style List dialog box. Choose <u>O</u>ptions, R<u>e</u>trieve, and then enter the file name (and path) of your Report file and choose OK. When asked whether you want to overwrite current styles, answer Yes. The retrieve operation will then be completed.

I want to add Table of Contents markings to a style but I can't figure out how to do it. You can add Table of Contents markings to any paired style. At the Styles Editor window, select the Show 'Off Codes' check box option. Select only the comment code ([Codes to the left...]). Choose <u>T</u>ools, Ge<u>n</u>erate, <u>T</u>able of Contents. Choose the level you want by choosing one of the Mark buttons on the Table of Contents feature bar that appears at the bottom of the screen. [Mrk Txt ToC] codes now surround the comment, and will surround any text that is formatted with the style.

CHAPTER 10

Using Tables and Graphics

Now that you've learned how to create WordPerfect documents, format them, and work with long documents, you may want to "spice up" your documents with elements like tables, clip art, and watermarks.

Corel WordPerfect provides simple ways to include these design features in your documents. You will also find many features that ship with Corel WordPerfect, including attractively designed lines, borders, and pictures that can also be used to enhance your documents. ■

Create a table

Make tables to display information in your documents, or create attractive forms for data entry.

Create graphics lines and add borders to paragraphs, columns, and pages

Create graphics lines and borders to set off headers and footers, section headings, or other design elements in your documents.

Create and edit graphics boxes that contain pictures or charts

Include clip art, charts, and drawings in your documents.

Use drop caps and watermarks

Create drop caps and watermarks that make your documents stand out in the crowd as something special.

Working with Tables

Corel WordPerfect's Tables feature offers many practical uses. Tables can illustrate, define, and explain text; they can enhance your documents and make them more effective.

A table also gives you a convenient way to organize text. Use a table to organize columns of numbers, produce forms, or add spreadsheets to your documents. There are many formatting options you can apply to a table to make it visually appealing. Corel WordPerfect even provides a Table Expert to let you preview and apply a table style (a set of formats) to your table all at once.

A table consists of columns and rows that form a grid of cells. You can fill cells with text and/or graphics. When you type text into a cell, the text wraps automatically from one line to the next, and the cell expands vertically to accommodate your text.

TIP Several Corel WordPerfect templates, including the expense report, invoice, and calendar templates, are forms that are based on tables.

An example of a Corel WordPerfect table is shown in Figure 10.1.

FIG. 10.1
Enter columns of text with automatic word wrap by placing the text in a Corel WordPerfect table.

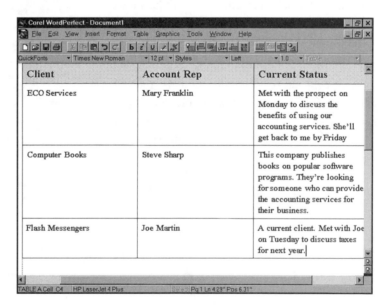

Creating a Table

A table can be inserted at any point in a document. You can create a table either with the Table menu or with the Table QuickCreate button on the Power Bar.

N O T E The quickest way to create a table is by pulling down a grid from the Table QuickCreate button on the Power Bar, and dragging through the number of columns and rows that you want for your table. The size of the grid doesn't limit the size of your table; the grid expands as you drag past its edge. ▨

To create a table with the Table menu, take the following steps:

1. Position the insertion point where you want the table to begin.

2. Choose Table, Create. The Create Table dialog box is displayed, as shown in Figure 10.2.

FIG. 10.2
Specify the number of columns and rows when you create a table.

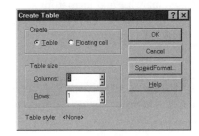

3. Enter the number of Columns and Rows that you want.

4. Choose a style for your table, if desired, with the SpeedFormat button. For information on using this feature, see the section "Using Table SpeedFormat to Enhance a Table" later in this chapter.

N O T E It's easy to add rows to a table after you create it. See the section "Inserting and Deleting Columns and Rows" later in this chapter. ▨

5. Click OK. A table with the specified number of columns and rows (and predefined style, if any) is inserted in your document. The table spans the width between the left and right margins. All columns have the same width.

Moving Within a Table   The easiest way to move within a table is to use the scroll bars until the part of the table you want is visible on the screen, then click with the mouse in the desired cell.

 When the insertion point is positioned in a table, Corel WordPerfect automatically displays the Tables toolbar for you.

You can also move within a table using the keyboard, as shown in Table 10.1.

Table 10.1   Keyboard Commands for Moving in a Table

Command	Result
Tab (or Alt+Right Arrow)	Next cell
Shift+Tab (or Alt+Left Arrow)	Previous cell
Alt+Up Arrow	Up one row
Alt+Down Arrow	Down one row

Entering Text Within a Table   As you enter text into your table, consider each cell a miniature document with its own margins and formatting. As you enter text, words wrap automatically to a new line and the row increases in depth. Press Enter only when you need to force words to wrap to the next line.

▶ **See** "Typing Text," **p. 87**

When you have completed entering text for a cell, press Tab to move to the next cell. When you reach the last cell of the table, pressing Tab will create a new row so that you can continue entering data.

Editing Table Design

A table has a very flexible structure. When you first create a table, it has a specified number of columns and rows, and every column has the same width. While you work with the table, you can adjust the column width to suit your taste, and you can add or delete columns and rows. You can even join cells to create a single cell, or you can split a cell into rows or columns.

When your insertion point is in a table, you see the Tables toolbar. This toolbar has a number of buttons that make editing your table design a snap.

Selecting Table Cells   Many design editing operations can be performed more quickly if you select the group of rows, columns, or cells that you want them to apply to. Follow these guidelines for selecting table elements:

- Turn on row/column indicators with the Row/Column Indicators button on the Tables toolbar.
- To select a *single cell*, position the mouse pointer against any edge of the cell so that it becomes a white arrow as shown in Figure 10.3, then click the mouse button. The entire cell should be highlighted.

FIG. 10.3
Position the mouse pointer against the edge of a cell so that it becomes a white arrow, then click to select the cell.

White arrow pointer —

Client	Account Rep	Current Status
ECO Services	Mary Franklin	Met with the prospect on Monday to discuss the benefits of using our accounting services. She'll get back to me by Friday
Computer Books	Steve Sharp	This company publishes books on popular software programs. They're looking for someone who can provide the accounting services for their business.
Flash Messengers	Joe Martin	A current client. Met with Joe on Tuesday to discuss taxes for next year.

TABLE A Cell A3   HP LaserJet 4 Plus   [Select] Pg 1 Ln 2.57" Pos 2.22"

Part
II

Ch
10

■ To select *several cells*, position the mouse pointer in the cell that is in the upper-left corner of all the cells that you want to select. Drag through the cells that you want to select. The cells should be entirely highlighted.

■ To select *columns or rows*, click or drag in the row/column indicators. The columns or rows in your selection should be entirely highlighted.

Figure 10.4 illustrates a table after column A has been selected. Row/column indicators have been turned on (from the Tables toolbar) to make selection easier.

Changing Column Width   To change the column width in a table, you can drag the column border or use the Size Column to Fit button.

To adjust column width by dragging a column border, take the following steps:

1. Position the mouse pointer against the right edge of the column you want to adjust, so that the pointer becomes a cross with horizontal arrowheads.

 TIP It's a good idea to start with the leftmost column that you're going to adjust and work your way to the right.

2. Drag the border to a new position. As you drag, a dotted vertical line appears and the exact position is indicated on the status bar, as shown in Figure 10.5.

 TIP Alternatively, you can drag a Column Break icon on the Ruler Bar to adjust the width of a table column.

FIG. 10.4

You should select table cells before formatting those cells.

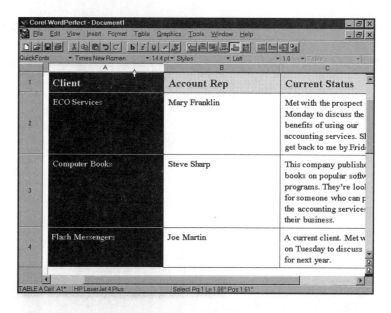

FIG. 10.5

Drag a column border to adjust the column's width.

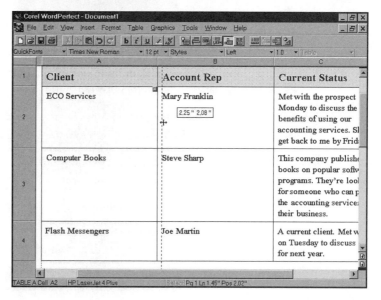

You can also adjust column width with the Size Column to Fit button. To adjust a column's width so that it's just wide enough for its widest entry, place the insertion point anywhere in the column and click the Size Column to Fit button on the Tables toolbar.

N O T E   Alternatively, you can set a precise width for a column from a dialog box. Position the insertion point in the column you wish to adjust. Click the Table SpeedFormat button, and choose the Column tab. Enter the exact measurement you need in the Width box, then click OK. ▓

Inserting and Deleting Columns and Rows   What if you enter several rows of information in your table and you realize that you need a new row in the middle of the table? No problem. You can insert a row (or column) anywhere in the table without disturbing what's already there.

To insert new rows (or columns) in a table, take the following steps:

1. Position the insertion point in the row (or column) next to where you want a new row or column.

2. Choose Table, Insert; or right-click, then choose Insert from the QuickMenu. The Insert Columns/Rows dialog box is displayed as seen in Figure 10.6.

Part II Ch 10

FIG. 10.6
Use the Insert Columns/Rows dialog box to indicate how many rows or columns to insert before the current column or row.

3. Choose Columns or Rows, then specify how many to insert.

4. If desired, adjust the Placement from Before to After.

5. Click OK.

N O T E   New rows and columns will contain the same formatting as the current row (or column). ▓

 T I P   Insert a row just above the current row by pressing Alt+Insert. Delete the current row by pressing Alt+Delete.

You can add a new row at the bottom of a table with the Tab key. Position the insertion point in the last cell of the table and press Tab to create a new row. If you're entering a list of names and addresses into your table, you can press Tab to add a new row just before you add the next name and address.

You can delete rows and columns just as you can easily insert them by following these steps:

1. Position the insertion point in the row or column that you want to delete or select the rows or columns that you want to delete (see the section "Selecting Table Cells" earlier in this chapter).

2. Choose T<u>a</u>ble, <u>D</u>elete; or right-click, then choose <u>D</u>elete from the QuickMenu. The Delete dialog box is displayed, as shown in Figure 10.7.

FIG. 10.7

Delete selected rows or columns with the Delete dialog box.

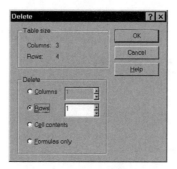

3. Choose <u>C</u>olumns or <u>R</u>ows. If you selected rows or columns before accessing the Delete dialog box, click OK. If you positioned the insertion point before accessing the Delete dialog box, you can specify how many rows or columns to delete, then click OK.

Joining Cells   What do you do when you want a title centered between the left and right edges of your table? You join table cells. When you first create a table, it has the same number of cells in every row and in every column. It doesn't have to stay that way; you can select the cells that you want to join and tell Corel WordPerfect to join them. The top row of the table shown in Figure 10.8 has a single cell that was created by joining adjacent cells.

To join table cells, take the following steps:

1. Select the cells that you want to join.

2. Choose T<u>a</u>ble, <u>J</u>oin, <u>C</u>ell; or, from the QuickMenu, choose <u>J</u>oin Cells.

FIG. 10.8

Join cells in the top row to create an attractive title row.

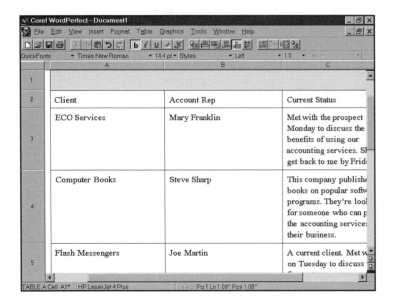

Splitting Cells On occasion, you may find it useful to split cells. You can split a cell into two or more cells either vertically or horizontally. The second row of the table shown in Figure 10.9 has a single cell that was split into three cells.

To split table cells, take the following steps:

1. Select the cells that you want to split.

FIG. 10.9

Split cells to create multiple cells where needed.

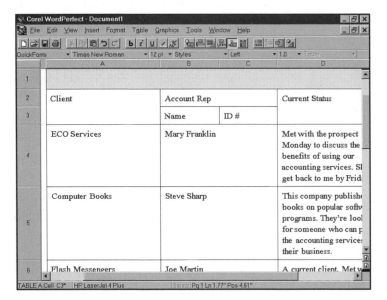

Part

II

Ch

10

2. Choose Table, Split, Cell.

3. Select whether you want to split the cell into Rows or Columns, and the number of cells that should be created.

4. Click OK to split the cells.

Formatting a Table

Use Table Format options to specify justification, text attributes, column margins, and so on for table cells. You can specify formatting either before or after you enter text in cells; in either case, the text is formatted according to the cell format.

N O T E   A table format is overridden by a column format; a column format is overridden by a cell format. You could, for example, format an entire column for decimal alignment, and the cell at the top of the column for center alignment. ◼

Formatting cells could be a matter of changing the alignment in the cells, of applying attributes such as bold or underline to text in cells, or of specifying header rows within the table. In this section, formatting table cells is used to mean formatting that is applied to any table element, whether that element is a cell, column, row, or the entire table. To format table cells, follow these steps:

1. Select the cell(s) or column(s) that you want to format.

2. Open the Properties for Table Format dialog box by clicking the Table Format button on the Tables toolbar; by choosing Format from the QuickMenu; or by choosing Table, Format. Figure 10.10 illustrates the Format dialog box with Table format options displayed as tabs (types of format options are Cell, Column, Row, and Table).

3. Choose the tab for the option type that you want to format: Cell, Column, Row, or Table.

4. Make the desired formatting changes. Your changes might include items in the following list:

   • When you format cells or columns, you can adjust the alignment with the Justification option. Cells containing numbers should be decimal-aligned.

   • When you format cells, you can lock cells to keep the insertion point from moving into the cells. You can also set vertical alignment, rotation, and place diagonal lines in cells.

   • When you format cells, you can specify that cell contents will be ignored in calculations (you might have to do this if you're adding a column that has a number in its column header).

FIG. 10.10

The Properties for Table Format dialog box with Table format options is displayed.

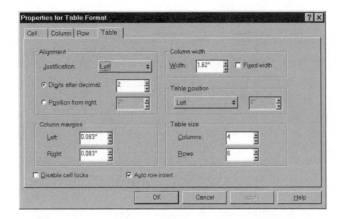

- When you format the table, you can adjust the Table Position relative to the page margins.

- When you format rows, you can designate the selected row to be a header row if desired. When a table spans a page break, header rows print at the top of each page.

- When you format rows, you can specify a fixed row height. This feature is useful when you create a table with "boxes" (cells) that should have a fixed height, regardless of any text they contain; for example, when you create a calendar. Unless you specify a fixed row height, the row height is a function of the number of text lines in the row.

5. Click OK to exit the Format dialog box and apply the specified changes to your table.

Changing Borders, Lines, and Shading in a Table

Give your tables visual appeal by changing table borders and lines, and adding shading to cells. Your "desktop publishing" efforts can make the table more attractive and easier to read. For example, when you shade every other row in a table, it's easy to read across a row.

The lines around a table are called its *border.* Lines around cells are called *lines.* By default, tables have no border and single lines around each cell. Borders and lines are created and formatted separately, and borders mask lines. Thus, if you have single lines around each cell, but a double-lined border, you will see the double line around the table, not the single line.

In addition to formatting table borders and lines, you can apply a fill style to table cells. Fill styles range all the way from standard gray shading to gradient patterns with blended colors.

You can use Table SpeedFormat to apply a set of changes for you, or you can make your own changes to table borders, lines, and shading.

Using Table SpeedFormat to Enhance a Table   The fastest and easiest way to make changes to borders, lines, and shading in a table is to apply a table style (a set of changes) all at once with Table SpeedFormat.

 T I P   You can Undo the effects after you apply a table style with Table SpeedFormat by choosing Edit, Undo.

To use Table SpeedFormat, take the following steps:

1. Position the insertion point anywhere in the table.

 2. Click the Table SpeedFormat button on the Tables toolbar; or, choose Table, SpeedFormat. The Table SpeedFormat dialog box appears, as shown in Figure 10.11.

FIG. 10.11

Apply a set of formats to your table in the Table SpeedFormat dialog box.

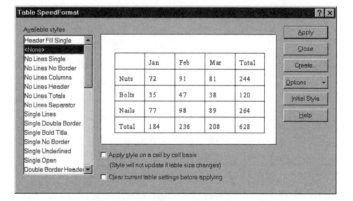

3. Examine the available styles, if desired, by selecting a style and looking at the preview area.

4. Select the style you want to apply.

 T I P   To set the current table style as a default style for all new tables, access the Table SpeedFormat dialog box, choose Initial Style, then choose Yes.

5. If you have already applied changes to borders, lines, or shading, you may want to check the Clear Current Table Settings Before Applying check box.

6. When you finish making selections in the Table SpeedFormat dialog box, choose Apply.

Making Your Own Table Enhancements   To make your own changes to table borders, lines, or shading, take the following steps:

1. Position the insertion point in the table, or select the cells for which you want to change borders or lines or add shading (see the section "Selecting Table Cells" earlier in this chapter).

2. Click the Lines/Fill button from the Tables toolbar; choose Table, Lines/Fill, or choose Lines/Fill from the QuickMenu. The Table Lines/Fill dialog box is displayed.

3. If you want changes to affect the entire table, select the Table tab at the top of the dialog box. Figure 10.12 illustrates the Properties for Table Lines/Fill dialog box with the Table options displayed.

FIG. 10.12

The Properties for Table Lines/Fill dialog box with Table options displayed.

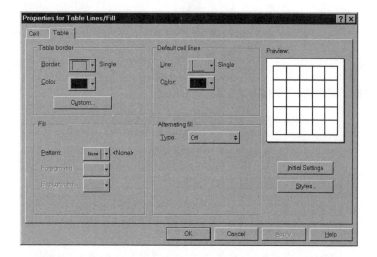

4. If the Table tab is selected, you can select or change the border for the table by displaying the Border palette of border styles. To add a table border, choose any border style other than <None>. Change the default cell lines in the Table tab as well, by changing the Line and Color options in the Default Cell Lines group.

5. To format lines or shading for selected cells, choose the Cell tab. Options in the dialog box now apply to the current selection, as shown in Figure 10.13.

6. With Cell options selected, change the line style for the sides you want to change (left, right, top, bottom, inside, or outside) from the pull-down palette of line styles.

7. With either Table options or Cell options selected, you can display a palette of fill styles and select a style. If the selected fill style has only one color, select a Foreground color, if desired. If the selected fill style has two colors, you can choose Foreground and Background colors.

8. Click OK to return to the table.

FIG. 10.13
The Properties for Table Lines/Fill dialog box with the Cell tab displayed.

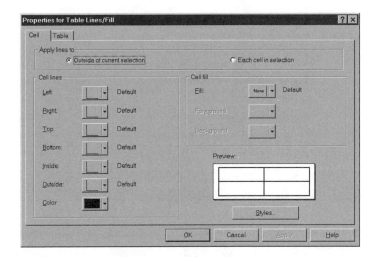

TROUBLESHOOTING

My table has cells with paragraphs of text in them. One row has an extra blank line at the bottom and I don't know how to get rid of it. Turn on the display of non-printing characters by choosing <u>V</u>iew, Show¶. Look for a ¶ somewhere in the row and delete it.

I inserted several rows in the wrong place. Click the Undo button to remove the unwanted rows. Then position the insertion point in a row right next to where you want a new row or rows. Choose Ta<u>b</u>le, <u>I</u>nsert. Specify how many rows you want and make sure that you choose the correct placement (before or after the current row).

I removed all of the lines in my table and now it's hard to tell which part of the table I'm working in. Choose <u>V</u>iew, Table Grid<u>l</u>ines to display dotted gridlines at the edges of cells. When table gridlines are displayed, you see gridlines at the edges of cells, regardless if any lines are defined for the cells. To view the table again as it will print (without the gridlines but with any defined lines or shading), choose <u>V</u>iew, Table Grid<u>l</u>ines again.

Working with Graphics

Take advantage of Corel WordPerfect's graphics features to add visual pizzazz to your documents. You can add lines, borders, shading, and pictures. Use graphics to call attention to your document, break the monotony of straight text, emphasize text, and pique the reader's interest.

You can add a line above (or below) headings to make them stand out or to help divide information on the page. Create a box with a border and enter text in the box, or add clip art to make a document more interesting. Use the Drop Cap feature to enlarge and emphasize the first letter in a paragraph. Use the Watermark feature to add a logo or clip art image or text behind the printed document text.

Working with Graphics Lines

WordPerfect enables you to add horizontal or vertical graphics lines through the Graphics menu and through buttons on the Graphics toolbar. To display the Graphics toolbar, right-click the toolbar and select Graphics.

The default graphics lines are thin lines that extend from margin to margin (left to right, or top to bottom). You can tell Corel WordPerfect how thick to make the line, what the color should be, how long it should be, or exactly where it should be on the page. Alternatively, you can use the mouse to adjust the thickness, length, and position of the line.

Figure 10.14 illustrates the use of a default horizontal graphics line to separate headings in a memo from the body of the memo.

Part
II
Ch
10

FIG. 10.14
Click the Horizontal Line button to create a horizontal graphics line that effectively separates the headings in a memo from the body of the memo.

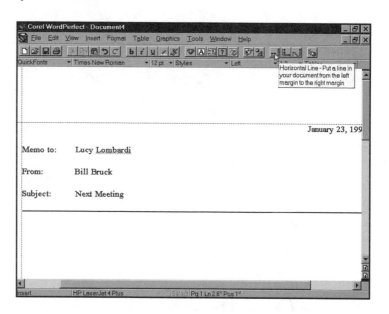

 Creating Instant Lines   You can instantly create a horizontal graphics line by clicking the Horizontal Line button on the Graphics toolbar, or by choosing Graphics, Horizontal Line. The result is a thin line that extends from margin to margin at the baseline of text on the current line.

Correspondingly, you can instantly create a vertical graphics line by clicking the Vertical Line button on the Graphics toolbar, or by choosing Graphics, Vertical Line. The result is a thin vertical line that is placed at the insertion point and extends from the top margin to the bottom margin.

Creating a Custom Line   To create a custom line, take the following steps:

1. If the line is to be a horizontal line, position the insertion point where you want the horizontal line. If you want the line to be placed slightly below a line of text, insert a hard return between the text and the horizontal line.

2. Choose Graphics, Custom Line. The Create Graphics Line dialog box is displayed, as shown in Figure 10.15.

FIG. 10.15

Customize a graphics line in the Create Graphics Line dialog box (or in the Edit Graphics Line dialog box).

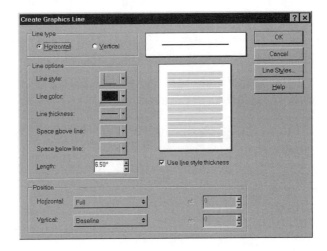

3. Adjust settings for the line as desired. For example, use the Horizontal Position option to adjust the length of the line. When you finish adjusting settings, click OK.

4. If the line you created is a horizontal line, you probably want to insert a hard return after the line.

N O T E   The Create Graphics Line dialog box becomes the Edit Graphics Line dialog box when you edit a line. ▪

Editing a Graphics Line   Edit a graphics line either with the mouse or through the Edit Graphics Line dialog box. The mouse is quick and easy to use, but not as precise as the dialog box.

To edit a graphics line with the Edit Graphics Line dialog box, take the following steps:

1. Click the line to select it. You see small square dots called *handles* around the selected line.

2. Choose Graphics, Edit Line. The Edit Graphics Line dialog box appears (it looks like the Create Graphics Line dialog box shown earlier).

 TIP You can also access the Edit Graphics Line dialog box by double-clicking the selected line, or right-clicking the line and choosing Edit Horizontal (or Vertical) Line from the QuickMenu.

3. Change any settings as desired and click OK.

To edit a line with the mouse, select the line first. To move the line, place the mouse pointer against the line so that the pointer becomes a four-headed hollow arrow. Then drag the line to a new position. To adjust the thickness or length of the line, position the mouse pointer against a selection handle so that the mouse pointer becomes a two-headed hollow arrow. Then drag the handle to adjust the thickness or length.

Part
II

Ch
10

Creating Borders

A graphics border is a box that surrounds text, emphasizes your message, separates text, or adds pizzazz to the page. You can use a paragraph border to call attention to one particular paragraph of text in a letter, for example; or you can add a page border to each page of a report to guide the reader and to create consistency within the report.

 TIP You can use a variety of line styles and thicknesses with page and paragraph borders.

Figure 10.16 illustrates a newsletter with a paragraph border, a page border, and a column border.

Creating Paragraph Borders A paragraph border is a frame that surrounds an individual paragraph or selected paragraphs. The border can include a fill style. Corel WordPerfect gives you a choice of many border styles and fill styles.

To add a paragraph border to your document, take the following steps:

1. Place the insertion point in the paragraph to which you want to apply a border, or select the paragraphs to which you want to apply a border.

2. Choose Format, Border/Fill, Paragraph. The Paragraph Border/Fill dialog box appears as shown in Figure 10.17.

3. In the Border tab, choose an Available Border Style to put a border around the selection, and select a color, line style, and shadow if desired.

FIG. 10.16

The page border dresses up the page. The paragraph border emphasizes the announcement about a new course offering.

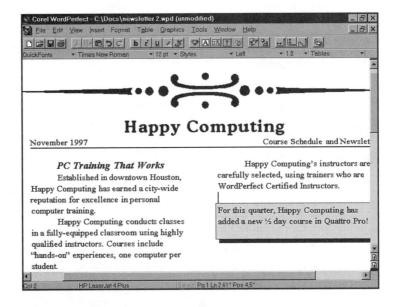

FIG. 10.17

Use the Paragraph Border/ Fill dialog box to add a paragraph border (and a fill, if desired) that calls attention to specific text.

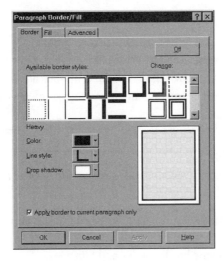

4. To frame the current paragraph and all subsequent paragraphs, ensure that the Apply Border to Current Paragraph Only check box is not selected.

5. To add a fill to your border, choose the Fill tab, then pick a style from the Available Fill Styles. Choose a foreground color, a background color, and a pattern if desired.

6. Click OK.

Creating Page Borders   A page border can add style to any document. Usually, you repeat the page border on all pages of a document, but you can choose to apply it to the current page only.

 T I P   Use Page view to see page borders on-screen; you can't see them in Draft view.

To add a page border to your document, take the following steps:

1. Position the insertion point on the first page where you want to apply a page border.

2. Choose Format, Border/Fill, Page. The Page Border/Fill dialog box is displayed as shown in Figure 10.18.

FIG. 10.18
To apply your page border to the current page only, click the box in the lower left corner of the Page Border/Fill dialog box. To remove the border from the current page, click the Off button.

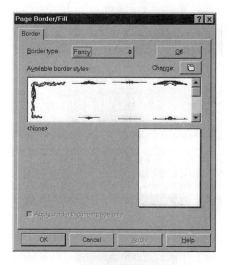

3. Select Fancy or Lines as the Border Type.

4. In the Available Border Styles area, select a border style.

5. Click OK.

N O T E   To remove a page border, place the insertion point on the page where the page border begins. Access the Page Border/Fill dialog box and choose Off. ▨

Creating Graphics Boxes

A graphics box is a box that holds an image or text—for example, clip art, a drawing, a callout, a text file, an equation, or a table. The contents of the document are adjusted to make room for the box. The box can be selected and moved or resized. A graphics box has its own contents and its own border; a paragraph or page border, on the other hand, is simply an ornamental frame surrounding text that is already in your document.

Adding graphics boxes to your documents illustrates the text, draws attention to the message, and adds interest to the document. Images, for example, help the reader understand the text, while text callouts attract the reader's attention to the text and break up "gray space" on the page. Corel WordPerfect enables you to add several types of graphics boxes to your documents, each with a style and purpose of its own.

Understanding Graphics Box Styles   Each of Corel WordPerfect's graphics box styles is designed to work best with one particular type of image or text. For example, the Image, Figure, and User styles work well with graphics images; and the Text Box and User styles work well with text. Any box, however, can hold any type of image, text, table, equation, and so on. The box style is simply a suggestion for the box's use. One aspect of the box style is its line style (width and type of border line). Other aspects of the box style include its placement (how it is attached or anchored to the document), its caption style, and the amount of space allowed both outside and inside the box. When you choose a box style, you choose the default settings for that box style. The style of an individual box, however, can be customized.

The following list describes each graphics box style and its default settings:

- *Image*. No border or fill, anchored to the page, suitable for graphics images.
- *Figure*. Single line border, anchored to the paragraph, suitable for graphics images.
- *Text Box*. Thick line on top and bottom, no fill, anchored to a paragraph, suitable for text.
- *Equation*. No border or fill, anchored to a paragraph, suitable for equations.
- *Table*. Thick line on top and bottom, anchored to a paragraph, suitable for a table or text.
- *User*. No border or fill, anchored to a paragraph, suitable for graphics images.
- *Button*. Button border with Button Fill, no outside border space, anchored to a character, suitable for text or images.
- *Watermark*. No border or fill, anchored to the page, contains images or text that is screened at 75 percent brightness so that it creates a background for text on the page.
- *Inline Equation*. No border or fill, anchored to a character, suitable for equations.
- *OLE 2.0 Box*. No border or fill, anchored to a page, used for data that is linked and embedded in a document.

Examples of a graphics box containing an image and a graphics box containing text are shown in Figure 10.19.

FIG. 10.19

Add graphics boxes to your document for visual interest.

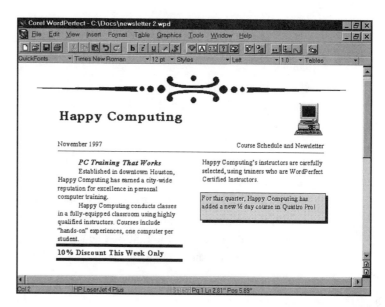

Part

II

Ch

10

Table 10.2 describes how each type of placement works and for what it is suited:

Table 10.2   Graphics Placement

Placement (Anchor Type)	How It Works	Suitable For
Paragraph	The box stays with the paragraph that contains it.	Boxes that are associated with text in the same area.
Character	The box is treated like a single character on a particular line of text.	Very small boxes that are associated with a line of text.
Page	The box stays in a fixed position on the page, regardless of editing changes to the text.	Boxes that are meant to stay in the same place on the page, such as a masthead at the top of a newsletter page.

Creating a Graphics Box   To create a graphics box, take the following steps:

1. To tell Corel WordPerfect that you want to position and size the box with the mouse when you create it, choose <u>G</u>raphics, then put a check mark by Drag <u>t</u>o Create. You see an explanation box. Click OK to proceed.

2. Click the Image, Text Box, In-line Equation, or Custom Box button.

3. Drag from the upper-left corner to the lower-right corner of where you want the box to be.

4. If you choose to create a box in the Text Box style, you are placed in the Text Box, where you can enter and format text. Click outside the box when you are finished editing it.

5. If you choose to create a box in the Image style, you are taken to the Insert Image dialog box, where you can choose an image to insert in the box. Select the image you want and choose Insert to return to the document. The box that you just created is selected.

6. To adjust the size or position of the box with the mouse, ensure that the box is selected (has handles around it), and use the two-headed sizing pointer or the four-headed moving pointer. If the graphic box is not selected, click it to select it.

 7. To edit the box, ensure that it is selected, then click the Edit Box button on the Graphics toolbar. You see the Edit Box floating dialog, as shown in Figure 10.20. Options within this menu are explained in Table 10.3.

 TIP To contour text around the image in a box, click the Wrap button on the feature bar. Choose Contour, then OK.

 TIP To quickly edit the text or the actual image in a graphics box, double-click the box.

Table 10.3 Edit Graphics Box Options

Option	What It Does
Border	Specifies the line style that surrounds the graphic box.
Fill	Specifies the color, shading, or pattern that fills the graphics box.
Wrap Text	Specifies whether text will wrap around or go through the graphics box. If it will wrap, specifies which side(s) it will wrap on, and the shape of the wrap (contour, square, and so on).
Attach To	Character: the box moves along a line like a text character does; Paragraph: the box moves up and down a page as paragraphs are added or deleted before it; Page: the box is on a fixed position on the page.
Position	Where the box is located relative to the margins or edges of the page.
Box Styles	Image, text box, and so on (as discussed previously).
Save Style As	Allows you to create a new graphic box style based on the settings for the current box.
Caption	Attaches a caption to the graphics box.

Option	What It Does
Content	Specifies a file or text to be included in the box; specifies that the WordPerfect document embeds or links to the file; specifies options for how the graphic object will be located within the graphic box.
Size	Specifies the size of the box.
Image Tools	Provides drawing and painting tools to adjust the image.
Prev/Next	Advances to previous or next graphics box in document.

FIG. 10.20

The Edit Box floating dialog allows you to change how the graphic box appears in the document.

8. When you finish working with the graphics box, deselect it by clicking outside of the box.

 To remove a graphics box, select it and then press the Delete key.

N O T E Choose Graphics, Custom Box to select a style for a box before you create the box. The box is created using default formatting options for your selected style. ■

 Double-clicking a graphic allows you to edit the graphic image using Corel Presentations 7.

Part
II

Ch
10

Creating Drop Caps

Corel WordPerfect's Drop Caps feature puts desktop publishing within everyone's reach. Now it's easy to add visual interest to your text by creating an oversized character at the beginning of a paragraph, like the one in Figure 10.21.

FIG. 10.21

Drop caps add interest and visual appeal to text.

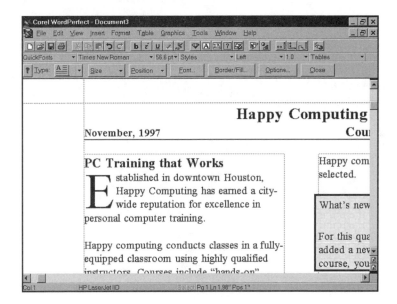

To create a drop cap, take the following steps:

1. Position the insertion point in the paragraph in which you want a drop cap.

2. Choose Format, Drop Cap. Corel WordPerfect creates a drop cap three lines deep using the first character in the paragraph, and displays the Drop Cap feature bar above the text area on-screen.

3. Adjust the drop cap, if desired, by using buttons on the feature bar. For example, if you want the drop cap to drop down through four lines of text instead of three, click the Size button, then select 4 Lines High.

4. Choose Close from the feature bar.

Creating Watermarks

A *watermark* is a special type of graphics box that contains either text or graphics, but prints in the background. The contents of the watermark box screens lightly so that the text you enter in the foreground is readable.

There are many uses for watermarks. You can dress up a letter to a client with your company logo, you can add text ("Draft") to the background of reports, and so on. You can use any of Corel WordPerfect's watermark files, create your own images or text to use as watermarks, or use images and text from other applications.

Using a Text Watermark   Most of Corel WordPerfect's watermark files (CLASSIFI.WPG, DRAFT.WPG, DUPLICAT.WPG, OVERDUE.WPG, and so on) consist of text that has been saved as a graphics image. You can use Corel WordPerfect's watermark text, or you can create your own text (it doesn't have to be saved as a graphics image). Figure 10.22 illustrates one of Corel WordPerfect's watermarks (DRAFT) in a draft copy of a newsletter.

FIG. 10.22
You can place a watermark with text to indicate the nature of your document.

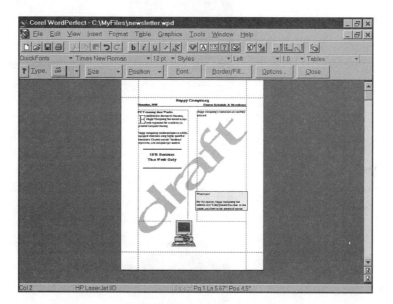

Using Images as Watermarks   You can use images created in other applications, or you can use any of the images in Corel WordPerfect's Graphics folder as a watermark image. The image you use doesn't have to be designed specifically as a watermark image. Figure 10.23 illustrates one of Corel WordPerfect's image files (COMPUTER.WPG) used as a watermark in a newsletter.

Creating a Watermark   Before creating a watermark, enter and format all document text. When the watermark appears on-screen, text editing slows considerably. To add a watermark to a document, take the following steps:

1. Position the insertion point on the first page that is to have a watermark (the watermark will appear on that page and on every subsequent page).

FIG. 10.23

You can also use an image, such as a computer, for your watermark.

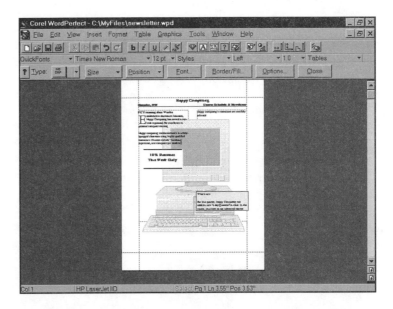

2. Choose Format, Watermark. In the Watermark dialog box, choose Create. You are placed in the Watermark A editing screen shown in Figure 10.24. The Watermark feature bar appears above the text area at the top of the screen.

FIG. 10.24

You can create watermarks that appear behind the text on each page.

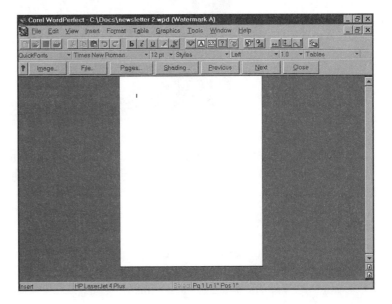

3. If you're going to create a watermark from text, you can type the text directly on the screen. You'll probably want an extremely large font size, however. Double-click

the Font Size button on the Power Bar. At the Font dialog box, double-click in the Font Size text box and type the size that you want (for example, type **150**). Click OK. Type (and format) the text that you want as a watermark. Then click the <u>C</u>lose button on the Watermark feature bar to return to your document.

4. To create a watermark that contains an image, click the I<u>m</u>age button on the Watermark feature bar and choose an image. The image you choose is automatically sized to fill the entire page. If you want to edit the image, choose <u>E</u>dit Image from the QuickMenu. Click the <u>C</u>lose button on the Watermark feature bar to return to your document.

TROUBLESHOOTING

I keep on creating a page border but no matter what I do I can't see it on-screen. Change the view from Draft view to Page view by choosing <u>V</u>iew, <u>P</u>age.

My page border only prints on the first page, and I have to specify it again and again on every page. When you create the page border on the first page, be sure that the <u>A</u>pply Border to Current Page check box is not selected.

My watermark is too dark. Edit your watermark by choosing Fo<u>r</u>mat, <u>W</u>atermark, <u>E</u>dit. Choose <u>S</u>hading to display the Watermark Shading dialog box. Adjust the percent of the text or image shading as needed and choose OK. Click the <u>C</u>lose button on the Watermark feature bar to return to your document.

I created a box and placed an image in it and now I'd like to change the border lines. Right-click your graphic and choose <u>B</u>order/Fill from the QuickMenu; or choose <u>B</u>order/Fill from the Graphics feature bar, if shown. Make whatever changes you want at the Box Border/Fill Styles dialog box, and click OK. Click outside of the box to deselect it.

Automating with Macros and Merge

Corel WordPerfect supplies many features that enable you to complete your work quickly and efficiently. Two of these features are macros and merge. Both of these features save you time by automating your work.

You can automate your work with macros, or miniprograms, by recording your keystrokes and commands, saving the recording, and then playing back the recording any time you need to repeat the same keystrokes and commands.

Corel WordPerfect's merge feature also saves you time and work. If you have ever had to send the same letter to a number of people, you know how much work this can be. Corel WordPerfect enables you to merge (combine) fixed information (the text in the letter) with variable information (the names and addresses). The form letters are produced all at once in a single merge operation. ■

Using Macros

Macros can save you time by performing repetitive tasks automatically. You can, for example, record a macro that types a closure to a letter. You can use macros to speed everyday formatting and editing, to automate an elaborate set of tasks, or to combine several commands into one (the one that plays the macro).

In addition to using the macros that you create yourself, you can use macros that Corel WordPerfect provides for you. Macros that Corel WordPerfect provides include: ALLFONTS.WCM, which prints a document with a sample of all available fonts; PLEADING.WCM, which creates a sample pleading for legal offices; and FILESTMP.WCM, which places the file name and path of the current document in a header or footer.

T I P   To see a description of the macros that are included with Corel WordPerfect, choose <u>H</u>elp, then look up Macro in the index and select Macros Included With Corel WordPerfect.

You can make a macro easy to use by assigning it to a button on a toolbar. Another way to make a macro easy to use is by naming it with the Ctrl+key method. See the "Creating a Macro" section, later in this chapter.

This section introduces you to playing macros, recording macros, and making simple editing changes to macros. It also shows you how to make a macro easy to use by assigning it to a button on a toolbar.

N O T E   Corel WordPerfect enables you to save macros inside templates, or as files on the disk. In the former case, they are saved as part of the template file, and are available only when you are using the appropriate template. In the latter case, they are saved as standalone files, and are always accessible.

Template macros are accessed by choosing <u>T</u>ools, Tem<u>p</u>late Macro; while the other macros are accessed by choosing <u>T</u>ools, <u>M</u>acro. Other than the location in which they are saved, they work the same way. The remainder of this chapter discusses macros, but the discussion applies as well to template macros. ■

Playing a Macro

When you play a macro, you execute the keystrokes and commands that are saved in the macro. The macro may type in text. It may perform formatting functions. It may even ask for your input and then perform certain steps depending upon your input.

T I P Once you have played macros, you can play recently played macros again easily. Choose Tools, Macro, then choose a recently played macro listed at the bottom of the Macro menu.

To play a macro, take the following steps:

1. Choose Tools, Macro, Play. The Play Macro dialog box appears, as shown in Figure 11.1.

FIG. 11.1
Select a macro to play in the Play Macro dialog box. A description of the selected macro appears at the bottom of the dialog box.

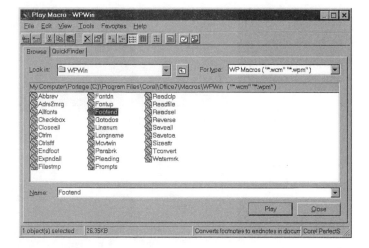

N O T E Corel WordPerfect automatically lists macros in the default directory specified for macros through File Preferences. To change this directory, choose Edit, Preferences, Files, Merge/Macro. ▨

2. Select a macro name, or enter a (path and) file name in the Name text box.
3. Choose Play. If this is the first time that you have played the macro, it compiles before it plays, and it takes a little extra time to get going.

Stopping a Macro

When you're testing a macro, it's a good idea to save any open documents before you play the macro. If something goes wrong during playback (for instance, if the macro adds text to the wrong part of your document), you'll want to cancel macro execution. You can usually stop a macro during playback by pressing the Esc key; however, the Esc key could be disabled or assigned to a specific function by the macro. After you cancel macro execution, you can always close all open documents without saving and then reopen them.

Part
II

Ch
11

Creating a Macro

Creating a macro is simply a matter of starting the macro recorder, performing the actions that you want recorded, and ending the recording session.

To record a macro, take the following steps:

1. Choose Tools, Macro, Record. The Record Macro dialog box appears (see Figure 11.2).

FIG. 11.2

Enter a name for your macro in the Record Macro dialog box.

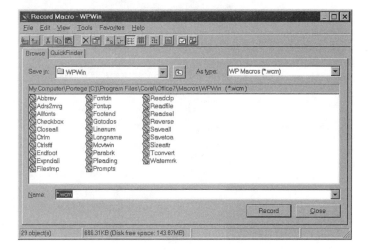

2. Enter a name for your macro. Corel WordPerfect assigns a .wcm extension to the name.

3. Choose Record. The macro recorder is activated, the Macro feature bar is displayed at the top of the screen, and Macro Record is displayed on the status bar, as shown in Figure 11.3.

4. Perform the actions that you want the macro to record. You can enter text from the keyboard, and you can choose commands from menus (with the keyboard or the mouse). You cannot use the mouse to move the insertion point or to select text while the macro recorder is active.

5. To finish recording, click the Stop Record button on the Macro feature bar; or choose Tools, Macro, Record. The Macro Record message disappears from the status bar and the macro is saved to disk. You can close the document window without saving changes after you stop recording, because the macro was saved when you stopped recording.

FIG. 11.3

The Macro feature bar displays while a macro is being recorded.

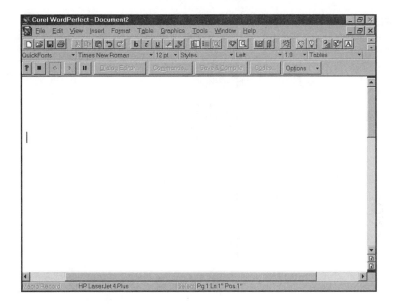

Making Simple Editing Changes to a Macro

Don't be afraid to make simple editing changes to a macro. If you decide, for example, that you want to add a middle initial to a closure that is typed by a macro, you can add the text without having to learn macro syntax and commands.

Take the following steps to make simple editing changes to a macro:

1. Choose Tools, Macro, Edit. The Edit Macro dialog box appears (it looks similar to the Record Macro dialog box).

2. Select the macro that you want to edit, then choose Edit. The macro file is opened into an editing window and the Macro feature bar appears just above the text window, like the macro being edited in Figure 11.4.

3. Use normal editing techniques to make simple editing changes.

    For example, to add a middle initial to the signature in the MACRO1.WCM macro, insert the middle initial in the appropriate place in the Type command. To remove one of the blank lines before the signature line, select a HardReturn( ) command and press Delete. To add a blank line above the signature line, type the command **HardReturn()**, or copy and paste a HardReturn( ) command.

    While you're editing the macro, you can press Enter (or Tab, or the spacebar) to separate commands; this formats the macro so that it's easier to read, but it doesn't affect what happens when you play the macro. Be careful, however, not to press Enter when the insertion point is positioned in the middle of a command; the Enter key signals the end of a macro command.

Part

II

Ch

11

FIG. 11.4

You can edit macros like you would edit any other Corel WordPerfect document.

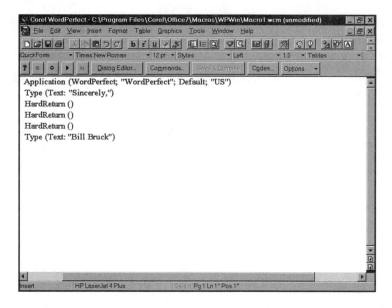

4. When you finish editing the macro, click the Save & Compile button on the Macro feature bar. The save and compile process begins; if there are no errors, the process is completed and the macro remains on-screen. If Corel WordPerfect detects errors during compilation, a dialog box appears describing the error and its location. You can then cancel compilation, correct the error, and try the save and compile operation again.

5. Once the macro successfully saves and compiles, choose File, Close to close the document window.

N O T E   Corel WordPerfect provides extensive on-screen help information about macros. For help with a specific macro command, chose Help, Help Topics. In the Contents tab, choose Macros, Macro Programming. ■

Adding a Macro to a Toolbar

For one-button access to a favorite macro, create a toolbar button that plays the macro. You can then play back all of the keystrokes and commands in the macro by clicking this button.

To add a macro to a toolbar, take the following steps:

1. Access the Toolbar Preferences dialog box by right-clicking the toolbar and choosing Preferences. The Toolbar Preferences dialog box is displayed, as shown in Figure 11.5.

FIG. 11.5
Begin the process of adding a macro button to a toolbar by selecting the toolbar that you want to edit and choosing Edit.

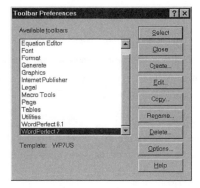

2. Select the toolbar that you want to edit and choose Edit. The Toolbar Editor dialog box appears.

3. Choose the Macros tab. The Toolbar Editor dialog box now looks like Figure 11.6.

FIG. 11.6
Choose Add Macro in the Toolbar Editor dialog box to add a macro to a toolbar.

Part
II

Ch
11

4. Choose Add Macro. The Select Macro dialog box is displayed.

5. Select the macro for which you want to create a button, and then choose Select. You are prompted with the Save macro with full path? message. Answer Yes. A Macro button is added to the toolbar and you are returned to the Toolbar Editor dialog box.

N O T E You only see button text if you have set toolbar preferences so that button text is displayed. By default, only a picture is displayed; you can ask for either or both. For information on changing toolbar preferences, see Chapter 8, "Customizing Corel WordPerfect." For more information on toolbars, see Chapter 35, "Customizing Toolbars and Menus." ■

6. Choose Close to return to the document window.

TROUBLESHOOTING

I'm recording a macro to move the insertion point and select text; however, I can't use the mouse to move the cursor within the text. The macro recorder cannot record mouse actions within document text, such as moving the insertion point and selecting text. Use the keyboard to record these actions.

I'd like to type some commands into my macro when I'm editing it, but I don't know the syntax. While you're editing a macro, you can click the Begin Record button on the Macro feature bar and record commands (this is easier than looking up the syntax and typing in the command). When you turn on the macro recorder, you access a new document window where you can choose the commands you want to record in the macro, either through the menu, the toolbar, or the Power Bar. When you finish recording, click the Stop Record button on the Macro feature bar; choose Tools, Macro, Record; or press Ctrl+F10 to return to the editing window for the macro. The steps you performed while recording are added to the macro at the insertion point. You can also press Ctrl+M while you are editing your macro to see a dialog box of macro commands.

I added a macro to the toolbar, but I can't tell what the macro does by looking at the button. Remember that when you position the mouse pointer on the button, you see the QuickTip (just under the button) and the Help text (in the title bar). To enhance the QuickTip or the Help text, edit the toolbar and double-click the button you want to edit in the Toolbar Editor dialog box. In the Customize Button dialog box, you can modify the button text and the Help Prompt.

Using Merge

Using Corel WordPerfect's Merge feature, you can mass-produce letters, envelopes, mailing labels, and other documents. When you merge a form letter with a list of names and addresses, each resulting document contains a different name, address, and company name. The process of merging a form letter with names and addresses is sometimes referred to as a mail merge. Because the names and addresses are saved in a separate file (the data file), you only have to enter them once—when you create the data file. You can use that same data file over and over again when you perform a merge.

Not only can you perform a merge in Corel WordPerfect using a data file, but you can also perform a keyboard merge. A keyboard merge merges a form file with input from the keyboard rather than from a data file. The result of a keyboard merge is a single, filled-in form document.

In this section, you learn to create the data file and form file that are used to perform a merge. You also learn to create the form file for a keyboard merge and to perform a keyboard merge.

What Is a Merge?

A *merge* is the process of combining fixed information and variable information. The fixed information—a form letter, for example—is in a file referred to as a *form file*. Every merge has a form file. The variable information can come from another file (referred to as a *data file*) or it can come from user input at the keyboard. A data file could be a Corel WordPerfect data file, or it could be a file from a database program such as Paradox, dBASE, or Access.

To create a merge data file or form file, or to perform a merge, access the Merge dialog box. Choose Tools, Merge. You see the Merge dialog box shown in Figure 11.7.

FIG. 11.7
Create a merge file or perform a merge in the Merge dialog box.

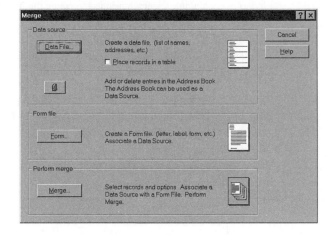

Performing a Merge

Performing a simple merge is a matter of creating a data file with variable information, creating a form file that asks for information from the data file, and performing the merge.

Creating a Data File

When you create a data file through the Merge dialog box, Corel WordPerfect guides you through the process of creating the file.

A Corel WordPerfect data file can be either a text file or a table. In either form, the data file is organized into fields and records. A *field* is one category of information, for example, a name or a phone number. A *record* contains all of the information about one person and is comprised of a complete set of fields.

To create a data file, take the following steps:

1. In an empty document window, choose Tools, Merge. The Merge dialog box appears. If you want your data records placed in a table, select the Place Records in a Table check box.

 T I P If you already have a table that is formatted as a list, you can use the table as a data file. You can also click the Address Book icon to use your Address Book as the data file for the merge.

N O T E If you have text in the active document window when you choose Data File, Corel WordPerfect displays a Create Merge File dialog box that asks if you want to use the file in the active window or open a new document window to create the data file. Choose New Document Window if you want to create the data file from scratch. ■

2. Choose Data File. Once Corel WordPerfect knows that you want to create a data file, the Create Data File dialog box appears.

3. In the Create Data File dialog box, create a field name list by typing each field name and pressing Enter to add the name to the list. Figure 11.8 illustrates the Create Data File dialog box after field names have been defined.

FIG. 11.8

Define field names in the Create Data File dialog box.

4. When you finish creating the field name list, click OK to close the Create Data File dialog box and open the Quick Data Entry dialog box.

5. At the Quick Data Entry dialog box, enter the data for each record, pressing Enter between each field and record. Figure 11.9 illustrates the Quick Data Entry dialog box with a filled-in record.

FIG. 11.9
Enter data records in the Quick Data Entry dialog box.

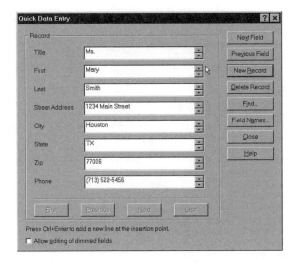

N O T E A field can have more than one line. An address field, for example, could have one or more lines for the street address and a line for the city, state, and zip code. In general, though, it's easier to sort and select records when fields are broken down into small categories. If you do want to enter more than one line of data in a field, press Ctrl+Enter before each subsequent line. Scroll arrows at the right end of the field box let you see different lines in the field. ■

6. Choose <u>C</u>lose when you finish entering records. Corel WordPerfect then prompts you to save the data file. You don't have to type an extension for the file name unless you want to. Corel WordPerfect automatically supplies a .dat extension.

7. Choose <u>Y</u>es to save the data file. Then specify a file name and click OK. If your data file is in a text format (rather than a table format), you see something like the illustration shown in Figure 11.10. At the top of the data file are the field names, followed by a page break. The end of each field is marked with an ENDFIELD code, even if the field is empty (the phone field in the second record is empty). The end of each record is marked with an ENDRECORD code and a hard page break. The Merge feature bar is displayed at the top of the screen.

Editing and Printing a Data File

You can edit your data file after creating it to add more records or to change existing data. You may want to print the data for verification. To edit a data file if it's not already in the active window, open it like any other file. When Corel WordPerfect opens the file, it recognizes it as a data file and displays the Merge feature bar at the top of the screen.

Part
II

Ch
11

FIG. 11.10

A text data file with records created in the Quick Data Entry dialog box.

Merge feature bar

Quick Entry button

Options button

The empty phone number field still has an ENDFIELD code

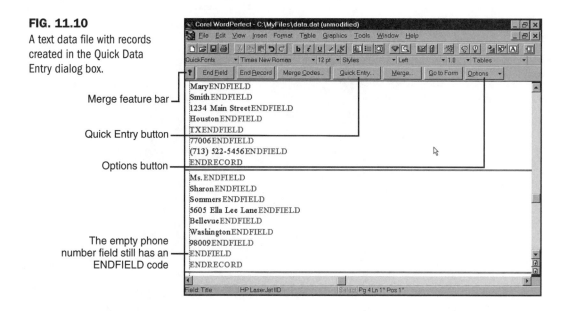

Adding Records

When you don't have time to enter all of your data file records at once, or you don't have all of the information when you create the data file, you'll want to reopen the file later and add records.

To add more records to the data file in the active window, follow these steps:

1. Select the Quick Entry button on the feature bar.

2. In the Quick Entry dialog box, choose New Record. An empty record form appears.

3. Enter new records until you're finished, and then choose Close.

4. When Corel WordPerfect prompts you to save your file, answer Yes and then save it to its existing name.

 It's easier to read the data on-screen if you choose Options on the feature bar, then select the Hide Codes option.

Editing Records

When you need to update the information in your data file—for example, when someone's address changes—reopen the data file and take the following steps:

1. Position the insertion point anywhere in the first record that you want to change, then choose Quick Entry, or position the insertion point at the beginning of the document and choose Quick Entry.

2. If the record that you want to change isn't displayed in the Quick Entry dialog box, choose Find. A Find Text dialog box appears. Enter the text that you want to find and choose Find Next. The first record that contains matching text is displayed in the Quick Entry data form (you may have to perform more than one find operation).

3. When the record you want to edit appears in the data form, make the desired changes and choose Close.

Printing the Data File

It's often helpful to have a printout of your data file. Corel WordPerfect makes it easy to print your data in a readable format. To print your data, follow these steps:

1. With the data file that you want to print on-screen, choose Options. To suppress the display of codes in the printout, make sure that Hide Codes is selected.

2. Then, from the Options menu, choose Print. Corel WordPerfect asks you to confirm that you want to print with no page breaks between records.

3. Click OK; the data file is printed.

Part

II

Ch

11

Creating a Form File

Every merge has to have a form file; the form file controls the merge. The form file contains merge codes that ask for information from another source; it should also contain any text, formatting, and graphics that you want in the final merged documents. When the merge is executed, the text, formatting, and graphics, if any, in the form file appear in every merged document. Merge codes in the form file are replaced by information from the data file or from the keyboard.

To create a form file, take the following steps:

1. If you already have a document with the fixed information for your form file, place the document in the active window.

2. Choose Tools, Merge. The Merge dialog box appears.

3. Choose Form. Corel WordPerfect asks you whether you want to use the current document window for your form file, or whether you want to create the form file in a new, empty window. Make the appropriate choice.

4. Corel WordPerfect then prompts you for the name of the data file to associate with your form file, as shown in Figure 11.11. The associated data file is the file that is merged with the form file. Enter a name for the data file, or select it after clicking the list button to the right of the text box.

FIG. 11.11

Associate a data file with your form file in the Create Form File dialog box.

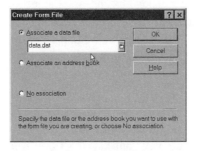

5. Alternatively, if you are in your Data Source file, to create a form file click the Go to Form button on the feature bar. You see the Associate dialog box shown in Figure 11.12. Choose Create to create a form file.

FIG. 11.12

The Associate dialog box allows you to create or open a form file to associate with the data file.

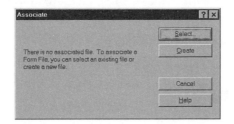

6. Type, edit, and format any text that should appear in your form file. Formatting text is described further in Chapter 6, "Formatting Text and Documents."

7. Position the insertion point where you want to insert the first merge code. If the form file is a form letter, for example, you might want to merge in the computer date at the top of the letter.

8. To insert a Date merge code, choose the Date button.

9. To insert a Field merge code, choose the Insert Field button. The Insert Field Name or Number dialog box appears, displaying a list of field names from the associated data file. Select the desired field name and choose Insert. The field merge code is inserted in the document and the dialog box is still on-screen. Figure 11.13 shows a form file just after inserting a date merge code and the first field merge code.

FIG. 11.13

The insertion point is placed after the merge code that was just inserted in a form file.

Insert Field button ──

Date button ──

Insertion point ──

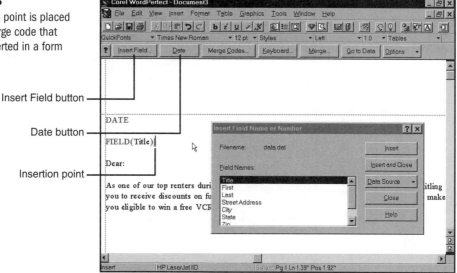

10. Position the insertion point where you want another merge code; or type, edit, and format text until the insertion point is where you want to insert the next merge code. Place commas and spaces between merge codes on the same line as appropriate. For example, if you have just inserted a field code for the City in the inside address of a form letter, press the comma key and then the spacebar.

T I P If the Insert Field Name or Number dialog box obscures your view of the form file, drag it to a new position.

11. When the insertion point is positioned where you want another merge code, select it from the list and choose Insert.

12. Repeat Steps 10 and 11 until you have entered all of the merge codes that you want to enter. When you finish, close the Insert Field Name or Number dialog box. The finished result may appear as illustrated in Figure 11.14.

13. Save and close the form file as you would any document. You don't have to type a file name extension; Corel WordPerfect automatically adds an .frm extension to the file name.

Performing the Merge

When you have a form file and a data file, you have the ingredients for a merge.

FIG. 11.14

A sample form file includes the form letter and the inserted fields.

A space separates
fields on this line

A comma and a space
separate the City and
State fields

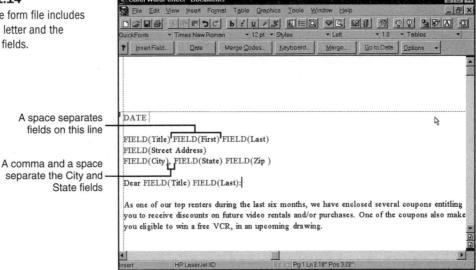

To perform a merge, take the following steps:

1. If you are not in the Form or Data file, choose Tools, Merge, then choose Merge from the Merge dialog box. Otherwise, if you are in the Form or Data file, select Merge from the feature bar. The Perform Merge dialog box appears as shown in Figure 11.15.

FIG. 11.15

The Perform Merge dialog box allows you to specify options for the merge.

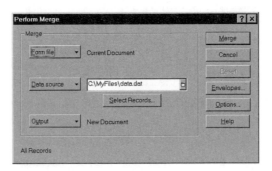

2. If they do not already appear, enter the names of your form file and data file, or use the list button for each option to select the name from a list.

N O T E To create merged envelopes at the same time that you create merged form letters, see the next section, "Creating Envelopes." ▪

TIP You can select specific records from your data file or address book for your merge. See help on Records (merge), Select in the Corel WordPerfect Help Index.

3. Choose <u>M</u>erge to perform the merge. When the merge has completed, the insertion point is positioned at the end of the last merged document. Page breaks separate each document.

4. Scroll through the merged documents to verify the success of the merge. If there are any problems, close the window containing the merged documents (don't save), edit the file that is causing the problem (either the form file or the data file), resave the corrected file, and perform the merge again.

5. When the merge has completed without problems, you can save the results, if desired, and print the merged documents all at once.

Creating Envelopes

Corel WordPerfect simplifies a merge by making it possible to create merged letters and envelopes all at once. When the merge is completed, both the form letters and the envelopes are in the active document window, ready to print.

To create merged envelopes and form letters in a single merge operation, take the following steps:

1. Enter the names of the form file and data file in the Perform Merge dialog box (see the previous section).

2. Choose <u>E</u>nvelopes. The Envelope dialog box is displayed.

3. Place your insertion point in the Mailing Address box, then click the F<u>i</u>eld button. Select the field you want to insert and choose I<u>n</u>sert and Close. Position the insertion point for the next field, then repeat this step until you have added all fields for your envelope. A completed Envelope dialog box is shown in Figure 11.16.

4. Add a bar code, if desired, through the Option<u>s</u> button.

5. Specify a return address, if desired. You can pick your return address from the address book by clicking the Address Book button.

6. When you finish working in the Envelope dialog box, click OK to return to the Perform Merge dialog box.

7. Choose <u>M</u>erge to perform the merge. Merged letters and envelopes are created in the designated output file (usually a new document). The insertion point is positioned at the end of the last letter; the envelopes are below the letters.

FIG. 11.16
To create merged envelopes,
enter field merge codes in
the Mailing Addresses area.

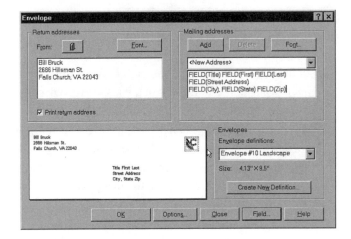

8. As with any merge, check the results before printing or saving. If there are problems, close the current window (don't save), edit and resave the problem file (it could be either the form file or the data file), and perform the merge again.

9. When the results are successful, you can save the output file, if desired, and print it all at once.

Filling in a Form with a Keyboard Merge

You can pause the merge operation to fill in information that is unique to each record. You can even create a form file that has no references to data file fields, but only has pauses for you to enter information. Creating and merging such a file is called a *keyboard merge*.

 Many of Corel WordPerfect's templates are automated merge forms. The Fax Expert, for example, prompts you for keyboard input and then places your input in appropriate places on the fax form.

You can use this technique to quickly create forms that require you to enter text in specific areas. All you have to do is start a merge and enter information as prompted. You don't have to move the insertion point to the next place that needs input; Corel WordPerfect does it for you. You even get help on what to input (from the prompt that is associated with each keyboard merge code).

Creating a Form File for a Keyboard Merge

When you create a form file for a keyboard merge, it's usually easier to create the document text first and add the merge codes later. You can, however, add the merge codes while you create the text.

Take the following steps to create a form file for a keyboard merge:

1. Create a boilerplate document containing all of the fixed information and formatting that should appear in every merged document.

2. Choose Tools, Merge. In the Merge dialog box, choose Form. In the Create Merge File dialog box, choose Use File in Active Window. Click OK.

3. At the Create Form File dialog box, choose No Association (to indicate that there is no associated data file), then click OK.

4. In your form file, position the insertion point where you want input from the keyboard. Choose Keyboard. The Insert Merge Code dialog box appears (this dialog box appears whenever you insert a merge code that requires additional information, such as a prompt).

5. Enter a prompt for the user to see when he inputs information at this specific place on the form. An example of the Insert Merge Code dialog box with a filled-in prompt is shown in Figure 11.17. When you finish entering the prompt, click OK.

FIG. 11.17
Remind the user what he should do while filling in variable information from the keyboard.

Part
II

Ch
11

N O T E It's helpful to tell the user which keystrokes to press to continue the merge after filling in data at the current location. For example, include the prompt "Type recipient's name, then press Alt+Enter to continue." ■

6. Continue to enter keyboard merge codes wherever you want input from the keyboard. A completed form might look like the illustration shown in Figure 11.18.

7. Save and replace the completed form file.

Performing a Keyboard Merge

When you perform a keyboard merge, you fill in the blanks in your form file from the keyboard while the merge occurs. The result is a single merged document. Once the form is filled in, you can print the results and save them.

To perform a keyboard merge, take the following steps:

1. In an empty document window, choose Tools, Merge. In the Merge dialog box, choose Merge. In the Perform Merge dialog box, specify a form file, then make sure that the Data File text box is empty. Choose Merge to begin the merge.

FIG. 11.18

This is a completed form file for a keyboard merge.

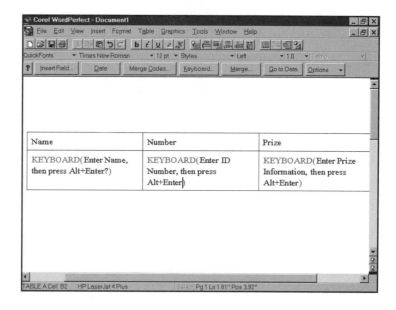

2. A merge feature bar appears at the top of the screen. When the merge pauses at the first keyboard merge code (see Figure 11.19), the prompt that is associated with that particular keyboard code appears in the center of the screen. Type the appropriate information. When you finish typing, press Alt+Enter or choose Continue from the feature bar. This tells Corel WordPerfect that you have finished entering information here and that you are ready for the merge to move on.

FIG. 11.19

A merge is paused for input at a keyboard merge code. What you type is entered at the insertion point.

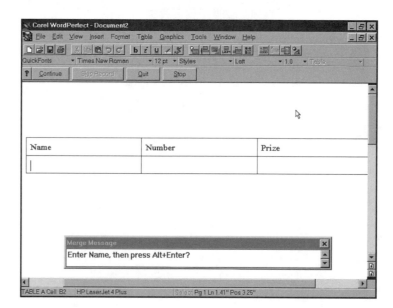

3. The merge moves to the next keyboard code, if there is one, and prompts you for input. As long as you are being prompted for input, the merge is in process. You must tell Corel WordPerfect to move on from each keyboard merge code, whether or not you type input at that code.

 You can type as many lines as necessary at a keyboard prompt. You can also add or correct any formatting on previous entries.

4. When the merge is complete, you can print the document on-screen and save it, if desired.

TROUBLESHOOTING

I created a data file and a form file and then I performed a mail merge, but the city, state, and ZIP code are all jammed together in the inside address. In a normal letter, you have a comma and a space separating the city and the state in an inside address. In a form file, you need the same text (a comma and a space) between the field code for the city and the field code for the state. Correspondingly, you need spaces between the state and ZIP code fields.

I performed a merge and asked for envelopes, but they're not there. When a merge completes, the insertion point is beneath the last form letter, but above the envelopes. Scroll downward to see the envelopes after you perform the merge.

I created a keyboard merge form file but when I performed a merge, I pressed Enter and the merge didn't move on to the next place that needed keyboard input. Then I didn't know what to do. When you get into a mess like this the best solution is to cancel the merge (press Esc), close the document window without saving, and start again. The only way you will move on from the current keyboard merge code during a merge is by choosing Continue or by pressing Alt+Enter. You must repeat this action for every keyboard merge code in the form file in order for the merge operation to come to a normal termination.

CHAPTER 12

Integrating Corel WordPerfect 7 with the Internet

Corel WordPerfect 7 helps you extend your desktop into the Internet or corporate intranet by allowing you to browse the Web, download text and images from the Web into your WordPerfect documents, create active links from your documents to the Web, or even publish your documents to the Web in a variety of ways.

If you are not familiar with the Web and Web documents, you might consider reading Chapter 26, "Using Corel WordPerfect Suite on the Internet" before you read this chapter. Even if you have experience with the Web, this chapter may have useful information of which you are not aware. ■

Publishing on the Internet

Understand some of the limitations of Internet publishing.

Using information from the Web

Learn how to pull information off the Web to incorporate into your word processing documents.

Create Web documents

Find out how to use the Internet Publisher to create complex Web documents.

Publish Web documents

Learn to view your Web documents in a Web browser or upload them to the Internet.

Convert Web documents

Understand how to convert Corel WordPerfect 7 documents into HTML, and vice versa.

Publish documents with Envoy

Learn how to convert your Corel WordPerfect 7 document into an Envoy document that retains all the formatting but can be read with the free Envoy viewer.

Publish documents with Barista

See how your Corel WordPerfect 7 can be converted into a Java applet that can be viewed with Web browsers, yet retains your formatting information.

Browsing the Web from WordPerfect

 The first way that you can extend your desktop is by browsing the Web from WordPerfect. Whenever you want to access the Web, click the Browse The Web button. You are taken into Netscape and from there automatically to Corel's site. From there, you can obtain assistance with Corel products or jump to anywhere else on the Internet.

Using Information from the Web in Your Documents

You cannot only reach out *to* the Web from WordPerfect, you can also bring information *from* the Web into your WordPerfect documents.

Because many companies have Web sites that advertise their wares, you can perform "environmental scans" by downloading their sites, and copying relevant information to a weekly report you prepare for internal use.

You can often download schedules of classes and even selected syllabi from local universities—a boon for students who want to keep organized and plan ahead. Whether it's recipes, technical support instructions, or IRS instructions, you will find it useful to be able to capture text from Web sites to integrate into WordPerfect documents you create.

Of course, if your Web is a corporate intranet, you may find many documents that are stored on your Web expressly *for* your use. Sections from corporate capability statements, résumé information, or the annual report can easily be incorporated into proposals or other documents you create in WordPerfect.

> **CAUTION**
>
> The information contained on Web sites is often copyrighted, and will in any case be protected by relevant copyright laws. Always attribute quoted text, and strongly consider establishing a company policy regarding use of information obtained from the Internet after advice from legal counsel.

▶ **See** "Understanding the Implications of Publishing on the Internet," **p. 534**

There are three ways you can incorporate text from Web pages into your documents. You can:

■ Save Web documents to your local disk, then convert them to Corel WordPerfect.

- Copy information from a Web page to your Corel WordPerfect document.
- Create a link from your Corel WordPerfect document to information on a Web page.

Saving and Converting Web Documents

The first way to incorporate information from the Web into your WordPerfect document is to save and convert the Web document. You can do this by first browsing to the document using Netscape, and then choosing File, Save As to save it to your local disk.

▶ **See** "Browsing," **p. 539**

▶ **See** "Saving Web Pages," **p. 544**

Then you can convert the Web page into a WordPerfect document. Once the document is converted into WordPerfect, you can edit it, or copy or move sections of it into another WordPerfect document you are working on.

▶ **See** "Converting HTML into Corel WordPerfect 7," **p. 267**

▶ **See** "Copying and Moving Text," **p. 92**

Copying Web Information into a Document

Alternatively, you can copy selected text directly from a Web document into your WordPerfect document. To do so, use Netscape to browse to the document you want to copy text from.

▶ **See** "Browsing" **P. 539**

When you are looking at the desired document, drag with your mouse over the text you want to select, then choose Edit, Copy to copy the text to the Clipboard. Switch to Corel WordPerfect, click where you want the text to appear, then choose Edit, Paste.

> **CAUTION**
>
> Viruses can be downloaded in program, data, and macro files. Be very careful about indiscriminately downloading files from the Web. The wrong virus can make every single file on your computer unusable. Practice "safe computing" by getting a virus protector (for individual machines or on a network) before getting set up to go out on the Web.

Using Hypertext Web Links

You can create links in your WordPerfect document that will take you to specific sites on the Web when you click them. For example, you might have a WordPerfect document on the network that discusses current industry trends. As you make points in your report,

Part
II
Ch
12

the supporting evidence can be links that readers can follow to see the Web-based data that led you to your conclusions.

▶ **See** "Adding Links and Bookmarks," **p. 256**

CAUTION

Web sites change frequently. If you are responsible for Corel WordPerfect documents that contain links to Web pages, be sure to check the links regularly to make sure that they still work.

Understanding Web Publishing

Everyone who has electricity has heard about the Internet now, and most people in business are sure it's a "good thing," but many people still do not honestly know why they might want to create Web documents.

There are two types of Webs that one might publish documents to, and they each have different purposes: The World Wide Web, which is part of the Internet; and private, corporate Webs called intranets.

Publishing to the World Wide Web

The World Wide Web is part of the global Internet. Information published on it is available to the public. There are many types of Corel WordPerfect documents you may want to put where the public can see them.

▶ **See** "Understanding Internet Basics," **p. 524**

Individuals create *personal Web sites* that are a little bit like a telephone white pages listing except that they tell the public more about you. Personal Web sites often contain information about your interests, your family, your work, and ways to contact you. Personal Web sites can be created using Corel WordPerfect templates.

Companies create *corporate Web sites* on the Internet as a matter of public relations. They not only can establish a corporate presence on the Internet, they can sell products, deliver technical information, or provide white papers on topics of interest to their industry. Corel WordPerfect is not the best software to create a sophisticated *home page* (the initial page you see at a company's site, often with sophisticated graphics). It is excellent, however, for creating the other Web pages, because technical information, white papers, and so on often *already* exist in WordPerfect.

A key to Web publishing is understanding that it is a public pronouncement. It's like standing on a box in the middle of Times Square and telling passersby what your opinions are.

You don't know who is going to read it, and it may be more permanent than you think. Even if you change what's on a Web page, someone else may well have saved the original version to their disk.

Publishing to a Corporate Intranet

Increasingly, corporations are using intranets as the method of choice to publish internal documents. The nature of the intranet means that only corporate employees can access it. The nature of the Web, however, also implies that employees with many different types of computers can see Web documents with all their formatting, allowing for inexpensive cross-platform integration.

For these reasons, corporations are publishing WordPerfect documents to their intranets such as:

- *Internal corporate documents.* All sorts of corporate documents, such as employee manuals, insurance application instructions, corporate policies, and the like are being published to intranets from their original WordPerfect format. Often, they are no longer being produced in hard copy to save money.

- *Knowledge bases.* Because search tools can search the text of all documents published to the intranet, more technical files, résumé files, and historical documents are being published to internal Webs to create searchable "knowledge bases" that can be accessed by personnel.

  ▶ **See** "What Are Intranets?," **p. 526**

Corel WordPerfect 7 provides three ways to publish your documents:

- Creating HTML Web documents that can be uploaded to the Internet or a corporate intranet,

- Creating Java applet Web documents, and

- Using Envoy, which creates documents with full Corel WordPerfect 7 formatting that can be viewed by anyone having the free Envoy viewer.

Part
II

Ch
12

Creating Web Documents

The Web is a part of the Internet that supports graphic and multimedia files that are written in HTML format. What's this all about?

The Internet only supports the transmission of text files, not the complex binary files that make up applications and data files, and contain complex format coding (such as Corel WordPerfect 7 documents).

To get around this shortcoming, complex coding systems have been developed to translate programs and data files into plain text. One of these mechanisms is the HyperText Markup Language (HTML). Using HTML, bold text is denoted by *tags* —ASCII codes that denote <b> the beginning of bold, and </b> the end of bold. Similarly, <H1> denotes the Heading 1 style, and </H1> denotes the end of it.

N O T E ASCII is a fancy name for the characters on a typewriter keyboard—A-Z, 0-9, and a few others. When you read ASCII, you can generally substitute "plain text." ▨

In the past, you had to learn HTML codes to create documents that could be published on the Web. Now, the Internet Publisher takes care of this for you, and you merely need to format your document using familiar Corel WordPerfect 7 commands.

Internet Publisher is a part of the Corel WordPerfect 7 program. It is a set of functions that allow you to create Web documents, save them in HTML format, and even convert existing Corel WordPerfect 7 documents to HTML and vice versa. You can create an empty Web document or use an Expert to create a simple Web home page for yourself. In addition, the Internet Publisher allows you to add and format text, create links, insert graphics, and add tables to your Web document.

When you publish a series of interlinked HTML documents on the Web, they become a Web site, and each document is called a Web page. The main page on your site that a person would usually go to first is called the *home page*.

For ease of writing, however, the following terms are used in this chapter to mean essentially the same thing: HTML document, Web document, and Web page.

N O T E Java is another, newer, coding system with which Web pages can be created. For an explanation of how Java works, see Chapter 20, "Using the Internet with Corel Quattro Pro." For creating Java applet pages from WordPerfect documents, see the section "Publishing Documents with Barista" later in this chapter. ▨

Making a Basic Web Document

To start making a Web page:

1. Choose File, Internet Publisher. You see the Internet Publisher dialog box shown in Figure 12.1.

2. Click the New Web Document button. You see the Select New Web Document dialog box shown in Figure 12.2.

FIG. 12.1
You can click the New Web Document button in the Internet Publisher dialog box to create Web documents such as home pages for yourself or your business.

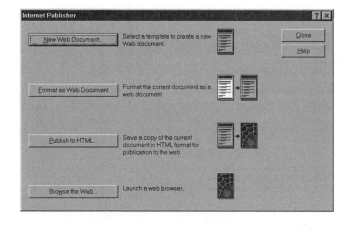

3. Select Create a Blank Web Document.

4. Choose Select. An information message appears, then you see a blank editing screen like the one shown in Figure 12.3.

FIG. 12.2
You can create a blank Web document or use the Web Page Expert to assist you.

N O T E Corel WordPerfect 7 supports HTML 2.0 tags. If your site supports a later version of HTML, newer tags must be inserted using custom HTML. You may want to refer to Que's *Special Edition Using HTML* for further information on codes in later HTML versions. ■

5. Add text, graphics, tables, styles, and other elements to the Web page as described in the next section.

N O T E You must save your document in HTML format before it can be uploaded to the Web. This procedure is discussed later, in the section "Publishing HTML Documents." ■

Adding and Formatting Text

Once you have created a Web page, you will want to add text to it, and format the text so that it appears attractive when seen in a Web browser such as Netscape. With the Internet

FIG. 12.3

When you create a Web document, you begin with a blank editing screen. In the toolbars, you only see active buttons for features that are supported in HTML 2.0.

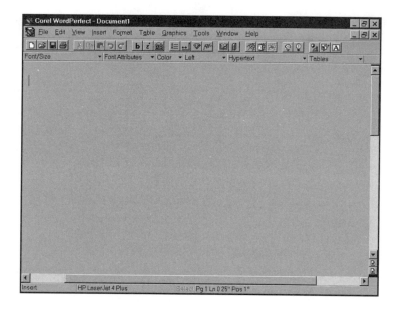

Publisher, not only can you do this easily, but you can also copy text into your Web page from other Corel WordPerfect 7 documents.

Adding Text   To add text to your Web page, type it in as you would in any other Corel WordPerfect 7 document. All the normal editing commands are available to you, just as they are in any other Corel WordPerfect 7 document. Move around the document with your mouse or keyboard, insert and delete text as you normally would, and even cut and paste text from one part of the document to another.

Formatting Text   When you are in the Internet Publisher, only the formatting features supported by HTML (the underlying "language" that Web documents are written in) are available to you. Notice that the toolbar and Power Bar change, as shown in Figure 12.4. Menu items that are not supported in HTML are removed as well.

Format your text as you normally would, recognizing that not all the formatting commands you are accustomed to will be available. For instance, to bold a sentence, you will highlight it, then click the Bold key. To create a bulleted list, click the Bulleted list button at the beginning of a new line, then type the bulleted items.

One major difference you will experience in formatting text with the Internet Publisher is in setting the font and size of your text. While the latest HTML standards support specifying fonts and font sizes, earlier standards do not; nor does the Internet Publisher.

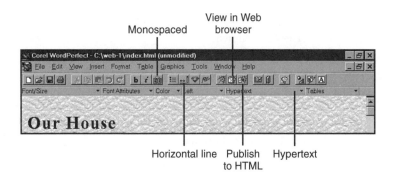

FIG. 12.4
When you create Web pages, your toolbar and Power Bar change to provide you with specialized options for your Web document.

When you click the Font/Size button on the Power Bar, you see a variety of styles that can be applied to your text, as shown in Figure 12.5.

To change the font or size of text, click anywhere in the paragraph to be formatted, then click the Font/Size button. Select a style for your paragraph. The entire paragraph is formatted in the selected style.

FIG. 12.5
Apply fonts and sizes from the drop-down list of styles in the Internet Publisher.

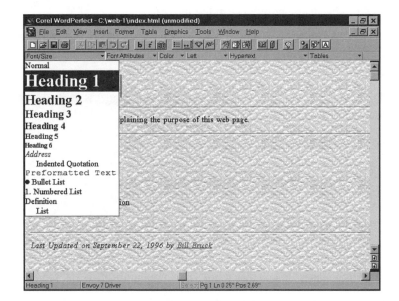

Part
II

Ch
12

Copying Text   To copy text into your Web document, open the document containing the text, select it, then choose Edit, Copy. Switch back to your Web document, place your insertion point where you want the text to appear, and choose Edit, Paste. The text is copied into your Web document, just as if you had copied it into any other Corel WordPerfect 7 document.

Inserting Graphics

Many Web pages contain graphics—either clip art or graphic elements such as lines, fancy bullets, graphic buttons, and the like. You can import all of these into your Web pages with the Internet Publisher.

Using Horizontal Lines   The simplest graphic element that you can use to spice up your Web page is a horizontal line.

 To insert a horizontal line into your Web page, position your insertion point where you want the line to appear, then click the Horizontal Line button. You see a line in your Web document.

You can also edit the appearance and attributes of horizontal lines. To do so, select the line to be edited by clicking it, then choose Graphics, Edit Line. You see the Edit Graphics Line dialog box shown in Figure 12.6.

Specify the Horizontal position of the line (left, center, right, or full), the line's Length, and the Thickness of the line, then click OK.

FIG. 12.6
Specify the position, length, and thickness of horizontal lines in your Web document.

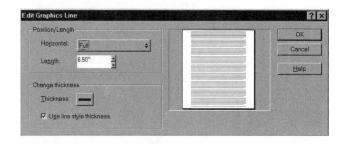

 Inserting Clip Art   To insert clip art into your Web page, click the Image button. You see the Insert Image dialog box shown in Figure 12.7.

Navigate to the folder containing the image you want to use, then double-click it. You see the image in your document, as shown in Figure 12.8.

> **N O T E**   The Web only supports images saved in two formats: GIF and JPG. Your image will be converted to GIF format when you save your document as an HTML document, described as follows. ■

FIG. 12.7

The Insert Image dialog box enables you to insert Corel WordPerfect 7 graphic files into your Web page, as well as files available through the Internet and other vendors.

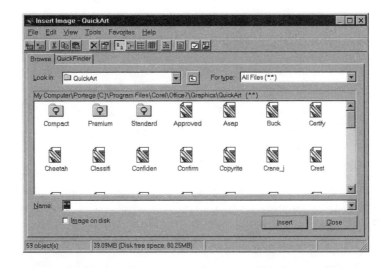

FIG. 12.8

Images appear in your document when you select them, and are automatically converted to GIF format when you save your document as an HTML file.

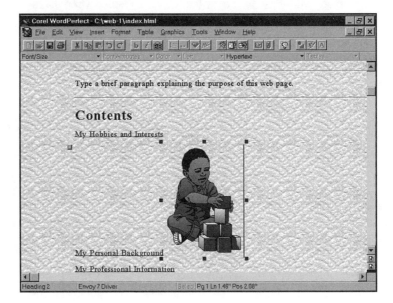

Part

II

Ch

12

To move your image, select it by clicking it so that you see handles around it. Position your mouse pointer inside the image, and notice that the pointer changes to a four-way arrow. Drag the image to its new location.

Similarly, you can size the image by selecting it, then positioning your mouse pointer on one of the handles. The mouse pointer becomes a two-way arrow. Drag the handle to resize the image.

TIP You can't wrap several lines of text around a graphic like you can in a Corel WordPerfect document. The box moves with the words in the line. You can change the position of the box on the line, but you can't change how several lines of text wrap.

To edit the image, you can double-click it to open Corel Presentations (or your default graphics editor for this file). Alternatively, you can right-click it to bring up the QuickMenu and use the same image editing tools you use for other images in Corel WordPerfect 7 documents.

When those browsing the Web are in a hurry, they sometimes choose the option to have their browser not automatically load graphics. This can decrease the amount of time it takes for their system to load the information on the page so they can view more pages faster. Additionally, some users do not have a browser that will permit the viewing of graphics of any sort, so they can only see text.

If you would like to specify text that will display when users do not use a graphical browser, or when users do not choose to automatically load graphics, do so as follows:

1. Select the image, then right-click it. You see the QuickMenu.

2. Choose HTML Properties. You see the Box HTML Properties dialog box shown in Figure 12.9.

FIG. 12.9
In the Box HTML Properties dialog box, you can specify text that will display in place of the image box if a user is not using a graphical browser.

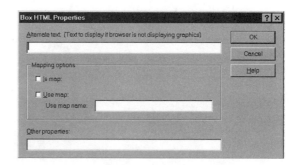

3. Type the text in the Alternate Text box, then click OK.

NOTE Users who are familiar with HTML documents can also use this box to add ISMAP images—images that activate links when a specific part of the image is clicked. ■

Adding Links and Bookmarks

Your Web document becomes a full-fledged member of your intranet or the Internet when it provides links to other documents. You can easily add links to other documents, or to specific bookmarks within these documents. The links can be highlighted terms, or they can be small graphics that the user will click.

N O T E The link feature is most often used in conjunction with the Internet Publisher. It is, however, a part of Corel WordPerfect 7 itself. Thus, you can create links from *any* Corel WordPerfect 7 document using the procedures described in this section. ■

Creating and Editing Links   To create a link to a document on your disk or the Web, follow these procedures:

1. Open the document where you want the link to be located.

2. Select the term that should be displayed for the text link or included in the link button.

3. Click the Hypertext button on the Power Bar, and choose Create Link. You see the Create Hypertext Link dialog box shown in Figure 12.10.

FIG. 12.10
In the Create Hypertext Link dialog box of Internet Publisher, you can quickly create hypertext links to documents on your disk, your local intranet, or the Internet.

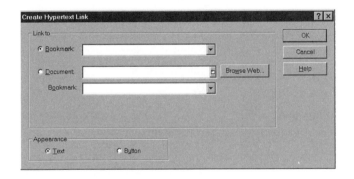

4. In the Document box, type the name of the file you want to link to. If it is a document on the disk, use the full path to the document, such as C:\Myfiles\Web\Index.htm. If it is a document on the Web, use a complete URL, such as **http://www.corel.com/index.htm**.

Alternatively, click the Browse Web button. Your default browser will be launched, and you can navigate to the Web site that you want to link to. When you switch back to Corel WordPerfect 7, the URL for the Web site will appear in the Document box.

CAUTION
Be careful about using links to Internet documents that you don't control. You may link to an URL that is here today and gone tomorrow, so you need to think about how long the document created with a link will be available. You also need to be willing to check regularly to make sure that links in your documents are still working.

5. If you want the link to take you to a specific bookmark in the destination document, type the name of the bookmark in the Bookmark box. (Creating bookmarks is discussed in the next section.)

6. If you would like the link to be a button, click the Button radio button.

7. Click OK. You return to your Web page and see the link term in blue, or see the link button.

 Many Internet servers are case-sensitive. To get to an URL on these servers, you must type the link in with the correct case. Because you don't know which servers are case-sensitive, it's good practice to always use the exact case that you see.

You can edit the link once it is created by right-clicking it, then choosing Edit Hypertext/ Web Link. You see the Edit Hypertext Link dialog box, which has identical functionality to the Create Hypertext Link dialog box discussed previously.

Creating Bookmarks   A bookmark is a marked place or section of text in a document that has a name. You can use bookmarks to go directly to a specific place in a document. You can create bookmarks in your Web documents—or in regular Corel WordPerfect 7 documents—so that links can take you to a specific place in your document, rather than merely to the beginning of the document.

In Web page design, a long Web page will often have a table of contents at the top, then bookmarked positions throughout the document. Clicking the table of contents link terms will take you to specific sections of the document.

 You can go to a bookmark in a document by pressing the GoTo shortcut key Ctrl+G, and specifying the bookmark you'd like to go to.

To create a bookmark, do the following:

1. Open the Corel WordPerfect 7 document or Web page that you want to put a bookmark in.

2. Place the insertion point at the position where you want to have a bookmark.

3. Choose Insert, Bookmark; alternatively, if the document is a Web page, click the Hypertext button on the Power Bar, then choose Bookmark. You see the Bookmark dialog box shown in Figure 12.11.

4. Click the Create button. You see the Create Bookmark dialog box.

5. Type the name of the new bookmark in this dialog box, then click OK. You return to the document.

FIG. 12.11

Using the Bookmark dialog box, create bookmarks in your document so that links can take the user to a specific place in the document.

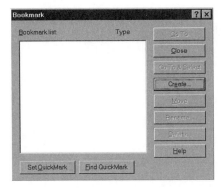

To use the bookmark, create a link to the appropriate file, including the bookmark, as was discussed in the previous section.

 There is no visible prompt that a bookmark has been created. However, you can press Alt+F3 to see the bookmark in Reveal Codes, if you like.

Including Tables

Increasingly, Web pages are being used to provide data to clients, customers, and employees. Catalogs and other similar information are often best displayed in a table. With Corel WordPerfect 7's Internet Publisher, you can insert a table into your Web page in the same way you would into a document.

To insert a table into your Web document using Internet Publisher, do the following:

1. Open the Web page and position your insertion point where you want the table to appear.

2. Click the Tables button on the Power Bar, and drag down to the appropriate cell for the number of rows and columns you want in your table. You see the table in your document, as shown in Figure 12.12.

3. Enter data in the table. Press the Tab key to advance to the next cell, and Shift+Tab to go to the previous one. If you press the Tab key at the last cell in the table, a new row will be created.

4. To format your table:

   • Select the appropriate cells or columns, then choose Table, Format.

   • Alternatively, right-click in the table and choose Format.

   • Click the hot spot and choose Format from the pop-up Tools window. You see the Properties for Table Format dialog box shown in Figure 12.13.

FIG. 12.12
With the Internet Publisher, you can put tables in your Web page to display a variety of information.

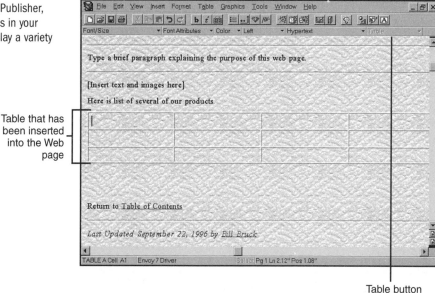

Table that has been inserted into the Web page

Table button

FIG. 12.13
In the Properties for Table Format dialog box, you format your table by cell, column, or entire table.

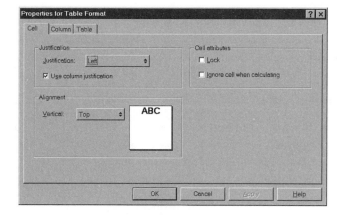

Publishing HTML Documents

Once you have created and edited your Web page using Corel WordPerfect 7's Internet Publisher, the result is still a Corel WordPerfect 7 document, *not* an HTML (i.e., Web) document. To publish it on the Web, you will need to save it as an HTML document. You may also want to save another version of it as a Corel WordPerfect 7 document, so that you can more quickly open it and edit it, without needing to convert it from HTML into Corel WordPerfect 7 when you open it.

N O T E There are two meanings of the term "publish." The normal usage of the term, for example, "publish a Web document," means to *place* a document on the Web where people can see it. WordPerfect uses the term publish, however, in a different sense, to mean *converting* a WordPerfect document to HTML.

When used in this latter sense, the document will still reside on your disk rather than on the Web, and you will still need to copy it to the Internet so that people can see it.

The meaning of the term in this book can be derived from the context in which it's used. ■

In any case, publishing your document means saving it as HTML. When you do this, the Internet Publisher converts the binary Corel WordPerfect 7 file into an ASCII text file with HTML codes in it.

Before you do that, however, you might want to see how the HTML document will look in a real Web browser. (Remember, what Corel WordPerfect shows you is *close* to how the document will look in a browser, but not necessarily exact.)

Viewing Your Document

You can view your document whenever you want to, as you build it up and add more features to it. When you view your document, the Internet Publisher converts it to HTML and saves it as a temporary file, then opens the file in your default Web browser.

 To view your document, click the View in Web Browser button. Netscape (or your default browser) opens, and you see your Web page as it will look when it is published, as shown in Figure 12.14.

Part
II

Ch
12

FIG. 12.14
You can view your Web page in your default browser before you publish it, to ensure that it looks the same in the browser as it does in the Internet Publisher.

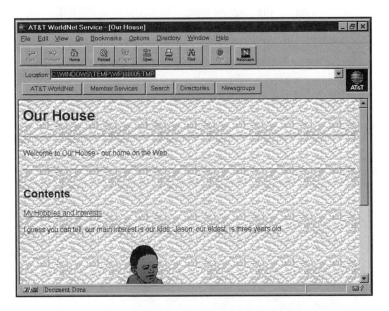

N O T E Web documents can appear differently depending on the browser used to access them. For instance, some older versions of standard browsers would not recognize a center code or an underline code. Many problems like this have been cleared up in the newer browser versions, but some people still have older browsers that have been purchased second-hand or passed down to them when new equipment was purchased for others. It is important to know who your most important customers are and the level of technology they have, and then set up pages to that standard. ■

Saving Documents as HTML

Saving your document as HTML creates a new file with an .htm extension. It is an ASCII text file, with HTML codes in it. If you have figures in your document, a folder is created with the same name as the document, and the figures are stored in this folder.

When you are satisfied with the Web page you have created, and want to convert it to an HTML document, do the following:

1. Save the document as a Corel WordPerfect 7 document, so that you can more easily edit it by opening the original Corel WordPerfect 7 document later, if you like, and so that you will have a backup of the file in case something happens to the version you will be putting on the server.

2. Click the Publish to HTML button on the toolbar. You see the Publish to HTML dialog box shown in Figure 12.15. If you have previously saved your document, you see the same document name, but with an .htm extension rather than a .wpd extension as the default choice.

N O T E Note that the Publish to HTML dialog box also indicates that graphics and sound files will be saved to a folder that has the same name as the file name, with the extension .htg. This folder is automatically created if you have graphic or sound files attached to your Web page. ■

FIG. 12.15
Use the Publish to HTML dialog box to save your document in HTML format.

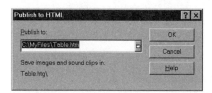

3. Edit the name that appears in the Publish To box or accept the default name, and click OK. A copy of the document is saved as an HTML file, with the extension .htm.

Interestingly, you do not see the HTML file on your screen. You still see the Corel WordPerfect 7 version of the file, as you can see by examining the title bar, which still shows the .wpd file.

Creating Your Home Page

When you have saved your documents in HTML format, you will want to set up your home page so that each page may be easily linked to by those browsing your site. The Web Page Expert will assist you in creating your INDEX.HTM page—your home page—and setting up the links to your other documents. To get assistance in creating your home page:

1. Choose File, Internet Publisher. You see the Internet Publisher dialog box shown previously in Figure 12.1.

2. Click the New Web Document button. You see the Select New Web Document dialog box previously shown in Figure 12.2.

3. Select <Web Page Expert>.

4. Choose Select. You see the first page of the Web Page Expert shown in Figure 12.16.

 TIP Another way to access the Web Page Expert is to run the Create Web Page QuickTask. It automatically launches the Expert.

FIG. 12.16
The Web Page Expert helps you create a folder in which to organize and store all of the Web pages that constitute your Web site.

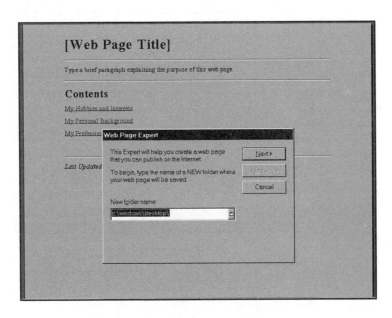

5. Type in the name of a new folder in which to save your Web pages. You need to type in a new folder name, since a series of files will be saved in this folder, including one that by default is always named INDEX.HTM.

6. Choose <u>N</u>ext. You see the second step of the Expert. Add a title for your Web home page, your name, and your e-mail address as requested.

7. Choose <u>N</u>ext. You see the third step of the Expert, shown in Figure 12.17.

FIG. 12.17
The Web Page Expert allows you to specify what Web pages will appear on the table of contents of the home page for your Web site.

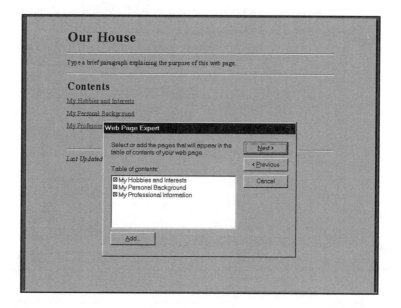

8. Check the pages you want to create, click <u>A</u>dd to add new pages that are not on the list, then click <u>N</u>ext.

 TIP You can also link to HTML pages that you have already created, rather than the default files listed. To do this, you must edit the hypertext link as discussed previously in this chapter in the section "Creating and Editing Links."

9. Choose a Color <u>S</u>cheme, <u>B</u>ackground Wallpaper, and <u>J</u>ustification style from the choices in the drop-down list boxes, then click <u>N</u>ext.

N O T E The color scheme is the colors that are used for various elements of your Web site. Background wallpaper is the image that is used for the background of your Web pages. ▨

10. Choose Finished in the last step of the Expert. Your home page is created, as shown in Figure 12.18, complete with links to any additional pages you selected to be included in the site.

FIG. 12.18

The Expert creates a professional-looking home page, complete with a background that you specify, and links to other pages.

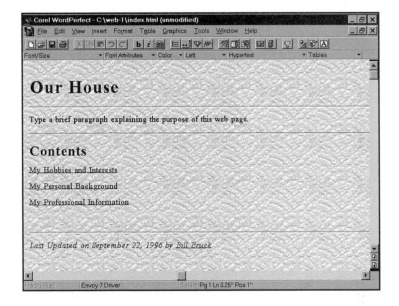

Copying Documents to Your Web Server

The last step in publishing your Web page is to copy it to the intranet server or Internet server where it will reside, literally, for possibly all the company (in the case of intranets) or all the world (in the case of the Internet) to see.

Uploading Files to the Internet An Internet server is often a UNIX-based computer that you cannot copy files directly to. Because UNIX is a different operating system than Windows, it is very likely that you cannot use a tool like Windows Explorer or Corel WordPerfect 7's File, Save As and specify the disk drive of your Internet Server as a destination for your files.

You may want to talk to your Internet Service Provider (ISP), your system administrator, or your Webmaster about the best way to upload files to the Internet. At the very least, these individuals will need to tell you where to upload them, and what permissions are needed.

▶ **See** "Connecting via an Internet Service Provider," **p. 527**

A common way to upload files to the Internet is to connect to the location of your Web site via File Transfer Protocol (FTP), which you can do through Netscape. If this protocol is supported, then you can upload files to the appropriate workspace on the Internet server.

To view the list of existing files and folders of your FTP site, you type in **FTP://** in front of the URL location in your Web browser (you can obtain the URL for your site from your system administrator). Figure 12.19 shows an example of an FTP site as seen through a browser.

FIG. 12.19

By connecting to an FTP site through your browser, you can see the names of the files and folders located at the site.

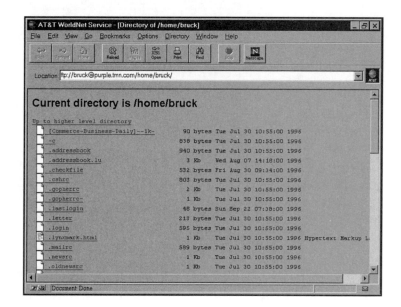

To upload your files to the server, do as follows:

1. Open Netscape.

2. Choose File, Open Location, and specify the FTP address of the location to which you want to upload your files. (You will probably need to get the FTP address from your system administrator.) You see a list of files in your FTP directory.

3. Choose File, Upload File. You see the File Upload dialog box shown in Figure 12.20.

4. Navigate to the folder containing the file to be uploaded, then double-click the file. You return to the main Navigator screen, and the file is uploaded to the specified directory.

5. After the upload is complete, you see the file listed in that directory by typing in your FTP site URL as you did previously to view the list of existing files and folders of your FTP site.

FIG. 12.20

Choose a file to upload to your FTP site from the File Upload dialog box.

Uploading Files to an Intranet   Similarly, if you are publishing to a corporate intranet, the intranet might be running on Windows 95, but more likely it is running on Windows NT, Novell Netware, or UNIX. Usually, directories where Web pages are located have limited access. You will want to talk to your system administrator about the best way to upload files to the intranet server. If you have sufficient permissions, you may be able to merely save your document to the intranet server with Corel WordPerfect 7; or Netscape's File, Upload command (as discussed in the previous section, "Uploading Files to the Internet") may work in your particular situation.

Converting HTML into Corel WordPerfect 7

Corel WordPerfect 7's Internet Publisher not only helps you to create *new* Web documents; you can also convert HTML documents into Corel WordPerfect 7 documents and edit them.

To convert an HTML document into a Corel WordPerfect 7 document, you first need to save it from the Web to your network or local computer. You can do this as follows:

1. Open Netscape.

2. Choose File, Open Location, and specify the URL of the Web document you want to copy. You see the Web page in Netscape, as shown in Figure 12.21. For more information about using Netscape, see Chapter 26, "Using Corel WordPerfect Suite on the Internet."

3. Choose File, Save As. You see the Save As dialog box shown in Figure 12.22.

4. Navigate to the folder in which you want to save the document, then click the Save button. The file is saved to your local computer or network drive.

Part
II

Ch
12

Once the file has been saved to a local drive, you can convert it to Corel WordPerfect 7 format by opening it as you would other documents:

1. In Corel WordPerfect 7, click the Open button. You see the Open dialog box shown in Figure 12.23.

2. Navigate to the folder containing the Web document to be opened.

FIG. 12.21

Use Netscape to save files from the Internet or a corporate intranet to your local computer.

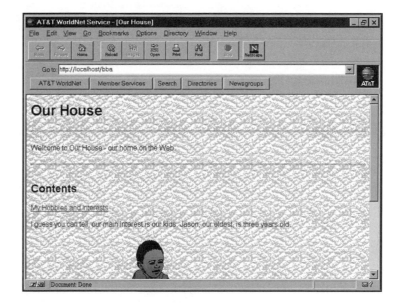

FIG. 12.22

With the Netscape Save As dialog box, you can save a Web file to your local computer or network drive.

 TIP Web documents will have an icon to the left of them that represents your default Web browser. If you are using the version of Netscape that comes with the Corel WordPerfect 7 Suite, you see an AT&T logo, because this version of Netscape is licensed to AT&T WorldNet.

3. Double-click the HTML file to be opened. You see the Convert File Format dialog box, and HTML appears in the Convert File Format From box.

4. Click OK. The file appears on your screen. You can now edit the file using the Internet Publisher as described earlier.

NOTE Using the preceding procedure, your document is still formatted using only Corel WordPerfect 7 functions supported in HTML. If you want to format the document as a true Corel WordPerfect 7 document, choose File, Internet Publisher, Format as WP Document. ■

FIG. 12.23
You can open Web documents in Corel WordPerfect as you would a standard Corel WordPerfect 7 document.

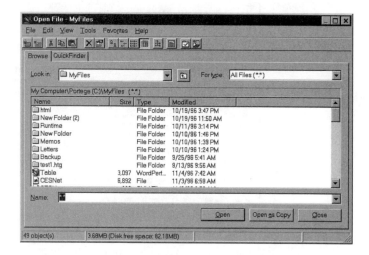

Converting Corel WordPerfect 7 into HTML

You can also convert documents the other way—from Corel WordPerfect 7 into HTML format. To do this, open the Corel WordPerfect 7 document, then choose File, Internet Publisher, Format as Web Document.

You see the menus and toolbars of the Internet Publisher, and your document loses any formatting features that are not supported in HTML.

You can now publish your document in HTML by clicking the Publish to HTML button as described previously, so you can upload it to the Web.

Publishing Documents with Envoy

Another way to publish your Corel WordPerfect 7 document is to publish it with Envoy. This creates a file that anyone with Envoy or the Envoy Viewer can read. You can then keep the document on your internal network, maintain it on a corporate intranet, or copy it to the Internet.

To publish your document with Envoy, ensure that your document has been saved and is displayed on the screen, like the one shown in Figure 12.24.

FIG. 12.24

A document in Corel WordPerfect 7, ready to be published in Envoy.

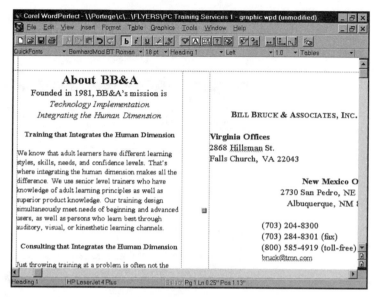

Choose File, Publish to Envoy. Your file is printed to the Envoy printer driver, which "prints" it to an Envoy file, then automatically opens Envoy so that you can see the document, like the one shown in Figure 12.25. For more information on the capabilities and uses of Envoy, see Chapter 28, "Using Envoy."

FIG. 12.25

The same document shown after being published in Envoy.

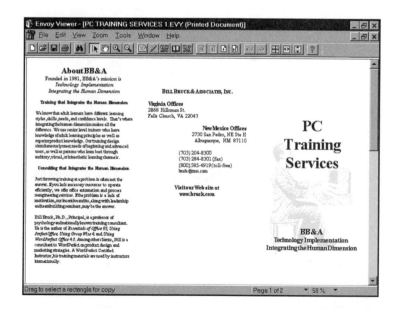

Publishing Documents with Barista

Corel WordPerfect Suite 7 incorporates a new feature called Barista—a technology that permits publishing documents in Java on intranets or the Internet.

Java is a programming language that creates simple applications (called applets) that can be included in Web pages. Assuming that your browser supports Java, the applet is automatically downloaded when you access a Web page that contains it.

Barista takes pages exactly as they are and makes Java applets out of them, putting in HTML code required to run the applet.

Barista is an alternative to the Internet Publisher for publishing your WordPerfect documents to the Web. The advantage is that the Java applet approach transcends the rigid, limited coding of HTML and permits documents to be created that look much more like the original WordPerfect document than is possible with standard HTML codes.

The disadvantage is that the files are larger and take longer to download and, because a Java applet is used, additional time is taken in processing the Java "program" that builds the page.

When you publish a page with Barista, two files are created. An HTML file is made, which calls the Java applet. The Java applet is contained in a second file called a class file. Both of these files must be copied to the Web server for the page to be seen.

The conversion process also allows you to choose whether to publish a multi-page document to several different Web pages, or to one long one.

The process of publishing a file using Barista is very straightforward:

1. Create or open the WordPerfect file to be converted.
2. Choose File, Publish To, Corel Barista. You see the Publish to Corel Barista dialog box shown in Figure 12.26.

Part II

Ch 12

FIG. 12.26
Corel Barista allows you to publish complex documents to the Web and retain their formatting.

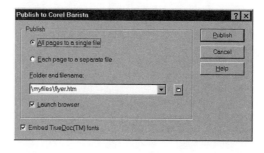

3. Choose whether to publish All Pages to a Single File, or Each Page to a Separate File. To ensure that the fonts on your Web page will be the same as in your WordPerfect document, make sure that Embed TrueDoc(TM) Fonts is checked.

4. Specify a folder and file name for your Web page(s), then choose Publish. Your Web pages are created and, if Launch Browser was checked, your Web browser will be launched so you can see them.

N O T E   For more information, see Que's *Special Edition Using Java.* ■

 T I P   You can find more information on Barista in the help system by choosing Help, Help Topics, Index, Barista, Publish To.

Using Corel Quattro Pro

CHAPTER 13

Getting Started with Corel Quattro Pro 7

Corel Quattro Pro 7 is the spreadsheet component of the Corel WordPerfect Suite 7. This chapter introduces Corel Quattro Pro 7, and prepares you to begin using this powerful tool quickly to analyze data, prepare reports, and graph results. Once you learn the basics, you'll be ready to apply your skills to creating your own Quattro Pro spreadsheets.

This chapter assumes you are familiar with standard Windows techniques and file management operations. If you are not comfortable with your knowledge in these areas, read Part I, "Working with Corel WordPerfect Suite 7" before continuing. ∎

Corel Quattro Pro

This chapter shows you what Corel Quattro Pro adds to your WordPerfect Suite 7 toolbox.

Access the correct commands

Learn how to save hours of work by knowing where to find the most often used and helpful commands.

Learn about important shortcuts

Learn about Corel Quattro Pro's many shortcuts that will enable you to perform tasks quickly with simple keystrokes or a few clicks with your mouse.

Get expert help from Corel Quattro Pro itself

See how you can use the built-in Experts to make learning and using Corel Quattro Pro easy and even fun.

Understanding Corel Quattro Pro

Corel Quattro Prois a *spreadsheet* program. You might like to think of a spreadsheet program as an electronic notebook, one that can quickly calculate the results of any formulas you enter. Corel Quattro Pro is a very capable electronic notebook, with hundreds of built-in features designed to make creating your spreadsheets as easy as possible.

What Can You Do with Corel Quattro Pro?

Even the most powerful tool is useless if you don't know what it can do and how you use it. Fortunately, even though Corel Quattro Pro is one of the most advanced spreadsheet programs available, it is also very easy to understand and use. You don't have to be an accountant or a computer whiz to use Corel Quattro Pro. In only a short time you'll be able to create Corel Quattro Pro notebooks that solve some of your problems with ease.

 TIP Use Corel Quattro Pro instead of your calculator. That way you'll learn Corel Quattro Pro more quickly.

A typical, traditional use for a spreadsheet is to prepare accounting reports. By automatically performing all of a report's calculations with complete accuracy, a spreadsheet makes quick work of the task. If you run a small business, you probably perform many different calculations on a daily basis. You might, for example, want to keep track of the receipts for a video rental business you recently began. To know whether the new business is worthwhile, you probably want to know whether you're making a profit after paying for the new movies, plus your utilities, and maybe even the cost of hiring someone to help keep the store open in the evenings.

Even if you don't consider these calculations to be standard accounting reports, wouldn't it be nice to have the calculations done quickly and accurately—the way Corel Quattro Pro can? How about calculating the cost of refinancing your mortgage and determining how long it will take to make up for the fees your lender may charge? Would it be useful to know which products you sell bring the highest profits, and when those products are most likely to be sold? Finally, suppose you needed to calculate the cost of building permits that were based on many different combinations of features for each property. Wouldn't it be nice to just enter the proposed building's size, type, and quantity of fixtures and have a totally accurate bill printed instantly?

These are but a small sample of the things you can do with Corel Quattro Pro. Spreadsheets aren't just for accountants; they also do real work for real people.

Starting Corel Quattro Pro

When you start Corel Quattro Pro, a new, blank notebook named NOTEBK1.WB3 appears (see Figure 13.1). This new notebook is your starting point for creating your own applications. You can use a more descriptive name when you save your notebook in a file on disk.

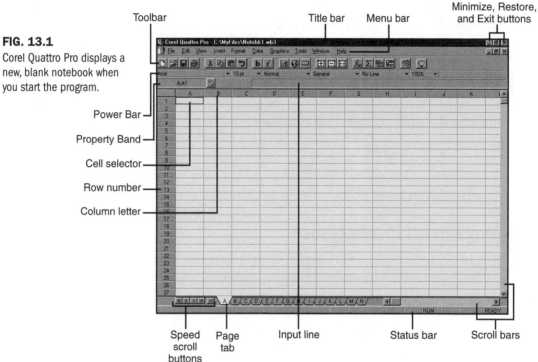

FIG. 13.1
Corel Quattro Pro displays a new, blank notebook when you start the program.

Toolbar · Title bar · Menu bar · Minimize, Restore, and Exit buttons

Power Bar · Property Band · Cell selector · Row number · Column letter

Speed scroll buttons · Page tab · Input line · Status bar · Scroll bars

TROUBLESHOOTING

My screen shows NOTEBK2.WB3 instead of NOTEBK1.WB3. Corel Quattro Pro starts new notebooks using sequential numbers. If you create a new notebook, it automatically is named NOTEBKxx.WB3, with xx replaced by the next higher number. When you save the notebook, you'll be prompted for a new name, so the default name really doesn't matter.

Each Corel Quattro Pro notebook provides a very large workspace—much larger than you can see on the screen at one time. Each notebook has 256 pages (indicated by the lettered page tabs at the bottom of each page), 256 columns on each page (indicated by the column letters along the top edge of each notebook page), and 8,192 rows on each page (indicated by the row numbers along the left edge of each notebook page). The intersection of each row and column on each page is a *cell*, the place where you store data, formulas, or labels. A Quattro Pro notebook has an incredible 536,870,912 cells—many more than you will ever need no matter how complex a report you want to produce.

Cells are identified by the page letter, column letter, and row number. The cell in the first row of the first column on the first page of a notebook is designated by the cell address A:A1. If you're referring to a cell on the current page, you don't have to include the page letter, but can instead refer to this same cell address as simply A1.

 TIP Always check the active cell before entering data.

The location of the current, or *active* cell is indicated by the *cell selector*—a darker outline around the cell. In Figure 13.1, the cell selector is in cell A:A1, making this the active cell. You can only place data, formulas, or labels in the active cell. To place anything in a different cell, you must first make the new cell the active cell by clicking it with the mouse. In addition to locating the cell selector, you can also see the address of the active cell in the cell indicator box at the left end of the input line near the top of the screen.

Moving Around in a Notebook

To do anything effective in a Corel Quattro Pro notebook, you must be able to move the cell selector. When you want to enter data, formulas, or labels in a different cell, you must first move to that cell. There are several methods you can use to move around in a notebook, and the best method often depends on your destination.

You can use the *direction keys* (the up-, down-, left-, and right-arrow keys), the Pg Up (or Page Up), Pg Dn (or Page Down), and Home keys to move the cell selector between cells. These direction keys work just about the way you would expect—if you press the down-arrow key, the cell selector moves down to a lower row. Table 13.1 describes the functioning of the direction keys.

Table 13.1 The Direction Keys

Key(s)	Action(s)
→ or ←	Moves right or left one column
↑ or ↓	Moves up or down one row
Ctrl+←	Moves left one column
Ctrl+→	Moves right one column

Key(s)	Action(s)
Ctrl+End+Home	Moves to the lower-right corner of the active area on the last active page
Ctrl+F6	Makes the next open notebook window active
Ctrl+Home	Moves to cell A1 on the first notebook page
Ctrl+PgDn	Moves to the notebook page immediately below the current page (from page A to page B)
Ctrl+PgUp	Moves to the notebook page immediately above the current page
End+→ or End+←	Moves right or left to a cell that contains data and is next to a blank cell
End+↑ or End+↓	Moves up or down to a cell that contains data and is next to a blank cell
End+Home	Moves to the lower-right corner of the active area on the current page
F5 (Go to)	Moves to the cell you specify
Home	Moves to cell A1 on the current notebook page
PgUp or PgDn	Moves up or down one screen on the current notebook page

Because Corel Quattro Pro is a true Windows program, it is often quicker and easier to perform tasks such as moving the cell selector using the mouse instead of the direction keys. For example, to move from cell A:A1 to cell A:C4, you could press the right-arrow key twice and then the down-arrow key three times, or you could simply point to cell A:C4 and click the left mouse button. Of course, if you hold down an arrow key instead of quickly pressing and releasing it, the cell selector will move several rows or columns instead of just one. Even so, a single mouse click is often much faster than the equivalent keystrokes. Moving between pages with the mouse is even faster—just click the appropriate page tab. Use the tab scroll controls to display different page tabs if necessary.

You can also use the scroll bars at the right edge or bottom edge of a notebook to view other parts of the current notebook page. Click the scroll bar or drag (hold down the left mouse button as you move an object) the box on the scroll bar to bring a different part of the page into view.

TROUBLESHOOTING

The cell selector disappears when I use the scroll bars. The scroll bars only change the portion of the page that is visible. To move the cell selector, first use the scroll bars to display the destination cell, then click the destination cell to make it the current cell.

Part
III

Ch
13

Using the Menus

Many tasks you perform in Corel Quattro Pro require the use of a command. Commands help you analyze and organize data effectively, copy and move data, graph and format data, sort and manipulate databases, open and close spreadsheet notebooks, and use colors and fonts to customize spreadsheets.

The Corel Quattro Pro menu appears on the menu bar near the top of the screen. If you use the mouse to select commands, just click the command you want to use. To access a command on the menu bar with the keyboard, you must first activate the menu by pressing the Alt key. A reverse video highlight, the *menu pointer*, appears in the menu bar when you choose a command menu by highlighting it with the direction keys. You can also simply press the Alt key and the underlined letter (usually the first letter) of the command name.

Commands that are dimmed are currently unavailable.

Corel Quattro Pro has several different menus. The menus change depending on the type of task on which you're working. For example, when you work with normal data in a notebook the main menu appears. If you create or modify a graph, the menu changes to include commands appropriate to graphs. Most of the time, however, you see the main menu.

Learn Corel Quattro Pro's commands by moving the menu pointer through the menus. A description of the command appears in a tip box next to the menu.

Learning the Shortcuts

In any field, the most productive people are usually those who know the fastest way to get things done—the shortcuts. Corel Quattro Pro provides many different shortcuts you can learn and use to get things done more quickly. You don't have to learn all of them, but you will find some that you'll use quite often.

Using Toolbar Buttons   The Quattro Pro toolbar contains many useful buttons you'll find very helpful as you build your notebooks (see Figure 13.2). Table 13.2 points out several of these buttons, which we'll use later in this and several following chapters. See the Toolbars item on the Index tab of Corel Quattro Pro's online help for more information on the complete range of toolbar buttons.

Table 13.2 Toolbar Buttons and Their Functions

Button	Function
	Create a floating chart on the notebook page
	Show or hide drawing tools
	Create a map on the notebook page
	Create a QuickButton on the notebook page
	Insert blocks, rows, columns, or pages
	Delete blocks, rows, columns, or pages
	Adjust a column's width to its widest cell entry
	Build complex formulas with @functions
	Total values in the selected block
	Fill blank cells in the selected block
	Apply a predefined format to the selected block
	Connect to the World Wide Web
	Ask the PerfectExpert

Part
III

Ch
13

Using the Right Mouse Button Menus   In Corel Quattro Pro, almost everything you see is an object—something that has properties you can change. But instead of requiring you to search through Corel Quattro Pro's menus to find the commands necessary to change an object's properties, Corel Quattro Pro gives you another choice. When you point to an object with the mouse pointer and click the right mouse button, you will see either an *Object Inspector* or a *QuickMenu* associated with the object. Object Inspectors are dialog boxes that contain all of the property settings for the object. QuickMenus are short command menus containing only those commands most appropriate for the selected object. QuickMenus always include a properties selection at the bottom of the menu that displays the Object Inspector dialog box for the selected object.

FIG. 13.2

Toolbar and Power Bar buttons are another way to access the tools you need to create powerful notebook pages.

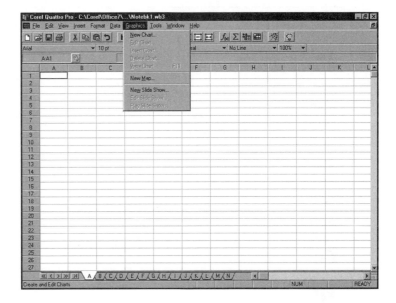

If you have not used them before, QuickMenus and Object Inspectors may be a little confusing at first. Once you begin using them, however, you'll find them to be very helpful. Figure 13.3 shows the QuickMenu that appears when you point to a notebook cell and press the right mouse button. The commands on this menu are also available if you search through several of Corel Quattro Pro's standard menus, but the QuickMenu has gathered several of the most frequently used commands that you might want to apply to a cell in one convenient place.

FIG. 13.3

QuickMenus gather commands from several menus into one convenient menu.

Notice the last item on the QuickMenu, "Block Properties." If you select this item, the Active Block Object Inspector dialog box is displayed (see Figure 13.4). You can also use the F12 shortcut key to display the Active Block Object Inspector dialog box directly. This dialog box contains 10 tabs that have every possible setting for a cell (or block of cells). In

Figure 13.4, the tab labeled Numeric Format is selected, so the settings pane of the dialog box displays all possible numeric format settings. As you select different options, such as a different numeric format, or a different property tab, such as Alignment, the settings pane of the dialog box changes and displays the available options.

FIG. 13.4
Object Inspector dialog boxes enable you to adjust object properties.

If you change a property setting, such as changing from <u>G</u>eneral to <u>D</u>ate format for displaying values, the name of the changed property tab will be displayed in blue letters rather than black as long as the dialog box is open, so that you can tell what changes you have made. You can adjust more than one property while the dialog box is active. Simply select OK when you've made all of your changes, or select Cancel if you decide you don't want to apply the changes. When you re-enter the dialog box the next time, all of the tabs will again be black, regardless of whether the change was accepted or canceled.

Table 13.3 shows some of the Corel Quattro Pro objects other than cells that you can inspect and adjust by pointing and clicking the right mouse button.

Table 13.3   Corel Quattro Pro Objects

Object	Action
Blocks of selected cells	Right-click in the selected area.
Notebook pages	Right-click the page tab.
Notebook	Right-click the notebook title bar if the notebook is in a window and not maximized.
Toolbar	Right-click the toolbar.
Graph objects	Right-click the object including drawn objects, titles, data series, and the graph background objects.
Corel Quattro Pro itself	Right-click the Corel Quattro Pro title bar.

Part
III

Ch
13

Important Shortcut Keys   Table 13.4 describes many of the more useful Corel Quattro Pro shortcut keys. To learn about even more shortcut keys, see the topic "key shortcuts" in the Corel Quattro Pro online help system.

Table 13.4   Important Shortcut Keys

Key(s)	Action(s)
F1	Displays a Help topic
F2	Places Corel Quattro Pro in Edit mode so that you can edit an entry
Alt+F2	Displays the Play Macro dialog box
F3	Displays block names in Edit mode in a formula
Alt+F3	Displays a list of functions
Ctrl+F3	Displays block names dialog box if pressed while a group of cells are selected
F4	Toggles formulas from relative to absolute and vice versa
Alt+F4	Closes Corel Quattro Pro 7 for Windows or a dialog box
F5	Displays the Go To dialog box
F6	Moves the cell selector between panes
Ctrl+F6	Displays the next open window
F9	In Ready mode, recalculates formulas; in Edit or Value mode, converts a formula to its current value
F10	Activates the menu bar
F11	Displays the current graph
F12	Displays Object Inspector for the selected object
Alt+F12	Displays application Object Inspector
Shift+F12	Displays active window Object Inspector
Ctrl+letter	Same as Tools Macro Play; executes a macro in Corel Quattro Pro
Ctrl+Break	Exits from a menu or macro and returns to Ready mode
Alt+Tab	Displays the Task List that enables you to switch from one Windows application to another
Ctrl+Esc	Activates the start menu on the start bar for Windows 95

TROUBLESHOOTING

Some Ctrl+letter shortcut keys don't perform the proper shortcut procedure. If you create macros that use the Ctrl+letter naming convention, Corel Quattro Pro runs the macro instead of using the key combination to run the shortcut. If the shortcut is one you use often, consider renaming the macro to restore the default shortcut.

Using Experts

Sometimes it's nice to get a little extra help. It would be very difficult, if not downright impossible, for any one PC user to know how to perform every task on his or her computer. When you're dealing with such a powerful and adaptable program as Corel Quattro Pro, it's even more difficult to know or remember exactly the correct sequence of steps that may be necessary, especially for those tasks you rarely perform.

Fortunately, Corel Quattro Pro includes some specialized tools—*Experts*—that can ease your way through learning Corel Quattro Pro and executing difficult tasks. In this section we'll have a quick look at the Experts.

Computer-based training isn't new; programs have included tutorials for years. But Corel Quattro Pro's Experts use a different approach to completing tasks. Instead of using a carefully preselected data set unrelated to the data you want to enter (as many tutorials do), the Experts allow you to use your own data. Not only that, but the Experts also allow you to save your work in a real Corel Quattro Pro notebook. When you complete a task, the notebook contains your data.

Experts provide the expertise to solve complex problems, while you provide the data. These Experts cover a broad range of topics, which are only hinted at by the Experts menu (see Figure 13.5). Table 13.5 provides a brief description of Corel Quattro Pro's Experts.

Part
III

Ch
13

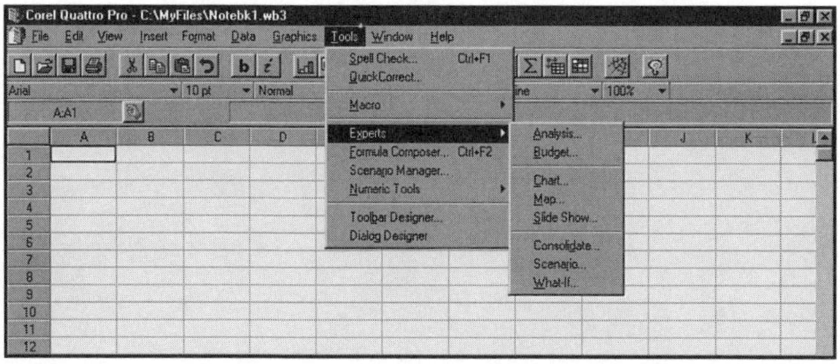

FIG. 13.5
Use the Experts to solve complex problems easily.

Table 13.5   Corel Quattro Pro's Experts

Expert	Description
Analysis	Helps you use the Analysis Tools
Budget	Helps you create and manage home and small business budgets
Chart	Helps you create graphs
Map	Helps you create maps of your data
Slide Show	Helps you create professional-looking slideshows
Consolidate	Helps you combine data from different sources such as different stores or company divisions
Scenario	Helps you create and manage scenarios—multiple groups of related data that enable easy what-if analysis
What-If	Helps you generate what-if scenarios

 TIP   Part IV, "Using Corel Presentations" shows you how to create slideshows using a tool specifically designed for the task.

For example, the Chart Expert leads you through the steps necessary to create powerful business graphics that will present your data in a highly effective visual manner. You don't have to be a graphics expert yourself; all you need to do is answer some questions and make a few selections along the way. The Budget Expert is another tool you'll probably find quite useful. Everyone knows the importance of a budget, especially in running a small business. The Budget Expert helps you prepare a Corel Quattro Pro notebook containing an individualized budget specific to your needs. ●

CHAPTER 14

Learning Spreadsheet Basics

This chapter presents information you need to use Corel Quattro Pro notebooks. If you are new to electronic spreadsheets, this chapter helps you learn to use a spreadsheet for basic data analysis. If you have used other spreadsheet programs, this chapter is valuable for learning the conventions and features of Corel Quattro Pro. ■

Enter and edit data

Learn how to enter and edit different types of data properly so that the data is recognized correctly.

Work with single and multiple notebook pages

Understand the three-dimensional arrangement of Corel Quattro Pro to help organize your work and make your spreadsheets much easier to use.

Link notebooks

See how to link Corel Quattro Pro notebooks so you can efficiently use data that comes from many different sources.

Document formulas, numbers, and data

Learn how proper documentation techniques will help you remember why you created complex formulas, and understand the assumptions used to create your models.

Add labels and headings

See how descriptive labels will help you change your raw data into useful information that can be shared more effectively.

Use the Undo feature

Learn to use the Undo feature to correct mistakes easily.

Understanding Notebooks and Files

In Corel Quattro Pro, a single spreadsheet is called a *page*—a two-dimensional grid of columns and rows. A file that contains 256 spreadsheet pages and an Objects page in a three-dimensional arrangement is called a *notebook*. Besides working with a single notebook, you also can work with several notebooks at the same time, and you can link notebooks by writing formulas that refer to cells in another notebook.

Using 3-D Notebooks

You will often need only a single page to analyze and store data. You can organize simple reports effectively on a single page without the added complication of including page references in your formulas. Page references are necessary, though, for accessing data that spreads across several pages.

TIP   Use multiple notebook pages to better organize your data.

Some situations, however, are well-suited to multiple notebook pages. Reports that consolidate data from several departments often work well as multiple-page reports—especially if one person produces the entire report. You can put a formula on one page that refers to cells on other pages.

You also can use multiple pages to separate different kinds of data effectively. You might place data input areas on one page, macros on another, constants on another, and the finished report on yet another page. This technique can provide some assurance that a spreadsheet isn't damaged by an inadvertent error. For example, a data entry error can write over formulas, or the insertion or deletion of a row or column can destroy macros or data tables contained on the same page. Building your notebook using several pages provides some protection against these all-too-common problems.

TIP   Protect important formulas and macros by placing them on separate notebook pages.

Spreadsheets that use multiple pages are called *3-D spreadsheets*. All Corel Quattro Pro notebooks are automatically 3-D notebooks whether you have data on one page or multiple pages. You don't have to manually add pages to a Corel Quattro Pro notebook as you do with most other spreadsheet programs.

Naming Notebook Pages   One good way to use multiple notebook pages is to place each month's data on a separate page and use a 13th page for the yearly totals. Because Corel Quattro Pro enables you to name individual notebook pages, you can name each page for one month so you can locate the correct page easily. Figure 14.1 shows a notebook that uses named pages to hold each month's sales data separately.

FIG. 14.1
Name notebook pages to indicate their purpose.

You can name a notebook page by pointing to the page tab and double-clicking the left mouse button. Simply type the new name directly on the tab after you double-click it. Alternatively, you can display the Active Page Object Inspector dialog box and select the Name tab. To display the Active Page Object Inspector dialog box, point to the page tab and click the right mouse button. Choose the Name tab (see Figure 14.2). Type the new name for the page in the Page Name text box, or select Reset to restore the original page letter.

FIG. 14.2
You can use the Active Page Object Inspector dialog box to name a notebook page.

Part
III

Ch
14

Page names can be up to 63 characters in length, but longer page names allow fewer page tabs to appear on-screen. You can use both letters and numbers in page names, as well as spaces and several special characters. If you have grouped notebook pages, you cannot use the same name for a notebook page and a group.

 N O T E   You group notebook pages so that any changes you make to one page, such as applying formatting, affect all pages in the group. You can group pages by holding down the Shift key while you click the page tabs for the first and last pages you want to group. A line appears under the page tabs of grouped pages. ▨

T I P   You can also name blocks of data. Learn more about this in the "Naming Blocks" section of Chapter 15.

Moving Between Pages   Multiple notebook pages wouldn't be of much value if there wasn't a quick way to move between pages. You have already learned that the key combinations of Ctrl+Page Down and Ctrl+Page Up allow you to move through the notebook one page at a time. In addition, you can point to a page tab and click the left mouse button to move to that page.

Sometimes, though, you may want to move to a page that has a tab not currently visible, such as a page far removed from the current page. The best method for moving to a distant notebook page is to use the Edit, Go To command (or press the shortcut key, F5) to display the Go To dialog box (see Figure 14.3). Select the page in the Pages list box, and press Enter or click OK.

FIG. 14.3

Use the Go To dialog box to move to a different notebook page.

 TROUBLESHOOTING

Selecting a page using the Edit, Go To command always moves the cell selector to cell A1 on the selected page. Create a block name (see the section "Naming Blocks" in the next chapter) and select the named block in the Block Names list box as the destination. The cell selector will then move to the upper-left corner of the named block.

Linking Notebooks

A single notebook, whether it uses multiple pages or is contained on a single page, is not always the best solution. Linking multiple notebook files with formulas is often a better solution than using a single notebook. Consolidating data from several departments or company locations may be easier when using multiple notebooks, especially if several people are producing the individual reports. The person producing the consolidated report can create a notebook that uses formula links to consolidate the data from each notebook.

 T I P Link notebooks with formulas rather than combining all the data into a single notebook.

When you work with data from several notebook files, you enter a formula in one notebook cell that refers to cells in another notebook. This technique is called *linking*. With this capability you easily can consolidate data from separate notebook files. You may, for example, receive data in notebooks from several departments or locations. A consolidation notebook can use formulas to combine the data from each notebook.

Figure 14.4 shows the notebook CONSRPT.WB3, which is used to consolidate data from three other notebooks: CARSRPT.WB3, SPARRPT.WB3, and RENORPT.WB3. Formulas link the notebooks. The formula in cell A:B5 of CONSRPT.WB3, for example, is:

+[CARSRPT]A:B5+[RENORPT]A:B5+[SPARRPT]A:B5

FIG. 14.4
You can use formulas to link
to data in other notebooks.

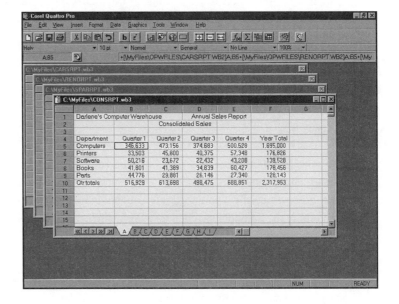

Part
III

Ch
14

This formula, as shown in the Input line of Figure 14.4, tells Corel Quattro Pro to add together the values in cell A:B5 of CARSRPT.WB3, cell A:B5 of RENORPT.WB3, and cell A:B5 of SPARRPT.WB3. In this case, the same cell in each notebook supplies the data for the formula, but that is not a requirement. You could, for example, create a linking formula that adds values from cell A:A1 in one notebook, and cell D:AA216 in another notebook. In most cases it is less confusing if each linked notebook uses a similar structure. However, when taking data from different departments or companies, you may not always have control over their spreadsheet structure development. Isn't it nice to know Corel Quattro Pro can allow for this?

Linking formulas can refer to notebooks that are open or closed. Corel Quattro Pro maintains the formula links even after the supporting notebooks are closed, but must be able to locate the supporting notebooks when the notebook containing the formula links is opened. If the supporting notebooks are not available, Corel Quattro Pro will not be able to determine a value for the linking formulas, and will display NA (Not Available) instead of a value in the open notebook.

 Use full path names to make certain Corel Quattro Pro can find the linked notebook.

When you open a notebook containing formula links to closed notebooks, Corel Quattro Pro offers three options: Open Supporting, Update References, or None. If you select None, Corel Quattro Pro changes the linking formula values to NA, but you can use the Edit, Links, Open Links or Edit, Links, Refresh Links commands to later update your linking formulas. See the section "Entering Formulas" later in this chapter for more information on creating formulas to link notebooks.

 If you don't need to see the values of linking formulas, select None when you open notebooks containing linking formulas. The linked notebook will open much faster.

Using Workspaces

In Figure 14.4, four different Corel Quattro Pro notebooks are open at the same time. If you are using notebooks that are linked, it may be convenient to open all of the linked notebooks, especially if you need to create additional formula links or enter data in more than one of the notebooks. When you work with multiple notebooks it is often handy to create a standard window arrangement, such as the cascaded windows in Figure 14.4, so you always know where to find each notebook.

Corel Quattro Pro has two commands (File, Workspace, Save and File, Workspace, Restore) that enable you to save the current notebook layout and then restore that same layout at a later time. When you use File, Workspace, Save, Corel Quattro Pro saves the current screen layout in a file with a WBS extension. You use File, Workspace, Restore to open the same group of notebook files and restore their screen layout in a single command. When restoring a workspace that has files that are linked, select Update References when the Hotlinks dialog box appears. If you select Open Supporting, the files will be opened full screen.

CAUTION

File, Workspace, Save does not save the notebook files, only their current screen layout. You must also save the individual notebook files to save any changes they may contain.

Entering Data for the First Time

A notebook isn't of much use until you enter data, whether that data consists of labels, values, or formulas. In this section you'll learn how to enter data in Corel Quattro Pro notebooks.

You can only enter data in the currently active cell, so to begin entering data you must first move the cell selector to the appropriate cell. Then, type the data and press Enter. As you type, the data appears in the input line and also in the current cell. If you enter data in a cell that already contains an entry, the new data replaces the existing entry.

 Always make certain the cell selector is in the correct cell before you begin entering data.

If you are entering a column of data, you can make the cell selector move down one row in the same column when you press Enter by selecting Move Cell Selector on Enter Key in the General tab of the Application Object Inspector dialog box. Right-click the Corel Quattro Pro title bar and select Application Properties, Edit, Preferences; or press Alt+F12 to display this dialog box. This default setting makes entering columnar data much faster and easier.

Editing Cell Entries

Sometimes you need to change an entry you have made in a Corel Quattro Pro notebook. You can edit cell entries several different ways. If you want to completely replace a cell entry, simply retype the entire entry (first make certain the cell selector is in the correct cell). When you press Enter or move the cell selector to another cell, your new entry replaces the existing entry. To cancel the new entry, press Esc before you press Enter or move the cell selector.

To replace part of a cell's current contents, press F2 (Edit) or double-click the cell with the left mouse button. You can then use the mouse pointer or the direction keys to place the insertion point at the point you want to add characters. Or, you can select the characters you want to replace and just type the new ones over them. Press enter or click another cell to confirm your edits. Press Esc to cancel any edits.

Understanding the Kinds of Data You Can Enter

If you plan to enter labels or values in more than one cell, you do not need to press Enter after each entry. Instead, you can enter the data, and then move the cell selector to the new cell with a direction key to complete the entry and move the cell selector in a single step. This technique does not work if you are entering formulas.

You can create two kinds of cell entries: labels or values. A *label* (or string) is a text entry, and a *value* is a number or formula. Corel Quattro Pro usually determines the kind of entry from the first character you type. The program always treats the entry as a value (a number or a formula) if you begin with one of the following characters:

> + — (@ # . $

If you begin an entry with a number, Corel Quattro Pro assumes you are entering a value unless you include any non-numeric character other than a single period. If you begin by typing any other character, Corel Quattro Pro treats the entry as a label.

Entering Labels

Labels make the numbers and formulas in a notebook understandable. In Figure 14.4, labels identify the departments and the time periods that generated the displayed results. Without labels, the numbers are meaningless.

 TIP Keep labels short so they can easily be displayed in the available space.

In Corel Quattro Pro, you can place up to 1,022 characters in a single cell. Although this allows you to create very long labels, remember that you will probably not be able to display nearly that many characters on-screen or in a single line of a report.

When you enter a label, Corel Quattro Pro adds a *label prefix*—a punctuation mark that controls the label's alignment in the cell—to the cell entry. The label prefix is not displayed in the spreadsheet, but does appear in the input line. By default, Corel Quattro Pro adds the label prefix for a left-aligned label, an apostrophe ('). You can change the way a label is aligned using one of the following label prefixes:

'	Left-aligned (default)
"	Right-aligned
^	Centered
\	Repeating (the same characters repeat as many times as necessary to fill the column width)
|	Non-printing (if the label is in the leftmost column of the print block)

N O T E Unlike older spreadsheet programs, Corel Quattro Pro allows you to enter labels that begin with numbers. If you use another spreadsheet program, you usually must begin label entries with a label prefix if the first character is a number. In Corel Quattro Pro, you only need to use a label prefix if you want to make a number by itself into a label. ■

Regardless of the label prefix you enter, any label longer than the column width is displayed as a left-aligned label. If a label is longer than the cell width, the label appears across empty cells to the right. A label that is too long to display on-screen appears in its entirety in the edit box when the cell is edited by double-clicking with the left mouse button.

 T I P You may also press F2 (Edit) to see a long label in its entirety.

If the cells to the right of a cell that contains a long label are not blank, Corel Quattro Pro cuts off the entry display at the non-blank cell border. The complete entry still is stored, however. To display more of the label in the spreadsheet, you can insert new columns to the right of the cell that contains the long label. Alternatively, you can widen the column by moving the cell selector to the cell that contains the long label and clicking the QuickFit button on the Toolbar. You can also use the <u>W</u>rap Text option on the Alignment tab of the Active Block Object Inspector dialog box to make text fit within the column width. (Press F12 or right-click the cell and select Block Properties to display the Active Block Object Inspector dialog box.) Unfortunately, if you select this option, the row height may automatically increase when the text wraps.

▶ **See** "Inserting Columns, Rows, or Pages," **p. 346**

 T I P You can also adjust column width by dragging the right border between the column letters when the mouse pointer changes to a double-headed arrow.

Part
III

Ch
14

Entering Numbers

Spreadsheets were originally designed to make calculation less time-consuming and easier to do. Most calculations involve numbers, so numbers will represent a large portion of the data you enter in your Corel Quattro Pro notebooks. To enter a number, type any of the 10 numeric characters (0 through 9) and certain other characters, according to the following rules:

- A number can start with a plus sign (+), but the plus sign is not stored when you press Enter. For example, **+302** is stored and displayed as **302**.

- If you start a number with a minus sign (–), the number is stored as a negative number. Negative numbers are usually displayed with the minus sign, but some numeric formats display negative numbers in parentheses. Therefore, **-302** may be displayed as -302 or **(302).**

- Numbers can include only one decimal point and no spaces.

- If you enter a number with commas, you must include the correct number of digits following the comma if you want Corel Quattro Pro to recognize the entry as a number. That is, **12,000** is recognized as a number, but **12,00** is entered as a label.

- If you include a currency symbol, such as a dollar sign ($), Corel Quattro Pro displays the currency symbol in the cell.

- If you end a number with a percent sign (%), the number is divided by 100, and the number appears as a percent.

- Numbers are stored with up to 15 significant digits. If you enter a number with more significant digits, the number is rounded and stored in scientific notation. That is, only 15 digits are retained, and any extra digits are dropped. Scientific notation uses powers of 10 to display very large or small numbers.

The appearance of a number in the notebook depends on the cell's format, font, and column width. If the number is too long to fit in the cell, Corel Quattro Pro tries to show as much of the number as possible. If the cell uses the default General format and the integer portion of the number does not fit in the cell, Corel Quattro Pro displays the number in scientific notation.

TROUBLESHOOTING

Corel Quattro Pro displays asterisks instead of the number entered in a cell. If the cell uses a format other than General or Scientific, or if the cell width is too narrow to display in scientific notation and the number cannot fit in the cell width, Corel Quattro Pro displays asterisks instead of the number. Use the QuickFit button on the Toolbar to change the column width, select a different numeric format, or change the font to a smaller size.

Entering Formulas

Formulas are the real power of a spreadsheet program like Corel Quattro Pro. Formulas enable the program to calculate results and analyze data. As you change or add new data to a spreadsheet, Corel Quattro Pro recalculates the new results. With little effort, you can quickly see the effects of changing information on the end results.

Formulas can operate on numbers, labels, or the results of other formulas. A formula can contain up to 1,022 characters, and can include numbers, text, operators, cell and block addresses, block names, and functions. A formula cannot contain spaces except in a block name, a quoted text string, or a note (see the section "Adding Reference Notes," later in this chapter).

N O T E Operators are symbols that represent mathematical operations, such as the plus sign (+) to indicate addition, or the asterisk (*) to indicate multiplication. ■

You can use Corel Quattro Pro as a calculator by typing numbers directly into a formula, as in **123+456**, but doing so ignores the real power of Corel Quattro Pro formulas. A more useful formula uses cell references or block names in the calculation. Figure 14.5 demonstrates this capability.

FIG. 14.5

Use cell references instead of the numbers in formulas.

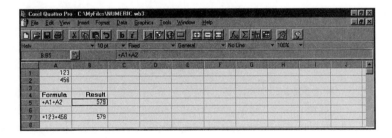

In this figure, the values 123 and 456 are placed in cells A1 and A2, respectively. In cell A5, the listed formula +A1+A2, which refers to these two cells, produces the same result as the formula 123+456 listed in cell A7—the value 579. (Notice that the formula in cell B5 begins with a plus sign—if the formula begins with a letter, not a plus sign, Corel Quattro Pro assumes that you are entering a label and performs no calculations.) Suppose, however, that the data changes and you discover the first value should be 124, not 123. If you used the cell reference formula, you just type **124** in cell A1 and the formula recalculates the new value of 580. If you used the formula with numeric values rather than the cell

Part

III

Ch

14

reference formula, you must edit or retype the formula to change the data and obtain the new result.

Corel Quattro Pro uses four kinds of formulas: numeric, string, logical, and function. The following sections briefly describe each type of formula.

Using Numeric Formulas   Numeric formulas are instructions to Corel Quattro Pro to perform mathematical calculations. You use *operators* to specify the mathematical operations and the order in which they should be performed. You use operators for addition, subtraction, multiplication, division, and exponentiation (raising a number to a power).

N O T E   Because Corel Quattro Pro attempts to evaluate simple numeric formulas that use division, such as 6/26, as a date entry, you must begin such formulas with a plus sign (+6/26). This tells Corel Quattro Pro you want to perform a calculation rather than trying to use the entry as a date. ■

Corel Quattro Pro evaluates formulas according to a set of defined operator preferences. That is, exponentiation is performed before multiplication or division, and all three are performed before any addition or subtraction. If the formula includes two operators of the same precedence, this portion of the equation is evaluated left to right. You can control a formula's evaluation order by placing portions of a formula within parentheses, because Corel Quattro Pro always evaluates items within a set of parentheses first.

For example, the formula 5+3*2 results in a value of 11, while the formula (5+3)*2 results in a value of 16. In the first formula, Corel Quattro Pro multiplies 3 times 2 and adds the result, 6, to 5. In the second formula, Corel Quattro Pro adds 5 and 3, and multiplies the result, 8, by 2. As you can see, a very small change in the formula produces quite different results.

Using String Formulas   A *string* is a label or the result of a string formula; it is text rather than numbers. Only two string formula operators exist: the plus sign (+), which repeats a string, and the ampersand (&), which *concatenates* (joins) two or more strings. String formulas use different rules than numeric formulas. String formulas always begin with the plus sign but cannot include more than one plus sign. To add two strings, you concatenate them using the ampersand.

Figure 14.6 shows several examples of string formulas. In the figure, cell C10 shows the results when the plus sign is used to repeat a string value. The formula to repeat a string or a numeric value is the same. C11 shows the result of concatenating two strings. Notice that no spaces exist between the two concatenated values. C12 and C13 demonstrate how to include spaces and commas in quoted strings to produce more attractive results.

FIG. 14.6

Use string formulas to join text.

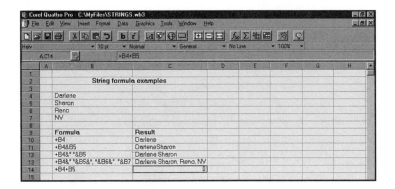

If you attempt to add two strings using the plus sign rather than the ampersand, Corel Quattro Pro treats the formula as a numeric formula rather than a string formula. A cell that contains a label has a numeric value of 0 (zero), so the formula +B4+B5 in C14 returns a value of 0. You can use the ampersand only in string formulas. Also, if you use any numeric operators (after the plus sign at the beginning) in a formula that contains an ampersand, the formula results in ERR.

Using Logical Formulas   *Logical formulas* are true/false tests. A logical formula returns a value of 1 if the test is true and a value of 0 if the test is false. Logical formulas often are used in database criteria tables and also to construct the tests used with the @IF function, discussed in the next section, "Using Function Formulas."

 Logical formulas are also called Boolean formulas.

Logical formulas provide a shortcut method of performing conditional calculations. Suppose that you want to include the value contained in cell A1 only if this value is greater than 100. The logical formula +A1*(A1>100) returns the result you want. In this formula, the logical test, A1>100, evaluates as 0 unless the value in A1 is greater than 100. If A1 contains a value over 100, the logical test evaluates to 1. Because any value multiplied by 0 equals 0, and any value multiplied by 1 is the original value, the logical formula returns the result you want.

Using Function Formulas   Although you can build many formulas using the numeric, string, or logical operators, some calculations are simply too complex to create with these simple operators. For example, if you want to calculate the interest due on a loan payment, you can simply multiply the beginning balance by the periodic interest rate. It's much more difficult, however, to calculate the actual payment amount necessary to pay off a loan in a series of equal payments.

Part

III

Ch

14

TIP   You can also use the Build complex formulas with @functions button to create function formulas.

Fortunately, Corel Quattro Pro provides a large number of built-in *functions*—preconstructed formulas that handle a broad range of calculations. These functions enable you to perform many different types of calculations by simply supplying the raw data. For example, to determine the payments on a loan, you can use the @PAYMT function. You supply the necessary data—the interest rate, number of payments, and the loan amount—and Corel Quattro Pro solves the problem.

Corel Quattro Pro includes nearly 500 powerful built-in functions that you can use in your formulas. Figure 14.7 shows an example of how the @PAYMT function calculates the loan payment on a slightly more complex loan, one with a balloon payment due at the end of the loan. In this case, a borrower wants to know the monthly payments on a loan with the following terms:

Principal	$100,000
Annual interest rate	9%
Term	15 years
Balance due at end of loan (balloon)	$10,000

FIG. 14.7
Function formulas quickly perform complex calculations using your data.

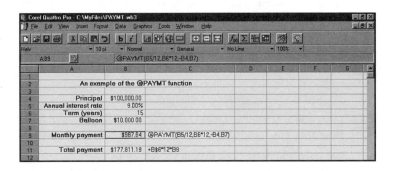

In this case, because the payments are made monthly, but the interest rate and term are stated in yearly amounts, the term must be multiplied by 12, and the rate must be divided by 12 to obtain the term in months and the monthly interest rate. The monthly loan payment, $987.84, is automatically adjusted if any of the raw data in cells B4..B7 is changed.

TIP   See the @Function Reference item on the Contents tab of the Corel Quattro Pro online help system for a complete listing of all built-in functions.

When you create formulas in a Corel Quattro Pro notebook, you can often combine functions with numeric, logical, and string formulas to produce the results you need. The section "Using Functions," in the next chapter provides much more information on functions.

▶ **See** "Building a Spreadsheet," **p. 309**

Creating Formulas by Pointing to Cells   Most formulas you create will contain operators and cell references. One way to enter a cell reference in a formula is to just type the cell address itself. However, you can also point to the cell by moving the cell selector to the cell with the mouse or the direction keys. When you move the cell selector as you are entering a formula, the Mode indicator at the right edge of the status line changes from VALUE to POINT, and the address of the cell selector appears in the input line (see Figure 14.8).

If the formula requires additional entries, type the next operator and continue entering *arguments*—the information you must supply to complete the formula—until you finish. Press Enter or click the Confirm button (the green check mark at the left of the input line) to place the formula in the notebook (see Figure 14.8). You can combine pointing and typing cell addresses—the result is the same.

FIG. 14.8
The Mode indicator changes from VALUE to POINT when a formula is entered into the cell.

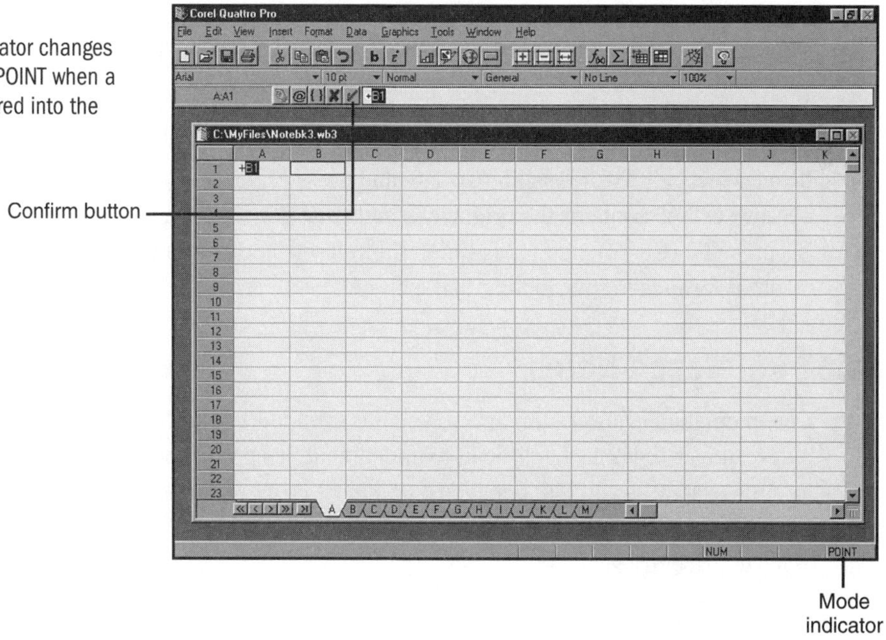

Confirm button

Mode indicator

To refer to a cell on another notebook page, include the page letter or name, followed by a colon and the cell address. To include the value of cell A13 from a page named EXPENSES, for example, type **+EXPENSES:A14**. To point to a cell on another page, click the page tab with the mouse and then point to the cell. You also can type + and then use the direction keys, including Ctrl+PgDn and Ctrl+PgUp, to move the cell selector to other pages.

Finding Formula Errors   Sometimes you may find your formulas display ERR or NA instead of the value you expected. ERR means the formula contains an erroneous calculation, such as dividing by zero. This can result from missing data or even from an error in entering a cell address. NA means some of the necessary information is currently not available, and can result from including a reference to a cell containing the @NA function, or from linking formulas that were not updated when the notebook was opened. Finding the source of such errors can prove to be difficult, especially in a complex formula. Corel Quattro Pro enables you to track down such errors using two different methods.

 TIP   Use the F5 (Go To) key to quickly move the cell selector.

To quickly find the source of an ERR or NA value, use the Go To feature. First move the cell selector to the cell displaying ERR or NA, and then press F5 (Go To) or select Edit, Go To. Do not select a destination, but simply press Enter or click OK, and the cell selector will move to the cell that is the source of the error. If the cell selector is already on the cell that is the source of the error, it will remain in the current cell.

To understand how this works, imagine that cell A5 contains the formula +1/A1, cell A10 contains the formula +A5, and cell A1 is empty. ERR will be displayed in both A5 and A10. If you select cell A10, press F5 (Go To), and press Enter, the cell selector will move to A5, because cell A5 contains the original formula that generates the error. If you select cell A5, press F5 (Go To), and press Enter, the cell selector will remain in A5, telling you that no other formula is contributing to the error.

Adding Reference Notes

Documentation is always important, and it is even more important when you create complex formulas that may be difficult to understand. It's pretty easy to forget why you built a formula exactly as you did, but even a brief note is often all you need to remind yourself. Corel Quattro Pro makes documenting formulas and values easy by allowing you to add notes to cell entries.

These reference notes don't appear when you print a report, but as Figure 14.9 shows, the notes appear on-screen in the edit box when you move the cell selector to a cell that contains a note and press F2 (Edit) or double-click the cell.

The note attached to the formula in cell C5 in Figure 14.9 clearly states the purpose of the formula—to show the combined total of sales of computers in each store during the second quarter.

FIG. 14.9
Add notes to formulas
to provide valuable
documentation.

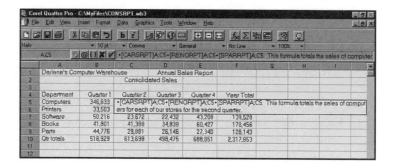

To attach a note to a cell containing data, type a semicolon immediately following the formula or value—don't leave any spaces before the semicolon—then type the note. You can include up to 1,022 characters in a cell, including the length of the formula or value and the note. Because these notes won't have any effect on your printed reports, they are a good method of creating internal documentation that will always remain with the notebook.

 TIP You can print the notes attached to formulas using the File, Print, Sheet Options, Cell Formulas command.

Correcting Errors With Undo

 When you type an entry, edit a cell, or issue a command (like Edit, Delete), you make changes in the notebook. If you make a change in error, you can usually choose the Edit, Undo command (or press Ctrl+Z) to reverse the previous change. You can also use the Undo button on the toolbar. If you type over an entry in error, you can undo the new entry to restore the previous entry. The Undo feature undoes only the last action performed, whether you were entering data, using a command, running a macro, or using Undo.

The Undo feature is powerful and using it can be a little tricky. To use Undo properly, you must first understand what Corel Quattro Pro considers to be a change that can be undone. A change occurs between the time Corel Quattro Pro leaves READY mode and the time it returns to READY mode. (Refer to Figure 14.8 to understand the location of the Mode indicator.) If you press F2 (Edit), Corel Quattro Pro enters EDIT mode. After you press Enter to confirm the edits, Corel Quattro Pro returns to READY mode. If you choose Edit, Undo, Corel Quattro Pro restores the cell contents that existed before you pressed F2 (Edit). To restore the last change, choose Edit, Redo (which replaces Edit, Undo until you make another change that can be undone). If a single command makes the change, the Undo feature can undo changes (such as Edit, Delete) made to an entire block of cells or even a complete notebook.

Part
III

Ch

14

N O T E The Edit, Undo and Edit, Redo commands inform you of the action that can be undone or redone by including a one-word description that changes with each type of action that follows the command. If you make an entry in a cell, for example, the command appears as "Edit, Undo Entry." If you use the Edit, Undo Entry command, the command then changes to "Edit, Redo Entry." ■

Corel Quattro Pro cannot undo some commands. Moving the cell selector, saving a notebook, and the effects of recalculating formulas are examples of commands that cannot be undone. Before you make a serious change to an important file, always save the work to protect against errors that Undo may not reverse.

Corel Quattro Pro has two levels of Undo command functionality. To ensure that the full Undo feature is available, make sure that the Undo Enabled check box in the General tab of the Application Object Inspector dialog box is checked (see Figure 14.10). To access this dialog box, right-click the Corel Quattro Pro title bar or press Alt+F12. If you don't enable the full Undo command, you will still be able to undo certain actions, such as entering data into a cell or changing a graph type or a graph title.

FIG. 14.10
Select Undo Enabled to ensure that the full Undo feature is available.

Saving Your Work

When you create a Corel Quattro Pro notebook, it first exists only in your computer's volatile memory—RAM. To make the notebook available for future use, you must also save the notebook in a file on disk. If you don't save new notebooks or changes before you quit Corel Quattro Pro, you lose your work. You must also save a notebook in a disk file if you want to share the notebook with other people. The notebook file remains on disk after you quit Corel Quattro Pro or turn off the computer.

Saving Notebook Files

To save your work, use File, Save or File, Save As, or the Save button on the toolbar. If you have not yet saved the notebook, Corel Quattro Pro suggests a default name—NOTEBK1.WB3. When you use File, New to open new blank notebooks, Corel Quattro Pro increases the numerical portion of the file name. The second new notebook is NOTEBK2.WB3, and so on.

 Quickly save your notebook by pressing Ctrl+S.

If you already have saved the active notebook and assigned a name, File, Save saves the active notebook to disk using the assigned name. If you choose File, Save As, Corel Quattro Pro saves the active notebook using a name you specify in the Save File dialog box (see Figure 14.11).

FIG. 14.11

Use the Save File dialog box to name your notebook files.

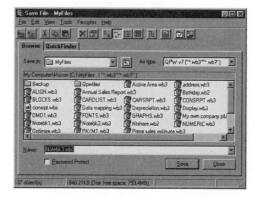

The standard extension for Corel Quattro Pro notebooks is WB3, but you can open or save notebook files in many different formats by selecting the appropriate type in the As Type list box in Figure 14.11. The standard extension for Corel Quattro Pro workspace files is WBS. When you type a notebook or workspace name to save, type only the descriptive part of the name. Corel Quattro Pro adds the appropriate file extension for you.

Protecting Files with Passwords   When you save a Corel Quattro Pro notebook in a disk file, anyone with access to your computer can open the file. While this isn't a problem in most instances, you may have some files that should remain confidential and restricted. To prevent unauthorized access to certain notebook files, you can apply a password to them when you save them. When a notebook is protected by a password, you must know the correct password before Corel Quattro Pro permits you to retrieve or open the notebook.

Part

III

Ch

To apply a password to a notebook file you are saving, select the <u>P</u>assword Protect text box in the Save File dialog box, type a file name, and select <u>S</u>ave. In the <u>P</u>assword text box, type a password of up to 15 characters. As you enter characters, Corel Quattro Pro displays graphics blocks rather than the password. After you choose OK to confirm the dialog box, Corel Quattro Pro displays the Verify Password dialog box. Retype the password using the same combination of uppercase and lowercase characters. Passwords are case-sensitive. Choose OK to confirm the dialog box.

TROUBLESHOOTING

Corel Quattro Pro reports that I used the wrong password when I attempted to open a password protected notebook file. Passwords are case-sensitive, and can be very tricky to use. **BRIAN** is not the same as **brian**. Try entering the password again with the case reversed (press the Caps Lock key before entering the password) or with only the first letter of the word capitalized.

Saving Files in Other Formats   Corel Quattro Pro can read and save files in many popular formats including: Lotus 1-2-3 for DOS, Lotus 1-2-3 for Windows, Corel Quattro Pro for DOS, Excel, Paradox, dBASE, and text. If you want to save a Corel Quattro Pro notebook in another format, select the correct file extension in the As <u>T</u>ype drop-down list box in the Save File dialog box. To save a notebook as a Lotus 1-2-3 for Windows file, for example, select the extension WK4.

TIP   Unless you need to share a notebook file with someone who does not have Corel Quattro Pro, always save notebooks using the Q<u>P</u>W v7("*.wb3""*.wb?") As type file format.

If you save a notebook in any type other than the default "QPW v7 WB3" format, any features unique to the newest version of Corel Quattro Pro will be lost. For example, because Lotus 1-2-3 Release 2.x spreadsheets cannot have multiple pages, only the first notebook page is saved if you use the WK1 file type.

Making Space on Your Disk   Each time you create a file, you use space on a disk—usually your hard disk. Eventually, you'll run out of disk space if you don't occasionally erase old, unneeded files from the disk. Even if you have disk space left, too many files make it difficult to search through the file list for a specific file.

Before you delete old files, consider saving them to a floppy disk in case you need them again. Corel Quattro Pro notebook files are quite space efficient, and you can store a large number of files on a single floppy disk. Corel Quattro Pro has no command for deleting files. You can use the Windows Explorer to delete old, unneeded files.

Using Automatic Backups

Many different types of problems can cause you to lose the results of your work. If there is a power failure, for example, any Corel Quattro Pro notebook that hasn't been saved to disk will be lost. If a program crashes and locks up your system, the same thing may occur. There's always the problem of the over-confident user, too. Have you ever lost work because you thought you already saved it, but then realized you hadn't because you were distracted? These are only a few of the many problems that present a danger to your notebooks and your data.

Saving your work frequently is the best insurance against losing a notebook or data to any of these problems. Unfortunately, it's pretty easy to forget to save your work often enough. When you're under deadline pressure, who remembers to select File, Save?

Fortunately, Corel Quattro Pro can quickly save your notebooks automatically at intervals you specify. That way, if a problem occurs, your notebook file on disk isn't too far behind and you won't lose too much work.

To activate the automatic backup feature, right-click the Corel Quattro Pro title bar and select Application Properties or press Alt+F12 to display the Application Object Inspector dialog box. Select the File Options tab (see Figure 14.12). Use the Timed Document Backup Every spin control to specify how often you want Corel Quattro Pro to automatically back up your notebook files. Select the Timed Document Backup Every check box to enable the automatic backup feature. Press Enter or select OK to close the dialog box.

FIG. 14.12
Use the automatic backup feature to automatically save your notebook files at specified intervals.

Part
III

Ch
14

How often should you have Corel Quattro Pro save your files? The best answer to that is another question: "How much work are you willing to do over?" Most notebook files can be saved quite quickly, so there isn't much of a delay as they save. A setting of 10 minutes between backups is probably a good compromise, but you can adjust the setting to one that suits your work style. ●

CHAPTER 15

Building a Spreadsheet

Building a Corel Quattro Pro spreadsheet can be fun. When you create a spreadsheet model, your computer performs the actions you specify. If you tell Corel Quattro Pro to use your business' past performance to predict future business, it will do just that. If you tell Corel Quattro Pro to analyze your investments, showing the poorest ones that you might want to reconsider, you can bet that's what Corel Quattro Pro will show you, too. Regardless of whether your uses for Corel Quattro Pro are these or perhaps something a little more ordinary, you must begin by building a spreadsheet, the subject of this chapter.

If you're new to Corel Quattro Pro, you may think that building a spreadsheet model sounds like quite a task. It's true that some models can be pretty complex, but most of the time you'll find them quite simple. Remember, you don't have to build a complete, complex masterpiece all at once. You don't even have to start with very complicated models, either. The best way to learn to build Corel Quattro Pro spreadsheet models is to start small, and then work your way up.

This chapter covers some of the basic subjects that will help you begin building your models. Don't be confused

Use basic Corel Quattro Pro commands

Learn which commands will help you perform the necessary tasks to create spreadsheet models that accomplish your goals.

Use blocks of cells as a unit

Save time by telling Corel Quattro Pro to perform the same actions on numerous cells at the same time.

Copy and move data

Learn how to use the same data in more than one place, or move data to more appropriate locations to make your spreadsheets far more useable.

Automatically fill blocks of cells with useful data

Corel Quattro Pro can easily automate the process of entering data, and it will enter many types of data for you.

Use built-in functions

Use built-in functions to leverage the power of Corel Quattro Pro in your notebooks and easily perform complex calculations.

if you see the terms *spreadsheet*, *model*, *worksheet*, and *notebook* used pretty much interchangeably; they all refer to the same thing in most cases. ■

Choosing Commands from Menus

Commands are used for almost everything you do in Corel Quattro Pro. Commands tell Corel Quattro Pro to perform a task, change the basic operation of Corel Quattro Pro, or operate on a notebook, a notebook page, a block of cells, or individual cells. Some commands are used every time you run Corel Quattro Pro; others are rarely, if ever, used. Some commands are general enough to apply to all notebooks; still others are specialized and apply to individual objects such as blocks or cells.

The Corel Quattro Pro main menu includes 10 options. Each option leads to a *drop-down menu* similar to the File menu (see Figure 15.1).

FIG. 15.1

The File drop-down menu on the Corel Quattro Pro main menu allows you to make changes that impact an entire file.

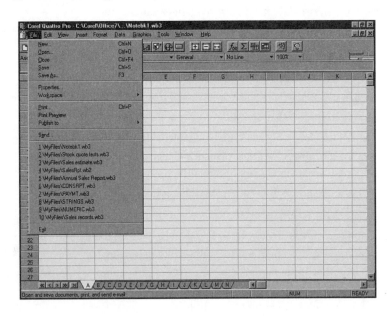

Each drop-down menu provides a series of commands you use to accomplish specific types of tasks. You'll save quite a bit of time if you understand the basic purpose of each main menu selection, because you won't spend so much time hunting for the correct command. Let's have a quick look at a summary of the main menu options.

■ The File commands enable you to save and open notebooks, print reports, set up your printer, and quit Corel Quattro Pro.

- The Edit commands enable you to undo commands; use the Windows Clipboard to copy, cut, and paste information; create links to other Windows applications; move the cell selector; customize Corel Quattro Pro's default settings; and search and replace.

- The View commands enable you to zoom in or out; control the display of screen elements; group pages; split the notebook into horizontal or vertical panes; lock rows or columns on-screen; and move between the notebook pages and the Objects page.

- The Insert commands enable you to insert and delete rows, columns, and pages; name blocks of cells; add a QuickButton onto a page; define, modify, or delete page groups; add functions to cells; add images or other objects to a notebook; and Insert page breaks.

- The Format commands enable you to create and modify styles; modify styles of blocks, pages, and notebooks; reformat text; apply SpeedFormats; use QuickFit; and adjust the position of objects added to a page.

- The Data commands enable you to convert formulas to unchanging values; Sort data; fill blocks with data and define customized fill series; use the Consolidator to combine data; extract and combine portions of notebooks; import and parse text files; Query or parse a notebook; use the Database Desktop and Data Modeling Desktop utilities, and use QuickColumn to rearrange text from a block or file into columns.

 T I P If you're not sure where to find the correct command, use the Help, Ask the PerfectExpert command.

- The Graphics commands enable you to create, view, and modify graphs; insert graph objects on notebook pages; create geographical maps; and create on-screen slideshows.

- The Tools commands enable you to check spelling; to use QuickCorrect; to create, run, and debug macros; use the Experts; create formulas using the Formula Composer; use Scenario Manager; perform what-if analyses; perform data regression and matrix manipulation; use the Optimizer and Solve For utilities; and create your own dialog boxes and toolbars.

- The Window commands enable you to create additional views of your notebooks, control the display of open windows, and select a window.

- The Help commands enable you to access the Corel Quattro Pro Help system, use the PerfectExpert, access help on the Internet, and display product and license information.

For more detailed information on Corel Quattro Pro's menus, you can use the Help, Help Topics command. You can also press F1 (Help) when a command is selected for context-sensitive help that explains how to perform the selected task.

TROUBLESHOOTING

Sometimes it's difficult to determine where to find the command necessary to perform a task. Try Help, Ask the PerfectExpert for help on how to perform a task. The PerfectExpert will show you a number of topics relating to the task, and you can select the one that seems to be the closest to what you want to do.

Using Blocks

A *block* is usually a rectangular group of cells in a notebook. In Corel Quattro Pro, a block also can contain several groups of cells defined by collections of rectangular blocks. That is, a single named block does not have to be rectangular, but can contain several smaller rectangular blocks. Figure 15.2, for example, shows one rectangular block in cells A1..B3; a nonrectangular block including B5..B6, B7..D9, and E7..F7; and a noncontiguous block that includes C14..D15 and E17..F18 (the blocks are shaded gray to make them easier to see).

Blocks are called ranges in Lotus 1-2-3 and Excel.

You specify a block address using cell addresses of any two diagonally opposite corners of the block. You separate the cell addresses with one or two periods and separate each rectangular block with commas. You can specify the nonrectangular block shown in Figure 15.2 by typing **B5..B6,B7..D9,E7..F7**, for example. You also can specify this block in several other ways, as long as you separate each rectangular block with commas.

A block can also span two or more notebook pages. This *three-dimensional* block includes the same cells on each page. When you use a three-dimensional block, you must include the page letter or page name with the cell addresses. For example, to extend the rectangular block in Figure 15.2 to a three-dimensional block, type **A:A1..C:B3**.

Selecting Blocks

Many commands act on blocks. The Edit, Copy Block command, for example, displays a dialog box asking for a From and a To block. To enter a block, you can type the address of the block, select the block with the mouse or the keyboard before or after you choose the command, or type the block name (to learn about creating a name, see "Naming Blocks" later in this chapter).

FIG. 15.2

You can create several different kinds of Corel Quattro Pro blocks on one page.

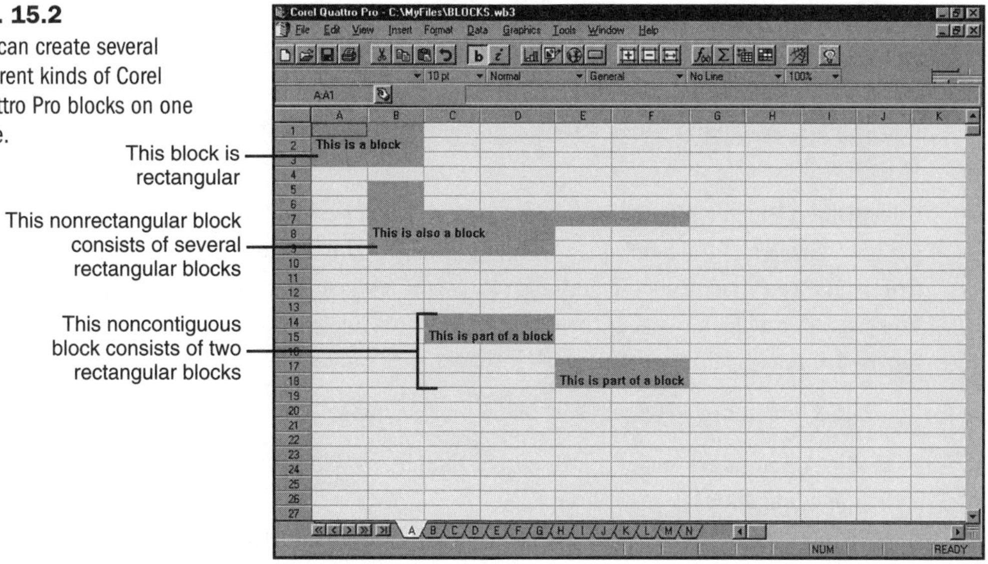

This block is rectangular

This nonrectangular block consists of several rectangular blocks

This noncontiguous block consists of two rectangular blocks

T I P You can specify a block address using any two diagonally opposite cells.

Typing the Block Addresses   If you want to type a block address, type the addresses of cells diagonally opposite in a rectangular block, separating each cell with a period. If the block is nonrectangular, you must specify each rectangular block and separate each block with a comma. To specify the block A1..C4, for example, you type **A1..C4**, **A1.C4**, **A4..C1**, or **A4.C1**. Corel Quattro Pro regards each of these addresses the same as A1..C4.

Selecting Blocks   The easiest method of specifying a block's cell addresses is usually selecting the block by pointing with the mouse or the keyboard. You can select a block before or after you issue a command. In a formula, however, you must select the block after you begin typing the formula. If you select a block before you issue a command, the block remains selected, allowing you to use the same block with more than one command without reselecting the block. To use the mouse to select a block, simply hold down the left mouse button as you drag the mouse across the block.

T I P If you use the keyboard to select a block, you can use the Shift+F7 keyboard shortcut as a method of anchoring a block selection. You can also anchor a block selection by pressing and holding down the Shift key while moving the cell selector.

When you preselect a block, the address automatically appears in the text boxes of any command dialog boxes. Some dialog boxes, however, require you to specify more than one block. For example, if you use the Edit, Copy Block command, you must specify both a From (source) and a To (destination) block. If you have selected a block before you issue the command, both the From and To text boxes will show the same block—the selected block. You can use the mouse or press Tab and Shift+Tab to move the highlight between the text boxes. Then enter the second block by typing its address or block name, or by pointing.

Specifying a Block with a Name   You also can specify a block in a dialog box using a name you assign to the block (see "Naming Blocks," later in this chapter). Whenever Corel Quattro Pro expects the address of a cell or a block, you can specify a block name. You can enter a block name in the Go To dialog box, for example, and Corel Quattro Pro moves the cell selector to the upper-left corner of the named block.

You gain a number of advantages by using block names:

■ Block names are easier to remember than block addresses—especially if a block is noncontiguous.

■ Typing a block name usually is easier than pointing to a block in another part of the notebook.

■ Macros that use block names rather than cell addresses automatically adjust after you move a block.

■ Block names also make formulas easier to understand. The formula +QTR_1_TOTAL (using the block name QTR_1_TOTAL) is easier to understand than the formula +B10.

Extending Block Selections   Extending a block selection to include a three-dimensional block or a group of blocks allows you to include more than a single two-dimensional block in a command or a block name. These extended blocks make some operations easier and faster because one command can replace a series of commands, such as applying numeric formats, adding shading, and choosing a text font.

T I P   Hold down the Ctrl key when selecting noncontiguous blocks.

Selecting noncontiguous blocks using the mouse is much easier than selecting noncontiguous blocks using the keyboard. You can select noncontiguous blocks using the mouse before or after you choose a command, but to select noncontiguous blocks using the keyboard, you must select the block after choosing a command.

If you use the mouse to extend a block selection that includes noncontiguous blocks, you can select the blocks before or after you choose a command. Use the following procedure:

1. Press and hold down the Ctrl key.
2. Select the first rectangular block.
3. Select each additional rectangular block.
4. Release the Ctrl key.

 TIP To work on noncontiguous blocks using the keyboard, choose the command first, then select the block.

To use the keyboard to extend a block selection that includes noncontiguous blocks, perform the following steps:

1. Choose the command in which you want to use the noncontiguous blocks.
2. Select the appropriate block text box by pressing the Tab key or, if the text box has an underlined letter, by pressing Alt plus the underlined letter.
3. Enter the block addresses by typing the addresses of rectangular blocks and separating each block with a comma. You also can point to the first cell of each rectangular block, press the period key to anchor the selection, and use the direction keys to select the block. Enter a comma and continue selecting rectangular blocks until you have selected each block.

Naming Blocks

Block addresses can be difficult to remember, and it's easy to type the wrong set of cell addresses when specifying a block. Corel Quattro Pro provides a very good solution to this problem: *block names*. If you name blocks, you can always substitute the block name for the block's cell addresses in commands and formulas, ensuring the correct block will be affected by the command or formula. Block names also make formulas much easier to read and understand, because Corel Quattro Pro will always substitute block names where appropriate in formulas—even if you didn't use block names when you created the formula.

Corel Quattro Pro does not distinguish between uppercase and lowercase letters; Block_1, block_1, and BLOCK_1 are equivalent block names.

You should follow certain rules and cautions when creating block names:

- You can use up to 63 characters to name a block.
- You can use block names in formulas, functions, commands, and macros.

■ Don't use the following characters in block names:

+ - * / & > < @ # ^ $ ( )

■ Although block names that start with numbers are valid, avoid starting block names with numbers because they may cause problems in formulas.

■ Don't create block names that also are cell addresses, column letters, or row numbers (such as A1, AA, or 199), names of keys (such as Edit), function names (such as @AVG), or advanced macro commands (such as WRITE).

■ Use descriptive block names.

■ Join parts of block names with the underscore (such as QTR_1_TOTALS) rather than spaces.

■ If you share spreadsheet files with users of other spreadsheet programs (such as Microsoft Excel, Lotus 1-2-3, or even older versions of Quattro Pro), limit block names to 15 characters.

Corel Quattro Pro provides several methods of creating block names. Each method uses the Insert, Block Names command (Ctrl+F3) to first display the Block Names dialog box (see Figure 15.3). The following sections describe the block naming options available through this dialog box.

> **CAUTION**
>
> Don't confuse the Insert, Block and Insert, Block Names commands. The Insert, Block command adds a rectangular block of cells to a notebook page, thus moving other cells down or to the right. The Insert, Block Names command creates block names.

FIG. 15.3
The Block Names dialog box provides several block-naming options.

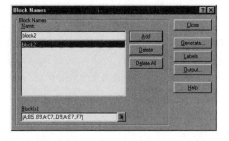

Creating Block Names with Insert, Block Names, Add   You can use the Insert, Block Names, Add command to assign a name to a cell or a block. To create a block name using this command, follow these steps:

1. Select the cell or block you want to name.

2. Choose Insert, Block Names (or press Ctrl+F3). The Block Names dialog box shown in Figure 15.3 appears.

3. Type the block name in the Name text box.

4. Select Add (or press Enter).

5. Select Close.

If you want to add more than one block name, repeat Steps 3 and 4 as necessary.

Creating Block Names with Insert, Block Names, Generate   You can also create block names automatically using the Insert, Block Names, Generate command. This command can generate block names for a row, a column, or for every cell in a selected block, using labels in the block. To create block names using this command, follow these steps:

1. Select the cell or block you want to name.

2. Choose Insert, Block Names (or press Ctrl+F3).

3. Select Generate to display the Generate Block Names dialog box (see Figure 15.4).

FIG. 15.4

You can create block names automatically using the Generate Block Names dialog box.

4. The check boxes in this dialog box determine which cells (in the selected block) the labels identify. Choose Under Top Row, Right of Leftmost Column, Above Bottom Row, or Left of Rightmost Column. For example, you might use labels to identify product lines and time periods.

5. To name all cells in the block using the label cells in combination, select Name Cells At Intersections.

6. Select OK to return to the Block Names dialog box.

The Name Cells At Intersections option creates block names by concatenating (joining) the column label, an underscore, and the row label. For example, if the column label is "Year Total" and the row label is "Software," the name generated for the intersecting cell is Year Total_Software.

Creating Block Names with Insert, Block Names, Labels   You also can use the Insert, Block Names, Labels command to create block names. With this command, you use labels already typed on a notebook page as block names for adjacent cells, such as to identify cells where users will input data. To create block names using this command, follow these steps:

1. Select the cell or block you want to name.

2. Choose Insert, Block Names (or press Ctrl+F3).

3. Select Labels to display the Create Names From Labels dialog box (see Figure 15.5).

FIG. 15.5

The Create Names From Labels dialog box is useful for creating block names.

4. The Directions check boxes determine which cells are named using the labels. Select the appropriate direction, Right, Left, Up, or Down.

5. Select OK to return to the Block Names dialog box.

The Insert, Block Names, Labels command ignores blank cells in the label block as it creates single-cell blocks. If you need to create multiple-cell blocks, you must use the Insert, Block Names, Add command.

Listing Block Names   A table of block names serves as important notebook documentation. Corel Quattro Pro creates a two-column table of block names and addresses using the Insert, Block Names, Output command. When you choose the Insert, Block Names, Output command, select an area with enough room for the block name table, because the table overwrites any existing data without warning.

TROUBLESHOOTING

The block name table doesn't seem to show the correct addresses for some blocks. If you change the definition of a block name, or add or delete block names, the block name table is not updated automatically. You must issue the Insert, Block Names, Output command again to update the table.

Some formulas don't show the correct results even though they appear to contain correct block names. Make certain your block names don't contain any mathematical operators, such as a plus or minus sign. Corel Quattro Pro may be confused if you include these operators in block names that appear in formulas.

Deleting Block Names   There's usually little reason to remove block names from a Corel Quattro Pro notebook. Block names don't use much memory, and the documentation they provide can be invaluable. Still, if you want to delete block names, Corel Quattro Pro has two commands that delete block names from the notebook. Use the Insert, Block Names,

Delete command to delete a single block name or several block names. You delete all block names at one time using the Insert, Block Names, Delete All command.

Copying and Moving Information

Few Corel Quattro Pro notebooks are masterpieces when first created. Most often, it's useful to copy or move data from one place to another. You might, for example, want to duplicate the appearance of an existing report, or you might simply find it's awkward to enter data correctly in the notebook's initial layout. Whatever your reason, you'll discover that Corel Quattro Pro offers several different methods of copying and moving data.

 TIP Chapter 16, "Changing the Display and Appearance of Data," shows you how to make your Quattro Pro notebooks look as good as they should.

The three primary methods of moving and copying data in Corel Quattro Pro are:

- the Edit, Cut; Edit Copy; Edit, Paste; and Edit Paste Special commands, which use the Windows Clipboard
- the Edit, Copy Block and Edit, Move Block commands, which do not use the Clipboard, and
- the mouse

In the following sections you'll learn the advantages and disadvantages of each, and why each method is important to you.

It is important to understand how moving data and formulas in Corel Quattro Pro differs from copying data and formulas. Table 15.1 describes what happens when the move or copy commands are used.

Table 15.1   Move and Copy Commands

Command	Description
Move data	Formulas that refer to moved data automatically move to new location.
Copy data	Formulas continue to refer to the data in the original location.
Move formulas	Do not change in new location.
Copy formulas	May or may not update, depending on types of references in the formula.

Copying and Moving Using the Clipboard

The Windows Clipboard is a feature shared by most Windows applications. Data stored on the Clipboard is available to any Windows program that knows how to use the data. Once you place data on the Clipboard, it remains there until new data replaces it, or until you exit from Windows. This permits you to make multiple copies of the same data without having to add the data to the Clipboard each time (as long as you don't use another command that places new data on the Clipboard).

Corel Quattro Pro follows the Windows convention of placing the commands that use the Clipboard in the top section of the Edit menu. These commands are Edit, Cut (Ctrl+X); Edit, Copy (Ctrl+C); Edit, Paste (Ctrl+V); and Edit, Paste Special. You will likely use the first three of these commands often; Edit, Paste Special is more specialized, and you probably won't use it too often. Most Windows programs have similar options on their Edit menus.

Using Edit, Cut   The Edit, Cut command removes—or *cuts*—data from the notebook and places the data on the Clipboard. Any existing Clipboard data is lost unless it has been saved elsewhere. Once you have placed data on the Clipboard, you can make as many copies of the data as you want using Edit, Paste.

> **CAUTION**
>
> The Edit, Cut command replaces any existing Clipboard data with new data. You cannot recover the old data, so be sure to use Edit, Paste to save the old data, if you will need it in the future, before you use the Edit, Cut command on the new data.

 Other programs may not always be able to paste every type of Corel Quattro Pro object.

You can place any selectable object on the Clipboard. If you select a single cell, the Edit, Cut command removes the data from the selected cell and places the data on the Clipboard. If you select a block of cells, the entire block is removed from the notebook and placed on the Clipboard. You can also use Edit, Cut to place other types of objects, such as graphs or drawn objects, on the Clipboard. Any object placed on the Clipboard using Corel Quattro Pro's Edit, Cut command can later be returned to the notebook using Edit, Paste, but other Windows applications may not be able to accept all types of Corel Quattro Pro objects.

 To use Edit, Cut, first select the object you want to cut, and then select Edit, Cut (Ctrl+X) or click the Cut button on the Toolbar. The selected object will disappear from the Corel

Quattro Pro notebook. If you cut an object in error, immediately select Edit, Undo before selecting any other commands.

Edit, Cut places any numeric formatting, alignment, or other object properties on the Clipboard along with the data. If you've used the Object Inspector dialog boxes to modify any of the properties for the selected object, these properties will be removed from the notebook along with the object, and placed on the Clipboard for possible use later.

Using Edit, Copy   The Edit, Copy command works very much like the Edit, Cut command, but there is one very important difference. When you use Edit, Copy, the selected object remains in your Corel Quattro Pro notebook, and an exact duplicate is created on the Clipboard. This duplicate shares all of the original object's properties, including any numeric formatting, alignment, and so on. Once the duplicate is placed on the Clipboard, however, the two objects—the original and the duplicate—are totally independent of each other. That is, any changes you make to the original object in your notebook are not reflected in the duplicate on the Clipboard. If you want the duplicate to match the changed original, use Edit, Copy to create an updated duplicate.

TIP   Edit, Copy adds a copy of the object to the Clipboard. You need to use Edit, Paste to add the copy to your notebook.

It's easy to become confused by the title of the Edit, Copy command. Although you might expect this command to make a copy of an object, the copy it produces isn't visible to you. The copy of the selected object only exists on the Windows Clipboard—ready to be pasted into another location in your Quattro Pro notebook, or into another document created in another Windows application.

 To use Edit, Copy, first select the object you want to copy, and then select Edit, Copy (Ctrl+C) or click the Copy button on the toolbar. You won't see any change in the notebook, but the Clipboard will now contain an exact duplicate of the selected object.

> **N O T E**   Objects placed on the Windows Clipboard are stored in your computer's memory until you use Edit, Cut or Edit, Copy to replace them with another object, or until you exit from Windows. Very large objects, such as bitmaps or sound files, can use quite a large portion of your system's memory, making your system operate at an unusually slow pace (especially if your notebook has lots of complex calculations). If you have copied a very large object to the Clipboard, but no longer need to store the object there, copy a single notebook cell to the Clipboard to free the memory for other uses. ■

Using Edit Paste   The Edit, Paste command places a copy of data contained on the Clipboard into your Corel Quattro Pro notebook. The object on the Clipboard is unaffected by this command, and can be pasted into more than one location using additional Edit, Paste commands. Corel Quattro Pro notebooks can contain most types of objects that can be placed on the Clipboard.

 To use the Edit, Paste command, first use Edit, Copy or Edit, Cut to place the object on the Clipboard. Next, position the cell selector at the location where you want to place a copy of the data, and select Edit, Paste (Ctrl+V) or click the Paste button on the toolbar.

The following guidelines enable you to determine the number and type of copies that will be created:

■ If the data moved to the Clipboard with the Edit, Copy or Edit, Cut command was from a single cell, one copy of the data will be added to each selected cell after you choose Edit, Paste.

■ If the data moved to the Clipboard with the Edit, Copy or Edit, Cut command was from several rows in a single column, one copy of the data will be added to each selected column after you choose Edit, Paste.

■ If the data moved to the Clipboard with the Edit, Copy or Edit, Cut command was from several columns in a single row, one copy of the data will be added to each selected row after you choose Edit, Paste.

■ If the data moved to the Clipboard with the Edit, Copy or Edit, Cut command was from several rows and several columns, one copy of the data will be added to the spreadsheet page starting at the selected cell after you choose Edit, Paste.

Three-dimensional data always creates a three-dimensional copy. If the source or destination data block includes more than one page, the same rules that apply to rows and columns also apply to the page dimension.

If you want additional copies of the same data, just reposition the cell selector and select Edit, Paste. Don't use any additional Edit, Copy or Edit, Cut commands if you want additional copies of the same data, because the Clipboard holds only the most recent Edit, Copy or Edit, Cut contents.

CAUTION

If you paste data to a block that already contains data, Corel Quattro Pro replaces the existing data with the new data. Use care when pasting data to avoid pasting data into cells that contain formulas or other data you don't want to lose.

Copying and Moving Data Using Edit, Block Commands

Corel Quattro Pro includes a second set of commands you can use to copy or move data from one place in the notebook to another. Edit, Move Block and Edit, Copy Block move and copy data directly within the notebook without using the Clipboard.

Because these commands don't use the Clipboard, any objects you've already placed on the Clipboard aren't affected by the Edit, Move Block and Edit, Copy Block commands. You can still use Edit, Paste to make copies of the unchanged Clipboard contents even after you use Edit, Move Block and Edit, Copy Block. This characteristic makes Edit, Move Block and Edit, Copy Block good complements to the Edit commands, which do use the Clipboard.

Using Edit, Move Block   When you use the Edit, Move Block command, the moved data includes the same formulas and values, as well as the same alignment, fonts, and numeric formats. Column widths and row heights do not move, however. The source cells still exist after the move, but they are empty.

To move data and formulas with the Edit, Move Block command, follow these steps:

1. Select the cell or block you want to move.

2. Choose the Edit, Move Block command. The Move Block dialog box shown in Figure 15.6 appears.

FIG. 15.6

Use the Move Block dialog box to move data and formulas.

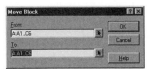

3. Press Tab or use the mouse to move the selection to the To text box. Use the mouse or the direction keys to select the destination for the data, or type the destination address in the text box.

4. Press Enter or click OK to confirm the dialog box and move the data.

 T I P   Use Edit, Move Block when you don't want to affect what is already on the Clipboard.

To specify the From and To blocks, you can type the cell addresses, select the blocks, or enter block names. After you preselect a block, as you just did in Step 1, the address appears in both the From and To text boxes. You can use the preselected block as the source or destination of the move.

Using Edit, Copy Block   When you copy data, the copy contains the same labels, values, formatting, and style properties as the original data. The data in the original location remains unchanged.

You can copy a single cell or a block to another part of the same notebook page, to another notebook page, or to another open notebook. You can make a single copy or multiple copies at the same time. To copy data with the Edit, Copy Block command, follow these steps:

1. Select the cell or block you want to copy. If you preselect a block, it appears in both the From and To text boxes.

2. Choose the Edit, Copy Block command. The Copy Block dialog box shown in Figure 15.7 appears.

FIG. 15.7
You can use the Copy Block dialog box to copy a single cell or a block of cells.

3. Press Tab to select the To text box.

4. Type the destination address, or use the mouse or direction keys to select the destination block.

5. Choose OK to confirm the dialog box and copy the block.

Corel Quattro Pro copies the data, overwriting existing data in the destination block.

You can use the Model Copy option to make a copy that uses the From block as a model for the To block. If you check Model Copy, formula references—even absolute references—adjust to fit the To block (see "Copying Formulas" later in this chapter for more information on formula references). In addition, if you check Model Copy, you can specify whether to copy Formula Cells, Label Cells, Number Cells, Properties, Objects, or Row/Column Sizes.

Copying and Moving Data Using the Mouse

Corel Quattro Pro offers yet another method of moving or copying data—one that takes advantage of the graphical nature of the Windows environment. This method, called *drag and drop*, uses the mouse and is by far the easiest way to move data short distances within a Corel Quattro Pro notebook.

To move data using the drag-and-drop method, perform the following steps:

1. Make sure the destination block—where the data is to be moved—does not contain any information of value, as it will be deleted by the block move.

2. Select the block of data you want to move. The block can be any size, including a single cell.

3. Point at the selected block and hold down the left mouse button until the mouse pointer changes to a hand.

4. Move the mouse pointer to the upper-left corner of the destination block. As you move the mouse pointer, Corel Quattro Pro displays an outline the size of the selected block. Any existing data within this outline will be written over.

5. Release the mouse button to drop the block of data in the new location.

To copy, rather than move, the selected block of data, hold down the Ctrl key when you point to the block in Step 3. A plus sign appears next to the hand-shaped mouse pointer when you are copying, rather than moving, data.

If the mouse pointer changes to a hand too quickly when you are selecting a block, adjust the Application Object Inspector dialog box General tab option, Cell Drag and Drop Delay Time. To do this, right-click the Corel Quattro Pro title bar or press Alt+F12 to display the Application Object Inspector dialog box. Select the General tab (see Figure. 15.8). The default delay time is 500 ms—one-half second. Try a slightly higher setting, such as 750 ms.

FIG. 15.8

The Application Object Inspector dialog box is where the cell drag-and-drop delay time may be changed.

Copying Formulas

Copying formulas in Corel Quattro Pro is more complex than copying data because of the way the program stores addresses in formulas. Addresses may be:

■ *Relative.* Refers to column, row, and page *offsets*—distances measured in columns, rows, or pages—from the formula cell;

■ *Absolute.* Always referring to a specific cell; or

■ *Mixed.* A combination of relative and absolute.

Relative Addressing   If you enter the formula **+B2** in cell C5, Corel Quattro Pro does not store the formula quite the way you may expect. The formula tells Corel Quattro Pro to add the value of the cell one column to the left and three rows above C5. When you copy this formula from C5 to D6, Corel Quattro Pro uses the same relative formula but displays the formula as +C3. This method of storing cell references is called relative addressing. After you copy a formula that uses relative addressing, Corel Quattro Pro automatically adjusts the new formula so its cell references are in the same relative location as they were in the original location.

Absolute Addressing   Sometimes you do not want a formula to address new locations after you copy the formula. You may, for example, create a formula that refers to data in a single cell, such as an interest rate or a growth factor percentage. Formulas that always refer to the same cell address, regardless of where you place the copy of the formula, use *absolute addressing*.

 You can use the F4 key to toggle cell addresses between relative and absolute modes.

To specify an absolute address, type a dollar sign ($) in the formula before each part of the address you want to remain absolutely the same. The formula +$B:$C$10, for example, always refers to cell C10 on notebook page B regardless of where you place the copy of the formula.

Mixed Addressing   You also can create formulas that use *mixed addressing*, in which some elements of the cell addresses are absolute and other elements are relative. You can create a formula, for example, that always refers to the same row but adjusts its column reference as you copy the formula to another column. To create a mixed address, use a dollar sign to indicate the absolute address portions of the formula, leaving off the dollar sign for relative addresses. The formula +$B1, for example, always refers to column B on the current notebook page, but adjusts the row reference relative to the current row.

Filling Blocks

Creating Corel Quattro Pro notebooks can seem like quite a task, especially if the model you want to build requires you to enter a series of data in a large number of consecutive cells. For example, a notebook based on an incrementing time series, such as a loan amortization schedule, may require you to include dates in monthly intervals. A notebook tracking results from each of your company's locations may require you to enter the location names, possibly in several different places. Entering the same data numerous times seems like a lot of work, doesn't it? Wouldn't it be nice if you could get someone else to do that sort of thing for you?

 Let Corel Quattro Pro work for you by automatically filling in data.

Fortunately, there is one thing computers are very good at—doing repetitive work. Corel Quattro Pro takes this concept a step further by providing easy-to-use methods of filling blocks automatically with either a number series, or groups of related labels. In the following sections you'll learn how to use two types of block-filling options.

Using Data, Fill

You use the Data, Fill command to fill a block with numeric values. This command offers a large range of options as seen in Figure 15.9. These commands are suitable for almost any instance needing an incrementing number series, such as a series of interest rates or budget percentages.

FIG. 15.9

The Data Fill dialog box is used to fill blocks with numeric values.

To use the Data, Fill command, follow these steps:

1. Select the block you want to fill.
2. Choose Data, Fill. The Data Fill dialog box appears (see Figure 15.9).
3. Enter the Start, Step (or increment), and Stop values in the appropriate text boxes.
4. If the block spans multiple rows and multiple columns, choose Column to begin filling the block in the first column, then the second column, and so on; choose Row to fill the first row, then the second row, and so on.
5. In the Series field, choose the type of fill. Table 15.2 summarizes the fill options.
6. Choose OK to confirm the dialog box and fill the block.

Table 15.2 Data Fill Types

Series	Type of Fill
Linear	Step value is added to start value.
Growth	Step value is used as a multiplier.
Power	Step value is used as an exponent.
Year	Step value is in years and is added to start value.
Month	Step value is in months and is added to start value.
Week	Step value is in weeks and is added to start value.
Weekday	Step value is in days with weekend days skipped and is added to start value.
Day	Step value is in days and is added to start value.
Hour	Step value is in hours and is added to start value.
Minute	Step value is in minutes and is added to start value.
Second	Step value is in seconds and is added to start value.

By default, Corel Quattro Pro uses 0 for the start number, 1 for the step (or increment), and 8191 as the stop number. Be sure to adjust these values to fit your needs. When filling a block, Corel Quattro Pro stops entering additional values when the specified block is filled or the stop number is reached.

TIP If you specify a start value larger than the stop value, no values enter the block.

If you want to fill a block with a sequence of dates, it's important to understand how Corel Quattro Pro enters date values. Corel Quattro Pro uses *date serial numbers* to determine dates. Date serial numbers increment by one for each day, starting with 1 for December 31, 1899.

N O T E For compatibility with Lotus 1-2-3 and Microsoft Excel, Corel Quattro Pro uses the value 61 for March 1, 1900, even though the year 1900 was not a leap year. Dates prior to March 1, 1900, are incorrect in Lotus 1-2-3 and Microsoft Excel. Dates prior to January 1, 1900, and dates after December 31, 2099, are not allowed in Lotus 1-2-3. Dates prior to January 1, 1900, and dates after December 31, 2078 are not allowed in Excel. Corel Quattro Pro correctly determines dates in the entire range of January 1, 1600, through December 31, 3199, using negative date serial numbers for dates prior to December 30, 1899. ■

Because date serial numbers increment by one each day, the default S̲top value is too small for most useful dates. For example, you cannot use D̲ata, F̲ill to enter a date such as June 26, 1997, which has a serial number of 35607, unless you remember to increase the stop value to a number at least as high as the serial number of the ending date you want.

Using QuickFill

 Another Corel Quattro Pro option for filling blocks is *QuickFill*. Unlike D̲ata, F̲ill, QuickFill can fill a selected block with a set of labels, such as month names or store locations. QuickFill also differs from the D̲ata, F̲ill command in another important way— you must activate the QuickFill button using the mouse, because there is no QuickFill menu command.

 TIP You can also use QuickFill to name a series of pages. Right-click an empty cell, select QuickFill, select a S̲eries Name, and choose T̲abs.

The QuickFill option functions two different ways, depending on whether the block you select already has sample values. If the block has sample values, these values are used as a *seed value*, or pattern for filling the block. If the block is empty, QuickFill presents a list of predefined fill series for selection.

Filling a Block Using Sample Values   To fill a block based on sample values you enter in the block (such as Jan, Feb, Mar, or Qtr 1, Qtr 2, Qtr 3), follow these steps:

1. First enter some sample values in the top-left corner of the block that you want to fill. If the first sample value is enough to define the series, you only have to enter one value. If you want to use an increment other than 1, you must enter at least two sample values.

2. Select the block you want to fill.

3. Click the QuickFill button.

Filling a Block Using a QuickFill Series   You can also use a predefined series to fill a block. To fill a block based on a predefined series, follow these steps:

1. Select the block you want to fill. The block should not contain any sample values.

2. Click the QuickFill button to display the QuickFill dialog box (see Figure 15.10).

3. Select the series you want in the S̲eries Name list box.

4. If necessary, select Co̲lumns, R̲ows, or T̲abs.

5. Press Enter or click OK.

FIG. 15.10
The QuickFill dialog box is
used to fill a block based on
a predefined series.

TROUBLESHOOTING

The Tabs option doesn't appear in the QuickFill dialog box, preventing the use of QuickFill to name page tabs. The Tabs option will only appear if an empty, single-cell block is selected when you click the QuickFill button. The Columns and Rows options only appear if an empty, single-cell block, or an empty, multiple-row and multiple-column block is selected. If the selected block consists of multiple cells in a single row or a single column, none of these options are available.

Creating a Custom QuickFill Series   Corel Quattro Pro includes several predefined QuickFill series for entering months, quarters, and days, but this limited set of options is really only a sampling of what you can do with QuickFill. This tool can really make the task of creating a Corel Quattro Pro notebook much easier by automatically entering any series of labels you want.

Imagine, for example, that you work for a company with 20 stores, and that you're often asked to create new analyses of sales data, advertising costs, or any other factors that affect your business' bottom line. Each time you create a new notebook, you have to enter each of the stores' names, the sales representatives' names, or even the region names associated with store groupings. Sounds like quite a job, doesn't it? Fortunately, by creating a custom QuickFill series, you can do the job once and, except for occasional modifications, simply use QuickFill to automatically enter the same series into any new notebooks.

 Create custom QuickFill series for data you must enter often.

Creating a custom QuickFill series is rather easy. You can enter the series as a set of labels in a dialog box, or you can even use a series of labels you've already entered in a notebook block. Modifying or deleting an existing series is just as easy. To create, modify, or delete a custom series, follow these steps:

1. Select Data, Define Fill Series to display the Define Fill Series dialog box (see Figure 15.11).

FIG. 15.11

The QuickFill Define Fill Series dialog box makes using existing series to fill blocks easy.

2. Select the Create, Modify, or Delete button to display the Create Series, Modify Series, or Delete Series dialog box. Figure 15.12 shows the Create Series dialog box.

FIG. 15.12

Use the QuickFill Create Series dialog box to easily create a customized series for filling blocks.

3. Use the options in the Create Series, Modify Series, or Delete Series dialog boxes to customize the fill series to suit your needs. For example, to create a custom series that automatically fills in the locations of your company's stores, enter each location in the Series Elements text box and then select Add. Continue until you have completed the series. Be sure to use a descriptive Series Name.

4. Select OK to confirm the dialog box.

N O T E If the cell selector is selecting an empty block, you can also access the Create Series, Modify Series, or Delete Series dialog boxes using the Create, Modify, or Delete buttons in the QuickFill dialog box. If you use this method to access the Create Series, Modify Series, or Delete Series dialog boxes, you can immediately use the new or modified series when you return to the QuickFill dialog box following Step 4. ■

To use an existing series of labels in the Create Series or Modify Series dialog boxes, select Extract in Step 3 and then specify the notebook block containing the labels you want to save as a custom QuickFill series. For example, if you already have the set of store names in cells A1..A20, select Data, Define Fill Series, Create, Extract and specify **A1..A20** as the block to use. Complete Steps 3 and 4.

Use custom QuickFill series to make repetitive notebooks entries, even if the fill series is not an incrementing series. When you create a custom QuickFill series, it will then be available for use in all of your Corel Quattro Pro notebooks. You don't have to save the custom QuickFill series—it is automatically saved for you.

Using Functions

As you learned in the last chapter, the real power of a Corel Quattro Pro notebook is its ability to perform calculations. You can create many different types of formulas, and perform many different types of calculations quickly and easily in Corel Quattro Pro. Using the built-in functions can make your formulas even more powerful, permitting you to perform calculations far too complex to build using simple arithmetic operators.

Understanding Functions

When electronic spreadsheets were first introduced in the late 1970s, the programs included a few limited built-in functions. The calculations you could perform using these functions were fairly simple, but they provided a glimpse of what might be possible. When Lotus 1-2-3 made spreadsheets a standard business tool in the early 1980s, the program offered nearly 100 different functions covering a wide range of calculations. Still, there were gaps in what the built-in functions offered, and PC users with specialized needs often had to resort to complex contortions, or had to turn to third-party developers to solve demanding equations.

Corel Quattro Pro sets a new standard in spreadsheets by offering nearly 500 built-in functions, covering the bases with specialized functions for many unique types of calculations. Some of these functions perform sophisticated financial calculations; others conduct engineering calculations, execute various statistical analyses, or analyze database records. The following sections briefly summarize the function categories included in Corel Quattro Pro.

 See the @Function Reference on the Contents tab of online help for a complete listing of the functions.

For example, you can use the @AMPMTI function to calculate the interest portion of the *n*th periodic payment of an amortized loan. You can use the @PRICEDISC function to calculate the price per $100 face value of a security that pays periodic interest.

Understanding Database Functions   You use database functions to perform statistical calculations and queries on a database. Each database function has an equivalent statistical function. Database functions differ from statistical functions in a very important way—database functions calculate values that meet criteria you specify, while statistical functions calculate all values in a block.

For example, @DAVG finds the average value in a field in a database, but only for records that meet specified criteria. @AVG finds the average value of all cells in a block.

Understanding Date and Time Functions   You use the date and time functions to perform date and time arithmetic. These functions enable you to easily calculate differences between dates or times, sort by dates or times, and compare a range of dates or times. Date and time arithmetic uses date/time serial numbers.

For example, to convert a date into a date/time serial number, you can use the @DATE function to convert a date given as a year, month, and day into a date/time serial number. You can then use this serial number in additional calculations. To find the number of business days between two dates, you can use the @BDAYS function.

 See Date and Time functions in the online @Function Reference for all date and time functions.

Understanding Engineering Functions   You use the engineering functions to perform calculations for solving complex engineering problems, perform binary, octal, decimal, and hexadecimal number manipulations, work with imaginary numbers, convert between numbering systems, and test results. The engineering functions return modified Bessel functions, join, compare, and shift values at the bit level, convert or modify a complex number (a number whose square is a negative real number), and return error functions or test the relationship of two numeric values.

For example, you use the @BASE function to convert a decimal number to another numbering system. You can use the @CONVERT function to convert between different systems of measurement, such as from miles to kilometers.

Understanding Financial Functions   You use the financial functions to discount cash flow, calculate depreciation, and analyze the return on an investment. These functions greatly ease the burden of complex financial and accounting calculations. They also provide tools allowing the average user to perform less complex, everyday financial computations.

 Chapter 17, "Analyzing Data," provides a look at some additional analysis tools that are a part of Corel Quattro Pro.

Understanding Logical Functions   You use the logical functions to add standard true/ false logic to the spreadsheet. The logical functions evaluate Boolean expressions, which are either true (returning a value of 1) or false (returning a value of 0). These functions can help to prevent errors that may occur if a cell used in a formula contains the wrong data, to test for the values ERR (error) or NA (not available), or to determine whether a specified file exists. These functions are important for decision-making when conditions elsewhere in the spreadsheet lead to different answers in the function results. Logical functions also control the operations of advanced macro programs.

For example, you can use the @IF function to select between different results based upon evaluation of an expression, such as including a value only if it is positive.

Understanding Mathematical Functions   You use the mathematical functions, which include transcendental (logarithmic) and trigonometric operations, to perform a variety of standard arithmetic operations, such as adding and rounding values or calculating square roots.

For example, you can use the @CEILING function to round a number up to the nearest integer, @RANDBETWEEN to generate a random number between two values, and @LN to calculate the natural logarithm of a number.

 See Mathematical Functions in the online @Function Reference for all mathematical functions.

Understanding Miscellaneous Functions   You use the miscellaneous functions to determine information about notebooks and cell attributes, current command settings, system memory, object properties, and Corel Quattro Pro's version number. You also use the miscellaneous functions to perform table lookups.

For example, you can use @CELL to determine whether a given cell is blank, contains a label, or contains a numeric value. You can determine the value contained in a given cell in a block using @INDEX. A single @ARRAY function can perform a series of calculations, producing many different results from a single formula.

Understanding Statistical Functions   You use the statistical functions to perform all standard statistical calculations on your notebook data, such as aggregation, counting, and analysis operations on a group of values. The statistical functions are separated into two subcategories, descriptive and inferential.

For example, you can use the @AVG function to determine the average of all numeric values in a list, and @COUNT to determine the number of nonblank cells in the list. You can use @CONFIDENCE to compute the confidence interval around the mean for a given sample size, using the normal distribution function.

 See Statistical Functions in the online @Function Reference for all statistical functions.

Understanding String Functions   You use the string functions to manipulate text. You can use string functions to repeat text characters, convert letters in a string to upper- or lowercase, change strings to numbers, and change numbers to strings. You also can use string functions to locate, extract, or replace characters. String functions can be important also when you need to convert data for use by other programs. They are invaluable when you need to read or write directly to ASCII text files.

@PROPER, for example, converts to uppercase the first letter of each word in a string and converts the rest to lowercase. @REPLACE changes specified characters in a string to different characters. @STRING changes a numeric value into a string, making it possible to use the value in a string formula.

Using the Formula Composer

If these short descriptions of Corel Quattro Pro's function categories have whetted your interest in using functions, you're probably wondering how you can ever build your own function formulas, especially with nearly 500 functions to select from. After all, a comprehensive description of each function, especially one with examples, would fill a complete book all by itself. How can you possibly get started, and how can you use the functions effectively in your formulas?

TIP The Formula Composer makes entering complex functions much easier.

One answer to learning and using Corel Quattro Pro's many functions is to turn to the *Formula Composer*—a calculator-like tool that helps you include functions in your formulas. Using this tool, you build formulas one step at a time, adding functions and supplying arguments as necessary. As you build a formula, you can even see an outline of the formula, so you can make certain you're creating exactly what you need to solve a problem.

To use the Formula Composer, select Tools, Formula Composer (Ctrl+F2) or click the Formula Composer button on the toolbar. This displays the Formula Composer dialog box (see Figure 15.13). You use this dialog box to build your formula with the Formula Composer.

The Formula Composer functions like a sophisticated scientific calculator, but has capabilities far beyond any calculator you can buy. If you want to use one of the Corel Quattro Pro built-in functions, simply click the @ button in the Formula Composer dialog box toolbar. Select the function you want to use, and the Formula Composer adds it to the formula. When you select a function, the right side of the Formula Composer dialog box describes the selected function as well as any arguments.

FIG. 15.13

Use the Formula Composer
dialog box to more easily
create formulas.

For example, suppose you want to enter a formula in cell A1 that calculates the number of
business days between June 26, 1997 and December 25, 1997. To make your formula
flexible—to allow you to use the same formula to determine the number of business days
between any other two dates—you place the two dates in cells A2 and A3. This enables
you to replace the dates in these two cells and instantly calculate new formula results. To
begin building your formula, follow these steps:

1. Select Tools, Formula Composer (Ctrl+F2) or click the Formula Composer button
   on the toolbar.

2. Click the @ button in the Formula Composer dialog box toolbar.

3. The Functions dialog box will appear. Select Date in the Function Category list box,
   and then BDAYS in the Function list box. As you select a function, the description
   pane at the bottom of the dialog box describes the selected function (see Figure
   15.14).

FIG. 15.14

The Functions dialog box is
where you select the function
to be used.

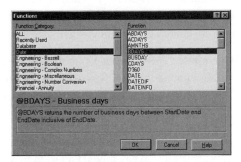

4. Press Enter or click OK to return to the Formula Composer dialog box. The dialog
   box changes to display the function pane, and describes the selected function as
   well as its arguments (see Figure 15.15).

FIG. 15.15
After you select a function, the Formula Composer dialog box displays the function pane where you fill in the required arguments.

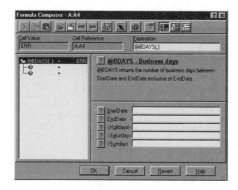

5. Fill in each argument by selecting the argument's text box, and then pointing to the notebook cell containing the argument. When you have entered the minimum required set of arguments, the dialog box displays the results of the calculation (see Figure 15.16). In this case, Holidays, Saturday, and Sunday are optional arguments, and do not require an entry.

FIG. 15.16
After you specify all required arguments, the Formula Composer dialog box displays the result in the Cell Value box.

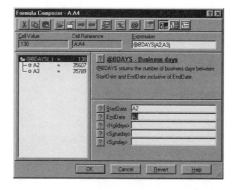

6. Click the OK button to return to the notebook and enter the formula in the cell.

To enter any of the required or optional arguments in Step 5, you can point to the cell containing the argument, or you can type an address or block name. If you want to use another function to specify the value for an argument, click the @ button.

TROUBLESHOOTING

It's often difficult to remember which cells hold each of the function arguments. Enter labels in the notebook to identify the arguments, and then use the Insert, Block Names, Labels command to name the cells. You can then use the block names instead of cell addresses in your formulas, making the formulas much easier to understand.

Functions really unlock the power of Corel Quattro Pro. The brief descriptions provided in these sections on using functions have only touched the surface of how powerful Corel Quattro Pro's set of built-in functions really are.

TIP   For more detailed information on using functions, you can use the Corel Quattro Pro Help, Help Topics, @Functions command.

CHAPTER 16

Changing the Display and Appearance of Data

Corel Quattro Pro provides you with a *WYSIWYG*— What You See Is What You Get—view of your data. If you change the on-screen appearance of a Corel Quattro Pro notebook, those changes will also be reflected in any printed reports you produce. In this chapter you learn to use the commands that control the appearance of data, both on-screen and in printed reports.

Producing clear and concise information from raw data can be as important as calculating correct answers. To make data understandable, you can control the *format*, the *style*, and the *alignment* of data. These commands change only the way data appears, not the value of the data when you customize its format. ◼

Adjust column and row characteristics

You learn how to use column width and row height adjustments to make your Corel Quattro Pro data much easier to understand.

Remove the excess

See how you can remove needless columns, rows, or pages from the notebook without destroying your data.

Lock data on-screen

Make it easy to see exactly which data you're using by keeping important information visible as you scroll to different areas of the notebook.

Change the appearance of data

Apply the available formats to improve the appearance of your data.

Use additional appearance improvements

Further enhance the appearance of your Corel Quattro Pro data using fonts, label alignment options, lines, colors, and shading.

Changing the Display

The Corel Quattro Pro display is extremely flexible, allowing you to select screen preferences. For example, you can zoom in to enlarge the on-screen appearance of a notebook on small screens. You can also control whether screen elements such as the toolbar, the Power Bar, or the Status line are displayed. These options exist for your convenience, but they don't really have much effect on the display of data or reports.

Some other options, such as adjusting the width of each column, or locking rows or columns on-screen as you scroll, directly affect your Corel Quattro Pro notebooks. Column widths, for example, determine whether numbers are displayed properly. Locked titles enable you to scroll the display to different locations in the notebook without losing track of which data should be entered in the individual cells. These options are covered in the following sections.

Adjusting Column Widths and Row Heights

When you start a new notebook, all the columns on each spreadsheet page are set to the default column width of approximately nine characters. All the row heights are set to a default height of 12 points (one-sixth of an inch).

N O T E Column widths are stated in characters, but are only valid for non-proportional (or *fixed-pitch*) fonts. Most Windows fonts are *proportional* fonts, allowing each character to have a different width, which is based on the actual space necessary to display a character. For example, the letter *m* requires more space than the letter *i*. In a proportional font, several *i*s will fit in the space required for a single *m*. ■

If columns are too narrow to display numeric data, asterisks appear rather than the numbers. If columns are too narrow for the length of labels, and the cell to the right contains data, the labels are truncated. If columns are too wide, you may not see all the columns necessary to view the complete data, and you may not be able to print reports on the number of pages you want.

Corel Quattro Pro automatically adjusts row heights to fit different fonts and point sizes, vertical orientation, or word wrap, but you can override the default to create special effects or to add emphasis. You can also adjust row heights in Corel Quattro Pro to make notebook entries easier to understand and more attractive.

Figure 16.1 shows why you must sometimes adjust column widths or row heights. Cells A1 and B4 contain the same number, 1234567890. Both cells are formatted to display the number using the comma numeric format with two decimals. Because column A is set to the default width, asterisks appear in place of the number in cell A1. The width of column B was adjusted to correctly display the number.

This number is too long to fit the default column width, so asterisks are displayed in place of the number

FIG. 16.1
Sometimes you must adjust column widths or row heights.

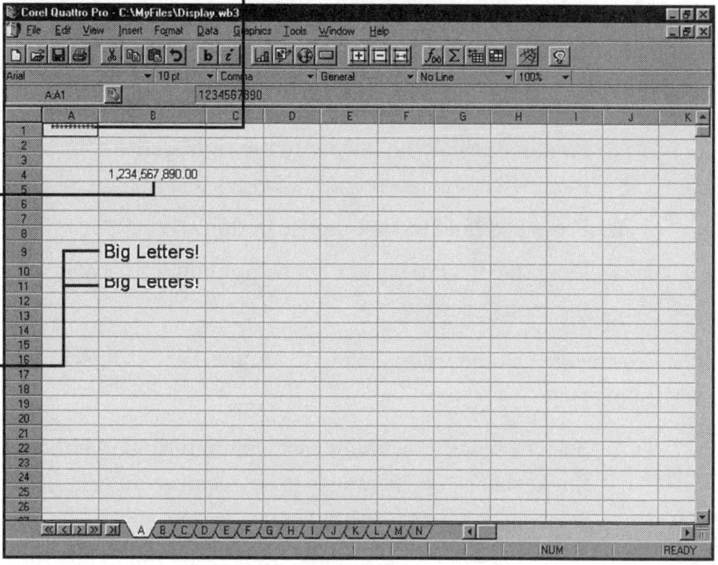

This number is also too long to fit the default column width, but when the column width is adjusted, the number displays correctly

Quattro Pro automatically adjusts row heights so larger font sizes are displayed correctly instead of being cut off

Even though Corel Quattro Pro automatically adjusts row heights to fit different fonts and point sizes, as shown in row 9 of Figure 16.1, you can make manual adjustments, too. In the figure, the height of row 11 was adjusted to show how Corel Quattro Pro cuts off the tops of characters if a row is too short.

Setting Column Widths   Whether a number fits in a cell depends on the column width, the numeric format, the font type, and font size. If a number appears as a series of asterisks, you need to change the column width, numeric format, font type, font size, or some combination of these factors.

TIP Column widths you set manually do not change if you later change the default column width for the page.

You can change the width of a single column or a group of columns. When you are adjusting the column width, Corel Quattro Pro displays a dashed line to indicate the position of the new column border. If you move the right column border to the left of the left border, you hide the column.

There are several methods you can use to set column widths. You can use the Active Block Object Inspector, the Fit button, or drag a column width using the mouse. Each method may be useful, depending on your needs.

To change column widths by dragging with the mouse, follow these steps:

1. If you want to adjust more than one column at a time, select the columns you want to adjust by pointing to the column letter in the notebook frame and clicking the left mouse button (drag the mouse pointer to select adjacent columns). If the columns are not adjacent, hold down the Ctrl key as you select the columns.

2. Point to the column border to the right of the column letter (in the spreadsheet frame). The mouse pointer changes to a horizontal double arrow.

3. Press and hold the left mouse button.

4. Drag the column border left or right until the column is the width you want. Release the mouse button.

To change column widths using the Active Block Object Inspector, perform the following steps:

1. Select a block containing each column whose width you want to adjust. You can use the keyboard or the mouse to select adjacent columns, but you can only select non-adjacent columns using the mouse.

2. Press the right mouse button to activate the Active Block QuickMenu, and then select Block Properties to display the Active Block Object Inspector dialog box. You can also press F12 to activate the Active Block Object Inspector dialog box.

3. Select the Column Width tab.

4. If you want to enter the column width in Inches or Centimeters rather than Characters, choose the appropriate radio button under Unit.

5. If you want to reset the column width, select Reset Width to return the selected columns to the page default column width.

6. If you want to set the column width automatically based on the length of data, select Auto Width. If you select Auto Width, you can specify (in the Extra Characters text box) that the column should be 0 to 40 characters wider than the data.

7. If you want to specify the column width, type the value in the Column Width text box.

8. Click OK to confirm the dialog box.

 You also can click the Fit button on the toolbar to adjust the widths of columns automatically. The width of columns set using the Fit button (or the Auto Width setting in the

Active Block Object Inspector dialog box) depends on the number of rows that are selected when you adjust the width. If you select a single row, the column width adjusts to fit the longest data below the cell selector in the entire column. If you select more than one row, the column width adjusts to fit the cell with the longest data below the cell selector in the same column.

 The Fit button can only be used on contiguous blocks.

Setting the Default Column Width for a Page   If you find yourself setting the column widths for most columns on a page, you can change the default column width for the entire notebook page. To select a new default column width for a page, follow these steps:

1. Point to the page tab and click the right mouse button. This displays the Active Page Properties dialog box.

2. Select the Default Width tab and enter the new default width in Characters, Inches, or Centimeters—depending on which Unit field radio button you choose.

3. Click OK to confirm the dialog box.

Each page in a notebook has its own default column width setting. You set each page individually.

TROUBLESHOOTING

Some columns don't adjust when a new default column width is set for a notebook page.
Column widths you set using the Fit button (or the Auto Width setting) remain at the current setting even when the length of data in the column changes. If you want the column width adjusted to fit new data, you must select the Auto Width setting or the Fit button again.

N O T E   You can also use the Fit-As-You-Go feature that automatically adjusts the column widths as you type data into the spreadsheet. Right-click the Corel Quattro Pro title bar, choose Application Properties, and make certain Fit-As-You-Go is selected on the General tab. ■

Setting Row Heights   You can adjust row heights in Corel Quattro Pro to make notebook entries easier to understand and more attractive. As you change fonts and point sizes, or apply vertical orientation or word wrap, Corel Quattro Pro automatically adjusts row heights to fit. However, you can override the default to create special effects or to add emphasis.

You can set the row height for an individual row or a group of rows at one time. You also can hide rows by setting their height to zero. You can set row heights using the Active Block Object Inspector dialog box, or by dragging the row height using the mouse. Because Corel Quattro Pro automatically adjusts row heights to fit, there is no equivalent to the Fit button for row heights.

To adjust the height of rows by dragging with the mouse, follow these steps:

1. Select the rows you want to adjust. If the rows are not adjacent, hold down the Ctrl key as you select the rows.

2. Point to the row border just below the row number (in the spreadsheet frame). The mouse pointer changes to a vertical double arrow.

3. Press and hold down the left mouse button.

4. Drag the row border up or down until the row is the height you want. Release the mouse button. When you are adjusting the row height, Corel Quattro Pro displays a dashed line to indicate the position of the new row border. If you move the lower row border above the top border, you hide the row.

 To reveal rows and columns once they have been hidden, select the rows or columns that surround the hidden rows or columns, right click, select Block Properties, choose the Reveal/Hide tab, select rows or columns, Reveal, and click OK.

To change the height of rows by using the Active Block Object Inspector dialog box, follow these steps:

1. Select the rows you want to adjust. If the rows are not adjacent, hold down the Ctrl key as you select the rows using the mouse. If you want to adjust the height of adjacent rows, place the cell selector in the first row you want to adjust, hold down the Shift key, and move the cell selector to select each of the rows you want to adjust.

2. Press the right mouse button to activate the Active Block QuickMenu, and select Block Properties to activate the Active Block Object Inspector dialog box. You can also press F12 to activate the Active Block Object Inspector dialog box.

3. Select the Row Height tab.

4. If you want to enter the row height in Inches or Centimeters, select the appropriate radio button under Unit.

5. If you want to reset the row height, choose Reset Height to return the selected rows to automatic.

6. If you want to specify the row height, type the value in the Row Height text box.

7. Press Enter or click OK to confirm the dialog box.

Removing Columns, Rows, or Pages

Sometimes you may want to delete sections from a notebook. Perhaps you made extra copies of some data while you were creating the notebook, or maybe you simply rearranged a notebook and have some unsightly gaps you'd like to eliminate.

Part
III

Ch
16

 TIP   Don't forget to use Edit, Undo immediately if you delete the wrong block in error.

You can remove part or all of a notebook in several ways. Any data that you remove is cleared from the notebook in memory but does not affect the notebook file on disk until you save the notebook file. Edit, Undo can restore the data if you use the command before making any other changes.

Some Corel Quattro Pro commands—such as Edit, Cut; Edit, Clear; or Edit, Clear Values— erase cell contents but leave behind blank cells. In contrast, after you delete a row, column, or page, Corel Quattro Pro deletes the row, column, or notebook page and moves remaining data to fill the gap created by the deletion. Cell addresses in formulas are also updated when you delete a row, column, or page.

To delete a row, column, or page, follow these steps:

1. Select the Edit, Delete command. Corel Quattro Pro displays the Delete Block dialog box (see Figure 16.2).

2. In the Block text box, specify the block you want to delete. You can type the address, select cells, or preselect the block.

3. Select the Columns, Rows, or Pages radio button.

4. Select the Entire or Partial radio button.

5. Click OK to confirm the dialog box and delete the block.

FIG. 16.2

Use the Delete Block dialog box to select the block dimension you want to delete.

N O T E Deleting a column, row, or page does not reduce the number of columns, rows, or pages in the notebook. Corel Quattro Pro replaces the deleted columns, rows, or pages at the end of the page or the notebook, so each page continues to have 256 columns and 8,192 rows, and each notebook has 256 spreadsheet pages. ▪

When you delete an area, Corel Quattro Pro moves data to fill the gap created by the deletion. If you delete a row, data below the deletion moves up on the current page. If you delete a column, data to the right of the deleted column moves to the left. If you delete a page, data on following pages moves forward in the notebook.

Formula references adjust to reflect the new addresses of the data. If you delete rows five and six, for example, the formula @SUM(A1..A10) becomes @SUM(A1..A8). If a formula refers specifically to a deleted cell, however, the formula returns ERR.

If you delete rows, columns, or pages that are part of a named block, the block becomes smaller. If you delete a row, column, or page that contains one of the block borders, the block becomes undefined and any references to the block return ERR.

You don't have to delete an entire row, column, or page. You may want to delete only part of a row, column, or page, and move remaining data to fill the gap. To accomplish this task, you choose the Partial radio button. When you specify Partial as the span, Corel Quattro Pro does not remove data from surrounding rows, columns, or pages.

Inserting Columns, Rows, or Pages

You also can insert rows, columns, or pages anywhere in the notebook. After you insert a row, column, or page, all existing data below, to the right, or on subsequent notebook pages moves to create room for the new data. Cell references in formulas and block names adjust automatically, but explicit cell addresses in macros do not adjust. If you make an insertion in the middle of a block, the block expands to include the new rows, columns, or pages. Formulas referring to that block automatically include the added cells.

N O T E Inserting a column, row, or page does not increase the number of columns, rows, or pages in the notebook. Each page continues to have 256 columns and 8,192 rows, and each notebook has 256 spreadsheet pages. If Corel Quattro Pro cannot delete the columns, rows, or pages at the end of the page or the notebook because data would be lost, an error message is displayed and the insertion fails. ▪

To insert a row, column, or page, perform the following steps:

1. Move the cell selector to the cell where you want to begin inserting.

2. Select the number of rows, columns, or pages you want to insert.

3. Choose the Insert, Block command and choose Rows, Columns, or Pages.

4. To insert a partial row, column, or page, select the Partial radio button.

5. Click OK to confirm the dialog box and make the insertion.

Locking Data On-Screen

Notebook pages often are too large to display at one time. As you move the cell selector to display different areas of the page, data scrolls off the opposite edge of the display. This can make it difficult to understand data, because you can't see the labels describing the data. To prevent titles from scrolling off the screen, you can lock a number of rows and/or columns so they remain on-screen as you move the cell selector.

Before you lock rows or columns to keep them on-screen, you need to position the cell selector to tell Corel Quattro Pro which rows or columns you want to remain visible. If you are locking horizontal titles, place the cell selector in the row below the last row you want locked. If you are locking vertical titles, place the cell selector in the column to the right of the last column you want locked. If you are locking both horizontal and vertical titles, place the cell selector in the row just below and the column just right of the intersection of the rows and columns you want to lock.

Once you have positioned the cell selector properly, select View, Locked Titles to display the Locked Titles dialog box (see Figure 16.3).

FIG. 16.3
Use the Locked Titles dialog box to keep specified rows or columns visible when you move the cell selector.

You can lock the rows above the cell selector by choosing the Horizontal radio button. To lock the columns left of the cell selector, choose the Vertical radio button. You can lock both horizontal and vertical titles by choosing the Both radio button. The Clear radio button unlocks titles.

Figure 16.4 shows a Corel Quattro Pro notebook containing an address database. In this figure, the cell selector was placed in cell B2 before issuing the View, Locked Titles command and choosing Both. The cell selector was then moved to cell H46, the last cell in the database. Column A and row 1 remain visible, enabling you to more easily understand the data, because you can see both the field names (row 1) and the value contained in the LAST_NAME field (column A).

FIG. 16.4
Titles locked on-screen can make data easier to understand.

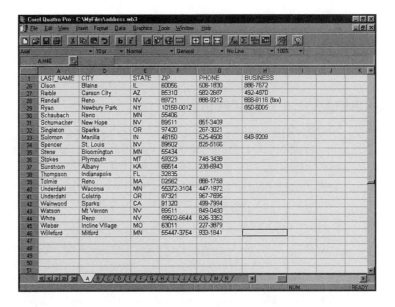

When rows or columns are locked on-screen, you can't move the cell selector directly into the locked rows or columns. Pressing the Home key moves the cell selector to the position below and to the right of the titles rather than to cell A1. You can't use the mouse or the direction keys to move the cell selector into the locked titles, either.

The only way to move the cell selector into the locked titles is to use the F5 (Go To) key, and specify an address in the locked rows or columns. If you do, you'll see an extra copy of the locked rows or columns. Use the direction keys to move at least one screen right and down to clear the duplicate display.

Changing the Appearance of Data

How your data appears in a notebook or in a report really doesn't affect the data, but it can have a major effect on how well people understand the data. Appearance can also make quite a difference in how people perceive your business. A well-prepared financial statement, for example, might not guarantee you that small business loan, but you'd probably feel more comfortable presenting your banker something that looked professional and polished.

A few simple steps can greatly improve the appearance of data. Simply applying the proper numeric format can change 1234567 into $1,234,567.00—changing raw data into a value anyone can quickly understand. In addition to numeric formats, you can use alignment, different fonts, borders, and shading to turn an ordinary report into something that is much more. The following sections show you some of the options you can use to improve the appearance of your Corel Quattro Pro notebooks.

Using Numeric Formats

You can display data in a cell in a variety of different numeric formats. Corel Quattro Pro offers a wide choice of numeric formats that you access through the Active Block Object Inspector dialog box. Most formats apply only to numeric data, although Text format can apply to string formulas, and Hidden format can apply to any type of data.

Formatting changes the appearance but not the value of data. The number 7892, for example, can be displayed as 7,892, $7,892.00, or 789200.0%, as well as many other formats. No matter how Corel Quattro Pro displays the number in a cell, the number remains the same.

To change the numeric format of a cell or block, follow these steps:

1. Select the cell or block.

2. Point to the cell or block, and click the right mouse button to display the Active Block QuickMenu.

3. Select Block Properties to open the Active Block Object Inspector dialog box (see Figure 16.5). You can also press F12 to display this dialog box.

FIG. 16.5

Select a numeric format from the Active Block Object Inspector dialog box.

4. Select the Numeric Format tab. If no numeric format has been assigned, the default General format is checked, as shown in Figure 16.5. Select the desired numeric format.

Part III

Ch 16

5. If you choose Fixed, Scientific, Currency, Comma, or Percent, enter the number of decimal places in the spin control that appears after you choose one of these formats. Corel Quattro Pro suggests a default of 2 decimal places, but you can type another number between 0 and 15.

6. Click OK to confirm the dialog box and apply the format to the highlighted cell or block.

The following sections briefly describe Corel Quattro Pro's numeric format options.

TROUBLESHOOTING

After formatting a block, some cells display asterisks instead of the values. If you apply a numeric format to a cell, the column width must be wide enough to display the cell's data in the format. Otherwise, asterisks display in the cell rather than the formatted value. You may need to adjust the column width to fit the new format.

Fixed Format   You use the Fixed format when you want to display values with a specified, fixed number of decimal points. Corel Quattro Pro displays values with up to 15 decimal places. Negative numbers have a minus sign, and decimal values have a leading zero. No punctuation is used to denote thousands.

Scientific Format   You use the Scientific format to display very large or very small numbers. Such numbers usually have a few significant digits and many zeros.

A number in scientific notation has two parts: a *mantissa* and an *exponent*. The mantissa is a number from 1 to 10 that contains the significant digits. The exponent tells you how many places to move the decimal point to get the actual value of the number.

Quattro Pro displays numbers in Scientific display format in powers of 10, with 0 to 15 decimal places, and an exponent from 308 to +308. If a number has more significant digits than the cell can display using the specified number of decimal places, the displayed value is rounded but the stored value is used in calculations.

Currency Format   Currency format displays values with a currency symbol, such as a dollar sign ($), or the British pound sign (£), and punctuation, depending on the current international settings. If you specify a currency symbol, the column width needs an extra position to display each character in the currency symbol. Values formatted as Currency can have from 0 to 15 decimal places. Thousands are separated by commas, periods, or spaces according to the current international settings. Negative numbers appear in parentheses.

Comma Format   Like the Currency display format, the Comma format displays data with a fixed number of decimal places and thousands punctuation. The thousands separator and the decimal point depend on the current international settings. Negative numbers appear in parentheses, and positive numbers less than 1,000 appear the same as Fixed display format.

If a value has more decimal digits than the cell can display using the specified number of decimal places, the displayed value is rounded but the stored value is used in calculations.

General Format   General format is the default format for all new notebooks. Numbers in General display format have no thousands separators and no trailing zeros to the right of the decimal point. A minus sign precedes negative numbers. If a number contains decimal digits, it contains a decimal point. If a number contains too many digits to the right of the decimal point to display in the current column width, the decimals are rounded in the display. If a number is too large or too small, it appears in Scientific display format.

+/– Format   The +/– format displays numbers as a series of plus signs (+), minus signs (–), or as a period (.). The number of signs equals the integer portion of the value. A positive number appears as a row of plus signs, a negative value appears as a row of minus signs, and a number between 1 and +1 appears as a period.

Percent Format   Percent format is used to display values as percentages with 0 to 15 decimal places. The number appears with its value multiplied by 100, followed by a percent sign (%). The number of decimal places you specify is the number displayed in the percent—not the number of decimal places in the value.

If a value has more decimal digits than the cell can display using the specified number of decimal places, the displayed value is rounded but the stored value is used in calculations.

Date Format   Date formats display date serial numbers as dates rather than numbers. Corel Quattro Pro stores dates as serial numbers starting with January 1, 1600, (which is –109571) and increases the number by one for each whole day. December 31, 1899 is counted as 1. The latest date Corel Quattro Pro can display is December 31, 3199, with a serial number of 474816.

If the number is less than –109571 or greater than 474816, a date format appears as asterisks. Date formats ignore decimal fractions; 34876.55 with a short international date format appears as 6/26. The decimal portion of a date serial number represents the time as a fraction of a 24-hour clock.

Corel Quattro Pro gives you a choice of five different Date display formats. Both Long Date Intl. and Short Date Intl. depend on the current international date format set using the Application Object Inspector dialog box.

Time Format   You use the Time formats to display date serial numbers as times. The decimal portion of a date serial number is a *time fraction*. The time fraction represents a fraction of a 24-hour day. For example, the time fraction for 8 a.m. is .33333…, the time fraction for noon is .5, and the time fraction for 3 p.m. is .675. When you use a Time format, Corel Quattro Pro displays the fraction as a time.

If a date serial number is greater than 1, the time formats ignore the integer portion. Both .5 and 33781.5 display 12:00:00 p.m.

Text Format   You use Text format to display the text of formulas rather than their results. Numbers in cells formatted as Text appear in General format. Unlike long labels that appear in blank cells to the right, formulas formatted as Text are truncated if they are too long to display in the column width. Corel Quattro Pro continues to use the value of formulas when you format them as Text.

Hidden Format   A cell or block formatted as Hidden always appears blank. You use Hidden format for intermediate calculations that you don't want to appear in a final report, or for sensitive formulas you don't want displayed. But the contents of a Hidden cell appear in the input line when you select the cell, so Hidden format offers little security.

User-Defined Format

Corel Quattro Pro enables you to define and apply your own numeric formats. User defined formats can include many different elements. For example, you can include text, the names of days or months, or leading zeros. For more information on creating your own numeric formats, see "Using Numeric Format Codes" in the Corel Quattro Pro help screens for details on the symbols you can use.

Avoiding Apparent Errors   Some formats display a number in rounded form. Even when the displayed number appears rounded, however, Corel Quattro Pro still stores and uses the exact value in calculations. If you format the value 1.5 as Fixed with zero decimal places, Corel Quattro Pro displays the number as 2 in a cell, but uses the actual value of 1.5 in calculations. This can make it seem as though Corel Quattro Pro is making arithmetic errors, such as 2+2=3. In fact, Corel Quattro Pro is correct, because the two values it is adding are 1.5 and 1.5, so the formula is actually 1.5+1.5=3. This apparent error is caused by rounding the display but not rounding the values.

CAUTION

You easily can create apparent rounding errors—especially when you produce cross-tabulated reports. To avoid apparent rounding errors, you need to round the actual value of the numbers used in

---

formulas, not just their appearance or format. To round the values used in a formula, use the @ROUND function to round each value before the value is used in the formula.

Aligning Data

Just as Corel Quattro Pro offers a very broad range of numeric format options, it also provides quite a few choices you can use to align labels and values. By default, labels are aligned to the left side of cells, and values are aligned to the right side of cells. These default alignments are easily changed. You can change alignment for both labels and values.

You can align labels and values to the left side of cells, center them in a cell or across a block, or to the right side of the cell. You can also align them to the top, center, or bottom of the cell. You can orient labels and values horizontally or vertically. Finally, you can wrap text on multiple lines in a single cell.

 TIP You can also change alignment using the Alignment button on the Power Bar.

To change the label alignment for existing labels or values, follow these steps:

1. Select the cell or block.
2. Point to the cell or block, and click the right mouse button to display the Active Block QuickMenu.
3. Select Block Properties to open the Active Block Object Inspector dialog box. You can also press F12 to display this dialog box.
4. Select the Alignment tab in the Active Block Object Inspector dialog box (see Figure 16.6).
5. In the Horizontal Alignment field, choose General to reset the alignment to the page default; or choose Left, Right, Center, or Center Across Block.
6. In the Vertical Alignment field, choose Top, Center, or Bottom.
7. In the Orientation field, choose whether you want horizontal or vertical orientation.
8. Select the Wrap Text check box to wrap labels on multiple lines within a single cell.
9. Click OK to confirm the dialog box and apply the selected alignment options.

Figure 16.7 demonstrates the various horizontal and vertical alignment and orientation options.

FIG. 16.6

Use the Alignment tab of the Active Block Object Inspector dialog box to specify data alignment.

Changing Fonts

Corel Quattro Pro applies the term *font* to the combination of *typeface*, *point size*, and *attributes* used for the characters displayed in your notebooks. A typeface is a type style, such as Arial, Courier New, or Times New Roman. Typefaces are available in a number of point sizes that represent character height. A standard 10 character-per-inch size usually is considered equivalent to a 12-point type size. Typefaces also have different attributes, such as weight (normal or **bold**) and *italic*.

FIG. 16.7

Corel Quattro Pro offers many horizontal and vertical alignment and orientation options.

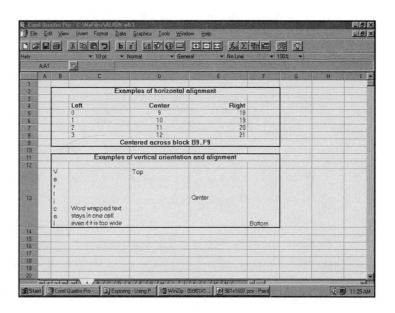

You can use the Font tab in the Active Block Object Inspector dialog box to choose different fonts. You can also use the Font and Font Size sections on the Power Bar to make these two selections, and the Bold and Italics buttons on the toolbar to apply either of these two attributes.

 Several factors determine which font options are available. If you have installed additional fonts on your system, you'll be able to select from a larger list of options. Scaleable fonts, such as TrueType fonts, greatly improve the quality of your reports. Corel includes more than 1,000 additional fonts on the Corel WordPerfect Suite 7 CD-ROM which you can install using the Bonus Application install option.

If you increase font size, Corel Quattro Pro enlarges the row height to fit the selected fonts. Column widths do not adjust automatically, however, so numeric data may not fit in a cell after you change the font, and the data may display as asterisks. Adjust the column widths as needed to display the data correctly. Figure 16.8 shows how several different typefaces, point sizes, and attributes change the appearance of your data (you probably will have a different selection of fonts installed on your system).

Adding Borders and Shading

If you really want to add a professional touch to your notebooks, *borders* and *shading* can do the trick. Borders are lines around a cell or block. Shading is a background tint within a cell or block.

FIG. 16.8
Different fonts change the appearance of data in your notebooks.

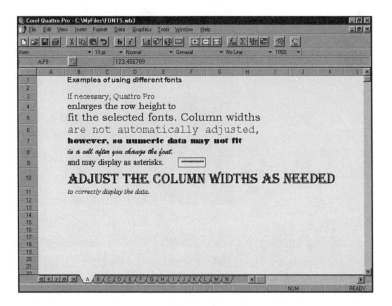

You can use borders to effectively isolate groups of data, making it easy to see all related data. You can also use borders as separators between report sections. Shading is most often used for emphasis, or to make certain that report data cannot be altered without the alterations being immediately apparent.

Adding Borders to Cells or Blocks   You can use the Line Drawing tab in the Active Block Object Inspector dialog box to draw lines above, below, on the sides, and around cells and blocks. You can also use the Underline section of the Power Bar to draw lines at the bottom of cells or blocks. Borders can be single lines, double lines, or thick lines.

To draw borders within or around a cell or block, follow these steps:

1. Select the cell or block.

2. Open the Active Block Object Inspector dialog box by clicking the right mouse button inside the cell or block and selecting Block Properties from the QuickMenu, or by pressing F12 (see Figure 16.9).

3. Select the Line Drawing tab.

4. Select the placement options you want using the Line Segments, All, Outline, and Inside options.

5. Select the Line Types you want.

6. Select the Line Color you want.

7. Click OK to confirm the dialog box and add the selected borders.

FIG. 16.9

Use the Line Drawing options in the Active Block Object Inspector dialog box to add borders to cells or blocks.

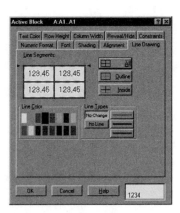

Adding Shading to Cells or Blocks   You can draw attention to cells or blocks by adding shading, a special effect that changes the background from white to a color. When you select shading, you also can select the blend of two colors.

To add shading, follow these steps:

1. Select the cell or block.

2. Open the Active Block Object Inspector dialog box by clicking the right mouse button inside the cell or block and selecting Block Properties from the QuickMenu, or by pressing F12.

3. Select the Shading tab (see Figure 16.10).

4. Select Color 1, Color 2, and the Blend (shading pattern). Corel Quattro Pro enables you to select from 16 colors for both the background and the foreground, and from seven different patterns.

5. Click OK to confirm the dialog box and apply the shading.

Part

III

Ch

16

FIG. 16.10

Use the shading options in the Active Block Object Inspector dialog box to add shading to cells or blocks.

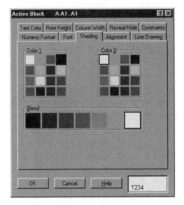

CAUTION

Not all printers can properly print text on a shaded background. Test printing shades on your printer.

Any borders or shading you add to cells or blocks print with the labels and values in a report. It's generally best to use light shading in cells or blocks containing values that must be visible in a printed report, or one that must be photocopied.

 Corel Quattro Pro also has several predefined formats that enable you to quickly set combinations of numeric and text formatting, lines, and shading. Click the Apply a Predefined Format to the Select Block button on the toolbar to view the SpeedFormat dialog box, which enables you to select from the available SpeedFormat options. ●

CHAPTER 17

Analyzing Data

Raw data is the foundation of every business report, but the most effective reports are those that efficiently analyze that data. Corel Quattro Pro provides you with a powerful suite of data analysis tools that enable you to solve complex problems, analyze results, produce cross-tabulation summaries, and work directly with external data. These tools are the subject of this chapter.

The concepts introduced in this chapter show you a glimpse of some of the more complex tools in the Corel Quattro Pro tool bag. Several of the functions provided by some of these tools were formerly only available in specialized and high-cost, stand-alone programs. These programs were not only specialized, but they were complex, usually difficult to use, and often required advanced training before you could use them effectively. As a part of Corel Quattro Pro, these tools are much easier to learn and use. This ease of learning and use hasn't come at the expense of power, though. The data analysis tools in Corel Quattro Pro provide the same level of powerful functions available in those stand-alone programs, but you don't have to pay extra to use them. ■

Find the best answers to problems

Use the Optimizer and Solve For tools to find the answers you need to solve complex and difficult problems.

Analyze data

Use What-If tables to analyze your data.

View complex relationships in data

Use the Data Modeling Desktop to view the complex and often hidden relationships in your data.

Access external database information

Use the Database Desktop to access external data in Paradox and dBASE files.

Using the Optimizer and Solve For

The Optimizer and Solve For tools are powerful utilities that help you create *What-If* scenarios with notebook data. What-If scenarios are a common way to analyze problems, using many different values for a set of variables to find optimal answers. What-If scenarios can be quite time-consuming, especially if done manually, because even problems with a limited number of variables have many possible solutions.

 TIP Use Solve For when you want to find an answer by changing one variable.

The Optimizer tool can analyze problems with up to 200 variables and 100 constraints to determine the best answer. The Solve For tool modifies a single variable to find a specified answer to a problem.

Solving Complex Problems Using the Optimizer

You use the Optimizer to determine a series of possible answers to a specific problem, and to select the answer that best fits your criteria. You can use the Optimizer, for example, to find the production mix that produces the highest profit, to analyze investment portfolios, to determine the least costly shipping routes, and to schedule your staff.

Each Optimizer problem must have one or more *adjustable* cells. Adjustable cells contain the variables that the Optimizer changes in searching for the optimal answer—and can contain numbers only. Adjustable cells might include production quantities, numbers of employees, or capital invested in a project.

Constraints are conditions that serve as problem limits, such as the range of acceptable values. Constraints are expressed as logical formulas that evaluate to true or false, and all constraints must be met before an answer is considered acceptable. Constraints might include limits on production levels, a requirement to produce a profit, or an obligation that at least one employee be on duty.

A solution cell contains the formula that defines the problem, and is optional. If you do not include a solution cell, the Optimizer finds answers that meet all the defined constraints. Solution cells might include formulas that calculate profits, overall costs, or the amount earned from different activities.

Using a Production Scheduling Notebook   Figure 17.1 shows a sample notebook that represents the costs involved in producing three different products. In this example, it is assumed that the factory can produce 50,000 total parts per month and that the production can be divided among the three parts in the most profitable manner.

FIG. 17.1

A notebook for computing optimal product mix.

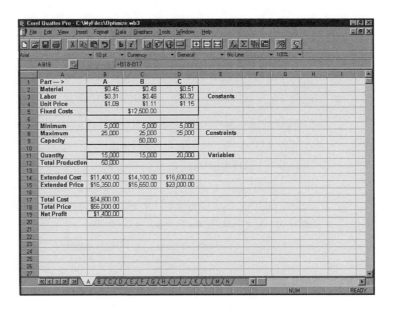

Part

III

Ch

17

 TIP Optimizer will find a solution more quickly if the initial values in the adjustable cells are a reasonable solution to the problem.

Several factors affect the final profit. In Figure 17.1, the production manager has scheduled the production run at 15,000 each for Parts A and B, and 20,000 of Part C. The net profit with this mix is $1,400. Of course, it would be possible to try other sets of values for each product's production quantity. Because each of the three values can vary between 5,000 and 25,000, however, the number of possibilities would be enormous.

CAUTION

Don't use logical (or Boolean) functions in Optimizer problems; they can make a solution very difficult or impossible to find.

To use the Optimizer to find a better solution, follow these steps:

1. Select Tools, Numeric Tools, Optimizer to display the Optimizer dialog box.

2. To make the production quantities of the three parts adjustable in the notebook, enter the cell addresses in the Variable Cells text box. In this example, you enter **B11..D11**.

   Next, define the constraints that the Optimizer must satisfy in solving the problem.

3. Select Add to display the Add Constraints dialog box.

The quantities of the parts (cells B11..D11) must be equal to or greater than the minimum quantity shown in cells B7..D7.

4. Enter **B11..D11** in the Cell text box, select the **>=** (greater than or equal to) radio button in the Operator group box and enter **B7..D7** in the Constant text box.

5. Select Add Another Constraint to enter additional constraints.

The quantities of the parts (cells B11..D11) must be equal to or less than the maximum quantity shown in cells B8..D8.

6. Enter **B11..D11** in the Cell text box, select the **<=** (less than or equal to) radio button in the Operator group box and enter **B8..D8** in the Constant text box.

7. Select Add Another Constraint to enter the last constraint. Cell B12 (total production) must be less than or equal to the value in C9 (capacity).

8. Select OK when all constraints have been entered.

9. Select the Solution Cell text box in the Optimizer dialog box and enter **B19**, the address of the formula cell. The dialog box should now look like Figure 17.2.

10. Select Solve to instruct the Optimizer to calculate the solution. Figure 17.3 shows the result in the production mix example.

FIG. 17.2
The Optimizer dialog box
shows the completed entries.

The Optimizer found a much different solution than the one proposed by the production manager. After redistributing production quantities, the total monthly profit jumped from $1,400 to $3,000. Although this example did not take all possible factors into account, it clearly demonstrates the value of applying the Optimizer to a What-If scenario.

TROUBLESHOOTING

Optimizer is unable to find an optimal solution to a complex problem, or sometimes produces different results when solving the same problem a second time. Try to supply initial values for the variables that you feel will be somewhat close to their final values. Optimizer usually has better success when it can start with a reasonable solution.

I can't tell whether the Optimizer's solution is the best solution to my problem. Use the Tools, Numeric Tools, Optimizer, Options, Reporting command to create an answer report. This report shows the values Optimizer used to find its solution.

FIG. 17.3

The notebook shows the optimal solution for the product mix example, as determined by the Optimizer.

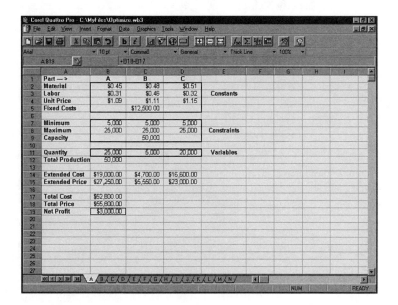

Solving for a Known Answer Using Solve For

Sometimes you know the answer you want, but don't quite know how to get there. The Solve For tool is a Corel Quattro Pro analysis utility that you use to find the value of a variable when you are seeking a specific goal. Rather than calculating an optimum answer by adjusting a block of variables, the Solve For tool adjusts a single variable to produce an answer you specify.

For example, suppose you know you can afford $325 as a monthly payment on an automobile, but don't know how large a loan you can receive for such a payment. The Solve For tool makes it easy to make this type of reverse calculation, where you already know the answer, but don't know the key to finding the answer.

To use Solve For to find the loan amount, follow these steps:

1. Create a Corel Quattro Pro notebook that uses the @PMT function to calculate the loan payment on a loan. For this example, enter a loan amount of **$10,000** in cell

C2, **9%** interest in cell C3, a term of **60** months in cell C4, and the formula, **@PMT(C2,C3/12,C4)** in cell C6.

2. Select <u>T</u>ools, <u>N</u>umeric Tools, <u>S</u>olve For.

3. Specify **C6** in the <u>F</u>ormula Cell text box. This is the cell that contains the formula whose value you want to specify.

4. Specify **325** in the <u>T</u>arget Value text box. This is the value you want to achieve in the goal cell.

5. Specify **C2** as the <u>V</u>ariable Cell, the cell whose value Solve For will adjust. Your screen should now appear similar to Figure 17.4 (in this figure, cells were formatted to display numbers correctly).

6. Select OK to execute the command and return to the notebook. Figure 17.5 shows the notebook with the solution.

FIG. 17.4

The Solve For dialog box is completed and ready to find the solution.

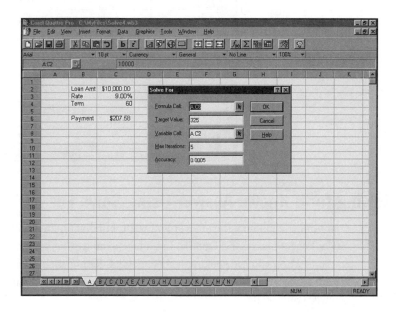

Your $325 monthly budget allows for payments on a loan of $15,656.35. Although you could probably find an answer close to this by trying several different values in cell C2, using Solve For makes the process both simple and fast.

T I P Save the notebook before you use Solve For so you can easily revert to the original values if necessary.

When you use Solve For, the adjustable value is permanently changed in the notebook. You can return to the previous value if you immediately select <u>E</u>dit, <u>U</u>ndo.

FIG. 17.5
The solved problem shows the answer you seek.

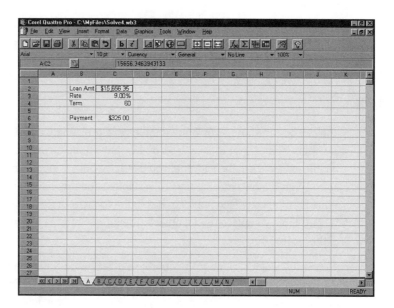

Using What-If Tables

In most notebook models, the variables your formulas use are known quantities. What-If tables enable you to work with variables whose values are unknown. Models for financial projections often fall into this category. For example, next year's cash flow projection may depend on prevailing interest rates or other variable costs you cannot predict exactly.

With the Tools, Numeric Tools, What If commands, you can create tables that show the results of changing one variable in a problem or the combined effect of changing two variables simultaneously. Another function of the Tools, Numeric Tools, What-If commands is to create *cross-tabulation tables*. A cross-tabulation table provides summary information categorized by unique information in two fields, such as the total amount of sales each sales representative makes to each customer.

Understanding What-If Tables

A *What-If table* is an on-screen view of information in a column format with the field names at the top. A *variable* is a formula component whose value can change. An *input cell* is a notebook cell used by Corel Quattro Pro for temporary storage during calculation of a What-If table. One input cell is required for each variable in the What-If table formula. The cell addresses of the formula variables are the same as the input cells. The formulas used in What-If tables can contain values, strings, cell addresses, and functions, but you should not use logical formulas because this type of formula always evaluates to 0 or 1, which is usually meaningless in a What-If table.

TIP Use One Free Variable What-If tables when you need to see the results from more than one formula.

You can build two types of What-If tables in Corel Quattro Pro. They differ in the number of variables, and the number of formulas that can be included. A One Free Variable What-If table can contain one variable, and can have one or more formulas. A Two Free Variables What-If table can contain two variables, but only one formula. In a One Free Variable What-If table, you place the formulas in the top row of the table. In a Two Free Variables What-If table you place the formula at the intersection of the top row and the left column of the table.

A common use for a One Free Variable What-If table would be to calculate both the interest and principal portions of each payment on a loan. A Two Free Variables What-If table might be used to calculate monthly payments on a given loan amount at different combinations of interest rates and terms.

Figure 17.6 shows a typical Two Free Variables What-If table. This table calculates monthly payments on a given loan amount at different combinations of interest rates and terms.

FIG. 17.6

The completed Two Free Variables What-If table of loan payment amounts.

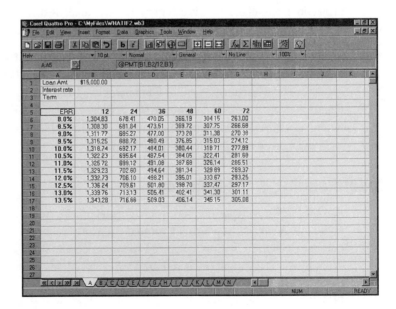

To create a similar What-If table, follow these steps:

1. Enter the loan amount of **$15,000.00** in cell B1.

2. For documentation purposes, place identifying labels in column A. In this case, enter **Loan Amt** in A1, **Interest rate** in A2, and **Term** in A3.

3. Enter the formula **@PMT(B1,B2/12,B3)** in cell A5. The formula will show ERR because it refers to blank cells, but Corel Quattro Pro will correctly calculate the What-If table.

4. Enter the interest rates in A6..A17. The fastest method of entering these rates is to enter **8%** in A6, **8.5%** in A7, select A6..A17, and click the SpeedFill button. (To improve the appearance of the table, format A6..A17 as Percent, 1 decimal.)

5. Enter the loan terms in B5..G5. Once again, you can use SpeedFill.

6. Select the table block A5..G17.

7. Select Tools, Numeric Tools, What-if.

8. Select Two free variables.

9. Enter **B2** as the Column input cell and enter **B3** as Row input cell.

10. Select Generate to calculate the What-If table values.

11. Click Close to confirm the dialog box and return to the notebook.

TROUBLESHOOTING

What-If tables don't display new values when the formula variables are changed. What-If tables don't recalculate when values change because the tables don't contain formulas. Select Tools, Numeric Tools, What-if, Generate to recalculate the What-If table values.

 You can also use QuickTasks to perform several types of analysis in your Corel Quattro Pro notebooks. See Chapter 33, "Integrating Your Work with QuickTasks," for more information.

Understanding Crosstabs

Crosstabs (or cross-tabulation tables) are tables that summarize the values in a database. For example, an address list showing customers in many different states might include information you could use to determine where you get most of your business, and therefore, where you should plan to spend your advertising dollars. You might also use a crosstab to see a sales summary by salesperson for each product line. Corel Quattro Pro can even generate a graph to quickly display the results of the analysis.

Part
III

Ch
17

Use crosstabs to evaluate database information.

The structure of a What-If table block for a cross-tabulation analysis is similar to the structure for a What-If analysis. If you are analyzing the effects of one variable, the upper-left cell may be empty, the top row contains the formula(s) that are to be evaluated, and the left column contains the sample values. If you are analyzing the effects of two variables, you place the formula in the upper-left cell of the table, and the two sets of sample values in the top row and left column of the table. In most cases, the formulas contain one or more database functions.

In addition, you must create one or two input cells, depending on the number of variables in the crosstab. For a crosstab analysis, you must place the input cells directly below cells that contain the corresponding database field names.

You also use the Tools, Numeric Tools, What-if command to create a cross-tabulation table. The sample values in the left column, or in the left column and top row are used to select the values displayed in the crosstab. The sample values for a cross-tabulation analysis are the values or labels that you can use as *criteria* for the analysis.

 If your data changes, remember to use the Tools, Numeric Tools, What-if command to recalculate the results.

After the What-If table has been calculated, each cell in the results block contains the result of the formulas. The formulas have been applied to those database records that meet the crosstab criteria.

Figure 17.7 demonstrates a crosstab analysis of a sales database. In this case, the crosstab is analyzing sales totals for each product line broken down by salesperson. The @DSUM database function is used to perform the analysis. Figure 17.8 shows how Corel Quattro Pro can quickly create a graphical representation of the crosstab analysis.

You use nearly the same steps to create a crosstab with the Tools, Numeric Tools, What-if command as you do to create a What-If table. Notice the similarities between the What-If table in Figure 17.6 and the crosstab in Figure 17.7. In both tables, the formulas are evaluated based on the values of the variables. The primary difference between the two types of tables is the data source. A What-If table generates new data, while a crosstab evaluates existing database data.

FIG. 17.7
A cross-tabulation displays an analysis of data.

The crosstab analysis of the sales database

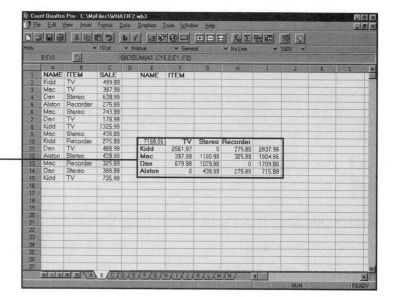

FIG. 17.8
Corel Quattro Pro displays a graph of the cross-tabulation analysis.

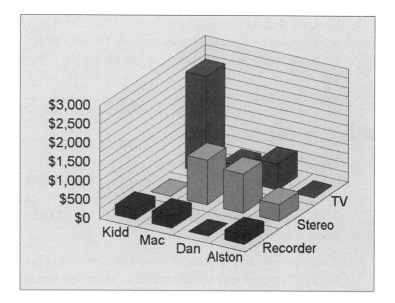

Using the Data Modeling Desktop

By now you can see that crosstabs can be a very effective data analysis tool. A crosstab can often display data relationships you might not otherwise be able to grasp quickly.

Unfortunately, creating a crosstab takes some planning and a lot of work. Not only that, but crosstabs created with the Tools, Numeric Tools, What-if command aren't too flexible—once you create a crosstab, it's difficult to change so you can see different data relationships.

Corel Quattro Pro includes another very powerful tool, the Data Modeling Desktop, which is a master at the art of creating crosstab data analyses. This tool is also much more flexible, and it's fun to use, too.

 T I P   Use the Data Modeling Desktop when you want more flexibility in your crosstabs.

Understanding the Data Modeling Desktop

Up until now, whenever you've created a crosstab, the finished crosstab was static and unchanging. You determined the data relationships you wanted to view, and created a crosstab displaying that view. If you wanted to see a different view, you had to go back to the beginning and start over.

The Data Modeling Desktop provides a much different approach to crosstab generation. Instead of a static and unchanging crosstab, the Data Modeling Desktop creates a *dynamic crosstab*—a crosstab you can quickly modify to display additional data relationships.

 T I P   Don't forget that you can use the Data Modeling Desktop to analyze data from an external database file, too.

The Corel Quattro Pro Data Modeling Desktop is quite similar to Lotus Improv and Excel Pivot Tables, but is easier to use because the Data Modeling Desktop is an integrated part of Corel Quattro Pro. Creating a data model for use in the Data Modeling Desktop is easy because you can use data already contained in a Corel Quattro Pro notebook or from an external database file.

When you first use a dynamic crosstab tool such as the Data Modeling Desktop, you may find that the appearance is quite similar to a standard spreadsheet, such as Corel Quattro Pro. You'll see the familiar row and column layout, but you'll also see some differences. Rows and columns aren't identified by numbers and letters, and individual cells don't contain formulas. Not only that, but there may be several rows of labels at the top of the Data Modeling Desktop workspace, or several columns of labels along the left side of the workspace. What does this all mean?

The Data Modeling Desktop analyzes data by using certain data sets as row or column labels, and a single numerical data set as the data being analyzed. The labels are used as selection criteria, to determine which values to include at the intersections of the labels. For example, if your database contained sales information, you might place the names of the salespeople as labels along the left side of the workspace, and items along the top. The intersection of the labels "John" and "Computers" would show the total of all computers sold by John.

Simple crosstabs such as the previous example really don't show the true power of the Data Modeling Desktop. Adding even one additional piece of data to the picture, though, really complicates matters. Suppose you decided to add time period data to the crosstab. You track sales by date, so you'd like to analyze how well each salesperson did each month, but you want to know how well they did in each product line, too. Now your crosstab is considerably more complicated, and you've only scratched the surface. Imagine that you'd rather change the focus and see how well each product line did each month, rather than each salesperson. The Data Modeling Desktop enables you to quickly make such changes in focus, so you can find the hidden relationships in your data.

Part

III

Ch

17

Creating a Dynamic Crosstab

To analyze data using the Data Modeling Desktop, you must organize the data in a fashion Data Modeling Desktop can use—using a layout identical to a typical Corel Quattro Pro notebook database. Data must be in tabular format, with each record in a single row, and field names in the top row.

N O T E The Data Modeling Desktop is not automatically installed along with Corel Quattro Pro. You must use the custom install and select Data Modeling Desktop to install this component. ▓

To send data you want to analyze to the Data Modeling Desktop, follow these steps:

1. Select the notebook database block—the block containing the data you want to analyze.

 2. Choose the Data, Data Modeling Desktop command or click the Create Dynamic Crosstab Reports button (on the Data Modeling toolbar) to open the Send Data to Data Modeling Desktop dialog box (see Figure 17.9).

3. Press Enter or click OK to display the Data Modeling Desktop window. If necessary, maximize the Data Modeling Desktop window so that you have a larger work area. Your screen should now be similar to Figure 17.10.

When you first start the Data Modeling Desktop, the screen looks similar to Figure 17.10. Several screen elements are similar to Corel Quattro Pro. The title bar shows the program title and the name of the current model. The menu bar has three familiar menus—File,

Edit, and Help—as well as four new menus—Build, Gadget, Font, and Preferences. The
third line has the Data Modeling Desktop toolbar. Below the toolbar is the Report Data
Area, which has three parts. The Top Label Bar Area and the Side Label Bar Area are the
areas where you place the field names of the data categories you want to tabulate. The
Report Data Area is the area where you place the data to summarize. The Source Window
holds the data you are transferring from Corel Quattro Pro.

FIG. 17.9
Use the Send Data to Data
Modeling Desktop dialog box
to specify the data to
analyze.

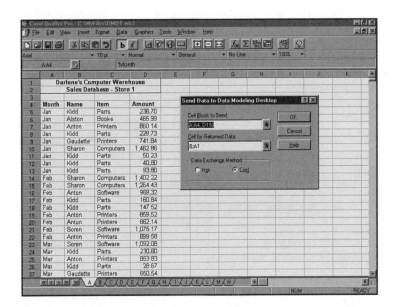

FIG. 17.10
The Data Modeling Desktop
Window.

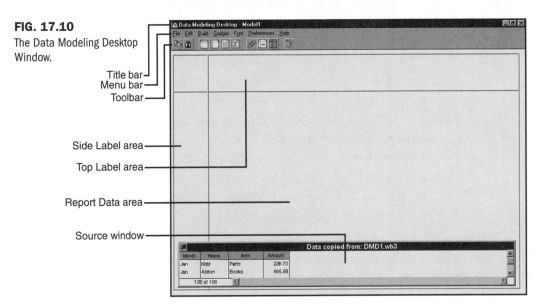

Adding Data to the Report The Side Label Bar and Top Label Bar areas on the Data Modeling Desktop hold the categories of data you want to analyze. Usually, the data categories you add to the Side Label Bar or Top Label Bar areas contain labels or dates, such as a month, item, or sales representative's name. The Report Data Area holds the summary data. In this case you want to summarize the sales for each month, showing which sales representatives sold which items. The data categories you add to the Report Data Area should contain numeric data that can be summarized mathematically, such as the sales totals.

 TIP Always add text data to the Top or Side Label areas, and numeric data to the Report Data Area.

To begin building the report, follow these steps:

1. Add the first field to the Side Label Bar by dragging the field to the Side Label Bar area.

   In this case, select the *Month* field, hold down the left mouse button, and drag it to the Side Label Bar area.

2. Select the next field you want to add and drag the field to the appropriate area.

   In this case, select the *Item* field and copy it to the top label area by dragging the field to the Top Label Bar area.

3. Select any other fields you want to add to the label bar areas and copy the fields to the appropriate area.

   In this case, select the *Name* field and copy it to the top label area. The top label area now contains two field labels, with the *Name* field displayed below the *Item* field.

4. Select the field containing the numeric data you want to summarize and copy the field to the report data area.

   In this case, select the *Amount* field and drag it to the report data area. The basic report now is finished and looks like Figure 17.11.

 TIP If you want a less cluttered work area, remove the Source Window after all the fields have been copied to the cross-tabulation report. To remove the Source Window, double-click the Source Window control menu. You can redisplay the Source Window at any time by clicking the Source Window button or choosing Build, Source Window.

TROUBLESHOOTING

Instead of numeric results, some cells in the crosstab say "Multiple Possibilities." You probably dropped a label field a little too low, making it a data item, rather than a top label. Click

continues

Part

III

Ch

17

continued

the handle for the field's label bar and then select Edit, Clear. Reselect the field in the Source window, and drag it slightly above the top label bar.

Numbers appear in one of the label areas instead of being shown in the Report Data area.
Always add numeric data to the Report Data Area, and the identifying data labels to the label areas. If you add numeric data to the label bars, or labels to the Report Data Area, your reports will be meaningless.

FIG. 17.11
The finished basic report shows the initial crosstab analysis.

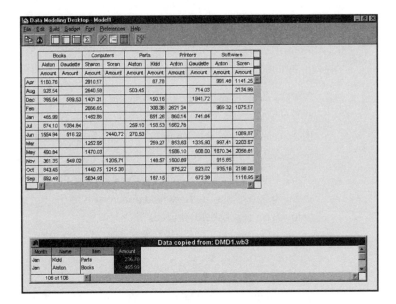

Modifying the Report   The real power of the Data Modeling Desktop becomes apparent when you learn how to rearrange the report by moving label bars. As you move the label bars, you change the entire basis of the report and can examine different types of relationships in the data.

 TIP   Change the importance of data by changing the order of the label bars.

You can move the label bars in two ways. You can *pivot* a label bar, changing it from a Side Label Bar to a Top Label Bar or from a Top Label Bar to a Side Label Bar. You also can change the *order* of the label bars in the Top or Side Label Bar area. Both types of changes have a profound effect on the cross-tabulation report.

The report created in the earlier example does a good job of summarizing the sales for each type of product, but the report does not summarize each sales representative's sales very well. Fortunately, with the Data Modeling Desktop, you can change the focus of the report quickly and easily. The first step is to pivot the label bar containing the sales representatives' names from the Top Label Bar area to the Side Label Bar area.

Follow these steps to pivot the label bar:

1. With the mouse, point to the *handle* for the Top Label Bar containing the sales representatives' names (the handle is the empty box to the right of the names).

2. Hold down the left mouse button and drag the label bar handle to the Side Label Bar area. As you drag the label bar handle, a dotted line shows the label bar pivoting.

3. Release the mouse button when the label bar handle is in the Side Label Bar area. The report changes to reflect the new cross-tabulation summary generated by the new positions of the label bars (see Figure 17.12).

FIG. 17.12

The report changes to reflect the new cross-tabulation summary.

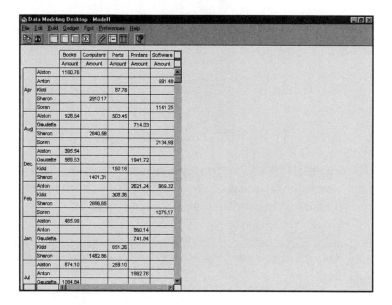

The new report shows the total sales for each sales representative for each month. You can easily see who had sales for each product line and who did not. This entirely new view of the relationships resulted from simply pivoting the label bar containing the names from the Top Label Bar area to the Side Label Bar area.

The report still does not focus on the individual results for each sales representative, but you can quickly move the label bar containing the names to change the cross-tabulation report again. Moving a label bar within the same label bar area changes the *level*, or importance, of the items in the label bars. If you move the names label bar to the left, the items in the names label bar become more important. To move the names label bar to the left, grab the handle for the names label bar, and drag it to the left of the months label bar. The report changes to reflect the new cross-tabulation summary generated by the new positions of the label bars (see Figure 17.13).

FIG. 17.13
Changing the position of the label bar changes its importance in the report.

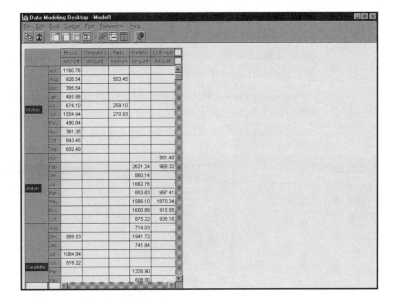

Pivoting label bars and moving label bars within the same label bar area completely change the focus of the cross-tabulation. You can try any number of combinations to see the many different relationships contained in your data. The Data Modeling Desktop enables you to examine every possibility easily.

 When your report is done, drag the month labels into calendar order for a more understandable report.

You can explore many more options in Data Modeling Desktop reports. You'll notice, for example, that the months are listed in alphabetical, rather than calendar order. You can drag individual labels to new positions within the same label bar, so it's easy to rearrange the months into calendar order. You can use Build, Add Total Element to add totals to the report; you can use Gadget, Formula to use a different type of summary; and you can use Build, Group Elements to combine items (such as combining months into quarters).

After you have created your cross-tabulation report in the Data Modeling Desktop, you copy the report to a Corel Quattro Pro notebook for formatting and printing. The report data copies to cells in the notebook, but any formatting (such as numeric format or lines) does not copy. Use the Edit, Copy to Quattro Pro command or click the Copy to Quattro Pro button to copy the current report to the Corel Quattro Pro notebook. You can then include the crosstab in a Corel Quattro Pro report, or even graph the data.

Using the Database Desktop

By now you've learned that data is extremely important. You also know that access to data in Corel Quattro Pro provides many options for analyzing data. Sometimes, though, you may want to use Corel Quattro Pro to analyze data that isn't already in a notebook file. For example, you may want to use data contained in a dBASE or Paradox database file.

Understanding the Database Desktop

NOTE If the Data, External Data, Database Desktop command is dimmed, use the Corel WordPerfect Suite 7 installation program to install the Database Desktop. ▪

Corel Quattro Pro can open many database files directly, treating them as though they were actually Corel Quattro Pro notebook files. This isn't always the best option, though, and if the database file is very large, may not be possible. To use a Corel Quattro Pro notebook, it must be loaded completely into your computer's memory. Database managers, such as Paradox, access database files differently. Instead of loading an entire database into memory, Paradox loads a few records into memory, leaving the rest of the records in the database file on disk. Because only a small portion of the database must fit into memory, disk-based databases can be much larger than databases in a Corel Quattro Pro notebook.

 The Database Desktop is a companion program to Corel Quattro Pro that enables you to access information in dBASE and Paradox database files. Through the Database Desktop, you can query a database, add new records to a database, modify existing records in a database, create a new dBASE or Paradox database, modify the structure of an existing database file, or delete records from a database.

NOTE The Database Desktop is closely related to Paradox for Windows. The Database Desktop lacks many of the more powerful features of Paradox for Windows such as scripts, forms, reports, and the ObjectPal programming language. You may find the Database Desktop a little more convenient to use with Corel Quattro Pro, however, because you can access the Database Desktop from the Corel Quattro Pro Data menu, or by simply clicking a toolbar button. ▪

Part III
Ch 17

Using Database Files

To load the Database Desktop into memory, select the Data, External Data, Database Desktop command. Your system briefly displays a message informing you of its progress loading the program, and then displays the Database Desktop (see Figure 17.14). If only the Database Desktop title bar appears, or if the Database Desktop does not fill the screen, click the Maximize button or select Maximize from the Database Desktop Control menu to provide the largest possible work area.

FIG. 17.14
Use the Database Desktop to access disk-based database tables.

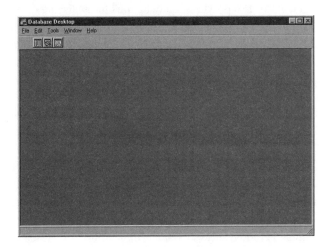

 Queries enable you to select the database records you want to see.

Rather than opening a database table and viewing the complete set of records, often you may want to view a subset of those records that you select by using specified criteria. You may want to search for records, for example, for a single customer, for records applying to sales over a specified amount, or for customers in a certain group of states. You use the Query commands in the Database Desktop to select specified records. You can then save the query, and use the saved query from Corel Quattro Pro to add the selected records into a Corel Quattro Pro notebook.

To create a new query, select File, New, QBE Query and choose the database table whose records you want to view. After you select a database table, the Database Desktop Query Editor appears. The Query Editor uses *Query by Example* (QBE) to build a database query; you place example values in the fields displayed in the Query Editor, and records are selected based on these values.

To build a query, you use symbols, operators, and reserved words. Query Editor *symbols* indicate the fields you want included in the answer table, whether to include duplicate values, and the default sort order. *Operators* select field values based on criteria you specify. The >= operator, for example, selects records that contain a value in the selected field greater than or equal to a specified value. *Reserved words* perform special database operations, such as inserting and deleting records.

Figure 17.15 shows an example of a query that selects books from a database. In this example, the query specifies that only those titles by Aristotle should be selected. The results of running the query appear in the Answer table.

FIG. 17.15
A query selects specific
database records.

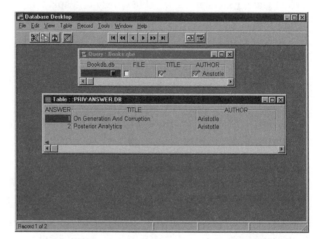

Part
III

Ch

17

In this case, the Answer table shows that the database contains 2 titles by Aristotle. By changing the comparison value and rerunning the query, you can produce different sets of answers. To reuse the same query in the future, use the File, Save or File, Save As command before you close the query or the Database Desktop. Queries you create in either the Database Desktop or Paradox are saved in text files that use the extension QBE. You can use such saved queries in the Database Desktop, Paradox, or through the Corel Quattro Pro Data, External Data, Table Query command.

 TIP If you want to save the results of a query, use the Query, Properties, Table name command and save the results in a table other than ANSWER.DB.

Sharing Results with Corel Quattro Pro

The Database Desktop stores the current answer in a temporary file called ANSWER.DB in your working directory. You can import this file into a Corel Quattro Pro notebook, but when you do, the imported information is static and is not updated when the database changes.

A better way to share database information between the Database Desktop and Corel Quattro Pro is to use the Database Desktop QBE file along with the Corel Quattro Pro Data, External Data, Table Query command. In this way, the information in your notebook is updated to reflect changes in the database. You can, for example, create and refine a database query, and then execute your fully developed query from within a notebook application.

To run a saved query from within a Corel Quattro Pro notebook, follow these steps:

1. Select Data, External Data, Table Query to display the Table Query dialog box.

2. Select Query in File to execute a query in a QBE file, or Query in Block to execute a query that you previously imported into a notebook block (remember, QBE files are text files).

3. If you select Query in File, specify the name of the QBE file. If you select Query in Block, specify the notebook block that contains the query.

4. Specify the Destination—the upper-left corner of the notebook block—where you want to place the database records.

5. Click OK to confirm the dialog box and execute the query.

The Database Desktop serves as a tool for creating more powerful Corel Quattro Pro applications that feature easy access to dBASE and Paradox database files. You could use a saved query to automatically update the information in a Corel Quattro Pro notebook to include the latest data—especially if you use shared database files on a network and need to make certain your notebooks are up-to-date. ●

CHAPTER 18

Using Charts

Corel Quattro Pro's presentation graphics features help you present data in an easier-to-understand manner. Instead of trying to understand countless rows and columns of data, a well-executed chart can enable you to see and analyze large amounts of information quickly. The most effective reports are those that efficiently analyze that data.

Corel Quattro Pro includes many powerful graphic capabilities. Because these graphics features are built-in, you will find that creating sophisticated graphics within Corel Quattro Pro is quite easy. You don't need to use a separate, dedicated graphics package to produce charts of your Corel Quattro Pro data. ■

Create charts

Learn how to create colorful charts from data in a notebook.

Select different chart types

Learn how you can use the many different types of Corel Quattro Pro charts to show your data in the most effective manner.

Enhance a chart

See how you can make changes to the appearance of your charts to greatly enhance their effectiveness.

N O T E Previous versions of Quattro Pro used the term *graph* to describe what Corel Quattro Pro calls charts. ■

Creating a Simple Chart

You can create extremely sophisticated, complex, and stunning charts with Corel Quattro Pro. You can even create on-screen slideshows that automatically change from one chart to the next at specified intervals using such fancy effects as dissolves, fades, wipes, or spirals. Learning all the intricacies of such fancy productions could use up all of your time for weeks or even months. For most of us, a relatively simple chart that effectively displays our data is a much more reasonable goal, so that's where you start—by learning how to create a simple chart.

  Create your basic chart in the spreadsheet and then use the Chart window to enhance the chart.

Although most of your work in Corel Quattro Pro is done in the spreadsheet, Corel Quattro Pro also provides a Chart window that gives you much more power and control over charting. The Chart window provides you with specialized commands and toolbars that are designed to help you enhance a chart. Before you can access the Chart window, however, you first must create a chart.

Starting a Basic Chart

The data you want to chart must be in a tabular format, similar to a typical Corel Quattro Pro notebook database. The requirements for data you want to chart aren't quite as strict as they are for a database, though, because you can use either rows or columns for similar data. A crosstab table is often a very good choice for the layout of data you want to chart, because a crosstab has labels identifying both the groups and the elements in your data.

▶ **See** "Creating a Dynamic Crosstab," **p. 371**

Figure 18.1 shows a notebook containing the annual sales report for a fictitious company. You use this notebook to demonstrate the steps in creating a Corel Quattro Pro chart.

You use the Graphics commands to create a chart that is linked to notebook data. With these commands, you can chart data from one notebook. The commands on the Graphics menu enable you to create a chart, view a chart, add an existing chart to the notebook, and view a slideshow. Before you create a chart in a notebook, most selections in the Graphics menu are dimmed. These commands are not available when a Notebook window is the active window and no chart currently exists, but they become available when the

Chart window is the active window, or when you have added a chart to a notebook and are editing the chart.

You use the Graphics, New Chart command to create a chart. By default, Corel Quattro Pro names the first chart Chart1, the second Chart2, and so on.

FIG. 18.1

A sample sales data notebook can be used for creating charts.

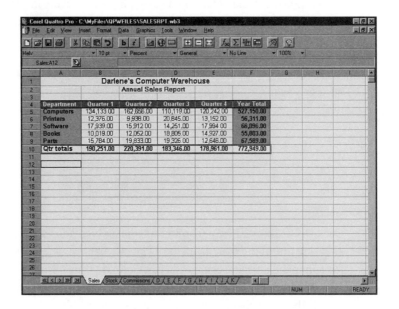

TIP Move the cell selector into the block of data you want to chart before you select Graphics, New Chart.

Corel Quattro Pro uses the currently selected spreadsheet block as the block to be charted. If you don't select a block, but the cell selector is located within a block of data, Corel Quattro Pro uses the entire block. If the block you want to chart is contained within a larger block of data, select the block of data to chart before selecting Graphics, New Chart. You can also click the Create a Floating Chart button on the toolbar to insert a chart directly onto the notebook.

To chart information from the sales data notebook, you need to know which data you want to plot and which data you want to use in labeling the chart. In Figure 18.1, time-period labels are listed across row 4. Category identifiers are located in column A. The numeric entries in rows 5 through 9, as well as the formula results in row 10 and column F, are suitable for charting as data points. For this example, however, the totals in row 10 and column F are not included in the charted data, because including these totals would make the other data very difficult to see by comparison. In this example, you should select the

Part
III

Ch
18

block A4..E9 before choosing <u>G</u>raphics, <u>N</u>ew Chart. The column and row labels can be used to label the points on the chart.

After you have selected a block to chart, choose <u>G</u>raphics, <u>N</u>ew Chart from the Corel Quattro Pro menu to display the New Chart dialog box (see Figure 18.2). If you want, you can change the default chart name by typing a new name in the <u>C</u>hart Name text box on the Name tab. If necessary, adjust the blocks shown in the text boxes on the Series tab.

FIG. 18.2
Use the New Chart dialog box to create a new chart.

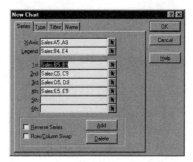

Click OK or press Enter to confirm the dialog box. You can change the chart type by choosing one of the options on the Type tab that appears by using the <u>C</u>hart, T<u>y</u>pe/Layout command after the chart is displayed in the Chart window. Figure 18.3 shows the basic chart as it appears in the Chart window. Later in this chapter, you learn how to modify the basic chart to improve its appearance.

FIG. 18.3
The default chart of the sales data spreadsheet shows basic information but could use improvement.

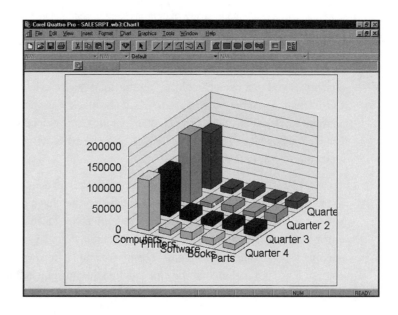

TROUBLESHOOTING

The new chart includes data I don't want to chart. Select the block you want to chart before you choose Graphics, New Chart. Otherwise Corel Quattro Pro includes the entire current block of data in the chart.

Most of the data values on a chart can't be determined because the Y-axis goes too high. Corel Quattro Pro automatically scales the Y-axis to show the largest values in the chart. You may need to select a smaller data block that doesn't include the largest values, or change the chart to a 2-D chart and chart the largest values on the second Y-axis.

Understanding the Chart Window

Note in Figure 18.3 that the command menu, the toolbar, and the Power Bar have changed. When you chart data from the notebook, Corel Quattro Pro displays the chart in a separate Chart window and automatically uses the Chart window menu, the Chart window toolbar, and the Chart window Power Bar. If you select Next (Ctrl+F6) on the Window control menu or select the notebook window from the Window menu, the screen changes and displays the Corel Quattro Pro Notebook menu, Notebook toolbar, and Notebook Power Bar.

Right-click the toolbar to select the toolbar containing the tools you want to use.

The Chart window has several toolbars that are specially designed for working with chart objects. The Chart Tools toolbar, for example, provides tools you can use to draw objects on charts. The Chart Colors toolbar enables you to select colors and patterns, and the Alignment Tools toolbar enables you to group and ungroup chart objects, change positions of chart objects so that they are in front of or behind others, and control object alignment. In addition, when the Chart window is active, the options on the Graphics menu are no longer dimmed as they were when the Notebook window was active, indicating that they now are available.

Understanding Common Chart Terms

Most charts (except for bullet charts, text charts, pie charts, and doughnut charts) have a *Y-axis* (a vertical left edge), and an *X-axis* (a horizontal bottom edge). In rotated charts, the Y-axis is the bottom edge, and the X-axis is the left edge. Corel Quattro Pro automatically divides each axis with tick marks and scales the numbers on the Y-axis, based on the

Part

III

Ch

18

minimum and maximum numbers in the associated data block. The intersection of the Y-axis and the X-axis is called the *origin*. The origin is zero unless you specify otherwise.

A chart is made up of one or more *data series*, each of which reflects a category of data. The first category of data is always series 1, the second is series 2, and so on. Some chart types use a limited number of data series; for example, pie and doughnut charts use one data series, and XY charts use two or more. Other chart types, such as line charts, can chart multiple data series.

 Use legends, titles, and labels to make your charts easier to understand.

Legends are text placed beside or below a chart that explain the symbols, colors, or fill used to denote each data series. *Titles* are text placed above the chart and along the horizontal and vertical axis that provide information about the overall chart. *Labels* are text entries used to explain specific data items or entries in a chart.

Understanding Chart Types

Corel Quattro Pro automatically selects a chart type when you use the Graphics, New Chart command. To change the type of chart Corel Quattro Pro displays, choose Chart, Type/Layout after you use Graphics, New Chart. When you choose the type of chart you want, Corel Quattro Pro changes the display to reflect your choice. You can also choose the chart type in the Chart Types dialog box (see the following section, "Selecting a Different Type of Chart").

Several types of charts are available in Corel Quattro Pro: Area/Line, Bar, Stacked Bar, Pie, Specialty, and Text. Each of the chart types also offers several variations.

Selecting a Different Type of Chart

You can change a chart to a different type in several different ways, but you can only change a chart's type if the chart is displayed in the Chart window, or if you first select the chart if it is displayed in a notebook.

To select a new type for a chart that is displayed in the Chart window or that has been selected in the notebook, point to an area in the chart outside any chart objects and click the right mouse button. Choose Type/Layout from the QuickMenu to display the Chart Types dialog box (see Figure 18.4). You can also display this dialog box by choosing Chart, Type/Layout.

FIG. 18.4
Use the Chart Types dialog box to select the type of chart to display.

As you select each basic type of chart from the Category drop-down list box, Area/Line, Bar, Stacked Bar, Pie, Specialty, or Text, small samples of each of the optional variations are shown in the dialog box. As soon as you select a new chart type and click OK, your chart is changed to the selected type. The following sections briefly describe the basic chart types.

Understanding Variations Within Chart Categories

Corel Quattro Pro offers many different variations within the different chart categories. These include 2-D (two-dimensional) charts, 3-D (three-dimensional) charts, rotated charts, and combination charts. To make the best choice of a chart for your needs, you should understand these variations.

Understanding 2-D Charts   2-D (two-dimensional) charts are the most common type of business charts. In this chart, data is plotted using an X-axis and a Y-axis or, in the case of column and pie charts, using no axis at all.

 T I P   If you want to chart some data using the second Y-axis, you must use a 2-D chart.

Understanding 3-D Charts   A 3-D chart plots data in three-dimensional perspective. Instead of just using an X-axis and a Y-axis, a 3-D chart adds a Z-axis. In some cases, 3-D charts do a better job than 2-D charts of showing the complex relationships between groups of data items.

 T I P   You may want to experiment with the Chart, Perspective settings to change the view of 3-D charts.

Understanding Rotated Charts   Sometimes you can create a more stunning visual effect by rotating a chart. *Rotated* charts place the X-data series along the left vertical axis and the Y-data series along the horizontal axis. Values are plotted as horizontal distances from the left axis instead of vertical distances from the lower axis.

Part
III

Ch
18

Don't overdo the use of rotated charts. Most people find rotated charts harder to interpret.

Understanding Combo Charts   Corel Quattro Pro enables you to mix chart types so that you can compare different sets of data. You can combine a bar chart and a line, area, or a high-low chart. You also can display multiple columns, 3-D columns, pies, 3-D pies, or bar charts.

 Charts that combine a bar chart and a line, area, or a high-low chart, are used to display data that is related, but that requires different types of plotting to best show different data series.

Charts that show multiple columns, pies, or bars show several different data series plotted as individual charts, but include each individual chart within a single-named chart in the notebook. When you use multiple columns or pies, each column or pie is the same size. You can compare how the data items within each data series relate as a percentage of the total of the data series, but you cannot determine the relative values of data items between series.

Understanding Area/Line Charts

Corel Quattro Pro offers several variations on the theme of area and line charts. These include the following types.

Line Charts   *Line charts* are the most common type of chart and one of the easiest to understand. Line charts plot values using individual lines to connect the data points for each data series.

Standard line charts plot data values using the height of the line above the bottom of the chart to indicate differences. Rotated line charts plot data value variations as distances from the left side of the chart.

 If one data set in a line chart has much higher values than the remaining data sets, consider plotting the out of proportion data set against the secondary Y-axis. Right-click the line plotting the data set, select Line Series Properties, and Se<u>c</u>ondary.

Area Charts   *Area charts* emphasize broad trends. Area charts plot the first data series closest to the X-axis, and stack additional data series above each other. Each data series line represents the total of the data series being plotted plus all lower data series. Area charts are filled between the origin and the plotted lines.

Area charts can also be displayed using either standard or rotated orientation, depending on your needs.

3-D Area Charts   *3-D area charts* are quite similar to 2-D area charts, except that 3-D area charts appear to have depth. This third dimension is not used to plot data, but rather to provide a more substantial appearance. 3-D area charts plot the first data series closest to the X-axis, and stack additional data series above each other. Each data series line represents the total of the data series being plotted plus all lower data series. 3-D area charts are filled between the origin and the plotted lines. Figure 18.5 shows a 3-D area chart of the sales data after the Row/Column Swap check box in the Chart Series dialog box was selected.

FIG. 18.5
Use 3-D area charts to emphasize trends in your data.

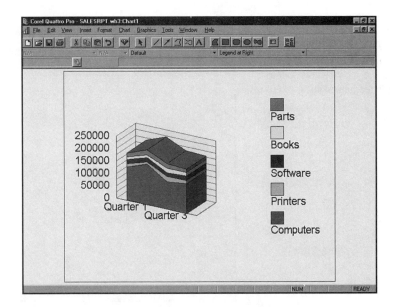

Part
III

Ch
18

T I P   To change the emphasis of your chart, select the Row/Column Swap check box in the Chart Series dialog box. Right-click an empty area in your chart and select Series from the QuickMenu to display this dialog box.

3-D Unstacked Area Charts   *3-D unstacked area charts* plot values using lines (which are stretched to add depth) to connect the data points for each data series, while filling the area between the lines and the origin. Because larger values in a 3-D unstacked area chart can hide lower values plotted behind them, this type of chart is best suited to displaying sorted data.

Ribbon Charts   *Ribbon charts* are similar to 3-D unstacked area charts; they plot values using lines (which are stretched to add depth) to connect the data points for each data series. Ribbon charts, however, do not fill the area between the lines and the origin. Ribbon charts are better than 3-D unstacked area charts at displaying unsorted data because larger values are less likely to hide lower values plotted behind them in a ribbon chart.

3-D Floating Marker Charts   *3-D floating marker charts* are also similar to 3-D unstacked area charts. Instead of using lines to connect the data points for each data series, however, small floating blocks are used to represent the data points. 3-D floating marker charts are quite good at displaying unsorted data since the floating blocks are unlikely to hide lower values plotted behind them. Figure 18.6 shows a 3-D floating marker chart of the sales data.

FIG. 18.6
The floating blocks in 3-D floating marker charts are unlikely to hide lower values plotted behind them.

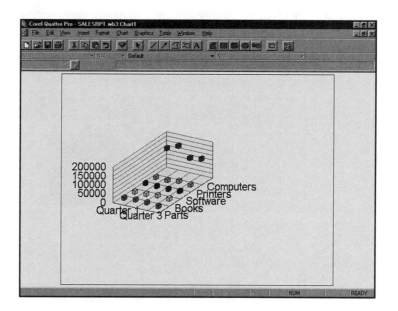

CAUTION
It may be difficult to see small differences in data values in 3-D floating marker charts.

Understanding Bar Charts

Corel Quattro Pro offers several variations of bar charts. These include 2-D, 2.5-D, 3-D, and several combo chart types.

Bar and Rotated 2-D Bar Charts   A *bar chart* shows data as a series of bars drawn next to each other. This type of chart is useful for showing how data categories compare over time. In addition to standard bar charts that plot data values as height above the X-axis, rotated 2-D bar charts plot data values as the distance from the left axis.

TIP In rotated charts, the left axis is the X-axis and the bottom axis is the Y-axis.

Variance Charts A *variance chart* is similar to a bar chart, except that the origin is adjustable to show how data varies from a specified value. Initially, a variance chart has the origin set to 0, and so the chart appears identical to a standard 2-D bar chart. After you create the basic variance chart, adjust the origin by pointing to the chart y-axis values, clicking the right mouse button, and choosing Y-Axis Properties; or by choosing Chart, Axes, Primary Y-Axis. Select the Zero Line At text box in the Scale tab of the Y-Axis dialog box, and enter a new value for the origin. Figure 18.7 shows the sales data plotted on a variance chart with the origin adjusted to 50,000.

FIG. 18.7
Use a variance chart to plot data with a non-zero origin.

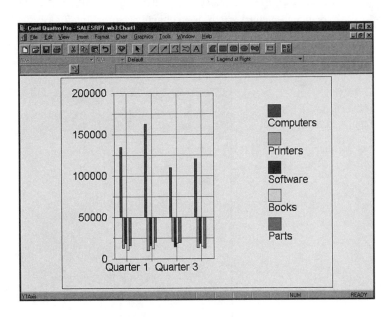

TIP Use variance charts to emphasize data that falls below targeted values.

2.5-D Bar Charts *2.5-D bar charts* show data as a series of deep bars drawn next to each other. A 2.5-D bar chart is not a true 3-D chart, because it does not use depth to portray a Z-axis value, but instead to add a third dimension to the bars. This type of chart is useful for showing how data categories compare over time.

Rotated 2.5-D bar charts are similar to standard 2.5-D bar charts with the data plotted as distances from the left chart axis.

Part
III

Ch
18

3-D Bar Charts   *3-D bar charts* show data as groups of bars plotted on a three-dimensional grid. Often a 3-D bar chart provides an easier-to-understand display of the relationship between the plotted data series than a 2-D bar chart can.

3-D bar charts can also be plotted using either standard or rotated orientation. Rotated 3-D bar charts may be more difficult to understand.

TIP   A 3-D bar chart may hide smaller values behind large values. Arrange the data series with the largest values first and the smallest values last. If this is not possible, consider using a 2-D chart to prevent data from being hidden.

3-D Step Charts   *3-D step charts* are nearly identical to 3-D bar charts, except that the bars in a step chart touch. Step charts are most useful for displaying data that changes in regular increments, rather than data that may change abruptly in either direction. Figure 18.8 shows the sales data plotted as a 3-D step chart.

FIG. 18.8
3-D step charts use bars that touch each other to plot data.

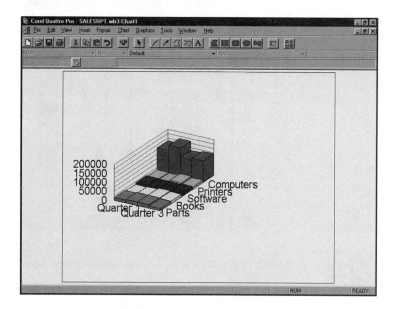

Combo Bar Charts   Corel Quattro Pro provides several types of charts that combine bars and other types of data markers.

- *Line-Bar.* Plot some data as lines and the rest as bars. This type of chart can be handy for showing trends such as temperature variations over a period of time.

- *High-Low-Bar.* Plot some data using High-Low markers (see the section "Understanding Specialty Charts" later in this chapter) and some as bars. This chart variation is often used to plot stock market data.

- *Area-Bar.* Combine area charts and bar charts. These charts can be used to display data that exceeds predictions, such as sales that are higher than expected. Because the area chart typically hides bars that fall below the level of the area chart, this type of combo chart can be more difficult to use than line-bar charts.

- *Multiple-Bar.* Display each data series in a separate bar chart. Each chart uses the same scale, so large values in one data series may reduce the size of the bars in the remaining charts.

 TIP All data series in multiple-bar charts are plotted against the primary Y-axis so each individual bar chart uses the same scale.

Understanding Stacked Bar Charts

Stacked bar charts are quite similar to area charts because all data is plotted together in a bar that represents the sum of the data values. There are several variations of stacked bar charts.

Stacked Bar Charts   A *stacked bar chart* shows data as a series of bars stacked on top of one another. This type of chart is useful for showing the portion that data categories contribute to a whole, as well as comparing changes in those contributions over time. Stacked bar charts not only show how each data item varies over time, but also how the total of all data items varies over the same time period.

Comparison charts are variations of stacked bar charts. For these chart types, the boundaries between the data segments in each bar are connected to the corresponding boundaries between the data segments in the next bar. These connecting lines can help you to spot trends more easily, but they may be difficult to understand if the bars contain too many data segments.

Both stacked bar charts and comparison charts can be displayed in standard or rotated format. Figure 18.9 shows the sales data plotted on a rotated 2-D comparison chart.

100% Stacked Bar Charts   A *100% stacked bar chart* is a variation of the stacked bar chart; in this type of chart, the bar is always full height, and the individual data items are shown as their percentage of 100 percent.

100% stacked bar comparison charts are also a variation of stacked bar charts. For these chart types, the bar is always full height, the individual data items are shown as their percentage of 100 percent, and the boundaries between the data segments in each bar are connected to the corresponding boundaries between the data segments in the next bar.

Part
III

Ch
18

FIG. 18.9
Rotated 2-D comparison charts use lines to connect the data segments on each of the bars.

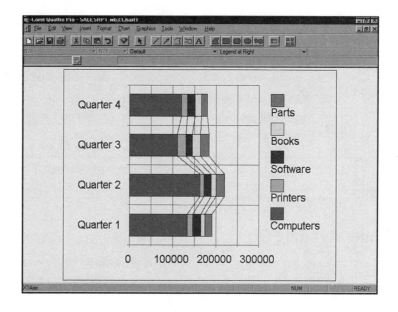

T I P 100% stacked bar charts quickly show percentage comparisons between the different data series.

3-D Stacked Bar Charts Similar to regular stacked bar charts, *3-D stacked bar charts* work best with small amounts of data in comparing sets of data over time. A 3-D stacked bar chart shows data as a series of 3-D bars stacked on top of one another. This type of chart is useful for showing the portion that data categories contribute to a whole, as well as comparing changes in those contributions over time. 3-D stacked bar charts not only show how each data item varies over time, but also how the total of all data items varies over the same time period.

3-D 100% stacked bar comparison charts show the data as a percentage. Both 3-D stacked bar charts and 3-D 100% stacked bar comparison charts can use either standard or rotated orientation. Neither 3-D stacked bar charts nor 3-D 100% stacked bar comparison charts are truly 3-D charts because neither uses the Z-axis to plot data.

Understanding Pie Charts

All pie chart variations compare values in a single set of data that contains only positive numbers. Each value appears as a slice of the pie, column, or doughnut and represents a percentage of the total. You can plot only one row or one column of numeric data in a pie chart unless you use the multiple pie or column chart options.

Each of the pie chart types can be displayed in 2-D or 3-D variations. Pie and column charts can also be plotted as multiple 2-D or 3-D charts if you need to display more than one data series.

Pie Charts   Pie charts plot data as wedges or pie slices in a circular chart, with each section representing one data value. You can *explode* a pie chart section to make it stand out from the pie by right-clicking the section you want to explode, choosing Pie Chart Properties, and selecting the Explode check box.

TIP If you attempt to plot too many data items, the wedges of the pie chart become too small to understand easily. Use column charts to plot data series with large numbers of individual items.

Doughnut Charts   A *doughnut chart* is a variation of a pie chart; unlike a pie chart, however, a doughnut chart has a center ring cut out. You use a doughnut chart exactly as you use pie charts.

Column Charts   A *column chart* compares values in a single set of data that contains only positive numbers. Each value appears as a section of the column and represents a percentage of the total. You can plot only one row or one column of numeric data in a single column chart. Column charts are very similar in function to pie charts, but column charts are more effective when you want to plot a large number of data items.

A *3-D column* chart compares values in a single set of data that contains only positive numbers. Each value appears as a section of the column and represents a percentage of the total. You can plot only one row or one column of numeric data in a 3-D column chart. 3-D column charts are very similar to 2-D column charts, except that the column is displayed with a third dimension: depth.

Part

III

Ch

18

TIP Use multiple column or pie charts to plot more than one data series.

Understanding Specialty Charts

Specialty charts provide you with several chart types that can plot certain types of data more effectively than any of the other types of charts.

Understanding XY Charts   The *XY chart*, often called a *scatter chart*, is a variation of a line chart. Like a line chart, an XY chart has values plotted as points in the chart. Unlike a line chart, an XY chart has its X-axis labeled with numeric values instead of labels.

Corel Quattro Pro always plots the independent variable (data you can change or control) on the X-axis, and the dependent variables (data you cannot control or change, and which is dependent on the independent variable) on the Y-axis. Thus, the independent data should be in the first row or column, and the dependent data should be in the second and succeeding rows or columns. Figure 18.10 shows an XY chart of the sine function for X-axis values from 0 to 360 degrees.

FIG. 18.10

XY charts plot the independent variable on the X-axis and the dependent variables on the Y-axis.

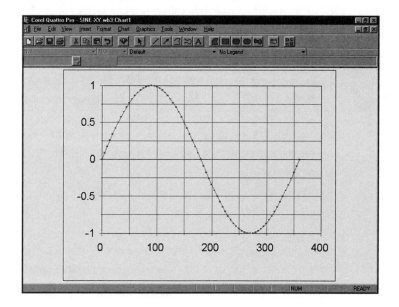

High-Low Charts *High-low charts* are sometimes called HLCO charts, which stands for high-low-close-open. A high-low chart is especially useful for charting data about the price of a stock over time. The high-low-close-open figures represent the stock's highest and lowest price in the given time period, the stock's price at the end of the time period, and the stock's price at the start of the time period.

 T I P High-low charts are the best choice for plotting stock market data.

Each set of data normally consists of four figures representing high, low, close, and open values. The set of data is typically represented on the chart as a vertical line with tick marks. The line extends from the low value to the high value. The close value is represented by a tick mark extending to the right of the line, and the open value is represented by a tick mark extending to the left. The total number of lines on the chart depends on the number of time periods included. If you have a fifth data series, it is plotted as a volume series against the second Y-axis.

Radar Charts   A *radar chart* plots data radiating out from a single center point. X-axis values appear as spokes in a wheel, and Y-axis data is plotted on each spoke. Radar charts may make spotting trends easier, depending on the type of data being charted.

3-D Surface Charts   *3-D surface charts* display data as lines connecting the data items for each series. The line for each data series is connected to the line for the next data series, and the area between the lines is filled in with different colors.

3-D Contour Charts   *3-D contour charts* are very similar to surface charts, except in the method used to color the surface plot. Instead of coloring the segments between each set of lines with a distinct color, contour charts apply color to show how far the surface lies above the origin. Contour charts can be used to show elevations, as in contour maps. Figure 18.11 shows how a 3-D contour chart can be used to display elevation data.

FIG. 18.11
3-D contour charts can be used to display elevations contained in topographical data.

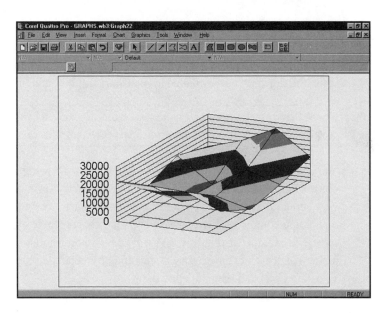

3-D Shaded Surface Charts   *3-D shaded surface charts* are another variation on surface and contour charts. The shaded surface chart uses a single color to create the surface, but applies different shading to show the slope of the surface between data points. Shaded surface charts may reproduce better than surface and contour charts on black-and-white printers.

Understanding Text Charts

Text charts are unlike the other types of Corel Quattro Pro because they are not used to display numerical data. There are two types of text charts, bullet charts and blank charts.

Bullet Charts   *Bullet charts* are a special type of chart often used in presentations. Instead of charting numerical data, bullet charts display notebook text in a special format. In a bullet chart, a title line is followed by one or more levels of bulleted text, usually presenting information in an outline style format.

To create a bullet chart, you use a block of text either two or three columns wide in the notebook as the source of chart data. The first column contains the chart title, the second contains the first level of bulleted text, and the third contains an optional second level of bulleted text.

Blank Charts   *Blank charts* are another special type of Corel Quattro Pro chart. Instead of plotting notebook data, blank charts enable you to create graphics objects that you can place anywhere you like in a notebook. Blank charts can contain text, objects you create using the drawing tools available in the Chart window, and imported graphics.

 T I P   Use the Drawing Tools toolbar to draw floating objects directly on a notebook page rather than using a blank chart. That way the chart pane won't cover your data.

You can also use the tools on the notebook window Drawing Tools toolbar to draw floating objects directly on a notebook page. Floating objects drawn on the notebook page are very similar to the objects you draw in a blank chart, except that floating objects drawn on the notebook page do not have an opaque chart pane to obscure other objects on the page. For example, if you draw an arrow directly on a notebook page, objects under the arrow's path are not covered by a rectangular box as they would be by an arrow drawn in a floating chart and then added to the page.

Enhancing a Chart

Corel Quattro Pro offers several options for improving the appearance of your charts and producing final-quality output suitable for business presentations. After you have created the basic chart, you use the Chart window menu commands to change the selection of chart blocks, types, and orientation; data labels and legends; X-, Y-, and optional second Y-axes; borders and grids; colors; hatch patterns; fonts; and lines.

Changing the Chart Orientation

The initial orientation Corel Quattro Pro selects for the rows and columns of data may not always be the optimal choice. A different chart layout may be more effective in representing your data.

By default, Corel Quattro Pro assumes that the first row or column of your data with labels contains the X-axis labels (the labels along the bottom of the chart that group the data series in comparable sets). To change the orientation of the data series, choose Chart, Series, Row/Column swap.

Adding Titles

When you chart data from a notebook, you can specify the titles after you create and view the chart. With the Chart, Titles command, you can create a Main Title, a Subtitle, an X-axis Title, a Y1-Axis Title, and a Y2-Axis Title (see Figure 18.12).

FIG. 18.12
Use the Chart Titles dialog box to add titles to your charts.

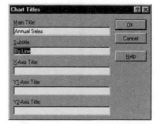

Part
III

Ch
18

You use the Main Title and Subtitle text boxes to create the first and second titles; they appear centered above the chart, with the first title in larger type above the second title. You use the X-axis Title, Y1-Axis Title, and Y2-Axis Title text boxes to add titles for the chart axes. You can move the main and subtitles, but you cannot move the X- or Y-Axis titles. Figure 18.13 shows the chart with main and subtitles added.

You can edit the titles and notes by choosing the Chart, Titles command and changing or editing the contents of the text boxes. When you have finished entering or editing the titles, click OK or press Enter to confirm the dialog box. You also can change the color, font, and text attributes of any title by using the Object Inspectors (point to the title you want to change, click the right mouse button, and choose the title's Properties selection).

 Right-click chart objects to see the many properties you can change in your charts.

Corel Quattro Pro offers many different options for enhancing charts. These sections have shown only a few of the possibilities. You'll also want to explore some other options such as changing the viewpoint for a 3-D chart, changing the fonts used to display text objects in a chart, and even using bitmaps (pictures) as backgrounds in your charts. To see the many possibilities, use the Object Inspectors to see the properties you can change. Point to an object, such as a data series, the chart background, or a title, click the right mouse button, and choose the object's Property selection. You'll find the Object Inspector dialog boxes provide literally thousands of option combinations you can use to fully customize your Corel Quattro Pro charts.

FIG. 18.13
The chart is much easier to understand after adding titles.

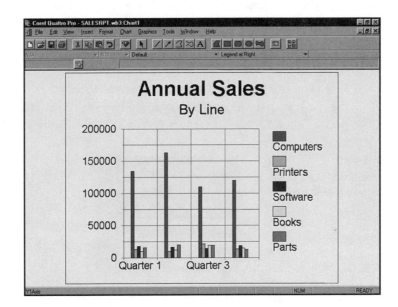

Displaying Charts in the Notebook

Corel Quattro Pro can print a chart from the Chart window or as part of a notebook report. In many cases, though, you'll find that adding a chart directly into a notebook-based report will be much more effective.

 Whenever you plan to print a notebook, you should first view it in File, Print Preview mode. You might, for example, find that you need to adjust the size of charts added to the notebook.

You add a chart to a notebook by using the Notebook menu Graphics, Insert Chart command. In the Select Chart list box of the Insert Chart dialog box, select the name of the chart. Click OK or press Enter to confirm the dialog box. Then select the notebook block where you want the chart displayed. Figure 18.14 shows a print preview view of a notebook with a chart added to the notebook. File, Print Preview changes the appearance of the notebook to Printer Preview mode and displays the notebook as it will appear when printed.

FIG. 18.14

A print preview of a chart added to a notebook block shows how your report will print.

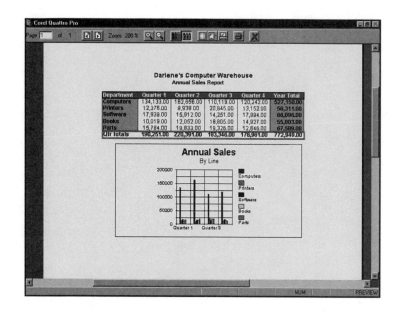

 TIP Corel Quattro Pro also has a Chart Expert QuickTask to help you create charts. See Chapter 33, "Integrating Your Work with QuickTasks," for more information.

Part
III

Ch
18

CHAPTER 19

Printing Reports

The final step in creating a useful Corel Quattro Pro notebook is to produce an effective, printed report. This step enables you to make good use of the data in your notebook and database files by sharing it with other people. This chapter introduces the commands and procedures you use to print Corel Quattro Pro reports. ■

Print Reports

Learn how to print your Corel Quattro Pro reports using the printing commands.

Preview reports

See how you can view your reports in print preview mode so you can discover and correct any problems before printing them.

Enhance reports

Learn how to improve your reports with headers and footers.

Control print margins

Learn to exercise more control over the final appearance of your reports using the margin setting options.

Select your printer

See how to choose between the available printers and also how to use Envoy to ensure other people can view your Corel Quattro Pro notebooks, even if they don't have Corel Quattro Pro installed.

Setting Up a Report

Setting up a report in Corel Quattro Pro can be quite simple. A very basic report, for example, requires only a few mouse clicks or commands to print. Usually, though, an effective report is a little more thought out. Corel Quattro Pro has many options that enable you to customize your printed reports so they look professional and convey the information properly.

The following sections show you how to print reports quickly and efficiently. Whether your report is a short report of a page or less, or a longer multiple-page report, you'll find the process is quite similar.

Selecting the Print Block

If you don't specify a block to print, Corel Quattro Pro automatically sets the entire *active area* of the current notebook page as the print block, so it's important to understand how Corel Quattro Pro determines the active area of a notebook page. The active area of a page is defined as the rectangular area between cell A1 and the intersection of the last column and the last row that contain entries. Figure 19.1 demonstrates how this works. In this figure, the active area extends from A1 to E14. Cell E14 does not contain any data, but is at the intersection of the last column and the last row used in the notebook. If you print the notebook shown in Figure 19.1, but don't specify a print block, Corel Quattro Pro will print the block A1..E14.

FIG. 19.1

Corel Quattro Pro automatically prints the active area of the current page if you don't specify a block.

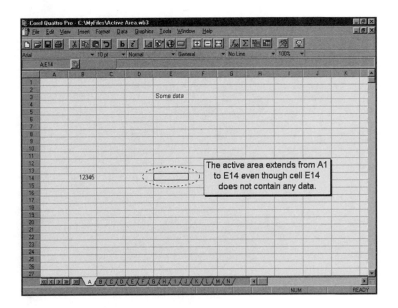

Printing a Single Block If you preselect a block, the selected block becomes the print block. Once a print block has been specified, Corel Quattro Pro remembers the specified block and uses the same block as the print block unless you specify a different block. If you forget to preselect the block to print, you can specify the block in the Block Selection text box of the Spreadsheet Print dialog box. You can select the block with the mouse or the keyboard, or you can type the block addresses.

 T I P If you don't want to print the entire active area of the notebook, be sure to preselect the desired print block.

To print a specified print block, follow these steps:

1. Select the block you want to print.

 2. Choose File, Print or click the Print a Notebook or Chart button to display the Spreadsheet Print dialog box (see Figure 19.2).

3. Click Print.

 T I P If your printer does not print in color, be sure the Adjust Image to Print Black and White check box is selected before you click Print.

FIG. 19.2
Use the Spreadsheet Print dialog box to specify what you want to print.

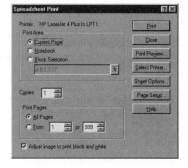

 ◆ **TROUBLESHOOTING**

Even though the correct print block is selected, text is cut off when a report prints. Long labels can spill over into empty cells to the right. If a label spills over to a cell outside the print block, only the text within the block is printed. Extend the print block to the right to include all the text, or adjust the width of the rightmost column of the print area to include the entire label.

The printed report includes blank pages. If the print area selection is Notebook, all pages will print even if some pages are blank. Use the Block Selection text box to specify the exact areas to print.

Printing Multiple Blocks   For many reports, a two-dimensional block—a single rectangular area on one notebook page—is all you need to print. Sometimes, though, you may need to print three-dimensional blocks or multiple two-dimensional blocks contained on one or more notebook pages.

A three-dimensional print block includes the same block on two or more notebook pages. You specify a three-dimensional print block by preselecting the block or by entering the block address or block name in the Block Selection text box of the Spreadsheet Print dialog box—the same way you specify a two-dimensional block (see the section "Using Blocks" in Chapter 15). After you have selected the block on the first page, hold down the Shift key and click the notebook page tabs to move to the final page of the block, or you can use Ctrl+PgDn or Ctrl+PgUp. When you have selected a three-dimensional block, Corel Quattro Pro draws a line under the page tabs to show the pages that are included in the block.

Multiple print blocks are two or more blocks that can be on the same or different notebook pages. You can use multiple print blocks when you want to print part of the information on a page, but don't want to include certain information that may be between the blocks you do want to print. To specify multiple print blocks, press and hold down the Ctrl key while you are selecting the blocks. To type the names or addresses of multiple print blocks, enter the first block name or address in the Block Selection text box of the Spreadsheet Print dialog box, type a comma, and type the next block.

When you specify multiple print blocks, previewing the printed output is always a good idea, so you may want to select File, Print Preview or File, Print, Print Preview. Press Esc or click the red X button to close Print Preview.

Figure 19.3 shows a notebook with four print blocks selected, and Figure 19.4 shows the result of selecting File, Print Preview to preview the printed output. If you are satisfied with the previewed printed output, click the printer button or press Esc to return to the notebook display.

You can specify any combination of two- and three-dimensional print blocks. Corel Quattro Pro prints the blocks in the order that you select the blocks or enter the block names or addresses.

Adding Enhancements to the Report

You can use Corel Quattro Pro's options to enhance your reports in many different ways. You select many printing options through the Spreadsheet Page Setup dialog box, which displays when you select File, Print, Page Setup. The Spreadsheet Page Setup dialog box includes tabs for specifying paper type, a header and footer, margins, print scaling, and for using named print settings (see Figure 19.5).

FIG. 19.3

If you only want to print selected areas of your notebook, preselect the print blocks before printing.

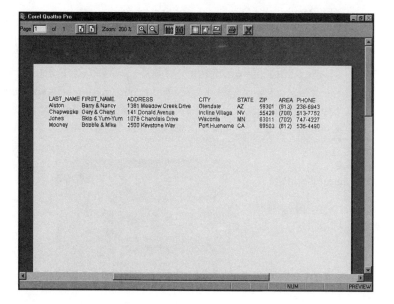

FIG. 19.4

Print Preview shows the printed report will contain only the preselected print blocks.

N O T E Use the Save Defaults button to save your settings so Corel Quattro Pro will automatically use them in the future. Use the Load Defaults button to return all settings to their default settings. ▨

FIG. 19.5
Use the Spreadsheet Page Setup dialog box Paper Type tab to specify the size and orientation of your paper.

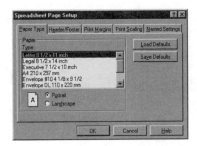

Selecting the Type of Paper   The Paper Type tab of the Spreadsheet Page Setup dialog box shown in Figure 19.5 enables you to select the type of paper and whether the report will print in Portrait or Landscape orientation. The Type list box has a scroll bar you can use to display the paper sizes available to fit your selected printer.

N O T E You may have to change the paper in your printer if you select a different paper size. The Type list shows the paper sizes your printer can use, not the sizes loaded into your printer. ▨

The Portrait and Landscape options are radio buttons—meaning you can select one or the other, but not both at the same time. The Portrait selection prints with the paper tall and narrow, the Landscape selection prints with the paper short and wide.

Printing a Header or Footer   A *header* is information printed in one or two lines at the top of each page of a report. A *footer* is information printed in one or two lines at the bottom of each page of a report. You specify a header or footer in the Spreadsheet Page Setup dialog box Header/Footer tab (see Figure 19.6).

FIG. 19.6
Use the Spreadsheet Page Setup dialog box Header/Footer tab to specify report headers and footers.

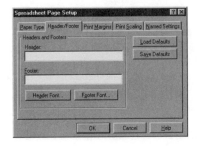

T I P Include the name of your Corel Quattro Pro notebook in the header or footer to make it easy to remember which notebook produced the report.

Each line of a header or footer can have up to three parts: a left-aligned, a centered, and a right-aligned section. When you enter header or footer text, separate the segments with a vertical bar (|). Segments that precede the first vertical bar are left-aligned; segments following the first vertical bar but preceding the second vertical bar are centered; and segments following the second vertical bar are right-aligned. To place the remaining segments of the header or footer on a second line, use **#n** in the header or footer at the point where you want to create the line break.

Table 19.1 describes the symbols you use to display information in headers and footers. You also can instruct Corel Quattro Pro to include the contents of a cell by entering a backslash (\) followed by the cell address or block name.

Table 19.1   Header and Footer Formatting Symbols

Symbol	Description
#	Current page number
#d	Current date in Short International format
#D	Current date in Long International format
#ds	Current date in standard Short format
#Ds	Current date in standard Long format
#f	Notebook name
#F	Notebook name with path
#n	Prints remainder of text on new line
#p	Current page number
#P	Total number of pages in printout
#p+n	Current page number plus the number n
#P+n	Total number of pages in printout plus the number n
#t	Current time in Short International format
#T	Current time in Long International format
#ts	Current time in standard Short format
#Ts	Current time in standard Long format
@	Current date
|	Left, center, or right-aligned text

Setting Print Margins   Print margins are the distance between the edges of the paper and the beginning of the area where Corel Quattro Pro can print. The Spreadsheet Page Setup dialog box Print <u>M</u>argins tab enables you to change margins (see Figure 19.7).

FIG. 19.7

Use the Spreadsheet Page Setup dialog box Print <u>M</u>argins tab to specify the size of margins.

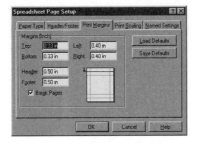

 Most laser and inkjet printers cannot print to the edge of a sheet of paper. See your printer manual to determine the minimum acceptable margins.

By default, Corel Quattro Pro reserves a margin that cannot be used for any printing: .33 inches at the top and at the bottom of each page, and .4 inches at each side of the page. In addition, another .5 inches is reserved between the top and bottom margins and any data for headers or footers.

The Spreadsheet Page Setup dialog box Print <u>M</u>argins tab contains six different text boxes you can use to set the page margins. The <u>T</u>op and Hea<u>d</u>er margins work together, as do the <u>B</u>ottom and F<u>o</u>oter margins. The Hea<u>d</u>er margin, for example, specifies the total distance between the top page margin and the beginning of the report text. The <u>T</u>op margin specifies the distance between the top of the page and the beginning of the header text.

Use the Bre<u>a</u>k Pages check box to specify whether Corel Quattro Pro should print continuously, regardless of margin settings, or start new pages on a new sheet observing the margin settings. This option only applies to printers using continuous forms that can print to the edge of the paper. If the Bre<u>a</u>k Pages check box is not checked, any header will print only on the first page, and any footer will print only on the final page.

Setting Print Scaling   You can reduce or enlarge the size of a printed report by using *print scaling*. This option enables you to specify an exact percentage, or to have Corel Quattro Pro automatically reduce the size of the print enough to fit the entire report on as few pages as possible. You use the Print <u>S</u>caling tab of the Spreadsheet Page Setup dialog box to specify print scaling (see Figure 19.8).

FIG. 19.8
Use the Spreadsheet Page
Setup dialog box Print
Scaling tab to reduce or
enlarge the scale of the
printed report.

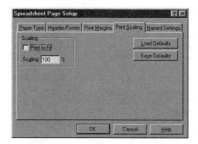

T I P If you use Print to Fit, select File, Print Preview before printing to preview the printed report, you can verify that the report will not be reduced to an unreadable size.

To fit all the printed output on as few pages as possible, select the Print to Fit check box. Corel Quattro Pro attempts to reduce the size of the print to fit the entire report on a single page. If the report still does not fit a single page, Corel Quattro Pro uses the maximum compression on all pages.

To control the exact level of compression, enter a percentage in the Scaling text box, and make certain the Print to Fit check box is not checked. To reduce the size of print by one-half, for example, enter **50** in the Scaling text box. You can expand the print also by entering a number larger than 100. To print the report three times the normal size, enter **300**.

TROUBLESHOOTING

Reports printed using Print to Fit print much too small, and leave large blank spaces at the right or the bottom of the page. Be sure to specify the print block. Corel Quattro Pro is probably printing the entire active area of the current notebook page.

Even though the correct print area is specified, the printed report is still too small to read. You may need to specify an exact percentage in the Scaling check box rather than using the Print to Fit check box. Your report may require more pages, but at least you'll be able to read it without a magnifying glass.

Using Named Print Settings   You can save current print settings under a unique name, recall the settings with this name, and reuse the settings without specifying each setting individually. You use the Named Settings tab in the Spreadsheet Page Setup dialog box to create or use named print settings (see Figure 19.9).

T I P Use named print settings to make certain your reports always have the same appearance.

FIG. 19.9

Use the Spreadsheet Page Setup dialog box Named Settings tab to save or reuse groups of print settings.

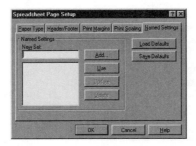

To assign a name to the current print settings, enter the name in the Ne<u>w</u> Set text box and select <u>A</u>dd. This will enable you to reuse the same group of print settings without going through all the steps to select each option. To change an existing named print setting, highlight the setting you want to change, and select Upda<u>t</u>e. To remove a named setting, select the setting you want to remove, and select <u>D</u>elete. To use an existing named setting, highlight the setting you want to use, and select <u>U</u>se.

Printing Row and Column Headings   Multiple-page reports can be difficult to understand. This is especially true when you cannot easily determine the correct column or row for data on pages after the first page. One improvement that can make multiple-page reports easier to understand is to include row or column headings, so each printed page includes the descriptive text that explains the data being presented. Setting headings in a printout has an effect similar to freezing titles on a notebook page.

> **CAUTION**
>
> Don't include any rows you designate as a <u>T</u>op Heading and any columns you designate as a Le<u>f</u>t Heading in the print block—they'll be printed twice.

To include row or column headings, select <u>F</u>ile, <u>P</u>rint, and then choose the Sh<u>e</u>et Options button to display the Spreadsheet Print Options dialog box (see Figure 19.10). For the <u>T</u>op Heading, select one or more rows of labels to print above each page of data. For the Le<u>f</u>t Heading, select one or more columns of data to print at the left of each page of data.

FIG. 19.10

Use the Spreadsheet Print Options dialog box to specify row or column headings and several other print options.

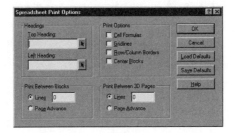

Using Additional Print Options   The Spreadsheet Print Options dialog box has several additional settings you can use to enhance your printed reports. These include:

- *Cell Formulas* prints cell formulas instead of the calculated results. This option is primarily for notebook documentation purposes.

- *Gridlines* prints the spreadsheet grid lines. This makes your report look more like the on-screen notebook page.

- *Row/Column Borders* includes the spreadsheet frame in your printed report. This is useful when you are developing a notebook, because the printouts show the location of data on the notebook page.

- *Center Blocks* prints the report centered between the page margins.

You use the Print Between Blocks and Print Between 3D Pages options to specify the separation you want between multiple or 3-D blocks.

Selecting Your Printer

You use the File, Print, Select Printer command to select or configure a printer, or to redirect print output to a file (see Figure 19.11). The choices in the Printer Setup dialog box depend on your system configuration.

FIG. 19.11
Use the Printer Setup dialog box to select your printer.

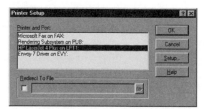

Part
III

Ch
19

To configure your printer, select Setup. When you make this selection, Windows displays a dialog box specific to your printer. Click OK to return to the Printer Setup dialog box.

If you want to delay printing, perhaps because you want to create a report you'll print on a printer that is temporarily unavailable, select the Redirect To File check box and specify a name for the print file. The print file will contain instructions specific to the selected printer, and will probably not print correctly on any other type of printer.

If you have installed Corel Envoy, you can also *publish* (or send the output) to Envoy instead of a printer. By publishing your file in Envoy format you create a file that can be viewed by other people, even if they do not have Corel Quattro Pro installed on their computer.

To publish your Corel Quattro Pro notebook in Envoy format:

1. Choose the File, Publish to, Envoy command to display the Spreadsheet Print dialog box.

2. Choose Print to publish your report.

   ▶ **See** "Publishing Documents with Envoy," **p. 269**

CHAPTER 20

Using the Internet with Corel Quattro Pro

The Internet is a big place, and most computer users want to be on the Internet. Sharing information is one of the best ways to use the Internet, and this chapter shows you what you can do with Corel Quattro Pro 7. ■

Create files for the Internet

Learn what you can do to save Corel Quattro Pro files for use on the Internet.

Use information from the Internet

See how you can access information on the Internet from Corel Quattro Pro.

Find help

Find out how to get more help by accessing resources on the Internet.

Publishing Corel Quattro Pro Files

Let's start by looking at the ways you can share, or *publish*, your Corel Quattro Pro files on the Internet. By doing so, you can provide easy access to information in your Corel Quattro Pro notebooks.

NOTE Technically, Corel Quattro Pro cannot publish files on the Internet. In fact, not even Corel WordPerfect can really publish files on the Internet. For that you'll need a *Web server*—the combination of a computer connected to the World Wide Web (commonly just called the Web) plus special software that enables users to access the information. Fortunately, you usually don't have to worry about setting up your own Web server. If your company has its own Web server, you also have someone who administers the Web server. If an outside company provides your Internet connection, it probably also administers the Web server. If you do have to create and administer your own Web server, you'll find that Que has a number of books that are useful. ▪

Understanding the Implications of Publishing on the Internet

It's been said that "just because you can do something doesn't mean you should do it." The same holds true for publishing information on the Internet. What does this mean exactly? You must realize that the Internet is like a big open book that millions of people can read whenever they like. When you publish information on the Internet, anyone who cares to can view the information at any time simply by connecting to your Web site. Whether you like it or not, what those people see creates their image of you (and your company if the Web site is identified with your company). If you place information on your Web site that creates a negative image, that's how people will view you.

> **CAUTION**
> Always consider whether publishing certain information might violate a copyright. If you didn't create the information yourself, you could be in trouble if you publish it without permission.

Let's say your company prides itself in its reputation as an environmentally conscious organization. It donates money to improve wildlife areas, is careful not to create pollution at its facilities, and generally is seen as a good corporate citizen. As an extra benefit to the employees, the company also allows employees to have home pages on the company's Web site. Imagine what the reaction would be if one of the employees decided to include a *link*—a shortcut to a location on the Internet—to an off-road motorcycling Web site that promoted racing motorcycles through an important prehistoric archeological site in an ecologically endangered desert area. Although your company might not support such activities as off-road motorcycling in sensitive areas, having the link on your Web site could appear to be an endorsement of them. It might not be either accurate or fair, but the company's image could suffer simply because someone wasn't careful about what they included on the Web site.

Inappropriate information isn't the only problem that can plague the Internet publisher. Some other problems you might inadvertently encounter could include copyright infringement, inaccurate information, and information that might be true, but could still result in legal action. For example, suppose you decide to improve the appearance of your Web site by including a cartoon. You found a cartoon in the newspaper that seems custom made for your Web site, so you scan it in and post it along with your other information. Unless you have obtained written permission from the copyright holder, publishing the cartoon on your Web page is a copyright violation and could cost you and your company a lot of money.

Next, imagine that you're creating a Web page that shows how well your company has been doing in selling its products. The company president has secret plans to run up the company stock, sell his shares, and move to the Caribbean, so he makes certain you aren't given the information about a couple of product lines that are causing big losses. While you may not realize your information is inaccurate, you'll probably have a tough time explaining that to the investigators after the president leaves for a warmer climate.

As you can see, it's very important to be extremely careful what you publish on the Internet. Still, there are valid reasons for placing information on the Internet, and you can use Corel Quattro Pro to quickly create documents in an Internet-compatible format.

Saving Files in HTML Format

 T I P View your HTML files by opening them in your Web browser (such as Netscape Navigator or Internet Explorer) to see how they'll appear on the Internet.

One reason the Internet has become so popular is that standards have developed that enable people using different types of computers and different types of software to all view the same information. *HTML*—HyperText Markup Language—is one of those standards. By saving documents in HTML format, you can make certain that other Internet users will be able to read your documents. For more information on HTML, see the section "Creating Web Documents" in Chapter 12.

In addition to the many standard spreadsheet formats it supports, Corel Quattro Pro can save notebooks in HTML format. When you've saved your Corel Quattro Pro notebooks in HTML format, you can then send the HTML file to your Web site administrator to be included on your Web site. To save a Corel Quattro Pro notebook file in HTML format, choose File, Save As, and select HTML from the drop-down As Type list box (see Figure 20.1). Enter the correct file name in the Name text box and choose Save.

N O T E When saving files for use on the Internet or on a company server that may not be able to correctly handle long file names, be sure to use file names that follow the DOS 8.3 file-name conventions. This will help prevent any confusion that may result if the server only shows shortened file names. ■

FIG. 20.1
Select HTML from the As Type list box to save your Corel Quattro Pro notebook in HTML format for publishing on the Internet.

 T I P Save your Corel Quattro Pro notebook in Corel Quattro Pro 7 format first to make certain you save all the formatting and features unique to Corel Quattro Pro 7.

When you attempt to save a Corel Quattro Pro notebook in a format other than as a wb3 file, features that are unique to Corel Quattro Pro 7 can be lost. This is certainly true when you try to save a Corel Quattro Pro notebook in HTML format. Therefore, you must always make sure to save any changes to a file as a Corel Quattro Pro v7 save before saving the file as an HTML file. Because of this potential for lost features, Corel Quattro Pro displays an information box (see Figure 20.2) which informs you that certain formatting of features may be lost if you don't save the file as a Corel Quattro Pro 7 file. Because you do want to save the file as an HTML file, choose HTML to continue.

FIG. 20.2
If you save your Corel Quattro Pro notebook in HTML format, you may lose formatting and features unique to Corel Quattro Pro 7.

Understanding the Limitations of HTML Format

The warning information shown in the dialog box in Figure 20.2 is extremely valid. While HTML is a true standard allowing easy exchange of information, it was never designed for the complexities of something like a Corel Quattro Pro notebook. Indeed, when you save a Corel Quattro Pro notebook in HTML format, you lose quite a bit of what makes a Corel Quattro Pro notebook useful. Figure 20.3 shows a typical warning you'll see when you attempt to save a Corel Quattro Pro notebook in HTML format. The exact warning you'll see will depend on the structure and makeup of your Corel Quattro Pro notebook.

FIG. 20.3

Corel Quattro Pro will warn you about some of the features you'll lose when you save your Corel Quattro Pro notebook in HTML format.

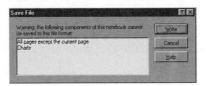

> **CAUTION**
>
> Corel Quattro Pro notebooks saved in HTML format lose a number of elements that are not listed in the warning in the Save File dialog box.

Unfortunately, the dialog box shown in Figure 20.3 really doesn't tell the whole story. In addition to losing all pages except the current page and any graphs, you also lose any formulas, any special formatting, any macros, and any links to other Corel Quattro Pro notebooks. For example, Figure 20.4 is a simple Corel Quattro Pro notebook that shows a sales report. To improve the notebook's appearance, the titles were centered across the columns of the report, different size fonts were used, some text was set to bold, lines were added to make data stand out, and formulas were added to summarize the data.

When you save the Corel Quattro Pro notebook in HTML format, many changes occur. Figure 20.5 shows the same Corel Quattro Pro notebook after it was saved in HTML format and opened in Netscape Navigator. As you can see, the basic information appears, but the appearance is not the same as the notebook's appearance in Corel Quattro Pro.

As a less obvious example, although totals for each column and row are listed in the HTML document, if a number is changed anywhere in the column or row, the total will not be updated in the totals cells because the formulas for calculation have been stripped from the notebook during the process of saving to HTML.

Because of the limited capability of HTML, you need to think of your HTML page as a snapshot of your spreadsheet at a given moment in time. The spreadsheet will no longer function as a "living document" on a Web site. Updating it will require saving the next version of the Corel Quattro Pro notebook each time it changes.

FIG. 20.4
A Corel Quattro Pro notebook as it appears in Corel Quattro Pro includes a number of formatting elements to improve the notebook's appearance.

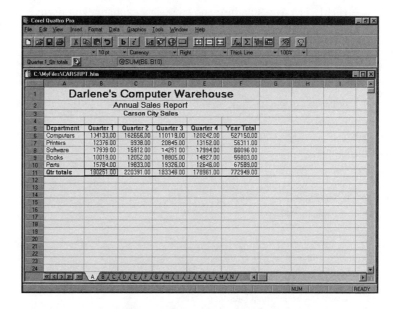

FIG. 20.5
After being saved in HTML format, a Corel Quattro Pro notebook looks much different after losing a number of formatting elements.

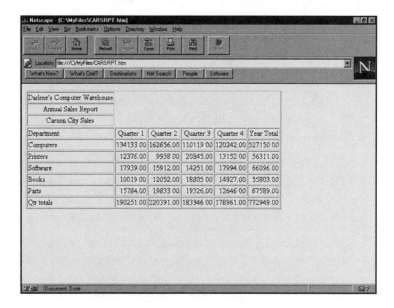

N O T E Don't forget that saving a Quattro Pro notebook in HTML format only saves the first page of the notebook. If you want to save other notebook pages in HTML format, move them to the front of the notebook before saving the file. ▪

Using Corel Barista for Better-Looking Documents

Although Corel Quattro Pro by itself doesn't produce very good-looking HTML files, there is a way to improve your image as a publisher of Corel Quattro Pro documents on the Internet. An add-in called Corel Barista enables you to create HTML files from your Corel Quattro Pro notebooks that look much more like the actual Corel Quattro Pro notebooks than a standard HTML file would. Corel Barista creates Java applets from your Corel Quattro Pro notebooks so that such features as graphs, fonts, and formatting are maintained.

Corel Barista uses *Java*—a programming language used to create applications on the Internet—to improve the appearance of Web pages, including those created from Corel Quattro Pro notebooks.

About Java

Java is a programming language based on C++. It is used to create small applications that enhance Web pages with features not available in standard HTML documents. Corel Barista creates HTML files that include the necessary Java applets to display your Corel Quattro Pro notebook on the Internet with an appearance very similar to the way Corel Quattro Pro itself displays the notebook.

Further coverage of Java topics is beyond the scope of this book. If you are interested in learning more about this interesting technology, extensive coverage can be found in *Special Edition Using Java*, published by Que.

To use Corel Barista to save your Corel Quattro Pro notebooks as HTML files, choose File, Publish to, Corel Barista to display the Publish to Corel Barista dialog box (see Figure 20.6).

Part

III

Ch

20

FIG. 20.6
Use the Publish to Corel Barista dialog box to save your Corel Quattro Pro notebooks in a much richer HTML format.

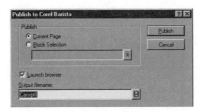

Specify whether you want to save the entire Current Page or the currently selected Block Selection. Enter the name for the Web page file in the Output Filename text box. To see how your Corel Quattro Pro notebook appears when it has been saved using Corel Barista, make certain the Launch browser check box is selected (this is the default). When you have completed your selections, click the Publish button to save the file in HTML format.

 T I P If you use Netscape Navigator, right-click the Download link and choose Save Link As to copy the Corel Barista file to your computer.

 ON THE WEB

If this is the first time you've used Corel Barista in Corel Quattro Pro, you may see a dialog box similar to the one shown in Figure 20.7.

If so, you must first download the Corel Barista file from the Corel Quattro Pro Web site at **http:// www.corel.com.** If you cannot find the Corel Quattro Pro Web site, call Corel Technical Support for assistance. Be sure to save the file in the Corel Quattro Pro program directory, which is usually C:\COREL\OFFICE7\ QUATTRO7.

FIG. 20.7
If this dialog box appears, you will need to download the latest version of Corel Barista before you can publish a file using the File, Publish to, Corel Barista command.

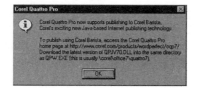

CAUTION
Make certain you save your files in Corel Quattro Pro 7 format before you publish them with Corel Barista. If you attempt to open an HTML file that was created by Corel Barista in Corel Quattro Pro, you'll find Corel Quattro Pro will display a blank notebook because Corel Quattro Pro doesn't understand the Java file code created by Corel Barista.

Figure 20.8 shows how your Corel Quattro Pro notebook appears when you use Corel Barista to save the file. Although the file still cannot include multiple pages, formulas, or macros, it can include important appearance items such as text formatting, lines, and even graphs.

FIG. 20.8
A Corel Quattro Pro notebook saved in HTML format using Corel Barista includes many of the formatting elements you used to improve the notebook's appearance.

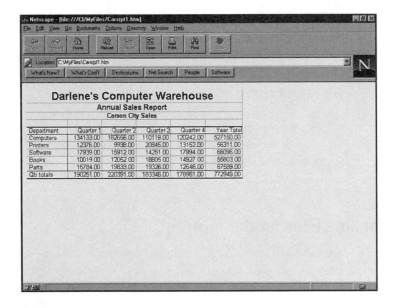

Publishing Documents with Envoy

You can also publish your Corel Quattro Pro notebooks using Envoy, Corel's *portable document format*, which enables users to view documents in their original format even if they lack the application that produced the document. When you save your Corel Quattro Pro notebooks using Envoy, other users will be able to view those notebooks even if they don't have Corel Quattro Pro.

To publish your Corel Quattro Pro notebooks using Envoy, choose File, Publish to, Envoy. Your file is printed to an Envoy file by the Envoy printer driver. For more information on the capabilities and uses of Envoy, see Chapter 28, "Using Envoy."

> **CAUTION**
> Because Envoy files are intended to display a large amount of document formatting on-screen, you may find that the files are too large to print on certain printers. Laser printers, for example, must load the entire page into memory before printing and may experience memory overflow problems when attempting to print Envoy files.

Part
III

Ch

20

Using Internet Files

Although sharing your information is useful, at some point you'll probably have the desire to get information from other people, too. In this section, we'll look at how you can use files on the Internet in Corel Quattro Pro.

N O T E You must be connected to the Internet before you can open files on the Internet or update links to Internet files. If you connect to the Internet through a dial-up connection, be sure to open that connection before you attempt to use Corel Quattro Pro to open or link to Internet files. ■

Opening Files on the Internet

You can easily open Corel Quattro Pro notebooks that are on the Internet. Suppose, for example, that your company has a master Corel Quattro Pro notebook containing the current pricing for all of your products. By making this notebook available on the Internet, your sales representatives could easily open the current file when they're visiting a customer and be certain that the pricing they're using is correct.

> **CAUTION**
>
> Unless your Web site administrator implements security measures limiting access to authorized users, anyone in the world who is browsing the Internet can access files you make available.

To open a Corel Quattro Pro notebook file located on the Internet, you must know the correct *Uniform Resource Locator* (URL) for the file. (See the section "What are Web Pages and URLs?" in Chapter 26 for more information on URLs.) Once you know the URL, you enter it in the <u>N</u>ame text box of the Open File dialog box instead of entering the name of a local file. For example, to open a Quattro Pro notebook located on a Web page:

1. Choose <u>F</u>ile, <u>O</u>pen.
2. Enter the URL of the notebook file in the <u>N</u>ame text box.
3. Choose <u>O</u>pen to open the notebook file. Figure 20.9 shows that the notebook looks just like a file you might have opened from your local hard disk.

N O T E The Quattro Pro notebook shown in Figure 20.9 is a real notebook that was created to assist small building departments in preparing building permits. It is available for free download and use, but the author retains the copyright. You may not modify or distribute modified copies of the notebook file. ■

FIG. 20.9
A notebook file opened from an Internet location looks just like a file opened locally.

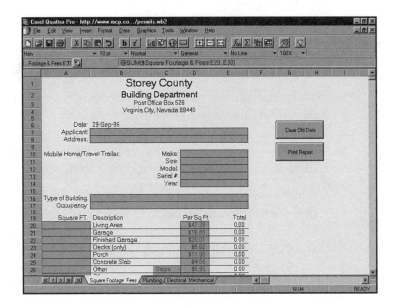

Saving Files from the Internet

You cannot save Corel Quattro Pro notebook files to Internet locations. If you attempt to save the PERMITS notebook, for example, Corel Quattro Pro will advise you that the file is read-only, and will offer to save the file on your computer. Once you save the file on your system, you can use it just like any other local file, but you should remember that the local file will not be automatically updated when the Internet file is updated. To update your local copy you must once again open the copy located on the Internet and then save it on your computer.

Linking to Internet Files

Rather than opening a complete Corel Quattro Pro notebook file on the Internet, you may want to simply create a link to a cell in a notebook file located on the Internet. You may find this a better choice if you need to both save data you've added to the notebook, and still make certain that you are always using the current information from a central source. For example, suppose you need to track how many pieces each customer orders of several different items, but your pricing is very volatile. If your home office maintains a master price list file in an Internet or intranet-accessible Corel Quattro Pro notebook file, you can link the pricing column to that file and simply update the links when you enter an order.

N O T E   *Intranet* is the term many people use to describe Internet-compatible networks within a company. See Chapter 26 "Using Corel WordPerfect Suite on the Internet" for more information on intranets. ■

T I P You may find security is easier if your users link to cells in a master Corel Quattro Pro notebook file on the Internet, rather than opening an entire file on the Internet because the master linking file can be considerably more obscure and simply contain data without any identifying labels.

Suppose, for example, that you wanted to always make certain that you were using the most current per square foot fees for living space in your local copy of the PERMITS notebook. Rather than entering an unchanging value in the notebook, you could link to the master copy by entering a formula that specified the correct cell in the master copy of the file on the Internet. In this case you would enter the following formula:

> **+[http://www.mcp.com/que/desktop_os/authors/underdahl/ permits.wb2]Square Footage & Fees:D20**

N O T E Although the URL shown in the formula was correct at the time this was written, the Internet is constantly changing and an address that is valid today, may disappear tomorrow. You should use this as an example of how to create your own links, rather than as an actual link that you will use. ▪

Once this linking formula was in place, you would have the option of updating the link at any time by choosing Edit, Links, Refresh Links. In addition, you would be given the opportunity to refresh the links whenever you opened the Corel Quattro Pro notebook file containing the link.

Using QuickButtons to Display Internet Documents

Sometimes you want to view information on the Internet, rather than using that information within a Corel Quattro Pro notebook. In some cases, a particular Web site (document) might contain information that would be useful in your Corel Quattro Pro notebook, but is not contained in a Corel Quattro Pro notebook, and therefore not available for linking to your local Corel Quattro Pro notebook.

For example, suppose someone had a Web site where they showed the current prices for computer memory, but the Web site was an HTML file (which cannot be linked to a Corel Quattro Pro notebook). You might want to visit this Web site often while you were working within Corel Quattro Pro, and then manually add the current pricing to your Corel Quattro Pro notebook. One way to automate this process is to use a QuickButton to open the document when you click the QuickButton.

 T I P You can use QuickButtons to open Internet documents even if they aren't in a format that can be linked to a Corel Quattro Pro notebook.

To create a QuickButton to open an Internet document:

1. Click the Create a QuickButton button on the notebook page toolbar.
2. Point to an empty place on the notebook page and click the left mouse button. Because the QuickButton will remain in the same location in the notebook, be sure to pick a location where the QuickButton will not interfere with any data, will not disrupt the appearance of your reports, and where it will be easy to find.
3. Right-click the new QuickButton and choose Button Properties from the QuickMenu.
4. On the Macro tab, choose Link to URL.
5. Enter the URL in the URL text box.
6. Choose OK, and then select the Label text tab.
7. In the Enter Text text box, enter a short descriptive label for the QuickButton.
8. Choose OK to complete the dialog box and return to the notebook.
9. Click a notebook cell to deselect the QuickButton.

To test your QuickButton, first make certain your Internet connection is open and then click the QuickButton. Your Internet browser will open and display the document specified in the URL text box. You may need to switch to your Internet browser to see the document.

 TIP Don't forget that information you copy to a Corel Quattro Pro notebook from an Internet document is static. You may want to update the information just before creating a report.

Once the document is displayed in your Internet browser, you can copy information to your Corel Quattro Pro notebook. The exact technique you'll need to use will vary according to which Internet browser you use, but the general steps are:

1. Select the information.
2. Use the Edit, Copy command in the Internet browser to copy the information to the Clipboard.
3. Switch to Corel Quattro Pro and use Edit, Paste to add the information to the notebook.

Downloading Internet Information into Corel Quattro Pro

Earlier in this chapter, you learned how to open a Corel Quattro Pro notebook on the Internet or link to a Corel Quattro Pro notebook on the Internet. Not all useful information is available in Corel Quattro Pro notebooks, however. Although you can manually copy information into your Corel Quattro Pro notebook, sometimes it's handier to automate the process. Unfortunately, Corel Quattro Pro has no direct way to automate this process, but with the help of a QuickTask, you can automate certain specific tasks. See Chapter 33, "Integrating You Work with QuickTasks" for more information on using QuickTasks.

Corel Quattro Pro has a QuickTask that can download Internet information into a Corel Quattro Pro notebook. This QuickTask is called Track My Stocks and we'll have a short look at it in the following section.

1. Start the Track My Stocks QuickTask by choosing Corel WordPerfect Suite 7, Accessories, Corel QuickTasks from the Start menu.

2. Choose Track My Stocks on the Internet tab.

3. Choose Run (you may then need to select Next if you haven't used Quicktasks before) to begin the QuickTask. Figure 20.10 shows the Track My Stocks QuickTask dialog box. For this example we'll use the sample stocks built into the Track My Stocks QuickTask, but you'll want to enter your own stocks.

FIG. 20.10

You can use the Track My Stocks QuickTask to enter stock market data into a Corel Quattro Pro notebook.

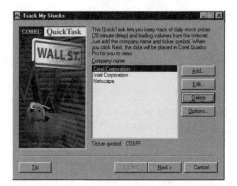

4. Choose Next to download the information and display it in your Corel Quattro Pro notebook. Figure 20.11 shows how the Track My Stocks QuickTask shows information downloaded from the Internet.

T I P If you want to examine the data more closely, be sure to save the Corel Quattro Pro notebook file by choosing File, Save before you select Cancel, because the Track My Stocks QuickTask will close the notebook when you select Cancel.

FIG. 20.11
The Track My Stocks QuickTask displays stock market data in a Corel Quattro Pro notebook.

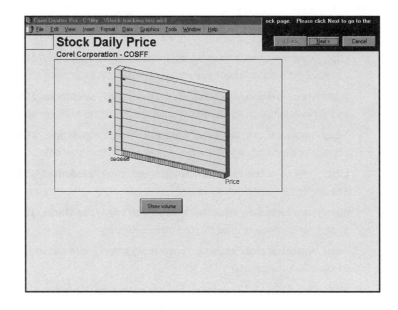

Finding Help on the Internet

 Corel Quattro Pro makes it easy to access help on the Internet. You can click the Connect to the World Wide Web button to access the Corel home page or you can choose Help, Help Online to go directly to the Corel Quattro Pro home page. The following On the Web section shows several Web pages you'll find useful.

CAUTION

The URLs in the following list are maintained by Corel Corporation and are for reference only. The nature of the Web is that it is ever-changing. Because of this nature, it cannot be guaranteed that any of these URLs will be available at any particular time, as systems are often taken down for repair or upgrading. It also cannot be guaranteed that any of these URLs will be available for any specific length of time as addresses are routinely changed as a system grows. The basic URL for Corel is listed in the first entry of the table. This URL is most likely to be available for the longest period of time and most of the others will probably be accessible through it in some way.

Part
III

Ch
20

 ON THE WEB

http://www.corel.com/   This is the Corel home page (reached by clicking the Connect to the World Wide Web button).

http://www.corel.com/products/ wordperfect/cqp7/tips&tricks/index.htm   Find tips and tricks for Corel Quattro Pro 7 at this address.

http://www.corel.com/products/ wordperfect/cqp7/tips&tricks/1020.htm See this address for information about entering data quickly into a spreadsheet.

http://www.corel.com/products/ wordperfect/cqp7/tips&tricks/1058.htm See this address for information about ready-made spreadsheets and forms.

http://www.corel.com/products/ wordperfect/cqp7/tips&tricks/1059.htm See this address for information about building a detailed budget or mortgage schedule.

http://www.corel.com/products/ wordperfect/cqp7/tips&tricks/1060.htm See this address for information about building a chart or map from your data.

http://www.corel.com/products/ wordperfect/cwp7/tips&tricks/1103.htm See this address for the macros user survey.

http://www.corel.com/products/ wordperfect/cwp7/tips&tricks/1027.htm See this address for information about ordering printed manuals.

http://www.corel.com/ customer/contactinfo.htm See this address for contact information for Corel customer service.

http://205.227.112.10/qp.htm See this address for information about the searchable knowledgebase of Quattro Pro answer documents.

http://www.corel.com/support/faqs/prqppdx.htm#QP70 See this address for information about Quattro Pro 7.0 for Windows 95 Frequently Asked Questions.

ftp://ftp.corel.com/pub/wordperfect/QuattroPro/Qpw70/ See this address for the Corel Quattro Pro 7 FTP site.

For more information on finding help on the Internet, see the section "Finding Help on the Internet" in Chapter 26. ●

Using Corel Presentations

CHAPTER 21

Getting Started with Corel Presentations 7

This chapter introduces Corel Presentations 7, a program you can use to create professional quality overhead, paper, 35mm slide, or on-screen presentations. In this chapter, you learn how to start Corel Presentations 7 and create a slideshow. You also learn the basic steps to entering and editing slide information, and a variety of ways to view the slide screen. ■

Start a new presentation

Learn about the Corel Presentations 7 screen and how to allow Corel Presentations 7 to walk you through the process of creating a new presentation.

Change views of the Corel Presentations 7 screen

See how you can zoom the presentation, show it in Draft Mode if you have a slower computer, or show margins on your drawing window.

Use Outliner to create a presentation

Learn about the Outliner view and how it permits you to type text into Corel Presentations 7 just as if you had a steno pad. Understand how to specify whether the text is automatically formatted as bullet slides or other slide types.

View slides in the Slide Editor

Find out how the Slide Editor allows you to select individual elements of your slide and format them, or add new slide elements as needed.

List and sort slides

Learn to rearrange your slideshow or specify transition effects if you are showing the presentation electronically using these two views.

Starting Corel Presentations 7

You start Corel Presentations 7 like you start any of the applications in Corel WordPerfect Suite 7—by clicking the Start button, then choosing Corel WordPerfect Suite 7, Corel Presentations 7 from the menu. Additionally, you can start Corel Presentations 7 from the Corel WordPerfect Suite 7 DAD (Desktop Application Director) by clicking the Corel Presentations 7 button on the taskbar.

The Corel Presentations 7 screen displays a dialog box that puts you to work immediately—the Document Selection dialog box. From this box, you choose the document type on which to work: you can Create a New Drawing, Create a New Slide Show, Create a New Slide Show Using PerfectExpert, Work on an Existing File, or Work on the Last File. Depending on your choice, Corel Presentations 7 displays other dialog boxes to help you along the way.

If you choose to Create a New Slide Show, Corel Presentations 7 displays a New Slide Show dialog box from which you can choose a Slide Master and Slide Template. The Slide Masters provide a consistent look and feel between all the slides of your presentation. They are made up of various colors, patterns, and graphic lines that make your slides attractive and professional-looking. The Slide Template defines the contents of each slide—bullets, charts, or text, for example.

N O T E   CorelFLOW 3, discussed in Chapter 30, "Using CorelFLOW 3," has many of the same graphics uses. It is not oriented toward a slide presentation format, but rather toward creating diagrams of various sorts. When you are creating a single graphic, you can use either Corel Presentations 7 or CorelFLOW 3. ■

Selecting a Presentation

When you start Corel Presentations 7, the Document Selection dialog box appears, as shown in Figure 21.1. From this dialog box, you choose to open or create a file, set preferences, or exit the program.

FIG. 21.1

You can choose to open or create a file, set preferences, or exit the program in the Document Selection dialog box.

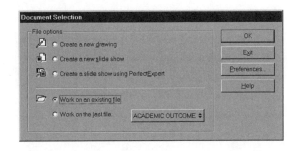

You may or may not want to continue to display this dialog box; Corel Presentations 7 gives you that choice in the Preferences dialog box. Table 21.1 describes the options in that dialog box.

Table 21.1 Document Selection Options

Option	Description
Create a New Drawing	Begin a new drawing (a single drawing).
Create a New Slide Show	Begin a new slideshow (a series of drawings linked together as a slideshow).
Create a Slide Show Using PerfectExpert	Begin a new slideshow using the PerfectExpert to receive step-by-step guidance.
Work on an Existing File	Displays the Open dialog box so you can open an existing file.
Work on the Last File	Select to open the last file you worked on; the file name appears in the box to the right of the option.
OK	Accept the choice in the File Options area and close the dialog box.
Exit	Close Corel Presentations 7.
Preferences	Open the Environment dialog box.
Help	View Help files describing available choices.

If you choose the Preferences command button, you see the Environment Preferences dialog box shown in Figure 21.2. In this box, you can choose various startup options. In the Startup Document Options area, choose Slide Show or Drawing if you do not want the Document Selection dialog box to appear each time you open the application. Instead, the program opens to a blank drawing screen or a new slide presentation screen. Click OK to close the dialog box and return to the Document Selection dialog box.

Using the Master Gallery

If you choose to create a new slideshow in the Document Selection dialog box, the New Slide Show dialog box appears (see Figure 21.3).

To create a new slideshow, you first choose a Master look and feel, and then choose a Template to specify the slide type for Slide 1.

A Master is a background for the slideshow that you can apply to one or all slides. Normally, you apply the same Master to all slides in the show to create consistency in the presentation.

FIG. 21.2

Choose how you want Corel Presentations 7 to start, using the Environment Preferences dialog box.

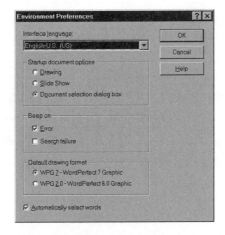

FIG. 21.3

In the New Slide Show dialog box, you choose a Master look and a Template for the first slide.

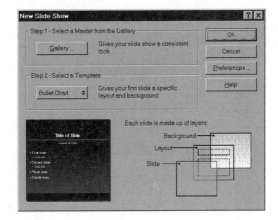

To use the Master Gallery, take the following steps:

1. To view the Masters that are available in the Gallery, click the Gallery button in the New Slide Show dialog box. The Master Gallery dialog box appears, as shown in Figure 21.4, with the available backgrounds you can use for your slides.

2. Additionally, the dialog box contains two important option buttons you can use:

   - *Category*. Choose to see the set of Masters appropriate to your presentation mode: Color (for color printers and electronic presentations), Printout (for printing with black-and-white printers), and 35mm (for sending to a slide service).

   - *Other File*. Look at the Insert Master dialog box and browse to a Masters file you would like to open.

FIG. 21.4
In the Master Gallery dialog box, you choose the Master that Corel Presentations will use consistently throughout all your slides.

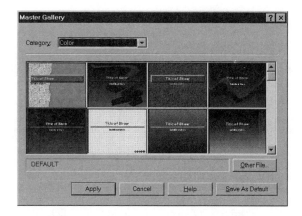

3. Choose a Master from the Master Gallery and click Apply. The Master Gallery dialog box closes and returns to the New Slide Show dialog box with the selected Master in the sample box. If you change your mind later, you can always change the Master by using this same simple process.

Selecting a Template

In Step 2–Select a Template (found on the New Slide Show dialog box), you choose the template or layout you want to use for the first slide in the New Slide Show dialog box. When you click the box in Step 2–Select a Template, a pop-up list appears, as shown in Figure 21.5.

FIG. 21.5
You can choose from among eight slide templates for your first slide in the New Slide Show dialog box pop-up list.

Select a slide type. Table 21.2 describes the slide types.

Table 21.2	Slide Types
Type	**Description**
None	Plain white background
Background	Background colors and lines only, no text boxes
Title	Background with formatted area for a title and subtitle

continues

Part
IV

Ch

21

Table 21.2 Continued	
Type	**Description**
Bullet Chart	Background with formatted area for a title, subtitle, and a list of bulleted text
Text	Background with formatted area for a title and paragraph text
Org Chart	Background with formatted area for a title and an organizational chart
Data Chart	Background with formatted area for a title and a data chart
Combination	Background with formatted area for a bulleted list and a data chart

After you choose the type of slide you want to use, click OK to close the dialog box and apply the background and layout to the slide on-screen.

N O T E   When you first create a drawing, the screen that is brought up automatically is blank, like a white sheet of paper, ready for you to fill with your ideas. When you first create a slideshow, to have a similar blank white screen, you must make a choice in the New Slide Show dialog box. In the Select a Template section, you must click the button and a drop-down menu will appear. Choose None from the list. ▨

  T I P   The template you choose applies only to the first slide; you select each additional slide's template when you add a slide using the Slide, Add Slides command.

N O T E   If you click the Preferences button in the New Slide Show dialog box, you can change the default options for slideshows, such as starting with a specific slide type, startup view, or page settings. ▨

Viewing the Corel Presentations 7 Screen

The Corel Presentations 7 screen includes many screen elements to help you complete your work. In addition to the common Windows 95 features—title bar, menu bar, Mini-mize/Maximize buttons, and so on—Corel Presentations 7 offers a toolbar, a Power Bar, and a Tool Palette to help you perform commands quickly, format your presentation, add elements, and move around your presentation with ease.

In addition to screen elements that help you in your work, Corel Presentations 7 offers a variety of views, or zooms, that enable you to look at your work in the best view for you.

Although the default view is the full page or slide view, you can, for example, zoom in to a specific part of the slide for a closer look. Figure 21.6 shows the Corel Presentations 7 screen, in Full Page view, with the screen elements labeled.

FIG. 21.6

Initially, you see the first slide in Slide view, which is valuable for selecting and editing specific elements on a slide.

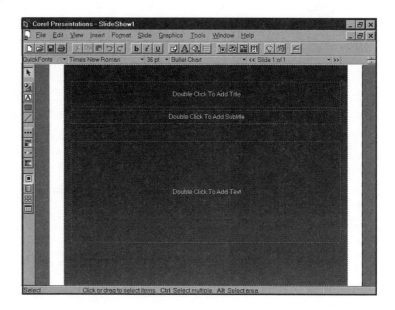

Using the Toolbar, Power Bar, and Tool Palette

The three icon bars on the Corel Presentations 7 screen help you complete your work by providing formatting, commands, and navigating shortcuts you use every day in your work. Using the Power Bar, for example, you can move to the next slide in the presentation, the toolbar is used to change text to bold, and so on.

Toolbar Table 21.3 identifies the icons, or buttons, specific to Corel Presentations 7 and describes their uses.

Table 21.3 Toolbar Buttons

Button	Function
	Shadow. Displays the Shadow Properties dialog box; choose shadow options.
	Font. Changes the properties of selected text.
	Object Properties. Changes the line and fill properties of selected objects.

Part

IV

Ch

21

continues

Table 21.3	Continued
Button	**Function**
	Bullet Chart Properties. Changes properties of bullets and numbers.
	Add Slides. Displays the Add Slide dialog box; adds one or more slides to the slideshow.
	Slide Transition. Displays the Slide Transition dialog box; defines slide transition and advance options, and adds sounds to slides.
	Master Gallery. Displays the Master Gallery dialog box; choose a slide background.
	Play Show. Displays the Play Slide Show dialog box; choose show options and play the show.
	Ask the PerfectExpert. Help feature allowing you to find solutions by asking questions using your own words.
	Web Browser. Launch your Web browser to access the Internet or your local intranet.
	ActionLink. Create buttons that play sounds, launch files, and take other actions.

N O T E If you cannot view all of the buttons on-screen at one time, you can click the scroll bar to display more buttons. ▪

Power Bar   The Power Bar, located directly below the toolbar, enables you to format text and edit slides. Figure 21.7 illustrates the Power Bar and Table 21.4 describes the buttons on the Power Bar.

FIG. 21.7
You can format slides with the Power Bar, which is located under the toolbar.

Power Bar

N O T E Depending on your screen resolution, you may see two more buttons on your Power Bar than the ones shown in these figures: the Slide Layers and Zoom Options buttons. ▪

Table 21.4   Power Bar Buttons

Button	Function
QuickFonts ▼	*QuickFonts.* Select from the last fonts used.
Times New Roman ▼	*Font Selection.* Assign a specific font to selected text.
36 pt ▼	*Font Sizes.* Assign a font size to selected text.
Bullet Chart ▼	*Slide Types.* Change the slide template of the current slide.
<<	*Move to Previous Slide.* Go to the previous slide.
Slide 1 of 6 ▼	*Slide Selection.* Choose the slide you want to move to.
>>	*Move to Next Slide.* Go to the next slide.
Slide Layer ▼	*Slide Layers.* Edit the slide background, the slide type, or the text layer.
54% ▼	*Zoom Options.* Change screen view to a percentage, such as 75% or 50%, or to Full Page, Margins, and so on.

Tool Palette   The Tool Palette is located along the upper-left side of the screen below the toolbar and Power Bar. Many of the tools on the Tool Palette present two or more choices when you click and hold the mouse button down. Table 21.5 lists the Tool Palette buttons and describes each tool. Additionally, when you choose a drawing tool and use it in the work area, the screen changes to the drawing view. The uses of these tools are described in the following sections, so don't worry if you don't understand some of the terms that are used in this table yet.

Table 21.5   Tool Palette Buttons

Button	Function
▶	*Selection Tool.* Click the item to select it; after the item is selected, you can perform actions such as copying, deleting, formatting, and so on.
📊	*Chart or Graphics Tools.* Choose a tool for creating charts, organizational charts, QuickArt graphics, or bitmap images.

Part
IV

Ch
21

continues

Table 21.5   Continued

Button	Function
	Text Object Tools. Choose a tool for creating text boxes, text lines, or bullet charts.
	Closed Object Tools. Create a rectangle, rounded rectangle, circle, ellipse, polygon, or a variety of other closed objects (objects that contain fills).
	Line Object Tools. Create a straight, curved, or freehand line, a Bezier curve, elliptical arc, or circular arc.
	Line Attributes. Choose a line style from the palette.
	Fill Attributes. Choose a pattern as fill for a closed object.
	Line Colors. Choose a line color from the color palette.
	Fill Colors. Choose a fill color from the palette.
	Slide Editor view. Change to Slide Editor view.
	Outliner view. Change to Outliner view.
	Slide Sorter view. Change to Slide Sorter view.
	Slide List view. Change to Slide List view.

Viewing the Presentation

The default view in Corel Presentations 7 Slide Editor is Margin Size view. You also can change the view to various magnifications. When you zoom or change views, the actual size of the objects, pages, text, and so on does not change; only the view of what you see on-screen changes.

To change the view, choose View, Zoom. A sub-menu appears. Table 21.6 describes each of the available views and lists the shortcuts you can use to switch views.

Table 21.6   Changing Screen Views

Screen View	Description
Zoom Area Ctrl+Shift+F5	Magnifies the view of a selected area; drag magnifying glass, drawing a rectangle across the area you want to enlarge.
Margin Size Alt+F5	Display the margins in the drawing window.
Screen Size	Displays the page as it will look when you play the slideshow.
Full Page Shift+F5	Displays the entire document.
Selected Objects	Magnifies the view of the selected objects.
Actual Size	Displays the page as it will look when printed.
Previous View	Displays the last view before you used Zoom.
Zoom In Shift+PgUp	Magnifies the view by 20 percent each time you use it.
Zoom Out Shift+PgDn	Reduces the view by 20 percent each time you use it.

Figure 21.8 shows the screen at Full Page view with the Zoom Area tool.

FIG. 21.8
You can define an area to zoom with the magnifying glass Zoom Area tool in a Corel Presentations slide.

Zoom Area tool —

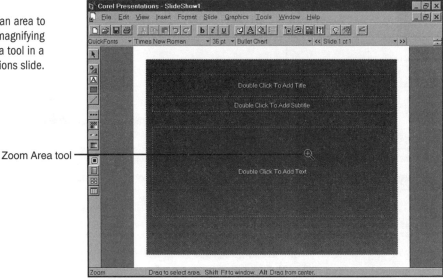

N O T E   Another view option is Draft Mode, found near the bottom of the View menu; you can use Draft Mode with any of the Zoom views. Draft Mode presents the slides without background color and objects with outlines instead of fill colors, patterns, and other attributes. Use Draft Mode to speed editing and working. To select Draft Mode, choose View, Draft Mode or Ctrl+F5. A check mark appears beside the command in the View menu. To turn Draft Mode off, choose the command again; the check mark disappears. ■

Part
IV

Ch
21

Using Outliner

The Outliner view is useful for entering text into your slideshow. You can add slides, create titles, text, bullets, and so on in Outliner view. Using the Outliner view enables you to plan and organize the slideshow, rearrange slides, and perfect the show before transferring it to slides, especially if your slideshow contains many bullet or text slides.

 To change to Outliner view, click the Outliner view on the Tool Palette or open the View menu and choose Outliner. Figure 21.9 shows Outliner view.

FIG. 21.9

Outliner view looks like a ruled sheet of paper on which you can organize your presentation.

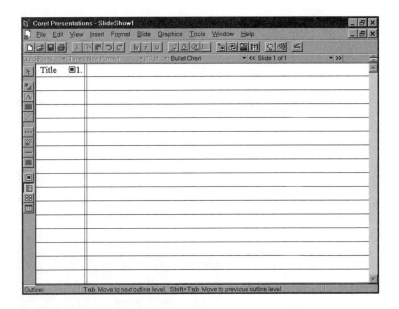

TIP In addition to entering your presentation outline in Outliner view, you also can insert a Corel WordPerfect file to use for an outline. Choose Insert, File and select the document and file type.

Adding Slides

You can add slides while in Outliner view with either the toolbar icon or the menu. Additionally, you can delete slides if you choose to. When you add a slide in Corel Presentations 7, you choose the slide type; alternatively, you can choose to add more than one slide at a time and choose the slide type as you enter the text for each slide.

To add a slide to a presentation:

1. In Outliner view, chose Slide, Add Slide, or click the Add Slide icon on the toolbar. The Add Slides dialog box appears, as shown in Figure 21.10.

FIG. 21.10
Add a slide to the slideshow in Outliner view through the Add Slides dialog box.

2. In the Number of Slides box, enter or select the number of slides you want to add.

3. In Template, choose the type of slide you want to add.

4. Click OK to close the dialog box and add the slide(s).

N O T E If you add two or more slides, they will all be the same type—Title, for example. You can change the type by clicking the slide number in the Outline and then clicking the Slide Types button on the Power Bar and choosing a type. ■

CAUTION
If you add too many slides or change your mind after adding, you can click the line in Outliner for the slide you want to delete, and choose Slide, Delete Slide. Corel Presentations 7 displays a message asking if you are sure; click Yes to delete or No to cancel. To delete more than one slide, select the lines in Outliner by dragging the mouse, and then select the Slide, Delete Slide command. When you delete a slide, you delete the entire outline family, including all sublevels.

Entering Text and Assigning Levels

Enter the text for your slides in Outliner so you can easily view, edit, and rearrange the slides before viewing them in Slide Editor view. As you enter the text, or even after entering it, you can assign various levels to the text, such as title, subtitle, bullets, and so on.

To enter text in Outliner:

1. Position the insertion point and type the text.

2. The first line of any slide type is a title. Press Enter to create a subtitle.

3. Press Enter again to create bullets. Each time you press Enter after creating the first bullet line, Outliner adds more bullets on the same level.

To change a level:

■ Press Tab to move down one level. You can create up to six levels of bullets by pressing the Tab key five times.

■ Press Shift+Tab to move up one level; for example, to change a bullet to a subtitle, press Shift+Tab. To change the subtitle to a title, press Shift+Tab again.

Part
IV

Ch
21

Figure 21.11 shows a sample outline with titles, subtitles, and two levels of bullets.

FIG. 21.11

You can create an outline of your slides with titles, subtitles, and bullets in Outliner, and easily arrange and rearrange the levels of the slide contents.

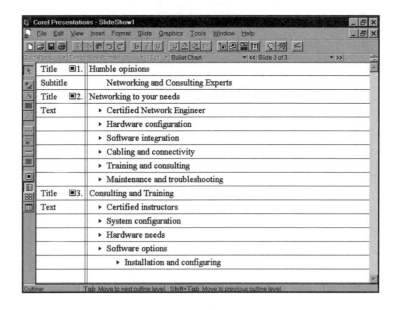

Rearranging Slides

As you create your outline, you can rearrange the slide order of the presentation in Outliner view. Change the slide order by dragging the slide title to a new position. All of the slide's text follows the title when you move it.

To move a slide:

1. Position the mouse pointer over the slide icon until the pointer changes to an arrow.

2. Drag the slide up or down to the new position. As you drag, the mouse pointer changes to a drag icon. Additionally, the screen will scroll up or down if you drag the icon past the window borders.

3. Drag the slide icon pointer to a line that holds another slide title. A short, horizontal line appears above the slide title to indicate the new slide will position ahead of it.

4. When you release the mouse button, the slide and the entire outline family slips into its new location.

Figure 21.12 illustrates a slide in the process of being moved to a new location.

FIG. 21.12
Move a slide and its contents
by dragging it to a new
position.

Line indicates
placement

Mouse pointer
with slide icon

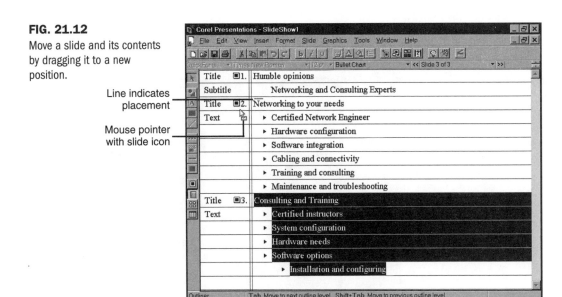

Using the Slide Editor

You use Slide Editor to view each individual slide as it will look in the slideshow or when
printed. You can switch to the Slide Editor after using Outliner to enter your text, or you
can create the text and other objects for the presentation directly in Slide Editor view.

 To switch to Slide Editor view, choose View, Slide Editor, or click the Slide Editor View
button on the Tool Palette to quickly switch views.

 TIP Use the Slide Selection button on the Power Bar to move to other slides as you work with the
presentation.

Adding Text

In Slide Editor view, text boxes appear that enable you to enter titles, subtitles, bullets,
and so on. You can enter, edit, and format the text in a text box. Additionally, you can
move the text box or resize it.

- To move or resize a text box, click the box once to select it; small handles appear on
  the corners and sides of the text box.

  Drag the box to a new position to move it.

- To resize the box, position the mouse pointer over any handle; the pointer changes
  to a double-headed arrow (see Figure 21.13).

Part
IV

Ch

21

Drag the handle toward the center to make the text box smaller, or away from the center of the box to make the box larger.

FIG. 21.13
When you resize or move a selected text box with its handles, the pointer changes to a double-headed arrow.

Handles —

Double-headed arrow —

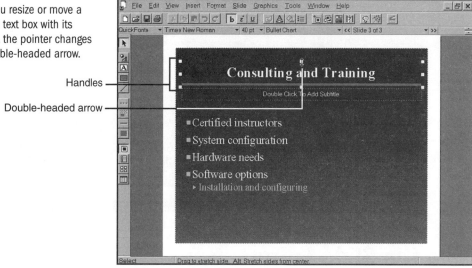

To enter text into a text box:

1. Double-click the box. The box changes to a text box with a blinking vertical cursor and a grayed outline (see Figure 21.14).

2. Type the text.

3. When you are done entering text, click outside the text box.

To edit the text in a text box, double-click the box and the cursor appears in the text box.

 TIP When you are finished typing in a text box, press the Esc key to indicate you are done typing. The box remains selected for moving or resizing.

To create a text box:

1. Click the Text Object Tools button on the toolbar.

2. Select the single line or the paragraph text tool and position the tool in the work area of the slide. The tool looks like a hand holding a rectangle.

3. Drag the hand to create the text block.

4. When you release the mouse button, the new text box appears with a blinking cursor, ready to receive text.

FIG. 21.14
You enter and edit all kinds of text—titles, subtitles, bulleted items, and body text—in the text box.

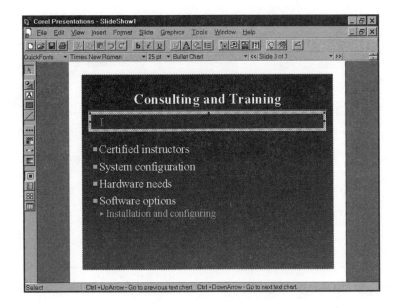

Formatting Text

You format the text in a text box similarly to formatting any text in other Corel WordPerfect Suite 7 applications, with one exception. In Corel Presentations 7, you must first double-click the text box and then drag the mouse to select the text; merely selecting the text box will not enable formatting of the text. After selecting the text, choose a font, size, or attribute.

After selecting the text:

- Use the Font Selection and Font Size buttons on the Power Bar to change font and size.

- Additionally, you can use the Bold, Italic, and Underline buttons on the toolbar to format text with attributes.

- Finally, you can use the Format, Font command to format text in text boxes.

Figure 21.15 shows the Font Properties dialog box where you can choose which options to apply to your selected text.

Part
IV

Ch
21

FIG. 21.15
Choose the font, size, and
attributes all at one time in
the Font Properties dialog
box.

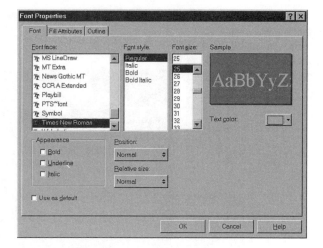

TROUBLESHOOTING

I switched from Outliner view to Slide Editor view and the text in my titles is too long, thus overlapping other text. You can do any of three things to solve the problem: Change the font size, edit the text, or move the text box on the page so the text does not overlap other text.

I can't move to another slide in Slide Editor view. You may be creating a drawing rather than a presentation. A drawing only has one "slide;" a presentation can have several. You need to create a new presentation, rather than a new drawing.

Listing and Sorting Slides

Corel Presentations 7 includes two other views, Slide List and Slide Sort, for you to use when creating and organizing your presentation. You will most likely use these two views when you are preparing to play a slideshow.

Slide Sort shows a mini-gallery of each slide so you can visually organize them. Slide List shows each slide's number, title, and other information to help you organize your presentation.

Using Slide Sorter

Slide Sorter view displays the slides in your presentation as small slides so you can see the visual impact of the overall presentation.

In addition, you can change the order of the slides in Slide Sorter view. To change the view to Slide Sorter, choose <u>V</u>iew, Slide <u>S</u>orter, or click the Slide Sorter View button on the Tool Palette.

Figure 21.16 shows the Slide Sorter view.

FIG. 21.16
Visually organize the slides in Slide Sorter view.

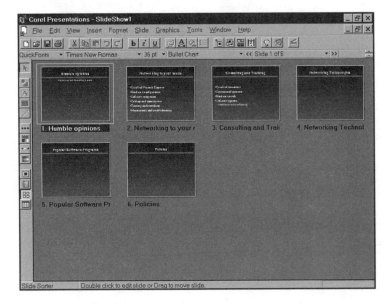

In Slide Sorter view, you can click and drag a slide to a new position.

Additionally, you can select more than one slide to move.

- To select consecutive slides, click the first slide, hold the Shift key, and click the last slide in the consecutive set of slides.
- To select non-consecutive slides, click the first slide, press the Ctrl key, and click the other slides you want to move.

Drag the selected slides to a new position to complete the move.

 T I P To edit a slide, you can double-click the slide and the slide appears in Slide Editor view.

Part
IV

Ch
21

Using Slide List

 In Slide List view, each slide in the presentation is identified by its display number, title, transition effects for moving from one slide to the other, and any advance options, such as a pause before advancing. Figure 21.17 shows Slide List view.

FIG. 21.17

Plan the slideshow in Slide List view.

Heading Bar ——

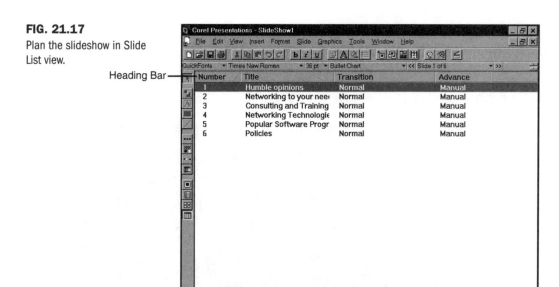

TIP In Slide List view, change the size of a heading bar and the column by positioning the mouse pointer over the right edge of the heading box that you are increasing, and dragging it to the right.

You can rearrange the slides in the Slide List view by:

1. Clicking the number of the slide and dragging it to a new position. The slide pointer and a horizontal line move to a new position.

2. When you release the mouse button, the slide moves in the list—and in the presentation.

To edit any slide, double-click while selecting the slide and the slide appears in Slide Editor view. ●

CHAPTER 22

Working with Data Charts

An effective presentation furnishes facts, figures, and brief statements that are quick to read and easy to understand. Strong titles and subtitles, descriptive bulleted lists, and interesting graphics, such as data charts, create a powerful, professional presentation. Data charts present information clearly by comparing parts to the whole or large sets of data, tracking trends over a period of time, or displaying the uniformity of data. ■

Create a data chart

Present information in your slides using bar, pie, and other types of charts. Enter data, import it from Corel Quattro Pro, and edit it using the datasheet.

Change chart types and layouts

Find out which type of chart is best for different applications, and how you can easily switch your chart from one type to another.

Add and edit titles, data labels, and legends

Learn how to quickly change the color, font, fill, or box around different chart elements, as well as set the scale for your chart's Y-axis.

Creating a Data Chart

A data chart is a chart created using figures you enter in a *datasheet*—similar to a table or spreadsheet. The chart visually represents the figures, contained in the datasheet, using column bars, pie pieces, lines, and so on. The chart type you choose depends on the data and how you want to represent it; comparing data, for example, is a common use for pie and bar charts.

Inserting a Chart

When you create a chart, you must first choose a chart type. After your selection has been made, you will enter the data. You can create a chart using the Data Chart slide type, the Insert menu, or the Chart Object Tool button on the Icon Bar. Following is a summary of the three methods of inserting a chart into a presentation:

- When you create a new slideshow, define a slide template as a data chart type, then double-click in the Add Data Chart area of the slide template; the Data Chart Gallery dialog box appears (see Figure 22.1).

FIG. 22.1

When you create an area for the chart, the Data Chart Gallery dialog box appears.

Chart Object Tool button

Data Chart slide type name

Graphic representation of Data Chart slide type

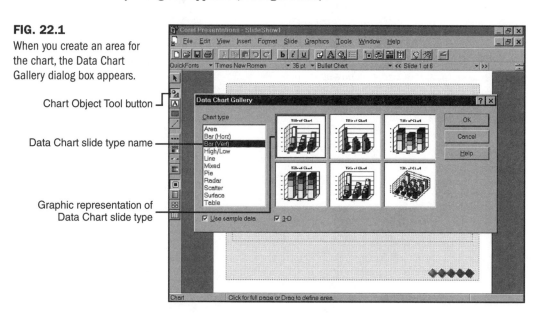

- Choose Insert, Data Chart. The mouse pointer changes to a hand holding a frame. Drag the hand on the slide or drawing to indicate the area designated for the chart. When you release the mouse button, the Data Chart Gallery dialog box appears (see Figure 22.2).

- Click the Chart or Graphics Tools on the Tool Palette and then click the Create a Data Chart button in the upper-left box of the popout menu that appears. The mouse pointer changes to a hand. Drag the hand on the slide or drawing to create the area for the chart. When you release the mouse button, the Data Chart Gallery dialog box appears. Figure 22.2 shows the Data Chart Gallery dialog box and the Chart or Graphics Tools button.

TIP 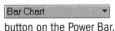 You can change the chart type at anytime by clicking the Chart Type button on the Power Bar.

Choosing the Chart Type

You choose the Chart type in the Data Chart Gallery dialog box. The type of chart you choose depends on the type of data you are planning to use and how you want to present it. Table 22.1 describes the chart types available in Corel Presentations 7 and their common uses.

Table 22.1   Data Chart Types

Chart Type	Description
Area	A chart that shows the height of all values with the area below the line filled with color or patterns. Use an area chart to compare several sets of data or trends over a period of time.
Bar	A chart that represents data by the height or length of the columns or bars; you can create horizontal or vertical bars. Use a bar chart to compare one item to another or to compare different items over a period of time.
High/Low	A chart that shows the high and low values compared over time using lines and bars. Use High/Low charts to track fluctuating data (stocks, commodities, and so on) over a period of time.
Line	A chart consisting of a series of data elements at various points along the axis; the points are connected by a line that indicates a trend or rate of change over a period of time.
Mixed	A chart that combines parts from a line, bar, or area chart so you can plot data in two forms on the same chart. Use a mixed chart to show a correlation between two or more data series.
Pie	A circular, pie-shaped chart with each piece (wedge) showing a data segment and its relationship to the whole. Use a pie chart to sort data and compare parts of the whole.

continues

Table 22.1   Continued

Chart Type	Description
Radar	A chart that starts from the center using a grid to represent the various data. Use a radar chart to show data over a period of time and to show variations and trends.
Scatter	A chart that plots two sets of data, placing a marker at each point where the data intercept. Use a scatter chart with extremely large amounts of data you want to plot along an interception course.
Surface	A chart that represents values to look like peaks and valleys, or landscape. Solid areas contour to the data, which is useful in tracking profits or losses.
Table	Not a graphical chart, but a representation of the data in rows and columns, similar to the datasheet.

To choose a chart type in the Data Chart Gallery dialog box, first choose an option in the Chart Type list. When you do so, the appropriate graphic views of the chart will be displayed. From the graphic views, select the view of the chart that will best represent your data to your audience (see Figure 22.2). Additionally, you can choose to make a chart three-dimensional by selecting the 3-D check box at the bottom of the dialog box. Click OK to accept the chart type and close the dialog box. When you close the dialog box, the datasheet appears.

FIG. 22.2
Select chart type options from the Data Chart Gallery dialog box. Note the difference in the graphic representation between the Line type here and the Bar chart type in the previous Figure 22.1.

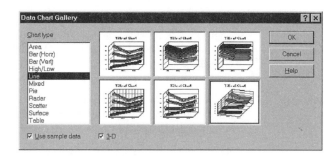

 T I P   Radar charts and tables cannot be created in 3-D.

N O T E   When you close the Data Chart Gallery dialog box, the datasheet appears with sample data already entered, by default. You can delete this data to enter your own, or you can de-select the Use Sample Data option in the Data Chart Gallery dialog box. If the option is not checked, a blank datasheet appears. ▪

Entering Data

After you choose the chart type, the datasheet appears with sample data (unless you chose to not display the sample data). Figure 22.3 illustrates the datasheet, sample data, and the chart created from the data. Additionally, the Data menu is added to the menu bar.

FIG. 22.3
The datasheet looks and acts like a spreadsheet.

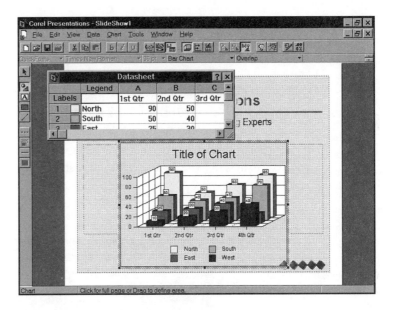

TIP If you cannot see all of the data, you can enlarge the datasheet by positioning the mouse pointer over a corner of the sheet and dragging to enlarge the window.

Inputting Data   To enter data in the datasheet:

1. Select the cells containing sample data by clicking the Select All button (see Figure 22.4).

Select All button

FIG. 22.4
The Select All button on the datasheet permits you to quickly select all information in the datasheet to apply new formatting or for deletion.

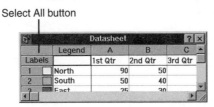

2. Press the Delete key. The Clear dialog box appears with the Data option selected (see Figure 22.5).

FIG. 22.5

Clear the data from the datasheet and fill in your own.

3. Click OK. The data in the datasheet is deleted.

4. To enter the values, enter the legend text, the data labels, and then the values.

5. The legend text will appear in a box near the chart and tell what each color or symbol in the chart's *data series* represents.

   The data series is a range of values in a worksheet and each data series is represented by a marker; for example, a column in a bar chart is a marker, as is a wedge in a pie chart. Data labels are names put along the vertical (Y-axis) or horizontal (X-axis) axis to describe the data, such as the year, quarter, dollar amounts, and so on.

   Figure 22.6 illustrates a sample datasheet and the resulting chart after the text and values are added.

FIG. 22.6

The bar chart displays the text and values after they have been entered into the datasheet.

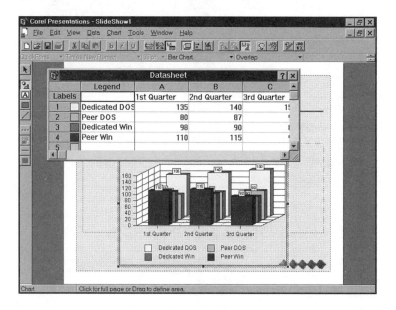

6. When you are finished entering the data, click the datasheet's Close button to close the window. You see the finished chart in your slide, with handles around it indicating that it is selected.

T I P You can edit the data in the datasheet at anytime by clicking the View Datasheet icon in the toolbar.

N O T E The first time you create a chart using your own data, it might be a good idea to take a few minutes and see what your data looks like when displayed in the different data chart types. Then compare each chart against its description in Table 22.1 listed previously. Make sure to try each chart type in both 2-D and 3-D. This will give you a better understanding of how each chart type displays your data, and a better idea of which chart types most effectively present the concepts you want to convey to your particular presentation audience. To change the chart type easily, click the Chart Type button on the Power Bar. ■

Importing Data   You can import data into the datasheet from a spreadsheet program, such as Corel Quattro Pro, by following these steps:

1. Select the cell in the datasheet where you want to import the data.

> **CAUTION**
>
> Make sure any cells that will be filled with data do not contain important data that you wish to keep. (If there is existing data in the destination cells of the datasheet, it will be written over.)

2. Choose Data, Import. The Import Data dialog box appears.
3. Choose the type of data you will import from the Data Type list.
4. Enter the path and file name in the Filename text box.
5. Specify a range, if you want, or you can import the entire worksheet.
6. Select Import at current cell if you want the new data to begin where you currently are in the datasheet.
7. Click OK. The data imports to the selected cell in the Chart Datasheet.

 T I P You can quickly and easily transfer data from another program by using the Windows Clipboard.

Editing a Chart

You can easily edit chart data or other chart options by double-clicking the chart. When you double-click the chart, the chart's border appears as a screened line to indicate it's selected. Additionally, the datasheet containing the charting data appears, the Data menu appears, new options appear on the menu bar, and several new buttons appear on the toolbars and Power Bar that pertain only to charts.

> **N O T E** If you click a chart once, small black handles appear on the chart's corners and sides, but its border remains a thin black line. When a chart is selected in this manner, you can move, resize, and copy or cut the chart. ■

Editing Data

 To edit the data in a chart, double-click the chart. The datasheet appears. Alternatively, select the chart and click the Datasheet button on the toolbar. Click the cell you want to edit and type the text or value. Press Enter and the chart changes to reflect the new data.

In addition to entering new text or editing text, you can format the values in the chart and sort the data in the cells of the datasheet.

Formatting Values   You can format a cell in a datasheet to contain specific data types, such as numeric, currency, or text. To format values:

1. Select the cells you want to format and choose Data, Format, or right-click the cells, then choose Format from the QuickMenu. The Format dialog box appears (see Figure 22.7).

FIG. 22.7
Format the data in selected cells using the Format dialog box.

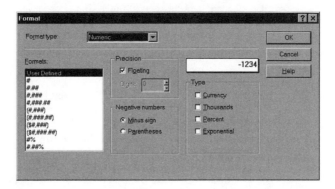

2. In Format Type, choose either General, Numeric, or Date. If you choose General, there are no options; otherwise, the options change depending on the Format Type.

3. Select the format you want to use and other options appear. The Numeric and Date options are described in Tables 22.2 and 22.3.

Table 22.2   Numeric Options

Option	Description
Precision Area	Choose only one option.
Floating	Decimal points and places appear only if needed.

Option	Description
Digits	Specify number of decimal places; option is only available if Floating is not selected.
Negative Numbers Area	Choose only one option.
Minus Sign	Displays a minus sign to indicate negative numbers.
Parentheses	Displays negative numbers in parentheses instead of with a minus sign.
Type Area	Choose any or all options.
Currency	Displays values with a dollar sign.
Thousands	Displays commas to indicate thousands.
Percent	Displays the percent sign with the number.
Exponential	Displays the exponent of the values.

Table 22.3   Date Options

Option	Description
Date Preview	Displays the selected date format.
Date/Time Formats	Choose a format to display date and/or time.
Custom	Create your own date format.

4. Click OK to close the dialog box.

 TIP The numeric format you choose in the Format dialog box changes the axis labels in your chart to the format you select.

Sorting Data   You can sort the data in a datasheet in a descending or ascending alphabetical or numerical order. Sorted data is more organized than data that is not sorted, and therefore makes a chart easier to read.

To sort in a datasheet:

1. Select the text or values in the datasheet to be sorted.

2. Choose Data, Sort; or right-click the cells, then choose Sort from the QuickMenu. The Sort Data dialog box appears (see Figure 22.8).

FIG. 22.8
You can Sort data by rows or
columns of the datasheet,
and in ascending or
descending order.

3. In the Sort Data dialog box, choose to sort the data by Rows or Columns and in either Ascending or Descending order. The Key column (the column or row by which the data will be sorted) shows the letter or number of the selected column by default, so you should not need to change this.

4. Click OK to close the dialog box and sort the data. Changes are reflected in the data chart.

Changing Chart Types

After you create a chart, you may decide a different chart type would better represent the data. You can change the chart type to pie, line, area, or any other available chart. To change a chart type, double-click the chart to select it. Choose Chart, Gallery, to view the larger variety of chart types, or choose Chart, Layout/Type to quickly select a type and edit the properties of the chart. Alternatively, click the Data Chart Types button on the Power Bar (see Figure 22.9). Choose the chart type you want and the selected chart changes.

FIG. 22.9
Choose a chart type from the
Power Bar data chart types
list.

Data Chart Types button ———

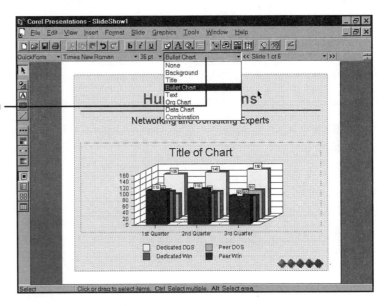

TIP You can choose the Show Table button to add the data to your chart in table format.

Modifying Layout and Series Options

You can edit the layout and the series of a selected chart to further modify the way the data is represented. Layout refers to the style, width, size, and general appearance of the chart's markers. The Layout options change depending on what type of chart you are working on. The Series options refer to each individual data series. You can change the color, type, and even the shape of each series in the chart to further represent the chart's data.

Changing Layout   To change the layout of the chart:

1. Select the chart by double-clicking it.

 2. Choose Chart, Layout/Type, or click the Layout button on the toolbar. The Layout/Type Properties dialog box appears (see Figure 22.10). The specific options you see depend on the type of chart selected.

FIG. 22.10

The Layout/Type Properties dialog box allows you to both select the type of chart you want and set properties for the chart.

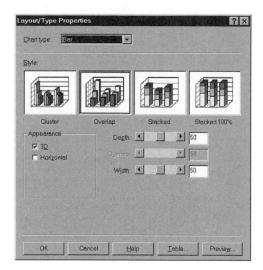

3. Change any of the options in the dialog box as described in Table 22.4. (The options that are available depend on the chart type that is selected, and not all the options in the table will be available at once.) Click the Preview button to view the change before accepting it. Click OK to accept the changes.

4. Click OK to accept the changes and close the dialog box.

CAUTION

Save your presentation *before* you modify the layout of a chart in case you change your mind about the changes; you can always revert back to the saved copy. Additionally, use the Preview button in the Layout/Type Properties dialog box before accepting the changes you make. If you make many changes, you may never be able to undo them all and the changes may not look good in your chart. If you use the Preview button first, you have the option of canceling the changes and trying again.

T I P

When using the Preview button in the Layout/Type Properties dialog box, click and drag the title bar of the dialog box to move it for a clearer preview.

Table 22.4   Layout/Type Properties Options

Option	Description
3-D	Applies a three-dimensional look to the markers in the chart.
Horizontal	Changes the direction of the markers from vertical to horizontal.
Table	Displays a table of the data in the chart box.
Width	Sets width percentages.
Depth	Sets depth percentages.
Height	Sets height percentages
Overlap	Sets overlap percentages.
Cluster	Groups each section of markers together so it can be better compared.
Overlap	Overlaps the markers.
Stacked	Stacks the markers on top of each other.
Stacked 100%	Stacks the markers so they are even along the top and bottom.
Line	Changes markers to lines.
Bar/Error Bar	Changes markers to bars with error indicators.
Error Bar	Changes markers to bars with top and bottom error markers.
Area	Changes markers to area markers.
Slice	Enter a number to indicate which slice you want to separate from the pie.
Distance	Enter the distance from the pie the exploded slice should locate.
Column	Changes pie slices to bar or column markers.

Option	Description
Sort Slice	Changes the positioning of the exploded slice(s).
Link	Indicate with lines the relative pieces of each pie.
Slice	Indicate the number of slices to link.
Radial	Displays on a radial grid.
Linear	Displays on a linear grid.
Depth	Sets the thickness of a pie chart.
Angle	Rotate the slices.
Size	Sets the size of the pie.
Tilt	Sets orientation.
Blend Range Colors	Blends colors of the area.
Label Dividers	Creates a heavy border under the titles row and to the right of the column titles.
Range Colors	Displays the table in the range colors.
Full Grid	Adds border lines to each cell in table.
Fill Color	Sets the color for the entire table chart.
Line Color	Sets the line color in a table.
Outline Color	Sets the color for the outline of the chart.
Outline Contours	Draws an outline around each area.

 TIP You can apply a style to a selected chart by clicking the Chart Style button on the Power Bar.

Changing Series   A series is a row of data in a chart. A series is represented by a column, pie slice, line, or other chart element, also called a marker. You can change how the series looks by setting series options.

 TIP Not all series options are available for all chart types.

To change the series options:

 1. Choose Chart, Series, or click the Series button on the toolbar. The Series Properties dialog box appears, as in Figure 22.11.

Previous   Next
button   button   Series box

FIG. 22.11
Open the Series Properties
dialog box to further
enhance and modify a chart.

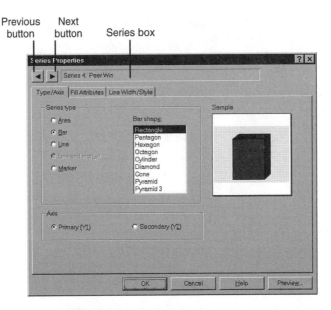

2. In Series box at the top of the dialog box, choose the Next or Previous button to select the series you want to edit.

3. On the Type/Axis tab, choose your Series type (Bar, Line, Marker, and so on), and the style or Bar Shape of the Series Type (Rectangle, Cylinder, Pyramid, and so on). Also, choose whether to use the Primary (Y1) or Secondary (Y2) Y axis.

 Click the Preview button at any time to see how the change looks.

4. On the Fill Attributes tab, choose Pattern, Gradient, Texture, or Picture to display a palette of fill choices. Select a new choice to apply to the current series.

5. In the Line Width/Style tab, choose the Line Width and Line Style as desired.

6. Use the Next or Previous buttons, if desired, to choose another series, then repeat Steps 3 through 6.

7. Click OK to accept the options and close the dialog box.

TROUBLESHOOTING

I made changes to the series of the selected chart, and I don't like the changes. Click the Cancel button before closing the Series Properties dialog box. Alternatively, you can click the Undo button on the toolbar to reverse the changes.

Changing the Grid and Axis

The chart's grid is formed by the horizontal and vertical lines behind the chart's markers. The grid enables you to better see the markers in conjunction with the axes labels and therefore, the lines make the data easier to read. You can add two grids to a chart: the major grid and minor grid. The minor grid further divides the values so you can better read the numbers.

A chart's axes are lines used as reference points for the chart data. The X-axis represents the horizontal line and the Y-axis represents the vertical. You can change axis options to help you define the data on the chart.

Changing the Axis   To change the axis options:

1. Select the chart and then the axis you want to change. Handles appear at either end of a selected axis. Choose <u>C</u>hart, <u>A</u>xis, then select <u>X</u>, <u>P</u>rimary Y, or <u>S</u>econdary Y. The Axis Properties dialog box appears (see Figure 22.12).

 TIP   Alternatively, double-click the axis you want to modify to display the Axis Properties dialog box.

FIG. 22.12
Double-click the axis to display the Labels tab of the Axis Properties dialog box for that axis.

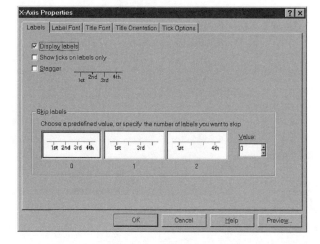

2. In the Labels tab (X-Axis), choose to display your labels in a variety of ways. This can make your chart readable if you have many labels, or if your labels are long.

   Alternatively, in the Scale/Labels tab (Y-Axis), choose the maximum and minimum for your labels.

3. Click the Label Font tab to specify the font and size for your labels.

4. In the Title Font tab, enter the title for your axis, and the font for that title. Change the orientation of the title, if desired, in the Title Orientation tab.

5. Ticks are short lines that are used to mark off values, such as dollars, distances, and so on. Major ticks are those lines that fall on a label, and minor ticks are lines that fall between labels. Set options for the ticks in the Tick Options tab, then click OK.

6. Select the other axis in the Axis area and set options for that axis, if desired.

TIP If you change the font style on one axis, your chart will look more readable and professional if you change to the same style on the other axis.

Changing the Grid   The grid in a data chart consists of horizontal and/or vertical lines that help to measure distance between the markers.

To change the grid options:

1. Select the chart, then choose <u>C</u>hart, <u>G</u>rids. The Grid Properties dialog box appears (see Figure 22.13).

FIG. 22.13
Open the Grid Properties dialog box to change the appearance of the chart's grids.

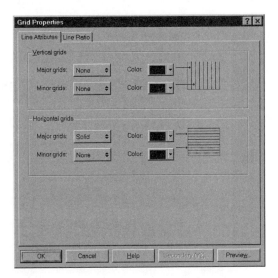

2. On the Line Attributes tab, choose appearance options for the vertical and horizontal grids.

3. On the Line Ratio tab, choose how many vertical and horizontal grids you want to display.

4. Click OK to accept the changes and close the dialog box.

TROUBLESHOOTING

I cannot see if I have made changes in the Axis Properties dialog box when I click the Preview button. Some options in the Axis Properties dialog box are codependent on options you set in the Grid Properties dialog box. Set grid and tick options and then come back to the Axis Properties dialog box.

After I make changes in the Grid Properties dialog box, the axis changes do not look right. Switch back to the Primary Y Axis Properties dialog box and change some of the options back to automatic by clicking the check box in front of the Minimum Value, Maximum Value, and Major Grid Value options.

Working with Titles and Legends

You can add and edit chart titles, a legend, and data labels to help identify the data in the chart. Titles name the subject of the chart; you also can add a subtitle and axis titles to your chart. The legend lists the colors, patterns, or symbols used for the chart markers and tells you what each represents. You can choose to show or hide the legend in a chart and if you choose to show the legend, you can set its placement, orientation, and various other attributes. Finally, you can edit the data labels in the chart. The labels show the numeric value, time period, or category of the markers.

Adding and Editing Titles

You can add titles to the chart and format the titles so they are easy to read. Editing titles is also quick and easy.

To add or edit titles:

1. Select the chart and choose Chart, Title. The Title Properties dialog box appears (see Figure 22.14).
2. Check the Display Chart Title box, and type in the title for your chart.
3. Use the tabs of the dialog box to specify the title's font, text fill, text outline, box type (for a box around the title), box fill, and position of the title relative to the chart.
4. Click OK to close the Title Properties dialog box.

FIG. 22.14

Use the Title Font tab of the Title Properties dialog box to enter the chart's title, and select its font style, size, and other attributes.

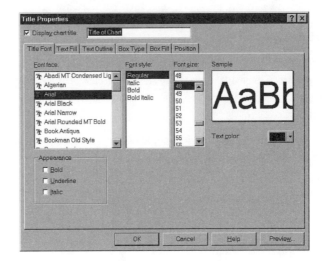

Editing Legends

You can show or hide the legend for the chart. If you choose to show the legend (the default), you can change the position, orientation, box style, and font of the legend box to suit your chart and data.

To modify a legend:

1. Select the chart and choose <u>C</u>hart, <u>Le</u>gend. The Legend Properties dialog box appears (see Figure 22.15)

FIG. 22.15

Use the Legends Properties dialog box to modify the legend for your chart.

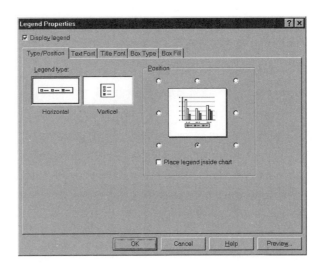

TIP With the datasheet on-screen, double-click the chart's legend to open the Legends dialog box.

2. Check the Display Legend check box to display the legend.

3. Use the tabs of the dialog box to specify the legend's type and position, font for the legend text, font for the legend title, box type (for a box around the legend), and box fill.

4. Click OK to close the Legend Properties dialog box.

 TIP If you prefer not to show the legend, deselect the Display Legend option in the Legend Properties dialog box so that no check mark displays in the check box.

Editing Data Labels

Data labels are tags that identify the tick marks or grid lines in a chart. You can show or hide the data label, plus change attributes, positions, and the fonts of the labels.

To edit the data labels:

1. Select the chart and choose Chart, Data Labels. The Data Labels dialog box appears as shown in Figure 22.16.

 TIP You can double-click a label in the chart to quickly open the Labels dialog box.

FIG. 22.16

Choose how to display the data labels in the Data Labels dialog box.

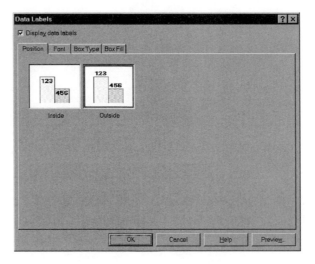

2. Check the Display Data Labels check box to display data labels.

3. Use the tabs of the dialog box to specify the data labels' position, font, box type, and box fill.

4. Click OK to close the Data Labels dialog box.

CHAPTER 23

Adding and Enhancing Objects

Corel presentations, whether printed on paper, overhead transparencies, or on-screen, are effective because of their visual impact. Your presentations are more powerful when you use brief titles and bulleted lists with charts, tables, pictures, and other graphics that are quick and easy to understand, as well as attractive and professional-looking. Corel Presentations 7 enables you to easily and quickly add a variety of graphic objects to your presentations. ■

Add lines and borders

Find out how to emphasize areas of your slide with colored lines and borders.

Add pictures and clip art

Learn how to match the medium to the message by adding visual appeal to your slides with pictures and clip art.

Add text from other sources

Understand how to pull in information from other files to cut down on your input time.

Use tables

If you're displaying data, you'll want to see how to create tables in your Corel Presentations 7 slides.

Add drawing objects

See how you can be artistic and draw your own objects with Corel Presentations 7.

Adding Lines and Borders

You can add a variety of lines and borders to any slide in your presentation to enhance text or other graphics, such as a logo or clip art picture. After adding the lines or borders, you can choose from a variety of line styles, colors, and thicknesses.

Creating Lines

To draw a line in Corel Presentations 7, use the Line Object tools on the Tool Palette (the Tool Palette is located along the upper-left side of the drawing area). You can draw a curved, arced, straight, or freehand line using the tools, and you can select the line, move the line, or change its attributes.

 Drawing Lines To create a line, click the Line Object Tools button and keep holding the mouse button down. You see the pop-up menu shown in Figure 23.1. With the mouse button still held down, move the mouse pointer over the type of line you want to choose and let go of the mouse button. Click and drag the tool in the work area to create a line. Each line tool looks like the line type that it creates. You will want to experiment with the tools to get a clear idea of how each works.

FIG. 23.1

Create a variety of lines to enhance text or graphics using the Line Object Tools buttons in the Tool Palette.

Line Object Tools ⎯⎯

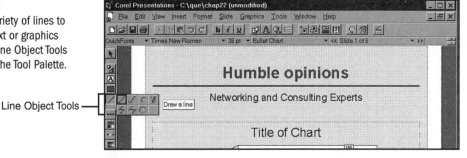

The Line Object tools are:

 Straight Lines. Create a straight horizontal, vertical, or diagonal line. Click and drag from the beginning to the end of the line.

Curved Lines. Draw soft curves. Click to begin the curve and then at each point you want the curve to change directions, click again. Double-click to end the line.

Sections of Ellipses. Draw arcs that are sections of an ellipse. Drag the tool to begin the arc. Release the mouse button to complete the arc.

Freehand Lines. Using the mouse, draw a line in any direction. Click and drag the tool as if the mouse were the pencil. Release the mouse button to end the line.

Angled Lines. Draw a line with several straight line segments. Click to begin the line and then at each point you want the line to change directions, click again. Double-click to end the line.

 Bezier Curves. Create Bezier curves, or curves with sectors you can edit and move independently. Click to begin the curve, then move the pointer to where the curve changes directions and drag the pointer to display the two handles. Move the handle to change the shape of the curve. Double-click the mouse to end the curve. You can go back and select the curve to display handles; then move the handles to edit the curve.

Sections of Circles. Draw arcs that are circular. Click at the beginning of the arc and hold down the mouse button. Drag the tool to the end of the arc and release the mouse button. Move the pointer to shape the arc, then click again to end the arc shape.

Part

IV

Ch

23

T I P You can constrain types of line objects with the Shift key. When you constrain a line, for example, you can only draw a vertical, horizontal, or 45-degree line. Look at the status bar for instructions on particular types of lines.

Modifying Lines   You can change line attributes such as line style, line width, and line color in the Line Attributes and Line Color palettes. To change line attributes:

 1. Select the line. Click the Line Attributes button on the Tool Palette, then select a type of line from the line attributes palette, as shown in Figure 23.2.

 2. Similarly, change the line color by selecting the line, then clicking the Line Color button on the Tool Palette, and choosing a color from the pop-up Line Color palette.

T I P You can invert certain types of line objects with the Alt key. When you invert an arc, for example, the arc you are drawing changes from an upward-facing arc to a downward-facing arc. Look at the status bar for instructions on particular types of lines.

---

3. Alternatively, change additional line properties by selecting the line, then choosing Format, Object Properties. The Object Properties dialog box appears (see Figure 23.3).

FIG. 23.2

Change the line thickness
and style from the pop-up
Line Attributes palette.

Line Attributes palette ————

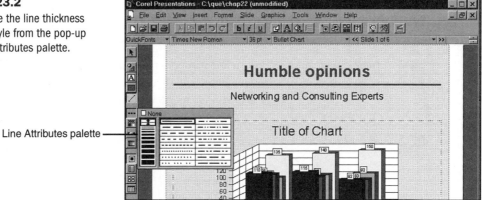

 T I P   If you don't select a line before going into the Object Properties dialog box, the new settings that
you choose will become the default for all new lines you draw for the rest of that editing session.

FIG. 23.3

Change line attributes for the
selected line in the Object
Properties dialog box.

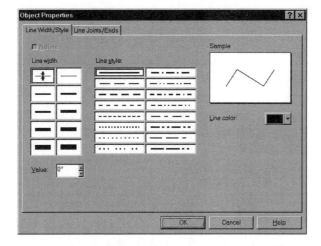

4. On the Line Width/Style tab, select the Line Width, Line Style, and Line Color you
   want to apply. Notice the Sample box updates to show you how your line will look.

5. On the Line Joints/Ends tab shown in Figure 23.4, choose from the following options:

   • *Joints.* Choose to join two line segments with a Bevel, Miter, or Round edge.

   • *Ends.* Choose to make the line endings Round, Flat, or Square.

   • *Arrowheads.* Choose to add an arrowhead to the Beginning or Ending of a line,
     to Both Ends of a line, or to None.

TIP The sample box shows you how the line will look as you change its formatting attributes.

 TIP Joints, ends, and arrowheads are more noticeable when the line thickness is greater than .05 inches.

FIG. 23.4

You can add arrowheads to lines, as well as specify how line segments are connected and how lines end on the Line Joints/Ends tab of the Object Properties dialog box.

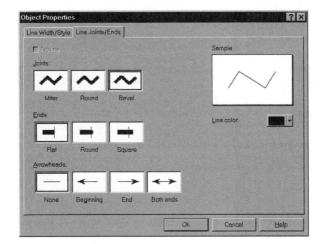

6. When finished with setting the line attributes, choose OK to close the dialog box.

TROUBLESHOOTING

I drew a freehand line, but it turned out too angled and rough. Freehand lines are very hard to draw smoothly; try using the Bezier curve line tool instead. After you draw the curve, double-click it to edit it, and then select a point (the mouse pointer will turn into a crosshair when it's over a point). Move the handles associated with that point by dragging them.

I drew a line, but I can't see it on the screen. Click the Line Attribute tool on the Icon Bar and deselect None so that no X appears in the check box.

Creating Borders

Many of the objects you draw, such as data charts, clip art, organizational charts, tables, and so on, enable you to add a border; however, you may also want to add borders to text or to a drawing you create. You can add a border by using the Closed Object tool on the Drawing toolbar.

Drawing the Border To draw a border shape, hold down the Closed Object Tools button to display the various closed object tools. You can select any shape after drawing it and drag one of its handles to change the shape.

The Closed Object tools are as follows:

 Rectangle. Click the tool and drag to create a rectangle.

 Rounded Rectangle. Click the tool and drag the mouse to create a rectangle with rounded corners.

 Circle. Click and drag the tool to create a circle.

 Ellipse. Click and drag the tool to create an ellipse.

 Polygon. Click to begin the shape and move the pointer to create one edge of the shape. Click, and the shape becomes closed; however, move the pointer to form the second edge and click again. Repeat until the shape is complete. Press the Shift key while drawing to make exact horizontal, vertical, or 45-degree angles. Double-click to complete the shape.

Closed Curve. Click once to begin the curved shape and at each place where the curve changes directions, click again. Double-click to complete the shape.

 Arrow. Click once to start the arrow, then move the pointer to where the arrow should end and click again. Releasing the mouse button after the second click creates a straight arrow; however, you can drag after the initial click and create a curved arrow shape.

Regular Polygon. Click the tool and drag to create a five-sided polygon. When you choose Regular Polygon, a dialog box appears in the upper-right corner of the screen which enables you to choose the number of sides your image will use.

 T I P Additionally, hold the Shift key while dragging to create a perfect square, circle, or 45-degree angle. Hold the Alt key while dragging to create the object from a center point instead of the edge.

Figure 23.5 shows an example of each of the closed object shapes you can use for a border.

FIG. 23.5

You can use any of these eight closed shapes for borders.

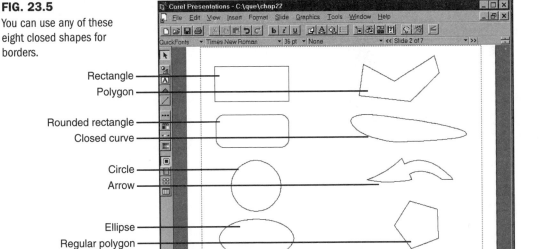

Rectangle

Polygon

Rounded rectangle

Closed curve

Circle

Arrow

Ellipse

Regular polygon

Modifying the Border When drawing a closed object, you can choose a fill color and pattern before drawing the object, or draw the object, select it, and then choose the fill and pattern. Additionally, you can change the line style, color, and thickness before or after drawing the object.

You can create a shape with no fill, so the shape's border line is all you see on-screen and its inside is transparent. Alternatively, you can create the shape with a fill color or pattern and make the fill transparent or opaque. If the fill is transparent, you can use color and still see what's behind the closed shape; if the fill is opaque, it blocks out what is beneath it.

To select a fill or change the fill to None with the Tool Palette:

1. Select the object.

2. Click the Fill Attributes button on the Tool Palette. You see the Fill Attributes pop-up palette shown in Figure 23.6.

3. Choose a fill type, or check the None box to turn off the object's fill.

> **TIP** Set the color of an object's fill by clicking the Fill Colors button on the Tool Palette, then choosing a color from the pop-up palette of colors.

To set the fill to a color or pattern from the menu:

1. Select the object, then choose Format, Object Properties, and ensure that the Fill Attributes tab is selected, as shown in Figure 23.7.

FIG. 23.6

Use the Fill Attributes palette to change the fill type.

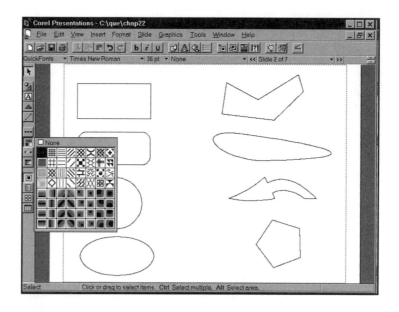

FIG. 23.7

You can set all Fill types and colors from the Object Properties dialog box.

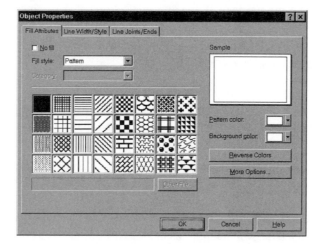

2. In the Object Properties dialog box, choose No Fill to remove any fill. Alternatively, in Fill Style, choose Pattern, Gradient, Texture, or Picture. Pattern creates a solid color, whereas Gradient produces a blend of two colors. Texture and Picture provide you with a selection of textures and pictures that you can fill your objects with.

3. If you chose Pattern, choose the fill pattern, then choose the Pattern Color and Background Color.

   If you chose Gradient, choose the gradient pattern, then choose the Gradient Color and a Background Color.

If you chose Texture or Picture, choose the Category you want to choose from, then select a specific texture or picture.

4. Choose More Options to set advanced options for any fill type.

5. Click OK to close the dialog box.

Figure 23.8 demonstrates various borders and fills.

FIG. 23.8
Use borders with fills and patterns to attract attention.

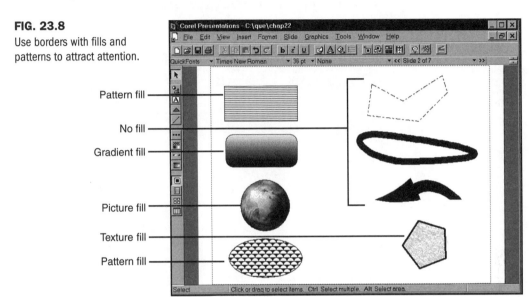

N O T E You can move a border around by selecting and dragging it to a new location. Additionally, you can select two or more items, such as a text box and a border by holding the Shift key as you click the items. ■

Adding Pictures

You can add pictures or clip art from the Corel WordPerfect Suite 7 suite of applications, or from other sources. Pictures help illustrate text and make a presentation more attractive. Corel Presentations 7 includes a QuickArt Gallery that provides various categories of clip art, such as animals, architecture, arrows, and so on. Alternatively, you can insert a file from another program, such as a bitmap or designer file.

Inserting a Corel Presentations 7 Picture

You can insert a Corel Presentations 7 picture using the QuickArt Gallery. First, you create the area for the picture, and then choose the picture you want to insert.

To insert a Corel Presentations 7 picture:

1. Choose Insert, QuickArt, or click and hold down the mouse pointer on the Chart or Graphics Tools button on the Tool Palette, then slide over to the Insert QuickArt tool and release the mouse button. The mouse pointer changes to a hand holding a frame. Drag the hand across the work area to create an area for the picture.

2. When you release the mouse button, the QuickArt Browser dialog box appears (see Figure 23.9).

FIG. 23.9

Insert a picture using the QuickArt Browser dialog box.

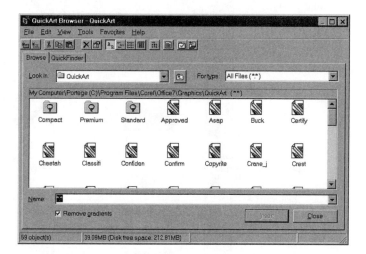

3. Double-click a graphic to insert, or double-click the Compact, Standard, or Premium folders (if available) to see additional QuickArt. You see folders containing categories of pictures. Double-click the desired category. You see additional folders for the subcategories of items.

 TIP The icon for each picture shows a thumbnail for the picture. If you click the Preview button, you see the selected picture at the right of the dialog box.

4. Select a picture and choose Insert. The picture appears in the work area and the mouse pointer changes to a Selection tool.

N O T E You can move, resize, cut and paste, add a border, and otherwise manipulate the picture as you would any object. To edit individual sections of the image, you may need to separate the image into sections by choosing Graphics, Separate. ■

Inserting a Picture from Another Program

If you have clip art, drawings, CorelFLOW diagrams, or other pictures you want to use from another program, you can insert them into a presentation slide.

To insert a picture from another program:

1. Choose Insert, QuickArt. The mouse pointer becomes a hand.
2. Draw an area for the art. The QuickArt Gallery dialog box appears.
3. In the dialog box, select For Type, and choose the type of file you are looking for; or choose All Files.

Part
IV

Ch
23

N O T E   It is usually not necessary to specify the file type. Corel Presentations 7 automatically interprets the file type for you. You will normally only use the file type function when you want to save your file in a format other than .SHW (for slideshows) or .WPG (for drawings). ■

4. Select the correct folder and then choose the file. Click the Insert button and the file is inserted into your work area.

Adding Pictures from the Web

You can also add pictures that you find on Web pages to your PowerPoint drawings or slideshows. The Web has many sites that have public domain images, and as you surf the Web you may find that you can easily increase your clip art library with these graphics.

CAUTION

While this is technically easy to do, you will usually be in violation of copyright laws if you take images from a public site without permission. Although many people do not know it, you cannot reuse photographs or clip art that you find in public sources without the permission of the creator.

Be sure to e-mail the administrator of the site where you find clip art and ask his or her permission prior to using images you find.

You can take images from a Web site to incorporate into your drawings or slideshows by saving them to your local computer using Netscape. To do so, take the following steps:

1. Using Netscape, browse to the site containing the image you want to use.

   ▶ **See** "Browsing the Web," **p. 539**

2. Right-click the image to be saved, and choose Save This Image As. You see a Save As dialog box.
3. Navigate to the folder in which you want to save the image, and choose Save. The image is saved to your local computer.

To import the image, use the procedure outlined in the previous section "Inserting a Picture from Another Program."

Inserting and Formatting Tables

You can create a table within Corel Presentations 7 that enables you to display data in rows and columns. Organizing numerical information in a table format makes it easier to read and comprehend. Additionally, you can display any chart data in table format by choosing Table as the chart type; you can change the table back to a chart when it better suits the presentation.

> **TIP** You can also copy a Corel WordPerfect 7 table to the Clipboard and paste it into a Corel Presentations slide.

When creating a table in Corel Presentations 7, you can choose from six table formats, including outlined, shaded, and plain table designs. Corel Presentations 7 enables you to add titles, subtitles, and range colors, and otherwise format the data within the table.

Adding a Table

You can create a table within Corel Presentations 7 in which you can enter, edit, and format the text, data, labels, and titles. You can also copy a table or table data from another program, such as Corel WordPerfect 7. After copying the table to the Clipboard, you can paste it into a Corel Presentations 7 slide.

To copy a table from another program, create the table. You can format the table text and alignment; however, Corel Presentations 7 does not retain the formatting when it is pasted into a slide. Next, select the entire table and choose Edit, Copy. Switch to the Corel Presentations 7 program and display the slide in which you want to paste the table. Choose Edit, Paste, and the table is embedded on the slide.

> **NOTE** When you embed a table in this way, it is created as an OLE 2.0 object in your slideshow or drawing. To find out more about OLE 2.0 objects (including how to edit them), see the section "Techniques for Linking and Embedding" in Chapter 34, "Transferring Data Between Applications." ∎

To create a table within Corel Presentations 7, follow these steps:

1. Hold down the Chart or Graphics Tools button in the Tool Palette, and let up the button on the Data Chart tool. The mouse pointer changes to a hand holding a square.

2. Drag the hand across the slide page to define the area for the table.

 TIP Make the original table box as large as possible; tables appear small on-screen, although you can enlarge the area later.

3. Release the mouse button. The Data Chart Gallery dialog box appears.

4. In Chart Type, choose Table. Six table formats appear from which you can choose, as shown in Figure 23.10.

Part IV Ch 23

FIG. 23.10
Choose Table as the chart type in the Data Chart Gallery dialog box to view various table formats.

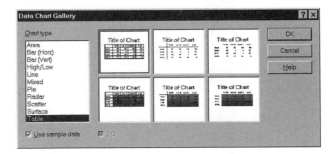

5. Choose a table format and click OK. The dialog box closes and the Datasheet appears next to the table in your slide, as shown in Figure 23.11.

FIG. 23.11
Use the Datasheet to define a table's contents in Corel Presentations 7.

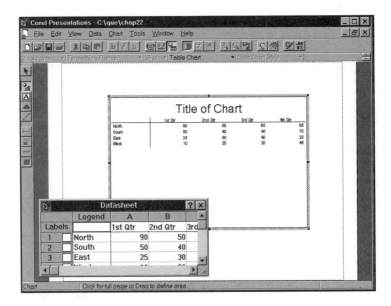

6. Enter the data into the Datasheet as you did when creating charts.

▶ **See** "Entering Data," **p. 457**

7. Close the Datasheet by clicking outside the blue hatch border that surrounds the chart object. The table appears in the designated area (see Figure 23.12).

FIG. 23.12

The table appears in the slide when you close the Datasheet after entering your data. The table object displays handles, indicating that it is selected.

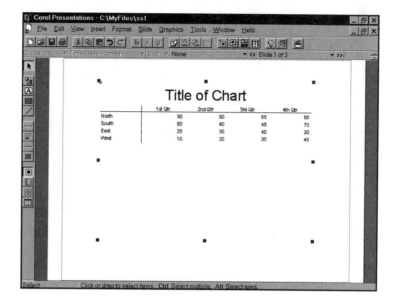

Editing a Table

You can edit the information in a Corel Presentations 7 table at any time, by editing the data in the table's Datasheet. To edit the data in a table, ensure that the table is not selected, then double-click the table to activate it. When active, the table's defining box displays a blue shaded border, and you may see the table's datasheet.

 If the Datasheet is not displayed, you can view it by clicking the View Datasheet button on the toolbar. The Datasheet appears. When you are finished editing, click the Close button in the Datasheet window. The edited data appears in the table.

Enhancing a Table

You can format the text and data in a table so the text is large enough to read easily during a presentation. When you format the text or data within the table, all of the text within the table reflects the format changes.

Additionally, you can add titles and subtitles to the table, and you can change the color of the table lines, background, font, and so on.

To format the text in a table, follow these steps:

1. Double-click the table to activate it, then click the View Datasheet button to close the Datasheet, if you prefer to have it out of the way.

2. Choose <u>C</u>hart, <u>L</u>ayout/Type. The Table Properties dialog box appears, as shown in Figure 23.13.

FIG. 23.13
Use the Table Properties dialog box to change the font and other table options.

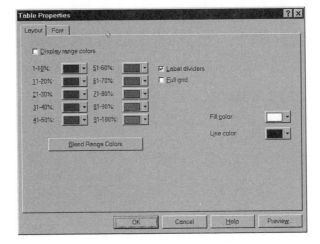

3. In the Layout tab, choose options as described in Table 23.1.

4. Choose font options by selecting the Font tab, then choosing the font face, style, size, color, and appearance attributes. The Sample box shows you how your fonts will look.

 TIP Change the type size to at least 36-point or even larger, so it can be read easily in the presentation slide.

5. Click OK to close the Table Properties dialog box; alternatively, you can choose Previe<u>w</u> to view the change before accepting it.

Table 23.1   Table Layout Options

Option	Description
<u>D</u>isplay Range Colors	Show or hide the selected colors to the table cells; this option fills each cell with the selected colors in the Range Colors area of the dialog box (see the following section, "Applying Range Colors").
<u>B</u>lend Range Colors	Allows you to blend a color chosen for the minimum with a color chosen for the maximum of the range (see "Applying Range Colors").

continues

Table 23.1   Continued

Option	Description
Label Dividers	Show or hide the table's formatted grid lines in a table.
Full Grid	Show or hide all grid lines in the table.
Fill Color	Choose one color to use for the table background.
Line Color	Choose one color to use for all grid lines.

Applying Range Colors

Corel Presentations 7 includes a useful feature that enables the reader to quickly discern the data in a table: *range colors*. Each range color represents a different value in the table; the range color is applied as background color for each cell. The lowest values, for example, may be represented in a red cell, whereas the highest values could be represented in a yellow cell. Using range colors enables the viewer to quickly see the number of high and low values on the table.

 Use grays if you are printing in black and white; use colors if your presentation is on-screen.

You choose the range colors in the Table Properties dialog box in the Range Colors area, by blending the colors or selecting specific colors for each range.

To blend colors, click the 1-10% box and a palette appears; choose the color to represent the first range in the table. Similarly, choose a color for the 91-100% box. Click the Blend Range Colors button to automatically fill in the remaining ranges with a blend of the two colors you selected.

 Don't use too many colors on a slide as it clutters it and obscures the information you're trying to convey. Be careful of dark colors that will hide the text/numbers in each cell of the table.

Figure 23.14 shows the table with a blend of grays applied to the ranges. Note that you must turn on the Display Range Colors option in the Table Properties dialog box.

Alternatively, You can choose a color for each range block by clicking the block and choosing a color from the palette.

 Keep the colors light enough so you can read all of the data in the table cells. Try making the text bold if it's hard to read. Also, keep the text style simple; stay away from italics and other fancy styles especially if you will be using the tables in a presentation.

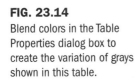

FIG. 23.14
Blend colors in the Table
Properties dialog box to
create the variation of grays
shown in this table.

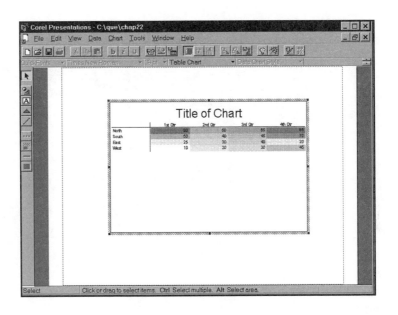

Part

IV

Ch

23

Adding Titles

Corel Presentations 7 enables you to add titles to your table. You can even format the title, if you want. When you create a table in Corel Presentations 7, it adds "Title of Chart" at the top of the table. Using the Title Properties dialog box, you can enter your own title or delete the title text altogether.

To add a title, follow these steps:

1. Click the chart to select it.

2. Double-click "Title of Chart." The Title Properties dialog box appears (see Figure 23.15).

3. Enter the title in the Display Chart Title text box.

4. To format the title font, ensure that you are in the Title Font tab, then choose the appropriate font options.

5. Choose the Text Fill or Text Outline tab to change the fill from solid to a pattern, or to specify the outline around the title letters. In the Text Outline tab, you need to deselect the No Line check box before other controls will become available.

6. Choose the Box Type or Box Fill tabs to change the type of box, or the pattern, gradient, fill, or texture that will fill the box. You need to deselect the No Box check box in the Box Type tab before other controls become available. The Box Type tab is shown in Figure 23.16.

FIG. 23.15

Use the Title Properties dialog box to add titles.

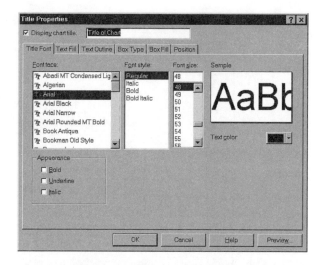

FIG. 23.16

Choose from a variety of boxes for your title in the Box Type tab of the Title Properties dialog box.

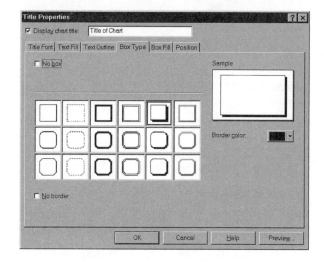

7. On the Position tab, choose whether to put your title at the top left, center, or right of the chart.

8. Click OK to close the Title Properties dialog box; then click the slide outside of the selected chart area to deselect the chart and close the Datasheet.

Working with Bitmap Images

There are two types of graphic images that you can incorporate in your documents: *vector* images and *bitmap* images.

A vector image is stored as a formula. For instance, a circle might be stored as several codes that specify the shape (a circle), the location of the center point, the diameter, the line width, style, and color. Vector images can be stored very efficiently, since there is very little information to store. They can also be resized and moved very easily, since you merely need to alter one or two elements in the stored formula. All the drawing objects you have worked with in this chapter so far are vector images, and vector images are the only type of images that many popular presentation packages can work with.

A bitmap image is stored as a series of dots (technically called *pixels*). When you scan a photograph into your computer, you are scanning (and saving) dots, not formulas. Thus, scanned images are stored as bitmaps. While bitmaps are thus important to be able to work with, they have limitations. They take up much more space, and resizing them is much more problematic, since they're not stored as a formula.

Programs that manipulate bitmap images are often called *paint programs*; programs used to manipulate vectors are often termed *drawing programs*. The types of tools used in paint programs are different than the ones in drawing programs. For instance, paint programs contain tools like paintbrushes, which spread a swath of color on your image (by changing the color of the pixels that you use the tool on). Other tools include spray brushes that let you smooth colors gradually on an image; for instance, to "air brush" a smooth complexion on a scanned image of a face.

With Corel Presentations 7, you can create and edit both vector *and* bitmap images, and even change your bitmap image to a vector image with a function that traces the bitmap and creates formulas that describe it.

Creating a Bitmap Image

 To add a bitmap image to a slide, hold down the mouse pointer on the Chart or Graphics tool on the Tool Palette, then select the Bitmap Image tool from the Chart or Graphics tools popout. The mouse pointer changes to a hand. Drag the hand across the slide work area to create a box for the image. The view changes to Bitmap Editing view (see Figure 23.17), and the toolbar, tool palette, and power bar all have different tools on them.

Use the text object tool, the closed object tool, and the line object tool to create your bitmap image just as you use them to create a vector image.

In addition, you can use Paint and Eraser tools to enhance your bitmap images.

 To paint a swath of color in your image, select the Paintbrush tool. Select a color with the Fill Colors button, and change the brush shape and brush width with buttons on the Bitmap Power bar, if desired. Your mouse pointer looks like the shape of the brush you have selected. Click and drag the paintbrush over the area of the slide to be painted.

FIG. 23.17

Corel Presentations 7 includes a complete bitmap editor where you can work with graphics at the pixel level.

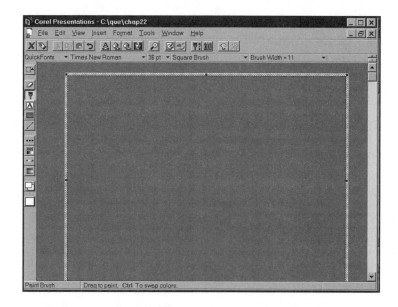

 Use the Spray Brush tool in a way similar to that used with the Paintbrush. Choose the tool, select the appropriate color, and change the brush shape and width, if desired. Repeatedly swipe the Spray Brush over the area to be colored to apply the color, just as you would with a real can of spray paint.

Use the Roller tool to instantly replace the color that you click with the selected color. For example, you can replace a white background with a blue background.

T I P You can use Edit, Undo to undo your last action.

 Use the Eyedropper tool to "dip into" a color to make it the active color. To use this tool, select it, then click an area of the drawing that has the color you want to duplicate. The color becomes the active color, and you can use one of the other tools to apply it to other areas of your drawing.

 There are two eraser tools you may find useful as well. The Erase tool erases the parts of the image that you drag it over. The Replace tool selectively replaces areas of the image that are in the foreground color with the background color.

When you are finished with your bitmap image, choose File, Close Bitmap Editor. Your bitmap image is inserted into your slide or drawing.

Editing an Existing Bitmap Image

To edit an existing bitmap image, double-click it. If the image was created in Corel Presentations 7, you will see the same bitmap editing screen that you saw when you created the image.

> **CAUTION**
>
> Depending on how your system is configured, if the image is a Windows icon (a BMP file), you may be taken into the Windows Paint program. In this case, your screen will look like the one shown in Figure 23.18.

Part
IV

Ch
23

FIG. 23.18
Edit BMP files using the Windows Paint menus items within Corel Presentations 7.

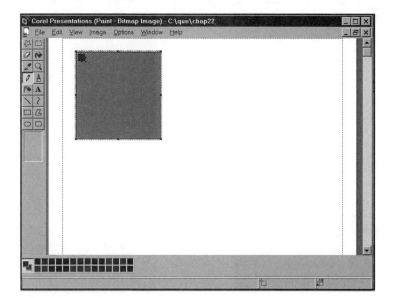

Tracing a Bitmap Image

You can trace a bitmap image to transform it into a vector image. This can be useful when you want to be able to size the image, as you might with a scanned signature.

To trace a bitmap image, click it once in the drawing or slide to select it. Choose Graphics, Trace Bitmap. The image is transformed into a vector drawing.

Using Corel Presentations versus CorelFLOW

When should you use Presentations and when should you use CorelFLOW for your drawing needs? Presentations and CorelFLOW share basic drawing functions, but they each have their unique features as well.

Presentations allows you to make a series of drawings (slides) that can be put together into a slideshow that contains transitions and animation. Presentations also has templates that provide backgrounds and text areas, automated bullet slides, and so on. When you are making a slide for a briefing or presentation, use Presentations. Presentations also has a wide selection of clip art, more powerful drawing tools, and the capability of editing bitmap graphics.

CorelFLOW has tools that make diagramming simple, including a much wider variety of simple objects that can be used as objects in diagrams. Its templates are oriented not toward presentations, but types of diagrams (family trees, org charts, etc.). It excels in creating connector lines between objects, even providing tools that automatically change the shape of connection lines as you move the objects in the diagram.

In short, use CorelFLOW for creating diagrams; use Presentations for slides and other types of drawings.

 Create your organizational charts and process flow charts in CorelFLOW. Export them from CorelFLOW to Corel Presentations Graphics format by using File, Export within CorelFLOW to save the diagram. Then, import the charts into Corel Presentations (as discussed in the previous section "Inserting a Picture from Another Program") when you need to present them to a group of people, or publish them in a series format on the Web.

CHAPTER 24

Printing and Displaying Your Presentation

Print the presentation

Learn how to preview your presentation so you won't waste paper, then select a printer and print presentation elements.

Create an electronic slideshow

Find out how to present your presentation electronically.

Add transitions and animation

Learn about spicing up your electronic slideshow with a variety of special effects, including transitions and animation.

When you're ready to show your presentation to others, you have several options. You can print the slideshow itself to paper, film, or transparencies. Additionally, you can print handouts, the outline, drawings, and other documents from the screen.

You may also want to show the presentation on-screen. Corel Presentations 7 enables you to run the show automatically, setting timing and transitions between the slides.

Whether you decide to print your presentation, make transparencies or slides, or present it as an electronic slideshow, you may want to have Speaker notes, handouts, and/or audience notes to accompany it. Speaker notes are pages that have one or more slides, along with notes that remind you of what you want to say while the slide is displayed. Audience notes are similar pages, but instead of notes, they display blank lines, like the one in Figure 24.1.

FIG. 24.1
Audience notes have blank lines where the audience members can write down important points as they listen to the presentation.

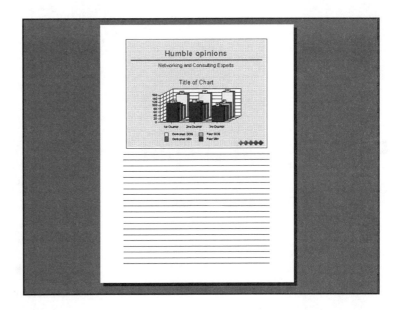

Handouts are merely pages with one or more slides printed on them, like the one shown in Figure 24.2.

FIG. 24.2
Handouts have the slides alone, with no lines or notes.

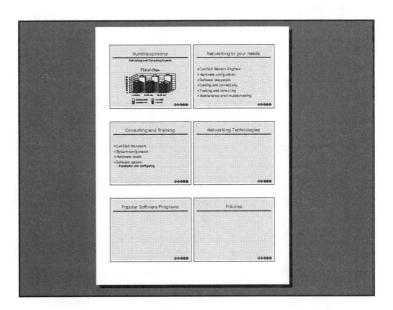

Audience notes and handouts can be printed at any time after you have created your slides. Because Speaker notes have additional text, you need to create them as a separate operation. To create Speaker notes:

1. In your open presentation, choose <u>S</u>lide, Speaker <u>N</u>otes. The Speaker Notes dialog box appears, as shown in Figure 24.3

FIG. 24.3
Enter comments and notes on the presentation in the Speaker Notes dialog box.

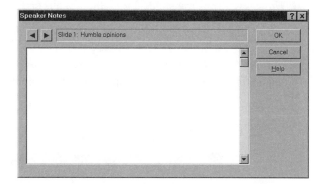

2. Using the left and right arrows in the dialog box, select the slide to which you want to add notes.

3. In the text box, enter the notes.

4. Repeat Steps 2 and 3 to enter notes to additional slides without closing the dialog box.

5. When you are done, choose OK to close the dialog box. ∎

Printing the Presentation

When you are ready to print, you can choose which presentation element you want to print—such as slides, Speaker notes, and so on—and you can choose the number of copies, binding offset, and other options before printing.

To choose printing options:

1. Choose <u>F</u>ile, <u>P</u>rint, and ensure the Print tab is selected. You see the Print dialog box shown in Figure 24.4.

TIP Choose Print Previe<u>w</u> in the Print dialog box as you select options to see how your printout will look.

2. In the <u>P</u>rint drop-down list box, choose the element you want to print:

- *Full Document.* Prints the full document.
- *Current view.* Prints only what you see on-screen; for example, if you are in a magnified view (zoom), Current view prints only that which is showing.

Part
IV

Ch
24

- *Slides.* Prints all or part of the slideshow.

- *Slide List.* Prints the list of slide titles and options for each slide.

- *Handouts.* Prints the slideshow as thumbnails on handout pages so the viewer can make notes as they watch the show. Enter the number of slides you want on each page in the Number of Slides per Page text box.

- *Speaker Notes.* Prints thumbnails, or small pictures, of each slide with any notes you entered as speaker notes (use the Slide menu, Speaker Notes command).

- *Audience Notes.* Prints thumbnails along with lines so that the audience can take notes as you talk.

FIG. 24.4

Choose Print Options in the Print dialog box.

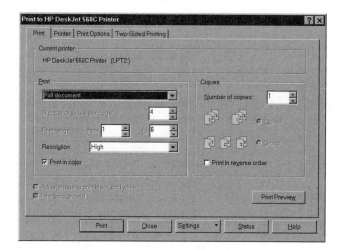

3. Select the number of copies, and (for more than one copy) whether you want to collate or group the copies, and whether to print in normal or reverse order.

4. Choose the Resolution, and whether to Print in Color or black and white.

5. If you want, you can click Print Preview to see how your document will look when it is printed.

You can also set other printing options from within the Print dialog box. By selecting the Printer tab, you can choose the printer and printer port you want to print to, and even set printer properties or add a new printer.

TROUBLESHOOTING

I want to stop the print job after I choose Print in the Print dialog box. Corel Presentations 7 displays the Printing dialog box until the print job leaves the print buffer in Corel Presentations 7.

You can cancel the print job by clicking the Cancel button in this dialog box. If you cancel a print job from Presentations that is partially completed, and you aren't able to delete it from the print queue, then a partial print job will come out of the printer. Alternatively, you can click the Printer icon on the taskbar to display the Printer dialog box after the print job has spooled to Windows, then highlight the print job and choose File, Purge Print Job.

My color graphics and text look an overall gray when I print to a black-and-white printer.
Choose the Adjust Image to Print Black and White option in the Print dialog box. If you are still unhappy with the results, return to the presentation and select the colored graphics you want to change. From the color palettes, you can choose from a variety of grays to assign text, chart markers, lines, fills, patterns, and so on. You may need to experiment with the grays to get the results you want.

NOTE If you have an HPGL plotter or a film recorder connected to your printer, you can print to either the same way you print to a printer. Using the Print dialog box, select the Print tab, then choose the printer you need from the Name drop-down list. Choose any other options as you did before and click Print. ■

Creating an Electronic Slideshow

With Corel Presentations 7, you can create a slideshow and display that show on your computer's screen—or project it from your computer via an LCD panel or projection device—for customers, employees, or other interested parties.

Electronic slideshows provide you a much greater opportunity to enhance the presentation by adding transitions between slides, having bullets appear one at a time, animating slide elements, or including sound and video to create a multimedia presentation.

Arranging Your Slides

When you print your slideshow, the arrangement of slides is not critical. You can shuffle your slides around and play them in any order that you desire. For electronic slideshows, however, you will need to ensure that your slides are arranged in the order that you intend to show them.

 If you have an initial slide that lists all your topics, consider copying this slide so that it is displayed before you start each new topic. This way, the audience will see how each topic fits into the presentation as a whole.

To rearrange your slides, switch to the Slide Sorter view by clicking the Slide Sorter View button. You see thumbnails of each of the slides in your slideshow. Select a slide by clicking it, or select several adjacent slides by clicking the first, then holding down the Shift key while you click the last. Drag the slide(s) you want to move to their new location. As you drag them, you see a vertical line that indicates where the slides will be placed, as shown in Figure 24.5.

FIG. 24.5
Rearrange slides by dragging them in the Slide Sorter view.

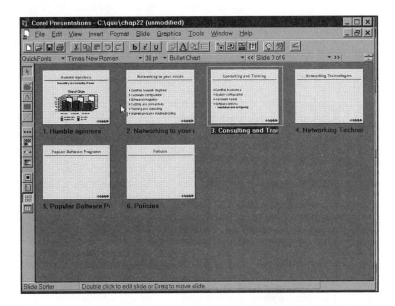

 Quickly copy a slide by holding down the Ctrl key while you drag it to its new position.

Adding Slide Transitions

The first option you will probably want to set for your electronic slideshow is the transition you will use from one slide to another. You can specify that Corel Presentations 7 should go from one slide to the next when you press a key or click the mouse; or you can set Corel Presentations 7 to move from one slide to another after a specified amount of time. You can set transitions and timing for all slides, or separately for each slide, if you like.

 If you use too many different types of transitions, the audience may become distracted. Set one transition for all slides, then vary it judiciously for a few slides in the presentation, if needed or for emphasis.

To set transitions:

 1. In your open presentation, choose <u>S</u>lide, Sl<u>i</u>de Transition; or click the Slide Transition button on the toolbar. The Slide Transition and Sound Properties dialog box appears (see Figure 24.6).

FIG. 24.6
In the Slide Transition and Sound Properties dialog box, you can choose from a variety of transition effects that govern how one slide moves to the next.

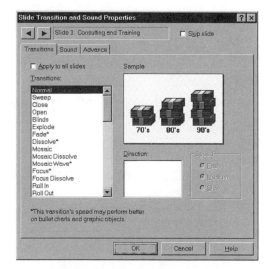

Part

IV

Ch

24

2. At the top of the dialog box, select the slide for which you want to set options. Click the right arrow to move to the next slide and the left arrow to move to the previous slide, or check <u>A</u>pply to All Slides.

 T I P If you have multiple slides selected before displaying this dialog, then the right/left arrows don't appear. Instead, the dialog box says "Multiple Slides Selected" in the static text box at the top of the dialog.

3. Select the transition from the <u>T</u>ransitions box. You see how the effect works in the preview window. Depending on the transition you select, you may also choose the <u>D</u>irection that it will occur.

4. Use the arrow keys to move to the next slide to which you want to add a transition, then repeat Step 3 as needed.

When you are finished setting transitions, choose OK to return to your slideshow.

5. Choose OK to close the dialog box and accept the changes in transition and timing.

▶ **See** "Playing Your Slideshow," **p. 506**

Adding Slide Timings

Often, you will want to manually advance from one slide to another so that you can spend as much or as little time needed on each slide.

Sometimes, however, you will want to have your slides advance automatically after a specified number of seconds. You may even want your slideshow to loop continuously, as when you play it at an entrance or convention table to advertise a product or service.

In this case, you will want to set timings for your slides. You can do so as follows:

To set timings:

1. In your open presentation, choose Slide, Slide Transition, then choose the Advance tab. The Slide Transition and Sound Properties dialog box appears (see Figure 24.7).

FIG. 24.7

You can have your slides advance from one to the next automatically after a specified number of seconds by setting options in the Slide Transition and Sound Properties dialog box on the Advance tab.

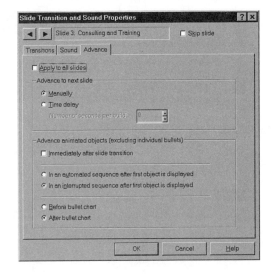

2. At the top of the dialog box, select the slide for which you want to set options. Click the right arrow to move to the next slide and the left arrow to move to the previous slide, or check Apply to All Slides.

3. If you want to automate the slide timing, choose Time Delay, and specify the number of seconds between slides.

4. Choose options for any animated objects you have on your slide. If you select Immediately After Slide Transition, then the animated object appears immediately after the slide has been drawn on-screen. If this option isn't selected, then the slide is drawn without the animated object, and you have to click again to have the animated object appear.

▶ **See** "Animating Slide Elements," **p. 503**

5. Use the arrow keys to move to the next slide to which you want to add a slide timing, then repeat Steps 3 and 4 as needed.

6. When you are finished setting timings, choose OK to return to your slideshow.

 TIP Set the seconds to delay higher for slides with a lot of information on them, so the viewer is sure to have enough time to read the information, even if you are going over it verbally.

N O T E You can add sound to a slideshow by using MIDI, digital audio, or CD audio sound files to one or more slides, if you have the sound hardware for the job. Choose the Sound button in the Slide Transition dialog box to display the Sound dialog box. Enter any options and click OK to return to the Slide Transition dialog box. ■

Part
IV

Ch
24

Animating Slide Elements

You can animate your slides further by having bullets appear one by one, with old bullets becoming dim. You can also have drawing objects fly in from the side, giving an animated appearance to your slideshow.

To cascade your bullets in bullet slides:

1. Select the bullets on any bullet slide.

2. Choose Slide, Object Animation. You see the Bullet Chart Animation Properties dialog box shown in Figure 24.8.

FIG. 24.8
Cascade bullets and have
them appear one at a time.

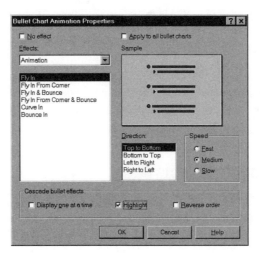

3. Deselect No Effect, then choose Display One At a Time.

4. Select the type of animation you want to use from the list box, and the Direction and Speed. If you want previous bullets to become dim, choose Highlight.

5. Click OK to exit the dialog box.

If you would like to animate drawing objects or QuickArt that you've placed on your slide, do the following:

1. Select the first object to be animated—the object that should appear first after the slide displays.

2. Choose Slide, Object Animation. You see the Object Animation Properties dialog box shown in Figure 24.9.

FIG. 24.9
In the Object Animation Properties dialog box, you can animate objects on your slide to have them fly onto the slide.

3. Uncheck No Effect, if it is checked, then choose Animation or Transition as the type of effect. Choose the specific animation or transition effect you want to use, and the direction and speed, if needed.

4. Click OK to return to the slide.

5. Select the next object to be animated, and repeat Steps 2 through 4. If you need to reorder the animated object, change its Object Display Sequence number.

6. Continue with this until all objects are animated.

Including Multimedia Effects

You can take your slideshow one step further by adding sounds to it, or even video files (if your hardware supports sound and/or video).

Insert Sounds on Your Slide   You can add short bursts of sound, like clapping hands, or longer melodies that you can play during the entire slideshow, or during the display of one or more specific slides.

To add sound to your presentation, do the following:

1. In your open presentation, choose Slide, Slide Transition. The Slide Transition and Sound Properties dialog box appears. Select the Sound tab if needed. You see the dialog box in Figure 24.10.

FIG. 24.10
You can add sound to your slides to make a multimedia presentation by choosing options in the Slide Transition and Sound Properties box.

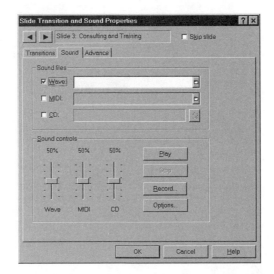

Part
IV

Ch

24

2. At the top of the dialog box, use the arrows to select the slide to which you want to attach the sound.

3. Select the type of sound you want to use (Wave, MIDI or CD), then click the folder button to browse the folders and find the right sound file.

4. If you would like the sound to loop and keep repeating, click the Options button and choose Loop Sound, then choose OK to return to the Slide Transition and Sound Properties dialog box.

5. Choose OK to close the dialog box and return to your slideshow.

TIP   To play a sound throughout your presentation, attach the sound to slide 1 and loop the sound.

Add Video Clips to Your Slideshow   To add a video clip to your slideshow, do the following:

1. Switch to the Slide Editor mode by clicking the Slide Editor View button, and navigate to the slide you want to attach your video clip to by using the left/right arrows on the Power Bar.

2. Choose <u>I</u>nsert, Ob<u>j</u>ect. You see the Insert Object dialog box shown in Figure 24.11.

FIG. 24.11
Use the Insert Object dialog box to add a video clip to your presentation.

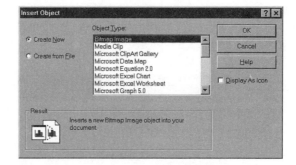

3. Choose Create from <u>F</u>ile, then click the <u>B</u>rowse button. You see the Browse dialog box.

4. Navigate to the video file you want to use, then double-click it. You return to the Insert Object dialog box. Click OK to return to the slideshow.

The video clip appears as an object on the appropriate slide, and will play when the slideshow reaches that slide.

Playing Your Slideshow

When you're ready to play your slideshow, Corel Presentations 7 offers you options for moving from slide to slide, using mouse pointers and highlighters to draw attention to aspects of your slide, and saving your show as a Quick File to eliminate pauses in your slideshow.

Playing a Slideshow   When you run the slideshow, Corel Presentations 7 clears the screen of tools, windows, menus, and everything except each slide.

To play a slideshow:

1. Open the slideshow. Choose <u>S</u>lide, <u>P</u>lay Slide Show, or click the Play Show button. The Play Slide Show dialog box appears, as shown in Figure 24.12.

2. In the <u>S</u>tarting Slide text box, enter the number of the slide you want to start the presentation with. You can also use the scroll bar to select slides.

3. In the Highlighter group, choose the <u>C</u>olor and the <u>W</u>idth of the marker you want to use during the presentation.

FIG. 24.12

Choose to play the slideshow and Corel Presentations 7 enables you to make a few last minute changes to some of the options.

TIP Draw on the slide by clicking and dragging with the mouse. Don't just click the mouse, because that will cause the slideshow to advance to the next slide.

4. In the Options group, choose to Repeat Slide Show if you want the show to run continuously.

5. Choose Play to start the show.

Play Options While you are playing your slideshow, you have several options.

If the show is set to manually advance the slides:

- Click the left mouse button; or press the right arrow or down arrow to advance to the next slide.
- Click the right mouse button; or press the left arrow or up arrow to advance to the previous slide.
- Press Esc to cancel the show at any time.

To show the cursor during your slideshow, move the mouse pointer. The cursor appears on your slide.

To highlight an area of your slide with an underline, move the mouse pointer to where the underline should start, then drag the mouse pointer to draw an underline.

Creating a QuickShow File Create a QuickShow file of your slideshow to speed up the display. When you create a quick file, you save the slideshow as bitmap and thus the display is much quicker; however, the file is much larger than a slideshow so make sure you have enough room for the show on your disk.

To create a quick file, choose Slide, Play Slide Show. The Play Slide Show dialog box appears. Choose Create QuickShow. If you haven't saved your file, you will be prompted to do so before the QuickShow is created. You see a Making QuickShow dialog box as the file is created.

When you play your slideshow in the future, you can choose to use the QuickShow file by checking the Use QuickShow box in the Play Slide Show dialog box.

Part
IV

Ch
24

TROUBLESHOOTING

I made a change in one of the slides and now the slideshow seems slower. If you saved the slideshow as a quick file and then made a change to the show, you must create a quick file again to speed up the display.

I am saving a copy of the slideshow to a floppy disk but I am worried the show is too large to fit on one disk. You can usually fit one slideshow onto a high density 3 1/2 or 5 1/4 floppy disk; however, if your show file is larger and fills up the disk, Corel Presentations 7 prompts you to insert a second disk.

Making a Runtime Slideshow

Making a runtime slideshow means to copy the show with all necessary program files to a disk so you can run the show on another computer that does not have Corel Presentations 7 installed.

To make a runtime file:

1. Open the slideshow or save the current show.

2. Choose Slide, Runtime Expert. The Runtime Expert welcome screen appears (see Figure 24.13).

FIG. 24.13
The Runtime Expert allows you to copy your presentation to a disk so that it may be run from a computer that does not have Corel Presentations 7 installed.

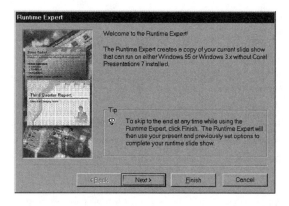

3. Choose Next. You see the second step of the Expert shown in Figure 24.14. Select the drive or folder you wish to make the runtime file in, then choose Next. (If you choose a folder that does not exist, you will be asked if you want the Expert to create it.)

FIG. 24.14
Choose whether to save your runtime slideshow to a floppy disk or a folder on your hard drive.

4. In the third step of the Expert, select whether your show will be played on a Windows 95 system or on both Windows 3.x and Windows 95 systems.

5. Choose Next. In the fourth step of the Expert, select whether the display of the system you will play your slideshow on matches yours, or whether it should be able to be played on any windows display.

6. The final step shows the choices you have made, as displayed in Figure 24.15. If any are incorrect, choose Back to revisit previous steps. If they are correct, choose Finish. You see the Making Runtime dialog box as your show is converted, then you return to the main PowerPoint window.

FIG. 24.15
After you choose options for your runtime slideshow, Presentations creates the runtime show automatically.

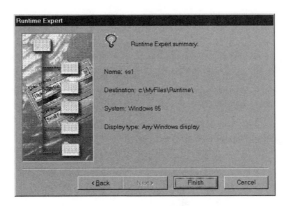

Copy the files in the show directory to a diskette, then copy them again (if desired) to the hard drive of the computer on which you will play your show.

To play the show, use Explorer in Windows 95 (or File Manager in Windows 3.1) and double-click the Show70 application. Choose the file you want to play. Corel Presentations 7 plays the show with your transitions and timing selections.

N O T E   If you choose to save the show so that it can be played in Windows 95 or Windows 3.1, you will experience certain limitations. All transitions will be normal, and animation will be removed. Slides with cascading bullets, however, will still play normally. ▩

CHAPTER 25

Integrating Corel Presentations 7 with the Web

Corel Presentations 7 helps you extend your desktop into the Internet or corporate intranet by allowing you to browse the Web, download images from the Web into your slideshows, create active links between your slideshows and the Web, or even publish your presentation to the Web in a variety of ways. ▪

Publishing on the Internet

Understand some of the best types of presentation information to publish on the Internet along with some of the limitations of Internet publishing.

Using information from the Web

Learn how to pull information off the Web to incorporate into your presentation slides.

Converting slideshows to Web pages

Find out how to convert your slideshow into a series of Internet Web pages.

Four types of Internet publishing

Corel Presentations 7 can publish your data on the Internet in four different ways. Learn what they are and when to use them.

Using Corel Presentations 7 with the Web

Corel Presentations 7 is no longer merely a desktop application. It allows you to browse the Web and download material such as clip art into your slideshows or drawings.

If you are not familiar with the Web and Web documents, you might consider reading Chapter 26, "Using Corel WordPerfect Suite on the Internet" before you read this chapter. Even if you have experience with the Web, this chapter may have useful information of which you are not aware.

NOTE Web integration works the same way with slideshows and drawings. For ease of reading, only slideshows will be referred to in this chapter, but everything applies equally to drawings you create with Corel Presentations 7. ▨

Using the Web Browser Button

 When you click the Web Browser button, you launch Netscape (or your default Web browser), and go automatically to Corel's Web site. You can browse this site for information on Presentations, or go anywhere else on the Internet that you prefer.

▶ **See** "Browsing the Web and Specifying Destinations," **p. 539**

Using Clip Art from the Web

The Internet can be a rich source for clip art to include in your slideshows. Using Netscape, it's easy to find and save clip art on your local computer, then import it into Presentations.

> **CAUTION**
>
> Images on Web sites are often copyrighted, and will in any case be protected by relevant copyright laws. Be sure to obtain permission from the copyright owner before using images from Web sites, and strongly consider establishing a company policy regarding use of information obtained from the Internet after advice from legal counsel.

▶ **See** "Understanding the Implications of Publishing on the Internet," **p. 534**

You can find free public domain clip art on the Internet. The easiest way to do so is to search for the term clip art using any of the popular search engines.

▶ **See** "Introducing Netscape Navigator," **p. 536**

Once you've found an image you like and have obtained permission to use it, you can copy a Web image into a Presentations slideshow easily by following these steps:

1. Open Netscape and browse to the Web site containing the image.

2. Right-click the image. You see a pop-up QuickMenu.

3. Choose Save This Image As. You see the Save As dialog box.

4. Specify a folder and file name for the image, then choose <u>S</u>ave. The image is saved to your local computer.

From Corel Presentations, you can insert this image into your slideshow as you do any other image on your disk.

▶ **See** "Inserting a Picture from Another Program," **p. 483**

Converting Slideshows to Web Pages

A slideshow can be an effective sales tool—getting your company's mission across to the public. It can be a learning tool, by using slideshows as a simple type of computer-based training. It can supplement other text-based Web pages by illustrating points with charts, diagrams, and tables.

Corel Presentations 7 includes a feature that allows you to convert your slideshow to one or more Web pages, so you can publish it on the Internet or on a corporate intranet.

▶ **See** "What Are Intranets?," **p. 526**

Understanding Web Page Formats

You can publish your slideshow in four different ways. If your readers will be using a browser that supports frames (such as Netscape Navigator 2.0 or Microsoft Internet Explorer 2.0), you can create Web pages like the one shown in Figure 25.1.

▶ **See** "Introducing Netscape Navigator," **p. 536**

N O T E There are two meanings of the term "publish." The normal usage of the term, for example, "publish a Web document," means to *place* a document on the Web where people can see it. Corel Presentations 7 uses the term publish, however, in a different sense, to mean *converting* a slideshow to HTML.

When used in this latter sense, the document will still reside on your disk rather than on the Web, and you will still need to copy it to the Internet so that people can see it.

The meaning of the term in this book can be derived from the context in which it's used. ■

Part
IV

Ch

25

FIG. 25.1

You can publish your slideshow in Web pages that have frames, if your readers' browsers support this.

Presentation Title frame ——

Frame separator bars ——

Table of Contents frame ——

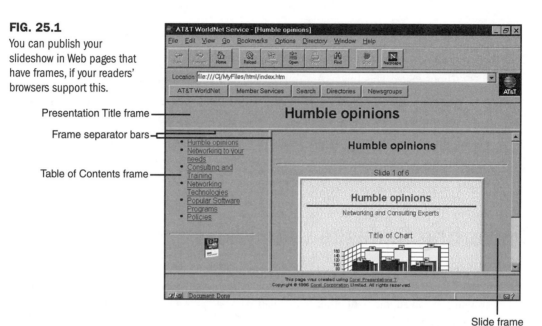

Slide frame

When frames are used, each slide has its own frame that is accessed from the Table of Contents frame.

If you want people to be able to read your slideshow even if their browser doesn't support frames, you can publish in multiple Web pages, with each slide on its own page, as shown in Figure 25.2.

FIG. 25.2

If you are not sure that everyone's browser supports frames, you may want to publish your slideshow with individual multiple pages.

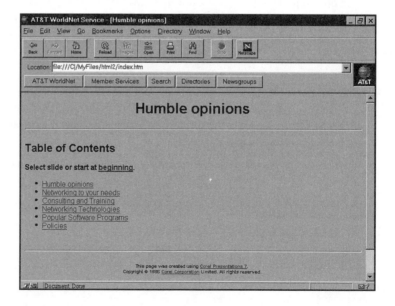

With this type of setup, the viewer can click the slide title in the Table of Contents and return to the Table of Contents after viewing each slide. Alternatively, you can set the slides up so that the viewer also has the choice of going on to the next slide without returning to the Table of Contents.

You can also publish your slideshow in one long Web page, with all the slides in the same page one after another, like the example shown in Figure 25.3.

FIG. 25.3

If you prefer, you can put all your slides on one Web page.

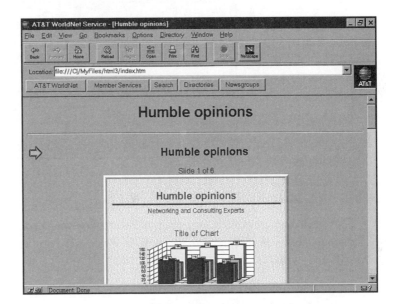

In this method, the viewer just uses the scroll bar to view one slide after the other.

Finally, you can publish thumbnails of your slideshow in one Web page, as displayed in Figure 25.4.

You can set this up so viewers just have access to the thumbnails, or so the thumbnails are buttons that the viewers can click, which will take them to a separate page with a larger version of the slide.

Part

IV

Ch

25

FIG. 25.4
You can also publish thumbnails of each slide; users can double-click a thumbnail to see the full-size slide.

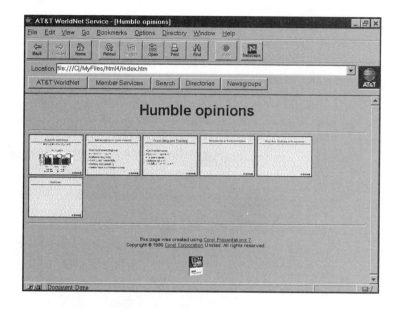

Converting Your Slideshow to HTML

When you convert your slideshow, it creates a series of files in a folder you specify. You should not try to save more than one slideshow in a particular folder, because many of the file names may be duplicates.

To convert your slideshow to Web pages, ensure that your slideshow has been created, finalized, and saved. Then follow these steps:

1. With the slideshow on the screen, choose File, Publish To, HTML. You see the Publish to HTML dialog box that allows you to choose from four different types of Web pages.

2. Choose Frame Enhanced Page, Multiple Pages, Single Page, or Single Gallery Style Page.

3. Depending on the choice you made, you will see some or all of the following options:

   - *Title Name.* Input a title for your presentation.
   - *Save File(s) To.* Specify the folder that you want to save your presentation in. Corel Presentations 7 will create the folder if it doesn't already exist. Remember to only save one presentation in a folder.

- *Include Slide Show File for Downloading.* If you mark this check box, a copy of the Corel Presentations 7 slideshow file will also be saved in the folder, and a link created to the file. In this way, people who visit this Web site and who own Corel Presentations 7 can click the link to download the file to their computer, where they can view it with Corel Presentations.

CAUTION

Keep in mind that those machines using Windows 3.1 and some networks either cannot cope with long names, or cope with them by truncating them—making identification of individual pages more difficult. For this reason, in many instances, it is best to stick with the DOS 8.3 naming convention.

- *Update HTML File(s) Only.* Allows you to change page arrangements or viewing order without regenerating the entire slideshow.
- *Page Numbers.* Put page numbers on each Web page.
- *Page Titles.* Put the title of the presentation on each Web page.
- *Speaker Notes.* Add the speaker notes to the bottom of each Web page.
- *Go to Slide Bar.* Add a navigation slide bar to the bottom of each slide.
- *Generate Table of Contents With.* Add a table of contents page (for multiple page slideshows) or frame (for frame-enhanced slideshows) that includes either the title of each slide or a thumbnail of each slide.
- *Color Options.* Use your browser's default colors, or specify colors for text, links, and so on.
- *Advance.* Create a self-running slideshow, rather than one with manual advances.
- *More Options.* Choose to publish your graphics in GIF or JPG format, select their width and height, change the file name of the initial page (INDEX.HTM by default), and specify footer information for each page.

NOTE Footer information should include Corel Presentations 7 copyright information, your e-mail address (so that viewers may contact you with questions or other information that may be of interest to you), the date the page was last updated (so viewers will know if it has been changed since the last time they looked), and any custom information.

Part

IV

Ch

25

4. Choose OK when you are finished setting options. You see a dialog box showing the process as each slide is converted, and the files are created in the folder you specified.

N O T E After you have published your slideshow as HTML, you should view it with your browser prior to uploading it to your Web site, to ensure that everything is as you want it to be. From within Netscape, choose File, Open File and specify the folder and file name of your presentation. If the presentation is not right, it's easier to fix it in Presentations and re-publish it, but you can edit the HTML files themselves if you need to. You may want to refer to Que's *Special Edition Using HTML* for further information on editing Web pages.

Publishing Corel Presentations with Barista

Corel Presentations incorporates a new feature called Barista—a Corel-developed technology that allows you to publish your presentations in Java on intranets or the Internet. For further information on how to use this technology, see the section "Publishing Documents with Barista" in Chapter 12, "Integrating Corel WordPerfect 7 with the Internet." For in-depth coverage of the Java language, see Que's book *Special Edition Using Java.*

Uploading Your Presentation

Before others can see your presentation, you will need to copy it onto the Internet or your corporate intranet.

Copying Your Presentation to the Internet   To copy the presentation to the Internet, you will need to use programs that are not included with the Corel WordPerfect Suite 7. Thus, this book cannot tell you *how* to do this; however, it is possible to specify *what* needs to be done.

To copy the presentation to the Internet, you must do the following:

■ Know the address of the file area you will copy the presentation to on your Internet server.

■ Have sufficient access permission to copy the files.

■ Create a subdirectory on the Internet server for the presentation.

■ Copy all files in your Web presentation folder to that subdirectory.

If you desire, you can create a link from another Web site to your presentation. The link should be of the form:

http://www.server.com/directory/subdirectory/index.htm

where **server** is the name of your Internet server, **directory** is the name of your main directory on that server, and **subdirectory** is the name of the new subdirectory you created for your presentation.

> **CAUTION**
>
> If you have changed the name of your table of contents page, that is the name that should be entered where it says INDEX.HTM in the previous URL.

Copying Your Presentation to a Corporate Intranet   Copying your presentation to a local Web site can entail any number of different methods, depending on how your site is set up. The basic procedure, however, is still the same as it is to copy your presentation to the Internet.

You must create a specific subdirectory on your Web server exclusively for the presentation, and copy all files from the folder in which you saved your Web presentation to this subdirectory.

If files on your Web site are accessible via your Windows 95, Windows NT, or Novell network, you may be able to create the directory (folder) and copy the files via Windows Explorer. More often, you will need to copy the files to a public workspace on your network, and your network administrator or Webmaster will take care of copying them to the appropriate locations on the Web server.

Publishing Presentations with Envoy

You can also publish your presentation with Envoy, creating a document that anyone with the Envoy Viewer can read.

To publish your presentation with Envoy, ensure that your presentation has been saved and is displayed on the screen.

Choose File, Publish To, Envoy. Your file is printed to the Envoy printer driver, which prints it to an Envoy file, then automatically opens Envoy so that you can see the presentation, like the one shown in Figure 25.5. For more information, see Chapter 28, "Using Envoy."

Part

IV

Ch

25

FIG. 25.5

When you publish your presentation in Envoy, you are taken to the Envoy Viewer to look at your presentation.

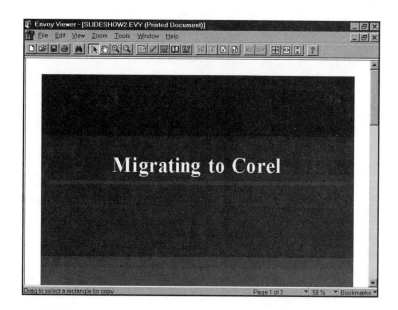

E-Mailing Your Presentation

As you are developing your presentation, you may want to e-mail it to reviewers or your supervisor prior to finalizing it.

If you are using a mail system that supports an e-mail standard called Simple MAPI, you will find the Send item on your File menu. If this is the case, you can e-mail your slideshow from within Corel Presentations 7.

NOTE Sometimes, networks that use compatible e-mail programs are not configured correctly, and the Send option does not appear on the File menu. Ask your system administrator to check if the Send item does not appear on your menu. ■

To e-mail your presentation, have the slideshow you want to send on the screen. Choose File, Send. You are taken into your e-mail system, and you will see a Send To dialog box, with the slideshow automatically included as an attachment to your (blank) message. Fill in the recipient(s), a subject, and a message, and send your message!

If File, Send is not available, go into your e-mail system and use the method appropriate for your system for attaching a file to an e-mail file. ●

PART

V

Using Internet Applications

CHAPTER 26

Using Corel WordPerfect Suite on the Internet

The Internet is a network comprised of millions of computers and computer networks that spans the globe. Because of its global reach, and because so many computers are connected to it, people are increasingly finding it to be an indispensable business tool, as well as being wonderful at home. ■

Understand Internet basics

Find out what all those funny terms mean: Internet, intranet, World Wide Web, URLs, browsers, and more.

Recognize implications of publishing on the Internet

When you publish to the Internet, the whole world can see it! Find out tips and tricks you should use.

Use Netscape

Learn how to "surf the Web" with AT&T WorldNet's version of Netscape Navigator, and how to "pull" information off the Web.

Get online help

Help on the Internet, Netscape, and Corel WordPerfect Suite is available on the Internet. Find out how to access it quickly and easily.

Understanding Internet Basics

People use the Internet in many ways to increase their productivity in business and access a wealth of information. Some of the most common uses of the Internet are:

- *To communicate*. Internet e-mail programs allow people to send and receive e-mail with anyone else who has an Internet connection, anywhere in the world. There are no long distance telephone charges for this; the only cost is your normal fee for connecting to the Internet. The Internet is also used for public discussions on topics ranging from using Corel WordPerfect 7 to sugarless baking recipes.

- *For information*. Computers on the Internet store a wealth of information. While some of it is private or for-fee, much is free to the public. You can access things including the Library of Congress card catalog, a nationwide telephone directory, maps to go from anywhere in the U.S. to anywhere else, the Commerce Business Daily, encyclopedias, dictionaries, and literally millions of other sources of data.

- *For commerce*. Increasingly, businesses are creating a presence for themselves on the Internet. Corporations advertise new products, provide customer support, and even sell products via the Internet.

N O T E Secure communication methods are just beginning to make their debut. Many companies allow you to purchase items with your credit card; unfortunately, security is not yet as tight as it could be, and cases of credit card fraud are becoming more common. ■

- *For business*. Businesses are using the Internet to create wide area networks, in which regional offices are connected together using the Internet rather than dedicated phone lines.

Physically, the Internet is comprised of a backbone of mainframe computers that are tied together with high-speed optical fiber cables. Networks "hook into" the backbone with fiber optic, copper, and even regular telephone lines. The Internet constitutes a complex web of these computers, where information may go from one place to another through any of thousands of routes, automatically bypassing computers that are out of service, or where the load is too heavy.

 T I P These Internet computers are often called *hosts* or *servers*, because they are the "hosts" for users, and "serve up" databases and other applications. Hosts and servers actually have technical meanings, but in general conversation they are used to refer to the Internet computers you log on to and link to.

N O T E If you're on a network, your Internet connection will provide faster or slower response time depending on how much "bandwidth" (or simultaneous information) your connecting line into the Internet supports. The slowest dedicated lines are 56k lines; they barely support one or two connections to the Web. Faster lines are T1, and T3 connections are even faster. If you're connecting to an Internet Service Provider via a modem, the speed of the modem is the limiting factor. ■

Computers on the Internet communicate by using *protocols,* or agreed upon ways of transferring information. The Internet is comprised of many types of computers, and these computers do not "speak each other's language" easily. Thus, they need to transfer information in a lowest common denominator—protocols that they can all adhere to. One of these basic protocols is TCP/IP, which is way of breaking down information into small chunks (called packets) that can be easily transmitted over the network. Another protocol you will learn about is HTTP—a way of transmitting files that contain graphics, sound, or video over the Internet.

What Is the World Wide Web?

The World Wide Web is a part of the Internet that supports graphic and multimedia files.

The protocols that are used on the Internet only support the transmission of ASCII text files, not the complex binary files that make up applications and data files like WordPerfect documents.

To get around this shortcoming, complex coding systems have been developed to translate programs and data files into plain text. One of these mechanisms is HyperText Markup Language, or HTML. Using HTML, bold text is denoted by "tags"—ASCII codes that denote, for example, <b> as the beginning of bold, and </b> as the end of bold. Similarly, <H1> denotes the Heading 1 style, and </H1> denotes the end of it.

N O T E HTML is actually a subset of a much more complex protocol called SGML (Standard Graphics Markup Language). SGML also uses tags to format ASCII text, but in addition supports rules that determine which text elements can follow which others (for example, a Heading 1 must immediately be followed by Heading 2) and the like.

WordPerfect supports SGML, although using SGML is beyond the scope of this book. If you are interested, Que's *Special Edition Using SGML* is an excellent and comprehensive treatment of this topic. ■

▶ **See** "Creating Web Documents," **p. 24**

HTML has one other important feature. It allows you to define *links*—highlighted areas of a document that, when clicked, take you to another document elsewhere on the Internet.

▶ **See** "Creating and Editing Links," **p. 257**

Part

V

Ch

26

The World Wide Web—often referred to as WWW or the Web—is comprised of Internet servers that support HTML. These servers constitute a web because they are not hierarchically organized. The links on one HTML document may take you to a variety of others, and the combined links resemble a spider web more than a hierarchical organizational chart.

When you publish a series of interlinked HTML documents on the Web, they become a *Web site*, and each HTML document, once it has been uploaded to the Web, is called a *Web page*. The main page on your site that a person would usually go to first is called the *home page*.

What Are Intranets?

The Web, in an earlier form, was originally begun by the United States government Department of Defense to permit contact between its departments and universities. As it grew, other universities and government agencies, and later corporations and other organizations, realized the power of the Web to communicate externally, and to tie together remote offices.

Then, the next logical idea that occurred to people was: If the Web could be used to communicate externally, why not use it to communicate *internally* as well? Intranets were born. An intranet is an internal Web, comprised of one or more Web servers that are connected to each other, but are not accessible to the larger Internet community. In effect, an intranet is just like a piece of the World Wide Web, except that outsiders generally cannot access the intranet (often, you must be physically logged into a computer at the site), and access to the Web from inside the intranet is sometimes limited as well.

Why have an intranet? Many organizations do not have standards for hardware and software. Often, employees will use a variety of software packages, so that putting a document up on a network is no guarantee that others will be able to read it or edit it. Similarly, if an organization has a variety of computers—Apples, PCs, UNIX-based computers, and Sun workstations, they may not be able to even access the same network to begin with. You can access the World Wide Web from virtually any type of computer, running almost any type of operating system. Thus, by setting up an internal Web—an intranet—the communication problem is solved.

The growth of corporate intranets is expected to be one of the biggest trends in computer use over the next two to three years. It is for this reason, as well as the ability to publish documents to the Internet, that Corel has built HTML functionality into all its major products. It has also developed Barista—a technology that permits publishing documents in Java on intranets or the Internet.

▶ **See** "Publishing Documents with Barista," **p. 271**

▶ **See** "Publishing Corel Presentations with Barista," **p. 518**

N O T E Java is a programming language that creates simple applications (called applets) that can be included in Web pages. Assuming that your browser supports Java, the applet is automatically downloaded when you access a Web page that contains it.

The first and simplest Java applications were ones that created animated figures or sound. Newer Java applets create interactive games on Web pages, allow you to search a database on the Web server that isn't stored as an HTML document, or show complex document formatting without the document being written in HTML. ▨

Connecting to the Internet

There are two main ways you connect to the Internet, by logging into a local area network (LAN) that is connected to the Internet, or individually, through an Internet Service Provider (ISP).

Connecting via a Network   If you work at an organization that has a LAN, it is probably connected to the Internet, or will be within a year or two at most. Alternatively, your LAN may be connected to a corporate intranet, which offers the same functionality (other than connecting to the rest of the Internet). In any case, if you are on a LAN, connecting to the Internet or an intranet is a simple matter of talking to your system administrator. They will tell you what (if any) connections are available, and how to access them.

Connecting via an Internet Service Provider   If you are not on a network, you can still access the Internet and the World Wide Web. To do so, you will need four things. You need a modem, a telephone line, software to access the Web with (a Web browser), and an account with an Internet Service Provider (ISP).

A *Browser* is an application that is used for looking at ("browsing") Web pages. Browsers do more than this, however. If you are like most people, your primary connection to the Internet will be via the World Wide Web, and your browser is your main tool for connecting to the Web. You can look at Web pages; move across links to other Web pages; save Web pages or download linked files to your local computer; or print Web pages. Browsers also include e-mail programs to send and receive e-mail over the Internet, and newsreaders to participate in public discussions called *newsgroups*.

One of the most popular browsers today is Netscape Navigator. A version of Netscape Navigator licensed to AT&T WorldNet Service is included as part of the Corel WordPerfect Suite 7.

Part
V

Ch
26

Different browsers support slightly different HTML feature sets, and earlier versions of browsers do not support as many HTML features as later versions of even the same browsers. For instance, some browsers support tables and forms, while others do not.

When you use the WordPerfect Suite to publish HTML documents, you should recognize that these documents may look slightly different in various browsers, and that some features may not be supported at all. Often, Web page creator will put notes on their Web pages, that say something like "This page is best viewed in Netscape 2.01 or later versions."

> **CAUTION**
>
> If you have access to different browsers, it's a good idea to look at documents you produce in each one to ensure that it can be read by the greatest number of people possible.

An ISP (Information Service Provider) is a company that has a computer connected to the Internet (an Internet host) and modems that subscribers can connect to. ISPs sell subscribers UserIDs with which they log on to the Internet host computer, and thereby access the Internet.

There are many different ISPs that service various regions of the country. Some are nationwide, offering local telephone numbers in major cities throughout the U.S. for those who travel.

Many ISPs provide you with free browser software with which to access the World Wide Web. The most common browser that is offered is Netscape Navigator.

Some are value-added ISPs, offering technical support, Web sites providing interesting information to subscribers, or automated processes for creating your own Web sites.

What About Other Online Services?

Many households are connected to online services, such as America Online (AOL) or CompuServe Information Services (CIS). These services originally started as completely separate networks that could be accessed from virtually anywhere in the U.S. Within the last two years, they have offered access to the Internet, and eventually may migrate entirely *to* the Internet, becoming sites that can be accessed for a fee, rather than maintaining a separate network infrastructure.

Online services offer a host of easy-to-use features and a friendly interface designed to help the novice get online and feel comfortable getting started. They are also much more expensive to use, if you are online extensively.

As of this writing, subscribers to online services use proprietary software to access them and, through them, access the Internet. Such proprietary software often does not support the full range of features found on many Web pages.

Your ISP will give you several items of information that you will need to connect to the Internet. These include your UserID and password, and several technical items required when you configure Windows 95 to dial to your ISP. You don't need to know what these mean, but you *do* need to get the following information: the phone number to dial, a primary and secondary Domain Name Server (DNS) address, an SMTP outgoing mail server name, a POP incoming mail server name, and the news server name.

The mail and news server names are used to configure your browser for e-mail and newsgroups, discussed in Chapter 27, "Communicating on the Internet."

N O T E   If you *are* on a LAN that is connected to the Internet, you probably have a fairly high-speed connection, and see graphic pages loading rather quickly (1-3 seconds, or even faster). If you use a modem to connect to the Internet, the connection is between 5 and 50 times slower than a LAN connection. Complex graphic pages may take as long as five minutes to load, though most will load in 5 to 30 seconds. ▪

Connecting via AT&T WorldNet Service   One ISP that you can use to connect to the Internet is AT&T's WorldNet Service. AT&T WorldNet Service offers toll-free connections to the Internet from most major metropolitan regions, and they advertise that the quality of their Internet connection is especially good. They have toll-free support lines open 24-hours a day. As of this writing, their pricing was about 25 percent higher than competitive pricing for other nationwide ISPs, unless you have AT&T long distance service, in which case you get a discount that makes their pricing equivalent to other ISPs.

AT&T WorldNet Service provides a free browser; it is a special version of Netscape Navigator 2.01 licensed to AT&T. Unlike virtually every other version of Netscape Navigator, it uses the AT&T icon on the desktop, and says AT&T WorldNet Service on the title bar, rather than Netscape.

This special version of Netscape is bundled with Corel WordPerfect Suite 7. It does not obligate you to use AT&T WorldNet Service as your ISP; you can connect to the Internet via your LAN or any ISP using this special version of Netscape as your browser.

If you use AT&T's version of Netscape bundled with Corel WordPerfect Suite, and do *not* choose AT&T WorldNet Service as your ISP, you will not be able to use most of the Directory Buttons on the Netscape Screen. The AT&T WorldNet button, the Member Services button, the Search button, and the Directories button, as well as all the options on the Directory menu, access **www.worldnet.att.net**—a site that you *cannot* access unless you are using AT&T WorldNet Service as your ISP.

Unfortunately, there is no indication of this when you use these buttons or menu items. The Status Bar says `Connect: Contacting host: www.worldnet.att.net`, and stays that way indefinitely. There is no indication that this is a restricted site, and you may think that there is merely a network delay in getting connected.

You may want to choose Options, Show Directory Buttons to turn off the display of directory buttons so that you don't inadvertently think you can use them.

N O T E   Throughout this chapter and the rest of the book, "AT&T WorldNet Service" will be used to refer to the AT&T Internet Service Provider. The AT&T version of Netscape will be referred to as Netscape, rather than as AT&T WorldNet Service, to prevent confusion between the browser and the ISP of the same name. ■

T I P   For further information about using AT&T WorldNet Service as your ISP, call the toll-free information number at (800) 400-1447.

Setting Up Your Internet Connection   Once you have signed up with an ISP, you may be provided with specific software and/or procedures to follow in setting up your Internet connection.

For example, to set up a connection to AT&T WorldNet Service, you can use the AT&T WorldNet Account Setup Wizard that is supplied with the Corel WordPerfect Suite.

CAUTION

The Internet Setup Wizard described here is only for use in creating an account with AT&T WorldNet Service.

You cannot use this Wizard if you are connected to a network. There is no other way, as of this writing, to obtain an AT&T WorldNet Service account (you cannot set one up by telephone). So, if you are connected to a network, you cannot set up an AT&T WorldNet Service account, and therefore some features of the version of Netscape that ships with Corel WordPerfect Suite will not work, as discussed previously.

To set up the connection, or to load the Netscape browser for use with other ISPs, do the following:

1. Put the Corel WordPerfect Suite CD in your computer's CD player. The Autorun feature will automatically bring up the screen shown in Figure 26.1.

2. Choose Internet Service Setup. You see the first step of the AT&T WorldNet Service Setup program shown in Figure 26.2.

3. Click Next to move to Step 2, which asks if the default directory should be used.

4. Click Next again. The Netscape browser, Internet Setup Wizard, and help files are installed on your computer. Restart your computer if you are prompted to.

FIG. 26.1

Set up Internet service with AT&T WorldNet Service from the Corel WordPerfect Suite 7 CD.

FIG. 26.2

The AT&T WorldNet Service setup program walks you through installing appropriate programs.

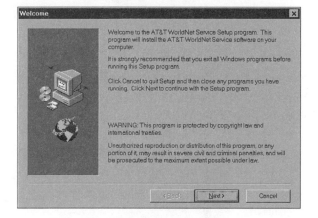

Part

V

Ch

26

N O T E If you are not going to use AT&T WorldNet Service as your ISP, you can stop here. The AT&T WorldNet Service version of the Netscape browser has been installed on your system. ▪

5. After installation, you see an AT&T WorldNet Service window like the one shown in Figure 26.3.

FIG. 26.3

If you are going to use AT&T WorldNet Service as your ISP, you can set up the account automatically by double-clicking the Set Up Account icon.

6. Double-click the icon that says Double-Click to Set Up Account. You see a Welcome to the Internet message.

7. Click Next. You see the first step of the Account Setup Wizard shown in Figure 26.4.

FIG. 26.4
The Account Setup Wizard steps you through the process of connecting to the Internet.

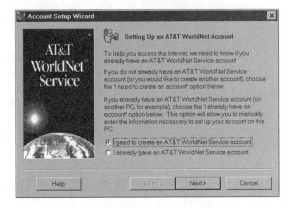

8. The Wizard will prompt you to enter personal and credit card information.

9. If you have not set up a modem, you will automatically be taken into the Modem Wizard to help you select the modem you have. You are taken to the final step of the Wizard shown in Figure 26.5.

FIG. 26.5
The Wizard creates your account from your modem connection without you having to do anything further.

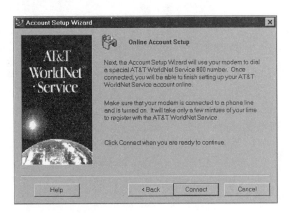

10. When finished, click the Connect button. You are connected to the WorldNet Service, and your account is created online.

What If You're Using Another ISP?

If you are using another ISP, you will need to create a dial-up connection in Windows 95 that will dial your ISP whenever you use Netscape, and will use the proper TCP/IP protocol to transform your files into packets that the Internet can recognize. You will need to know the DNS addresses that your ISP has provided when you create this connection.

Discuss this procedure with your ISP, or create it yourself with the assistance of Windows 95 by choosing Start, Help. Choose the Index tab, then type **Internet, connecting to** in the text box.

Understanding Internet Addresses

Before you start "surfing the Web" or sending Internet e-mail, you will want to know the addresses of sites you want to visit, or people with whom you want to exchange mail. It's easiest to do this by starting with e-mail addresses.

E-mail Addresses   A person's Internet e-mail address consists of three parts: their UserID, the @ symbol, and the name of the host computer on which they have an e-mail account. Typical e-mail addresses include:

> **bill.bruck@marymount.edu**
>
> **bbruck@phoenix.marymount.edu**
>
> **bruck@concentric.net**
>
> **bill@purple.tmn.com**

Notice that in all these addresses, there is a UserID, the @ symbol, and the name of a host computer.

The UserID is created by the rules (or vagaries) of the system administrator, and most often follows one of four conventions: full name, separated by a period (bill.bruck), first initial and last name (bbruck), last name only (bruck), or first name only (bill). This latter is for very small systems, or for the system administrators themselves, who most often get first choice of User IDs.

Part
V

Ch

26

The host name is comprised of two or more parts. The suffix, for Internet hosts in the U.S., refers to the type of organization: com (commercial), edu (educational), org (non-profit organization), net (network), gov (government), or mil (military). If the host is in another country, the suffix refers to a country code: ca (Canada), uk (United Kingdom), and so on.

The name preceding the suffix is usually the name of the organization: marymount (Marymount University), concentric (Concentric Corporation), tmn (The MetaNetwork), and so on.

Sometimes, an organization will have several Internet hosts. In this case, they may specify the name that the system administrator has given to the computer that your UserID is on: purple, phoenix, and so on. (System administrators have notoriously weird senses of humor, so be prepared for some unusual computer names.)

Note that all names are lowercase in these examples. Most names *will* be lowercase, but in any case, depending on the Web server, names may be case-sensitive. However you see the name, be sure to type it exactly that way, just in case.

Internet Site Addresses A site on the Internet to which you may go will also have an address. This address is technically called a Uniform Resource Locator, and is most usually referred to by its initials, URL, and spelled out or pronounced "earl."

Typical URLs include:

> **http://www.wordperfect.com**
>
> **http://www.corel.com/newfeatures/**
>
> **http://www.tmn.com/personal/bruck/bb&a.html**

The first term in these URLs—**http**—indicates that the site is an HTML file, i.e., a Web page. (Http stands for HyperText Transfer Protocol, and is used to refer to HTML documents in an URL.) Occasionally, you will access other types of sites, such as ftp:// or gopher://. These are used for older, pre-World Wide Web ways of accessing information on the Internet. Don't worry, your browser will still handle them.

The next term, **www.wordperfect.com**, is the name of the server that you are accessing. Although you don't see this, your browser looks for the files index.html, index.htm, home.html, or home.htm and displays whichever file it finds.

Sometimes, you will browse to a specific directory on a server, like the **/newfeatures/** directory in the third example. Again, the browser looks for the files index.html, index.htm, home.html, or home.htm in the specified directory.

Occasionally, you will browse to a specific file in a specific directory on the server, such as the **bb&a.html** file in the last example.

 URLs can be confusing, but don't worry about them. Usually, you will merely click a highlighted term to browse to a location. If you need to go to a specific URL, however, be sure to type it exactly as it was given to you, because URLs are case-sensitive.

Understanding the Implications of Publishing on the Internet

Creating a Web page can be technically easy, but there's far more to it than that from a legal and marketing perspective, so don't be naïve about it. Literally, the *whole world* is watching and can see what you put out there.

Several issues must be considered in publishing information on the Internet. One of these issues concerns taking information from another site and republishing in your own documents—to the Internet or an internal intranet.

- There are blatant copyright infringement implications (either individual or corporation/company ones) if another's information is copied to your Web documents and published to another site. Copyright is automatically implied and does not require registration for all pages on the Web. It's much better to link to a site than copy it into your own documents.

- Even if you are publishing on an internal intranet site, that information could still be taken by someone else and used on their site or in a brochure. For instance, say you see a great tip for using a product on the company's Web site. You cut and paste this tip into a document on Tips and Tricks. This is an internal document just for those in your company to view, so you don't see the need to worry about copyright issues. The Public Relations department sees your document, and decides that the best idea in there is the tip that you happened to get from the company itself. They pull that idea out and put it in one of their advertising brochures, which goes out to the world at large including, of course, to the company. The company then sees that their information was used and, at worst, another lawyer can meet his or her rent that month or, at best, customer confidence in your firm is jeopardized.

- The validity of the information that's out on the Internet may be hard to verify. Care should be taken as to how and when it is used. References to where it was obtained should always be included so that readers can make up their own minds as to its truth or accuracy.

- Another issue concerns linking to other sites. There is a matter of company policy and image. Say a company is a child-oriented entertainment company with their primary market being families with children under five years of age. This company has advertised that they are family sensitive and that their Web sites are safe for children. If someone within the company publishes a page with a link to a site that has material that is legal, but would be unacceptable for viewing by small children, the company might be financially or legally liable for damages by lawsuits of the families for false advertising. Or, worse, the word could get around about the connection and the company's business could go down the tubes because of word of mouth that they were not following the values that they had said they would. For this reason, many organizations have policies about clearing Web pages with the public relations, marketing, or legal department before posting information.

- You may also want to think about issues surrounding privacy of information. A phone book listing employees' work and home numbers may be customarily distributed in hard copy throughout the organization. If this same information is put on a Web site accessible to the world, the privacy of employees may be impinged on.

Part
V

Ch
26

While these issues are all real and important, they are by no means comprehensive. Many other similar issues exist, and would-be Web publishers need to think about legal, ethical, and practical considerations prior to uploading files that the whole world can see.

N O T E The fact that the Internet is composed of many types of computers has one other practical implication for publishing documents on the Internet. You should save your documents using DOS naming conventions (eight characters, no spaces). This eliminates problems that users of other computers have (such as Windows 3.1-based systems) with reading long file names, and with trying to figure out truncated file names. ▨

Introducing Netscape Navigator

Netscape Navigator is one of the most powerful and popular browsers you can buy—and you get it free with Corel WordPerfect Suite 7.

N O T E The WordPerfect Suite 7 comes with Netscape Navigator version 2.01E, licensed to AT&T WorldNet Service as AT&T WorldNet Service Internet Client Software, version 2.0. AT&T has chosen to use their own name on this version of Netscape Navigator. Thus, the title bar shows AT&T WorldNet Service; the mail feature is AT&T WorldNet Mail, and the newsgroup reader is AT&T WorldNet News.

Because the name most people use for the Netscape Navigator browser is "Netscape," the browser is referred to in this chapter as Netscape (which is actually the company name, not even the name of the product!). ▨

Using Netscape, you can access World Wide Web pages, and follow links from one Web site to another (this is called "browsing" or "surfing" the Web). You can also save files you browse to on your local computer or print them if you want. Additionally, you can download program or data files directly to your disk.

Netscape even has an e-mail program that allows you to exchange mail with people worldwide, and a newsreader that allows you to participate in public discussion groups. (These two features are discussed in the next chapter.)

 T I P You can access Netscape directly from your Corel WordPerfect Suite applications by clicking the Browse to Web button available on the Standard toolbar in Corel WordPerfect, Corel Presentations, and Corel Quattro Pro.

Figure 26.6 shows the Navigator screen. You can turn certain screen elements on and off, including the toolbar, location bar, and directory buttons, by choosing the appropriate

option from the View menu. Sometimes you will access Web pages where you cannot see the entire page from top to bottom, and the page is an integrated whole (not one you want to scroll through). In this case, turn off the display of one or more of these items to see the entire Web page.

FIG. 26.6
Corel WordPerfect Suite 7 comes bundled with Netscape Navigator 2.01.

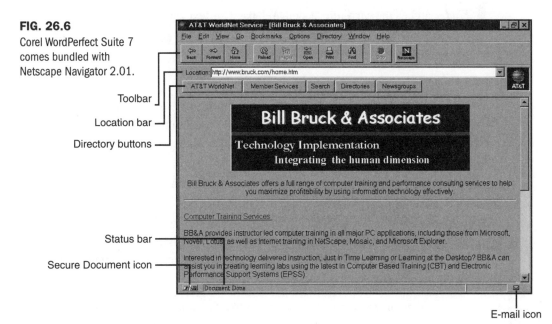

The screen elements that follow will help you browse the Web.

The toolbar contains buttons that permit you to easily accomplish the most common tasks you will do in Netscape:

- The *Back* button becomes active after you have moved through a link. It allows you to go back to the page from which the link originated.

- The *Forward* button becomes active after you have moved back through a link. It allows you to go forward through the same link without having to locate the link and click it.

- The *Home* button takes you to the site that you access by default when you open Netscape.

- The *Reload* button reloads the site. This can be useful if the page has changed, or if you interrupt the loading process before the page has loaded completely.

- The *Images* button loads the images at the site. (Netscape allows you to load the text portion of sites alone, which can be useful if you access graphics-intensive sites with a slow modem.)

■ The *Open* button shows you an Open Location dialog box, where you can type in the URL of a site you want to go to.

■ The *Print* button opens the Print dialog box, which allows you to print the current Web page.

■ *Find* searches the currently loaded Web page for text you specify.

■ *Stop* halts the loading of the page that is currently being accessed. Netscape takes you to Netscape's home page.

The Directory buttons also make navigating easier:

■ The *AT&T WorldNet* button on the Directory buttons bar takes you to the AT&T WorldNet home page. Similarly, the Member Services button takes you to a page listing services available to AT&T WorldNet subscribers.

■ The *Member Services* button takes you to an AT&T WorldNet Web page that offers special services to AT&T WorldNet subscribers. These services change from time to time.

■ The *Search* button takes you to a Web page listing several available search engines. The search engines available on this page change regularly, and the one that you see by default comes up randomly. You can use any of these search engines to look for documents anywhere on the Web that contain key words, names, or concepts.

TIP Search engines are one of the most powerful tools on the Web, but each one prioritizes the information it finds differently. Therefore, it's useful, when searching, to try several different engines for the most thorough search.

■ The *Directories* button takes you to a Web page listing several available directory services. You can use these services to locate people throughout the world that have Internet e-mail accounts or Web sites.

■ The *Newsgroups* button takes you to the Newsreader that allows you to access public conversations in news groups. This function is discussed in Chapter 27, "Communicating on the Internet."

Other elements that help you browse the Web are:

■ The *Location bar* shows you the URL of the site you are currently viewing. You can type the URL of a new site directly in the location text box and press Enter to go to that site.

■ The *Secure Document icon* informs you whether the document you are viewing is encrypted, or a document sent openly (in which case hackers or system administrators could more easily intercept the transmission).

■ *Messages* on the status bar tell you the process of a document that is being loaded, and when the loading is done.

■ The *E-mail icon* takes you to the e-mail program that allows you to exchange e-mail with others on the Internet. This function is discussed further in Chapter 27, "Communicating on the Internet."

Browsing the Web and Specifying Destinations

Browsing is the process of moving from one Web page to another through links on Web pages. You can actually go from one Web page to another in three different ways: by browsing (following links), by specifying the URL of a Web page you want to go to, or by using *bookmarks*.

 TIP Web pages are dynamic, not static. Corporations change their Web pages regularly to improve readership. Thus, many Web pages are here today, gone or changed tomorrow—without notice. The best surfing philosophy is if you see it and need it, grab it and print it or download it, as it may not be there the next time you go out.

Browsing the Web

Most Web pages contain *links*—codes that specify another location on the Web. Some links are text, in which case the text appears in a different color. Others are graphical— often icons or small pictures.

When you move your mouse pointer over a link—whether the link is text or a graphic image—the mouse pointer changes to a hand, as shown in Figure 26.7. The address to which the link points is also displayed in the status bar. When you click the link, the new page appears on your screen.

To browse the Web using links, click the link. You are taken to the Web page that the link points to.

To go back to the Web page from which you came, click the Back button. If you want to go through the link again, click the Forward button.

You can also go back to the default Web page—your *home* location—by clicking the Home button at any time.

Part
V

Ch
26

FIG. 26.7
When your cursor is on a
link, the mouse pointer
changes to a hand.

Back button ———

Forward button ———

Home button ———

Graphic link ———

Text link ———

Mouse pointer on a link ———

Going Directly to Web Pages

The second way to browse the Web is to go directly to a Web page by specifying its address—technically, its Uniform Resource Locator, or URL.

To go to a specific Web page, choose File, Open Location. You see the Open Location dialog box shown in Figure 26.8. Type in the URL and choose Open. You are taken directly to that location on the Web.

FIG. 26.8
Go directly to a Web page by
specifying its URL.

Open Location	☒
Open Location:	
	Cancel Open

T I P   You can also click the Location box, edit the URL there or type in a new one, and press Enter to go to a specific address.

If you have Web pages stored on your local or network drive, you can access them via Netscape as well. This can be very helpful when you are creating pages with the Corel WordPerfect Internet Publisher and want to see how they will look in Netscape. To open a Web page on your disk, choose File, Open File. You see the Open dialog box shown in Figure 26.9. Browse to the folder containing your Web page, then double-click it to open it in Netscape.

FIG. 26.9
You can open Web documents stored on your disk from the Open dialog box.

Using Bookmarks

After you've used the Web for a while, you will find certain sites that are particularly valuable, and that you'd like to be able to go back to quickly. Typing in URLs is a tedious process, and you can easily make a mistake.

For this reason, Netscape allows you to save the names and addresses of your favorite sites in a list of *bookmarks*. In fact, the AT&T WorldNet version of Netscape that ships with the Corel WordPerfect Suite 7 comes with an entire list of bookmarks already created for you.

N O T E The term "bookmark" has a different meaning in Netscape and in WordPerfect. In Netscape, bookmarks are favorite sites, saved in a file named bookmark.htm. In WordPerfect, a bookmark is a marked place in a document that you can quickly jump to. ▨

Using Existing Bookmarks To go to a location for which a bookmark already exists, choose Bookmarks. You see the Bookmarks menu, listing all the bookmarks you have created, or that come with Netscape. Some of the bookmarks have arrows to their right, indicating that they are actually bookmark categories. As you move your move pointer over a category, you see a cascading menu showing the bookmarks in that category, as shown in Figure 26.10.

Click the bookmark for the site you want to browse to. Netscape accesses that site and, assuming it's not out of service, you are taken to it.

T I P If you have more bookmarks than will display on the screen, More Bookmarks is the last entry in the list. Click it to see the rest of your bookmarks.

Create New Bookmarks To create a new bookmark, browse to the desired site using any of the methods discussed previously.

Part
V

Ch
26

FIG. 26.10

Go back to your favorite sites quickly by using bookmarks that you have created.

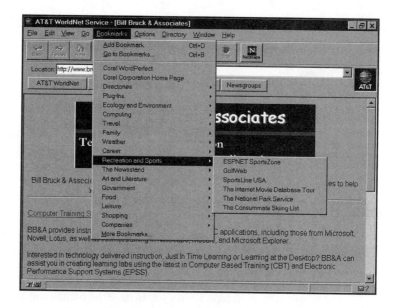

While you are at the site, and the URL for the site appears in the Location box of Netscape, choose Bookmarks, Add Bookmark. Your new bookmark is added to the end of the bookmark list, and you can access it whenever you want to.

N O T E   Your bookmarks are stored in a HTML file (a Web page type of file) named BOOKMARK.HTM. By default, it is stored in the WorldNet subfolder of the Program Files folder. ■

Editing Bookmarks   To edit your bookmark list, choose Bookmarks, Go to Bookmarks. You see the Bookmarks dialog box shown in Figure 26.11.

FIG. 26.11

You can create new category folders for your bookmarks, or move them from one folder to another in the Bookmarks dialog box.

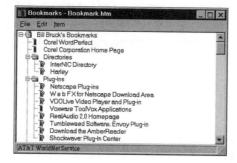

Edit your bookmarks as follows:

■ *Delete* a bookmark by selecting it, then pressing the Del key.

■ *Move* a bookmark from one folder to another, or to another place on the bookmark list, by selecting it and dragging it to its new location.

■ *Create* a new category folder for your bookmarks by selecting the bookmark below the new folder to be created, then choosing Item, Insert Folder. You see the Bookmark Properties dialog box shown in Figure 26.12. Type the name for your new folder, then click OK.

FIG. 26.12
Create new category folders to organize your bookmarks in the Bookmark Properties dialog box.

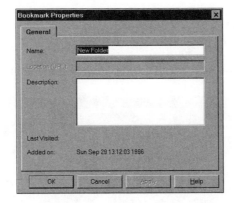

■ *Insert* a separator line underneath the current folder by choosing Item, Insert Separator. You see a Separator icon below the folder, and when you list your bookmarks again from the Netscape Bookmark menu, you will see a separator line underneath that folder.

■ *Combine* another bookmark file with the current bookmark file by choosing File, Import. You see the Import Bookmarks File dialog box shown in Figure 26.13. Browse to the folder containing the bookmark file you want to import, then double-click it.

Part
V

Ch
26

FIG. 26.13
Combine two bookmark files by importing one into the other in the Import Bookmarks File dialog box.

Printing, Downloading, and Executing Files

Once you've browsed to a Web site containing useful information, what's next? You may want to print the information, save it to a file on your own computer, or even execute certain types of applications.

Printing Files

To print a Web page, you merely need to browse to it, then choose File, Print. You see the Print dialog box shown in Figure 26.14.

Your Web page is printed to the selected printer, including graphics that are on the page.

FIG. 26.14
Print your Web pages, including graphics, using the Print dialog box to maintain them in hard copy if desired.

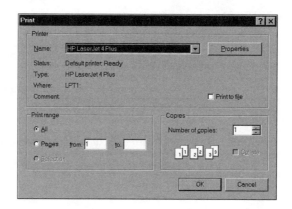

Downloading Files

You will often access the Web to obtain information. When you do, you may want to save the files you find to your local computer.

You can do this in two ways: saving Web pages that you browse to, and saving data files that Web pages point to.

Saving Web Pages   When you want to save a Web page, do so as follows:

1. Browse to the page in Netscape.

2. Choose File, Save As. You see the Save As dialog box shown in Figure 26.15.

3. Navigate to the folder in which you want to save the Web page, enter a name in the File Name box, and choose Save. Your file is saved in the designated folder.

Once you have saved a Web page, it is saved in HTML format. You can open this file in Corel WordPerfect and edit using Corel WordPerfect's Internet Publisher. You can even upload it back on to the Web, if you have the necessary permissions to upload files to that Web site.

FIG. 26.15
Save Web pages directly to your local computer through the Save As dialog box.

For more information about editing Web documents, see Chapter 12, "Integrating Corel WordPerfect 7 with the Internet."

Saving Data Files   Often, when you visit a Web site, there will be links to data files or even programs that you can download. If the data files are not in HTML format, your Web browser may not be able to view them directly—especially if the browser does not have an add-on viewer that is configured for that type of file.

When you click a link to a program file or a data file that your browser cannot view, you can opt to download it into your computer, where you can open it with the proper application, or even (in the case of a program file) execute it.

Clicking a link to an unknown file type shows the Unknown File Type dialog box shown in Figure 26.16.

FIG. 26.16
You can download a data file using the Netscape Unknown File Type dialog box.

If you think that the file is actually a data file that Netscape might be able to execute—like an audio file or a video file that needs a certain type of viewer in order to play, choose More Info. You are taken to a Netscape site where you can find procedures for downloading the proper viewer, as shown in Figure 26.17.

If, however, the file is a data file that you want to download, such as a Corel WordPerfect file, then save it in the same way as described in the previous section, "Saving Web Pages."

FIG. 26.17
You can download viewers to
play audio and video files.

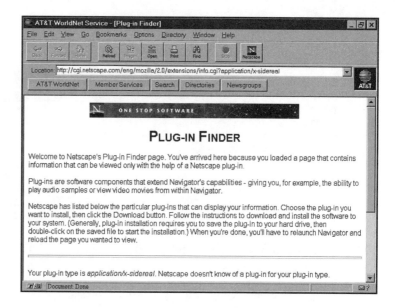

Customizing Netscape to Your Preferences

Usually, you will not need to change options in Netscape. Occasionally, however, you may
want to fine-tune your installation.

One set of preferences you may want to set is from the Options menu. Check or uncheck
Show Toolbar, Show Location, and Show Directory Buttons to display or hide the toolbar,
location bar, and directory buttons at the top of your Netscape screen. Hiding these can
provide more space for your Web pages.

To set these preferences, choose Options, General Preferences, Appearance. The most
common options you might want to set in the Appearance tab shown in Figure 26.18
include the following:

- *Toolbars*. Showing the toolbar as text only can give you more area to see your Web
  pages.

- *On Startup Launch*. If you check your mail whenever you enter Netscape, you might
  consider checking AT&T WorldNet Mail to launch the mail application automatically.

- Choose *Start With* to specify the Web site that you see initially when you open
  Netscape. By default, it is Netscape.com, but you may prefer to see a page from a
  favorite news service, your corporate home page, or even a personal startup page
  that you create, that includes links to your favorite sites.

FIG. 26.18

The Appearance tab of the Netscape Preferences dialog box allows you to choose which options are in force and which applications start when you open Netscape.

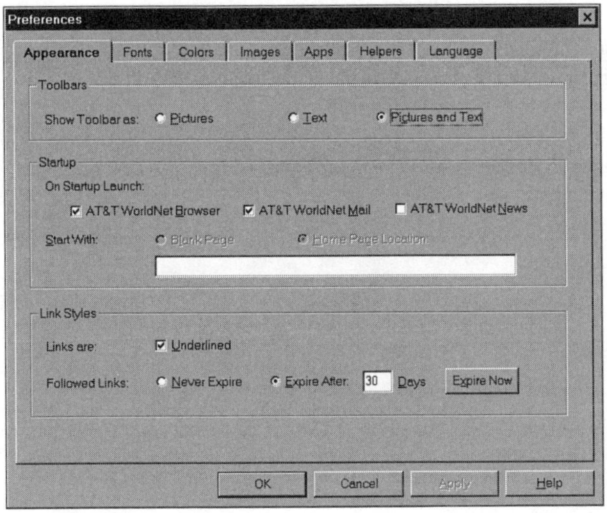

■ *Followed Links* allows you to specify how long a link stays colored after you follow it. Having the links you have followed appear in color helps you to find you way around the Web; it's a little like leaving a trail of bread crumbs!

You can also select the Fonts or Colors tab to change the font and color of text and backgrounds in the Web documents you browse to.

Another preference you may want to set is the amount of cache you use for saving old Web pages. If you are connecting via modem, graphic-intensive pages take a long time to load. For this reason, you can save pages you have visited in a cache—a place on your disk where temporary files are stored. This way, if you go back to a graphic-intensive page soon after visiting it, you may not need to reload it. Netscape will load it from your disk (which is very fast) rather than your modem (which is relatively slow). The price you pay, however, is that you are using up disk space.

To set your cache size, choose Options, Network Preferences, Cache. You see the Cache tab shown in Figure 26.19.

To make reloading Web pages as fast as possible, set your memory and disk caches to the maximum size that allows you to maintain enough free memory and disk space for other applications, then click OK to close the dialog box and save your changes.

Part

V

Ch

26

FIG. 26.19
Set your cache on the Cache
Tab of the Netscape
Preferences dialog box to
enable you to reload sites
from your computer's disk
rather than the Internet.

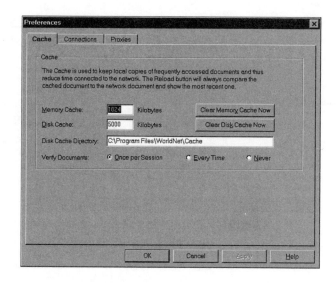

Finding Help on the Internet

You may want to get help on Netscape, on other Corel products, or on subjects unrelated
to Corel software.

▶ **See** "Using Help Online," **p. 40**

To obtain help in using Netscape, choose <u>H</u>elp, Netscape <u>N</u>avigator Handbook. You see
the Netscape Navigator Handbook shown in Figure 26.20. The handbook is actually a
number of linked HTML pages that are stored on your disk, as you can see from the URL
displayed in the figure.

N O T E   Non-AT&T WorldNet Service versions of Netscape use the same menu command to
access the handbook. However, in most other versions, you are connected to the
version of the handbook maintained at the Netscape Web site; thus, you connect to the Internet
to see the latest version of the handbook. ■

Browse through the contents to see help on all aspects of using Netscape.

 T I P   Click the Netscape button in the main Netscape window to connect to Netscape's home page.
Though this site changes regularly, you can browse through it to find more help on using
Netscape.

If you'd like to search the Web for help with virtually any other question you might want
to ask, the Web has powerful tools called search engines that can assist you. Want to know

the difference between a cocktail and a highball? The name of Dudley Dooright's horse in *The Rocky and Bullwinkle Show*? Search the Web to find out.

FIG. 26.20

The Netscape Navigator Handbook is included as a Web page on your disk.

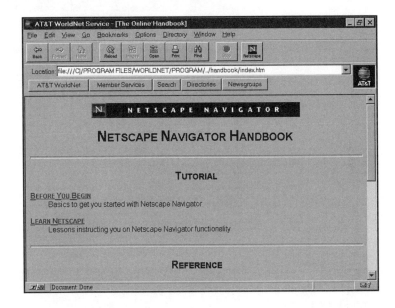

If you are using AT&T WorldNet Service as your ISP, you can click the Search button on the directory bar to access a Web page that lists popular search engines. Otherwise, click the Netscape button to access the Netscape home page. Scroll down until you see a link to search engines, called *Net Search*. When you click this button, you are taken to the Net Search page. Its exact appearance changes regularly, but it will resemble the site shown in Figure 26.21.

Part
V

Ch

26

There are several major search engines that compete for your business. Although they are free to you, you see advertisements for different vendors when you use them; this pays for the service.

The search engines shown in Figure 26.21 include Excite, Yahoo, Infoseek, Lycos, and Magellan. Each time you access Net Search, you will see a different one of these engines, randomly chosen. In Figure 26.21, it is Excite.

Choose the search engine you want to use, if it is not displayed, by clicking its button. Type the words you are searching for in the text box, and click the Search button.

Millions of documents on the Web are searched, and within a few seconds, you see a list of the documents that best match the terms you searched for, as shown in Figure 26.22.

FIG. 26.21
Net Search allows you to search the Web for information of interest.

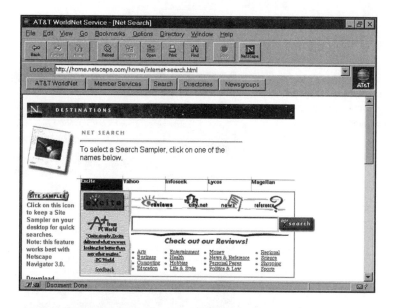

FIG. 26.22
Search engines show you the documents that best match the terms you searched for.

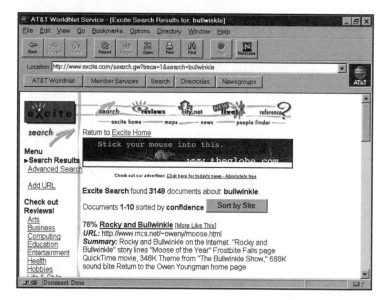

 TIP Different search engines often produce different results. As you start, use several of them with the same terms. You will eventually settle on one or two that best meet your needs.

Using Corel QuickConnect

The Corel WordPerfect Suite comes with QuickConnect—a handy application that resides on the taskbar that allows you to quickly connect with your favorite Web sites.

 Access QuickConnect by clicking the QuickConnect button on the taskbar. You see the Quick Connect window shown in Figure 26.23.

FIG. 26.23
The Browse Connection dialog box of QuickConnect allows you to connect to sites stored alphabetically in your bookmark list.

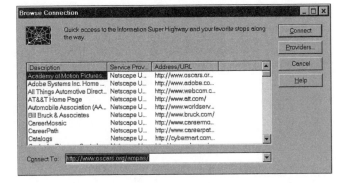

When you open QuickConnect, it reads the list of favorite sites you have stored in your bookmark list, and presents them alphabetically. If you are using more than one browser, it will read the bookmark list or list of favorite sites from each browser, and combine them in the list you see.

 T I P If you are using Compuserve (CIS) or America Online (AOL), you can also add sites used by the CIS or AOL software to this list of favorites, and the appropriate software (Netscape, CIS, or AOL) will be used to access the site you select.

Part
V

Ch
26

CHAPTER 27

Communicating on the Internet

The main use of the Internet is still for communication between people and organizations. Netscape enables you to speak privately with an individual or group via electronic mail, or e-mail. Mailing lists bring public discussions to your e-mail inbox. Newsgroups enable you to participate in on-going conversations that are categorized by topics and responses. This chapter will teach you how to use all three methods to communicate on the Internet. ■

Netiquette

Learn about the correct and not-so-correct ways of communicating in the new world of instant online messaging.

Use Netscape Mail

Learn how to send and receive mail and attachments, and maintain an address book for frequent contacts.

Join mailing lists

Find out how to use your Netscape Mail to participate in on-going discussion groups.

Subscribe to newsgroups

See how to use the newsreader to subscribe to on-going newsgroups.

Understanding Netiquette

Netiquette stands for network etiquette, and concerns rules of politeness or "correct behavior" when communicating electronically. The basic rule of netiquette is the same as the basic rule of etiquette: be considerate of the other party.

Some netiquette rules apply to all communication; others are more specific to the type of communication (private e-mail conversations versus public listserv and newsgroup conversations) you may have. See the section "Participating in Automated Mailing Lists" later in this chapter.

N O T E   The term "listserv" is used in this chapter for Internet mailing lists. ■

- Keep paragraphs short and to the point, and double-space between paragraphs. It is very hard to read long paragraphs if there is little or no white space in the text.

- DON'T SHOUT! Capitalized text is considered shouting. It's hard to read, and inconsiderate to your reader. Rather, use *asterisks* to emphasize points, or _underline at the beginning and ending of emphasized characters for such things as book titles.

- Would you say it to a person's face? This question is asked by Virginia Shea in her online book *Netiquette*. It serves as a nice criterion for whether you are being impolite.

- Use abbreviations and emoticons ("smiley faces") judiciously. Several abbreviations have become part of the "language" of the Internet; others are more obscure. Use only the abbreviations and emoticons that your recipients are likely to understand. Common abbreviations include IMHO (in my humble opinion), FYI (for your information), BTW (by the way), and PMFJI (pardon me for jumping in). The most common emoticon is :) which represents a smile, but there are many variants on this.

T I P   In Netscape, click the Search button, then search for emoticon to find sites that have entire pages filled with cute smileys.

N O T E   The Corel WordPerfect Suite 7 comes with Netscape Navigator version 2.01E, licensed to AT&T WorldNet Service as AT&T WorldNet Service Internet Client Software, version 2.0. AT&T has chosen to use its own name on this version of Netscape Navigator. Thus, the title bar shows AT&T WorldNet Service; the mail feature is AT&T WorldNet Mail, and the newsreader is AT&T WorldNet News.

Because the name most people use for the Netscape Navigator browser is "Netscape," the browser is referred to in this chapter as Netscape (which is actually the company name, not even the name of the product!). ■

- Don't flame. *Flaming* happens when content-oriented discussions take on a personal, ad hominem, flavor. Often, they resemble the feeding frenzy of sharks, as more and more people are drawn into the fray. Watch out for sarcasm and other forms of hostile humor; they don't translate well into print.

- Wait before responding in sensitive instances. It is *so* easy to respond with e-mail, that people often do so without thinking through what they are saying and the impact it will have. If you receive an e-mail that causes you to have a negative response, the best thing to do is to send the answer to yourself. Then wait several hours or overnight and reread it. If it still sounds okay, send it. But in many instances you may find you will want to reword it before you hit that Send button.

Understanding E-Mail Netiquette

E-mail is a private communication between you and one or more other people. Additional netiquette rules that apply to such mail include the following:

- Always enter a subject. When there is no subject in an e-mail message, the reader must open the message to see what it's even about. Many people receive scores of messages each day, and often want to open just the urgent ones when they only have a few minutes.

- Use quote-backs sparingly. Netscape, by default, inserts the entire original message in your reply. Making a person wade through their own words to see your response is impolite. If there's a specific question or point you are responding to, quote that sentence or paragraph—not the whole message. A method of incorporating relevant phrases that you want to respond to is described in the section "Reply to Mail" later in this chapter.

- Attribute things properly. It's easy to cut a person's words out of an e-mail message or a Web site and include them in your e-mail. If you do not attribute them to their source, it is impolite at best, and illegal (if the site is copyrighted) at worst. Similarly, be careful about forwarding personal mail someone sends you or posting it to public listservs or newsgroups.

There are a few other rules that you might want to consider when you're sending business e-mail:

- Business e-mail is a business communication. Use the same degree of formality or informality you would in any other mode of written business communication, like a letter or a memo.

Part

V

Ch

27

■ Consider using a signature block. If you do, this is a short (no more than three-line) trailer at the end of your message that identifies who you are, your company, and alternative ways of contacting you. Long signature blocks or promotional signature blocks are rude.

■ Focus your recipient list. Sending a promotional e-mail to several thousand people who are not selected on any basis other than availability may be good business, but it may generate more ill will than sales.

■ Weigh formality. The Internet makes doing business internationally easy, but remember, many people find Americans overly informal in their use of first names. When in doubt, error on the side of formality.

■ Keep it short. Try to keep general correspondence to two screens, or put your most important summary data up front. People tend to read a couple of screens and then decide they'll read the rest later—sometimes not getting back to it for quite a while.

■ Don't spam. *Spamming* is sending unwanted messages, most often ones that are self-promoting, off-track, and/or sent to hundreds of people.

Although we usually think of netiquette as rules of politeness between us and our e-mail recipients, there are also some netiquette rules regarding our e-mail and our system administrator that are cited by Arlene Ribaldi in *The Net: User Guidelines and Netiquette.* These include:

■ Check e-mail daily and respond as promptly as possible.

■ Delete unwanted messages immediately because they take up disk storage, and remain within your limited disk quota.

■ Keep messages remaining in your electronic mailbox to a minimum.

■ Mail messages can be downloaded or extracted to files, then to disks for future reference.

■ Never assume that your e-mail can be read by only yourself; others may be able to read or access your mail. Or, someone may forward your e-mail to others with your posting information still visible. Never send or keep anything that you would mind seeing on the evening news.

 T I P You can find many online "books" on netiquette, including Arlene Ribaldi's, by clicking the Search button in Netscape and searching for the word "netiquette."

Understanding Public Conversation Netiquette

Public conversations have a few different netiquette rules, because of the nature of the communication.

- Monitor the list. When you first join a conversation, listen for a while before jumping in. Often, you'll find that many of your questions are answered within a week or so by just listening to the on-going flow of conversation. This will also give you a sense of the social atmosphere of the conversation—how personal or formal it is, whether long or short postings are encouraged, and so on.

- Combine public and personal modes. If you have a response to someone's remarks that pertains to him or her only, consider responding by e-mail rather than publicly. Conversely, if a person asks a question to which you know the answer, and you suspect that others might benefit as well, post the answer in public.

- Know what to ignore. If remarks are off the subject or personal in nature, resist the temptation to jump in. This only adds to the fire (for personal remarks) or the amount of off-the-subject text.

- Have tolerance. If newcomers ask questions you regard as elementary, or mistakenly send a private message to an entire group of people, be tolerant. You probably made some of the same mistakes when you were starting out.

Setting Mail and News Preferences

Before you can start using mail or newsgroups, you need to identify yourself and your Internet server. To do so, obtain the following information from your system administrator or your Internet Service Provider:

- Your UserID
- Your Outgoing Mail (SMTP) server name
- Your Incoming Mail (POP) server name
- Your e-mail address
- Your News (NNTP) server name

Then, set up Netscape for mail and news as follows:

1. Open Netscape.
2. Choose Options, Mail and News Preferences, and select the Servers tab.
3. Fill in the Outgoing Mail Server, Incoming Mail Server, Pop user name (your UserID), Mail directory, News Server, and News Directory.
4. Choose the Identity tab.
5. Fill in your name, e-mail ID, reply-to address, and organization, as shown in Figure 27.1.
6. Click OK when you are done.

Part

V

Ch

27

FIG. 27.1
Finish setting mail preferences by filling in information about yourself in the Identity tab of the Preferences dialog box.

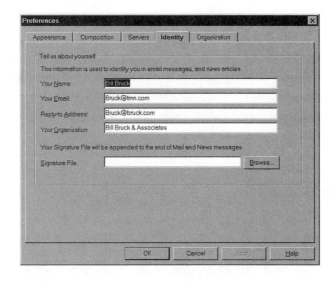

Using Mail

Once Netscape is configured, you can send and receive e-mail to and from anyone in the world via the Internet.

To access Mail, choose Window, AT&T WorldNet Mail, or click the Mail icon (the envelope at the bottom right of the Navigator window). The first time you enter Mail, you are prompted to enter a password. Enter the appropriate password and choose OK. You see the Mail window shown in Figure 27.2.

From the Mail window, you can send mail, receive mail, and organize it into folders. Before learning how to send mail, however, you'll want to know how to maintain a list of your frequent correspondents in the Address Book.

Using the Netscape Address Book

The easiest way to address mail is to store recipients' addresses in the Address Book. You can access the Address Book from either the main Navigator window or the Mail window, by choosing Window, Address Book. You see the Address Book window shown in Figure 27.3.

> **N O T E** The Netscape Address Book is a file containing e-mail addresses, used only in Netscape. This is different than Corel Address Book 7, which is a stand-alone application. ▪

FIG. 27.2

The Mail window allows you to send and receive e-mail, as well as store it in folders that you create.

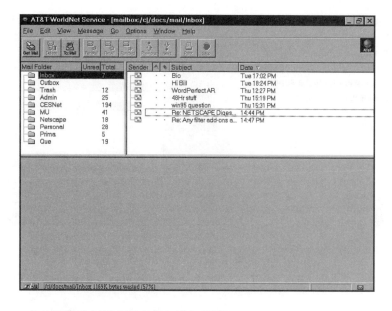

FIG. 27.3

The Address Book window allows you to see the list of your e-mail recipients.

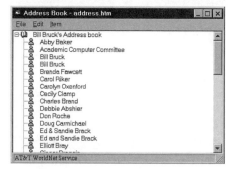

To add a user to your Address Book:

1. Choose Item, Add User. You see the Address Book dialog box shown in Figure 27.4.

2. In the Nick Name box, insert an optional nick name, ensuring that you use only lowercase letters. Put the person's name as you want it to appear in your messages in the Name box, and their e-mail address in the E-Mail Address box.

3. Click OK when you are done.

You can also create a list of users to whom you often send mail. To create the empty folder:

1. Choose Item, Add List. You see a similar Address Book dialog box, except that the E-Mail Address box is grayed out.

FIG. 27.4

With the Properties tab of the Address Book dialog box you can add a nickname to each user and make sending mail easier.

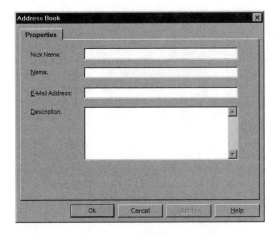

2. Enter an optional nickname and a name for the list.

3. Click OK. The folder is created in your Address Book, as shown in Figure 27.5.

FIG. 27.5

The Address Book dialog box shows the folders that contain lists of the users to whom you send mail.

To put users in the list, copy them into the folder. Hold down the Ctrl key, and drag the user's icon on top of the folder icon. The user appears in the folder, as shown in Figure 27.6.

FIG. 27.6

The names of users that you add to the list by dragging them onto the folder will appear underneath that folder.

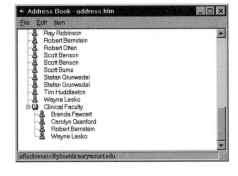

When you are finished editing your address book, click the Close button (the X in the right-hand corner) to close the Address Book window.

Reading Mail

To see any new messages you have received, click the Get Mail button on the toolbar. You see a message indicating that Navigator is connecting with your mail server on the status bar, and then subject lines for your new messages appear in the right pane of the Mail window, as shown in Figure 27.7.

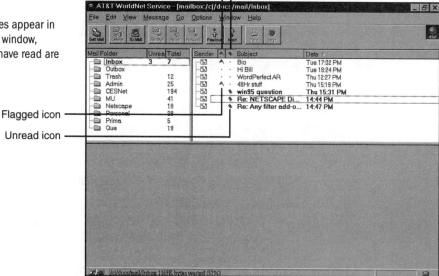

FIG. 27.7
Unread messages appear in bold in the Mail window, while ones you have read are in normal type.

Flagged icon ——
Unread icon ——

Messages you have not read appear in bold, with a small green icon in the Unread column, while ones you have read are in normal type. The text of the selected message appears at the bottom of the screen. You can use the scroll bars to scroll through the message titles or through the text of the selected message.

 You can also mark a message as unread by clicking it in the Unread column—this is the column in the Sender pane with a small green icon as the column heading.

Save or Print a Message   While Navigator stores messages internally until you delete them, you will occasionally want to save a message in your regular filing system. In addition, you may occasionally need to have a hard copy of a message to take into a meeting or give to a colleague who doesn't have e-mail.

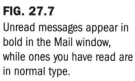

Part
V

Ch
27

To save a message:

1. Select its subject line so the message can be read in the lower window.

2. Choose File, Save As. You see the Save As dialog box shown in Figure 27.8.

FIG. 27.8

You can save a message to your regular disk filing system in the Save As dialog box.

3. Browse to the folder in which you want to save the file, and give the file a name.

4. Click Save.

Printing your message is just as simple. With the message showing in the lower window, click the Print button, or choose File, Print Message(s). You see the Print dialog box shown in Figure 27.9.

FIG. 27.9

You can print one or more messages, if you need hard copy, through the Print dialog box.

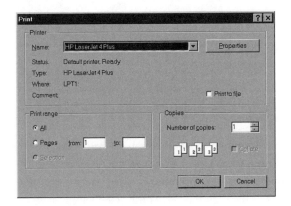

T I P   You can also select several messages by clicking one, then holding down the Ctrl key and clicking additional ones, before you click the Print button.

Add Name to Address Book   When you are reading your e-mail, it's a great time to add a name to the Address Book, if you think you'll be corresponding with that person in the future. To add a name to the Address Book, choose Message, Add to Address Book. You see the Address Book dialog box. The sender's name and e-mail address already appear in appropriate boxes. Enter a lowercase nickname, if desired, in the Nick Name box, and choose OK. The name is added to the address book.

Read Attachments   If you receive an attachment to your e-mail message, it will usually appear at the bottom of the message, in a box like the one shown in Figure 27.10.

FIG. 27.10

Attachments appear at the bottom of the Mail window. You can save attachments to your disk, then open them later with the appropriate application.

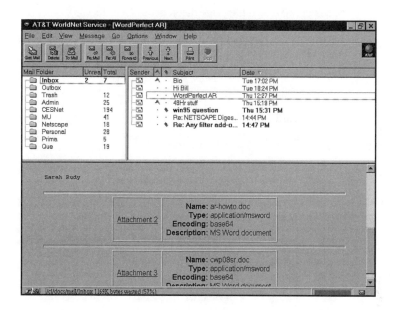

To save the message, click it. You see a Save dialog box. Determine the folder you want to save your message in, then click Save.

> **N O T E**   Occasionally, you may receive a message that looks garbled, with pages of codes and characters you can't read. You can download a program from the Internet like Stuffit to decode such files. ■

Reply to Mail   Many times, when you read your e-mail, you'll want to reply to it or, less often, forward it to someone else.

To reply to a piece of mail:

1. Select the e-mail you want to answer.
2. Click:
   - The Reply button (Re: Mail) to reply only to the original sender, or
   - The Reply to All button (Re: All) to reply to all recipients of the mail message.

You see the Reply window, with the sender's message copied with > signs in front of each line (denoting that these lines were from the original message).

Part
V

Ch
27

3. Delete the parts of the original message (the quote-back) that can be eliminated in your reply, then type your reply before or after the quote-back.

4. Click the Send button.

If you prefer, you can delete the original message first. The fastest way is to press Ctrl+A to select the entire message, then press Delete.

Alternatively, some people like to insert their reply as paragraphs between paragraphs of the original message, so that you can respond to specific points made by the original sender. To keep your e-mails shorter and easier to read, it is always advisable to delete any material not related to your response before sending.

Forward Mail   To forward mail you receive to another participant:

1. Select the received message.

2. Click the Forward button. You see the Forward window shown in Figure 27.11.

FIG. 27.11
You can forward your mail to someone else, in which case the original message becomes an attachment to the forwarded message.

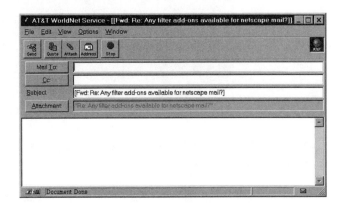

3. The subject of the forwarded message is the word Fwd: followed by the subject of the original message. The original message is included as an attachment to the forwarded message. Fill in the Mail To: box.

4. Send the message off, as is described in the next section.

Sending Mail

To send a message, do the following:

1. Open Netscape Mail.

2. Click the To: Mail button. You see the Message Composition dialog box shown in Figure 27.12.

FIG. 27.12

Send mail to anyone with an Internet address throughout the world by using the Message Composition dialog box.

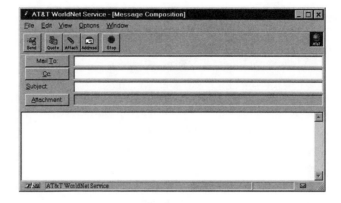

3. Type a valid Internet mail address in the Mail To: box, or click Mail To:. You see the Select Addresses dialog box in Figure 27.13.

FIG. 27.13

Send mail to anyone in your Address Book with the Select Addresses dialog box.

4. Select an addressee and click To:.

5. Repeat this process for any additional addressees.

6. Click OK when you are done. You return to the Message Composition dialog box.

7. Use the procedure in Steps 3 through 6 to select CC: (carbon copy) recipients, if desired.

8. Fill in a Subject for your message.

9. Type the text of your message in the message box. Use standard Windows formatting and text editing commands.

T I P You can cut and paste text from other applications into the text of your message, if desired.

10. Add an attachment if desired, as described below.

11. Click the Send button to send your message.

You can attach binary files to your message, like Corel WordPerfect documents, Corel Presentations slideshows, and the like.

Encoding Files

You can think of two types of files: text files (called ASCII files), which contain nothing but text; and binary files, which can be programmed files or data files containing formatting codes and the like. When you save a Corel WordPerfect document, Corel Quattro Pro spreadsheet, or Corel Presentations slideshow, it is saved as a binary file.

Unfortunately, the Internet does not directly support binary files; it only supports text files. However, it is possible to encode a binary file into a text file. This encoding process is done automatically by Navigator, and incoming encoded files are automatically decoded. This process works best when both parties are using standard Internet browsers such as Navigator or Microsoft Explorer. When one party is accessing the Internet via America Online or CompuServe Information Services, the encoding/decoding process often goes awry.

To attach binary files to your mail:

1. Access the Message Composition dialog box as described in the section immediately above.

2. Click the Attachment button. You see the Attachments dialog box shown in Figure 27.14.

FIG. 27.14

The Attachments dialog box of Netscape makes it easy to attach a Corel WordPerfect, Corel Quattro Pro, or Corel Presentations file to your e-mail message.

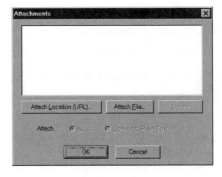

3. Click the Attach File button. You see the Enter File to Attach dialog box shown in Figure 27.15.

FIG. 27.15
In the Enter File to Attach dialog box, you browse to the file you want to attach, then double-click it.

4. Browse to the file you want to attach, then double-click it. You return to the Attachments dialog box, and see your file listed.

5. Repeat this step if you want to attach additional files, or click OK to return to the Message Composition dialog box.

Organizing Your Mail

After a while, your mail will tend to pile up. Not only will this make it harder for you to find particular messages, but you will also start using up a lot of disk space. For this reason, Netscape offers you several tools to organize your mail.

Delete Mail   One of the best is the Delete key. To delete a message, select its subject line and press Delete. The first time you delete a message, a new Trash folder is created. Deleting a message causes it to be moved to the Trash folder.

Emptying the Trash folder deletes the messages completely. Empty the Trash folder by choosing File, Empty Trash Folder. You should do this periodically to keep your messages from piling up and taking up disk space.

 To view items in Trash, click the Trash folder in the Mail Folder pane. To undelete a message, drag it from the Trash folder to another folder.

Flag Mail   You can flag a message for further attention by clicking in the Flag column of the message. Once you have flagged messages, you can quickly move between them.

- Choose Go, First Flagged to go to the first flagged message.
- Choose Go, Next Flagged to go to the next flagged message.
- Choose Go, Previous Flagged to go to the previous flagged message.

These options are grayed out if there are no flagged messages.

Part
V

Ch
27

T I P You can also choose Go, then First Unread, Next Unread, or Previous Unread to move between messages marked as Unread.

Sort and Thread Mail You may find it easier to find mail messages if they are sorted—either by date or by sender. You may also prefer to see replies linked to the original messages; this is called *threading* messages.

To sort your mail, choose View, Sort. You see the pop-up window shown in Figure 27.16, and can sort by a number of different categories.

 T I P You can also sort by Sender, Subject, or Date clicking in the appropriate column header.

FIG. 27.16
With the Sort menu, you can sort messages by date, subject, sender, or message number.

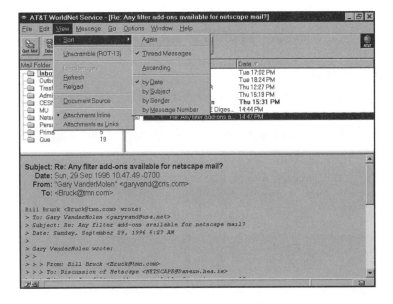

To thread your messages, choose View, Sort, Thread Messages. You will see replies linked to their original messages in an outline format like the one shown in Figure 27.17.

Using Folders When you first start using Netscape Mail, there is only one folder, the Inbox. This folder contains all your incoming messages, by default. After you send mail, you will see a Sent folder containing copies of messages you have sent. When you delete messages, a Trash folder is created containing those messages.

One of the best organizational tools is the folders feature. You can create any number of folders, and move your mail into them. The mail messages you see in the right pane of the Mail window are the subjects of mail messages contained in the folder selected in the left window.

FIG. 27.17
Threaded replies appear indented and linked to the original message in the Mail window.

Threaded message ———

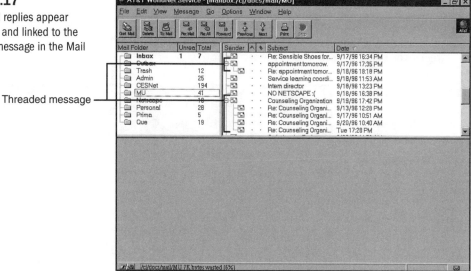

There are four main actions that are most used with folders:

- To create a new folder, choose File, New Folder. You are prompted to add the name for your new folder. Enter a name, then press Enter. You see the new folder in your folder list.

- To move a message into a folder, drag the icon to the left of the message to the folder you want. The message disappears from its current folder, and is displayed when you click the icon of the destination folder.

- You can also copy a message into a folder by holding down the Ctrl key while you drag it to the destination folder. The message then appears in both the original folder and the destination folder.

- To delete a message from a folder, select it and press the Delete key. To delete a folder, delete all the messages in it, then select the folder in the left pane and press the Delete key.

Compress Folders   If you want to keep a historical record of important messages in a particular folder, you will not want to delete them. However, recognizing that they do take up disk space, you may want to periodically *compress* a folder, thus reducing its size. While compressing a folder saves space, it does not affect how you read its messages.

To compress a folder, click its icon in the left window pane. Choose File, Compress this Folder. The items in the folder are compressed, thus saving disk space.

Part
V

Ch
27

Change Column Width   You can change the width of the columns in both the folder list and the message list. To do so, move your mouse pointer to the edge of one of the column headers. The mouse pointer changes to a resizing pointer. Drag the pointer right or left to resize the column, as shown in Figure 27.18.

FIG. 27.18
Resize a column width in the Mail window by dragging the edge of the column header.

Resizing pointer

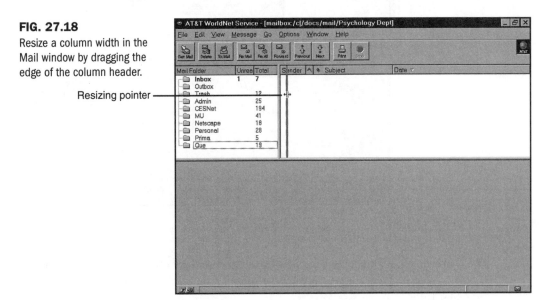

Participating in Automated Mailing Lists

One of the earliest ways that groups used Internet e-mail to communicate was by creating automated mailing lists. When you send a message to an automated mailing list, you are sending an e-mail to everyone on the list.

N O T E   There are several programs that automate mailing lists on the Internet. LISTSERV is a popular mailing list program, used primarily on IBM mainframe computers. Major-domo is another such program, running primarily on UNIX servers. Some mailing lists are served by the MailList program. In common terms, however, many people tend to refer to all mailing lists as listservs, just as they often call facial tissues Kleenex.

The discussion in this section will deal with LISTSERVs; however, the procedure for subscribing, unsubscribing, and sending mail is the same in all major automatic mailing list programs. ■

When you subscribe to a listserv, you are adding your name to the mailing list. You will receive a copy of any mail addressed to that listserv. When you send mail to the listserv, everyone who has subscribed to that listserv will get the message you post. Therefore, even though you are sending e-mail, you are engaging in a public conversation with any number of people all across the world.

> **N O T E** Listservs were one of the earliest forms of public conversation on the Internet and therefore, are technically the most primitive. Messages related to a certain topic or discussion thread are not categorized, but merely arrive as pieces of e-mail in your inbox. ■

CAUTION

Belonging to a listserv can fill up your mailbox very quickly. Many listservs get between 10 and 200 messages per day. It's easy to make a clean mail system into a nightmare, in which you must wade through hundreds of messages to get to your personal e-mail.

Some people arrange to have a second e-mail ID, and join all listservs with this ID; thus separating their personal mail from their listservs. Others are merely more selective about which listservs they join.

Subscribing and Unsubscribing to Listservs

You may already know of a listserv you would like to join, or you may want to find listservs where people have conversations about areas of interest to you. You can find a list of listservs by choosing Search in Netscape and looking up the word "listserv."

ON THE WEB

http://tile.net   As of this writing, this is an excellent site that lists all available listservs by category and alphabetically, and allows you to search the site for keywords.

The name of a listserv will have two parts: the listserv name itself, and the name of the computer where it is maintained (the host name). You'll want to know both of them.

Once you know the name of the listserv you're interested in, you will want to know how to *subscribe* to it (join it) and *unsubscribe* to it.

When you subscribe or unsubscribe to a listserv, you send a piece of e-mail to **listserv@server_name**—that is, a user named "listserv" at the computer that's hosting the listserv you're interested in. The body of the message will say:

      SUBSCRIBE listname first_name last_name

or

      UNSUBSCRIBE listname

Part

V

Ch

27

For example, if *Sam Williams* were interested in a listserv called *ponies* that is hosted at **horse.equestrian.com**, he would subscribe to the listserv by sending an e-mail. The To: line would have the following address:

listserv@horse.equestrian.com

The body of the message would simply say:

SUBSCRIBE ponies Sam Williams

Conversely, if he found that after a while he no longer wanted to be part of the listserv, he would send another e-mail to **listserv@horse.equestrian.com**. The body of this message would say:

UNSUBSCRIBE ponies

N O T E   If the ponies mailing list were maintained by majordomo rather than listserv, the subscribe command would be mailed to **majordomo@horse.equestrian.com**, as would other commands. ■

Setting Listserv Options

When you have subscribed to a listserv, you can set several options on the listserv. All of the options assume you are sending e-mail to **listserv@server_name**, as you did above.

- ■ *Query.* Returns information about your options on the listserv. Put **Query listserv_name** in the body of the message.

- ■ *Review.* Returns a description of the listserv, the owner of it, and a list of members. Put **Review listserv_name** in the body of the message.

- ■ *Register.* Registers your full name with a listserv server. Any listserv hosted on that computer will then use the name you register. Put **Register First_Name Last_Name** in the body of the message.

Responding to Listservs

Once you have subscribed to a listserv, you will receive all mail that anyone sends that is addressed to that listserv. It will appear in your inbox just like any other mail message.

 T I P   To stop listserv mail from driving you crazy, create a folder for each listserv you belong to and be sure that you move the listserv mail to the appropriate folder regularly.

To respond and participate in the listserv "conversation," you can merely reply to any message you receive. It will automatically be posted to the listserv.

If you want to manually address mail to a listserv, you address it differently than when you are sending commands to the listserv. When you are sending commands, you are talking to the listserv program, so you address the mail to **listserv@server_name**. When you are participating in the conversation, you are addressing the *people* in the listserv. Therefore, you address your mail to **listname@server_name**.

Thus, in our previous example, to post a response to the ponies listserv, you would address it to **ponies@horses.equestrian.com**. Everyone who has subscribed to ponies will see your message.

 Remember the distinction between sending commands to the listserv and participating in discussions. No one likes to keep reading "unsubscribe" commands that are accidentally sent to the entire list.

Using Newsgroups

A newer way to hold public conversations is via *newsgroups*. Newsgroups are structured conversations that are displayed as items with associated responses. After a newsgroup receives a certain number of responses, the oldest responses are discarded. Depending on how active the newsgroup is, you may be able to see a few days or a few weeks of conversation when you access it.

You read and participate in newsgroups via a *newsreader*. Netscape provides a newsreader, which in the AT&T WorldNet version is called AT&T WorldNet News.

There are thousands of newsgroups on the Internet for people who want to talk about virtually anything. To participate in newsgroups, you will want to know how to use the newsreader to list newsgroups, subscribe to ones you're interested in, read postings, and respond to them. Some newsgroups are moderated, and only certain postings are allowed; others are unmoderated, and anyone can join and post to them.

Before learning newsreader commands, however, it's important to understand the structure of newsgroups and how they maintain conversations. Your newsreader and newsgroups organize conversations in a hierarchical manner, as can be seen in the Netscape newsreader shown in Figure 27.19.

The top level of the hierarchy is the news server. This is the name of the computer (server) that maintains some or all of the newsgroups in storage, ready for you to access.

Part
V

Ch
27

FIG. 27.19

The newsreader allows you to view and participate in on-going conversations.

News server

Messages

Threaded responses

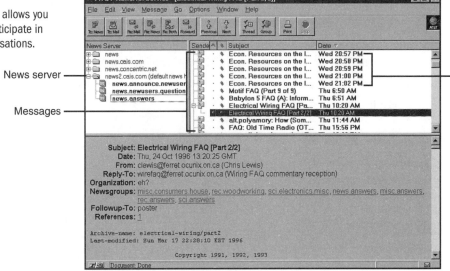

Normally, you will only see one news server, which is the folder in the top-left window pane of the screen.

N O T E   Some servers maintain all available newsgroups, while others do not make certain adult-oriented newsgroups available to the public. Ask your Internet Service Provider if you are unsure about the "news feed" that it supports. ▓

▶ **See** "Connecting Via an Internet Service Provider," **p. 527**

The next level of the hierarchy is a news category—a group of related newsgroups that share the same prefix, noted by folders in the left window pane. For instance, one of the largest categories of newsgroups is the "alt" newsgroups, which are unmoderated.

 When you first access the newsreader, you will only see three newsgroups. To see all available newsgroups, choose Options, Show All Newsgroups. Depending on the speed of your Internet connection, retrieving all the newsgroups may take a few minutes.

The third level of the hierarchy is an individual newsgroup—a series of conversations about a specific topic. These are denoted by icons representing sheets of paper.

Each newsgroup contains a series of messages. The subject lines of the messages for the selected newsgroup are shown in the right-hand pane. By default, these messages are *threaded*—that is, responses to a message are shown underneath the message. The text of the selected message is shown in the bottom window.

NOTE Messages do not remain in newsgroups forever. They scroll off periodically, and you cannot retrieve them once they are gone. The length of time a message stays in a newsgroup depends on how many new messages are added each day. ■

Subscribing to Newsgroups

You will usually not want to see the entire list of 15,000+ newsgroups. Instead, you will probably want to display only specific newsgroups you are interested in, by *subscribing* to these newsgroups.

To subscribe to newsgroups, do the following:

1. From Netscape, choose Window, AT&T WorldNet Newsgroups. You see the newsreader. Maximize the window if needed.

2. Show all newsgroups by choosing Options, Show All Newsgroups. You may need to wait a few minutes, then all newsgroups appear in the left window pane.

3. Position your mouse pointer on the right edge of the left window pane until it becomes a double-pointed arrow, then size the window like the one shown in Figure 27.20. You can now see the additional columns: the Subscribe column (denoted with a check mark), the Unread column showing how many unread messages are in the newsgroup, and the Total column, showing how many total messages are in the newsgroup.

FIG. 27.20
Size the newsgroup window pane to see the columns allowing you to subscribe to newsgroups.

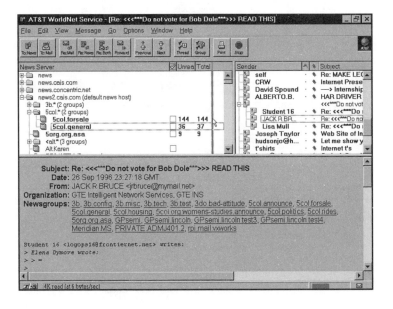

4. Expand newsgroup categories you may be interested in by clicking the plus sign to the left of the folder icon. You see the subcategories and newsgroups contained in them.

5. In the column with a yellow check mark (the Subscribe column), check the boxes of the newsgroups you want to subscribe to.

6. When you have finished subscribing to newsgroups, choose Options, Show Active Newsgroups to show only the newsgroups you have subscribed to that have unread items. Alternatively, choose Options, Show Subscribed Newsgroups to show *all* newsgroups you have subscribed to, whether or not they have unread items.

N O T E Subscribing to a newsgroup is different than subscribing to a listserv. Listservs actually have your name on a mailing list. You have to request to have your name on the list, and request it to be taken off. When you subscribe to a newsgroup, you are just checking which newsgroups you want your computer to display, but your name isn't really on a list anywhere. ■

Participating in Newsgroups

After you have selected your newsgroups, you will want to participate, either by reading the postings of others or by posting messages yourself.

To participate in newsgroups, open Netscape, and choose Window, AT&T WorldNet Newsgroups.

To read the messages in a newsgroup:

1. From the main Netscape window, open the newsreader by choosing Window, AT&T WorldNet Newsgroups.

2. Click the newsgroup you want to follow in the left pane. You see the messages headers in that newsgroup in the right pane.

3. Click a message header you want to read. The message is loaded, and displays in the bottom pane.

4. Use the scroll bar in the message pane to scroll through the message.

T I P Resize the three panes as needed by dragging the border between the panes. Similarly, resize the columns in the message header window if needed by dragging the edge of the appropriate column heading.

To mark a message as unread, click in the column with the green icon. The green icon denotes that the message has not been read.

Similarly, flag a message by clicking the column with the red icon. You can use the <u>G</u>o menu to move to the next or previous unread or flagged message.

To post a reply to a message:

1. Select the message you want to reply to.

2. Click the Re: News button. You see a dialog box like the one shown in Figure 27.21. The subject of your message is filled in, and you see the original message quoted back, with a > symbol at the beginning of each line.

FIG. 27.21

Reply either publicly to the newsgroup or privately to the individual who sent the original message.

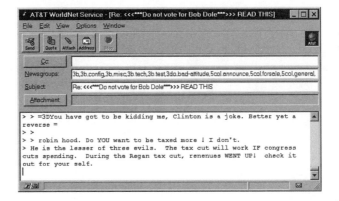

3. Delete as much of the original message as does not need to be repeated.

4. Type your reply in the message box.

5. Click the Send button. Your reply is posted to the newsgroup.

Posting a new message is similar to replying. Click the To: News button. You see a dialog box, without a message subject. Enter a subject and the text of your message, then click the Send button.

You can also reply privately to a posting by selecting the message, and then clicking the Re: Mail button. In this case, the automatic address of your message is not the newsgroup, but the individual who sent the message.

Similarly, if you use the Re: Both button, a reply is sent both privately via e-mail and posted publicly to the newsgroup. ●

Part
V

Ch
27

CHAPTER 28

Using Envoy

Corel positions the Corel WordPerfect Suite 7 as a total office solution. An important part of this total solution is *document publishing*. Document publishing means distributing a document electronically, in a form that is easily readable no matter what computer is used to read the document.

For many organizations, converting a Corel WordPerfect Suite data file to an HTML file is not the most efficient publishing solution. Often, the document is too complex, and converting it manually takes too much time. Envoy can be an excellent publishing solution in these instances. ∎

Create an Envoy document

Learn how to make an Envoy document from any Windows application.

Use the Envoy Viewer

Find out how to read an Envoy document and add annotations to it.

Use bookmarks and links

See how you can make an easily searchable Envoy document by creating a table of contents with bookmarks and hypertext links.

An Overview of Envoy

Using Envoy, you can create a document that:

- Can be read on both PCs and Macintoshes.
- Cannot be changed by readers.
- Can, however, be annotated by reviewers.
- Includes objects such as sound files or animated pictures.
- Contains bookmarks and hypertext links to help readers move through the document.

For example, you may want to maintain a technical manual that includes text, diagrams, and pictures. It is probably vital that users not make changes to this document, but it is equally important that they be able to jump quickly to procedures of interest.

Alternatively, you may want to route a contract to a variety of attorneys and representatives of the contracting parties for comment. It is important that the original document not be altered, but that reviewers be able to highlight important parts, put "sticky" notes on it, read others' comments, and identify who made which comment. In either of these cases, Envoy provides the solution.

Envoy consists of two parts: the Envoy printer driver and the Envoy Viewer. The Envoy printer driver is used to convert a document from its original format into an Envoy document. This driver enables you to create an Envoy document from any application that can send a job to a Windows printer. It even enables you to embed the original document's fonts in the Envoy document, ensuring that exact formatting is maintained.

> **CAUTION**
> You cannot view an Envoy file under Windows 3.1.

The Viewer enables the document to be read and annotated. It provides document security, allowing the creator to choose whether the document can be annotated, printed, or password protected against even being viewed. The Viewer is also the part of Envoy that enables the document creator to add bookmarks and hypertext links, and permits readers to annotate and/or highlight the document.

N O T E The runtime Viewer allows anyone who has Windows 95 to view Envoy files. If the recipient uses a Mac, the file should be saved as a regular Envoy file, and the recipient should use the Macintosh version of the Envoy Viewer to see the file. ▪

Creating Envoy Documents

You can easily create an Envoy document from any Windows application once Envoy has been installed. You can even create a runtime Envoy document, so that the reader does not need to have Envoy on their machine in order to read the document (they do, however, need to open the runtime Envoy document from within Windows).

Creating Envoy Documents from an Application

To create an Envoy document from within a Corel WordPerfect Suite application, such as Corel WordPerfect, Corel Quattro Pro, or Corel Presentations, choose File, Publish To, Envoy.

To create an Envoy document from within any other Windows-based application, follow these steps:

1. Open the application you want to use to create the Envoy document.

2. Open or create the document to be made into an Envoy document.

3. Use your application's commands to select the printer to which the document will be printed. For instance, in CorelFLOW, it is File, Print, Name.

4. From the list of available printers, choose Envoy 7 Driver.

 T I P If the Envoy printer driver does not appear on the list, Envoy has not been correctly installed. Reinstall it from the distribution disks or see your system administrator.

5. Print the file as you normally would from the application—often, by choosing OK. For instance, Figure 28.1 shows the CorelFLOW Print dialog box used to print a calendar to the Envoy printer.

You are taken into the Envoy Viewer, and your printed document is created as an Envoy file, as shown in Figure 28.2.

FIG. 28.1
You can create Envoy documents out of any program that prints using the Envoy printer driver.

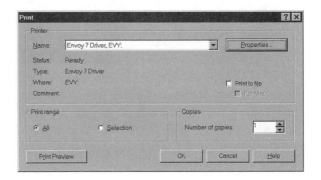

Part

V

Ch

28

FIG. 28.2

The Envoy document resembles its original counterpart almost exactly.

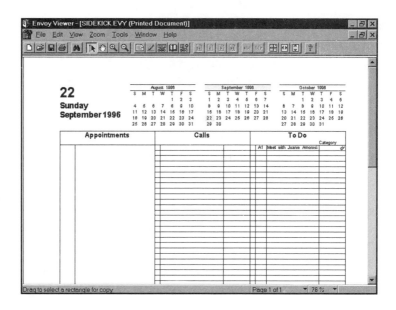

> **N O T E** When the Envoy printer driver is chosen, printing a document does not actually send it to a printer. Instead, it creates an Envoy file out of it. ■

6. Save the file as described in the section "Saving Envoy Files" later in this chapter, and close Envoy. You leave the Envoy viewer and return to your application.

Creating Envoy Documents from within the Envoy Viewer

You can also create Envoy documents from within the Envoy Viewer itself. To do so, follow these steps:

1. Open Envoy by clicking the Envoy button on the Task Bar.

2. Choose File, Import, File. You see an Import Document dialog box (see Figure 28.3).

3. Choose the file to be imported.

> **N O T E** In order to import properly, the document must have an extension that is registered in the Windows registration database. For instance, Corel WordPerfect documents must have the extension .WPD; Corel Presentations drawings must have the extension .WPG. ■

4. The application that created the file will open with the desired document loaded, and you see the Print dialog box of the application. Print the file, making sure that you are using the Envoy print driver.

FIG. 28.3
The Import Document dialog box enables you to convert existing documents into Envoy format from within the Envoy Viewer.

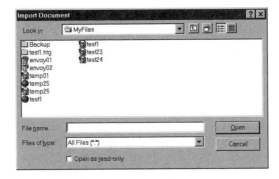

> **CAUTION**
> This feature is not completely stable, and may or may not work consistently, depending on your configuration.

5. The application will close, and you see the new Envoy document in the Envoy Viewer. Save the file as described in the section "Saving Envoy Files" later in this chapter.

Creating Envoy Documents with Drag and Drop

You can also create Envoy files with a drag-and-drop method. To do so, follow these steps:

1. Open the Windows Explorer, and make sure that it is not maximized.

2. Open Envoy (either minimized or in a window).

3. Drag the file of your choice from the File Manager onto:

   - The Title bar or menu bar area of the Envoy window

   - The minimized Envoy icon, or

   - The text area of the Envoy screen if there isn't a document currently open.

N O T E This method works best with files created by other Corel WordPerfect Suite 7 applications. Often files created with earlier versions of Corel WordPerfect—or with major applications from other vendors—will not import using this method. ■

 T I P If you drag the file into the text area of an existing Envoy file, you create an OLE object in that file, rather than creating a new Envoy file. (See the section "Inserting OLE Objects" later in this chapter for more details.)

Part
V

Ch
28

4. The application that created the file will open (minimized) with the desired document loaded, and you see the print dialog box of the application. Print the file, making sure that you are using the Envoy print driver.

5. The application will close, and Envoy will open with the new document in it. Save the file as described in the next section "Saving Envoy Files," and close Envoy.

Saving Envoy Files

You will save Envoy files as you do other files within Corel WordPerfect Suite 7 applications:

1. Choose File, Save. If the file has previously been saved, the modified file will replace the old file on the disk with no further prompting. Alternatively, if you want to save an existing file with a new name, choose File, Save As.

   If this is the first time you have saved the file, or if you chose Save As, you see the Save As dialog box (see Figure 28.4).

FIG. 28.4

You should save Envoy documents with a .EVY extension from the Save As dialog box so that Envoy can easily locate them.

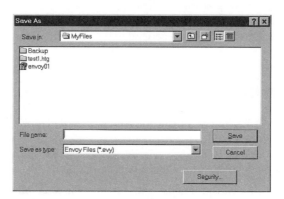

2. If you want to set security options, choose the Security button in the Save As dialog box. (Security options are discussed in the next section.)

3. Enter the file name and, if necessary, select a different drive or folder, and then click OK.

Setting Security Options

If you choose Security when saving a document, you see the Security Settings dialog box. You may choose from the following options:

■ *Password*. Users will be prompted for a password when opening the file, and will not be able to open the file without it.

■ *Document Access*. <u>U</u>nrestricted access is the default. Users can annotate the document and save their changes, and print the document. If you choose <u>V</u>iew and Print only, users can annotate and print the document, but they cannot save their changes. If you choose View <u>O</u>nly, they will also not be able to print it. In either case, they will not be able to copy contents to the Clipboard, nor can they use <u>F</u>ile, Save <u>A</u>s to save it with a different name.

> **CAUTION**
> Restricting document access makes permanent changes in the document that you cannot undo. Always save a copy of the document with no restrictions in addition to the restricted version.

Creating a Runtime Document

Sometimes, you may want to provide your Envoy document to a person who does not have Envoy on their computer. You can do this by saving the file as a runtime document. When you do this, a runtime version of the Envoy Viewer is saved with the file. The runtime Viewer works like the full Viewer, with a few exceptions:

■ The help files are reduced.

■ Only the document saved with the Viewer can be viewed.

■ You cannot create new Envoy files with the runtime Viewer.

 Saving a file as a runtime document adds approximately 1.1M to its size.

To create a runtime document when you save an Envoy document follow these steps:

1. Choose <u>F</u>ile, Save <u>A</u>s. You see the Save As dialog box (see Figure 28.5).

FIG. 28.5
You can create runtime Envoy documents by choosing Envoy Runtime Files as the file type from the Save As dialog box.

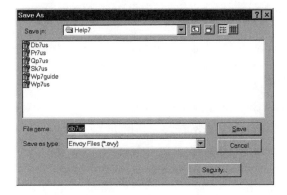

2. Choose Save as Type.

3. Choose Envoy Runtime Files (*.exe).

4. Enter the file name.

5. Click Save.

To open a runtime Envoy document, execute it just as you would any other Windows application, by using either of the following methods:

■ Double-click it from Windows Explorer, or

■ From the Start button, choose Run and specify its path and file name.

Embedding Fonts in Envoy Documents

Sometimes, it is vital to use the exact fonts that created the document to view the document—even if users don't have those fonts on their system. In this case, you can embed the original fonts in the Envoy document by following these steps:

 TIP If you don't embed fonts, Envoy will use intelligent font mapping to choose the font with the closest typeface and size to the original. Embedding fonts significantly adds to the size of the Envoy document.

1. Open the application you want to create the Envoy document from, then open or create the document to be exported to Envoy.

2. Use your application's commands to select the printer to which the document will be printed. For example, in CorelFLOW, it is File, Print, Name.

3. From the list of available printers, select Envoy 7 Driver.

4. Use your application's commands to edit the properties for the printer. Often this is a Properties button in the Print dialog box.

5. Select the Fonts tab. You see the Envoy 7 Driver Properties dialog box shown in Figure 28.6.

6. Choose each font that you want to save (embed) with the document, then click the right arrow to add it to the Fonts Available for Embedding list.

7. When you are finished, click OK to return to the Print dialog box from which you selected the Envoy printer driver.

8. Print the file to Envoy as you normally would from the application.

9. Save the file as described in the section "Saving Envoy Files," and close Envoy. You return to your application.

FIG. 28.6
You can embed original fonts within an Envoy document by choosing the Fonts tab in the Envoy 7 Driver Properties dialog box.

Viewing and Annotating Envoy Files

When you distribute an Envoy file, users may read, print, and/or annotate it, depending on the security options you have specified. Users need to know how to do several things to effectively use the Envoy Viewer:

- Open, close, and print Envoy files
- Set environment options
- Move through the document
- Annotate the document with highlights and notes
- Add bookmarks, hypertext links, and OLE objects to the document

Opening and Closing Envoy Files

You may open an Envoy file from the Windows Explorer or from Envoy itself.

To open an Envoy or a runtime Envoy file from the Windows Explorer, navigate to the folder containing the Envoy file, then double-click it.

To open an Envoy file from the Envoy Viewer, follow these steps:

1. Click the Envoy button on the DAD Bar to open Envoy, or choose Start, Corel WordPerfect Suite 7, Envoy. You see the Envoy Viewer shown in Figure 28.7.

2. Choose File, Open or click the Open icon. You see the Open dialog box shown in Figure 28.8.

Part
V

Ch
28

FIG. 28.7
You will view and annotate Envoy files from the Envoy Viewer.

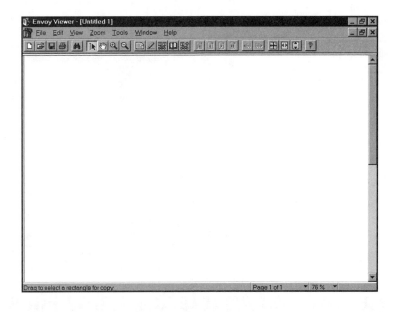

FIG. 28.8
The Open dialog box enables you to open Envoy files.

3. Choose the appropriate drive and folder, then double-click the file to choose it. The file is opened in the Envoy Viewer.

▶ **See** "Saving, Opening, and Closing Files," **p. 58**

To close a file, choose File, Close. If you have added annotations to the file, provided there are no security restrictions, you will be asked if you want to save it before closing. If you respond Yes, the file will be saved, replacing the old version with no further prompting.

TROUBLESHOOTING

When I view an Envoy file at home, equations are all messed up. The symbols are showing as boxes. What might be wrong? Apparently, you don't have the fonts at home that were used to create the document at work, and there are no similar fonts. You will need to re-create the Envoy file at work, embedding the appropriate fonts in it as described in "Embedding Fonts in Envoy Documents" earlier in this chapter.

Printing Envoy Files

To print an Envoy file, follow these steps:

1. Open the file in Envoy, as described in the preceding section.

2. Choose File, Print. You see the Print dialog box (see Figure 28.9).

FIG. 28.9
You can print Envoy documents from the Print dialog box of the Envoy Viewer, providing there are no security restrictions against printing.

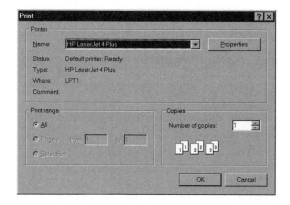

3. Select the printer, if necessary, in the Name box.
4. Set the Print Range and Number of Copies, if more than one is desired.
5. Click OK to print the document.

Changing the Viewer Environment

You can set environment options that determine how your file will look in the Envoy window, including the zoom factor and display of thumbnails.

Setting the Zoom Factor   The zoom factor is the degree of magnification that the Envoy file has on the screen. You can show an entire page, or just a few letters.

The quickest way to change the zoom factor is by using the Fit Width and Fit Height buttons on the toolbar:

■ The Fit Width button calculates the proper zoom factor to show the entire width of the page from side to side, including the white margins.

Part
V

Ch
28

■ The Fit Height button functions similarly, but shows the entire height of the page from top to bottom, including the white margins.

 T I P   When you click the Fit Height button, smaller text may be represented by shaded lines rather than letters. Often, the Fit Height button is used to show entire page layout or larger graphics, rather than regular text.

You can also set the zoom factor by choosing Zoom on the Menu bar. You can then choose specific zoom factors, such as 25%, 50%, 75%, 80%, 90%, and so forth.

 Finally, you can use the Zoom In and Zoom Out buttons on the toolbar to magnify selected areas of the document in two ways:

■ Click the Zoom In or Zoom Out button, and then click in the document window. The document will zoom in or out by selected amounts each time you click the button.

■ Click the Zoom In button, and then drag a rectangle in the document window. The document will be magnified so that the rectangle you drew occupies the entire window.

■ Click the Zoom Out button, then drag a rectangle in the document window. The contents of the document window will shrink to fit into the rectangle that you drew.

 T I P   After you click the Zoom In or Zoom Out button, the status bar reminds you of the options you have and the current Zoom percentage.

Displaying Thumbnails   Thumbnails are small representations of each page of a document that can be shown at the top or left of the Envoy screen.

 To show thumbnails, click the Thumbnails button on the toolbar. Repeatedly clicking this button scrolls you through the thumbnail display options. The first time you click, thumbnails appear at the top of the window (see Figure 28.10). The second time, they appear at the left. The third time, they disappear.

You may also show the page numbers below the thumbnails while thumbnails are displayed by choosing View, Thumbnails, Show Page Numbers. (If page numbers are already displayed, the last command changes to Hide Page Numbers.)

Moving Through Envoy Files

You can move through Envoy files in several ways:

■ Using the scroll bars

■ Using the toolbar or menu

- Using thumbnails
- Using the Scroll tool
- Using the Find command

FIG. 28.10

Thumbnails are small pictures of each page. They can appear at the top or left of the Envoy window.

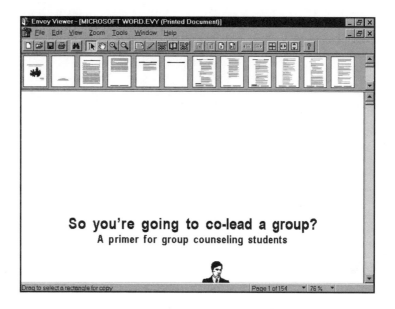

Perhaps the easiest way to move through the Envoy document for Windows users is by using the scroll bars.

You can also move between pages easily using the First Page, Previous Page, Next Page and Last Page buttons on the toolbar. Alternatively, you can choose View, then Last Page, Previous Page, Next Page, or Last Page.

You can go to a specific page by clicking the page number in the status bar. You see the Go To Page dialog box. Type in the number of the page you want to go to, and then choose OK.

If thumbnails are displayed, you can also go to a specific page by double-clicking the appropriate thumbnail.

You can also scroll through a document using the Scroll tool. When you choose the Scroll tool, the mouse pointer changes to a hand. You can then drag the page in any direction. Thus, if you drag it down, the text (and/or pages) above the current position starts to show. The Scroll tool is most useful when you want to show a little more of the document than what displays in the window.

Alternatively, you can search for specific text within the document or annotation.

Part
V

Ch
28

1. Choose Edit, Find. You see the Find dialog box (see Figure 28.11).

FIG. 28.11
You can search Envoy documents for selected words in the text, or in annotations using Find.

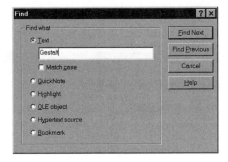

2. Choose whether to look for Text, QuickNote, Highlight, OLE Object, Hypertext Source, or Bookmark.

3. Type the text to be searched for in the Text box, if you chose Text in Step 2.

4. Click Find Next.

T I P See the following sections to find out more about notes, highlights, OLE objects, hypertext, or bookmarks.

Highlighting Text

You can highlight text while you are reading an Envoy document almost like you are doing it by hand with a highlighter.

■ To highlight text, click the Highlight button on the toolbar. The mouse pointer changes to a miniature highlighter. Drag the mouse pointer over the text to be highlighted. The highlighted text changes color, just as a paper copy would (see Figure 28.12).

■ Alternatively, you can drag over an area of the document that does not contain text. In this case, a rectangular area is selected.

To clear highlighting:

1. Make sure that the Highlight tool is selected.

2. Click anywhere in an area of highlighted text. The entire highlighted text is selected.

3. Press the Del key to remove the highlighting.

Alternatively, you can right-click the highlighted text, then choose Clear.

FIG. 28.12
Dragging the Highlight mouse pointer over text highlights it just as it would on paper.

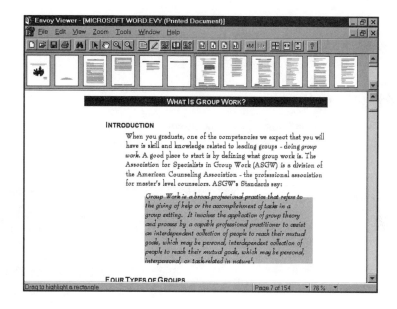

To change highlighting options:

1. Make sure that the Highlight tool is selected.

2. Right-click any area of highlighted text to see a QuickMenu.

3. Choose Highlight Properties. You see the Highlight Properties dialog box (see Figure 28.13).

FIG. 28.13
You can change highlighting options using the Highlight Properties dialog box.

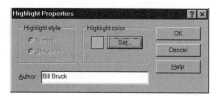

- You can change the highlight color or,

- If your printer prints it better, choose to have highlighted text struck out rather than colored.

You can also change the name of the highlight author.

 By default, the highlight author is the person who logged in (or installed Corel WordPerfect Suite 7, in the stand-alone version).

Part
V

Ch
28

Any changes you make become defaults affecting the present and future highlighted text—even in future work sessions. They do not, however, affect text that is already highlighted in the document.

Attaching QuickNotes

You can annotate Envoy documents by attaching what look like yellow sticky notes to them, as seen in Figure 28.14. These notes can be any size, and you can move and resize them at will.

FIG. 28.14

You can attach "yellow sticky notes," called QuickNotes, to Envoy documents to annotate them.

QuickNote ———

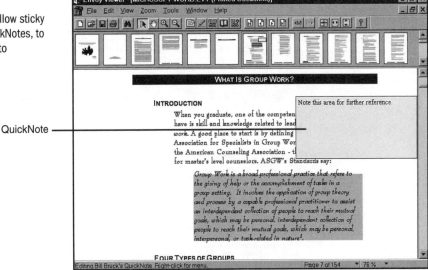

To create a QuickNote, follow these steps:

1. Click the QuickNote button on the toolbar. The mouse pointer changes to a note—a sheet of paper with the edge turned over.

2. Click the position where you want the note to appear. A standard size yellow note box appears.

 TIP You can create custom size notes by dragging the mouse pointer over the area the note should occupy, rather than clicking where the note should appear.

3. You see a blinking insertion point within the note box. Type the text of the note. Don't worry if there's too much or too little text for the note box—you can resize the box later.

4. When you are finished, click anywhere outside of the note box.

To edit the note, click the Select button on the toolbar. Rapidly double-click the mouse pointer anywhere inside the note box. You see a blinking insertion point, and can edit your text as you desire.

You can also move or resize a note box when it is not currently selected by using the following procedure:

1. Click the Select button on the toolbar.
2. Click anywhere in the note box. You see handles around it (see Figure 28.15).

FIG. 28.15
You can move or resize QuickNote boxes by using their handles.

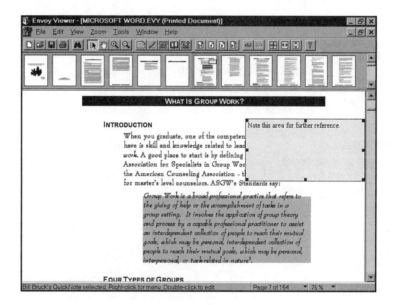

3. Move or resize the note box using the following procedures:
    - To move the note box, position the mouse pointer in the middle of the box, where the mouse pointer changes to a four-headed arrow, and then drag it to its new position.
    - To resize the note box, position the mouse pointer on one of the eight handles, where the mouse pointer changes to a two-headed arrow, and then drag the handle to change the box size.
4. Click anywhere outside of the box to deselect it.

You can also delete a note box. Select the box by clicking it with the Select tool, and then press the Delete key.

CAUTION

There's no Undo command in Envoy. Be careful!

You may not want to see these yellow boxes all over a document you are viewing. You can close a note, leaving only a note icon in the document to indicate where the note is.

■ To close a note, right-click it with the Select tool, then choose Close QuickNote.

■ To open a closed note, double-click the note icon with the Select tool.

To change note box options:

1. Make sure that the Select tool is selected.

2. Right-click the note box to see a QuickMenu.

3. Choose QuickNote Properties. You see the Note Properties dialog box (see Figure 28.16).

FIG. 28.16

You can reset the default note color, text font and color, and author's name with the Note Properties dialog box.

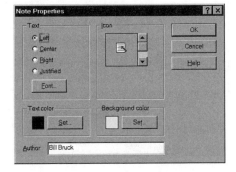

You can change the justification, font, and color of the text, the background color, and the author's name. You can also choose the icon to be displayed when the note is closed.

You can use the color and icons to easily show who is annotating a document. Just make sure that each reviewer uses a unique color (for open notes) and icon (for closed ones).

T I P You can easily see who wrote a note by positioning your mouse pointer on it. For a note written by Frank Owen, the status line will say "Click to select Frank Owen's QuickNote. Double-click to edit it."

N O T E Any changes you make in the Note Properties dialog box become defaults. They will affect future notes written in this document, and notes you enter from now on in other documents, until you reset the note properties again. ■

Adding Bookmarks

Bookmarks are an alphabetical list of *jump terms*—terms that enable you to move quickly to predefined places in your Envoy document. The creator of an Envoy document often creates bookmarks prior to saving the document, to assist readers in finding important places quickly.

To effectively use Bookmarks, you need to know how to create them, use them, and set bookmark options.

To create a bookmark, follow these steps:

1. Click the Bookmark button on the toolbar. The mouse pointer changes to a bookmark—a book with a place marker in it.

2. Mark the position that you want the user to move to when the bookmark is selected, in one of two ways:

    - Position the mouse pointer inside the text until the bookmark pointer displays an insertion point, then drag over the text to select it.

    - Position the mouse pointer where there is no text until the bookmark pointer displays crosshairs, then drag a rectangle to select the area.

3. You see the Bookmark Properties dialog box (see Figure 28.17). Fill in options as needed:

    - Type a label for the bookmark. (If you selected text, the first words of the selected text will be the label unless you change it.)

    - If you want the content of the bookmark to be selected after you jump to it—perhaps so that the reader can easily copy it to the Clipboard—choose Select Bookmark Content After Jump.

    - When you jump to the bookmark, choose whether the bookmark text should be centered in the window (Center Bookmark in Window) or whether the window should zoom to the size needed to fit the bookmark in the window (Fit Bookmark to Window).

FIG. 28.17
You can change default bookmark options with the Bookmark Properties dialog box.

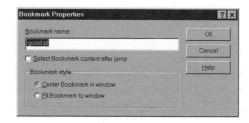

4. When you are finished selecting options, click OK.

5. The bookmark is added to the list, and the mouse pointer remains as a bookmark pointer. Create another bookmark or select a different type of pointer for another action.

To edit the properties of an existing bookmark follow these steps:

1. Click the Bookmark button on the toolbar.

2. Right-click anywhere inside the text of an existing bookmark to display a QuickMenu.

3. Choose Bookmark Properties to display the Bookmark Properties dialog box. You can edit the options of existing bookmarks with the Bookmark Properties dialog box.

4. Change options as needed, then click OK.

To jump to a bookmark, choose Edit, Go To Bookmark, or click the Bookmark button on the status bar at the bottom of the window. You see a list of available bookmarks. Double-click the desired one. You will jump to the area of the document defined in the bookmark.

Adding Hypertext Links

Hypertext links are buttons or jump terms within the document that allow you to jump to predefined places in your Envoy document, such as bookmarks. The creator of an Envoy document often creates hypertext links prior to saving the document. This is most easily done if the original document contains a table of contents, list of figures, index, or other logical place for hypertext links. You can even create hypertext links whenever an unfamiliar term exists in a document—assuming that you have the term defined somewhere else in the document.

To effectively use hypertext links, you need to know how to create them, use them, and set their options.

To create a hypertext link, follow these steps:

1. Click the Hypertext button on the toolbar. The mouse pointer changes to a hypertext pointer.

2. Choose from either of the following procedures, depending on whether you want to create a jump term or a hypertext button:

   - To create a jump term (a word or phrase that the user can click to jump through the link), position the mouse pointer inside text until the hypertext pointer displays an insertion point, then drag over text to select it.

- To create a hypertext button, position the mouse pointer where there is no text until the bookmark pointer displays crosshairs, and then drag a rectangle the size of the button.

  In either case, on the status bar, you see the message "Go to the destination," then drag the link on main view or thumbnails.

3. Move to the position that you want to jump to, then click the mouse, or drag the mouse over the destination.

4. To set options, right-click in the text, then choose Properties. If you do not want to set options, skip to Step 6.

5. Depending on whether you selected text or a rectangle, proceed as follows:

   - If you selected text, you see the Hypertext Properties dialog box shown in Figure 28.18. Select the source text style as Colored Text, Underlined Colored Text, or Underlined Only. Choose the source text color. When you jump through the hypertext link, choose whether the text should be centered in the window (Center Destination in Window) or whether the window should zoom to the size needed to fit the text (Fit Destination to Window). When you are finished selecting options, click OK.

FIG. 28.18
The Hypertext Properties dialog box for text enables you to change the color and underline of jump terms.

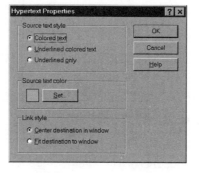

 Make hypertext jump terms green and underlined so they resemble jump terms in Windows help.

   - If you selected a rectangle, you see the Hypertext Properties dialog box (see Figure 28.19). Select the source text style as an Invisible Rectangle, Framed Rectangle, or Button. If you chose Framed Rectangle, choose the rectangle color. If you chose Button, use the button scroll bar to choose from pre-defined button types. When you jump through the hypertext link, choose whether the text should be centered in the window (Center Destination in Window) or whether the window should zoom to the size needed to fit the text (<u>F</u>it Destination to Window). When you are finished selecting options, click OK.

FIG. 28.19
The Hypertext Properties dialog box for rectangles enables you to specify the rectangle as invisible, framed, or a button.

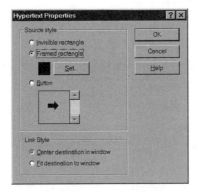

 T I P You can choose <u>I</u>nvisible Rectangle to make graphic objects in your document into jump terms.

---

6. The hypertext link is created, and the mouse pointer remains as a hypertext pointer. Create another link or select a different type of pointer for another action.

To edit the properties of an existing hypertext link, follow these steps:

1. Click the Hypertext button on the toolbar.

2. Right-click anywhere inside the text or area of an existing hypertext source. You see a QuickMenu.

3. Choose <u>P</u>roperties. You see the appropriate Hypertext Properties dialog box.

4. Change options as needed, and then click OK.

When you are using the Select tool and your mouse pointer is positioned on a hypertext source, it will change to a hand. This is true whether the source is text, a colored box, invisible box, or button.

To jump through to a hypertext link, position your selection pointer on a hypertext source. When the mouse pointer changes to a hand, click. You will jump to the area of the document defined in the hypertext link.

Inserting OLE Objects

You can insert objects into your Envoy document—such as sound clips, animated pictures, or links to spreadsheets and databases—by using Object Linking and Embedding (OLE).

▶ **See** "Understanding the Types of Data Transfer," **p. 722**

However, one special consideration applies to using OLE with Envoy documents: OLE enables you to create a link to the object (for instance, to a sound file), or embed the sound file in the Envoy document. When you create a link, the sound file exists on the disk, and when you click the sound file icon in the Envoy document, it reads the file from the disk. When you embed the sound file in the Envoy document, a copy of the sound file is placed in the Envoy document itself.

In most applications, linking is frequently preferred for two reasons: Linking keeps the Envoy file relatively small, whereas embedding can make the Envoy file rather large; and linking ensures that you are reading the latest version of the file, whereas embedding "locks" the then-current version of the file into the Envoy document.

However, Envoy documents are regularly distributed via the Internet, on a diskette or CD to viewers who may have no access to the disk to which an OLE object is linked. If you are creating an Envoy document that will be distributed in this manner, you may want to embed, rather than link, your OLE object.

 For you "techies" who are into the details of OLE; Envoy is OLE 2.0 enabled.

Part

V

Ch

28

Using Other Suite Applications

CHAPTER 29

Using Corel Address Book 7

Corel Address Book 7 is a deceptively simple address list manager. It integrates seamlessly with WordPerfect, allowing you to insert addresses in your WordPerfect documents, and serving as a data source for WordPerfect merges. It also integrates with Microsoft Exchange, allowing you to maintain your Exchange Personal Address Book in Corel Address Book 7, which offers much more functionality. ■

Integrate Address Book 7 with Exchange

Maintain your Microsoft Exchange personal address book using Address Book 7.

Maintain address lists

Use Corel Address Book 7 to maintain multiple address lists for home and business use.

Integrate with WordPerfect

Use Address Book 7 to insert names and addresses in WordPerfect documents and merges.

Understanding How Address Book Works

Corel Address Book interfaces closely with Microsoft Exchange, and to understand how Address Book works, you need to understand a few things about Exchange.

> **CAUTION**
>
> If Exchange is installed *after* Corel Address Book, then Address Book can error on startup. This occurs because Exchange overwrites information that Corel Address Book modifies on its install. If you have problems integrating the two, try uninstalling Corel Address Book, then reinstall it (after Exchange has been installed).

Understanding Microsoft Exchange Profiles

Exchange is the universal Inbox in Windows 95 that provides a central point for services including your faxes, Microsoft Mail messages, Internet e-mail, and Microsoft Network e-mail. If you have installed Exchange, you will have one or more of these services installed as well.

These services each use address lists. Microsoft Mail uses a Postoffice Address List. The other services can access the Postoffice Address list, but because it doesn't maintain much information, you will usually use the Personal Address Book that is created for you when you install Exchange.

Because more than one person might use a given computer, Exchange supports *profiles.* The Microsoft Exchange help system describes a profile as:

"…a set of configuration options used by Microsoft Exchange and other messaging applications that contains essential information, such as which information services you are using. This information includes the location of your Inbox, Outbox, and address lists, and the personal folder files available to you for storing and retrieving messages and files."

In short, you can think of a profile as the information needed to support an individual *user* of Exchange services.

Understanding How Corel Address Book Uses Profiles

When you install Corel Address Book, a new Exchange profile—the Corel Settings profile—is created. By default, the service that is set up in this profile includes the Corel Address Book. Depending on how Exchange was configured when Corel Address Book was installed, the profile may also include your Exchange Personal Address Book, and/or your Microsoft Mail Postoffice Address list.

When you open Corel Address Book, it looks at the last profile you specified. The address books you see will depend on the profile you use. If you create profiles for several people who use the same computer, each person will see only their own address books.

Usually, you will just use the default Corel Settings profile. If you need to add a profile, or add services to an existing one, you can do so as follows:

1. Right-click the Inbox icon in the Windows 95 desktop, then choose Properties. You see the MS Exchange Settings Properties dialog box.

2. Choose Show Profiles. You see the Microsoft Exchange Profiles dialog box shown in Figure 29.1.

FIG. 29.1
You can create new profiles and add new services to existing profiles.

3. Choose Add to create a new profile, or Copy to copy an existing one to a new one. (If you choose Add, you will need to use the Inbox Setup Wizard to configure the different Exchange services you want to include in the new profile.)

4. To add a service to an existing profile, select it, then choose Properties. You see the Corel Settings Properties dialog box shown in Figure 29.2. Select the service you want to add, then choose Add. The service may be added, or you may need to fill out a properties dialog box for that service, then click OK to add it.

T I P Use this procedure to add the Personal Address Book service to your Corel Settings profile if you do not see the Microsoft Exchange Personal Address Book as one of your address books in Corel Address Book 7.

N O T E To use a different profile with Corel Address Book 7, open Address Book, then choose Edit, Preferences. You see the Address Book Preferences dialog box shown in Figure 29.3. Select the profile you want to use, then click OK. The new profile will take effect the next time you open Corel Address Book 7. ■

FIG. 29.2
Add or remove a service
from an existing profile
with the Corel Settings
Properties dialog box.

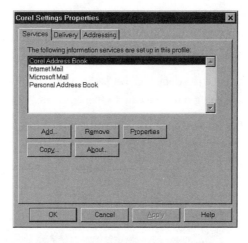

FIG. 29.3
The Address Book Prefer-
ences dialog box allows you
to specify the profile you
want to use the next time
you use Address Book.

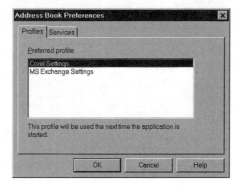

Creating Address Books

You can use just one address book if you prefer, or create as many address books as you like. You may find it useful, for example, to have one address book for personal addresses, and another for business contacts.

To create a new address book, choose Book, New. You see the Create new Address Book dialog box shown in Figure 29.4. Enter the name of your new address book and click OK. You see a new tab at the top of the Address Book window containing the new address book.

Once you have created more than one address book, you can select the appropriate one by clicking its tab.

FIG. 29.4
You can create separate
address books for your
personal and business
addresses.

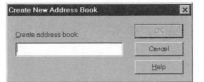

Adding Contact Information

Corel Address Book 7 maintains two types of records: records for individuals and records
for organizations. When you create a record for an individual, you can include their organization as one piece of information about them. If you enter an organization name that is
not in the address book, a record for that organization is created automatically, containing
only the organization name. If, when you create a record for an individual, you specify an
organization that is in the address book, the person's record is linked to the record for
that organization.

To add an organization to your address list, do the following:

1. From the main Address Book window, click the <u>A</u>dd button. You see the New Entry
   dialog box shown in Figure 29.5.

FIG. 29.5
Address book entries
are for either persons or
organizations.

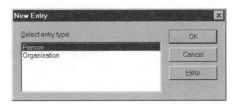

2. Select Organization and click OK. You see the New Organization Properties dialog
   box shown in Figure 29.6.

3. Enter information in each field. Press Tab to move to the next field; Shift+Tab to
   move to the previous one.

4. When you are finished, click Ne<u>w</u> to add another new record, or OK to return to the
   main Address Book window.

Use a similar procedure to enter a new person into the address book:

1. From the main Address Book window, click the <u>A</u>dd button. You see the New Entry
   dialog box.

2. Select Person and click OK. You see the Properties for New Entry dialog box shown
   in Figure 29.7.

FIG. 29.6

Insert the main number and address for the organization in the New Organization Properties dialog box.

FIG. 29.7

Insert specific information about the individual, such as their telephone extension, department, and so on in the Properties for New Entry dialog box.

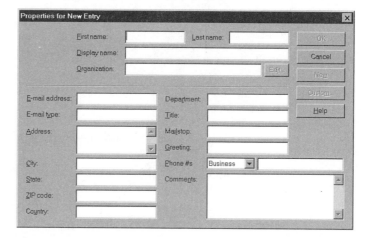

3. Enter information in each field. Press Tab to move to the next field; Shift+Tab to move to the previous one.

4. When you are finished, click New to add another new record, or OK to return to the main Address Book window.

You can edit an existing contact in a similar manner. Select the person or organization whose record you want to change, then choose Edit. You see the Properties For dialog box that has the same functionality as the dialog box used to create the record. Make changes in the appropriate fields, then click OK.

Creating Custom Fields

You can also create custom fields that are maintained for each person or organization. For instance, you might want to have a field for organizations called Web Site, in which you can record the URL for their organization's Web site. To do so, create a new record or edit an existing one to access the Properties dialog box for the organization or an individual. Choose Custo<u>m</u>. You see the Custom Fields dialog box shown in Figure 29.8.

FIG. 29.8
The Custom Fields dialog box allows you to add new fields for persons or organizations.

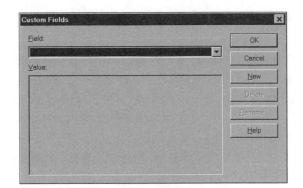

Choose <u>N</u>ew. You see the New Custom Field dialog box. Put the name of the new field in the <u>N</u>ew Field Name box and click OK. You see the Custom Fields dialog box, and the field is available through the <u>F</u>ield drop-down list. Click OK to return to the Properties for New Entry dialog box.

To use custom fields, create or edit a record. You see the Properties for New Entry dialog box. Choose Custo<u>m</u>. You see the Custom Fields dialog box. Select the field from the drop-down list, then enter the value for the field in the <u>V</u>alue box.

Importing Contacts

You can also import your contact list from another application. This can be especially handy when you have already created a contact list in another application, and don't want to have to manually re-enter your entire address list.

The first step is to save your address list in comma separated value (CSV) format. (Corel calls this format ASCII Delimited Text.) The commands you will use for this differ, depending on the program, but commonly there is a File, Export command. Occasionally, instead, you will use File, Save As, and specify CSV as the Save As Type. Check the documentation for your particular program for details.

N O T E CSV format puts each record on a separate line, with each field contained in quotes and separated by a comma, as shown here:

"Smith","Joe","555-1212"

"Jones","Mary","666-1313"

The CSV format is a "lowest common denominator" that most address list programs can all export to and import from. ▓

Once you have saved your information as a CSV file, you can import it into Corel Address Book as follows:

1. Choose Boo**k**, **I**mport, and ensure that A**S**CII Delimited is selected. You see the first step of the Import Expert, shown in Figure 29.9.

2. Choose Next. In the second step of the Expert, enter the file name in the **S**elect a File box, or choose Bro**w**se to select the file from the Address Book Import dialog box.

FIG. 29.9
You can import text from other address books by saving them in a common format like Comma Separated Value.

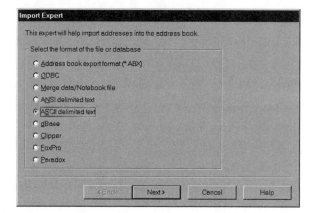

3. Choose Next. In the third step of the Expert, choose whether the first line of the file contains field names (such as First Name, Last Name) or the first person's information (like John, Jones).

4. Choose Next. In the fourth step of the Wizard, shown in Figure 29.10, specify the Field Separator character as a comma, and the Encapsulation Character as a quotation mark.

FIG. 29.10
Specify what character separates fields (usually a comma), and which encapsulation characters should be stripped out of the file (usually quotation marks).

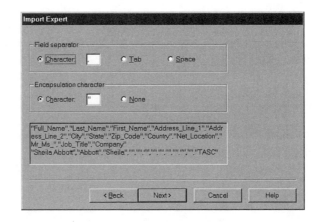

5. Choose Next. In the fifth step, shown in Figure 29.11, you see a list of fields in the database being imported, and you can associate (map) them to the Address Book fields. Fields with the same name are mapped together automatically; and fields that don't have a corresponding Address Book name have IGNORE FIELD, indicating that they will be ignored unless you specify which field they correspond to. To specify a field that doesn't have a corresponding name, select it in the left column, then click the field in the right column containing the Corel Address Book fields. Notice that the Corel field name appears in the left column next to the name of the field being imported.

FIG. 29.11
Map fields between the two databases. If fields have the same name, they are mapped together automatically.

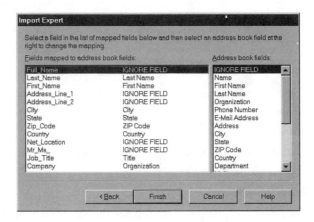

6. Choose Finish. The database is imported, and you return to the Address Book main window.

TIP You can import addresses into the Microsoft Exchange Personal Address Book using Corel Address Book so that the names and addresses you have in Sidekick or other PIMs can be imported into your Microsoft Address Book.

Creating Address Lists

You can create address lists, which are groups of persons or organizations contained in the address book. These groups are part of the address book, and can be created, deleted, edited, or renamed when necessary.

To create an address list, follow these steps:

1. Select the address book you want to add an address list to.

2. Click the Address List button. You see a new text box at the right of the Corel Address Book window, as shown in Figure 29.12.

FIG. 29.12
You can create address lists to easily send mail to several people.

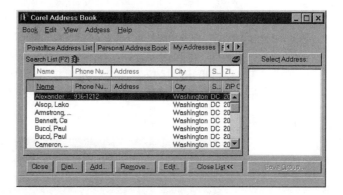

3. Select one or more names you want to add to the new address list. To select multiple names, click the first name, then hold down the Ctrl key while clicking additional names.

4. Choose Select Address. You see the selected names in the text box at the right side of the Address Book window.

5. If desired, select additional names by repeating Step 3.

6. Click the Save Group button. You see the Save Group dialog box shown in Figure 29.13.

7. Enter a name in the Save Group As box, then click OK. The group is added to the Address Book list, denoted by a group icon, as shown in Figure 29.14.

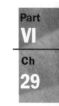

FIG. 29.13
Give your group a name in the Save Group dialog box.

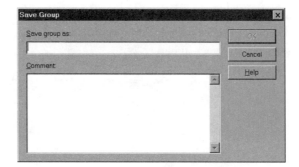

FIG. 29.14
Groups and organizations are denoted by special icons in the address list.

Organization icon ——

Group icon

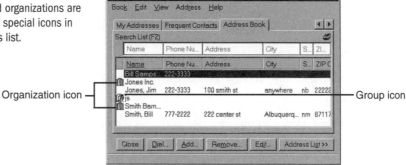

You can use a group just as you use any other name in the address list.

Using the Address Book

To use the address book, you will want to access appropriate records, and edit, delete, or copy records. You may also want to use your address book in conjunction with Word, dialing phone numbers from an address book, or using an address book for e-mail addresses.

Finding and Filtering Records

You can arrange the records in your address book by last name, first name or by first name, last name. To do so, choose View, Name Format, then choose First Last or Last, First. You may need to wait a few seconds, but your list will be re-sorted by the desired field.

If you want to look up a name by text that exists in any field, click in the column heading of the field in which the text exists, then type the text. The first name matching the typed letters is selected, as shown in Figure 29.15.

FIG. 29.15

You can search for text in any field by typing the text in the appropriate field heading.

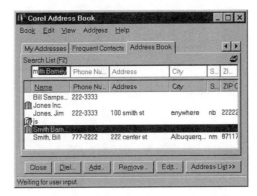

You can also create a filter for your address list that will show only the records meeting specified criteria.

To do so, choose View, Define Filter. You see the Building a Filter dialog box shown in Figure 29.16.

FIG. 29.16

You can create a filter that shows only specified records.

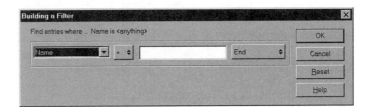

Choose the field you want to filter the list by from the drop-down list, then choose the operator (by default, it is the equal sign). Type the criterion text in the right text box. If you want to add another criterion, click the End button, and change it to And or Or, and enter additional criteria. Click OK when you are finished. You see the filtered list like the one shown in Figure 29.17.

Editing, Deleting, or Copying Records

Once you have located the appropriate record, you can edit, delete, or copy it. To edit a record, select it, then double-click it; or choose Edit. You see the appropriate Properties dialog box, and can make the appropriate changes.

FIG. 29.17
You can filter the list by any combination of criteria.

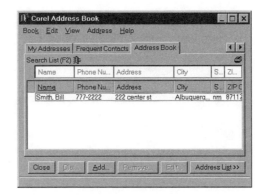

To delete a record, select it, then press the Del key or click the Remove button. The record is removed from the address list.

To copy a record, select it and then choose Edit, Copy. Switch to the desired address list, if needed, then choose Edit, Paste. If the operation creates a duplicate record, you will be warned, then the duplicate record will be created.

 T I P You may find this to be an easy way to create records for related persons, or persons in the same organization that share many fields of information.

Using the Dialer

If you have a modem attached to your computer, and a telephone on the same line, you can use the Address Book to dial a phone number. You will also need to ensure that the Windows 95 Phone Dialer application is loaded.

 T I P If the dialer application is not loaded, you can choose Start, Help and look up help on the Dialer to find instructions on how to load it.

Once these basics are taken care of, you can dial a number as follows:

1. Open the Address Book and choose the appropriate address book tab.
2. Select the name of the person you want to dial.
3. Choose Dial. You see the Dial Number dialog box shown in Figure 29.18.
4. Select the number in the Available Phone Numbers box and click OK. You see the Dialing dialog box as the number is dialed, then you see the Call Status dialog box shown in Figure 29.19.

FIG. 29.18

Use the Dial option to dial numbers directly from the Address Book.

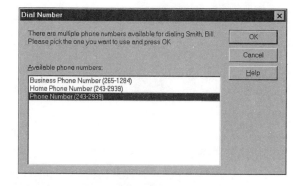

FIG. 29.19

The Call Status dialog box allows you to log your calls if you like.

5. Click the **T**alk button. You see the Active Call dialog box, which will display while you are on the call.

6. Choose Hang **U**p when you are done. The name of the person you called is placed in the Call Log of the Windows Dialer program.

To display the call log, choose Start, **P**rograms, Accessories, Phone Dialer. You see the Windows 95 Phone Dialer dialog box shown in Figure 29.20. Choose **T**ools, Show **L**og. You see a log of your calls, including the name of the person called, the date and time of the call, and its duration.

FIG. 29.20

The Windows 95 Phone Dialer maintains a log of your calls.

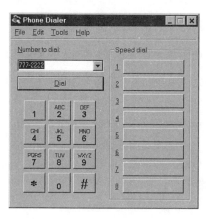

Integrating the Address Book with WordPerfect

You may find that you access the Address Book more from WordPerfect than you do as a stand-alone application, once you get used to its easy functionality.

Inserting Names and Addresses into WordPerfect

Your address books can be used to quickly insert a name and address into a WordPerfect document, or to serve as the data source for merge operations.

 To insert a name and address in a WordPerfect document, open WordPerfect and create or open the document. Position your insertion point where you want the name and address to be inserted, then click the Address Book button. You see the Address Book window shown in Figure 29.21.

Address Book button

FIG. 29.21
Quickly insert a name and address from the Address Book by clicking the Address Book button from within WordPerfect.

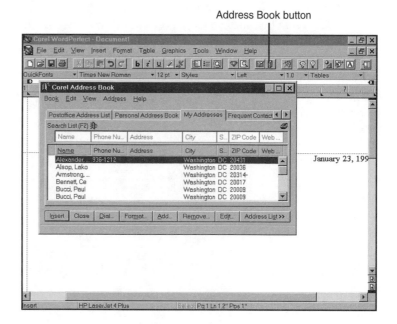

Choose the appropriate address book, then select the desired person or organization. Double-click the person's name. You see their name and address in your WordPerfect document.

 If you select an address group, all the names and addresses will be brought into your document.

If you like, you can specify which fields will be imported into your WordPerfect document. While the Address Book is open, click the For<u>m</u>at button. You see the Format Address dialog box shown in Figure 29.22. Pick from the five default formats, or add a format that includes just the fields you want by choosing <u>C</u>ustom and creating a new format.

FIG. 29.22
Choose the fields you want to use in the Address Book from the Format Address dialog box.

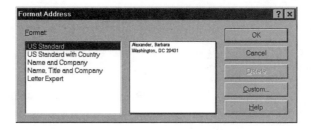

You can also use your address books as data sources for merge operations. When you choose <u>T</u>ools, <u>M</u>erge in WordPerfect, you see the Merge dialog box shown in Figure 29.23. From this dialog box, you can click the Address Book button to view, edit, or add entries to an address book.

▶ **See** "Using Merge," **p. 230**

FIG. 29.23
Address Books can be used as the data source for WordPerfect merges.

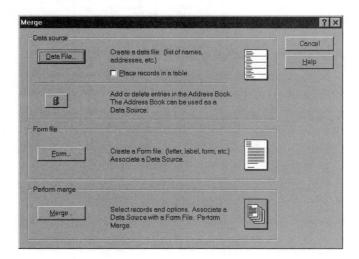

To use an address book as the data source, do not click the <u>D</u>ata File button; this is used to *create* a data source. Instead, choose <u>F</u>orm. After you choose whether to create the form in the active window or a new window, you see the Create Form File dialog box shown in Figure 29.24. Choose Associate an Address <u>B</u>ook, then choose from existing address books in the drop-down list box that becomes active.

FIG. 29.24
You are given the option of using an address book as the data file when you create the form file.

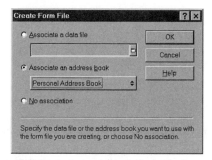

Using Frequent Contacts

The Frequent Contacts address book is created automatically and updated as you use Corel Address Book to insert addresses into WordPerfect, or use your Corel Address Book as a data source for a WordPerfect merge.

The Frequent Contacts address book is shown in Figure 29.25. It can be very useful because it contains copies of the records of people you contact most often, and people you have contacted lately. To sort the list by either one of these fields, drag the appropriate field header (Last Reference or Reference Count) to the left of the header bar. The list is re-sorted by the appropriate field.

FIG. 29.25
Sort the Frequent Contacts address book by the last contact date, or by the number of contacts.

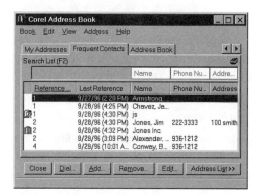

TROUBLESHOOTING

I entered my personal information the first time I used a template and now I want to change it. Choose File, New, then click the Personal Information button in the Select New Document dialog box. Select your entry in the Address Book then click the Edit button. Edit the entry, then click OK to return to the Address Book. Click Close to return to the Select New Document dialog box, and then click Close to return to the main editing window.

Printing an Envelope

Corel WordPerfect's Envelope feature automatically formats and addresses your envelope for you. If you have already typed the inside address into a letter, and you want an envelope for the letter, just choose Format, Envelope.

To address an envelope after typing a letter, follow these steps:

1. Choose Format, Envelope to open the Envelope dialog box shown in Figure 29.26.

FIG. 29.26
Corel WordPerfect's Envelope feature automatically formats and addresses your envelope.

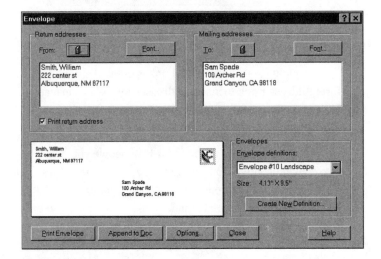

2. Check Print Return Address, then click the Address Book icon in the From box and select your address for the return address.

3. To change the font face or size used in the return address, choose the Font button in the return address section.

4. To enter or add a mailing address (if the mailing address is not automatically selected), click the Address Book icon in the To box to choose your recipient from the Address Book, or type the recipient's name in the To box.

5. As with the return address, you can change the font face or font size used in the mailing address.

6. If you want a USPS bar code printed on the envelope, click the Options button, and select whether you want the bar code printed above or below the address.

7. To print the Envelope immediately, choose Print Envelope; to add the envelope to the document, choose Append to Doc.

N O T E The font on an envelope is automatically taken from the document initial font (Format, Document, Initial Font). To save the document text in the Envelope window, make sure that the document initial font is what you want both for the letter and the envelope. ■

CHAPTER 30

Using CorelFLOW 3

CorelFLOW 3 is an application that makes creating diagrams a breeze. Whether you need to make an organizational chart, a family tree, a flow chart of a business process, or a diagram of an electrical circuit, CorelFLOW 3 is for you.

CorelFLOW combines standard drawing tools with a variety of specialized drawing shapes and a method of creating lines between these shapes that automatically takes the best route and avoids other objects. This makes creating a variety of documents quick and simple. ■

Create a diagram

Create diagrams like process flow charts, tables of organization, and time lines.

Use Smart Libraries

Find out about the 25 libraries of diagram icons available in CorelFLOW.

Use connectors

See how CorelFLOW provides intelligent connecting lines.

Understanding CorelFLOW

CorelFLOW is used for creating drawings called *diagrams*. A diagram is a drawing that contains a series of boxes or shapes that are connected by lines. Diagrams are used for showing tables of organization, time lines, family trees, electronic circuits, business processes, and so on. Typical business diagrams that CorelFLOW can make are shown in Print Preview mode in Figure 30.1 and Figure 30.2. Whatever the type of diagram you need to use, CorelFLOW makes creating it painless.

FIG. 30.1
In CorelFLOW, you can create computer network documentation like this diagram of a local area network.

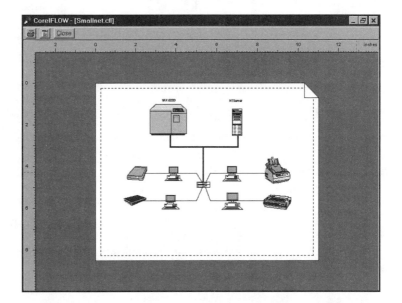

 Both the LAN and the business process diagrams are samples that ship with CorelFLOW. You can open them by choosing File, Open. They are named smallnet.cfl and Flowchrt2.cfl.

Which Product Is for You?

When should you use Corel Presentations and when should you use CorelFLOW for your drawing needs?

Corel Presentations and CorelFLOW share basic drawing functions, but they each have their unique features as well.

Corel Presentations allows you to make a series of drawings (i.e., slides) that can be put together into a slideshow that contains transitions and animations. Corel Presentations also has templates that provide backgrounds and text areas, automated bullet slides, and so on. When you are making a slide for a briefing or presentation, use Corel Presentations. Corel

Presentations also has a wide selection of clip art, more powerful drawing tools, and the capability of editing bitmap graphics.

CorelFLOW has tools that make diagramming easy, including a much wider variety of simple objects that can be used as objects in diagrams. Its templates are oriented not toward presentations, but types of diagrams (family trees, organization charts, and so on). It excels in creating connector lines between objects, even providing tools that automatically change the shape of connection lines as you move the objects in the diagram.

In short, use CorelFLOW for creating diagrams, use Corel Presentations for slides and other types of drawings.

FIG. 30.2
This diagram of a business process comes packaged with CorelFLOW.

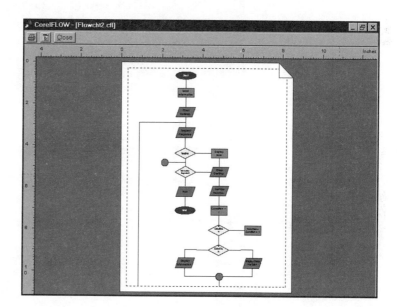

Starting CorelFLOW

When you open CorelFLOW by choosing Start, Corel WordPerfect Suite 7, CorelFLOW 3, you see the Welcome to CorelFLOW introductory screen shown in Figure 30.3 asking what you would like to do (unless you have previously turned off the display of this dialog box).

When you choose Start a New CorelFLOW diagram, you see the CorelFLOW window shown in Figure 30.4.

The window resembles that of other drawing programs like Corel Presentations. You see standard elements like the Title Bar, Status Bar, Rulers, and scroll bars. The Standard toolbar and the Text toolbar closely resemble the Standard toolbar and Formatting toolbar seen in other Corel WordPerfect Suite applications, and the Color Palette resembles the color palettes seen in other drawing programs.

FIG. 30.3
The CorelFLOW introductory screen allows you to start by choosing the task you want to do.

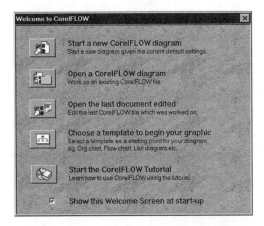

FIG. 30.4
The main CorelFLOW window has tools specifically geared to creating diagrams.

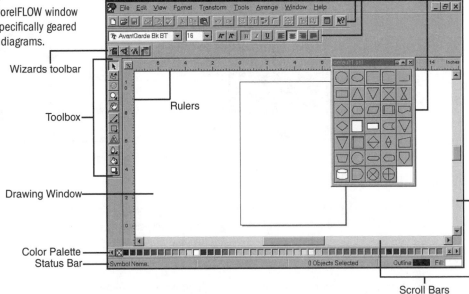

TIP CorelFLOW also includes a tutorial that consists of linked CorelFLOW diagrams. To run this tutorial, select the option from the Welcome to CorelFLOW dialog box when the program is initiated, or choose Help, Tutorial.

Understanding CorelFLOW Tools

There are a few additional tools you see on the screen, however, that assist you in creating professional-looking diagrams. These include Smart Libraries and Wizards. In addition, there are a few tools you don't see on the screen, like templates, projects, and connection tools (for connecting objects with lines).

Smart Libraries   When you first create a new CorelFLOW diagram, you see a floating palette of icons containing a number of different boxes and shapes. This palette is a Smart Library. CorelFLOW comes with 25 Smart Libraries. You can drag objects from the Smart Library to your diagram, and display or edit Smart Libraries to meet your needs, as described later.

Part
VI
Ch
30

Templates   All CorelFLOW diagrams are based on templates. A template is a master diagram that contains page formatting information, as well as the Smart Libraries that should display by default.

Wizards   CorelFLOW comes with four Wizards, comparable to QuickTasks in other Suite applications, which create sample diagrams for you: a calendar, a family tree, an organization chart, and a time line.

To use a Wizard, click the appropriate button in the Wizards toolbar. The Wizard asks you to fill out pertinent information, like the number of departments and levels in the Organization Chart Wizard shown in Figure 30.5.

 TIP   If you had a CD or Workstation installation, you will not see the Wizard buttons. In this case, choose Tools, Run Wizard/Script, and choose the appropriate Wizard from the Run Script dialog box.

FIG. 30.5
The Organization Chart Wizard asks you questions regarding the structure of your organization.

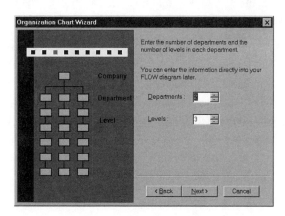

It then creates a finished diagram, like the one shown in Figure 30.6.

FIG. 30.6
The Organizational Chart
Wizard uses information you
enter to create a finished
organization chart, which you
can edit or enhance to suit
your needs.

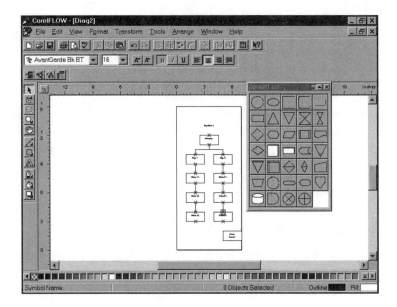

While you may be able to use the Wizards for diagrams you will create, they are also an
excellent way for new users to see some of the functions that CorelFLOW can perform.

TIP   Spend five minutes running each of the four Wizards to see the various types of diagrams
CorelFLOW can make. It will be worth your time.

Projects   You can save information about a related group of diagrams as a project. A
project file, like the one shown in Figure 30.7, allows you to organize your diagrams, and
even classify them into folders within a given project.

▶ **See** "Organizing Diagrams into Projects,"**p. 645**

Connection Tools   CorelFLOW provides several tools that help you connect objects
together to form diagrams. These include Connector Pins and Connector Points, which
act like magnets that attract both connector lines and other objects to it. You can also
create *autorouted* lines that automatically find the "best route" between one object and
another, avoiding "obstacle" objects as needed.

FIG. 30.7
Project files permit you to organize related diagrams together into folders.

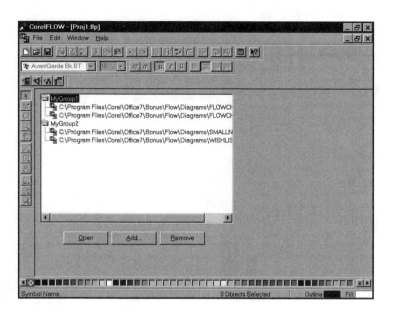

Managing Diagrams

In using CorelFLOW, you'll want to be able to create a new diagram, save and close your diagram, and open existing diagrams. After you've created a new diagram, you'll also want to be able to set up your drawing area for both the printer and the type of diagram you are making.

Creating a New Diagram

You can create a new empty diagram based on the general purpose default template. To do so, click the New button on the Standard toolbar, or choose File, New, Diagram. You see an empty diagram along with the default Smart Library, as shown in Figure 30.8.

You can also create a new diagram based on a different template. This can be helpful if you are diagramming a business process, a network, or the like, because the other templates display page layouts and Smart Libraries that are geared toward these specialized diagram types.

To create a new diagram from another template, choose File, New, From Template. You see the Template dialog box shown in Figure 30.9. Select the appropriate template and choose Open.

FIG. 30.8

When you create a new diagram using the default template, you see the default Smart Library as well.

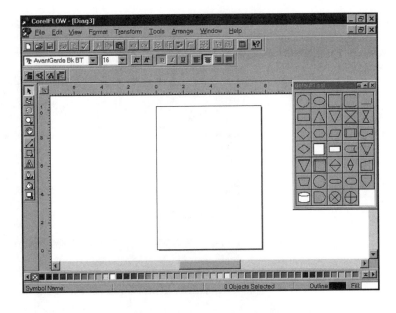

FIG. 30.9

Specialized templates designed for special types of diagrams are opened using the Template dialog box.

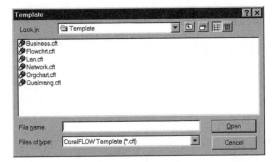

You see the appropriate page layout and Smart Libraries, like the ones shown in Figure 30.10, which creates a new document based on the Network template.

Setting Up the Drawing Area

Before putting objects in your new diagram, you should take a few minutes to set up your drawing area.

To start, when you have a new diagram on the screen, choose File, Page and Diagram Setup. You see the Page and Diagram Setup dialog box shown in Figure 30.11.

Set your page size and margins in the Layout tab. Choose autorouting settings, such as how close autorouted lines will come to "obstacle" objects they encounter. In the Options tab, set default folders for Smart Libraries, and make other default settings for such elements as objects and grids.

FIG. 30.10
Each template utilizes a different page layout, and opens the appropriate set of Smart Libraries, some of which remain rolled up until you access them.

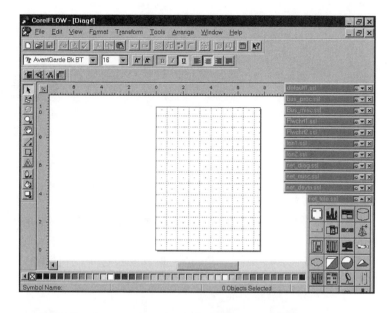

FIG. 30.11
Specify initial settings for your diagram in the Page and Diagram Setup dialog box before you start adding objects to it.

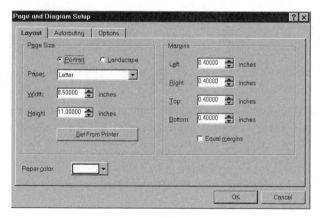

Choose Tools, Options to set additional defaults related to tool use, file management, display options, and object placement. You see the Options dialog box shown in Figure 30.12. In the General tab, specify options for the working folder, Tooltips, and the initial Welcome screen. In the Objects tab, select where duplicates should be placed, how objects should be displayed, and which key (Ctrl or Shift) to use for constraining the sizing of objects. In the Advanced tab, you can set backup options including selecting the directory to which files should be backed up, and the frequency with which your diagrams are automatically backed up.

FIG. 30.12
Choose a variety of display, tool use and file management options in the Options dialog box.

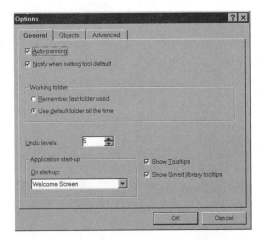

Choose Format, Grid & Ruler Setup to display the Grid & Ruler Setup dialog box. Use this dialog box to set preferences for the scale used in rulers, how large grids should be, and whether to display the grid.

Saving, Closing, and Opening Diagrams

When you are finished with your work, you will want to save it to the disk. You will also want to save it periodically in case of power failure, or in case you want to go back to an earlier version because of mistakes you made in creating the diagram.

- To save the diagram, choose File, Save or click the Save button. You are prompted for a name for your diagram in the Save As dialog box. Provide a name and choose Save. The file is saved to the disk.

- To save the document periodically or when you are finished working with it, use the same procedure described previously. You will not be prompted for the file name again.

- If you would like to save the diagram with a different name, choose File, Save As. You will be prompted for a new name for your diagram in the Save As dialog box. Provide the name and choose Save.

To close your document, choose File, Close. If you have unsaved editing changes, you will be prompted to save the diagram before the application closes.

NOTE When you close a diagram, the associated Smart Libraries remain open. This can be a little confusing if you then create or open a new diagram that uses different Smart Libraries. You may want to close any open Smart Libraries by clicking the Close button on their Title Bars before you create or open the next diagram. ▪

To open a diagram, choose File, Open, or click the Open button. You see the Open dialog box shown in Figure 30.13. Double-click the desired diagram to open it.

NOTE By default, CorelFLOW searches for diagrams in the Open dialog box. To open other types of files, choose Template, SmartLibrary, or Project in the Files of Type box. ▪

FIG. 30.13
Open new diagrams, templates, Smart Libraries, or Projects from the Open dialog box.

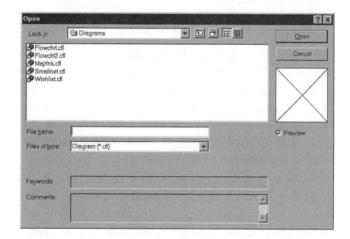

 CorelFLOW ships with five sample diagrams. Open each of these to see professionally created diagrams that demonstrate CorelFLOW's capabilities.

Exiting CorelFLOW

To exit CorelFLOW, click the Close button on the title bar. If you have open diagrams that have unsaved editing changes, you will be prompted to save each diagram that has unsaved revisions before the application closes.

Using CorelFLOW Drawing Tools

Before you begin creating flow charts or business process diagrams, it's worthwhile to spend a few minutes getting familiar with CorelFLOW's basic drawing tools. Then the more sophisticated diagramming tools will make more sense.

Part
VI

Ch
30

CorelFLOW is a complete drawing package, having the same functionality as Corel Presentations for making complex vector graphics. You will want to understand how to:

- Create objects
- Select objects
- Set object properties
- Move and copy objects
- Arrange objects

Two Types of Graphics

There are two types of graphic images that you can incorporate in your documents: *vector* images and *bitmap* images.

A vector image is stored as a formula. For instance, a circle might be stored as several codes that specify the shape (a circle), the location of the center point, the diameter, the line width, style, and color. Vector images can be stored very efficiently, because there is very little information to store. They can also be resized and moved very easily, because you merely need to alter one or two elements in the stored formula. All the drawing objects you have worked with in this chapter so far are vector images, and vector images are the only type of images that many popular presentation packages can work with.

A bitmap image is stored as a series of dots (technically called *pixels*). When you scan a photograph into your computer, you are scanning (and saving) dots, not formulas. Thus, scanned images are stored as bitmaps. While bitmaps are thus important to be able to work with, they have limitations. They take up much more space, and resizing them is much more problematic because they're not stored as a formula.

You cannot edit bitmap images with CorelFLOW. You can, however, use Corel Presentations 7 to work with bitmap images.

▶ **See** "Working with Bitmap Images," **p. 490**

Creating Basic Drawing Objects

To create a basic drawing object, or *shape*, you will use the tools provided on the Toolbox. You can create a variety of shapes including lines, curves, rectangles, circles, ellipses, and text boxes.

Start by creating or opening the diagram, as discussed above. Ensure that the Toolbox is displayed. Your blank diagram will look like the one pictured in Figure 30.14.

FIG. 30.14
The CorelFLOW Toolbox provides a number of tools used in creating simple drawings.

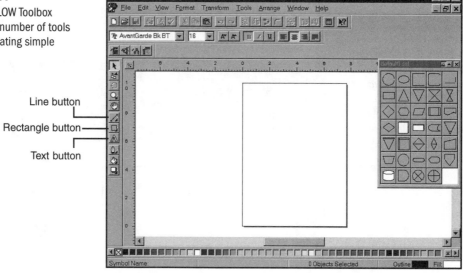

Line button
Rectangle button
Text button

The Toolbox provides three main drawing object tools:

- The Line button contains the Line tool, the Autorouted Line tool, the Curve tool, and the Freehand tool.

- The Rectangle button contains the Rectangle tool, the Ellipse tool, and the Polygon tool.

- The Text tool button is used for making text boxes.

The line and rectangle buttons have small black triangles in their lower-right corners. Click this triangle to see the pop-up *flyout* (the palette of icons that pops up) containing the other tools in the tool family, then click the appropriate tool to select it.

 T I P Drawing tools stay selected after you use them, so you will need to click the Pick tool when you are done adding shapes.

You can insert shapes into your diagram as follows:

- To create a line, select the Line tool. Click where the line should begin, then double-click where it should end. To create a segmented line, click where the line should begin, then click at each point where a new line segment should start. Double-click at the end of the line.

  N O T E The autorouted line, discussed later in this chapter, is used to connect diagram objects. ■

■ To create a curve, select the Curve tool. Click where the curved line should begin, then click where the curve should peak. Finally, double-click where the curved line ends, as shown in Figure 30.15.

FIG. 30.15

Create a curve by clicking at the start of the curved line, clicking at the peak of the curve, then double-clicking where the curved line ends.

Peak of curve

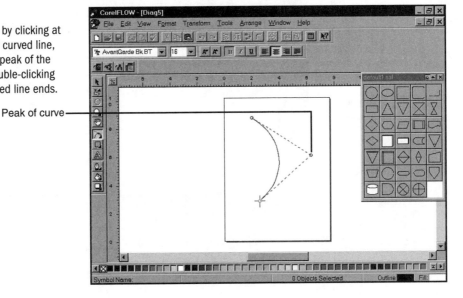

■ To draw a freehand shape, select the Freehand tool. Click and drag to use the Freehand tool like a pencil. Let up on the mouse button when you are finished drawing the freehand shape.

■ To draw a rectangle, select the Rectangle tool. Click and drag from the beginning of the rectangle to the end.

■ To draw an ellipse, select the Ellipse tool. Click and drag from the beginning of the ellipse to the end.

■ To draw a pentagon, select the Polygon tool. Click and drag from the beginning of the pentagon to the end.

TIP Hold down the Shift key while drawing a line to constrain it to a vertical or horizontal line. Hold down the Ctrl key to constrain a rectangle to a square, or an ellipse to a circle. Hold down the Shift key to have a rectangle or square be centered on the starting point.

Selecting Objects

Selecting objects follows the usual Windows conventions for object selection in graphics programs. First, start by selecting the Pick tool. Then select objects as follows:

- To select one object, click it. You see handles (eight small black squares) around the object, and an unfilled black square (the Connector Pin) in the middle of it.

- To select another object while the first one is selected, hold down the Shift key and click it. You see eight handles around the area encompassed by *both* objects, and a Connector Pin in the middle of each of the objects that are selected.

- Alternatively, to select several adjacent objects, click and drag an imaginary rectangle around the outside of the area that they are in. Corel terms this *marquee selecting*. You see eight handles around the objects, and an XXX inside each one.

Part

VI

Ch

30

T I P To delete one or more objects, select them and then press the Del key. To deselect objects, click in an empty area of the diagram.

Setting Object Properties

Once you have created drawing objects in your diagram, you can specify how they should appear. You can set the objects' color, outline, fill, and shadow.

To set an object's properties, first start by selecting the object or objects. Then, to set an object's color, click the appropriate color on the Color Palette (the color buttons at the bottom of the screen).

N O T E To remove color from an object, select the No Color button at the left—the white button with an X in it. To display more colors, click the Up Arrow at the right of the Color Palette. You see three rows of colors, rather than the default one.

T I P If you set a tool's properties when no object is selected, you will be resetting the default properties for the selected tool. These properties will be applied to new objects.

 To change an object's outline, select the object(s), then click the triangle on the Outline tool on the Toolbox. You see a number of available outline styles on the Outline flyout, as shown in Figure 30.16. Click the outline style you want to apply to the object(s).

To change an object's fill, select the object(s), then click the triangle on the Fill tool on the Toolbox. You see a number of available uniform, pattern, and fountain fills on the Fill flyout, as shown in Figure 30.17. Click the fill style you want to apply to the object(s). Alternatively, click the X for no fill.

To add a shadow to an object, select the object, then click the triangle on the Shadow tool on the Toolbox. Click the shadow style you want to add to the object from the Shadow Flyout, as shown in Figure 30.18.

FIG. 30.16
Change an object's outline style from the styles available in the Outline flyout.

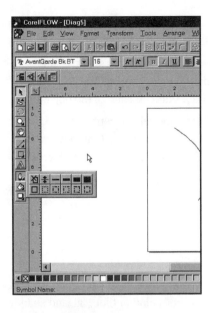

FIG. 30.17
Change an object's fill style from the styles available in the Fill flyout.

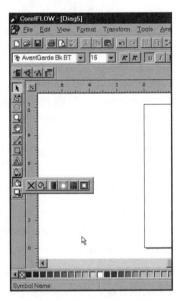

Moving and Copying Objects

You can easily move or copy objects on your diagram using the mouse. To do so, select the item(s) to be moved or copied. To move an object, position your mouse pointer inside the object (but not on a handle), then drag the object to its new location. To copy it, hold down the Ctrl key while you drag it.

FIG. 30.18
Change an object's shadow
style from the styles
available in the Shadow
Flyout.

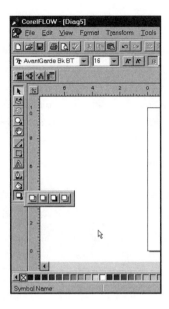

Arranging Objects

You can put objects in front of or behind each other, creating *layers* in the diagram. You can also *combine* or *group* objects to create complex objects.

- To arrange objects in front of or behind other objects, select the object(s) that are to be rearranged. Choose Arrange, In Front Of to move the object one layer forward, or Arrange, Behind to move it one layer back.

- To move an object in front of all other objects, select it and choose Arrange, To Front. To move it behind all others, select it and choose Arrange, To Back.

- To combine two or more objects into one, more complex object, select all the objects to be combined, then choose Arrange, Combine, or choose Arrange, Group.

- To separate combined objects, select the object, then choose Arrange, Break Apart. To separate a grouped object, select it and choose Arrange, Ungroup.

Using CorelFLOW Diagramming Tools

Creating a diagram is very much like creating a simple drawing using the basic drawing shapes discussed in the last section. You merely need to start using two additional tools: Smart Libraries and Connectors.

Using Smart Libraries

Usually, you will want to use objects from your Smart Libraries rather than creating simple drawing objects. Smart Library objects have Connector Pins that make connecting them together a breeze (as described later). To insert an object from a Smart Library into your document, ensure that the Smart Library is displayed, then drag the desired object into your document. The object appears with handles around it, like the one shown in Figure 30.19. You can move it or size it as you do any other graphics object (as described previously).

FIG. 30.19

Drag objects from Smart Libraries into your document.

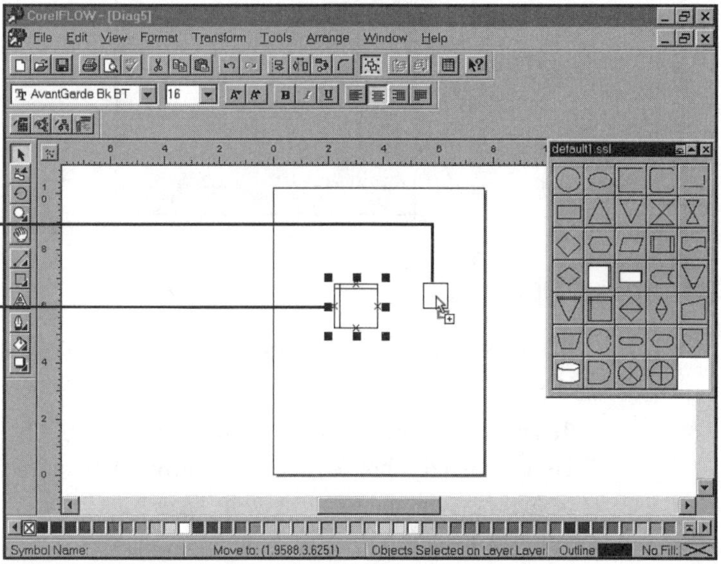

Smart Library icon being moved

Icon after move is complete

TIP Rest your mouse pointer on an icon in a Smart Library to see a description of the icon. This can be helpful for symbols whose use you are unfamiliar with.

If the appropriate Smart Library is not displayed, you can display it by clicking the SMARTLIB Open button. This displays the Open dialog box with Smart Library chosen as the type of file to search for, as shown in Figure 30.20.

You can add or delete icons from visible Smart Library palettes. To add an object in your diagram to a Smart Library, drag it from your diagram to the Smart Library palette to which you want to add it. To delete an icon from your Smart Library, right-click the icon and choose Delete. No changes are written to the disk unless and until that library is saved.

FIG. 30.20
Display as many Smart Libraries as you want by opening them in the Open dialog box.

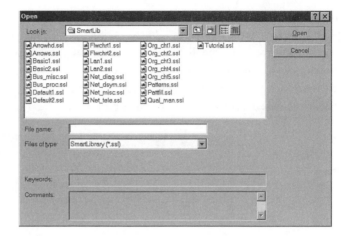

Using Connectors

CorelFLOW provides several tools that help you connect objects together to form diagrams.

- Each CorelFLOW object has a Connector Pin, represented by a small white box that is initially in the center of the object. The Connector Pin acts like a magnet that attracts both connector lines and other objects to it.

- In addition, there is another type of "magnet" that objects can have—Connector Points. Connector Points are "magnetic points" that you can place anywhere on the border of an object (or inside or outside the object) that attract Connector Pins or Lines.

- Connector Lines are lines that connect objects together. They go from a Connector Point of one object to the Connector Point of another. You can create autorouted lines that automatically find the "best route" between one object and another, avoiding "obstacle" objects as needed.

- You can also connect objects directly together to form one object, by using the Connector Pins and Connector Points. The connection can weld the two objects together, show the intersecting area of the objects, or trim away the overlap of the objects.

T I P Although the Connector Pins and Points display on the screen, they do not print.

You can use a variety of different methods to connect objects in your diagram. The simplest way to connect two objects is to select them both, then click the Connect button. This creates a straight line that connects the two objects. As you move the objects, the line moves as well, continuing to connect the two objects. Further, the end-points of the line will move along the border of the objects so that it connects the two points of the objects that are closest to each other, as shown in Figure 30.21.

FIG. 30.21

Lines adjust to connect the nearest points of the two objects that they connect.

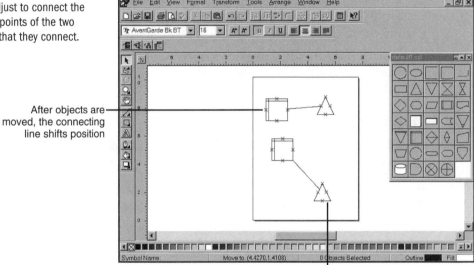

After objects are moved, the connecting line shifts position

Objects connected at nearest point

You can also connect objects with an *autorouted* line that automatically routes itself around objects that lie between the two objects to be selected. To do so:

1. Select the Autorouted Line tool.

2. Click in the middle of the first object.

3. Double-click in the middle of the second icon. A line is created that automatically avoids intervening objects, as shown in Figure 30.22. As you move the objects, the line moves automatically to continue avoiding intervening objects.

FIG. 30.22
Autorouted lines automatically avoid intervening objects.

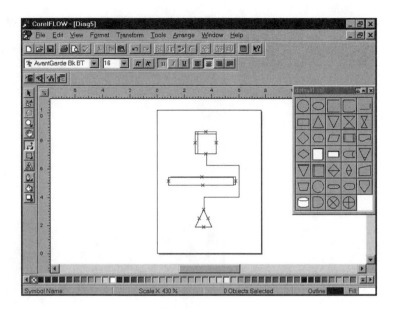

Part
VI

Ch
30

Organizing Diagrams into Projects

If you have a number of related diagrams, you can group them together into a *project*. A project is a file containing file names, optionally organized into folders, that allows you to quickly access related diagrams.

To create a new project, choose File, New, Project. You see a new project on the screen, shown in Figure 30.23.

To add a diagram to your new project:

1. Click Add.

   You see the Select New Item dialog box shown in Figure 30.24, displaying the default group to which diagrams will be added, and the diagrams in the default folder.

2. Double-click a diagram in the list box, or click Browse to navigate to the folder containing your diagrams.

3. Add other diagrams as required.

To delete a diagram from the project, select it and choose Remove. Deleting a diagram from a project does not delete it from the disk.

FIG. 30.23
You can organize your related diagrams into projects.

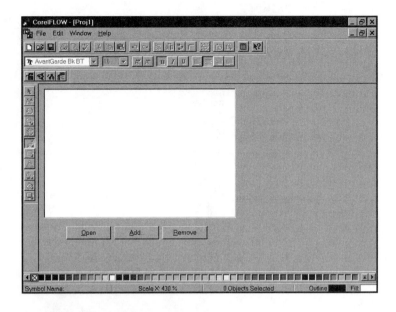

FIG. 30.24
Any existing diagrams are listed in the Select New Item dialog box.

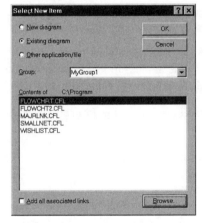

To add a new group:

1. Click the Add button.

2. Type a new group name in the Group box of the Select New Item dialog box and click OK.

3. You see the new group folder in the Projects window. When you add additional diagrams in the Select New Item dialog box, select the group from the Group drop-down list box. You see your diagrams in the appropriate group folders, as shown in Figure 30.25.

FIG. 30.25

Arrange your diagrams in groups to further organize your projects.

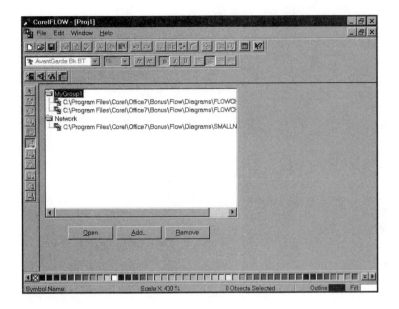

Part

VI

Ch

30

4. When you are finished, save your project by clicking the Save button, just as you would save a diagram.

N O T E Open a project just as you open a diagram, but be sure to select Projects in the Files of Type box in the Open dialog box. ▪

CHAPTER 31

Using Sidekick

Sidekick 95 is a complete Personal Information Manager (PIM) developed by Starfish Software, and included with Corel WordPerfect Suite 7.

Sidekick has seven main features that help you organize your day and keep track of where you have to be, what you have to do, and who you need to keep track of. These features include:

- *Cardfile.* Cardfiles are used to maintain your address lists. You can create several different cardfiles (for business use, personal use, and so on), and customize the fields that they contain.

- *Calendar.* The calendar maintains your appointment book electronically. You can associate appointments with individuals in your cardfiles, and even create recurring appointments.

- *To Do.* The to do list keeps track of what you need to accomplish, and helps you prioritize tasks. You can even create long-term tasks—called *goals*—to remind you of future objectives. You can also associate tasks with individuals in your cardfiles and create recurring tasks.

Understand Sidekick

Learn how Sidekick can be a complete Personal Information Manager for you, with address list, calendar, and task and phone call management.

Maintain a contact list

Find out how you can maintain your address books and contact lists with Sidekick.

Create calendars

Learn to maintain an electronic appointment book with Sidekick.

Keep a To Do list

See how to prioritize your daily tasks and phone calls, and keep track of them with Sidekick.

- *Calls.* The call feature allows you to maintain a list of priority calls in a single location. You can note your call attempts, and take notes on a call as you make it. Again, you can associate calls with individuals in your cardfile and create recurring calls. You can even dial your calls directly from Sidekick.

- *Write.* The write feature provides a mini word processor for jotting down and organizing your notes on various subjects. You can associate these notes with individuals, and even create customized Quick Letters that you can rapidly create for anyone in your cardfile.

- *Expense.* The expense feature allows you to keep track of travel and other business expenses for tax purposes.

- *Reminder.* The reminder screen brings together all your appointments, tasks, and calls for a given day, week, or other time period. ■

Understanding the Sidekick Window

To open Sidekick, choose Start, Corel WordPerfect Suite 7, Sidekick 95. When you open Sidekick for the first time, you see the Calendar view shown in Figure 31.1. The calendar itself allows you to schedule appointments, record tasks, and track calls. There are also elements common to all the Sidekick views that enable you to use Sidekick easily.

FIG. 31.1
By default, you see the Calendar view in Sidekick.

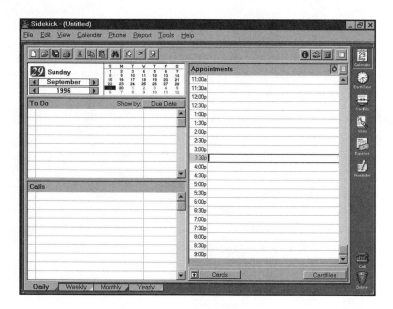

Common Window Elements

At the right of the window, you see a group of six icons, then two more icons below them. The top six icons are used to switch between the six views that Sidekick provides. These are discussed later.

The bottom two icons are the Call icon and the Delete icon. The Call icon automatically dials the number of anyone in your cardfile (if you have a modem). The Delete icon (trash can) drags items from the various windows and views to the trash can for deletion.

The <u>V</u>iew menu allows you to display or hide four screen elements. Figure 31.2 shows the window with all elements displayed:

FIG. 31.2
You can display or hide four screen elements in the <u>V</u>iew menu.

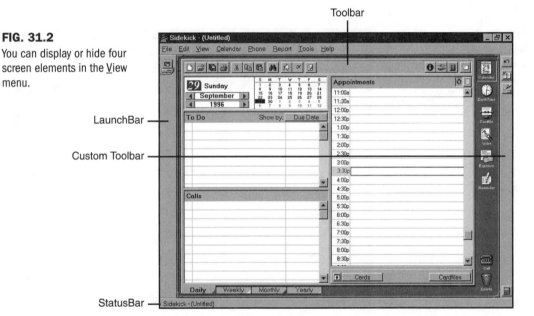

- ■ *Toolbar*. A standard Windows toolbar can be displayed or hidden. This toolbar appears on-screen by default. Toolbar buttons vary with each Sidekick view.

- ■ *Custom Toolbar*. You can display an additional toolbar at the right of the screen for toolbar buttons that you add yourself. To add tools to the custom toolbar, choose <u>T</u>ools, Custom <u>T</u>oolbar Setup.

- ■ *LaunchBar*. You can display a special toolbar called a Launch Bar at the left of the screen to launch applications directly from Sidekick. To add applications to the Launch Bar, choose <u>T</u>ools, <u>L</u>aunchBar Setup.

- ■ *StatusBar*. You can display a status bar at the bottom of the screen that indicates the name of the active file that Sidekick is using.

N O T E Sidekick saves data in a number of different files. For example, separate files are used to save each cardfile, your appointment book, your expenses, and so on. ■

Calendar View

The Calendar view is shown in the preceding Figure 31.2. It is used to maintain your appointment book, to do list, and call list. You can even create several calendars for different people.

There are four different tabs within the Calendar view that allow you to display a daily, weekly, monthly, or yearly calendar. For example, Figure 31.3 shows the Monthly calendar view.

FIG. 31.3

You can display a daily, weekly, monthly, or yearly view of your calendar. The Monthly view is displayed here.

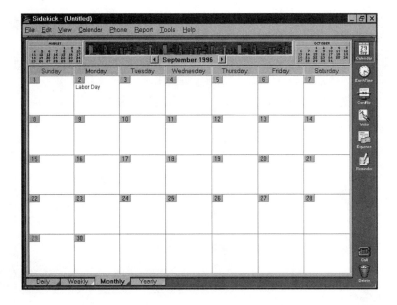

The up arrow to the left of the Cards button at the bottom of the daily calendar allows you to display a list of your contacts (called *cards*, in keeping with the cardfile metaphor). You can see the daily calendar with the pop-up cards displayed in Figure 31.4. When cards are displayed, the up arrow becomes a down arrow. Clicking the arrow hides display of your cards.

If you click the Cardfile button, you can switch between available cardfiles to display. If you click the Card button, you see a pop-up menu allowing you to switch between a list of cards, your contact log, or your goals list (discussed in the following section).

FIG. 31.4
You can display a list of cards, so that you can quickly drag a card onto the calendar, to do list, or call list to create an item associated with that person.

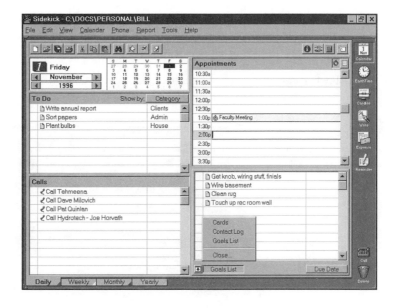

Earth Time View

The Earth Time view displays a map showing time zones throughout the world, as shown in Figure 31.5.

FIG. 31.5
The Earth Time view shows a map displaying the current time in different areas of the world.

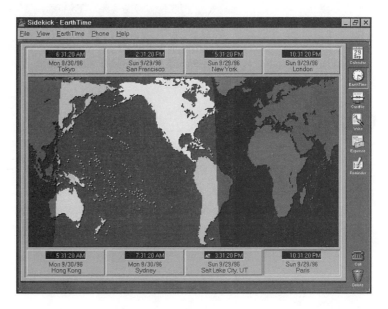

The time for eight cities is displayed at the top and bottom of the view. You can display a different city by right-clicking a city, and choosing Change City. You see the Change City dialog box, providing a list of over 350 cities to choose from.

If you right-click a city and choose Facts About City, you see the Facts About City dialog box shown in Figure 31.6, providing simple facts about the city.

FIG. 31.6
Sidekick provides simple
facts on all cities in its list.

Similarly, you can also right-click the city and choose Time Difference. You see the Time Difference dialog box, and can obtain information on the time difference between any two cities of your choice.

Cardfile View

The Cardfile view is shown in Figure 31.7. Tabs at the bottom allow you to quickly switch between cardfiles. You see a list of all your cards on the left, and the full text of the selected card on the right.

The down arrow at the bottom of the Cardfile view allows you to display a list of your appointments, calls, to do items, contact log, or goals list. It works exactly as it does in the Calendar view, as described previously.

FIG. 31.7

The Cardfile view has tabs at the bottom that allow you to quickly switch between your cardfiles.

Write View

Use the Write view shown in Figure 31.8 like a small notebook that is always with you (at least, while you are in Sidekick). You can create a new note on any subject by clicking the Add Note button. Give the note a name in the Subject box, then write your thoughts in the right-hand window. Subjects of notes you create will be listed in the left-hand windows. You can sort them by choosing Write, Sort Documents, or search for specific text in them by choosing Edit, Find.

You can create additional note files by choosing File, New. Your Write files appear as tabs at the bottom of the Write view.

Exiting Sidekick

To exit Sidekick, choose File, Exit, or click the Close button on the right side of the title bar. You will be prompted to save any work you have done in your calendar, cardfile(s), or Write documents. These are saved in separate files on your disk.

FIG. 31.8
The Write view acts like a small notebook. It's useful for jotting down ideas you have, or notes about meetings and conversations.

Add Note button

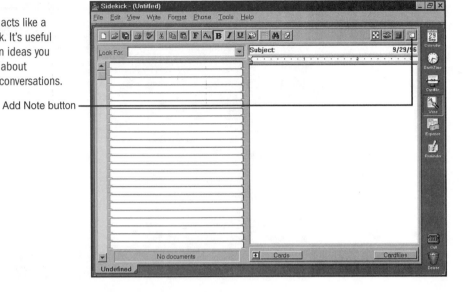

Using the Sidekick Cardfile

The Sidekick Cardfile feature can serve as your address book and contact manager, maintaining a variety of data on each of your friends, business associates, or sales leads. You can even customize the information fields that you maintain for each contact.

Sidekick allows you to maintain several cardfiles, each containing a list of names, addresses, and contact information. You can maintain one cardfile for business contacts, and another for your personal address list.

You can even copy contacts from one cardfile to another. Thus, you could keep one cardfile for sales leads, and copy them to your business contacts cardfile when they become clients. You can even use your cardfile information to address letters in WordPerfect automatically.

To access the cardfile, open Sidekick, then click the Cardfile icon. You see the Cardfile view, with one untitled cardfile, as shown in Figure 31.9.

Add button

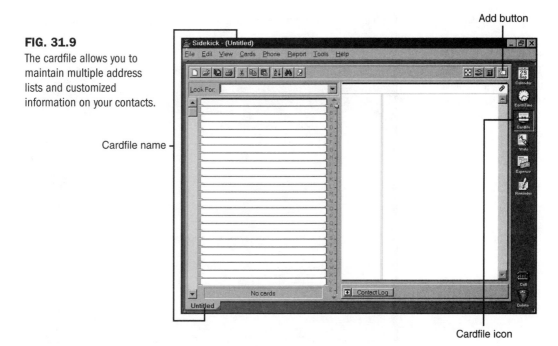

FIG. 31.9
The cardfile allows you to maintain multiple address lists and customized information on your contacts.

Cardfile name

Cardfile icon

Defining Cardfile Fields

Before you can start using your cardfile, you must define the cardfile fields. You can use the predefined sets of fields—called *templates*—that ship with Sidekick, and modify these by deleting ones you don't need and adding new ones that you do.

To define cardfile fields, do the following:

1. Choose Cards, Define Cardfile Fields. You see the Select Cardfile Template dialog box.

2. Select the template that best describes the type of cardfile you are creating from the Cardfile Template drop-down list. You see the fields listed in the dialog box, as shown in Figure 31.10.

FIG. 31.10
Templates allow you to create cardfiles that have the appropriate fields for different uses, such as a business address book, personal address book, and so on.

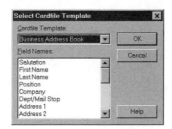

3. Click OK. You return to the main window, and you see the fields listed on the right side of the cardfile window, as shown in Figure 31.11.

FIG. 31.11

After you select a template, the cardfile fields appear in the right window.

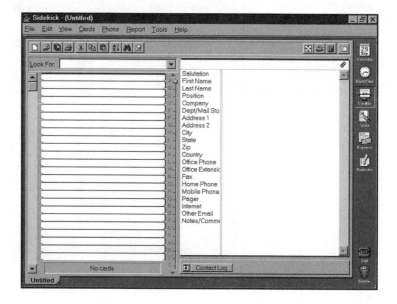

To modify the fields, do the following:

1. Choose Cards, Define Cardfile Fields. You see the Define Cardfile Fields dialog box shown in Figure 31.12.

FIG. 31.12

Once a template has been selected, you can add, modify, and remove fields as needed in the Define Cardfile Fields dialog box.

2. To delete a field, select it and click the Delete button.

3. To change the name of a field, select it, then type the new name in the Field Name box. The Change button becomes active. Click the Change button. The field name changes in the list of field names.

4. To add a field, select the field that the new field should appear before or after. Type the name of the new field, then click <u>A</u>dd to add the field after the selected one, or Add <u>B</u>efore to add it before the selected one.

5. To choose the field that the list will be sorted by, click the <u>S</u>ort By button. You see the Sort Cardfile dialog box shown in Figure 31.13. Use the double-left arrow to remove a field from the <u>S</u>ort By list, and the double-right arrow to add a field to the <u>S</u>ort By list. Click OK to return to the Define Cardfile Fields dialog box.

> **TIP** You can sort by up to three fields in case of ties. For instance, you can sort by last name, then by first name, then by middle initial.

6. Click OK twice when you are finished defining the cardfile fields, to return to the main Sidekick window.

FIG. 31.13
In the Sort Cardfile dialog box, you can sort the cardfile by up to three fields.

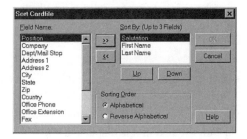

> **NOTE** You can also access the Sort Cardfile dialog box by clicking the Sort button from the main Cardfile window. ■

Adding, Finding, and Editing Contacts

 Once you have defined your cardfile fields, you can add contacts. To add a contact, click the Add button. You see the Add Cards dialog box shown in Figure 31.14. Fill out the information for your contact, and choose <u>A</u>dd. The contact is added to your cardfile.

Part
VI

Ch
31

FIG. 31.14

After clicking the Add button, you can add a new contact in the Add Cards dialog box.

To find the card of a specific individual, you can type their name in the Look For box located in the main window. As you type their name, the cardfile scrolls to display the first name that starts with the letters that you have typed.

You can also click a letter A through Z in the letter area to see all the names that start with the specified letter.

 Alternatively, if you want to find a card that has text in a different field than the primary sort field, click the Find button. You see the Find Text dialog box shown in Figure 31.15. Type the text you want to find, then select Cards as the area in which to search, and click Find. The first record with the text in it is displayed, and the text you searched on is selected. Click the Find button, then choose Find again to see the next record with the desired text in it.

FIG. 31.15

After clicking the Find button, the Find Text dialog box permits you to search for contacts that have specified text in any field.

Once you have selected a record, editing it is as easy as changing the information in the right-hand window of the cardfile using normal text-editing procedures.

Saving Your Cardfile

Once you have created your cardfile, you will want to save it periodically while you work with it to avoid data loss.

To save your cardfile, choose File, Save Cardfile. You see the Save As dialog box shown in Figure 31.16. Navigate to the folder you want to save the file in, enter a name in the File Name box, and click Save.

T I P The default folder for cardfiles may be the Windows/Desktop folder. If you save your cardfiles here, you will see an icon on your desktop for each cardfile you save in this folder. Many people don't like having too many icons on their desktop. If you're one of them, save the cardfiles to a different folder.

FIG. 31.16
Save your cardfile in the Save As dialog box as you would any other file in WordPerfect Suite applications.

To save all your cardfiles, choose File, Save All. All open cardfiles are saved.

 T I P Use short names for your cardfiles. The name appears on the cardfile tab, and if the name is too long, you can't see many cardfile tabs at once.

Using Multiple Cardfiles

You can create as many cardfiles as you like, because each one is saved as a separate file on the disk. Often, people have at least two cardfiles—one for personal addresses, and another for business contacts.

You can even use different templates and custom fields in each cardfile. This can be handy because personal contacts generally have fields such as spouse and children names that business contacts don't, and vice versa. Be aware, however, that if you use different names in your different cardfiles, the process of copying a card from one file to another will not be as automatic as if the cardfiles all have the same fields and same names.

Creating Multiple Cardfiles   To create multiple cardfiles, create additional cardfiles by choosing File, New Cardfile. You will see the Select Cardfile Template dialog box, and can choose the template and fields for your new cardfile as described earlier. You can also create new cardfiles by importing information from other programs, as described later. If you create new cardfiles while other cardfiles are open, you will see each cardfile as a tab at the bottom of the Sidekick window.

> **CAUTION**
>
> Be sure to save all cardfiles that are displayed before attempting to create a new one, because Sidekick only supports using one unnamed cardfile at a time.

Open additional cardfiles by clicking the Open button, then double-clicking the cardfile to be opened. Switch between cardfiles by clicking the appropriate tab.

Copying Cards Between Cardfiles   You can copy a card—a record or the information on one person—between two cardfiles whenever you need to. This can be handy when one person is both a personal friend and a business associate.

> **N O T E**   You cannot copy a card into a Microsoft Exchange card file—in other words, a card file that was imported from Microsoft Exchange. ▓

To copy a card from one cardfile to another, start to drag the name from the left-hand pane to the tab of the destination cardfile, and while you are dragging the name press and hold the Ctrl key, as shown in Figure 31.17.

FIG. 31.17
Copy a card by dragging it from the left pane to the tab of the destination cardfile.

> **T I P**   You can *move* a card from one cardfile to another by dragging it without holding down the Ctrl key.

If you have any field names that are not identical in the two cardfiles, you see the Match Cardfile Fields dialog box shown in Figure 31.18. Click the field name in the left list, and the associated field name in the right list, then click the Match button in the middle of the dialog box. Repeat this procedure for any other field names as needed, then click OK when you are done.

FIG. 31.18
Using the Match Cardfile Fields dialog box, you can match fields with different names to ensure that all information is transferred accurately.

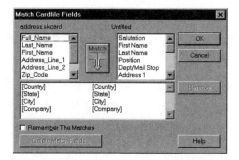

Part
VI

Ch
31

Importing Contacts

If you are already using another address book or contact management system, you can import your address information into Sidekick. In fact, you can automatically create a cardfile based on a Microsoft Exchange mailing list or the Corel Address Book 7.

Creating a Cardfile from Exchange or the Corel Address Book   If you are already using Exchange or the Corel Address Book, you can create a cardfile based on the contact information from these other applications. You can create a cardfile from the Frequent Contacts or My Addresses contact lists that are created automatically by Corel Address Book 7, as well as any other contact list that you have created in Address Book. Similarly, you can create a cardfile from the Schedule+ Address Book, or from your Postoffice Address List (if you are using Microsoft Mail in conjunction with Microsoft Exchange), or from any other address list maintained in Microsoft Exchange.

▶ **See** "Understanding How Address Book Works," **p. 606**

To create such a cardfile, open Sidekick and switch to the Cardfile view. Be sure that you have saved the cardfile that you are working with. Select File, MS Exchange Cardfile. Depending on your Windows configuration, you may see the Choose Profile dialog box. If so, choose Corel Settings and click OK. You see the MS Exchange Address Book dialog box shown in Figure 31.19. You will see different address lists in the list box, depending on whether you are using Exchange and/or Corel Address Book, and what address lists you have created in those applications.

FIG. 31.19
Create a read-only cardfile based on any address list you have created in Microsoft Exchange or Corel Address Book.

Select an address list, and click OK. You see a new cardfile tab at the bottom of the window, and the information in your Exchange or Address Book is displayed in the new cardfile. Save the cardfile as described earlier.

N O T E The new Sidekick cardfile is not linked to the old address list. Additions or changes you make to your Sidekick cardfile will not be reflected in the address book or address list in Microsoft Exchange or Corel Address Book and vice versa. ▮

Creating a Cardfile by Importing Information   If you are using another address book manager, such as Act, Organizer, or Ecco, you can import your address list into Sidekick as well.

The first step is to save your address list in comma separated value (CSV) format. (Microsoft calls this format Comma Delimited, but it's still the same format.) The commands you will use for this differ, depending on the program, but commonly there is a File, Export command. Occasionally, you will use File, Save As, and specify **CSV** as the Save As Type. Check the documentation for your particular program for details.

N O T E CSV format puts each record on a separate line, with each field contained in quotes and separated by a comma, as shown here:

"Smith","Joe","555-1212"

"Jones","Mary","666-1313"

The CSV format is a "lowest common denominator" that most address list programs can all export to and import from. ▮

Once you have saved your information as a CSV file, you can import it into Sidekick as follows:

1. Open Sidekick and switch to the Cardfile view.

2. Save any unsaved cardfiles.

3. Choose Tools, Import Cardfile. You see the Import Cardfile dialog box shown in Figure 31.20.

4. Choose Comma Delimited in the File Types box in the Source group box.

FIG. 31.20
Using the Import Cardfile dialog box, you can import cardfiles from popular software packages such as Act, Ecco, or Organizer.

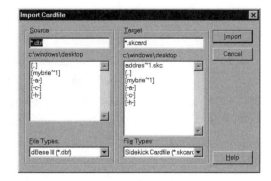

5. In the folder list box in the Source group, navigate to the folder containing the exported CSV file. Select it, then click Import. You see the Field Selection dialog box shown in Figure 31.21.

FIG. 31.21
In the Field Selection dialog box, select which fields from the CSV file you wish to import.

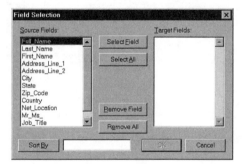

6. Choose the fields you want to import by double-clicking them, or by selecting them and clicking the Select Field button.

7. Choose the field by which you want to sort the new cardfile by selecting it, then clicking the Sort By button.

8. Click OK. The file is imported, and you see a dialog box asking if you want to import another file. Unless you do, choose No. You return to the Sidekick window.

9. Choose File, Open Cardfile, to open the new file, if desired.

Printing Your Cardfile

Sidekick allows you to print your cardfile in a number of ways. You can print cards, mailing labels, envelopes, or an address book. Each of these methods uses the metaphor of a label, where there is a defined printing area for each card, and you can specify which fields are to be printed in that area. In fact, the address book option allows you to print in a number of popular formats for Day-Timers, Day Runners, and the Franklin Planner.

Printing Cards   The Print Cards feature prints one or more of your cards on plain paper, in any of a number of formats you can specify. Print cards as follows:

1. Open Sidekick, switch to the Cardfile view, and select the appropriate cardfile tab.

2. If desired, select multiple cards to be printed by clicking the first one, then holding down the Ctrl key while you click additional ones. Alternatively, mark cards by selecting them, then choosing Cards, Mark Current Card.

3. Choose File, Print, Print Cards. You see the Print Cards dialog box shown in Figure 31.22.

FIG. 31.22

From the Print Cards dialog box you can print cards to plain paper in a variety of formats.

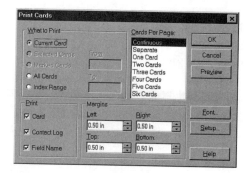

4. In the What to Print group, select the cards you want to print.

5. In the Print group, select what to print—the Card (information about the person), the Contact Log (a history of contacts with that person as described below), and/or Field Name (the printed name of each field).

6. In Cards Per Page, select the format you want to use. Click Preview to see how each format looks when printed.

7. In the Margins group, change the margin settings if desired.

8. Click OK. Your cards are printed.

Printing Labels   Use the Print Labels feature to print one or more of your cards on mailing labels, in a number of popular Avery formats, by following these steps:

1. Open Sidekick, switch to the Cardfile view, and select the appropriate cardfile tab.

2. If desired, select cards to be printed by clicking the first one, then holding down the Ctrl key while you click additional ones. Alternatively, mark cards by selecting them, then choosing Cards, Mark Current Card.

3. Choose File, Print, Print Labels. You see the Print Labels On dialog box shown in Figure 31.23, with four steps labeled.

4. In Step 1, Select Cards to Print, select the cards to be printed.

FIG. 31.23
You can print mailing labels in a variety of Avery formats using the Print Labels dialog box.

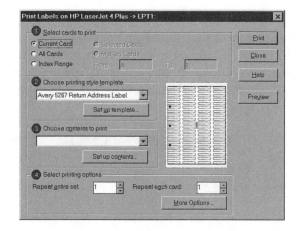

5. In Step 2, Choose Printing Style <u>T</u>emplate, select the type of Avery label you will be using from the Choose Printing Style Template box. If your label is not listed, you can click Set <u>U</u>p Template to define a new label style in the Set Up Template dialog box.

6. In Step 3, Choose C<u>o</u>ntents To Print, specify which fields are to be printed on each label. The first time you use this feature, no pre-defined set of fields exists. Click the Set Up Co<u>n</u>tents button. You see the Set Up Contents dialog box shown in Figure 31.24.

FIG. 31.24
Specify the fields to be printed on each label with the Set Up Contents dialog box.

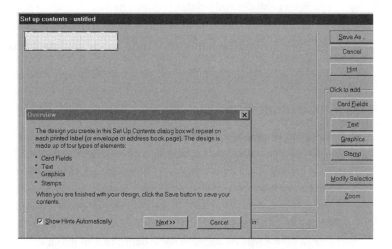

7. If you'd like instructions on the process, click <u>N</u>ext repeatedly in the Overview wizard that appears inside the Set Up Contents dialog box. You see a number of screens of information about the process.

8. To add fields, click the Card Fields button. You see the Edit Label Text dialog box shown in Figure 31.25. Add fields by double-clicking them, and add new lines, spaces, or commas by clicking the appropriate button. Click OK when you are finished. You return to the Set Up Contents dialog box, and you see the fields in the label preview area. Drag fields to move them, or right-click them to change their font.

FIG. 31.25

Add fields to your label with the Edit Label Text dialog box.

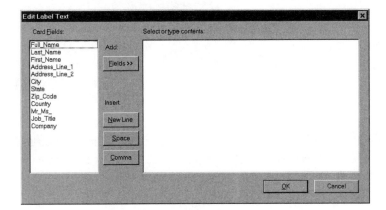

9. Click Save As. You see the Save As dialog box. Give your field set a name and click OK. You return to the Print Labels On dialog box.

10. Select any desired printing options in Step 4, such as how many times the set of labels should be printed, and how many times each label should be repeated.

11. Click the Preview button, if desired, to see how the labels will look, then click Print to print them.

TROUBLESHOOTING

Information on my labels is truncated; I can't see the last few letters of the city. Ensure that you have chosen a label that is sufficiently big enough to provide space for all fields. Right-click the city name field in the Set Up Contents dialog box, and choose a smaller font size to see the entire field contents.

Printing the Address Book   The Print Address Book feature permits you to print one or more of your cards on address book pages that fit into a variety of Day-Timer, Day-Runner, or Franklin Planner books. Printing address books is very similar to printing labels. Make address book printouts as follows:

1. Open Sidekick, switch to the Cardfile view, and select the appropriate cardfile tab.

2. If desired, select cards to be printed by clicking the first one, then holding down the Ctrl key while you click additional ones. Alternatively, mark cards by selecting them, then choosing Cards, Mark Current Card.

 TIP You can also mark cards by right-clicking them.

3. Choose File, Print, Print Address Book. You see the Print Address Book On dialog box shown in Figure 31.26, with four steps labeled.

FIG. 31.26
From the Print Address Book On dialog box, print an address book in a variety of daily planner formats.

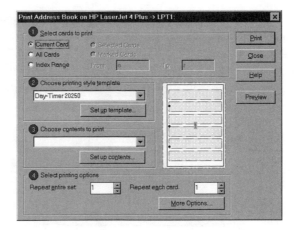

4. In Step 1, Select Cards to Print, select the cards to be printed.

5. In Step 2, select the type of address book you will be using from the Choose Printing Style Template box. If your address book is not listed, you can click Set Up Template to define a new address book style in the Set Up Template dialog box.

6. In Step 3, Choose Contents To Print, you will specify which fields are to be printed for each card. Use the same procedure for choosing contents as previously detailed in printing labels.

7. Select any desired printing options in Step 4, such as how many times the set of labels should be printed, and how many times each label should be repeated.

8. Click the Preview button, if desired, to see how the address book will look, then click Print to print it.

Printing Envelopes   You can also print envelopes with Sidekick. Again, printing envelopes is very similar to printing labels. Print envelopes as follows:

1. Open Sidekick, switch to the Cardfile view, and select the appropriate cardfile tab.

2. If desired, select cards to be printed by clicking the first one, then holding down the Ctrl key while you click additional ones. Alternatively, mark cards by selecting them, then choosing Cards, Mark Current Card, or right-click the cards to mark them.

3. Choose File, Print, Print Envelope. You see the Print Envelopes On dialog box shown in Figure 31.27, with four steps labeled.

FIG. 31.27

Print envelopes in a variety of envelope formats using the Print Envelopes On dialog box.

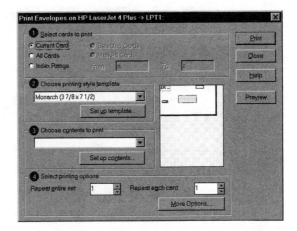

4. In Step 1, Select Cards to Print, select the cards to be printed.

5. In Step 2, select the type of envelope you will be printing on from the Choose Printing Style Template box. If your envelope size is not listed, you can click Set Up Template to define a new envelope size in the Set Up Template dialog box.

6. In Step 3, Choose Contents To Print, you will specify which fields are to be printed for each card. Use the same procedure for choosing contents as is detailed previously for printing labels.

7. Select any desired printing options in Step 4, such as how many times the set of labels should be printed, and how many times each label should be repeated.

8. Click the Preview button, if desired, to see how the envelopes will look, then click Print to print them.

Dialing a Number

Once you have created a cardfile, you can use it to automatically dial the number of a person you want to call.

N O T E This procedure assumes that you have a modem attached to your computer and set up in Windows 95. If you need to set up your modem, choose <u>P</u>hone, Set<u>u</u>p. ■

To use Sidekick as a phone dialer, first define which field contains the phone number you will use to dial your contact. From the Cardfile view, choose <u>P</u>hone, <u>S</u>peed Dial Field. You see the Setup Default Speed Dial Field dialog box shown in Figure 31.28. Highlight the field containing the phone number, and click OK.

FIG. 31.28

The Setup Default Speed Dial Field dialog box allows you to select the field containing the phone number you want to dial.

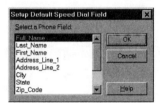

 To dial a number, select the name of the person you want to call, then click the Call icon, or choose <u>P</u>hone, <u>C</u>all. You see the Phone Dialer dialog box displayed in Figure 31.29.

FIG. 31.29

With the Phone Dialer dialog box, you can dial a person using the predefined field, or type in the number you want to dial.

 While you are on the phone, you can log the time of your call or make a note about it. To log the time of your call, click the Timer button. You see the time of your call in the dialog box. To log the call, write a summary note about the call's subject, then choose <u>L</u>og Notes. The time and duration of the call, along with the note, is kept in the call log file.

Part
VI

Ch
31

To see your call log for this contact, click the button at the bottom of the card (it says Contact Log by default, but will display the last item chosen). If needed, choose Contact Log from the pop-up menu, shown in Figure 31.30.

FIG. 31.30

Using the pop-up menu, you can view your call log to quickly review the subject of your last calls with the contact.

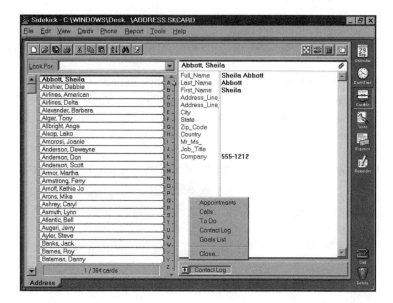

Click the up arrow to the left of this button. You see a window displaying a log of all your calls to this contact, as shown in Figure 31.31.

FIG. 31.31

The contact screen displays the call log.

Using the Calendar

The calendar is your "home base" for tracking day-to-day objectives—appointments you need to keep, things you need to do, and calls you need to make. The daily calendar shown in Figure 31.32 is especially handy, because it also displays your to do list and call list.

FIG. 31.32

The Daily Calendar also shows your To Do items and calls.

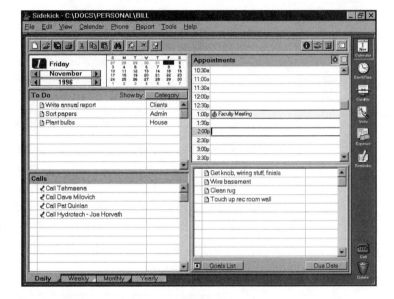

Part

VI

Ch

31

If you are only worried about yourself, you'll probably only need one calendar. You can, however, create any number of calendars, by choosing File, New Calendar, or clicking the New button. When you exit Sidekick or open a different calendar, you'll be prompted to save the new one.

You can easily switch between your calendars by choosing File, Open Calendar, and selecting the desired calendar from the Open dialog box. Unlike cardfiles and write files, however, only one calendar can be open at a time.

To move between dates in the calendar in the Daily view, click in any date displayed in the monthly calendar at the top left of the window. To move between months or years, click the arrows to the right and left of the month and year at the top left of the window.

Similarly, in the Weekly, Monthly, and Yearly views, there are arrows to the right and left of the current week, month, or year displayed at the top center of the calendar.

Scheduling Appointments

You may want to schedule an appointment with someone in your cardfile, or schedule an appointment that isn't linked to anyone in particular.

 T I P If you link an appointment to a person in your cardfile, that appointment is also listed in the contact manager, and you can quickly see a history of all your contacts with that person.

To create an appointment that is not linked to anyone, type the text of the appointment into the appropriate slot in the calendar. Alternatively, double-click the time to the left of the text box, when the mouse pointer looks like a hand over a mouse, to display the Appointment dialog box. You can enter information in more detail using this dialog box, as described later.

To schedule an appointment that is linked to a person in your cardfile, do the following:

1. If contact cards are not displayed at the bottom-right corner of your window, look at the button at the bottom of your window, next to the up arrow. If the button does not say Cards, click the button and select Cards from the pop-up menu.

2. If you are using several cardfiles, click the Cardfiles button in the Calendar window and select the appropriate cardfile from the list of cardfile files.

3. Click the up arrow next to the Cards button. You see a list of cards at the bottom of the screen, as shown in Figure 31.33.

FIG. 31.33

You can drag a contact from the card list to the calendar to create an appointment linked to that person.

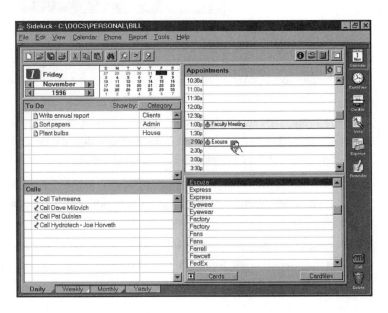

4. Scroll through the list of cards, if needed, then select the appropriate name.

5. Drag the name from the card list to the appropriate time on the calendar above it. Don't worry if the time isn't exactly right, you can fix it later. You see the person's name in the calendar.

6. Double-click the person's name in the calendar to edit the appointment. You see the Appointment dialog box shown in Figure 31.34.

7. If necessary, adjust the date of the appointment in the When box, and the beginning and ending time in the Start Time and End Time boxes. Choose whether or not to play an Alarm and, if so, how far in advance it should alert you using the Lead Time box. Mark the appointment Unconfirmed or Completed, as needed, and select whether or not to Enter In the Contact Log.

N O T E You can also create recurring appointments and predefined activities in the Appointment dialog box, as described next. ■

FIG. 31.34
Edit the appointment in the Appointment dialog box.

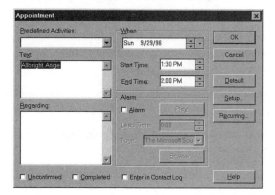

Modifying Appointments

To modify an appointment, you double-click it in the Daily view. You see the Appointment dialog box. Edit the text or time of the appointment as needed.

You can also schedule recurring appointments from this dialog box, or create predefined activities that allow you to quickly enter common text for your appointments.

Scheduling Recurring Appointments To schedule an appointment that recurs regularly, create it as you normally would, then access the Appointment dialog box by double-clicking the appointment. Then do the following:

1. Choose Recurring. You see the Recurring Appointment dialog box shown in Figure 31.35.

FIG. 31.35

The Recurring Appointment dialog box permits you to schedule recurring appointments for meetings that happen regularly, like staff meetings or board meetings.

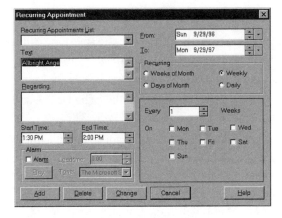

2. Edit the Text of the appointment. Make any notes in the Regarding box, if needed, and alter the time of the meeting if necessary.

3. Enter recurring information in the Recurring group. The specific options you have depend on which type of recurring appointment it is:

   - Choose Weeks of Month if the appointment is on a specific day, but only on certain weeks, such as the second Monday of the month, or the first Tuesday and Thursday of the month.

   - Choose Weekly if the appointment is on the same day or days each week, such as every Friday.

   - Choose Days of Month if the appointment is on a specific date, such as the 15th of each month.

   - Choose Daily if the appointment happens every day, every fifth day, and so on.

4. Select any additional options that are specific to the type of recurring appointment you have chosen.

5. Click Add to add this appointment to the list of recurring appointments. Add additional recurring appointments or click OK to exit back to the Appointments dialog box.

Creating Predefined Activities   You can also create phrases of text that can be combined with names from your contact list to make your appointment subjects more meaningful, like "Meeting with John Smith," "Performance Review with John Smith," or "Supervision with John Smith." These predefined activities combine a phrase that you enter with the field names you want to use from the cardfile.

You can create a predefined activity from the main window or from the Appointment dialog box. From the main window, choose Calendar, Personal List Setup, Predefined

Activities. Alternatively, from the Appointment dialog box, choose Setup. You see the Personal List Setup dialog box shown in Figure 31.36.

FIG. 31.36
Using the Personal List Setup dialog box, you can create predefined activities that make the subject of your appointments more descriptive.

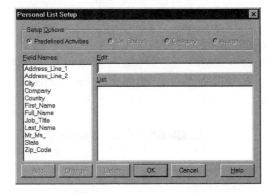

To create a new activity, type the text in the Edit box, such as **Supervision with**. Enter a field you want to use by double-clicking it. Remember to insert spaces and commas as needed to make the activity readable. Choose Add to add it to the list, like the one shown in Figure 31.37.

FIG. 31.37
Predefined activities listed in the Personal List Setup dialog box combine text you enter with fields in your cardfile.

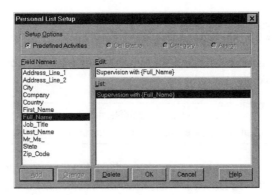

Once you have added activities to the list, you can select them and choose Delete to remove them, or select them and edit them in the Edit box, then click Change to modify them. Click OK to exit the Personal List Setup dialog box.

To use a predefined activity, click the correct person's name in the Cardfile list. Double-click the appropriate time in the calendar. You see the Appointment dialog box. Select Predefined Activities. Activities you have listed appear in the drop-down list box. Choose the one you want to use; you only see field names, and not the actual name of the contact. Click OK. You return to the main window and see the text of the predefined activity, including information from the cardfile, in the appointment.

TIP There are two small buttons above the calendar. The one that looks like a clock causes all time slots to be displayed, even if they have no appointments. The other one that represents an appointment book causes only the appointments themselves to be displayed.

N O T E You can create multi-day appointments to record vacations or business trips by choosing Calendar, Multi-Day Event. You see the Multi-Day Event dialog box in Figure 31.38.

You can also mark holidays and other similar events by choosing Calendar, Special Day. This can be a handy way to remember birthdays and anniversaries. ▮

FIG. 31.38
Use the Multi-Day Event
dialog box for entering
conferences, business trips,
or vacations.

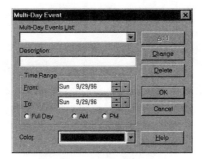

Using the Task and Call Lists

Create tasks and list calls you have to make from the Daily Calendar view, in a similar fashion to making appointments.

 TIP If you link a task or call to a person in your cardfile, that item is also listed in the contact manager, and you can quickly see a history of all your contacts with that person.

To create a to do item or a call that is not linked to anyone, type the text of the item into an empty line of the To Do list or Calls list. Alternatively, double-click the right column of the list to display the To Do or Call dialog box. You can enter information in more detail using these dialog boxes, as described next.

To create a to do item or call that is linked to a person in your cardfile, do the following:

1. If contact cards are not displayed at the bottom-right corner of your window, look at the button at the bottom of your window, next to the up arrow. If the button does not say Cards, click the button and select Cards from the pop-up menu.

2. If you are using several cardfiles, click the Cardfiles button in the Calendar window and select the appropriate cardfile from the list of cardfile files.

3. Click the up arrow next to the Cards button. You see a list of cards at the bottom of the screen, as shown in Figure 31.39.

FIG. 31.39
You can drag a contact from the Cards list to the To Do list or Calls list to create an item linked to that person.

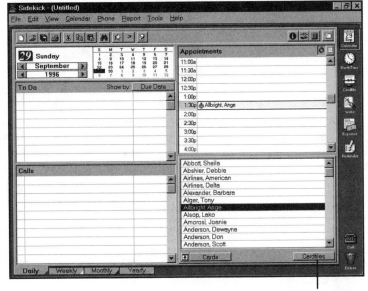

Cardfile button

4. Scroll through the list of cards, if needed, then select the appropriate name.

5. Drag the name from the card list to an empty line in the to do list or calls list. You see the person's name in the list.

6. Double-click the right-hand column to edit the item. You see the To Do dialog box shown in Figure 31.40 (or the Call dialog box, as appropriate).

FIG. 31.40
Edit the task in the To Do dialog box.

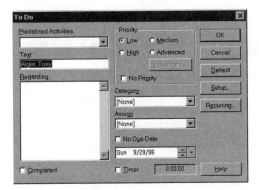

7. If you want, choose Predefined Activities and select a pre-defined activity from the list. (Setting up pre-defined activities is described earlier.)

8. Edit the options for the to do item. These include the priority of the item, its category, who it's assigned to, and its due date. You can also mark it Completed or start a Timer for the item.

   Alternatively, if the item is a call, edit options including the Call Status, whether it is Completed, and whether it is Urgent.

 N O T E   If you want to use categories or assign to do items to other people, or if you want to create call status categories, you must set up the appropriate items. Do this by choosing Setup. You see the Personal List Setup dialog box. Add categories or people in the same way you add predefined activities, described earlier. ■

9. If it is a recurring event, click the Recurring button and set the options for recurring events. (These options were described previously.)

10. Click OK to return to the main calendar window.

T I P   You can also add an appointment, task, or call from the calendar by clicking the Add button, and choosing Appointment, Call, or To Do.

N O T E   You can also create a special kind of to do item, called a Goal, for long-term projects that you need to do someday, but you don't want to have cluttering up your day-to-day to do list. Create a goal by choosing Calendar, Goal List. You see the Goals dialog box, which is similar to the To Do dialog box. Enter a goal the same way you enter a to do item.

To move a goal to the to do list, select Goals List as the item that should be displayed at the bottom of the calendar, then drag the goal to the to do list. ■

Using the Sidekick Contact Manager

If you have linked your appointments, tasks, and calls to individuals in your card file, you can quickly see a contact history for that individual.

1. Select the appropriate person from the contact list by clicking on them.

 2. Click the Contact Manager button. You see the Contact Manager dialog box shown in Figure 31.41.

3. Choose the Date Range as Today, Tomorrow, This Week, Next Week, This Month, Next Month, or Pick a Date Range.

4. You see the contacts displayed in the contact manager.

FIG. 31.41
The Contact Manager dialog box displays all your contacts with the selected individual.

5. View your contact list, or select an activity and choose <u>G</u>o To to switch to that activity. Choose Close when you are finished.

Using the Reminder View

While the Contact Manager selects all your contacts for a specific person, the Reminder view selects all your obligations (appointments, tasks, and calls). To see your reminders, click the Reminder button at the right side of the Sidekick window. You see the Reminder view shown in Figure 31.42.

FIG. 31.42
Reminders consolidate your appointments, tasks, and calls.

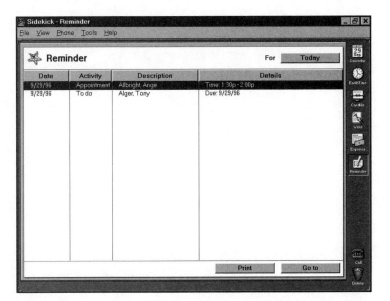

Choose the range of days for which you'd like to see reminders by clicking the For button in the upper-right corner, then choosing a range of days. You see all your upcoming obligations in one place. Double-click any item to go to that day's calendar.

N O T E Sidekick also offers a complete set of reports from the Report menu available in the Cardfile and Calendar views. These include reports on your cardfile, calendar, to do list, and contact log. You can even choose Report, Free Time to print a report showing which of your time slots are free. ▓

CHAPTER 32

Using Dashboard

Dashboard is a utility that enhances your control over Windows 95. If you're a person who likes to drive a stick shift because you really feel like you're *driving* the car rather than being driven, then Dashboard is for you. In fact, the name Dashboard refers to the dashboard of a car, with its gauges, instruments, and controls. ∎

View system resources

Learn how to use Dashboard to see available memory, disk space, and system resources.

Set alarms

Find out how to use Dashboard as an alarm clock, or to run applications at preset times.

Create virtual desktops

See how Dashboard's Extended Screens feature allows you to create up to nine virtual Windows desktops.

Organize applications

Understand how to use Dashboard to organize your applications into meaningful groups, and access them with one or two mouse clicks.

Understanding Dashboard

Dashboard 95 is a Windows 95 utility program created by Starfish Software (who also makes Sidekick 95), and bundled with Corel WordPerfect Suite 7.

Dashboard is designed to give you immediate information about how Windows 95 is running, and to provide instant control over both Windows 95 and your application. Like the dashboard of a car, Dashboard provides you with gauges and controls that let you monitor and operate your computer. Unlike your car's dashboard, however, Dashboard can be custom-built to display as simple or as complex a set of gauges and controls as you like.

N O T E The control panel is referred to as "the Dashboard," rather than "the Dashboard window" or "the Dashboard dialog box." This assists you in furthering the metaphor of the Dashboard as the Windows control panel. ■

To start Dashboard, choose Start, Corel WordPerfect Suite 7, Accessories, Dashboard. You see the default Dashboard, like the one shown in Figure 32.1. It consists of three types of controls:

- ■ *Menus.* Three pull-down menus provide access to different commands.
- ■ *Panels.* Controls on the Dashboard are grouped into panels. These panels can be "snapped" on or off the Dashboard, displayed or hidden, or even resized on the Dashboard.

N O T E Snapping a panel off the Dashboard means making it a floating window, independent of the Dashboard. The other panels of the Dashboard then expand to take up the space left by the snapped off panel. Snapping it on the Dashboard is returning the panel onto the Dashboard. ■

- ■ *Buttons.* The buttons at the right and left of the Dashboard allow you to snap panels on and off the Dashboard, launch programs, and access the Customize dialog box.

Menus

FIG. 32.1
The default Dashboard has panels, menus, and buttons that allow you to monitor and control Windows and your applications.

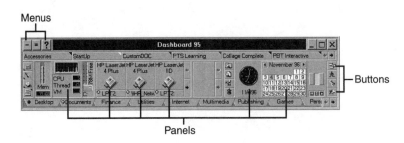

Panels

Learning About Dashboard Panels

Dashboard panels are groups of controls that enable you to customize Windows and perform common tasks. Panels are the heart of Dashboard. These panels can be contained in the Dashboard, or separated as separate windows. Separating panels is called "snapping" them off the Dashboard, and can be done by right-clicking a panel, then choosing Snap Off from the QuickMenu. To understand how Dashboard works, let's look at each panel separately.

Quick Launch Panel

The Quick Launch panel allows you to quickly access and run your frequently used applications. You can use it while it is snapped onto the Dashboard, or you can snap it off to see it as a floating palette of program icons by right-clicking in the panel and choosing Snap Off.

When you first install Dashboard, the program looks for applications on your computer, and inserts shortcuts to them in groups such as Desktop, Documents, Multimedia, Finance, Utilities, Games, Internet, Publishing, Tools, and Perfect Office.

You see these groups as tabs at the bottom of your Dashboard, as shown in Figure 32.2.

Part

VI

Ch

32

FIG. 32.2
The tabs at the bottom of the Dashboard allow you to select program groups for the Quick Launch panel.

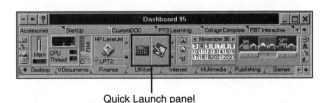

Quick Launch panel

To launch a program, click the appropriate program group tab. You see the buttons for the applications in that program group in the Quick Launch panel. Click the appropriate button to launch the application.

To put a program icon on the Quick Launch panel, click the tab for the program group you want to add the program to. You see icons for the applications in that program group in the Quick Launch panel. Click the menu at the top of the Dashboard that contains the program you want to add. When you see the program on the menu, drag its icon from the menu to the Quick Launch panel.

T I P
You can also drag and drop items from the Windows 95 desktop onto the Quick Launch panel.

You can customize the display and options of the Quick Launch panel as follows:

1. Right-click the panel, then choose Customize. You see the Customize dialog box shown in Figure 32.3.

FIG. 32.3
You can use the Customize dialog box to modify the display of the Quick Launch panel, as well as set the options for the programs it can launch.

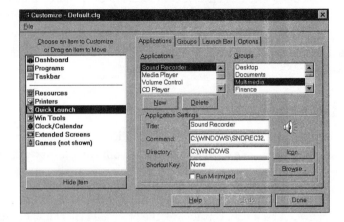

2. To add or delete applications from a program group, ensure that the Applications tab is selected.

3. Choose the appropriate group in the Groups list box, then select options as follows:

   • To delete an application, select it in the Applications list box and choose Delete.

   • To modify an application, select it and change options in the Title, Command, Directory, or Shortcut Key text boxes. You can use the Browse button to locate an application.

   • To add a new application, choose New, then fill in appropriate values in the Title, Command, Directory, and Shortcut Key text boxes.

   • To change an application's icon, click the Icon button, and select from available icons.

   • Choose Run Minimized if you want to have the application run in the background.

4. To make modifications to the program groups, click the Groups tab. You see the Groups tab shown in Figure 32.4.

   • To delete a group, select it in the Groups list box and choose Delete.

   • To add a new group, choose New and specify a name for the new group.

   • To rename a group, select it and enter the new name in the Name box.

   • To display or hide the three default groups (Desktop Tab, Documents Tab, and Layouts Tab), mark the appropriate check box(es).

FIG. 32.4
Use the Groups tab in the Customize dialog box to add, delete, or change the name of program groups.

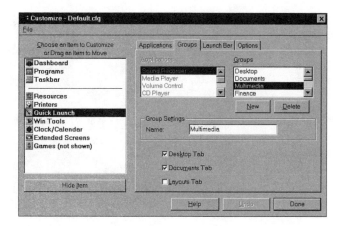

5. Use the Launch Bar tab to determine how the Launch Bar will be displayed when it is snapped off the Dashboard. Use the Options tab to specify the button style, and how groups are sorted.

6. Click Done when you are finished.

 TIP You must snap off the Launch Bar before most options on the Launch Bar tab become active. If the Launch Bar isn't snapped off, most options are dimmed.

Win Tools Panel

The Win Tools panel provides instant access to your most used Windows utilities. By default, these are Windows Explorer, Find Files, Control Panel, and Task Manager.

You see the four buttons comprising this panel in Figure 32.5.

FIG. 32.5
The buttons in the middle of the Dashboard provide access to common Windows utilities.

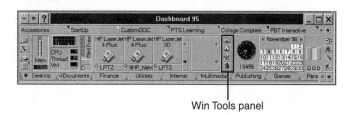

Win Tools panel

NOTE Depending on your screen resolution, you may see either three or four tools in the Win Tools panel. ▨

You can choose which tools appear on the Win Tools panel by right-clicking the panel, and choosing Customize. You see the Customize dialog box shown in Figure 32.6.

FIG. 32.6

Use the Customize dialog box to choose the four Windows utilities that should appear in the Win Tools panel.

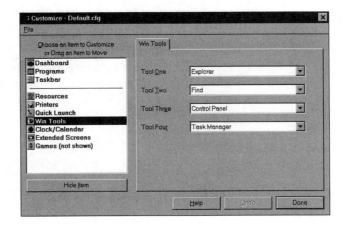

For Tool One through Tool Four, use the drop-down list box, and choose the utility that should be associated with the button in the Win Tools panel. Click Done when you are finished.

Resources Panel

Have you ever found that Windows 95 was slowing down, and wondered exactly which application might be causing the difficulty? The Resources panel can help you keep track of exactly what's going on with your system.

By default, the Resources panel appears as shown in Figure 32.7. The Resources panel includes the following:

- *Resource Gauge.* The Resource gauge shows how much memory is available in your system, both digitally and in a bar gauge. Lack of available memory is the most frequent reason that applications terminate abnormally.

- *CPU Meter.* The CPU meter is a rolling bar chart showing what percent of CPU processing power is being used. The current percent is also displayed digitally. You also see a digital count of threads—that is, simultaneous activities your CPU is engaging in.

- *Drive Watch.* This shows the amount of free disk space you have, both digitally and with a bar gauge.

You can see more information on your resource usage by double-clicking the Resource Panel. When you double-click the CPU Meter, you see the Resources dialog box shown in Figure 32.8. You see different resource utilization information, depending on which item you select to view:

CPU meter — Drive Watch

FIG. 32.7

The Resources panel keeps track of your available memory, CPU use, and free disk space.

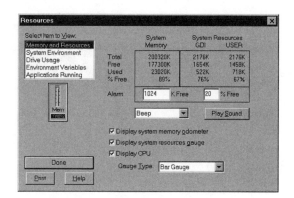

Resource gauge — Odometer

FIG. 32.8

The Resources dialog box provides more details on resource usage than you see in the Resource panel.

- *Memory and Resources.* View information on system memory, as well as GDI and User resources being utilized. You can specify that an alarm sounds when less than a predefined amount of memory is free by choosing the minimum amount of memory (K free) or percent of memory (% free). You can also specify whether to display the system memory odometer (digital part of the Resource Gauge), system resources gauge (bar chart of the Resource Gauge), and CPU (CPU meter). Finally, you can determine whether the memory gauge should display as a bar gauge, a fuel meter, or resources. If you choose resources, you see the percent of Memory, GDI, and User resources that are free.

- *System Environment.* This option does not change the way the Resource panel displays, but shows you essential elements of your system, such as the main processor type, display type, language, network, operating system, and so on.

- *Drive Usage.* This option shows how much space is available on each drive, and how much is free. You can also choose whether or not the drive watch window should display in the Resource panel. Remove or add the drive watch window by clicking the appropriate drive in the list box, then click the Remove or Add button.

- *Environment Variables.* This lists the DOS and Windows environment variables that are defined.

■ *Applications Running.* This option lists the applications that are currently running, along with their process priority, heap size, and the name of the executable application.

When you are finished, click Done. You return to the main Dashboard.

Clock/Calendar Panel

The Clock/Calendar panel looks by default like the one shown in Figure 32.9.

FIG. 32.9
The clock/calendar panel shows the time as well as the current month's calendar.

You may not see the Clock/Calendar panel when you open Dashboard, because if there is not enough room to see all panels, the clock/calendar will not display. If you want to see it, snap off other panels until you see the Clock/Calendar panel by right-clicking the panel you want to snap off, then choosing Snap Off.

To see more clock/calendar options, right-click the Clock/Calendar panel. You see a pop-up shortcut menu. Options include:

■ Digital changes the clock to a digital clock; the pop-up menu then shows the Analog option that changes the clock back to analog.

■ Hide Clock and Hide Calendar remove the display of the appropriate item; the menu item then changes to Show Clock and Show Calendar.

■ Change Date/Time allows you to change the system date and/or time.

■ Customize reveals the Customize dialog box shown in Figure 32.10. Use this dialog box to change the default display preferences for your clock and calendar.

You can also use the Clock/Calendar panel to set alarms. Double-click the Clock/Calendar panel. You see the Clock Alarms dialog box, which lists all alarms you have set. Choose Add. You see the Alarm Settings dialog box shown in Figure 32.11.

Specify the date and time for your alarm, and whether to play a chime for the alarm. You can even identify a program that should be run at the specified time, such as a backup or a fax program. Click OK twice to close the two dialog boxes when you are finished.

FIG. 32.10
Use the Customize dialog
box to change the default
preferences for the clock
and calendar.

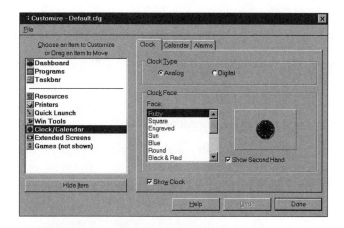

FIG. 32.11
Use the Alarm Settings
dialog box to set alarms with
Dashboard and remind you
of things you need to do.

Part
VI

Ch
32

Printers Panel

The Printers panel allows you to view the status of the printers and fax drivers attached to
your system, and to set printer options.

To display the printers more visibly, right-click the Printers panel and choose Snap Off.
You see the Printers panel separated from the Dashboard, as shown in Figure 32.12.

 You can also click the Snap Off Printers button at the left of the Dashboard.

FIG. 32.12

You can display the Printers panel separate from the rest of the Dashboard.

You can control printing functions in several ways using this panel:

- To print a file, drag its icon from Windows Explorer to any printer icon in the Printer panel. The file is printed on the selected panel. Similarly, if you want to fax a file, drag it to a fax driver icon in the Printer panel. If you want to create an Envoy document, drag the file to the Envoy printer icon in the Printer panel.

- To set a printer as the default printer, click the printer "port" at the bottom of the printer icon. A green dot denotes the selected printer.

- To set printer properties, click the icon for the printer. You see the Properties dialog box for the selected printer, like the one for the HP LaserJet 4 Plus shown in Figure 32.13.

FIG. 32.13

Set printer properties with the Properties dialog box.

You can also set defaults for the way printers are displayed in the Printer panel. To do so, right-click the Printer panel, and choose Customize. You see the Customize dialog box shown in Figure 32.14. From this dialog box, you can:

- Hide the display of a printer by selecting it, then clicking Hide Printer.

- Change the description of a printer by selecting it, then typing desired text in the Description box.

FIG. 32.14
Customize the display of printers with the Customize dialog box.

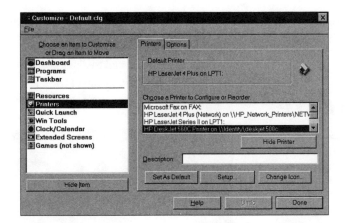

Extended Screens Panel

The Extended Screens panel is one of Dashboard's most exciting features. It provides you with three or more virtual Windows desktops (or "extended screens") that you can alternate between. You will see the standard icons on each desktop, as well as any applications that you define as "sticky" applications—ones that should appear on every desktop.

In this way, you can have one application or a group of applications in each virtual desktop, and are able to alternate between the different screens using hotkeys.

The Extended Screens panel can be displayed in compact or full size. To alternate between them, right-click the panel, then choose Compact Size or Full Size.

To alternate between extended screens, click the extended screen you want to access in the Extended Screens panel shown in Figure 32.15.

T I P The Extended Screens panel can show three icons or, if the Dashboard is displayed in Compact Size, three bars.

FIG. 32.15
Alternate between extended screens by clicking the screen you want to access in the Extended Screens panel.

Extended Screens panel

You can easily launch a program in an extended screen by dragging its icon from the Quick Launch panel to the appropriate extended screen icon. When you switch to the screen you dragged the icon to, you will see the program running in that screen.

Part
VI

Ch
32

To maximize the use of the extended screens, however, you will want to customize them. To do so:

1. Right-click the Extended Screens panel to display the shortcut menu, then choose Customize. You see the Screens tab of the Customize dialog box shown in Figure 32.16.

FIG. 32.16
Choose the number of screens and specify their appearance in the Screens tab of the Customize dialog box.

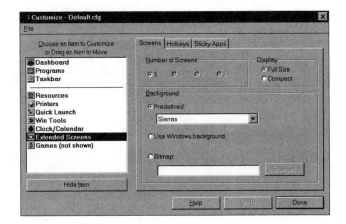

2. Choose options as follows:

   • Choose the number of extended screens as 3, 5, 7, or 9.

 T I P You can only choose 3 extended screens when you are displaying them in Full Size.

   • Choose whether you want to display the extended screens in Full Size or Compact format.

   • Select a background from the predefined backgrounds supplied with Dashboard, the default Windows background, or specify a bitmap image to use.

3. Click the Hotkeys tab to define hotkeys. You see the Hotkeys tab shown in Figure 32.17.

4. Type a number or letter for the hotkey in the appropriate Screen # box. The number or letter will be combined with Alt and Ctrl to create the hotkey. In other words, if you type the number 1 in the Screen #1 box, then you can switch to extended screen 1 by pressing Ctrl+Alt+1. Use the Delete or Backspace key to set the hotkey to None.

FIG. 32.17
Use the Hotkeys tab of the Customize dialog box to define a hotkey for each extended screen.

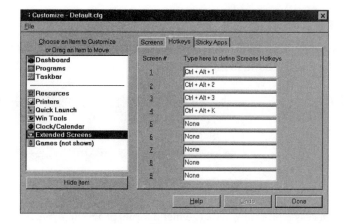

5. You can define any open application as a sticky application—an application that will appear in each extended screen. To do so, ensure that the application you would like to define as a sticky application is open, then select the Sticky Apps tab shown in Figure 32.18. Your currently selected Sticky Apps are listed in the text box.

6. To add a new one, choose <u>A</u>dd. All your currently open applications are listed. Click the one you want to define as a Sticky App, then choose OK.

7. Click Done when you are finished customizing your extended screens.

FIG. 32.18
Sticky Apps are applications that appear in every extended screen.

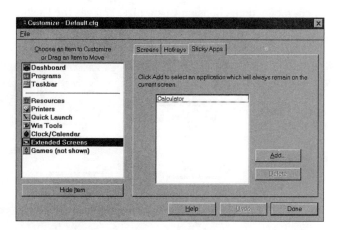

Once you have customized your extended screens, you can open an application or a set of applications in each one, then switch between the extended screens by pressing the appropriate hotkey.

TIP You can save frequently used combinations of extended screens as a layout, and even define a layout that will be loaded automatically when you start Dashboard as discussed in the section "Creating Layouts" later in this chapter.

Programs Panel

The Programs panel consists of a series of menus at the top of the Dashboard, under the Title Bar, as shown in Figure 32.19.

FIG. 32.19
The Programs panel of the Dashboard provides all the functionality of Windows 3.1 program groups.

Programs panel

Snap On Programs Panel button

To access a program, click the menu for its program group, then pick the desired program from the drop-down menu. To display a group in its own window, click the group to open its menu, then click in the group name at the top of the menu to open it as a stand-alone window.

As with other panels, you can snap it on or off the Dashboard with the appropriate button on the Dashboard by right-clicking it, then choosing Snap On or Snap Off.

To customize your Programs panel, do the following:

1. Access the Customize dialog box by right-clicking the panel to display the short-cut menu, then choosing Customize. You see the Customize dialog box shown in Figure 32.20.

FIG. 32.20
The Customize dialog box allows you to change the appearance of the Program panel, or to add, delete, and rearrange groups.

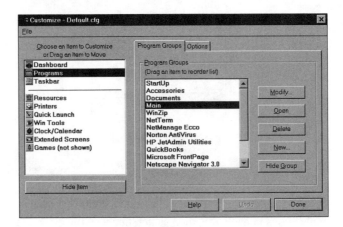

2. Choose options including:

- Drag a group to change its position in the list.

- Delete a group by selecting it, then clicking Delete.

- Create a new group by choosing <u>N</u>ew, then entering a Group <u>D</u>escription and choosing a color.

- Hide a group by selecting it, then choosing Hide <u>G</u>roup. Make it visible again by selecting it and choosing Show <u>G</u>roup.

- Sort the groups by clicking the Options tab, then choosing Sort <u>A</u>lphabetically or Sort by Co<u>l</u>or.

- Reread the groups from the Windows system files by clicking the Options tab, then choosing Reread Groups from <u>S</u>ystem.

3. Choose Done when you are finished.

Creating Layouts

Layouts are arrangements of application windows that you can save in Dashboard. Layouts enable you to customize Windows to the way you work. For instance, one task you might do during the week is financial, and you might want to have Quicken and Corel Quattro Pro open in tiled windows. At another time, you might be writing, and need to have easy access to Explorer and Corel WordPerfect. Throughout the day, you might want to have Sidekick open in another extended screen where it's out of the way, but easily accessible.

Using layouts, you can save these arrangements of windows. Dashboard will open and size the windows as you have specified in the layout. You can even specify one layout as an arrangement that should be used when you start Dashboard. If you put Dashboard in the Startup group, then when you start your computer, your most-used applications will open in the appropriate extended screens.

 To create a layout, open the appropriate applications and arrange them in extended windows the way you want them. Click the Layouts button on the Dashboard, and choose <u>S</u>ave Layout. You see the Save Layout dialog box shown in Figure 32.21 that lists open applications. Enter a name for the layout. If necessary, select an open application and choose <u>D</u>elete to delete it, or <u>E</u>dit to open the Edit Layout dialog box allowing you to modify the application's name, command line, working directory, parameters, or window size. If you want, you can click the L<u>o</u>ad Layout on Startup check box to have the layout automatically load when you start Dashboard and open the appropriate programs.

Part

VI

Ch

32

FIG. 32.21

Open applications and arrange them as you want, then save them in a layout using the Save Layout dialog box.

You can also manage the layouts you create. To do so, click the Layouts button on the Dashboard, and choose Manage Layouts. You see the Manage Layouts dialog box shown in Figure 32.22.

FIG. 32.22

The Manage Layouts dialog box enables you to create new layouts of application windows.

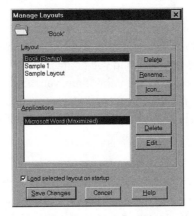

Select options including:

- To delete a layout, select it and choose Delete.
- To rename a layout, select it and choose Rename, then enter a new name for the layout.
- To change a layout's icon, select it and choose Icon, then select a new icon from the list of icons you see.
- To edit the contents of a layout, select it. You see the applications included in the layout in the Applications box. Select the application to be changed, then choose Delete to delete it, or Edit to modify its name, command line, working directory, parameters, or window size.

Layouts you create will appear at the bottom of the shortcut menu that you see when you click the Layouts button. To select a layout, click the Layouts button, then choose the appropriate layout from the bottom of the shortcut menu.

Using Dashboard Run

Dashboard Run provides similar functionality to the Windows Run feature you access by clicking Start, Run. You can use Dashboard Run to enter DOS commands or run DOS programs.

 To access Dashboard Run, click the Dashboard Run button. You see the Dashboard Run dialog box. Type the desired command in the Command Line box and click Run. You see the results in the lower text box. For instance, the result of several DOS commands are shown in the Dashboard Run dialog box shown in Figure 32.23. Click Done when you are finished.

FIG. 32.23
The Dashboard Run feature allows you to run DOS commands, and shows you the results in the Dashboard Run dialog box.

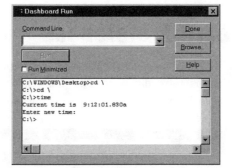

Using the Dashboard Taskbar

The Dashboard taskbar provides information on currently running applications, and allows you to switch to them by clicking them (as does the Windows 95 taskbar). Additional information provided on applications includes:

 TIP If the Dashboard taskbar is not visible, click the Snap On Taskbar button at the bottom left of the Dashboard.

- Find out information on a task by right-clicking the taskbar, then choosing Tasks. You see the Dashboard Task Manager dialog box shown in Figure 32.24. Select a task and choose Task Info to see information on the selected task.

- Snap off the taskbar using the Snap Off Taskbar button to create a floating taskbar. Right-click the floating taskbar and choose Left, Right, Top, or Bottom to dock it to an edge.

- Choose whether to show icons and/or labels in the buttons by right-clicking the taskbar, and choosing Customize from the shortcut menu. Choose the Settings tab, then set options for Button Style and Button Options.

FIG. 32.24
Use Dashboard Task
Manager to end tasks
or see information on
selected tasks.

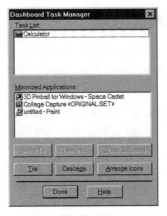

Setting Dashboard Preferences

To set overall options for Dashboard, right-click in the Dashboard Title Bar and choose Customize. You see the Customize dialog box shown in Figure 32.25. Some of the most commonly used options include:

FIG. 32.25
Set overall Dashboard
options by right-clicking in
the Title Bar and choosing
Customize to display the
Customize dialog box.

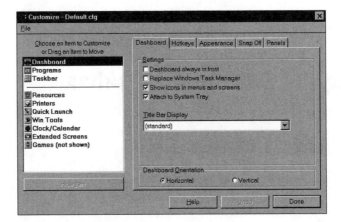

■ Choose whether the Dashboard Title Bar should display just the Dashboard title (standard), the clock/calendar information, or system resource use information.

TIP Because the clock is already on the Windows taskbar, this is usually sufficient. Displaying system resources on the Dashboard Title Bar can save valuable space on the Dashboard.

■ Click Attach to System Tray to have the Dashboard icon migrate to the system tray on the taskbar when the Dashboard is minimized.

- In the Hotkeys tab, you can specify a hotkey that will restore the Dashboard when it is minimized, giving you quick access to its features. Additionally, you can specify a hotkey for Windows Explorer and for Dashboard Run.
- Use the Appearance tab to specify colors and fonts for the Dashboard.
- The Snap Off tab permits you to identify which (if any) panels should be snapped off by default.
- The Panels tab displays the panels that are in use by Dashboard. If there are panels you do not use, you can remove them from the panels in use list, saving Dashboard space.

Part
VI

Ch
32

Integrating and Customizing Corel WordPerfect Suite 7

CHAPTER 33

Integrating Your Work with QuickTasks

Use QuickTasks

Learn to use QuickTasks to perform over 60 common office and home functions.

Manage QuickTasks

See how to create categories for your QuickTasks, and move or copy your QuickTasks to the categories you prefer.

Create QuickTasks

Learn how to easily create a QuickTask that integrates Corel WordPerfect, Presentations, and Quattro Pro.

Part of what makes Corel WordPerfect Suite 7 the "perfect way to work" is its task-orientation. For you, this means that as you use Corel WordPerfect Suite 7, you should be able to focus on getting your work done, rather than on learning specific applications. Instead of focusing on features of Corel WordPerfect or Quattro Pro, for example, you can think about the job, or *task*, that you need to accomplish.

The principle feature that integrates applications in the Corel WordPerfect Suite is QuickTasks. Corel WordPerfect Suite 7 contains over 60 QuickTasks that automate many of your day-to-day tasks.

▶ **See** "Using QuickTasks," **p. 44** ◼

Learning About QuickTasks

At the heart of Corel WordPerfect Suite 7 is the concept that a suite is more than just a box full of otherwise unrelated products. Suite products need to be *integrated*. In the past, integration meant more work for you. Integrated products could "talk" together, but it was up to you to start the conversation.

Moderating the conversation required you to learn the nitty-gritty details of cross-application communication, such as DDE, OLE 2.0, or in-place editing. Just the terminology is enough to make a person search for the Excedrin bottle.

While most of us enjoy technology, we *use* software to get our work done, not simply for technology's sake. QuickTasks reflect your need to do work rather than merely play with technology.

So what is a QuickTask? It is an automated routine that does work for you. It takes you through the task, step-by-step, from start to finish. Most QuickTasks involve two or more applications—but to you it is application-independent. You don't need to know which applications are required. You need not start the applications at all. You simply choose a task, click its button, and the QuickTask does the work for you.

Accessing QuickTasks

 You access QuickTasks from a special button on the Desktop Application Director (DAD). When you click the QuickTasks button, you see a dialog box that contains all of the available QuickTasks, shown in Figure 33.1. You can also access QuickTasks from the Windows 95 Start menu. Choose Start, Corel WordPerfect Suite 7, Accessories, Corel QuickTasks.

▶ **See** "Introducing DAD," **p. 24**

As you can see, QuickTasks are divided into categories. By default, there are categories for QuickTasks related to creating correspondence, financial matters, connecting to the Internet, getting organized, publishing various types of documents, and miscellaneous utilities. There are two other special categories. The All category lists all your QuickTasks. The Favorites category is initially empty, but you can move or copy frequently used QuickTasks into it, as described later.

 When you select a QuickTask, a description of what it does appears in the Description box below the list.

FIG. 33.1
The QuickTasks dialog box, which you can access from DAD, contains over 60 predefined tasks.

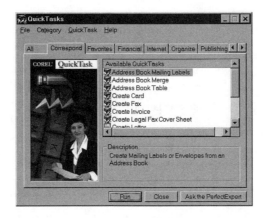

Reviewing Default QuickTasks

Corel WordPerfect Suite 7 includes more than 60 QuickTasks to automate your work. The tasks are listed in Table 33.1.

Part
VII

Ch
33

Table 33.1 WordPerfect Suite 7 QuickTasks		
Category	**Name**	**Description**
Correspond	Address Book Mailing Labels	Create mailing labels or envelopes from Address Book.
	Address Book Merge	Create merge data file from Address Book.
	Address Book Table	Create a table based on information in an Address Book.
	Create Card	Create a card in Corel WordPerfect.
	Create Fax	Create a fax in Corel WordPerfect.
	Create Invoice	Create an invoice in Corel WordPerfect.
	Create Legal Fax Cover Sheet	Create a legal fax cover sheet in Corel WordPerfect.
	Create Letter	Create a letter in Corel WordPerfect.
	Create Memo	Create a memo in Corel WordPerfect.
	Create Resume	Create a resumé in Corel WordPerfect.
	Send File	Use e-mail to send a file to someone.
	Send Message	Send an e-mail message to someone.

continues

Table 33.1   Continued

Category	Name	Description
Financial	Calculate Loan Amortization	Calculate loan amortization in Corel Quattro Pro.
	Create Balance Sheet	Create a balance sheet in Corel WordPerfect.
	Create a Budget	Use the Corel Quattro Pro expert to create a budget.
	Create Expense Report	Create an expense report in Corel WordPerfect.
	Create Income Statement	Create an income statement in Corel WordPerfect.
	Create Invoice	Create an invoice in Corel WordPerfect.
	Create Purchase Order	Create a purchase order in Corel WordPerfect.
	Extra Payment Analysis	Calculate savings seen by making extra payments.
	Loan Refinance Calculation	Calculate loan refinancing in Corel Quattro Pro.
	Track My Investments	Track your investment portfolio.
	Track My Stocks	Track daily prices and volumes of selected stocks.
Internet	Create Web Page	Create a Web page in Corel WordPerfect.
	Read My Web Pages	Browse your favorite Web pages.
	Track My Investments	Track your investment portfolio.
	Track My Stocks	Track daily prices and volumes of selected stocks.
Organize	Address Book Mailing Labels	Create mailing labels or envelopes from Address Book.
	Address Book Merge	Create merge data file from Address Book.
	Address Book Table	Create a table based on information in an Address Book.
	Create an Agenda	Create an agenda in Corel WordPerfect.

Category	Name	Description
	Create a Calendar	Create a calendar in Corel WordPerfect.
	Create a Grading Sheet	Create a grading sheet in Corel WordPerfect.
	Create a Numbered List	Create a numbered list in Corel WordPerfect.
	Create an Organization Chart	Create an organization chart in Corel Presentations.
	Create a Time Line	Create a time line using CorelFLOW.
	Create a Time Sheet	Create a legal time sheet in Corel WordPerfect.
	Create a Journal	Maintain a journal, diary, or personal history.
Publishing	Create Brochure	Create a brochure in Corel WordPerfect.
	Create Business Card	Create a business card in Corel WordPerfect.
	Create Card	Create a card in Corel WordPerfect.
	Create Certificate	Create a certificate of achievement in Corel WordPerfect.
	Create Exam	Create an exam in Corel WordPerfect.
	Create Graph Paper	Create graph paper in Corel WordPerfect.
	Create New	Create a new Corel Office document.
	Create Newsletter	Create a newsletter in Corel WordPerfect.
	Create Phone Message	Create blank phone message sheets in Corel WordPerfect.
	Create Pleading	Create a legal pleading in Corel WordPerfect.
	Create Press Release	Create a press release in Corel WordPerfect.
	Create Report	Create a report in Corel WordPerfect.
	Create Sign	Create a sign in Corel WordPerfect.

Part
VII

Ch
33

continues

Table 33.1   Continued

Category	Name	Description
	Create Table	Create a table in Corel WordPerfect.
	Create Term Paper	Create a term paper in Corel WordPerfect.
	Open Document as Copy	Create a new Corel WordPerfect document from an old one.
	Open Notebook as Copy	Create a new Corel Quattro Pro notebook from an old one.
Utilities	Add Header/Footer/Watermark	Add a header, footer, or watermark to a Corel WordPerfect document.
	Archive a File	Copy a file to an archive directory.
	Build a New Quick Task Project	Create a new QuickTask Project for Visual Basic.
	Calculate Statistical Analysis	Perform numerical and statistical analyses with Corel Quattro Pro.
	Chart Expert	Create a chart with Corel Quattro Pro.
	Create WordPerfect Template	Create a new Corel WordPerfect template.
	Create Family Tree	Use CorelFLOW to create a family tree.
	Create Map	Create a map in Corel Quattro Pro.
	Finish Document	Choose common document finishing options.
	Notebook Consolidation	Consolidate data from several sources.
	Notebook Scenario Analysis	Perform analyses on different scenarios in Corel Quattro Pro.
	Share Data between Applications	Copy or link data from one application to another.
	What-If Analysis	Perform what-if analyses in Corel Quattro Pro.

 TIP The All category lists all of the QuickTasks alphabetically, so you do not need to search through the various tabs to find the one you want.

Taking a Guided Tour of Some QuickTasks

Enough about how QuickTasks work—or do your work for you. Now it's time to experiment with a few of the more common QuickTasks. We'll take a guided tour through three specific tasks that automate common things you have to do.

Using the Create Letter QuickTask

The Create Letter QuickTask guides you through writing a letter from start to finish:

1. Click the QuickTasks button on the Task Bar, and select the Correspond tab in the QuickTasks dialog box. Select the Create Letter task, then choose Run. The task will start and display an introductory dialog box that introduces the QuickTask.

N O T E The first time a template is run in WordPerfect, you see a dialog box allowing you to enter personal information. You will not see this after you have filled it in the first time. ■

2. Choose Next. You see the Letter Expert dialog box shown in Figure 33.2, which allows you to modify different elements of your letter. Type in the recipient's name and address or click the Address Book button to choose it from your Address Book.

FIG. 33.2
The Letter Expert allows you to modify all the different parts of your letter.

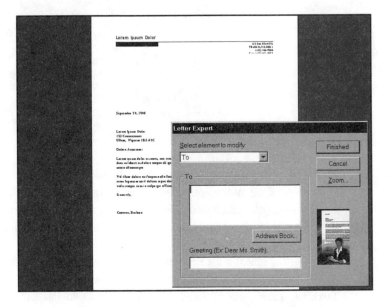

Part
VII

Ch
33

T I P At any point, click the Zoom button to alter how the letter you are creating looks in the background.

3. Click the down arrow in the Select Element to Modify drop-down list box. Choose From and, if needed, click Change to access the Address Book to enter or modify your personal information.

4. Similarly, use the Select Element to Modify drop-down list box to select whether you want a Subject or Reference line, your preferred letterhead style and text format, the closing information you desire, courtesy copy information, the date format, whether you prefer formal or informal punctuation (a colon versus a comma after the salutation), and whether you want the letter centered top to bottom.

5. Click the Finished button when you are done. You see the letter in Corel WordPerfect, with a dialog box in the upper-right corner of the screen that advises you to make any changes you want, then click Continue.

6. Click Continue after entering the text of the letter. The Finish Document QuickTask is started, and you see the options shown in Figure 33.3.

FIG. 33.3
The Finish Document QuickTask provides you with several options for finishing your letter.

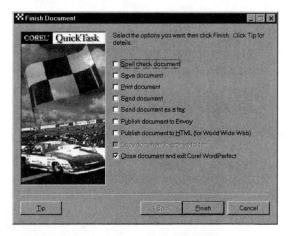

7. Select the options you want, then choose Finish. Actions are taken on your letter depending on the options you select. For instance, the spelling checker may run, or you may be taken into your e-mail program or fax program to send the letter electronically. When the actions are completed, the QuickTask ends.

N O T E   The options in the Finish dialog box appear in the order they are actually carried out. Selecting Spell Check Document, Save Document, and Print Document will cause the QuickTask to spell check, then save, then print the document. This applies to all Finish dialog boxes, regardless of the specific items in the list. ■

TROUBLESHOOTING

When I run a QuickTask, the dialog box flashes on the screen then disappears. If a
QuickTasks window or dialog box disappears, it is usually just hidden behind another window,
typically the application's main window. Use the Alt+Tab keys to find and switch to the current
QuickTask.

Using the Extra Payment Analysis QuickTask

If you have a home mortgage, you've probably heard that making just a little extra payment each month will shorten your mortgage life considerably. How much "little extra" is
enough? How much will it really shorten the mortgage? The Extra Payment Analysis
QuickTask can give you useful information.

1. Click the QuickTasks button on the Task Bar, and select the Financial tab in the
   QuickTasks dialog box. Select the Extra Payment Analysis task, then choose Run.
   The task will start and display an introductory dialog box that introduces the
   QuickTask.

2. Choose Next. You see the Extra Payment Analysis dialog box shown in Figure 33.4
   that allows you to enter required elements for the analysis. Enter the Loan Amount,
   Interest Rate, Loan Term, Loan Start Date, and Extra Payment Amount. When you
   are finished, choose Next.

3. Corel Quattro Pro opens, and you see the Extra Payment Analysis workbook. In the
   foreground, the Finish Document QuickTask starts, and you can make choices for
   finishing your document, as described next.

Part
VII

Ch

33

FIG. 33.4
The Extra Payment Analysis
dialog box assists you with
entering all the elements you
need for the analysis.

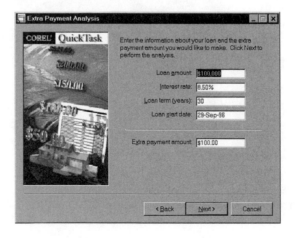

Using the Finish Document QuickTask

The Finish Document QuickTask automates tasks you typically do once your document is complete.

What if you want to "finish" a document (or spreadsheet, slideshow, or other type of file) that was not created by a QuickTask? Both the Create a Letter and Extra Payment Analysis QuickTasks incorporate a final step called the Finish dialog box. This QuickTask can be run for any open document—even if it wasn't created via another QuickTask.

While the concept is simple, this QuickTask is actually quite powerful and can involve several applications. As usual, the whole process is application independent. Here are the steps to finish a document:

1. Choose the Finish Document QuickTask from the Utilities tab of the QuickTasks dialog box and then choose run.

2. The QuickTask detects which Corel WordPerfect Suite 7 applications are running and asks whether you want to use a document from an open application or from a file on disk. Click the appropriate radio button for the proper document type (see Figure 33.5).

   If you choose a file from disk, you'll need to enter the document name or click Browse.

   ▶ **See** "Saving, Opening, and Closing Files," **p. 58**

FIG. 33.5

The Finish Document QuickTask operates on any disk file or document currently open in Corel WordPerfect, Quattro Pro, or Presentations, as well as any file on disk.

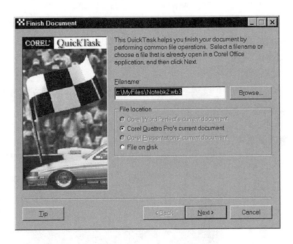

3. Select Next. You see the Finish Document dialog box. The Finish Document QuickTask has a large list of actions it can perform on the document (see Figure

33.6). Some of these actions are simple, some complex. Some of the actions, such as Index and Archive, are complete QuickTasks by themselves. Rather than trace through the dialog boxes for each of these actions, they are described in the text that follows:

FIG. 33.6
The Finish Document QuickTask gives you a simple way to "finish" a file. Finishing means any task you would perform with a completed file, such as printing, e-mailing, or indexing.

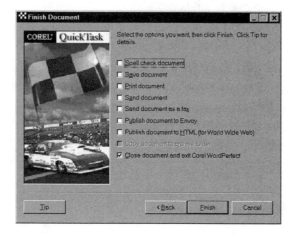

- *Spell Check Document.* The task will run the Spelling Checker, just as if you had chosen Spell Check from the application's menu.
- *Save Document.* If you choose a currently open document, this brings up the Save As dialog that allows the user to save to disk.
- *Print Document.* Prints the document to the default Windows printer.
- *Send Document.* The QuickTask looks for an existing e-mail system and enables you to send the document.
- *Send Document as a Fax.* This action is enabled only if the QuickTask finds a fax driver installed on your system. If one is installed, the QuickTask faxes through your fax driver.
- *Publish Document to Envoy.* "Prints" the document to Envoy for sharing with others in a work group.
- *Publish Document to HTML.* Uses the publish to HTML feature of the application to convert the file to an HTML file, for uploading to the World Wide Web.

  ▶ **See** "Checking Your Spelling," **p. 48**
  ▶ **See** "Saving Files," **p. 59**
  ▶ **See** "An Overview of Envoy," **p. 580**

Part

VII

Ch

33

- *Copy Document to Archive Folder.* Makes a backup copy of the file to an archive location you specify, often on a network drive, with simple versioning control—in other words, archiving the file repeatedly does not overwrite the previously saved file. There is a separate Archive QuickTask that Finish uses to complete this action.

- *Close Document and exit Corel WordPerfect.* Closes document after other actions are completed.

4. Select the boxes for the actions you want, and click Finish. Each action is then carried out in sequence. The specific dialog boxes you'll encounter depend on the steps you choose.

 T I P   To exit the Finish dialog box without taking any actions, click the Cancel button.

Managing QuickTasks

You can rearrange Quicktasks into any category you prefer; in fact, QuickTasks can be in more than one category. You can even create new category names or modify the existing ones.

You can also create new QuickTasks and edit the ones you create. You cannot, however, edit the QuickTasks that ship with Corel WordPerfect Suite 7.

Copying, Moving, and Renaming QuickTasks and Categories

To copy a QuickTask from one category to another, ensure you are not in the All tab, then select the QuickTask and choose QuickTask, Copy. You see the Copy QuickTask From Current Category dialog box shown in Figure 33.7. Select the destination category in the Destination drop-down box, then click OK. The QuickTask appears in both categories.

FIG. 33.7
You can copy a QuickTask to another category, such as the Favorites category, to put your most frequently used QuickTasks together in one place.

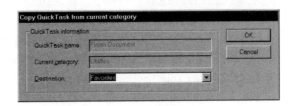

 T I P   If you type a new name for a category while copying or moving a QuickTask, that category will be created.

Move a QuickTask from one category to another in a similar fashion. Select the QuickTask and choose QuickTask, Move. You see the Move QuickTask From Current Category dialog box. Select the destination category in the Destination drop-down box, then click OK. The QuickTask is moved to the new category.

To rename a category, click the appropriate tab, then choose Category, Modify. You see the Modify a Category dialog box shown in Figure 33.8. Enter the new name and/or description for the category, then click OK. The changes are reflected in the QuickTasks dialog box.

FIG. 33.8
Rename a category using the Modify a Category dialog box.

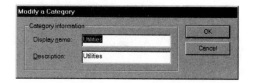

Similarly, to add a category, choose Category, Add. You see the Add a Category dialog box. Enter the new name and description for the category, then click OK. The new category appears in the QuickTasks dialog box.

You can also modify the name, description, and file name of a QuickTask by selecting it, then choosing QuickTask, Modify. You see the Modify a QuickTask dialog box shown in Figure 33.9. Change the name, description, or file name of the QuickTask as needed, then click OK.

Part
VII

Ch
33

FIG. 33.9
You can modify the name, description, or file name of an existing QuickTask. You cannot, however, edit the QuickTasks that ship with Corel WordPerfect Suite 7.

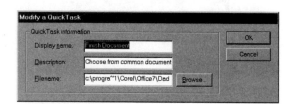

Creating a QuickTask

You can also create a new QuickTask that uses Corel WordPerfect, Quattro Pro, or Presentations. To do so, follow these steps:

1. Ensure that you are not in the All tab, then choose QuickTask, Create. You see the Create a QuickTask dialog box shown in Figure 33.10.

FIG. 33.10

Create new QuickTasks just as you would create a macro in Corel WordPerfect, Quattro Pro, or Presentations.

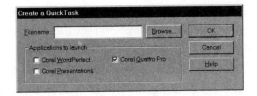

 TIP If the QuickTask works with an existing presentation, open Corel Presentations before starting the QuickTask creation process. Otherwise, the QuickTask will record the actions needed to get past the initial Document Selection dialog box seen when you first open Corel Presentations.

2. Enter a name for the QuickTask in the Filename text box, and check the boxes for the applications that will be used in the QuickTask.

3. Click OK. The required applications open, and you see the Create QuickTask dialog box as shown in Figure 33.11.

FIG. 33.11

While you create a QuickTask, the Create QuickTask dialog box appears in the foreground.

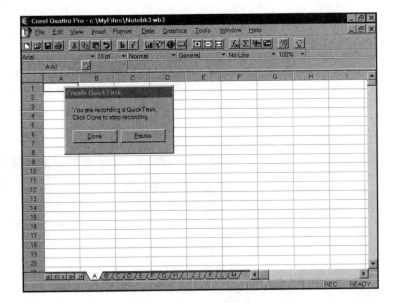

4. Perform the necessary commands, taking note of the following:

   - Access menu commands as needed.
   - You cannot use the mouse to scroll through a document, or select text in a document.
   - You can use the keyboard to scroll through or select text in a document.
   - Use Shift+Tab to switch between applications, or click on them in the taskbar.

5. When you are finished, click the Done button in the Create QuickTask dialog box. You see the QuickTask Complete dialog box shown in Figure 33.12.

FIG. 33.12
Complete the QuickTask by entering a display name, description, and category.

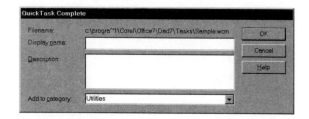

6. Enter the Display Name, Description, and Category for the QuickTask, then click OK. The new QuickTask appears in the QuickTasks dialog box.

N O T E The QuickTasks you create are macro files that can be edited by noting where you are saving them, then opening them in Corel WordPerfect. You must understand the PerfectScript macro language to make any major modifications in your QuickTasks, though you can correct simple misspellings and the like pretty easily.

You cannot edit the QuickTasks that ship with Corel WordPerfect Suite 7. ■

Part
VII

Ch
33

CHAPTER 34

Transferring Data Between Applications

One of the benefits of working within a suite environment is the ability to think about your work, rather than the applications that you are using to get your project done. Behind the scenes, however, data often needs to be transferred between applications for you to obtain a finished result. For instance, a final report may be a Corel WordPerfect 7 document incorporating a Corel Quattro Pro 7 spreadsheet or a Corel Presentations 7 chart.

As you begin to use more than one Corel WordPerfect Suite 7 application and integrate applications to do your work, you'll find that you need more information about what occurs when data is transferred from one application to another.

Before talking about "how to do it," though, it's vital that you understand what's going on with data transfers, and the three very different ways that data is transferred. ■

Corel WordPerfect Suite 7's data transferring strategies

See the three ways the Suite permits you to transfer data between applications, and understand the benefits and drawbacks of each.

Moving and copying data

Learn how to move and copy data between your applications with ease.

Linking and embedding

Find out the difference between copying, linking, and embedding data—and when you should do each one.

Understanding the Types of Data Transfer

There are three basic ways that data can be transferred between documents:

- Moving/copying
- Linking
- Embedding

Before you learn the different commands and methods used to transfer data, it's a good idea to get a conceptual understanding of what's happening with the different processes.

▶ **See** "Copying and Moving Text," **p. 92**

Understanding Moving and Copying

Most people are familiar with moving and copying data, using the cut-and-paste metaphor. When you move a sentence from one Corel WordPerfect paragraph to another, or move a Corel Quattro Pro cell to another location, you do two operations. First, you cut the data, which removes it from the original location. Then, you paste the data to its new location. Copying works the same way, except that a copy of the data is left in the original location as well. You move data by copying it to the Clipboard, then paste it where you want to move it.

N O T E   When you cut or copy data, it goes to the Windows Clipboard. This is a temporary storage area that holds the last item that you cut or copied. The data stays in the Clipboard until you either exit Windows or copy something else into the Clipboard.

There are a few important implications:

- The same Clipboard is used in all Windows applications, enabling you to move data from one application to another.
- Because the Clipboard only holds one item, if you put something else in the Clipboard, the first item is erased.
- You can paste the same copy of the data from the Clipboard multiple times—until you copy something else into the Clipboard. ■

Moving and copying data between applications works the same way as it does within applications. The data is moved or copied to the Windows Clipboard, from which it is retrieved when you paste the data in the destination application.

N O T E When you move or copy data using the drag-and-drop method discussed in previous chapters, the data is not put into the Clipboard, nor are the contents of the Clipboard affected. However, because the data is not in the Clipboard, you cannot repetitively paste multiple copies of it. ▓

Understanding Linking

Linking data adds another dimension to the copying process. For example, when you link a range of spreadsheet cells in Corel Quattro Pro to a Corel WordPerfect word processing document, the spreadsheet information is displayed in the word processing document. This means the word processing document maintains information that specifies where the linked data is to be obtained: the application that created it, the path and file name, and the selected information in that file. When you link data, you thus create a pointer from the file where you want the data to appear to the file in which that data exists.

N O T E You might want to become familiar with the technical terminology used for linked and embedded data (see the following table).

In this chapter, the terminology *source application* and *destination application* are used, rather than *server* and *client*, for purposes of clarity. ▓

Term	Refers to
Object	The data that is linked or embedded
Source file	The file from which the object comes
Source application	The application in which the source file is created
Server	Another term for source application
Destination application	The application in which the object appears
Client	Another term for the destination application
Destination file	The file in which the object appears

Because a link consists of a pointer to a source file, when the option for data updating is set to automatic, the object that appears in the destination file is always the latest version. When you or someone else changes the source file containing the object, the object in the destination file is updated with the new information. For example, if someone changes the Corel Quattro Pro file, which affects the cells that are linked to Corel WordPerfect, the spreadsheet cells appearing in your word processing document immediately reflect this change.

Alternatively, you can specify that the link be updated manually. In this case, the object remains static (containing the old information) unless you manually update it.

Part
VII

Ch
34

TIP When creating a link, first ensure that your source document has been saved so that information about the link can be stored. If the document has not yet been saved, you won't be able to create the link.

Windows applications use different technologies to create links. Three of the most common are DDE, OLE 1.0, and OLE 2.0. DDE, the oldest, stands for Dynamic Data Exchange. It allows for linking, but not embedding. DDE was later subsumed under OLE, Object Linking and Embedding.

The major differences between OLE 1.0 and 2.0 are that OLE 2.0 allows for dragging and dropping data between applications, and allows you to edit the source data from within the destination application. Corel WordPerfect Suite 7 applications support OLE 2.0 where possible. However, you may have links to other applications that only support OLE 1.0. If you double-click a linked object, you stay in the destination application and the menus change to those of the source application; the link is an OLE 2.0 link. If, on the other hand, you double-click and the original application opens up, the link may be OLE 1.0 or 2.0.

N O T E OLE and DDE are quite complex; usually the method being used for linking and embedding is immaterial to the user. However, if you *are* interested in the details, Corel WordPerfect 7 is an OLE 2.0 server, meaning that you can link WordPerfect information to Quattro Pro 7 or Corel Presentations 7, for example. It is *not*, however, an OLE 2.0 in-place server. Thus, when you double-click Corel WordPerfect 7 objects that are embedded in Corel Quattro Pro 7, you will not be able to use in-place editing. ■

Understanding Embedding

Embedding data is like copying it, with one difference. When you embed an object, a copy of it is stored in the destination file, just as it is when you copy it. However, because OLE is used to transfer the data, you can edit the embedded data using the source application by double-clicking the embedded data. For example, if you have a Corel Quattro Pro spreadsheet embedded into a Corel WordPerfect document, you can double-click the spreadsheet inside Corel WordPerfect, then use Corel Quattro Pro to edit it.

Depending on the specific applications involved, when you double-click an embedded object to edit it, a window may open enabling you to edit the object using its source application. Alternatively, the title bar, toolbar, and menus may change to those of the source application, enabling you to edit the object in-place from within the destination document.

For instance, when you double-click an embedded Corel Quattro Pro object within Corel WordPerfect, the title bar, menu bar, and toolbar change to those of Corel Quattro Pro, enabling in-place editing. However, when you double-click an embedded Corel

WordPerfect object within Corel Quattro Pro, Corel WordPerfect is launched in a separate window, enabling you to edit the Corel WordPerfect object. Because Corel WordPerfect is an OLE 2.0 server, it is not an "OLE 2.0 in-place server" that allows for in-place editing.

Comparing the Methods of Transferring Data

In summary, the differences between the three methods of transferring data can be seen in the following table:

Method	Copies Data to Destination	Allows Editing Using Source Application	Updates When Source Changes
Copying/ Moving	Yes	No	No
Linking	No	Yes	Yes
Embedding	Yes	Yes	No

Having looked at the principles behind the three methods of transferring data, let's see how to actually do it.

Learning the Techniques for Moving and Copying

You can use several methods to move or copy data between applications. These include using menus and toolbars, keyboard shortcuts, and drag and drop.

Moving and copying data using the menus, toolbars, and keyboard shortcuts is the same whether you are transferring the data within or between applications:

1. Open the source application, and select the data to be moved or copied.

2. Choose Edit, Cut or Edit, Copy; or click the Cut or Copy button on the toolbar, if one is visible. Alternatively, right-click the data to be moved, then choose Cut or Copy from the QuickMenu that pops up.

 TIP You can also use hotkeys for cutting and pasting: Ctrl+X for cut; Ctrl+C for copy; and Ctrl+V for paste.

3. Open the destination application, and place the insertion point where the data should go.

Part
VII

Ch
34

4. Choose Edit, Paste, or click the Paste button on the toolbar, if one is visible. Alternatively, right-click at the insertion point, then choose Paste from the QuickMenu that pops up.

Learning Techniques for Linking and Embedding

To effectively work with linked and embedded data, you need to be able to:

■ Create links and embedded data.

■ Edit a linked object.

■ Edit the link itself.

Creating Links and Embedding Data

Creating links and embedding data take an extra step than merely copying data, but you'll soon find that you can accomplish them efficiently by following these steps:

1. Open the source application and select the data to be linked or embedded. (If you are going to link the data, the file must be saved before you cut or copy the data.)

2. Cut or copy the data as described previously.

3. Open the destination application, and place the insertion point where the data should go.

CAUTION

In Corel Quattro Pro 7, you need to clear a space for the information, or the new information could overwrite the old information in the destination cells.

4. Choose Edit, Paste Special. You see the Paste Special dialog box (see Figure 34.1).

FIG. 34.1
The Paste Special dialog box enables you to both embed and link objects, as well as specify the object type.

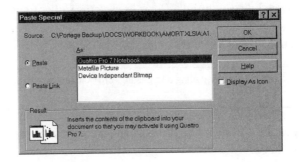

5. To embed the data, choose <u>P</u>aste; to link it, choose Paste <u>L</u>ink.

6. Select a data type as discussed in the following section "Choosing Data Types," then click OK. The data appears in your destination application.

Alternatively, if the windows for both applications are simultaneously visible on the Windows desktop, you can drag selected text or objects from one application to another. An easy way to embed an object while keeping it in the source application is to open both application windows, select the data, then hold down the Ctrl key while dragging the data from one window to another. Follow these steps:

1. Make sure both the source application and the destination application are open.

2. Right-click a blank area of the taskbar, then choose Tile <u>V</u>ertically or Tile <u>H</u>orizontally. Alternatively, move and size the application windows until you can see both the data to be moved in the first application and the destination for that data in the other application.

3. Select the text or object in the source application, and position your mouse pointer inside it.

4. Embed the object and remove it from the source application by dragging it to the appropriate position in the destination application. Alternatively, embed the object and keep it from the source application by holding down the Ctrl key and dragging it to the appropriate position in the destination application.

Alternatively, link the object by holding down Ctrl+Shift while you drag it to the destination application (see Figure 34.2).

FIG. 34.2
In this example, Corel WordPerfect data is being dragged into a Corel Quattro Pro spreadsheet.

Source document with selected data that is to be transferred

Destination document with drag-and-drop cursor in place

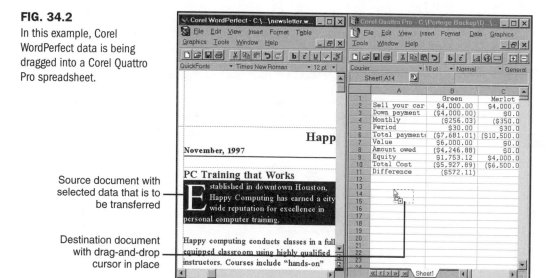

TROUBLESHOOTING

Why is it that sometimes I can drag text from a non-Corel WordPerfect Suite 7 application into Corel WordPerfect, and sometimes I can't? If the other application is OLE 2.0-compliant, you can drag and drop objects into Corel WordPerfect (which is also OLE 2.0-compliant). If the other application is not compliant, you may still be able to cut and paste data using the Edit menu. However, some Windows applications do not use the Windows Clipboard in a standard way. You won't be able to move or copy data from these applications at all.

Choosing Data Types　When you are linking or embedding an object in the Paste Special dialog box, you see a number of different object types from which you can choose. The list you see depends on the characteristics of both the source and destination application.

In general, the first data type on this list is the file type of the source application. Thus, when you link or embed a Corel Quattro Pro file into Corel Presentations, the first data type on the list is Corel Quatto Pro 7 Notebook, as you see in Figure 34.3. Similarly, when you link or embed a Corel Presentations drawing into Corel WordPerfect, the first entry on the list is Corel Presentations 7 Drawing. Choosing this option is often advantageous, because it offers full OLE 2.0 functionality.

FIG. 34.3
The first data type listed usually provides the best way of linking data. If the Display As Icon option is active, it indicates that the data type provides an OLE 2.0 link.

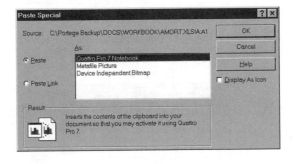

　TIP　When you choose OLE 2.0 data types, the Display As Icon option becomes active. This can be particularly useful when you attach sound files or background text files to a document.

Other data types that you can choose may include:

■ *Rich Text Format.* This data type is useful in transferring data from one word processor to another, when you want to retain the maximum formatting information possible.

■ *Unformatted Text.* This data type is useful in opposite situations, when you want to merely transfer text and no formatting.

■ *Picture, Metafile, or Device Independent Bitmap.* These options convert the object into different graphic formats.

When embedding an object, you'll often see options such as Quattro Pro 7 Notebook, Rich Text Format, QB1, or WordPerfect 7 Document. These options enable you to paste the object into your document in a slightly different, often earlier, format than that of the current version of the source application.

> **N O T E** You often have more options when embedding a file with the Paste option than when linking it with Paste Link. This makes sense, because a link must usually be established with the file in its original format. ■

Inserting Objects You can also embed an object by choosing Insert, Object from the menu of Corel WordPerfect Suite 7 applications such as Corel WordPerfect, Corel Presentations, and Corel Quattro Pro. You see the Insert Object dialog box shown in Figure 34.4.

FIG. 34.4
The Insert Object dialog box enables you to create new embedded objects in your file using a variety of OLE-compliant applications, by choosing Create New.

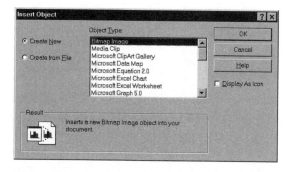

This dialog box provides two choices for embedding an object. If you choose Create New, you see a list of OLE object types that are supported on your system.

> **T I P** If you have installed applications from other vendors that are OLE-compliant, they may also appear on this list.

This option enables you to create a new object using one of the listed types of objects. When you choose an Object Type, the appropriate application opens. If the source application is an OLE 2.0 in-place service, you use in-place editing. Otherwise, it opens in its own window, and you can create the new object there. See the next section for details on editing linked objects.

Alternatively, you may want to embed an object that already exists as a file on the disk. In this case, choose Create from File while you are in the Insert Object dialog box. The dialog box changes to the one shown in Figure 34.5. You can type the name of the desired

Part
VII

Ch
34

file, or use the Browse button to see a Corel Office Open dialog box, then choose the file from there.

FIG. 34.5

You can embed or link an entire file into your document by choosing Create from File in the Insert Object dialog box.

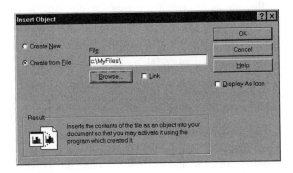

 TIP When you create an object from a file, you have the option of creating it as a link, rather than embedding the object or displaying it as an icon.

Editing a Linked Object

One of the nicest things about linking objects is that you can go back through the link to edit the source file in the source application that created it.

When you double-click a linked object, another application window opens on the screen. This is the source application that created the object, and you see the source file in that window. Edit the object within the application window and save it as you normally would. When you're finished, choose File. There is an option such as the one shown in Figure 34.6 that enables you to exit and return to the destination application.

Editing a Link

When you have linked one or more objects into your documents, you can edit the link information. You may want to edit the links in your document for a number of reasons:

- To redefine the link if the source file is renamed or moved
- To break the link so that the object no longer changes in your document
- To change the link from automatically updated (whenever the source file changes) to manually updated (when you specify)
- To update a manual link

To edit a link in Corel WordPerfect or Corel Presentations, choose Edit, Links. The Links dialog box appears (see Figure 34.7). All the links in your document are listed.

FIG. 34.6

When you edit linked objects, that object's application window opens, enabling you to edit it. An option on the File menu enables you to return to your original application.

Object in destination file in destination application —

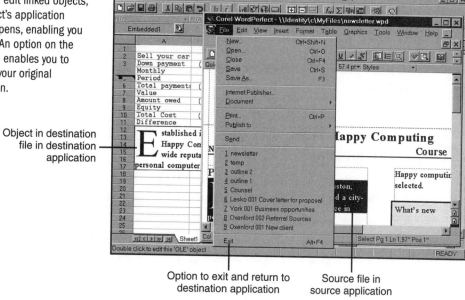

Option to exit and return to destination application

Source file in source application

N O T E Corel Quattro Pro handles this differently. On the Edit menu is a Linked Object menu. The word "Object" may change dynamically, depending on the object you currently have selected. For example, it may read "Linked Document" if the object is a Word document. After clicking the Linked Object option, there is a cascading menu with more options. ▪

FIG. 34.7

The Links dialog box lists all links in your document, and enables you to edit them, break them, or specify their update as manual or automatic.

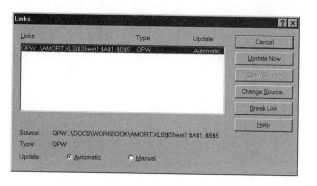

The Links dialog box provides the following options that affect links that you have selected:

■ *Update Automatic and Manual.* Choosing Automatic causes objects to be updated as soon as they are changed. Choosing Manual causes objects not to be updated until an Update command is given.

- *Update Now.* This option causes all selected manual links to be updated—that is, the objects are refreshed from the latest versions of the source files.

- *Open Source.* This option opens the source file in the source application.

- *Change Source.* When you choose this option, the Change Source dialog box appears. You can then change the file name and (in the case of spreadsheets) the cell range.

- *Break Link.* This option breaks the link between the object and its source file.

TROUBLESHOOTING

Why is the Li<u>n</u>ks option grayed out on the Edit menu? The Li<u>n</u>ks option is only active if you have links in your document. If you have embedded objects, rather than linked objects, the option is not active.

Why is it that sometimes changes in my source document aren't reflected in my destination document? The source document may not be available, either because it no longer exists, has been moved, or you cannot establish a connection to it on the network. In this case, the last copy of the object will display in your destination document.

Alternatively, the link may be one that is manually updated, rather than updated automatically.

In either case, you can examine the link information and make necessary changes.

CHAPTER 35

Customizing Toolbars and Menus

Set toolbar preferences

Find out how to display toolbars on any side of the screen, and how to change their display preferences.

Set Desktop Application Director preferences

Learn how to add and remove Corel WordPerfect Suite 7 icons from the taskbar.

Customize menus

See how to add macros, text scripts, and commands to create your own customized menus.

Certain Suite applications, like Corel WordPerfect 7 and Corel Presentations 7, enable you to create and edit toolbars in an identical manner, with a few variations. You can even create and edit menus in a similar manner. This chapter discusses how to modify "standard" Corel WordPerfect Suite 7 toolbars and menus, such as those found in Corel WordPerfect and Corel Presentations. ■

Customizing Toolbars

Corel WordPerfect and Corel Presentations enable you to create multiple toolbars, edit their buttons, and position them in several different places on-screen.

To effectively customize your toolbars, you need to know how to:

- Display and hide toolbars
- Select different toolbars
- Access the Toolbar Preferences dialog box
- Control toolbar display options
- Position the toolbar in the window

NOTE Corel Quattro Pro 7 and Envoy 7 behave somewhat differently, and do not yet permit the standard toolbar and menu modification techniques to be used effectively within them. In future versions of the Corel WordPerfect Suite, Corel is committed to increasing the level of standardization throughout the Suite. ■

Displaying, Hiding, and Selecting Toolbars

You can control the display of the toolbar in Corel Presentations 7 by choosing View, Toolbar. There will be a check mark by the Toolbar entry if the toolbar is displayed. In Corel WordPerfect 7, control the display of the toolbar by choosing View, Toolbars/Ruler. You see the Toolbars dialog box, and can check or uncheck the WordPerfect 7 Toolbar item to display or hide the toolbar.

 TIP To hide a toolbar, right-click it, and then choose Hide Toolbar.

To select a different toolbar to display, ensure that a toolbar is displayed, then right-click it. You see a pop-up QuickMenu that displays the names of available toolbars. Click the name of the toolbar that you want to display.

Setting Toolbar Preferences

To control toolbar display options, or to create, edit, copy, rename, or delete a toolbar, you must access the Toolbar Preferences dialog box. To do so, use the following procedure:

1. Make sure that the toolbar is displayed, and then right-click it. You see a QuickMenu that displays the names of available toolbars, and selections including Edit, Preferences, and Hide Toolbar.

2. Select Preferences. You see a Toolbar Preferences dialog box (see Figure 35.1).

FIG. 35.1
You can select different toolbars, as well as create and edit new ones, from the Toolbar Preferences dialog box.

3. Highlight the toolbar that you want to select, edit, copy, rename, or delete.
4. Choose an option from the following list:
   - *Select*. Use this to display the selected toolbar.
   - *Create*. Use this option to create a new toolbar (see "Creating Toolbars and Menu Bars," later in this chapter).
   - *Edit*. Use this option to edit an existing toolbar (see "Editing Toolbars and Menu Bars," later in this chapter).
   - *Copy*. Use this option to copy an existing toolbar. The option works slightly differently depending on the application (see "Copying Toolbars," later in this chapter).
   - *Rename*. This option enables you to rename an existing toolbar.
   - *Delete*. Use this to delete a toolbar. Certain default toolbars noted with <> symbols cannot be deleted.
   - *Options*. This option enables you to set display preferences, as described in "Setting Toolbar Display Preferences" later in this chapter.
   - *Help*. This provides context-sensitive help.
5. When you have finished with whichever option you have selected, choose Close in the Toolbar Preferences dialog box. This option completes any operations you have made and returns you to the application.

Part
VII

Ch
35

TIP You can quickly edit the currently displayed toolbar from the QuickMenu by choosing Edit.

N O T E By default, when you edit the toolbar in Presentations, you will be prompted to make a copy of the <Drawing> toolbar, which is the only toolbar available, and cannot be directly edited. You can, however, edit the copy of the drawing toolbar that you made, and save it with a different name. ■

Setting Toolbar Display Preferences

You can specify options regarding the appearance and location of your toolbars. The selections you make affect any toolbar that you select, and are retained in future work sessions until you reset them. To set display preferences, use the following procedure:

1. Access the Toolbar Preferences dialog box as described in the previous section, by right-clicking a toolbar, then choosing Preferences.

2. Choose Options. You see the Toolbar Options dialog box (see Figure 35.2).

FIG. 35.2

The Toolbar Options dialog box enables you to change the appearance and location of your toolbar.

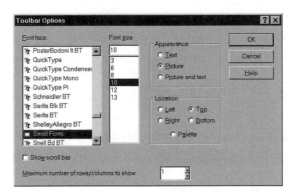

3. Select display preferences (not all preferences are available in all applications):

- *Font Face and Font Size*. Choose the font and size for toolbars that display text.

- *Appearance*. Toolbars can display Text (text only), Picture (icon only), or Picture and Text.

T I P If you choose Text or Picture and Text, display your toolbars at the left or right side of the window; otherwise, you will not have room for many buttons.

- *Location*. You can specify that toolbars display to the Left, Right, Top, Bottom of the window, or as a floating Palette.

- *Show Scroll Bar*. Click this check box to have a scroll bar appear on the toolbar so that you can have more buttons than appear in the window.

- *Maximum Number of Rows/Columns to Show.* You can display more than one row or column of buttons by entering a number greater than 1 in this option.

4. When you are finished selecting preferences, click OK. You return to the Toolbar Preferences dialog box.

5. You can now set further toolbar preferences or choose Close to return to the application.

Moving Toolbars with the Mouse

Another easy way to position toolbars bars is by moving them with the mouse, as outlined in the following steps:

1. Ensure that the toolbar is visible on the screen.

2. Position the mouse pointer in an area of the toolbar that does not contain buttons—either in the space between buttons or below or after the buttons. The mouse pointer changes to a hand.

3. Drag the toolbar to the desired edge of the window. Alternatively, display the toolbar as a palette by dragging it into the middle of the window.

4. When you release the mouse button, the toolbar moves to its new position.

 You can also move a toolbar that appears as a palette in the middle of the screen by dragging its title bar, or close it by double-clicking its Control button.

Copying Toolbars

Copying a toolbar is handled differently by Corel Presentations and Corel WordPerfect. In Corel Presentations, you see a Copy Toolbar dialog box that merely asks you for the name of the new toolbar.

In Corel WordPerfect, toolbars are stored in templates. To copy a toolbar:

1. Display the Toolbar Preferences dialog box as described above.

2. Choose Copy. You see the Copy Toolbar(s) dialog box (see Figure 35.3).

3. Specify the template containing the toolbar you want to copy.

4. Specify the toolbar in that template to be copied.

5. Specify the template to copy the toolbar to.

6. If the copying operation will result in overwriting the name of an existing toolbar, you are prompted to overwrite the toolbar or provide a new name for it. (You see this prompt, for instance, when you copy a toolbar to the same template it comes from.)

Part
VII

Ch
35

FIG. 35.3

In Corel WordPerfect, you copy a toolbar from one template to another using the Copy Toolbar(s) dialog box.

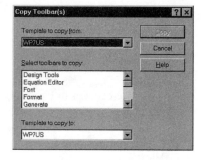

7. Click the Copy button to copy the toolbar.

Customizing Menu Bars

In Corel WordPerfect and Corel Presentations, you can create multiple menu bars and edit their contents—just as you can with toolbars.

To effectively customize your menus, you need to know how to:

- Select different menu bars
- Access the Menu Preferences dialog box
- Create and edit menus

Selecting Menu Bars

To select a different menu bar to display, right-click the current menu bar. You see a QuickMenu that displays the names of available menu bars (see Figure 35.4). Click the menu that you want to display.

FIG. 35.4

When you right-click a menu bar in Corel WordPerfect or Corel Presentations, you see a QuickMenu enabling you to choose different menus or to set menu preferences.

 TIP In Corel WordPerfect, you can hide the menu bar and all toolbars by choosing View, Hide Bars. To restore the menu bar, press the Esc key.

Setting Menu Preferences

To create, edit, copy, rename, or delete a menu, you must access the Menu Bar Preferences dialog box. To do so, use the following procedure:

1. Right-click the menu. You see a QuickMenu.

2. Choose <u>P</u>references. You see a Menu Bar Preferences dialog box (see Figure 35.5).

FIG. 35.5
The Menu Bar Preferences dialog box enables you to customize menus just as you customize toolbars.

3. Highlight the menu that you want to select, edit, copy, rename, or delete.

 TIP Menus that are enclosed in angle braces (<>) are default menus that cannot be edited, renamed, or deleted. You can copy these menus, however, and then edit them.

---

4. Choose an option from the following list:

   - *<u>S</u>elect*. Choose this to display the selected menu.
   - *C<u>r</u>eate*. Choose this option to create a new menu. See the section "Creating Toolbars and Menu Bars" later in this chapter for details.
   - *<u>E</u>dit*. Choose this option to edit an existing menu. See the section "Editing Toolbars and Menu Bars" later in this chapter for details.
   - *Co<u>p</u>y*. Choose this option to copy an existing menu. The option works slightly differently depending on the application. See the section "Copying Menu Bars" later in this chapter for details.
   - *Re<u>n</u>ame*. This option enables you to rename an existing menu.
   - *<u>D</u>elete*. Choose this to delete a menu from the list of available menus.
   - *<u>H</u>elp*. This option provides context-sensitive help on menus.

5. When you have finished with whichever option you have selected, choose <u>C</u>lose in the Menu Bar Preferences dialog box. This option completes any operations you have made and returns you to the application.

Part
VII

Ch
35

Copying Menu Bars

Copying menu bars is handled differently by Corel Presentations and Corel WordPerfect. In Corel Presentations, you see a Copy Menu Bar dialog box that merely asks you for the name of the new menu. By default, the new menu has the same entries as the menu se-lected in the <u>M</u>enu Bars list.

In Corel WordPerfect, menus are stored in templates. To copy a menu bar:

1. Access the Menu Bar Preferences dialog box as described previously. Choose Co<u>p</u>y. You see the Copy Menu Bars dialog box (see Figure 35.6).

FIG. 35.6

The Copy Menu Bars dialog box in Corel WordPerfect enables you to copy menus from one template to another.

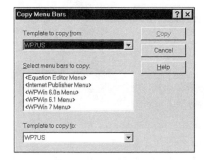

2. Specify the template containing the menu you want to copy.

3. Specify the menu in that template to be copied.

4. Indicate the template to copy the menu to. If the copying operation will result in overwriting the name of an existing menu, you are prompted to overwrite the menu or provide a new name for it. (You see this prompt, for instance, when you copy a menu to the same template it comes from.)

5. Click the <u>C</u>opy button to copy the menu.

T I P In Corel Presentations, you can quickly edit the currently displayed menu by right-clicking the menu, and then choosing <u>E</u>dit from the QuickMenu, if the menu's name is not enclosed in angle braces.

Creating and Editing Toolbars and Menu Bars

The process of creating and editing toolbars is almost identical to creating and editing menus. This is because the same elements can be added to toolbar buttons as to menu items. Thus, these are considered here in the same section.

Creating Toolbars and Menu Bars

Creating a new toolbar or menu bar involves two basic steps: giving the toolbar or menu bar a name, and then adding buttons or items to it. To create a new toolbar or menu bar, follow these steps:

1. Access the Toolbar Preferences or Menu Bar Preferences dialog box as before, by right-clicking the menu or toolbar. You see the QuickMenu.

2. Choose Preferences. You see a Toolbar or Menu Bar Preferences dialog box.

3. Choose Create. You see a Create Toolbar or Create Menu Bar dialog box like the Create Menu Bar dialog box shown in Figure 35.7.

FIG. 35.7
The Create Menu Bar dialog box is used to create menu bars.

4. Give the toolbar or menu a descriptive name, and then click OK.

N O T E In Corel WordPerfect, toolbars and menu bars are saved in a template, rather than as a separate file on the disk. You can specify which template the new toolbar or menu will be saved in by choosing Template from the Create Toolbar or Create Menu Bar dialog box. In the resulting Toolbar or Menu Bar Location dialog box, you can specify either the current document's template or the default template. If you choose the latter, your toolbar or menu will be available in all documents. ■

5. You see the Menu Editor dialog box similar to the one in Figure 35.8, or a similar Toolbar Bar Editor dialog box.

FIG. 35.8
You can add, move, and delete buttons from a menu bar using the Menu Editor dialog box.

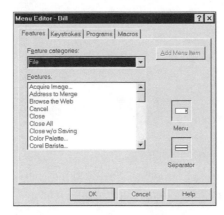

Part
VII

Ch
35

6. Add, move, and delete buttons as described in the section "Editing Toolbars and Menu Bars" later in this chapter.

7. When you are finished, click OK. You return to the Toolbar or Menu Bar Preferences dialog box. Your new toolbar or menu is on the appropriate list.

8. You can set further preferences or choose <u>C</u>lose to return to the application.

TROUBLESHOOTING

Sometimes I don't know what the toolbar buttons mean. My office mate's machine gives a little yellow prompt when she puts her mouse pointer on a button. How can I do that? Turn on QuickTips by choosing <u>E</u>dit, Pr<u>e</u>ferences, <u>E</u>nvironment, then checking the Sho<u>w</u> QuickTips option.

Editing Toolbars and Menu Bars

Editing a toolbar or menu bar involves adding, deleting, moving, and customizing buttons or items. To edit an existing toolbar or menu bar, follow these steps:

1. Access the Toolbar Preferences or Menu Bar Preferences dialog box as before, by right-clicking the menu. You see the QuickMenu.

2. Choose <u>P</u>references. You see a Toolbar or Menu Bar Preferences dialog box.

3. Select the toolbar or menu to be edited.

4. Choose <u>E</u>dit. You see a Toolbar or Menu Bar Editor dialog box similar to the one shown in Figure 35.9. (The Menu Editor has similar functionality.)

FIG. 35.9

By using the Toolbar Editor dialog box for a specific toolbar, you can add, move, delete, or customize buttons.

5. You can now do the following:

   • Add buttons to the toolbar or menu items as described in "Adding Toolbar Buttons and Menu Items" later in this chapter.

- Move toolbar buttons or menu items by dragging them to a new position on the toolbar or menu.

- Delete buttons or items by dragging them off the toolbar or menu.

- Customize buttons and items as described in "Customizing Toolbar Buttons and Menu Items" later in this chapter.

6. When you are finished editing the toolbar or menu bar, click OK. You return to the Toolbar Preferences or Menu Bar Preferences dialog box.

7. You can now set further preferences or choose <u>C</u>lose to return to the application.

Adding Toolbar Buttons and Menu Items

Toolbar buttons and menu items are extremely powerful. One of their simplest uses is to invoke program features. But toolbar buttons and menu items can perform four different types of tasks:

- *Activate a feature.* Each application has specific features that can be assigned to a toolbar button or menu item. These are the features that are seen on the default menus of the application. This option enables these menu items to be assigned to toolbar buttons, and permits menus to be rearranged to your liking.

- *Play keystrokes.* You can use a keyboard script to store a sequence of keystrokes. These keystrokes are played back when you click the button or choose the menu item that contains the keyboard script. Keystroke sequences can contain text and extended characters. They can also contain function key and hotkey keystrokes. Thus, you can record simple macros that do anything that can be done by a sequence of keystrokes (but not mouse movements or mouse clicks).

- *Launch a program.* Toolbar buttons and menu items can launch any application on your disk—both Corel WordPerfect Suite and non-Corel WordPerfect Suite programs.

- *Play a macro.* You can also create a button or menu item that will run a macro. (The macro must already have been created and saved on the disk.)

In order to add a button or item to your toolbar or menu, access the Toolbar or Menu Bar Editor dialog box by creating or editing a toolbar or menu as described earlier. What you do next depends on what type of button or menu item you want to add.

Adding a Feature   To add a button or menu item that calls a feature:

1. From the Toolbar Editor or Menu Editor dialog box, choose the Features tab. The dialog box shows options for F<u>e</u>ature Categories and <u>F</u>eatures.

2. Click the down arrow to the right of the Feature Categories text box. You see a list of available feature categories (see Figure 35.10). These parallel the main menu options. Some applications may have additional feature categories.

FIG. 35.10
In the Menu or Toolbar Editor, you can assign buttons or menu items to application features that parallel default menu items.

3. Depending on the category you select, a different list of features appears. Select the feature you want to associate with the button, then choose Add Button or Add Menu Item.

4. A new button or item appears on the toolbar or menu, and you remain in the Edit Toolbar or Menu Editor dialog box so you can make further additions, or accept the change you have made and exit the dialog box by clicking the OK button.

 T I P New menu items are added as main selections on the menu bar. Move them by dragging them to their appropriate place on a menu.

Adding a Keystroke Sequence   If you want a button or menu item to play a keystroke sequence, follow these steps to create it:

1. From the Toolbar or Menu Editor dialog box, choose the Keystrokes tab. The Keystrokes tab of the Toolbar or Menu Editor dialog box shows a text box for the keyboard script (see Figure 35.11).

2. Choose Type The Keystrokes This Button (or Menu Item) Plays. An insertion point appears in the text box.

3. Type the keystrokes that the button should play. Function keys are entered with braces—for example, **{Shift+F7}**.

FIG. 35.11

In the Toolbar or Menu Editor dialog box, you can enter the keystroke sequences that create toolbar buttons and menu items for text, function keys, or menu choices.

4. When you are finished, choose <u>A</u>dd Keystrokes. A new button or item appears on the toolbar or menu, and you remain in the Toolbar or Menu Editor dialog box so you can make further additions.

 TIP By default, a new keyboard sequence item has the name of the first word in the script. To change this name, double-click the menu item while you are editing the menu bar.

Launching a Program To create a button or menu item that will launch a program, you must know the name of the program file, and the folder in which it resides. Then, create the button or item as follows:

1. From the Toolbar or Menu Editor dialog box, choose the Programs tab.

2. Click the <u>A</u>dd Program button. You see the Open dialog box (see Figure 35.12).

FIG. 35.12

Assign an application to a toolbar button or menu item using the Open dialog box.

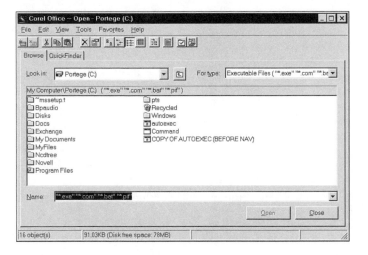

Part

VII

Ch

35

3. Navigate to the folder containing the program, and double-click the appropriate program file.

▶ **See** "Saving, Opening, and Closing Files," **p. 58**

A new button or item appears on the toolbar or menu, and you return to the Toolbar or Menu Editor dialog box so you can make further additions.

TIP   By default, a new application launch menu item has the name of the application. To change this name, double-click the menu item.

Running a Macro   If you would like to assign a macro to a toolbar button or menu item, use the following steps:

1. From the Toolbar or Menu Editor dialog box, choose the Macros tab.

2. Click the Add Macro button that appears in the dialog box. You see an Add Macro or a Select Macro dialog box, like the one shown in Figure 35.13, enabling you to choose the macro to be assigned to the button or menu item.

N O T E   In Corel WordPerfect, you can also choose Add Template Macro. This adds a macro that is stored in a template to a button or menu item, as opposed to one stored on the disk. In this case, you see a list of macros stored in the current template, and you can choose a macro from this list. ▨

FIG. 35.13

Through the Select Macro dialog box, you can access macros that you can also assign to toolbar buttons and menu items.

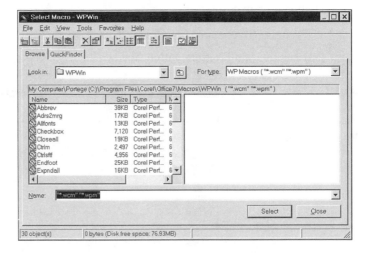

3. Navigate to the appropriate folder, then double-click the macro file.

A new button or item appears on the toolbar or menu, and you return to the Edit Toolbar or Menu Editor dialog box so you can make further additions.

Customizing Toolbar Buttons and Menu Items

You may customize a button or menu item by double-clicking it while you are editing or creating a toolbar or menu bar.

If you double-click a toolbar button, you see the Customize Button dialog box (see Figure 35.14).

FIG. 35.14
The Customize Button dialog box enables you to change the properties of specific buttons on the toolbar.

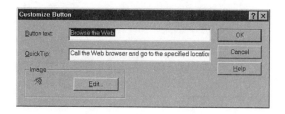

If you double-click a menu item, you see the Edit Menu Text dialog box (see Figure 35.15).

FIG. 35.15
The Edit Menu Text dialog box enables you to change the text of the menu item and the help prompt that appears on the title bar.

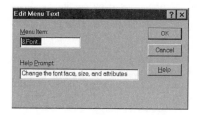

These dialog boxes provide options including:

■ *Button Text and QuickTip (for toolbar buttons).* The text that pops up when you hold the mouse pointer on a toolbar button.

■ *Menu Item (for menu items).* The text of the menu item.

■ *Help Prompt.* Additional help text for the menu item.

■ *Edit (toolbar buttons).* Enables you to edit the image of the button. Choosing Edit displays an Image Editor dialog box (see Figure 35.16).

- Select the colors that you can paint with the left and right mouse buttons by clicking the appropriate colors with the respective buttons.

- If Single Pixel is selected, click either button to fill small rectangles with the appropriate color, one at a time.

- If Fill Whole Area is selected, clicking a cell changes the color of that cell and all contiguous cells of the same color.

- You can also use the Copy and Paste commands to copy images from one button to another.

Part
VII

Ch
35

FIG. 35.16
Corel WordPerfect Suite 7 includes an image editor that enables you to change the appearance of toolbar buttons.

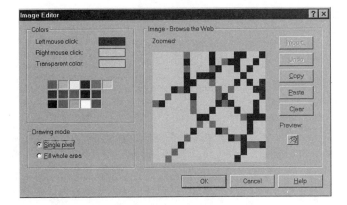

TROUBLESHOOTING

I've created three toolbars that I like. Can I show them all on the screen at once? Unfortunately, only one toolbar can be displayed at a time in most applications. Toolbars can, however, display more than one row or column of buttons. (See "Setting Toolbar Display Preferences" earlier in this chapter). In Corel WordPerfect, there is another special toolbar called the Power Bar that can also be displayed while a "regular" toolbar is displayed. The Power Bar can be edited just like any other toolbar. In Corel Presentations, there is also a second toolbar showing buttons specific to the mode you are in. This toolbar can be moved, but not edited.

Setting Additional Properties

When you edit toolbars and menu bars, and double-click a button or menu item, you may see a Properties button.

This option enables you to change certain aspects of the command invoked by the button or menu item. How it works depends on what the button or menu item does:

- For buttons or menu items that invoke a feature, no Properties option is available. There is also no Properties option available for Corel WordPerfect toolbar buttons that invoke macros stored in the template.

- If the button or menu item plays a keyboard script, choosing Properties displays a Script Properties dialog box that enables you to edit the script.

- Choosing Properties for buttons or menu items that launch a program displays an Application Launch Properties dialog box. You can use this dialog box to specify the Command Line, Working Folder, and whether to Run the program minimized.

- Choosing Properties for buttons that launch macros located on the disk enables you to edit the path and name of the macro.

Index

G

M

Q

X

Y

Z

Broaden Your Mind
And Your Business
With Que

The *Special Edition Using* series remains the most-often recommended product line for computer users who want detailed reference information. With thorough explanations, troubleshooting advice, and special "Techniques from the Pros" sections, these books are the perfect all-in-one resource.

Launching a Business on the Web, Second Edition
0-7897-0871-X
$39.99 USA
Pub Date: 8/96

Special Edition Using Netscape 2
0-7897-0612-1
$49.99 USA
Pub Date: 12/95

Creating and Enhancing Netscape Web Pages
0-7897-0876-0
$49.99 USA
Pub Date: 8/96

For more information on these and other Que products, visit your local book retailer or call 1-800-772-0477.

que

Source Code ISBN:0-7897-0999-6

Check out Que® Books on the World Wide Web
http://www.mcp.com/que

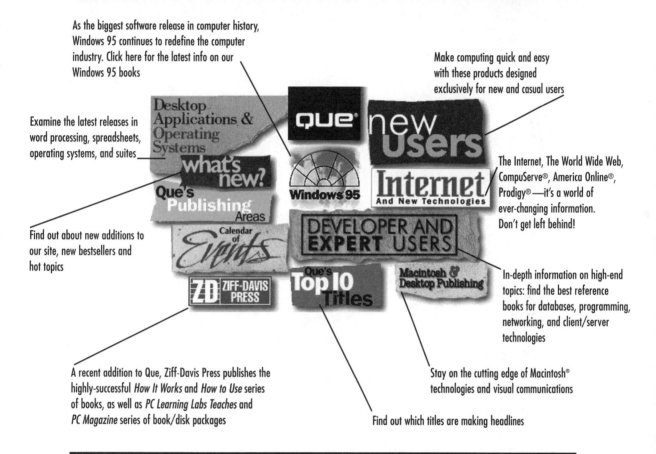

As the biggest software release in computer history, Windows 95 continues to redefine the computer industry. Click here for the latest info on our Windows 95 books

Examine the latest releases in word processing, spreadsheets, operating systems, and suites

Find out about new additions to our site, new bestsellers and hot topics

A recent addition to Que, Ziff-Davis Press publishes the highly-successful *How It Works* and *How to Use* series of books, as well as *PC Learning Labs Teaches* and *PC Magazine* series of book/disk packages

Make computing quick and easy with these products designed exclusively for new and casual users

The Internet, The World Wide Web, CompuServe®, America Online®, Prodigy®—it's a world of ever-changing information. Don't get left behind!

In-depth information on high-end topics: find the best reference books for databases, programming, networking, and client/server technologies

Stay on the cutting edge of Macintosh® technologies and visual communications

Find out which titles are making headlines

With 6 separate publishing groups, Que develops products for many specific market segments and areas of computer technology. Explore our Web Site and you'll find information on best-selling titles, newly published titles, upcoming products, authors, and much more.

- Stay informed on the latest industry trends and products available

- Visit our online bookstore for the latest information and editions

- Download software from Que's library of the best shareware and freeware

Complete and Return this Card
for a *FREE* Computer Book Catalog

Thank you for purchasing this book! You have purchased a superior computer book written expressly for your needs. To continue to provide the kind of up-to-date, pertinent coverage you've come to expect from us, we need to hear from you. Please take a minute to complete and return this self-addressed, postage-paid form. In return, we'll send you a free catalog of all our computer books on topics ranging from word processing to programming and the internet.

Mr. ☐   Mrs. ☐   Ms. ☐   Dr. ☐

Name (first) ☐☐☐☐☐☐☐☐☐☐☐☐   (M.I.) ☐   (last) ☐☐☐☐☐☐☐☐☐☐☐☐☐☐☐☐☐

Address ☐☐☐☐☐☐☐☐☐☐☐☐☐☐☐☐☐☐☐☐☐☐☐☐☐☐☐☐☐☐☐☐

☐☐☐☐☐☐☐☐☐☐☐☐☐☐☐☐☐☐☐☐☐☐☐☐☐☐☐☐☐☐☐☐

City ☐☐☐☐☐☐☐☐☐☐☐☐☐☐☐   State ☐☐   Zip ☐☐☐☐☐ ☐☐☐☐

Phone ☐☐☐ ☐☐☐ ☐☐☐☐   Fax ☐☐☐ ☐☐☐ ☐☐☐☐

Company Name ☐☐☐☐☐☐☐☐☐☐☐☐☐☐☐☐☐☐☐☐☐☐☐☐☐☐☐

E-mail address ☐☐☐☐☐☐☐☐☐☐☐☐☐☐☐☐☐☐☐☐☐☐☐☐☐☐☐

1. Please check at least (3) influencing factors for purchasing this book.

Front or back cover information on book .... ☐
Special approach to the content .... ☐
Completeness of content .... ☐
Author's reputation .... ☐
Publisher's reputation .... ☐
Book cover design or layout .... ☐
Index or table of contents of book .... ☐
Price of book .... ☐
Special effects, graphics, illustrations .... ☐
Other (Please specify): _____ ☐

2. How did you first learn about this book?

Saw in Macmillan Computer Publishing catalog .... ☐
Recommended by store personnel .... ☐
Saw the book on bookshelf at store .... ☐
Recommended by a friend .... ☐
Received advertisement in the mail .... ☐
Saw an advertisement in: _____ ☐
Read book review in: _____ ☐
Other (Please specify): _____ ☐

3. How many computer books have you purchased in the last six months?

This book only .... ☐   3 to 5 books .... ☐
books .... ☐   More than 5 .... ☐

4. Where did you purchase this book?

Bookstore .... ☐
Computer Store .... ☐
Consumer Electronics Store .... ☐
Department Store .... ☐
Office Club .... ☐
Warehouse Club .... ☐
Mail Order .... ☐
Direct from Publisher .... ☐
Internet site .... ☐
Other (Please specify): _____ ☐

5. How long have you been using a computer?

☐ Less than 6 months   ☐ 6 months to a year
☐ 1 to 3 years   ☐ More than 3 years

6. What is your level of experience with personal computers and with the subject of this book?

	With PCs	With subject of book
New	☐	☐
Casual	☐	☐
Accomplished	☐	☐
Expert	☐	☐

Source Code ISBN: 0-7897-0999-6

7. Which of the following best describes your job title?

Administrative Assistant .... ☐
Coordinator .... ☐
Manager/Supervisor .... ☐
Director .... ☐
Vice President .... ☐
President/CEO/COO .... ☐
Lawyer/Doctor/Medical Professional .... ☐
Teacher/Educator/Trainer .... ☐
Engineer/Technician .... ☐
Consultant .... ☐
Not employed/Student/Retired .... ☐
Other (Please specify): _____ ☐

8. Which of the following best describes the area of the company your job title falls under?

Accounting .... ☐
Engineering .... ☐
Manufacturing .... ☐
Operations .... ☐
Marketing .... ☐
Sales .... ☐
Other (Please specify): _____ ☐

Comments: _____
_____
_____

9. What is your age?

Under 20 .... ☐
21-29 .... ☐
30-39 .... ☐
40-49 .... ☐
50-59 .... ☐
60-over .... ☐

10. Are you:

Male .... ☐
Female .... ☐

11. Which computer publications do you read regularly? (Please list)

_____
_____
_____
_____
_____
_____
_____
_____
_____
_____
_____

Fold here and scotch-tape to mail.